Collaboration and the Semantic Web:

Social Networks, Knowledge Networks, and Knowledge Resources

Stefan Brüggemann
Astrium Space Transportation, Germany

Claudia d'Amato
Università degli Studi di Bari "A. Moro", Italy

Managing Director:	Lindsay Johnston
Senior Editorial Director:	Heather A. Probst
Book Production Manager:	Sean Woznicki
Development Manager:	Joel Gamon
Development Editor:	Hannah Abelbeck
Acquisitions Editor:	Erika Gallagher
Typesetter:	Nicole Sparano
Cover Design:	Nick Newcomer, Lisandro Gonzalez

Published in the United States of America by
Information Science Reference (an imprint of IGI Global)
701 E. Chocolate Avenue
Hershey PA 17033
Tel: 717-533-8845
Fax: 717-533-8661
E-mail: cust@igi-global.com
Web site: http://www.igi-global.com

Library of Congress Cataloging-in-Publication Data

Collaboration and the Semantic Web: social networks, knowledge networks and knowledge resources / Stefan Bruggemann and Claudia d'Amato, editors.
    p. cm.
  Includes bibliographical references and index.
  Summary: "This book showcases cutting-edge research on the intersections of Semantic Web, collaborative work, and social media research, exploring how the resources of so-called social networking applications, which bring people together to interact and encourage sharing of personal information and ideas, can be tapped by Semantic Web techniques"--Provided by publisher.
  ISBN 978-1-4666-0894-8 (hbk.) -- ISBN 978-1-4666-0895-5 (ebook) -- ISBN 978-1-4666-0896-2 (print & perpetual access) 1. Semantic Web. 2. Online social networks. 3. Internet--Social aspects. I. Bruggemann, Stefan, 1978- II. d'Amato, Claudia, 1977-
  TK5105.88815.C64 2012
  025.04'27--dc23
                                            2012001349

British Cataloguing in Publication Data
A Cataloguing in Publication record for this book is available from the British Library.

All work contributed to this book is new, previously-unpublished material. The views expressed in this book are those of the authors, but not necessarily of the publisher.

Editorial Advisory Board

Table of Contents

Section 1
Introduction: The Importance of Knowledge Sharing and
Collaborative Environment

Section 2
Exploiting Semantic Technologies and Principles for
Supporting Collaborative and Social Environments

Section 3
Acquiring, Querying, and Discovering Knowledge from
Collaborative and Social Environments

Section 4
Applications

Detailed Table of Contents

Section 1
Introduction: The Importance of Knowledge Sharing and
Collaborative Environment

Chapter 1
    Eva Zangerle, University of Innsbruck, Austria
    Wolfgang Gassler, University of Innsbruck, Austria

The creation of content within semistructured, collaborative information systems imposes the problem of having to deal with very heterogeneous schemata. This is due to the fact that the semistructured paradigm does not restrict the user in his choice of nomenclatures for the data he intends to store within the information system. As many users participate in the creation of data, the structure of this data is very heterogeneous. In this chapter the authors discuss two main movements that aim at dealing with heterogeneity. The first approach is concerned with efficiently avoiding structure heterogeneity within collaborative information systems by providing the users with suitable recommendations for an aligned schema during the insertion process. The second approach is mainly focussing on overcoming structure heterogeneity by providing efficient means for querying heterogeneous data.

Chapter 2
    Brian D. Goodman, IBM Corporation, USA

Individuals are the generators and consumers of content, and in doing so, make up a substantial presence in the literate internet, above and beyond the formal media outlets that make up the minority. Accelerating the explosion of content are Web 2.0 interactions, where participants are encouraged to engage with primary content. These social spaces are a platform, supporting often-overlooked micro-interactions referred to in this chapter as digital fingerprints. In parallel, companies construct web experiences that uniquely deliver Internet inspired experiences. However, the competition that divides popular Internet destinations is absent in well run intranets. Collaboration and cooperation among internal web properties offer a unique opportunity to organize people and information across disparate experiences. An example of such a solution is IBM's Enterprise Tagging System, a collaborative classification and recommendation service that knits employee identities and destinations together through fingerprints. The benefit of creating such a common service also exhibits the side effect and power of the relative few participants. It introduces the desperate need to consider how actions and relationships affect user experiences. The success of social systems requires a high level of diverse participation. This diversity is what ensures the mediation and influence of co-creation and collaborative filtering is not overly narrow.

Chapter 3

Stefan Thaler, STI-Innsbruck, University of Innsbruck Austria
Elena Simperl, AIFB, Karlsruhe Institute of Technology, Germany
Katharina Siorpaes, STI-Innsbruck, University of Innsbruck, Austria
Stephan Wölger, STI-Innsbruck, University of Innsbruck, Austria

A multitude of approaches to match, merge, and integrate ontologies, and more recently, to interlink RDF data sets, have been proposed over the past years, making ontology alignment one of the most active and at the same time mature area of research and development in semantic technologies. While advances in the area cannot be contested, it is equally true that full automation of the ontology-alignment process is far from being feasible; human input is often indispensable for the bootstrapping of the underlying methods, and for the validation of the results. The question of acquiring and leveraging such human input remains largely unaddressed, in particular when it comes to the incentives and motivators that are likely to make users invest their valuable time and effort in alignment tasks such as entity interlinking and schema matching, which can be domain-knowledge-intensive, technical, or both. In this chapter, the authors present SpotTheLink, a game whose purpose addresses this challenge, demonstrating how knowledge-intensive tasks in the area of the Semantic Web can be collaboratively solved by a community of non-experts in an entertaining fashion.

Chapter 4

Salman Iqbal, Massey University, Manawatu Campus, New Zealand
Hayati Abdul Jalal, Massey University, Manawatu Campus, New Zealand
Paul Toulson, Massey University, Manawatu Campus, New Zealand
David Tweed, Massey University, Manawatu Campus, New Zealand

Organisational culture plays an important role for enabling the process of knowledge sharing. Organisational culture is not only reflected in the visible aspects of organization such as structure, mission, and objectives, it is also embedded in the behaviour of people. The purpose of this chapter is to close research gaps present in knowledge sharing success by examining the linkages between employees' knowledge-sharing through collaboration, perceived values of involvement, trustworthiness, and formal recognition. The research data was collected by using simple random sampling techniques from a population of knowledge workers in Malaysian IT organisations. The findings highlight the importance of organisational culture for successful knowledge sharing within organisations. The results of factor analysis show the emergence of four new cultural values extant in the Malaysian context. These values are involvement, trustworthiness, formal recognition, and independence. Successful knowledge sharing is significantly related to the perceived value of involvement, trustworthiness, and formal recognition. This chapter will be beneficial for researchers, practitioners, scholars, and organisations (leaders and employees); it will also be helpful for those interested in organisational structure and relationships across organisations in knowledge contexts.

Section 2
Exploiting Semantic Technologies and Principles for
Supporting Collaborative and Social Environments

Chapter 5

Federico Bergenti, Università degli Studi di Parma, Italy

Enrico Franchi, Università degli Studi di Parma, Italy

Agostino Poggi, Università degli Studi di Parma, Italy

In this chapter, the authors describe the relationships between multi-agent systems, social networks, and the Semantic Web within collaborative work; they also review how the integration of multi-agent systems and Semantic Web technologies and techniques can be used to enhance social networks at all scales. The chapter first provides a review of relevant work on the application of agent-based models and abstractions to the key ingredients of our work: collaborative systems, the Semantic Web, and social networks. Then, the chapter discusses the reasons current multi-agent systems and their foreseen evolution might be a fundamental means for the realization of the future Semantic Social Networks. Finally, some conclusions are drawn.

Chapter 6

Rabeeh Ayaz Abbasi, Quaid-i-Azam University, Pakistan

In today's social media platforms, when users upload or share their media (photos, videos, bookmarks, etc.), they often annotate it with keywords (called tags). Annotating the media helps in retrieving and browsing resources, and also allows the users to search and browse annotated media. In many social media platforms like Flickr or YouTube, users have to manually annotate their resources, which is inconvenient and time consuming. Tag recommendation is the process of suggesting relevant tags for a given resource, and a tag recommender is a system that recommends the tags. A tag recommender system is important for social media platforms to help users in annotating their resources. However, many social media platforms support other media features like geographical coordinates. These features can be exploited for improving tag recommendation. In this chapter, a comparison of three types of social media features for tag recommendation is presented and evaluated. The features presented in this chapter include geographical-coordinates, low-level image descriptors, and tags.

Chapter 7

Simon Scerri, DERI, National University of Ireland, Galway

Digital means of communications such as email and IM have become a crucial tool for collaboration. Taking advantage of the fact that information exchanged over these media can be made persistent, a lot of research has strived to make sense of the ongoing communication processes in order to support the participants with their management. In this chapter, a workflow-oriented approach is pursued to demonstrate how, coupled with appropriate information extraction techniques, robust knowledge models, and intuitive user interfaces, semantic technology can provide support for email-based collaborative work. While eliciting as much knowledge as possible, the design concept in this chapter imposes little to no changes and/or restrictions to the conventional use of email.

Section 3
Acquiring, Querying, and Discovering Knowledge from Collaborative and Social Environments

This chapter aims to set out relevant discourse and approaches to consider when planning strategies for acquiring and building knowledge for formal ontology construction. Action Research (AR) is offered as a key means to help structure the necessary reflexivity required to enrich the researcher's understanding of how they know what they know, particularly within a collaborative research setting. This is especially necessary when revealing tacit domain knowledge through participation with actors and stakeholders: "In this kind of research it is permissible to be openly normative and to strive for change, but not to neglect critical reflection" (Elfors & Svane 2008, 1).

For large-scale data mining, utilizing data from ubiquitous and mixed-structured data sources, the extraction and integration into a comprehensive data-warehouse is usually of prime importance. Then, appropriate methods for validation and potential refinement are essential. This chapter describes an approach for integrating data mining, information extraction, and validation with collaborative knowledge management and capture in order to improve the data acquisition processes. For collaboration, a semantic wiki-enabled system for knowledge and experience management is presented. The proposed approach applies information extraction techniques together with pattern mining methods for initial data validation and is applicable for heterogeneous sources, i.e., capable of integrating structured and unstructured data. The methods are integrated into an incremental process providing for continuous validation options. The approach has been developed in a health informatics context: The results of a medical application demonstrate that pattern mining and the applied rule-based information extraction methods are well suited for discovering, extracting and validating clinically relevant knowledge, as well as the applicability of the knowledge capture approach. The chapter presents experiences using a case-study in the medical domain of sonography.

Recently, social bookmarking systems have received surging attention in academic and industrial communities. In fact, social bookmarking systems share with the Semantic Web vision the idea of facilitating the collaborative organization and sharing of knowledge on the web. The reason for the apparent success of the upcoming tools for resource sharing (social bookmarking systems, photo sharing systems, etc.) lies mainly in the fact that no specific skills are needed for publishing and editing, and an immediate benefit is yielded to each individual user, e.g., organizing one's bookmarks in a browser-independent, persistent fashion, without too much overhead. As these systems grow larger, however, the users address the need of enhanced search facilities. Today, full-text search is supported, but the results are usually simply listed decreasingly by their upload date. The challenging research issue is, therefore, the development of a suitable prediction framework to support users in effectively retrieving the resources matching their real search intents. The primary focus of this chapter is to propose a new, context aware tag query prediction approach. Specifically, the authors adopted Hidden Markov Models and formal concept analysis to predict users' search intentions based on a real folksonomy. Carried out experiments emphasize the relevance of the proposal and open many issues.

While building and using a fully semantic understanding of Web contents is a distant goal, named entities provide a small, tractable set of elements carrying a well-defined semantics. Generic named entities are names of persons, locations, organizations, phone numbers, and dates, while domain-specific named entities includes names of for example, names of proteins, enzymes, organisms, genes, cells, et cetera, in the biological domain. An ability to automatically perform named entity recognition (NER) – i.e., identify occurrences of NE in Web contents – can have multiple benefits, such as improving the expressiveness of queries and also improving the quality of the search results. A number of factors make building highly accurate NER a challenging task. Given the importance of NER in semantic processing of text, this chapter presents a detailed survey of NER techniques for English text.

Section 4
Applications

This chapter gives a comprehensive overview of ongoing research about semantic approaches for Collaboration Engineering. The authors present a new ontology-based approach, where each concept of the ontology corresponds to a specific collaboration step or a resource, to collect, manage, and share collaborative knowledge. The chapter discusses the utility of the proposed ontology in the context of a real-world example where the authors explain how collaboration can be modelled and applied using their ontology in order to improve the collaboration process. Furthermore, they discuss how well-known ontologies, such as FOAF, can be linked to their ontology and extend it. While the focus of the chapter is on semantic Collaboration Engineering, the authors additionally present methods of reasoning and machine learning to derive new knowledge about the collaboration process as a further research direction.

A software project is developed by collaboration of some expert people. However, the collaboration puts obstacles in the way of software development when the involved people in the project are scattered over the world. Although Internet has provided a collection of scattered islands in which the denizens of the islands are able to communicate with each other, it lacks full requisite qualifications for the collaboration among the denizens. The emerging idea is that a supportive environment should be developed on the Web for providing full requisite qualifications and facilitating collaboration. Towards providing such an environment, this chapter aims to present a framework exploiting Open Hypermedia System (OHS) and a Web-based collaboration protocol. OHS assists in saving and restoring artifacts constructed by the scattered people, and the protocol provides channels to concurrent communication and distributed authoring among the people.

Due to a higher need for healthcare provision, and due to the decreasing number of contributors in the German healthcare system, the market situation has changed over the last years. The resulting competitive and cost pressure forces the executives to tap potentials in a competitive manner. Analytical Information Systems as part of business intelligence can be used to receive information from several integrated data sources that may be used in the decision making process. However, the system's complexity of use can be seen as problematic so that unskilled business users, unlike power users, are not able to execute analyses for their issues in an adequate way. The focus of the presented approach lies on a semantic metadata layer, which is capable to import and manage modeled semantic metadata. Based on this layer, the metadata is supposed to be used for further analyses support functionalities in order to allow a business user information self-service.

Knowledge workers in specific professional domains form the fastest increasing workforce in OECD countries. Since this fact has been realised by management researchers, they have focussed on the question of how to measure and enhance the productivity of said workforce. According to the author's cross-industrial research undertaken in five different knowledge-intensive organisations, it is, however, not productivity in the traditional meaning of the term which is to be regarded as the crucial performance indicator in knowledge work. There rather exist multiple performance indicators, each of which is, moreover, differently graded as to its importance by different stakeholders. These findings, firstly, indicate the need for an alternative definition of productivity when the term is applied to knowledge work. Secondly, they indicate the need for alternative definitions of the specific challenges that might be involved in making knowledge workers productive. Thirdly, they imply different consequences for the management of knowledge workers. This chapter closes abovementioned research gaps by summarising the indicators employed in five knowledge-intensive organisations from different business sectors for the assessment of knowledge workers' performance, by subsequently deducing the specific challenges involved in the management of knowledge workers and by further delineating consequences for the management of knowledge workers – consequences affecting various knowledge-intensive industries.

Foreword

Semantic knowledge representation formalisms and technologies have a great potential to make collaboration more efficient and effective. Ontologies, for example, can be employed to structure knowledge in a certain domain and provide a conceptual framework for the collaboration. Reasoning can help knowledge workers to gain new insights by revealing implicit information from collaboratively created knowledge bases. Triple stores provide the base infrastructure to manage data and knowledge being the result of collaboration. Using the Linked Data paradigm, knowledge can be published on the Web in structured form and easily reused and integrated from various sources. Semantic user and authoring interfaces such as Semantic Wikis represent tools, which enable new forms of collaboration.

This book, edited by Stefan Brüggemann and Claudia d'Amato, addresses the synergistic combination of collaboration and the semantic web through paradigms such as social networks, knowledge networks and knowledge resources. The book is of paramount importance, since large scale semantic collaboration is still not a reality on the Web. The goal of the book is to showcase research on the intersection of Semantic Web, Collaborative Work, and Social Media. The rationale of this book was to find answers to research questions such as: How can richly structured Semantic Web data and existing Semantic Web technologies together build next-generation systems for collaborative work? How could knowledge management techniques contribute to the full realization of integrated semantic applications? What are the challenges for developers of social systems with integrated semantic web data?

As a result, the book comprises 15 chapters, which range from foundations and base technologies over strategies for integrating various aspects of collaboration and semantic technologies to systems and concrete applications.

Some foundational questions addresses by the chapters of this book are in particular: a survey of "Techniques for Named Entity Recognition," an approach for integrating data mining, information extraction and validation with collaborative knowledge management and capture in order to improve the data acquisition processes ("Data Mining, Validation and Collaborative Knowledge Capture"), and the use of "Hidden Markov Models for Context-Aware Tag Query Prediction in Folksonomies."

There are a number of chapters addressing cross-cutting, social, and conceptual problems of semantic collaboration. These are: "Dealing with Structure Heterogeneity in Semantic Collaborative Information Systems," "Ontological Collaboration Engineering," and "Collaborative mediation," "What is productivity in knowledge work?," "The Reflexive Practitioner: Knowledge Discovery through Action Research," as well as the view on "Knowledge Management" from an organizational perspective.

There are two chapters that particularly address the social dimension of collaboration namely: "Exploiting Social Media Features for Automated Tag Recommendation" and "Enhancing Social Networks with Agent and Semantic Web Technologies."

Last but not least the book is complemented by chapters that describe concrete application scenarios, systems, and use cases with "Developing a Web-Based Cooperative Environment to Software Project Development," "Knowledge Based Business Intelligence for Business User Information Self- Service," "Semantic Technology for Improved Email Collaboration," and "SpotTheLink: A Game-Based Approach to the Alignment of Ontologies."

Altogether the book represents an excellent compilation of recent advancements, challenges, and insights in the area of collaborative semantic applications. It is of great use to advanced students, researchers, and practitioners aiming to research and develop collaborative systems and applications that build on semantic technologies.

Sören Auer
Universität Leipzig, Germany

Preface

Collaborative work has been increasingly viewed as a good practice for the organizations to achieve value for money and efficiency. Organizations that work well in collaboration may have access to new sources of funding, deliver new, improved, and more integrated services, and make efficiency savings costs that could be shared. Working in collaboration can strengthen organizations of all levels and allow them to share knowledge, information, and expertise. As such, collaborative working environments have been developed for providing the capabilities of sharing information and exchanging views in order to reach a common understanding. Some examples are instant messaging, email, application sharing, videoconferencing, collaborative workspace and document management, task and workflow management, Wikis, and blogging.

Over time, the collaborative view has moved from the typical organizational context to the everyday life, generating an increasing attention to the so-called social networking that is a social structure made up of individuals or organizations, which are connected by one or more specific types of interdependency, such as friendship, common interest, financial exchange, dislike, business, or professional interests. Although social networking is possible in person, especially in the workplace, universities, and high schools, it has known a wide development as an online web-based service, platform, or site that focuses on building and reflecting of social networks or social relations among people.

A social network service essentially consists of: a representation of each user as a profile, the specification of the social links among the users (profiles), and a variety of additional services. These services/sites cover specific interests such as Flickr (for photo sharing), Blogster (for the blogging community), Delicious (for Social bookmarking allowing users to locate and save websites that match their own interests), LinkedIn (for Business and professional networking), or general interests such as Google+, Facebook, and MySpace. Overall, the common goal is bringing people together to interact with each other (for instance by offering searching services for finding other users with similar interests) to encourage sharing of personal information and ideas. For this aim, easy-to-use publishing tools are generally provided. Furthermore, profiles that can be potentially connected to a given user are also suggested by the use of social network analysis methods.

Among the others, a service that is widely offered in the context of social network websites is tagging. A tag is a keyword (or term) assigned as an annotation to a piece of information or to a resource such as Internet bookmark, image, file, picture. A tag is a kind of metadata that is used for describing an item and allows it to be found again by browsing or searching. Tags are generally chosen informally and personally by the creator of an item and/or by its viewer (indeed annotations can be added on the personal profile or also on other connected profiles/resources). For instance, Delicious provides a way for its users to add tags to their bookmarks (as a way to help find them later) and also provides browseable aggregated views of the bookmarks of all users featuring a particular tag; Flickr allows its users to add free-form tags to each of their pictures, constructing flexible and easy metadata that make the pictures highly searchable. Tags expressed by the users are useful both to them and to the larger community. Websites that include tags often display collections of tags as tag clouds. The adoption of tags in a collective or collaborative way is named folksonomy. Thus, a folksonomy is a system of classification derived from the practice of collaboratively creating and managing tags to annotate and categorize content. This practice is also known as collaborative tagging, social classification, social indexing, and social tagging.

Tags may be a bottom-up type of classification, opposite to the hierarchies that are top-down. Indeed, in a traditional hierarchical system (taxonomy), a limited number of terms are considered to be used for classification, and there is almost one correct way to classify each item. In a tagging system, there are several ways to classify an item, and there is no wrong choice since instead of belonging to one category, an item may have several different tags. The flexibility of tagging allows users to classify their collections of items in the ways they find useful. However, the personalized variety of terms that can be used as tags can constitute a potential issue when searching and browsing. Even if there are some studies which prove that the distributions of the tags tend to converge over time to stable distributions that could be considered for assessing stable vocabularies, the absence of any standard still represents a source of issues. Indeed spelling errors, tags that can have more than one meaning, or unclear tags due to synonym/antonym confusion could by hardly retrievable or erroneously retrieved. This is because, in a typical tagging system, there is no explicit information about the meaning (semantics) of each tag. The adoption of the Semantic Web principles, technologies, and techniques could be of help in solving this problem, besides potentially opening interesting perspectives in collaborative and social networking.

The Semantic Web is the new vision of the Web, introduced in the last decade by Tim Berners-Lee. The main goal is to make the Web contents machine-readable and processable in addition to being human-readable. In this way, the available knowledge can be reused and/or integrated in different contexts. For achieving this goal, resources are enriched with metadata, namely semantic annotations referring to shared ontologies. An ontology is the formal conceptualization of a certain domain that is shared and reused across domains, tasks, and group of people. An ontology acts as a shared metadata vocabulary, making semantics explicit. Hence, the Semantic Web is not a separate Web but an extension of the current one, in which information is given well-defined meaning, better enabling computers and people to work in cooperation. This peculiarity is missing in the collaborative and social environments.

The primary goal of this book is to showcase the cutting edge research on the intersection of Semantic Web, collaborative work, and social media. Social media and the Semantic Web mainly co-existed in the past, but when these developments became massively popular, they began to have an influence on collaborative working. Learners and online workers now have a variety of knowledge resources at hand. Integrated semantic applications, linked data, social networks, and networked digital solutions can now be used in collaborative learning environments and present participants with the context-aware information that they need. Semantic technologies have shown their potential for integrating valuable knowledge bases and information systems, and they are being applied to the composition of digital learning and working platforms. These semantic technologies not only have potential for solving the semantic heterogeneity of knowledge resources, trust, and accountability, but also provide solutions for contemporary data quality management cycles, which are necessary to ensure the high-quality integration of shared knowledge resources.

The vision of the book is to put together social and collaborative environments with the Semantic Web principles and techniques to improve both contexts. Specifically, the Semantic Web could benefit from the collaborative and social environment in addressing important problems such as ontology learning. For instance, given the tag clouds emerging from a folksonomy, they can be clustered and an intentional definition for them could be learnt. The result can be considered a sketch of an ontology that could be aligned with an existing domain ontology. In this way an enriched ontology can obtain with the advantage of having a knowledge base that is emerging from the behavior of the users or annotators. On the other hand, collaborative and social environments could benefit from the availability of semantic tools, for instance, for annotating resources with a controlled vocabulary emerging from the social and collaborative environment. Furthermore, suitable semantic tools for matching requests and offers in collaborative environments could be also realized (i.e. finding a CV that is suitable for a specific job requirement), resulting in useful tools for several domains such as education, healthcare, and business-to-business activities.

Following this twofold perspective, the book is organized as follows. Section 1 introduces on the importance of knowledge sharing and collaborative environment focusing on collaborative paradigms for creating and managing knowledge and information. Section 2 focuses on the adoption and exploitation of semantic technologies and principles for supporting and improving collaborative and social environment. Section 3 focuses on knowledge acquisition from collaborative and heterogeneous sources of information and on querying and discovering knowledge from collaborative and social environments. Section 4 concludes the book by considering specific applications, specifically: the exploitation of ontologies for improving collaborative software engineering, the adoption of ontologies for supporting the decision making process, and measuring the productivity in collaborative environment.

The book is intended for researchers and practitioners in the fields of Semantic Web, knowledge management, and collaborative and social networking by summarizing recent research results in the fields.

Stefan Brüggemann
Astrium Space Transportation, Germany

Claudia d'Amato
Università degli Studi di Bari "A. Moro", Italy

Acknowledgment

This book could not be realized without the precious contributions of several researchers in the field that actively collaborated for the selection and revisions of the chapters for creating this book. We are very grateful to Sven Abels, Sören Auer, Nicola Fanizzi, Chiara Ghidini, Agnieszka Lawrynowicz, Jens Lehmann, Jochen Meyer, Kunal Patel, Tassilo Pellegrini, Beatrix Perez-Valle, Sebastian Rudolph, Thomas Scharrenbach, and Joannis Vlachakis, and also to Hannah Abelbeck for providing her expertise in all phases of this project.

Stefan Brüggemann
Astrium Space Transportation, Germany

Claudia d'Amato
Università degli Studi di Bari "A. Moro", Italy

Section 1
Introduction:
The Importance of Knowledge Sharing and Collaborative Environment

Chapter 1
Dealing with Structure Heterogeneity in Semantic Collaborative Information Systems

Eva Zangerle
University of Innsbruck, Austria

Wolfgang Gassler
University of Innsbruck, Austria

ABSTRACT

The creation of content within semistructured, collaborative information systems imposes the problem of having to deal with very heterogeneous schemata. This is due to the fact that the semistructured paradigm does not restrict the user in his choice of nomenclatures for the data he intends to store within the information system. As many users participate in the creation of data, the structure of this data is very heterogeneous. In this chapter the authors discuss two main movements that aim at dealing with heterogeneity. The first approach is concerned with efficiently avoiding structure heterogeneity within collaborative information systems by providing the users with suitable recommendations for an aligned schema during the insertion process. The second approach is mainly focussing on overcoming structure heterogeneity by providing efficient means for querying heterogeneous data.

INTRODUCTION

Most online, collaborative information systems, such as wiki systems, provide means to easily add, modify and delete information, which does not have to adhere to any predefined schema or structure. In contrast, traditional (relational) databases are strictly-structured and enforce the user to store information in a predefined schema. Such structured data stores provide the big advantage of structured access, which enables complex query capabilities. Traditional wiki systems only support full-text search which is not feasible for complex

DOI: 10.4018/978-1-4666-0894-8.ch001

queries such as "Which Austrian cities have more than 10.000 inhabitants and have a female mayor who has a doctoral degree?" Nevertheless, wiki systems are able to cope with very large amount of collaboratively created information with very heterogeneous structures and schemata.

Weikum et al. (2009) observed that modern information systems have to be able to support both structured and unstructured data to combine the advantages of both worlds and be able to answer such complex questions. This need of combination initiates the development of collaborative, semistructured information systems. They provide mechanisms for the combination of both unstructured and structured storage of data. Semistructured data features a structure without having to specify a fixed schema. As this paradigm does not restrict the user and the used schema at all, the massive collaborative creation and editing of content by hundreds or thousands of users obviously leads to the usage of very heterogeneous schemata and structures in collaborative environments. Even Wikipedia, which has a very committed community dealing with heterogeneity, is also not able to avoid heterogeneity within its schema.

In the following sections we discuss the problem of heterogeneity in semistructured information systems and show approaches which are able to deal with heterogeneous schemata, data and the collaborative paradigm of creating and managing knowledge and information.

Schema and Heterogeneity

Modern collaborative Information Systems mostly use the semistructured paradigm, as it features the possibility to structure information without having to adhere to a predefined schema. The most popular example of a semistructured data format is RDF which is often used in the underlying storage layer of semantic, collaborative information systems. RDF consists of triples with the form <subject,predicate,object>. For example

information about the subject Albert Einstein can be stored by using the triples shown in Listing 1.

Listing 1. Semistructured description of Albert Einstein

<AlbertEinstein,name,Albert Einstein>
<AlbertEinstein,born,1897/03/14>
<AlbertEinstein,bornIn,Ulm>
<AlbertEinstein,wonAward,Nobel Prize>
<AlbertEinstein,wonAward,Max Planck Medal>

RDF distinguishes between URIs which describe resources and literals for specifying values. For reasons of simplification, the URI prefixes are omitted in the example in Listing 1. RDF can also be represented as a graph $G = (N, L, E)$ where N contains all nodes. The edges of the graph are defined in the set E with $e\,(n_1, n_2)$ and $n_1, n_2 \in N$. The possible labels of edges are denoted by L. In the graph representation, subjects and objects are modelled as nodes. The predicates are modelled as labels and the triple $< s_i, p_i, o_i >$ itself is defined by an edge $e\,(s_i, o_i)$ with the label p_i.

The schema or structure of a graph is defined similar to a classical relational database schema. A database schema is defined by the columns - also called attributes - of a relation. Each row also called record of a relation has to conform to a predefined schema. As semistructured data or RDF data are not restricted in any way, each record can consist of arbitrary many attributes. In the context of RDF a record is called subject and attributes are called predicates. The schema or structure of a RDF subject S_i is defined by the used attributes

$$Schema_{S_i} = \{p \mid p \in L, e(S_1, n) \ with \ label \ p\}$$

In contrast to classical relational databases each record can constitute its own schema. Exactly this feature of RDF is one of the most important advantage and at the same time a big disadvantage. Massive collaborative information systems have to store data of many different and heterogeneous domains. Therefore, RDF is best suited as each subject can use its own attributes and schema.

This freedom of the semistructured paradigm leads at the same time to a proliferation of schemata and structures as even subjects of the same domain may be stored with different schemata. Every single user in a collaborative environment has his own view of structuring information and uses his own terminology. Furnas et al. (1987) already showed in the 1980s that two people would spontaneously choose the same word for an object with a probability of less than 20%. The resulting proliferation of structures, schemata and vocabulary results in a very heterogeneous schema and therefore impedes a common schema, which is essential for structured access and complex queries. For example, a query like "Which persons won a Nobel Prize, were born in a German city and also lived in Austria?" is only possible if the information of all persons in an information system is stored with the same schema.

The example in Listing 2 describes Barack Obama in a well-structured way. In comparison to the stored information about Albert Einstein, as shown in the RDF example above, semantically similar information are described with completely different attributes and thus result in very different schemata. Such different schemata may already arise if only two users enter information. In massive collaborative information systems thousands of users enter information and structure their data very differently if there is no restriction on the schema at all.

Listing 2. Semistructured description of Barack Obama

```
<BarackObama,knownAs,Barack Obama>
<BarackObama,dateOfBirth,1961/08/04>
<BarackObama,placeOfBirth,Honolulu>
<BarackObama,hasAward, Nobel Prize >
<BarackObama,hasAward,Grammy Award>
```

Consider the infoboxes within Wikipedia articles, which are perfect examples of semistructured data and can also be extracted as RDF triples (Auer et al., 2007). The infoboxes are manually created, tabular aggregations of the most important facts within an article and consist of multiple properties and according values. For example an infobox about New York City contains the property-value pairs area metropolis: 468.9 sq mi and elevation: 33 ft. These property-value pairs – together with the article URL itself – constitute RDF-triples. The schema of such infoboxes is specified by a predefined template. However, Wikipedia has to cope with a big heterogeneity problem. Wu & Weld (2007) showed that even schemata of template-based infoboxes – which are supervised and enforced by the community – are divergent and noisy. Moreover, Boulain et al. (2008), revealed that only 35% of all edits within Wikipedia are related to content, whereas all other edits are concerned with the structure of articles to avoid the proliferation. These facts imply that even with the support of a huge committed community, the proliferation of schemata within a multi-user information system cannot be prevented.

The intersection of the two computed schemata of the examples shown in Listing 1 and Listing 2, $Schema_{Einstein} \cap Schema_{Obama} = \varnothing$ results in the empty set as they do not share any attributes. Nevertheless, the stored information in these heterogeneous schemata can be perceived by a human being very easily. A human being is also able to align the information to a homogenous schema without great effort. The automatic alignment of schemata, however, is a very complex, error-prone and difficult task. The successful performing of such an alignment task can be realized in restricted domains where domain-specific thesauri and other ontologies or meta-information is provided. Even in the environment of a very restricted domain, the alignment is often realized in a semiautomatic way. In such semiautomatic alignment applications, the system proposes mappings between schemata or attributes to a user. In most cases the user is a specialist in the respective domain and can decide whether the mapping is correct or has to be revised. In contrast, large collaborative information systems, such as Wikipedia, cover hundreds or thousands of domains, thus the automatic alignment of structures is hardly impossible.

Besides the automatic alignment process, which is not feasible in large collaborative systems, there exists two movements to cope with the heterogeneity.

- The consideration of the heterogeneous data during the query and search process.
- Recommendations during the insertion process to prevent heterogeneity

The first approach does not touch the stored data at all but tries to enhance the query process to cope with the heterogeneity. The query process aims at discovering relations and semantically similar information which are not specified by the query.

The second approach is meant to support the user during the insertion process by recommending tiny adaptions to the data to conform to a common schema. Thereby, the common schema is computed on the fly, uses the wisdom of the crowd and does not need any predefined configuration or any external maintenance.

Both approaches can incorporate the user in the process of insertion or querying to exploit the fast human cognition capabilities and the extensive knowledge of the user. The rest of the chapter is focused on these two movements and describes important representative approaches in this respective area of research.

QUERYING OF HETEROGENEOUS DATA

The main goal of information systems is to satisfy the information needs of their users regardless of the structure of the underlying data. The formulation of precise queries within homogeneous data is the most efficient means of satisfying a user's information needs. However, the user does not have sufficient information about the schema to be able to formulate such precise queries. For example, an inexperienced user cannot know if he has to place a restriction on the attribute <birthday> or <dateOfBirth>. Therefore, information systems have to offer support to the user to enable him to still query the data in an intuitive and efficient way without having to know details about the underlying schema. Hence, the following approaches presented in this section are mainly concerned with tackling these problems and provide so-called agnostic search facilities. These schema agnostic search facilities allow the user to efficiently create structured queries without having any knowledge of the underlying heterogeneous structure.

In the following section, different approaches for efficient search facilities within data featuring heterogeneous schemata are discussed. The one thing these approaches all have in common is that they are all based on an initial keyword search aiming at retrieving a starting point for a further refinement of the query or the respective result set. The presented search paradigms are illustrated in Figure 1. These three keyword-based approaches comprise the Browsing of the desired information in search of the desired information, the Faceted Search paradigm and Query Completion, an approach aiming at supporting the user in the formulation of precise queries.

Keyword Search

The vast amount of information available in the internet demands for simple and efficient means

Figure 1. Overview of keyword-based search paradigms

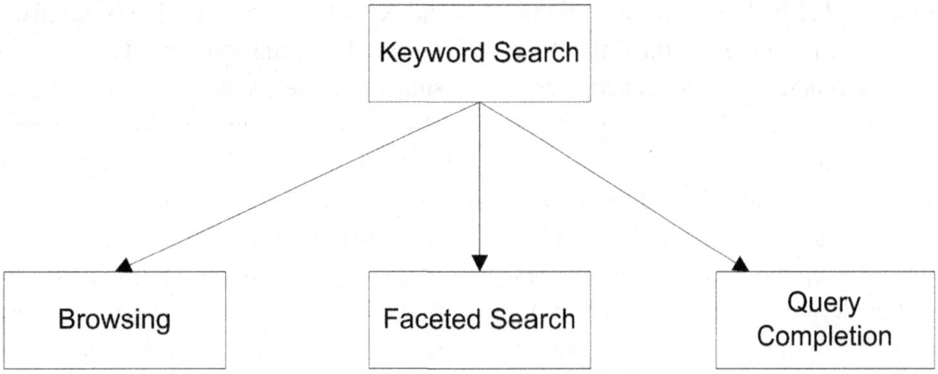

to search through this information. The most popular paradigm when searching information online is keyword search where the user specifies a relatively small set of keywords which are then used as input for the search process. The biggest advantage of this approach is its simplicity as the user is able to express his query by simple keywords. Beside this simplicity, everybody is accustomed to using search engines such as Google or Yahoo. Furthermore, this keyword search paradigm also features the big advantage that the user does not have to have any knowledge about the data or structure of the data underlying the search facilities. By stating one or more keywords, the user describes the documents or information he intends to find. Based on this information, the search engine scans its index for the desired information and returns links to the most relevant documents to the user. The user is then able to browse through these documents and scan them for the desired chunk of information. Frequently, such a keyword search is only the starting point in a search process and the users refine their search keywords based on the documents retrieved from the first search attempt.

The amount of semantic information such as RDF available online as both documents and through SPARQL endpoints is increasing steadily. Due to this fact, the Semantic Web also demands for efficient and easy-to-use search facilities. As

for simple information needs, keyword search is also feasible in the context of the Semantic Web. However, when having to deal with complex information needs, more sophisticated querying mechanisms frequently make use of keyword search to reach a starting point, which marks a first direction for the further search process. There have been quite a few successful approaches for keyword search within Semantic Web data which are described in the following section.

The creation of a search engine for the Semantic Web basically is very similar to the steps which have to be taken to create a traditional online search engine. The main steps are:

1. Crawl sources in order to gather relevant information for the index
2. Create an index based on the crawled information
3. Use the index for the computation of results for keyword queries

The first step in the creation of a search engine for the Semantic Web is the creation and maintenance of a search index. To do so, the Semantic Web has to be crawled as all relevant information has to be gathered before it can be added to the index. Modern semantic web search engines crawl both online (RDF) documents and SPARQL endpoints.

The fundamental approach for the creation of an index for online HTML documents is straight-forward. The search engines extract the text within the page and add the words (except stop words) to the index. The index itself basically is an inverted list which features the word itself and the document it is contained in. The crawling of the Semantic Web can be realized in a very similar way by storing the according properties and values of a defined URI. However, RDF documents may be highly interlinked and stored decentralized within many different sources. For example, information about Albert Einstein can be found in many different RDF documents on the Web. Therefore, the URIs have to be resolved and matched between the crawled subgraphs in order to be able to provide the most complete information about a certain subject. To tackle these challenges, the various search engines all use different approaches which are described in the following section.

Sindice (Tummarello et al., 2007) is an index for the Semantic Web. In particular, all occurring literals and especially the URIs and Inverse Functional Properties as identifiers are indexed. The Inverse Functional Property specifies that if a predicate is declared to be inverse functional, then the subject can be determined solely by the object within the triple. For example, the ISBN property and the according object of a book are able to fully identify the respective subject. Additionally, all literals within the detected graphs are added to the index. The index itself is kept within SOLR, a stand-alone full-text index based on Apache's Lucene index.

Falcons (Cheng & Qu, 2009) is another keyword-based search engine for the Semantic Web. The authors of the Falcon search engine propose to firstly create a virtual document for each subject which is to be indexed. These virtual documents are created by extracting terms from the RDF document. The extracted terms are either the local name of the subject's URI (URI without the namespace prefix, unique within its namespace) or literals which are connected with the object. The index itself is an inverted index based on the terms within the virtual documents and the respective subjects these terms belong to. Technically, the index is realized by the Apache Lucene full-text search engine. Besides querying this index based on a virtual document for each subject, the authors also propose to refine the search results by recommending suitable ontologies to the user. If a user chooses such an ontology, the search result is reduced to a set of concepts which are contained in this ontology. Furthermore, a refinement of queries based on class hierarchies is also provided by the Falcons search engine. This way, the system provides the user with suitable subclasses of the current object for a further refinement. Consider the following example: Albert Einstein is of type: person. Therefore, the system could automatically suggest to further restricting the search results to type: researcher to narrow down the result set. Such class hierarchies can also be used for the creation of a broader result set, namely by selecting a superclass of the current object and therefore extending the result set. These features are realized by creating a second inverted index which basically contains all subjects and the respective super- and subclasses.

In contrast to the other presented search engines, the index of the keyword-based Semantic Web Search Engine (SWSE) (Harth et al., 2007) is based on YARS2, which basically is a RDF store with extensive indexing, storage, querying and ranking facilities. The triples are stored as quadruples consisting of subject, predicate, object and context where the context basically describes the provenance of the triple. Furthermore, YARS2 allows for distributed query processing. The crawler underlying the SWSE search engine is very versatile as it is able to crawl RDF, RSS feeds, HTML and also Postscript and PDF-files. The indexed entities are additionally consolidated and interlinked. The search engine provides means for keyword search, filtering of results by entity type and navigation between entities. Furthermore,

SWSE also provides for searching of external live data sources. This is done by wrappers which can be plugged into the system. Each wrapper is responsible for a certain data format and the creation of an appropriate index for this external data source. The wrapper provides the information to the query processor and therefore makes the plugged in data source searchable.

However, simple keyword search does not fully exploit all the characteristics of Semantic Web information. Thus, the user is not able to express complex information needs just by specifying keywords. Complex, structured queries like "Which Austrian cities have more than 10.000 inhabitants and have a female mayor who has a doctoral degree?" are not feasible by simple keyword matching within the underlying data. Furthermore, the structure of Semantic Web documents is not exploited in order to provide the user with efficient search facilities. Therefore, more sophisticated search paradigms evolved for the Semantic Web. Some of these paradigms originate from traditional web search and have only been adapted to the need of the Semantic Web. The most dominant paradigm within traditional web search is browsing. The adaption of browsing for the Semantic Web and especially for RDF graphs is discussed in the following section of the chapter.

Browsing

The probably most natural way of exploring highly interlinked data such as RDF is browsing and navigating through the graph representation of the data. Users are accustomed to browse through interlinked website and documents online and therefore, such navigation through the RDF graph is very intuitive. However, this paradigm imposes the problem of scalability. Providing a visual representation of large datasets basically means representing large, browsable graphs.

VisiNav (Harth, 2009) is a system which allows its users to systematically browse and navigate through the result set of a keyword search. The

system furthermore provides means to restrict the result set by faceted search. The main focus lies on the visual formulation of complex queries. Essentially, six basic operations are provided to the users. These operations comprise:

- **Keyword Search:** This operation basically is responsible for the definition of an initial result set. The user specifies a small number of keywords in order to define the context of further operations.
- **Object Navigation:** The navigation through the graph is based on the traversal of links within the RDF graph. Based on the visual representation of the data as a graph, the user is able to simply click on a certain node to focus on it.
- **Facet Selection:** The system also provides means for restricting the result set by facets (see next section for an in-depth description of faceted search).
- **Path Traversal:** The traversal of a certain path within the graph is another way of creating the result set within the VisiNav system. This operation basically comprises navigating along predicates of subjects within the RDF graph aiming at the creation of a result set.
- **Projection:** Within a tabular representation of the result set, users are able to select only certain values based on their datatype properties which are then displayed.
- **Sorting:** This operation is also created for tabular representations of the result set. Within this set, the user is able to sort the elements based on certain criteria.

As already mentioned, the graphical representation of large graphs and the browsing of such large graphs are hardly efficient. In contrast, the Faceted Search paradigm is able to deal with huge amounts of data. This approach is presented in the following section.

Faceted Search

Keyword search is often used to retrieve a starting point for an exploratory search. From there, the user is able to browse through the results and restrict these results further. In this case, the restriction is based on facets. Faceted search describes the process of navigating through and exploring data by dividing the search space based on facets. These facets are orthogonal dimensions where each dimension features multiple values. These (mostly predefined) facets divide the information space into multiple subsets. Thus, the user is able to restrict the result set by applying constraints on the values of the facets step by step, like e.g. on the amazon.com website, where also inexperienced users are able to narrow down the possible large number of search results based on the prices of items, the category to which the items belong to (e.g. books or DVDs) or the star rating of the items the user is searching for. This is a typical example of faceted search within online shops.

A faceted browsing approach is also very suitable for Semantic Web data at large scale. This is due to the fact that RDF is already structured and can directly be used for the creation of facets. Thus, users do not have to have knowledge about the underlying structure. Instead, users are able to formulate queries based on a visual interface by progressively placing restrictions on the facets. This process is simplified by the fact that facets are considered to be predefined for the user and only have to be used by browsing through the various facets and their values. This way, the user is able to drill down and roll up along certain dimensions – without any special knowledge about the structure of the underlying data. According to Oren (2006), faceted search features the following advantages:

- An unknown dataset can easily be explored by facet navigation.
- Faceted search features a visual interface; therefore the user does not have to actually write queries. The user is able to construct a query by browsing and adding constraints.
- Results are visible immediately and further restrictions are proposed by the system.
- "Dead-end queries" are avoided, the user is only provided with restrictions which still lead to a minimum number of search results.

As for RDF data, such a faceted approach features placing restrictions on predicates as facets and the according objects are used as restriction values. E.g. a facet for the predicate <bornIn> could be used for restricting the value of the place of birth of e.g. persons. The according values for the predicate <bornIn> within the underlying dataset serve as the values upon which the restriction can be placed. The selection of predicates used as facets can either be predefined or computed dynamically if the schema of the underlying dataset is changing frequently.

As another example, (Hahn et al., 2010) propose to use Faceted Search for Wikipedia data in order to be able to answer complex queries. As structured queries like "Which Austrian cities have more than 10.000 inhabitants and are located above 1000m sea level?" can only be answered correctly based on structured knowledge, the authors make use of the Dbpedia dataset (Auer, 2007). The Dbpedia dataset contains structured information which was previously extracted from Wikipedia infoboxes. This data forms the basis for the creation of facets for Wikipedia data which enable the user to narrow down the search results by placing restrictions on the facets. By placing such restrictions, the user is able to easily find information corresponding to such a structured query.

Such an approach for structured data has also been facilitated in BrowseRDF (Oren, 2006). This application supports a variety of operations which are all based on facets and restrict the result set in any given way. The authors essentially propose to support the following operations for facetted search:

- **Basic Selection:** This operation places a simple restriction on the nodes of the underlying graph. E.g. the result set can be restricted to contain all persons who are older than 30 years.
- **Existential Selection:** The basic motivation for this operation is verifying whether a certain property exists or not within the given data set. The system also provides for checking for non-existence of properties, such as retrieving all researches who have not won any prize.
- **Join Selection:** This operation is proposed due to the graph nature of RDF. It basically determines a restriction based on properties of connected nodes, like e.g. "somebody connected to someone via another resource". Such path relations can be determined recursively by this operator and the join can be performed on arbitrary properties along the path.
- **Intersection:** This is the standard way of combining the result set of multiple restrictions within BrowseRDF. This way, more complex constraints like e.g. all people above 30 years who are also married can be placed on the data set.
- **Inverse Selection:** All previously mentioned operations are also provided as inverse operations which allows for formulating queries in the backward direction like <object> <inversePredicate> <subject>, e.g. <NobelPrize> <wonBy> ?person.

Furthermore, the authors propose to use metrics for the ranking of the quality of facet candidates. This approach allows for an automatic detection of facets for any arbitrary RDF dataset. This way, facets do not have to be predefined manually. The authors propose to distinguish two different types

of facets: descriptors and navigators. Descriptors are those facets that describe the data best (e.g. knownAs) while navigators are those facets which enable the users to navigate through the dataset in an optimal way (e.g. category). Determining descriptors basically requires semantic knowledge about the meaning of the specific facets which can hardly be done automatically. In contrast, navigators can be determined efficiently as they should be present in every document and split the search space (e.g. category). The authors propose to represent the navigation through facets as the traversal of a decision tree. Within the decision tree, facets are represented by edges and nodes are values of the corresponding edges. A path within the tree represents the order in which the facets are used for constraining the result set. During each step, new facets for further suitable restrictions are computed dynamically. The order in which the facets are used for constraining the result set is not crucial as facets always are orthogonal and therefore are not dependent on each other in any way. However, using a different order of facets results in a different decision tree as the order of nodes and the respective edges changes. Based on this tree, the quality of facets in regards of their role as navigators is determined for every new step during the traversal of the tree. The computation of this metric is based on the following factors:

- **Predicate Balance:** The more balanced a decision tree is, the more efficient it is. This is due to the fact that the branching within a well-balanced tree is optimal in regards of the decision power within each branch.
- **Object Cardinality:** The number of distinct object values is also crucial for the selection of the predicate as a facet. If there are too many options in terms of different object values, the user might be confused.
- **Predicate Frequency:** The higher the number of occurrences of a certain predicate, the higher is its benefit in terms of

dividing the information space. This is due to the fact that a predicate which is used for many different resources is able to significantly constrain the result set as the restriction is applicable to a huge number of resources.

The combination of these three metrics then results in a ranking of facet candidates. Obviously, the computation of these metrics has to be repeated after every restriction step as the result set gets smaller and more constrained within every step.

Another approach is to exploit the hierarchies within facet in order to be able to use facets together which are not directly related. GFacet (Heim, 2010) is such a faceted search interface which provides the possibility to exploit the hierarchical structure of facets. It basically makes use of hierarchical relationships between facets where the user is able to make restrictions based on all levels of the hierarchy. For example, the user is able to restrict a result set of researchers by specifying the country of birth to Austria. Thereby, the country of birth is reasoned automatically via the hierarchical path "?researcher <bornIn> ?city <locatedIn> ?country". The authors of gFacet propose to use tree visualizations for displaying the hierarchies within all facets. Thus, the user is able to easily navigate through all abstraction levels within the displayed facets.

/facet (Hildebrand, 2006) is a RDFS (Resource Description Framework Schema) browser which provides exploratory and faceted browsing. /facets allows for multi-type facet browsing which basically means that the users are able to define constraints on multiple types of facets which is especially useful when dealing with very heterogeneous data sets. The only prerequisite for the facets of different types is that the types have to be semantically related. The big advantage of this approach is that the user is able to construct complex queries which may also cover different types of resources. In contrast to the BrowseRDF approach, facets within the /facets system are predefined in a configuration file and are not selected dynamically during the search process. Other projects relying on faceted search are mspace (schraefel, 2005), Humboldt (Kobilarov, 2008) and Longwell (Simile project, 2011).

Query Completion

All previously described approaches use keywords to retrieve a most appropriate result set of matching data. A completely different approach is proposed by Tran et al. (2009) which uses keywords to find matching queries rather than matching results. The queries are graphs which characterize the searched data in a descriptive way. As a first step, the user is asked to enter some keywords in the same way as all previously described approaches. In the next step query candidates regarding the entered keywords are computed and proposed to the user. Subsequently, the user can analyse the proposed queries, refine them or just accept a query which is used for the final search process. (refer to Figure 2). The additional step of refining or accepting a proposed query maps the unstructured keywords to a structured search query which takes the data's structure into account and therefore increases the quality of search results. Still the user doesn't need to know anything about the stored data's structure or it's labelling. Consider the example in Figure 3, which shows a computed query based on the input keywords Nobel, Prize and Germany. The query searches for all Nobel Prize winners, who were born in a German city. The variables are marked with a ? and its possible configurations in the graph constitute the final result.

The computation of the appropriate queries is realized using three steps. The first step – Keyword Matching – searches for nodes and attributes in the graph, which match with the specified keywords. The Graph Exploration phase computes paths between the found nodes and spans the query subgraphs as shown in Figure 3. Potentially, the resulting set of possible subgraphs can be very large and cannot be shown to the user in its entirety. Therefore the last step computes the most appropriate queries by using different scoring and ranking methods. The implementation of all three steps and the underlying index techniques are discussed in the following part.

Keyword Matching

The Keyword Matching process takes the keywords entered by the user as input. Subsequently, the keywords are mapped to elements in the graph. As the keywords are not limited in any way, the matching task has to incorporate not only nodes (subjects, objects) but also edges (predicates) in the graph. Therefore the matching process is realized by using a Keyword Index, which conceptually returns all elements in the data graph which match with a given keyword. The keyword index is implemented as an inverted index. Furthermore, the search algorithms have to cope with the problem that the users do not know the exact labelling of the information in the graph. In the area of information retrieval there are many approaches which try to tackle these problems. In the first step a lexical analysis is performed which removes stop words and reduces the search space by stemming the used labels to their stem or base form. Furthermore, labels in the graph which consist of more than one word are split into multiple terms to increase the result set of matching terms. Another severe challenge is constituted by using semantically similar labellings or keywords. It is obvious that in collaborative systems synonyms, homonyms or hypernyms are used very often and therefore impede the search and matching process. This problem can be solved by using a thesaurus, such as WordNet (Fellbaum, 1998), which contains references between semantically similar terms. Thus, the search process is extended to search not only for the entered keywords but also keywords which are semantically related to the entered keywords and are referenced in the thesaurus. In order to incorporate syntactic similarities caused by e.g. typos or failed stemming processes, the

Edit Distance metrics are often used. Tran et al. (2009) uses the very popular Levenshtein distance to find syntactically similar terms during the search process. In many approaches (also Tran et al. 2009) the mature Information Retrieval engine Lucene is used as it provides all important features such as lexicographic analysis or imprecise matching facilities.

Graph Exploration

In the next step, the output of the previous Keyword Matching process is taken as input. The goal of the Graph Exploration process is to find substructures that connect the matching nodes in the graph in a very fast and efficient way. Old approaches used the entire data graph for the exploration task which might be very expensive and time consuming. To decrease the complexity of this task, Tran et al. (2009) introduced the Graph Schema Index which provides an abstract and smaller representation of the original data graph. The final queries, which are proposed to the user, should represent the structure of the graph. Therefore, only the structure / schema of the graph is needed for the graph exploration and the instances can be omitted or aggregated to reduce the size of the graph.

A summary graph G' of the original data graph $G = (N, L, E)$ is defined as $G' = (N', L', E')$ with $N' = N_C \cup \{Thing\}$, $L' = L_R \cup \{subclass\}$ and E' of type $e\ (n_1, n_2)$ with $n_1, n_2 \in N'$ and $e \in L'$. N_C consists of all class nodes, which represent the type and class hierarchy of the data and an universal node Thing. L_R contains all labels, which are used to connect two subject nodes and the label subclass to be able to construct the class hierarchy. Every node $n' \in N_C$ represents an aggregation of all nodes having the type n'', $\llbracket n' \rrbracket := \{n \mid type(n, n'') \in E\}$. The node Thing is used for all nodes which do not have any assigned type in the original data graph. All nodes, edges and labels, which are not used by the given definition, are deleted from the original data graph. The resulting graph after the aggregation and deletion step constitutes the final summary graph which only contains the schema information of the data graph. The grey nodes in Figure 2 constitute an exemplary summary graph in the domain of researchers.

As the graph exploration process aims at finding connections between any nodes (also attributes and values), the summary graph has to be augmented to contain also nodes to which the keywords are mapped to. The summary graph can be computed offline whereas the augmentation has to be done in real time, as only mapped nodes (matching a keyword) are augmented to the summary graph to keep the search space as small as possible. The resulting graph which consists of the schema nodes and the keyword mapped nodes is subsequently explored. Figure 2 shows an augmented graph, where the white boxes represent the matched keyword nodes (from the keyword query "Nobel Prize Germany") which augment the grey summary graph. The problem of finding substructures respectively connections is a very common problem in the research area of data-

bases, XML and trees and therefore influences the approaches to find substructures in graph data (Bhalotia et al, 2002; He et al, 2007; Kacholia et al., 2005). The exploration task in Tran et al. (2009) starts with a set of keyword elements and subsequently decides which next exploration step in the graph would be the "cheapest" one regarding the costs (see Scoring below) of this step. This procedure of exploration is repeated until the maximal defined depth is reached, a connection is found or the current path is too "expensive" to be in final result of top-k paths (see Scoring below). An exemplary resulting structured query, which was computed by the given keywords "Nobel Prize Germany" and the summary graph in Figure 2 is shown in Figure 3.

Scoring

The computation of appropriate queries can result in a very large result set of queries which cannot entirely be shown to the user. Therefore, only the Top-k queries regarding the entered keywords are presented to the user. To compute the Top-k queries, a scoring of each computed query is required to perform a ranking on the result list.

Figure 2. Augmented summary graph

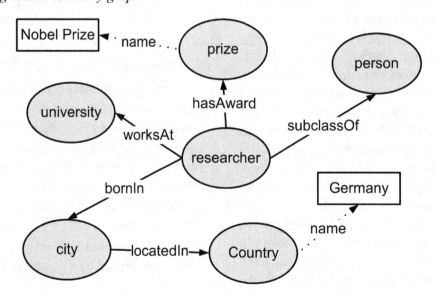

Common metrics in the research field of graphs are the PageRank algorithm to compute the scoring of nodes in the graph. The shortest distance is often used to score paths in the graph. Both metrics can be computed in advance and can be reused during the search process. The TF/IDF can be used as a score regarding the entered keywords and therefore has to be computed on-the-fly.

These scoring techniques are also used in an adapted way in Tran et al. (2009). They propose a cost function to score each appropriate query respectively subgraph. The cost function C is defined as the sum of the costs of all paths P in the subgraph G, $C_G = \sum_{p_i \in P} C_{p_i}$. C_{p_i} denotes the costs of each path p_i and is defined by $C_{p_i} = \sum_{n \in p_i} c(n)$. Depending on the metric, $c(n)$ denotes the score of one subpart of the path of the respective query. Tran et al. (2009) uses the metrics Path Length, Popularity Score and Keyword Matching Score. The metric Path Length is implemented by just counting the node jumps between two keyword matching nodes. The Popularity Score takes the number of aggregations of the summary graph into account. The higher the popularity value, the more nodes have been aggregated to the current node. If a summary node represents many nodes of the original data graph, the costs of this node are lower. This metric is very similar to the PageRank algorithm but can

be computed much faster. The Keyword Matching Score incorporate the syntactic and semantic similarity between the matched node and the entered keyword. The higher the matching score respectively the higher the similarity, the lower should be the contribution to the cost. The evaluations in Tran et al. (2009) showed that the incorporation of the Keyword Matching Score leads to the best suitable results in all test settings.

The global cost, which is gathered from all costs of paths of a subgraph and its subpaths, can subsequently be used to rank the final result set of queries. In the approach of Tran et al. (2009), the task of scoring is merged with the graph exploration task as both processes are operating on the augmented summary graph. Furthermore, the exploration task can omit paths if the scoring is computed on-the-fly after every step during the exploration phase. These measures can increase the performance which is also shown in the evaluation part in Tran et al. (2009).

Conclusion

The previously approaches all provide an agnostic search interface which uses keyword search as an entry point. Keyword search is used as it provides simple means for the specification of the context of further querying steps – even without knowing anything about the underlying structure of data.

Figure 3. Structured query

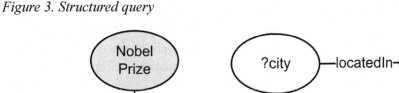

Additional computations such as the hierarchical reasoning and the choice of restricting facets propose the user possibilities to refine the result set based on the specified keywords. Most approaches also provide browsing facilities to explore the result set in the most natural way. The last discussed approach computes appropriate structured queries based on the user's specified keywords and the structure of data. These queries are ranked by various metrics and can further be refined by the user. All approaches are able to satisfy the user's information needs and provide a very simple but powerful search interface, although, they are limited when considering heterogeneous schemata. For example the problem of subjects which are described by synonyms like <birthday> and <dateOfBirth> is still present. An approach, which tackles this problem already during the creation of content by exploiting the human knowledge of the inserting user about synonyms, is described in the next section.

AVOIDING SCHEMA HETEROGENEITY DURING INSERTION TIME

Another approach of dealing with structure heterogeneity is directly related to the process of storing information in a collaborative, semistructured information system. The previously described approaches all are aimed at the correct computation of query results despite a very heterogeneous schema within the underlying data.

In contrast, the Snoopy approach (Gassler, 2010) aims at creating a homogeneous schema already during the insertion process. Therefore, the querying facilities are able to fully exploit the homogeneous schema and provide the users of the system with the best possible search results independent of the used query engine. Furthermore, the proposed approach also aims at "snooping" more information from the user. This "snooping" process increases the quality and quantity of stored information as it encourages the user to enter more information and refine and enrich the information in the system.

Basically, the Snoopy approach allows users to enter information grouped into a so-called collection. A collection is concerned with one subject, e.g. Albert Einstein. On each subject, the user is able to enter an arbitrary amount of key-value pairs which are concerned with this subject. This combination of subject, key and value forms triples similar to RDF triples, like e.g. <Albert Einstein> <dateOfBirth> <1897/14/03>. The semistructured paradigm allows users to arbitrarily choose the names of subject, key and value. Such a modelling of information as semistructured data still features structure without restricting the schema. To cope with the problem of heterogeneity within semistructured data, the Snoopy approach aims at guiding the user already during the insertion process in order to avoid heterogeneous schemata within the system. The guidance is based on recommendations which suggest tiny adaptions on the inserting information or appropriate keys which conform to a common, dynamically computed homogeneous schema in the system.

Recommendations

Recommender Systems (Resnick, 1997) are traditionally used within online shops. The computed recommendations are used to provide the users of the shop with suggestions of additional items the customer might be interested in. Also, recommender systems are used for the recommendation of movies for the users of a movie database.

Such recommendations are computed based on all previously stored data about the items available and the customers of the system. The recommender system aims at detecting items similar to previously purchased items. These similar items are then recommended to the customer. A second approach is based on the detection of customers with a similar profile as the current customer. The items these similar customers bought are then recommended to the user.

Computation of Recommendations within the Snoopy System

Within the Snoopy approach, recommendations are used for the creation of a homogeneous schema already during the insertion of data. Essentially, the user is provided with various recommendations, which are concerned with:

- Structure/Schema
- Avoidance of Synonyms
- Semantic Refinement of the Entered Information

The computation of the recommendations is based on all information which has been stored within the system previously. Therefore, the Snoopy approach does not rely on any predefined schema, configurations or external sources, which are domain specific. The different types of recommendations used within the Snoopy systems are described in detail within the next section.

Structure Recommendations

Structure recommendations are the main type of recommendations within the Snoopy system which contribute to a common schema. These recommendations are mainly focused on suggesting further suitable keys to the user during the insertion of data. Consider the example of a user entering information about Albert Einstein. The user already entered the following information:

<Albert_Einstein> <dateOfBirth> <1897/03/14>
<Albert_Einstein> <placeOfBirth> <Ulm>

Based on this information, the system is able to deduce appropriate keys which occur in collections with a similar structure and recommends this set of keys to the user. Suppose that many

other users, who have also entered information about a person, used the keys <dateOfBirth> and <placeOfBirth> and additionally specified the date of death and the awards won by this specific person. This information leads to a recommendation of <dateOfDeath> and <award> to the user who is just entering information about Albert Einstein. To contribute to a common structure, an additional ranking algorithm is proposed by the authors, which ranks the recommendation candidates according to their popularity and suitability for the currently entered information. All these computations are always performed on-the-fly as with every new key-value pair the user enters, the recommended keys are refined. The algorithm to compute recommendations takes all previously entered keys and values of any user into account. Therefore, the computed schemata are based on the wisdom of the crowds as all users are considered and the common schemata are created in a democratic way. This fact allows the system to react to changes immediately in terms of the adaption of the recommended keys. If there arises a new and important key, such as the CO_2 emission of cars, which was not relevant a few years ago, the key is immediately recommended to other users during the insertion. This exploitation of the already stored information enables the system to be used in any arbitrarily domain or even large collaborative systems which deal with a huge amount of different domains. The system adapts itself to the stored information respectively to its users.

Besides the guidance to a commonly used schema, the recommendations constitute another big advantage. The user is pointed to missing bits of information, which has already been entered by other users on similar collections. Consider the example of Albert Einstein and the recommended key <award>. Maybe the user did not plan to insert information about Albert Einstein's awards or simply did not think about it. In most cases, considering e.g. the users of Wikipedia, the users are experts in the domain of their created collections. Therefore, the suggested key is often sufficient to encourage the user to enter the additional information and increase the amount of information in the system (Gassler, 2011).

Avoidance of Synonyms

Synonyms are a crucial factor for the proliferation of schemata. Consider the example of the keys <dateOfBirth> and <birthdate>. These two keys are semantically equivalent, however they differ syntactically. If users are entering information based on these two keys, the schema within the system suffers from proliferation as more different keys are used. In many cases, the usage of synonyms can be already avoided by the structural recommendations as described above. Consider a user who plans to insert information about the birthday and wants to use the key <birthday>. If the key <dateOfBirth> is suggested at an early stage, the user can simply accept the recommendation and might not even get to the point to insert the synonymous keyword <birthday>.

Furthermore the user is provided with an intelligent auto-completion feature, which recommends suitable keys during typing. Besides the usual suggestion of completed terms which are already present in the system, the suggestions also consist of semantically equivalent keys which are syntactically different. In the previously mentioned example, a user who just entered <birthdate> would be provided with a recommendation for the synonym <dateOfBirth> which has been used by the majority of other users. Besides synonymous keys, also synonymous values can infer the search capabilities of an information system. Consider the example of a structured query, which searches for all persons with a Swiss citizenship, which basically is a query searching for subjects featuring the key-value pair <citizenship> <Swiss>. All persons in the system which are described by the key-value pair <citizenship> <Switzerland> are not contained in the result set due to the use of

the synonyms Swiss and Switzerland. To avoid such cases, users are provided with recommendations of exemplary values for the given keys. The specification of the key <citizenship> results in the recommendation of possible values, such as Australia, Austria, etc., which are present in the system. Therefore, dead-end queries which lead to an empty result set are prevented. The same intelligent auto-completion feature as described above is also used for the recommendation of values and reduces the usage of synonyms in the system. The recommendation of synonyms, which should be preferred as they are used more often in the system, is realized by using an external thesaurus, such as WordNet (Fellbaum, 1998). Such an approach features the advantage that the recommendations based on a thesaurus are additionally verified by a human user and therefore semantically incorrect mappings can be eliminated. This way, synonyms can be avoided and a further proliferation of the schema and values can be prevented. Still the user is free to ignore the recommendation and insist on the originally entered information.

Semantic Enrichment of the Entered Information

Another important pillar of the Snoopy concept is the semantic enrichment of data which is essential for its semantic correctness. The semantic enrichment of entered information is mainly concerned with the entered values in collections. The simplest enrichment - which is done semiautomatically - is the determination of the data type of each newly entered value, e.g. the value for the key <dateOfBirth> is asserted to be a date value. Vice versa, if a key is added that already exists, has a data type assigned and is used by the majority of key instances, the user is advised to enter values according to the data type. The detection of data types is very important as it is crucial for range queries, such as "Find all persons who were born between 1800 and 1900". Furthermore, the data type of a value can lead to a special behaviour of the user interface, such as a date picker, calendar views, audio playback or editing features, a content-based image search or even a slider for integer values.

The system additionally suggests linking entered values to already existing subjects. This way, the semantic correctness of homonyms can be dealt with. Consider a user who enters information about Freiburg, the twin city of the city of Innsbruck. Semantically, this information is not precise as it is not clear whether this information is concerned with the city Freiburg in Germany or Freiburg in Switzerland. By suggesting the user to link the value "Freiburg" to one of the already existent collections "Freiburg, Germany" or "Freiburg, Switzerland", this semantic disambiguation can easily be resolved.

The Snoopy approach has been implemented within a prototypical implementation called SnoopyDB. A screenshot of the prototype can be seen in Figure 4. In this example, information about the University of Innsbruck is entered. The user already entered information about the foundation of the university, the number of professors employed at the university and the URL of the website address. The three further lines in light grey are structure recommendations. The screenshot also shows how exemplary values are shown for each of the additional recommended keys. Further recommendations of additional appropriate keys are shown in the box on the right. Information about the implementation details of the recommendation algorithm can be found in Zangerle et al. (2010).

Conclusion

The Snoopy approach aims at avoiding heterogeneity in collaborative semistructured information systems by guiding the user during the insertion process to commonly used schemata. This is realized by different recommendations which suggest the user appropriate keys, which are often used in the system in the respective semantically context and avoid the usage of synonyms. Furthermore, the extensive knowledge of the user about the data is exploited by encouraging the user to insert more information and specify further semantic enrichments, such as data types or interlinking. However, the user is not forced to accept any recommendations or align its information to any schema. Gassler et al. (2011) showed in their evaluations that the Snoopy approach increases the amount of information while at the same time

Figure 4. Screenshot of the SnoopyDB prototype

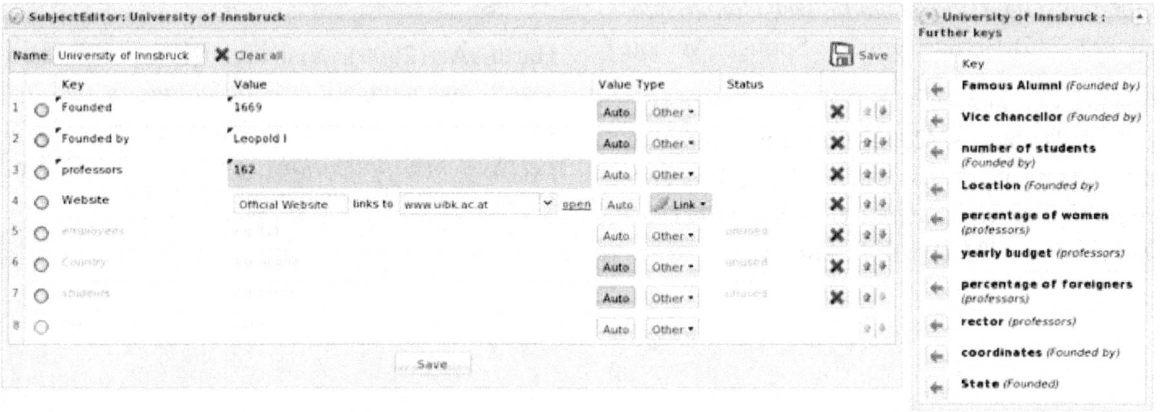

the recommendations contribute to much more homogenous structure in the evaluated test system.

CONCLUSION

In this chapter we showed that collaborative, semistructured information systems are confronted with the problem of structure heterogeneity within the stored data. Such heterogeneity can seriously influence the querying capabilities of the system. We showed two different approaches which are able to deal with this problem within collaborative, semistructured information systems. The first type is the adaption of querying facilities to the heterogeneous nature of the stored data. Therefore, we showed how keyword search, faceted search and query completion are able to deal with heterogeneous. In contrast, the second approach is focused on the creation of a homogeneous schema within the system by providing the users with useful and suitable recommendations which contribute to a homogeneous schema and encourage the user to insert more information and enrich it semantically.

REFERENCES

Auer, S., Bizer, C., Kobilarov, G., Lehmann, J., Cyganiak, R., & Ives, Z. (2007). Dbpedia: A nucleus for a web of open data. *Proceedings of the 6th International The Semantic Web and 2nd Asian Conference on Asian Semantic Web Conference*, (pp. 722–735). Berlin, Germany: Springer-Verlag.

Bhalotia, G., Hulgeri, A., Nakhe, C., Chakrabarti, S., & Sudarshan, S. (2002). Keyword searching and browsing in databases using banks. *Proceedings of the 18th International Conference on Data Engineering 2002*, (pp. 431–440).

Cheng, G., & Qu, Y. (2009). Searching linked objects with falcons: Approach, implementation and evaluation. *International Journal on Semantic Web and Information Systems*, 5(3), 49–70. doi:10.4018/jswis.2009081903

Fellbaum, C. (Ed.). (1998). *WordNet: An electronic lexical database*. Cambridge, MA: The MIT Press.

Furnas, G., Landauer, T., Gomez, L., & Dumais, S. (1987). The vocabulary problem in human-system communication. *Communications of the ACM, 30*(11), 964–971. doi:10.1145/32206.32212

Gassler, W., Zangerle, E., & Specht, G. (2011). The snoopy concept: Fighting heterogeneity in semistructured and collaborative information systems by using recommendations. *Proceedings of the 2011 International Conference on Collaboration Technologies and Systems (CTS 2011)*, Philadelphia, PE.

Gassler, W., Zangerle, E., Tschuggnall, M., & Specht, G. (2010). SnoopyDB: Narrowing the gap between structured and unstructured information using recommendations. In M. H. Chignell & E. Toms (Ed.), *Proceedings of the 21st ACM Conference on Hypertext and Hypermedia 2010*, (pp. 271–272).

Hahn, R., Bizer, C., Sahnwaldt, C., Herta, C., Robinson, S., Bürgle, M., & Scheel, U. (2010). *Faceted Wikipedia search. Business Information Systems* (pp. 1–11). Berlin, Germany: Springer-Verlag.

Harth, A. (2009). VisiNav: Visual Web data search and navigation. *Proceedings of the 20th International Conference on Databases and Expert Systems Applications*, (pp. 214–228). Berlin, Germany: Springer-Verlag.

Harth, A., Hogan, A., Delbru, R., Umbrich, J., ORiain, S., & Decker, S. (2007). SWSE: Answers before links. *Proceedings of Semantic Web Challenge 2007.*

He, H., Wang, H., Yang, J., & Yu, P. S. (2007). Blinks: Ranked keyword searches on graphs. *Proceedings of the 2007 ACM SIGMOD International Conference on Management of Data,* (pp. 305–316). New York, NY: Springer-Verlag.

Heim, P., Ertl, T., & Ziegler, J. (2010). Facet graphs: Complex semantic querying made easy. In Aroyo, L. (Eds.), *The Semantic Web: Research and applications, LNCS 6088* (pp. 288–302). Berlin, Germany: Springer-Verlag. doi:10.1007/978-3-642-13486-9_20

Hildebrand, M., van Ossenbruggen, J., & Hardman, L. (2006). Facet: A browser for heterogeneous Semantic Web repositories. *The Semantic Web-ISWC, 2006,* 272–285. doi:10.1007/11926078_20

Kacholia, V., Pandit, S., Chakrabarti, S., Sudarshan, R. D., & Karambelkar, D. (2005). Bidirectional expansion for keyword search on graph databases. *Proceedings of the 31ˢᵗ International Conference on Very Large Databases 2005,* (pp. 505–516). Trondheim, Norway: VLDB Endowment.

Kobilarov, G., & Dickinson, I. (2008). *Humboldt: Exploring linked data.* Linked Data on the Web Workshop (LDOW 2008), Beijing, China.

Oren, E., Delbru, R., & Decker, S. (2006). Extending faceted navigation for RDF data. In Cruz, I. (Eds.), *The Semantic Web - ISWC 2006, LNCS 4273* (pp. 559–572). Berlin, Germany: Springer-Verlag. doi:10.1007/11926078_40

Resnick, P., & Varian, H. (1997). Recommender systems. *Communications of the ACM, 40*(3), 58. doi:10.1145/245108.245121

Schraefel, M. C., Smith, D., Owens, A., Russell, A., Harris, C., & Wilson, M. (2005). The evolving mSpace platform: Leveraging the Semantic Web on the trail of the Memex. *Proceedings of the ACM Hypertext Conference,* (pp. 174–218). New York, NY: ACM.

Simile Project. (2011). *Longwell website.* Retrieved February 24, 2011, from http://simile.mit.edu /wiki/Longwell

Tran, D. T., Wang, H., Rudolph, S., & Cimiano, P. (2009). Top-k exploration of query candidates for efficient keyword search on graph-shaped (RDF) data. *Proceedings of the 25th International Conference on Data Engineering 2009,* Shanghai, China.

Tummarello, G., Delbru, R., & Oren, E. (2007). Sindice.com: Weaving the open linked data. *Proceedings of the 6th International The Semantic Web and 2nd Asian Conference on Asian Semantic Web Conference,* (pp. 552–565). Berlin, Germany: Springer-Verlag.

Weikum, G., Kasneci, G., Ramanath, M., & Suchanek, F. (2009). Database and information-retrieval methods for knowledge discovery. *Communications of the ACM, 52*(4), 56–64. doi:10.1145/1498765.1498784

Wu, F., & Weld, D. (2007). Autonomously semantifying Wikipedia. *Proceedings of the Sixteenth ACM Conference on Conference on Information and Knowledge Management,* (pp. 41–50). New York, NY: ACM.

Zangerle, E., Gassler, W., & Specht, G. (2010). Recommending structure in collaborative semi-structured information systems. *Proceedings of the Fourth ACM Conference on Recommender Systems,* (pp. 261–264). New York, NY: ACM.

ADDITIONAL READING

Elliott, A., Hearst, M., English, J., Sinha, R., Swearingen, K., & Yee, K. (2002). Finding the flow in website search. *Communications of the ACM, 45*(9), 42–49.

Hearst, M. (2008). UIS for faceted navigation: Recent advances and remaining open problems. *Proceedings of the 2008 Workshop on Human-Computer Interaction and Information Retrieval,* (pp. 13-17).

Ricci, F., Rokach, L., Shapira, B., & Kantor, P. B. (Eds.). (2011). *Recommender systems handbook*. Berlin, Germany: Springer-Verlag. doi:10.1007/978-0-387-85820-3

Chapter 2
Collaborative Mediation:
How the Power of Collaboration in Social Computing Demands Greater Thought Diversity

Brian D. Goodman
IBM Corporation, USA

ABSTRACT

Individuals are the generators and consumers of content, and in doing so, make up a substantial presence in the literate internet, above and beyond the formal media outlets that make up the minority. Accelerating the explosion of content are Web 2.0 interactions, where participants are encouraged to engage with primary content. These social spaces are a platform, supporting often-overlooked micro-interactions referred to in this chapter as digital fingerprints. In parallel, companies construct web experiences that uniquely deliver Internet inspired experiences. However, the competition that divides popular Internet destinations is absent in well run intranets. Collaboration and cooperation among internal web properties offer a unique opportunity to organize people and information across disparate experiences. An example of such a solution is IBM's Enterprise Tagging System, a collaborative classification and recommendation service that knits employee identities and destinations together through fingerprints. The benefit of creating such a common service also exhibits the side effect and power of the relative few participants. It introduces the desperate need to consider how actions and relationships affect user experiences. The success of social systems requires a high level of diverse participation. This diversity is what ensures the mediation and influence of co-creation and collaborative filtering is not overly narrow.

DOI: 10.4018/978-1-4666-0894-8.ch002

INTRODUCTION

People residing and employed in an Internet connected country having awareness to MySpace, YouTube, Facebook and Flickr experience a duality of their personal versus business persona. With the growing and changing generations, those identities are often blurred where the appropriateness of content cross networks unintentionally but often with some consequence. (Horowitz, 2006; Morello et al., 2006; de Zengotita, 2004; Florida, 2002; Howe et al., 2000) Individuals leverage these social spaces to create, share and manage content about themselves, their family and their friends. Increasingly, they have similar technology counterparts in their workplace. As they engage with the wide variety of primarily web-based social spaces, they rate, tag and comment on these assets, leaving digital fingerprints – "not only was I here, but I have something to contribute!" The attitude that what any individual thinks is worthy of persisting, in of itself, raises the volume of everyone's voice. Participants are the generators and consumers of content and in doing so make up a substantial presence in the literate internet, above and beyond the formal media outlets that make up the minority.

Casual compilation of statistics from 2009 shows MySpace touting 130 million unique users monthly, making it one of the giant profiling information sharing sites. (Stelter, 2009) Consider that Facebook in the same year, a competitor to MySpace, attracts 222 million unique users monthly contributing over 28 million photos per day, larger than social spaces focusing on photo sharing such as Flickr. (Facebook, 2009) Delicious, a social book marking site has at least 53 million posts covering 25 million URLs tagged with approximately 125 million tags. (Keller, 2007) Technorati, a blog-tracking site, monitors over 110 million blogs and over 250 million pieces of tagged social media. (Technorati, 2007) While current statistics as recent as 2010 show

fluctuations in active users and traffic, overall the amount of content and places to create content has only increased.

Several offerings introduced and created by IBM's Technology and Innovation team correlate with external social experiences, specifically around wikis, blogs, media sharing and profiling. The Company's wiki platform has over 360,000 employees participating in 26,000 wikis, managing over 500,000 pages. IBM's internal media library has serviced over 6.7 million downloads in its first 18 months, by 200,000 employees contributing over 29,000 pieces of media. Adoption is rampant although these services are not supported directly by the corporate IT function, rather nurtured and matured through IBM's Technology Adoption Program. (Chow et al., 2007; Orlov, 2005)

The Digg community, a network of internet users who vote for what is hot, is 56% controlled by 100 of the users. (Saleem, 2007; Seomoz, 2006) Wikipedia contains millions of articles that match or rival traditional encyclopedic references and yet 50% of the content is created by 2.5% of the users. (Horowitz, 2006) Social offerings within IBM reflect similar ratios of a contributor to a beneficiary. The active participant has a disproportionate impact on the community in a variety of ways. We have a confluence of massive content generation, critical core communities and the digital fingerprints that a wider number of users generates.

Social spaces are the platform where people leave digital fingerprints, sharing who they are and what they are interested in experiencing. Content creation is extended beyond traditional digital media (i.e. blogs, wikis and forums) to include social and interaction fragments (i.e. rating, tagging and commenting). Each of these interactions creates relationships between people, activities and content. In a world of increasingly virtual interactions (including activities in 3D worlds) in an ever-increasing fragmentation of spaces, how might define, interchange, harvest, connect and open up, these collaborative digital fingerprints to improve social spaces by surfacing collective wisdom?

This chapter will establish a common lexicon around social spaces as a platform, supporting the often-overlooked micro-interactions that follow. Digital fingerprints will be defined, introducing a new way of thinking about collaborative content creation. It will highlight one technology, IBM's Enterprise Tagging Service that addresses the fundamental problems of the proliferation of siloed experiences, describing the high-level approach and end-to-end experience of interaction to fingerprint to self-mediated experience. Finally, we will posit the future work required to knit the digital self together.

COLLABORATION LOOSELY JOINED: SOCIAL SPACES AS A PLATFORM

What once began as a hypertext platform, the web has evolved to house not only the content people seek, but the applications they use. The web became a platform the minute JavaScript and XML HTTP Request allowed web developers to construct experiences that felt more like the desktop applications they knew so well. (Raman, 2009) The biggest difference was that the rich level of interaction was in the context of content and services, not yet another application with its own conventions. This richer experience is a portion of what people have come to refer to as Web 2.0, but it does not stop there. (O'Reilly, 2005) In addition to single context experience – web sites that deliver content and updates without navigating away from the current URL – community interaction broke out. Commenting, sharing, tagging and rating are only some of the aspects that turned the reader into a participant. While the Internet has always been filled with discussion forums and instant messaging, this new level of micro-participation

spawned an era of social computing. Suddenly, using the web as a platform, developers could deliver lightweight interactions alongside their content. Viewers became participants and participants communities. Social spaces are platforms that focus on enabling individuals to interact with content and people in new ways, often generating original web content in the process adding to the exponentially growing web.

Collaboration is often thought of as the process by which two or more individuals work toward one or more common goals. People share, learn and create new artifacts that intend to resolve to at least in part, a shared end goal. There is an intention presumed in the definition of collaboration, where in all parties are engaging directly. The Internet affords a full spectrum of interaction, from real-time video chat to the more passive reading of content. In the latter, there is still an exchange, but the author is little aware of who and how much they have spoken to. The web enables one to many communications effortlessly and this more passive collaboration is at the heart of what is making systems smarter and people more connected. We are becoming socially networked because the technology we use is enabling us to connect in ways that appeal to all of our personas and the implicit communities our interactions create.

The basis for collaboration is cooperation, intent to find common ground motivating us to work together. We often think of our online interactions being synchronous (i.e. instant messaging or screen sharing) or asynchronous (i.e. email or document editing). More recent applications such as Flickr, an online photo sharing site, blur the lines with synchronous and asynchronous bringing together so many people that the actions of many independent, loosely joined participants leave feeling the spaces they occupy are evolving in real-time, which they are! Applications such as Facebook have recently included a site wide awareness component, letting users know who else they know is on the site with them. It takes the massive contributions of many and technologies to knit them together to make what is literally an asynchronous activity and transforms it into a reality that feels very intimate despite the distances. Social spaces, in particular, are platforms for a specific kind of asynchronous collaboration. It occurs as participants engage with the space, leaving digital fingerprints. These spaces, in particular, are able to facilitate a social web between people, content and other people.

DIGITAL FINGERPRINTS

Graduated levels of participation engage a broader audience. If the primary goal of a web application is to share content, then allowing account holders to comment only on that content is a way of keeping individuals engaged without requiring them to be a part of the core activity. Engaging a community is one of the most critical aspects of creating a healthy organic online experience and providing relatively simple avenues to participate allows for broader inclusion. Digital fingerprints represent micro-events supporting a primary "hand print" activity.

Flickr is a popular site for sharing photographs. The primary activity is to enable a user to share their photos with family, friends and the rest of the web-connected world easily. This is the "hand print" activity. Participating in the primary activity is a first-degree relationship to the participant. Photos are posted with titles, descriptions and other metadata. This content is associated directly and describes something about the individual.

Activities such as rating, favorite-ing, commenting, tagging, sharing or recommending a product create smaller associations to occur. Flickr allows viewers of images to connect with images they appreciate in a variety of micro-event ways. For example, a participant may choose to mark a photo as a favorite, allowing them to keep track of imagery they have enjoyed in the past. Users are able to comment directly on a photograph to annotate a shared event or simply offer praise. These events create a triple connection between the person sharing the content, the content and the observer. Fingerprints are smaller and come in higher volumes. By reducing the barrier of entry for participation, not only are sites encouraging more engagement, they are automatically increasing the number of events taking place. Smaller events are just as important as large events, especially if the goal is to make sense of all the data as a collaborative view that enriches everyone's experience.

In Figure 1, the fingerprints describe four key views: the first person, the content, the second person and in the aggregate, the community. The second person is the obvious relationship to draw upon. This is the individual that is commenting on the photograph. They are literally leaving a mark on the first person's contribution. This action describes that they are now related, however superficially, to the content and the first person, the contributor. The next obvious connection is the content, which is directly being annotated. If the second person, the observer, marked the image as a favorite, they are establishing that this photograph among all other photographs is worth remark. The third annotation is that of the first user, the one sharing. The two individuals may not know each other, but once the second interacts with the work of the first, a relationship is created. It is possible to understand the first person by understanding the people they attract. Finally, there is a powerful insight derived by reviewing activity in aggregate – the community. By looking at micro-events in the aggregate, we get the fingerprint of the community. For example, several hundred people are engaging in the same photographs of buildings in New York City. This example also illustrated that the larger community can easily be subdivided into smaller communities. Understanding communities finally helps describe the individuals and the associated content. Taken together, fingerprints establish metadata that allows people and systems to so some very special things. Fingerprints can be thought

Figure 1. Examples of graduated levels of collaboration and participation

of in six ways: as a collaboration activity, as an expression of interest, as connective tissue, as a community builder, as organizing content and as a filter of information.

Collaborating with People and Information

Many of the web applications associated with Web 2.0 fame leverage the "wisdom of crowds." (Fuxman et al., 2008; Weiss 2005) Sites such as Digg or Delicious require the participation of a core few to help drive the content they present to the larger audience. (Saleem, 2007; Horowitz, 2006) For example, Digg allows participants to express appreciation for content found in other online spaces. A user submits the URL to the content often through clicking a button encourag-

ing people to "dig it." The site then keeps track of the content and displays the totals and ranking to the larger audience. If you want to see what is currently hot on the net, Digg is one place to go. The appeal here is that the "newspaper" at Digg is driven by the populous, not an editorial board. People trust the recommendations that come from "friends" over those of formal experts or systems. (Sundar et al., 2008) In this example, the collaboration of many, while relatively few, is driving the construction of web importance. The publication reflects the community's interests.

Delicious is a social book marking site that allows individuals to keep track of sites and content that they find on the Internet. Users are able to bookmark from the context of their browser, editing the title, adding a description and most importantly classifying using tags. Tags are keywords that help describe something. They are an informal taxonomy, often referred to as a folksonomy. While community generated categorizations lack the hierarchy associated with formal taxonomies, fingerprints are a critical social collaborative artifact. As individuals bookmark and tag the same resources a web is created between people, the resource and the associated words. The more people bookmark an item, the more important it becomes. Furthermore, the more the same tags are applied to the item, the more definitively users and the system understand what is important about the item. For example, if a URL has been bookmarked one hundred times it has more perceived value. Additionally, the top tags associated across all the bookmark activities tell users and the system the major keywords associated. Research has been done around using tags as quality indicators, so the repeated action of many is a basis for inferring rank. (Lee et al., 2008) Understanding the collaborative behavior of the community allows the system to recommend additional content intelligently that may be of interest. The recommendation is generated based on the collaboration with all. Consider work from Krishnan et al. that looked into who predicts better, humans and an online recommendation system. While collaborative filtering algorithms outperform humans on average, humans on average outperform systems on specific tasks. (Krishnan et al., 2008) Some users were notably better than the system. Either way to review these findings, collaborative filtering is powerful.

Expressing Interest

In general, most people are browsers, or lurkers on the Internet. The majority of people are looking and reading. As Web 2.0 sites introduced additional levels of participation a shift towards a more collaborative web began. There is more content than is possible to consume, and so it will remain, most people are reading, not collaborating. When someone does participate, the relationship triple is

a precious indicator of interest. A prior example reviewed the ability for a user to mark a photograph as a favorite. This is an explicit indicator of interest, however, commenting, tagging rating are all expressions connecting individuals with content. Given all the content that could garner interaction, the ones that actually do, reflect the interest of the community. While systems may never truly understand what is so interesting about a given item, they do know the individuals and their interest levels. In the aggregate, systems are able to understand users, items and how interesting either is. Fingerprints are expressions of interest.

Connecting People and Information

Prior examples discuss the power of the relationships created through interactions. The side affect of these interactions are connections between people because of information. For example, in the Flickr examples, people are interacting with photographs contributed by other individuals. They likely do not know the person. While commenting on a photograph establishes a first tier connection to the image, a second tier relationship is captured between the individuals. Sites like Flickr have ways of making this connection explicit where users can keep track of others. This capability is often couched with words like "follow" (as in to follow) or "friend." Web 2.0 applications build communities not simply facilitate the collaboration around content. Fingerprints connect people and information.

Creating ad hoc Communities

Organizations are formal expressions of communities. They often have a leadership team and a membership base. They have mission statements and sponsor activities. Organizations are sometimes made up of smaller communities called teams. These teams range in size, but often express different aspects of the larger community. Communities are the foundation of collaboration.

Introducing multiple avenues for members to participate, communities facilitate higher levels of engagement. These micro-events establish connections among people and information. In the aggregate, communities are formed that may not have the formality of traditional communities, but are no less important. For example, the fury of bookmarking on Delicious around wedding content likely increases in the spring, when many choose to wed. The implicit community is wedding related. Within that, there are other communities, such as individuals that do not want a white dress, or people considering wedding venues. These are all ad hoc groups with no formal organization. Systems often simply allow the navigation of content via tags. Other systems, such as Flickr, offer exploration of "clusters." (Flickr, 2009) The system leverages the tagged data, but then attempts to display collections of photographs based on metadata relation. Images that share common tags are closer than those that share none. In this example, communities are being formed through content. One could just as easily imagine a view that showed related people. Fingerprints create ad hoc communities, facilitating loosely connected serendipitous collaboration.

Organizing People and Content

A few collaborative activities help organize content. When participants rate or tag, they are adding metadata that overlays organization. Amazon is a powerhouse of five star ratings, where customers rate the products for sale. (Sundar, 2008) Amazon displays the average rating associated with an item and the rating entered for each buyer. These ratings can drive confidence in the merchant and the item for sale. They also provide queues as to what buyers like. Many users leverage this attribute as a method for sorting a collection of potential items. A buyer might search for inkjet printers and then sort by most highly rated. Amazon uses an individual's rating of items as a method for organizing which items of interest to display.

Tagging is a more obvious method of organizing content. Users are asked to add keywords that they associated with a given item. The words applied most and by many drive classification and confidence around the content. There is also a powerful element of findability embedded in tagging. Because it is a social and collaborative activity using language that is natural to the community, finding content is eased. Specifically, a user might describe a book differently as technical and business. Users sharing the same ad hoc community attributes will use similar language to find that book. Tags also allow differences among communities to surface the same items. For example, technical professionals often use different words to describe the same things when compared to business professionals. Each imparts a valid and accurate lexicon, and each is accessible to their specific audience. Some fingerprints help organize people and content (see Figure 2).

Filtering Socially Collaborative Information

Social artifacts are created from collaborative interactions with information. Emphasis is often placed on the connections created between people and content. In the prior examples around tagging, one user is tagging content submitted by a second user. Other web experiences have people tagging people. (Guy et al., 2008) These micro-events create connections, but also enable a graduated level of content filtering. The Amazon five star rating example illustrated how collaborative rating is used to filter search results. In the example of Delicious, users can browse through links by tag, filtering results that have the same keyword. Flickr provides an alternative view of browsing images by tag cluster. (Flickr, 2009) Each of these is an obvious notion of collaborative filtering. Consider the overlay of other fingerprints from individuals and their communities and how those can be a filter for information. Digg provides an overt expression of what the community thinks is

Figure 2. The relationship between people, things, and tags

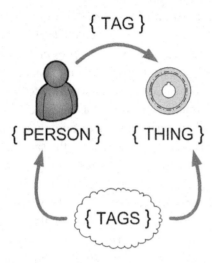

interesting. If tags, ratings and comments indicate items of interest related to an individual, and those relationships between information and people create ad hoc communities, then together content that matches or is of interest to those communities is likely to be of interest to the individual. Fingerprints are also used as collaborative filters of people and information.

COMMON COLLABORATIVE TAGGING WITH AN ENTERPRISE TAGGING SERVICE

Collaborative social tagging has become a prevalent model for marking content for collection, retrieval and classification – moving the focus from the ivory tower to the individuals that know best. In 2007, IBM fundamentally changed the nature of intranet search, applying one of their latest innovations, an enterprise wide collaborative social tagging system to influence how people track, classify and discover information and colleagues. (CXO Media Inc., 2008)

Searching an intranet is a radically different challenge and the expectations created by internet search engines compound people's frustrations. When was the last time you found what you were looking for inside your enterprise? Most search engines rely upon a variety of techniques where the number of links to a given website determines a page's importance. (Brin et al., 1998) However, intranet searches are often reduced to keyword and concept matching, forcing people to learn search techniques. IBM's Enterprise Tagging Service (ETS) changes this model completely, enabling people to collaboratively associate words that describe the information. they find meaningful.

ETS was completed in late December 2006, offering employees the ability to tag and categorize web pages. These tags reflect the community's context, culture and language. Users select tags in a pattern consistent with personal information management goals and not because of social influence. (Rader, 2008) As the community evolves, so does its language. Through a variety of widgets, an employee can add tags, see their colleague's tags, and view related content and related people. This simple interaction enables employees to classify content using words that come naturally, instead of the more ridged traditional taxonomy where the language is predefined. This also means people see what and how others have previously tagged. This means people can indirectly help each other find related content and other people, transcending corporate jargon, geographical and cultural biases. The people define the web, and ETS makes those connections meaningful, dynamically connecting information. ETS centralizes all the social tagging data in a single place allowing services to leverage the social knowledge of all employees, across the intranet. Even if a website was designed not to share tagging data, ETS opens up the closed system, accepting a feed of the data. The more people participate the smarter ETS becomes, surfacing related information dynamically (refer to Figure 3).

The integration of social tagging with enterprise search dramatically improves an employee's ability to locate information, increasing productivity, and satisfaction, while reducing costs as the system grows. Social filters are the future of improving information discovery and expertise location.

IBM's Enterprise Tagging System is an investment in research and development of a social tagging system offering a variety of capabilities around collaboration, information discovery and expertise location. The expectation of investing in the integration of ETS and IBM's intranet search was an improved rate of findability due to the introduction of collaboratively tagged content. Employees benefit from quicker and more accurate access to corporate information, and this results in significant improvements on productivity and employee satisfaction. A secondary goal was to create an easy reusable model to offer an enterprise service to new applications to facilitate employees to enter tags to classify their data. This collection of web applications feed their data "tags" into the ETS databank. This model created direct cost avoidance and reusability that improved the corporate "data folksonomy."

Empowering employees via "collaborative social tagging" and integrating it with core intranet search services created a new innovative value proposition for the enterprise. Part of the value is to accelerate the classification of data within specific business context as well as demonstrate the measurable value of Web 2.0 technologies. Web 2.0 and Social networking tools - with its collaborative participatory capabilities- presented an opportunity to improve enterprise search. Finally, it delivered the key value to the business unit, improving employee productivity through faster better information discovery, increased employee satisfaction and quicker enablement with reduced cost through the extension of a service oriented architecture with reusable interactive widgets.

Specifically measured and imperative to the CIO's office where the following:

1. Improve potential productivity for employees – spend less time by streamlining information discovery.
2. Enable IBM employees to find more of the information and people they need.
3. Lower the cost of re-implementing known components and services
4. Engage employees the collaborative creation of a meta-web.

Understanding the impact of helping employees find information and people, more effectively is a necessarily complex endeavor. In an attempt to balance what often seems to be over hyped estimates, metrics and models were purposefully conservative.

In the measure of potential productivity gains, it was estimated that time on the task was reduced 12 seconds. IBM's enterprise search receives on average 286,568 search visits per week, yielding a total of 955 hours per week in time reduction. In estimating, the dollar value saved this model used the average hourly rate for an employee at $100/hr, which results in $95,528 saved per week ($100/wk x 955 hrs/wk) Extend that figure out, assuming 40 hours per week and 48 weeks per annum results in almost $4.6 million in potential productivity gain.

It is hard to base line finding the right information or the right person at the right time – it is often worth far more than the pennies associated with an online ad click. To help model the value associated with the early click-though data, we adopt the ad click approach to this situation. The premise is that for an individual to click on an advertisement is similar to clicking any other link. The person is attracted and feels there might be the value on the other end of the link. There may not be and so this model describes the minimum the click was worth, the cost to have placed the ad and received the click. An average cost per click ad is very conservatively around 32 cents. Averaging the click-through patterns during the first few months of usage (July, August and Sep-

Figure 3. Early versions of the ETS tag cloud and add tag widgets

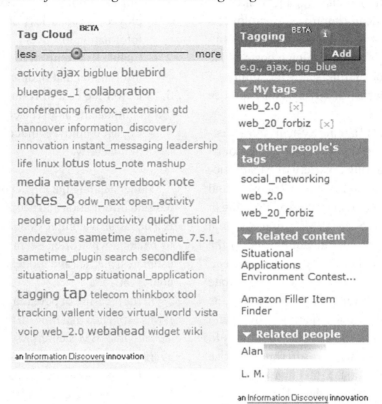

tember), 130,338 clicks were made on employee tagged URLs. This results in $41,708 per month and over $500,000 per annum as a minimum valuation in the value of the information found. One could argue this figure is much hire With 50% of searches ending in a collaboratively tagged link, the data suggests that the value is much higher or employees would continue to seek out additional search results.

Determining the value of reusing a common service can be measured by the cost of having to create the capability. In the case of adding tagging, it was conservatively estimated that it could be added to an application at the rate of $24,360. This includes all the traditional development costs such as design, development, testing, etc. and equivalent capabilities in the core tagging engine and similar AJAX widgets. In this model, the hourly rate for a

developer is $85 and the time to develop is placed at 280 hours or just around seven weeks. One could argue that less needs to be developed, but the reuse of the common service would benefit from these capabilities and as such needs to be taken into account. At the end of 4Q2007, around 100 applications were contributing to ETS, leveraging the service, widgets or both contributing to $2.4 million in cost avoidance.

With at the end of 2007 having over 250,000 URLs, 75,000 unique tags and 25,000 unique taggers in the environment it is not hard to imagine IBM is at the beginning of understanding the entire impact of this work. With the initial investment being well under one million dollars, the very conservative $7.5 million dollar benefit is astounding ($4.6M + $500K + 2.4M = $7.5M). With 50% of searches ending in socially tagging URLS and 70% of all traffic to a high profile innovation site coming from socially tagged widgets, ETS's and more importantly employees, contribution to IBM's enterprise search and information discovery is remarkable.

Key Design Points

There are three key design points that make ETS powerful as a collaborative information organization tool. First, it is a common service allowing flexible integration across a variety of systems. ETS offers three approached to integrations, RESTful programming APIs, an AJAX widget enabling exploiters to integrate ETS into their existing site and scheduled imports (push or pull) of third party data. ETS is an aggregation point for fingerprints captured by disparate systems and thus a hub for collaborative data. Second, ETS works with multiple formats of metadata (e.g. ratings as well as tags) and is designed around a basic triple store. Any triple relationship could be aggregated in a similar way, allowing for the collaborative web overlay to continue and increase in complexity. Finally, its integration with query interfaces such as search engines completes the cycle from collaborative filtering to the recommendation of people and content. These three design points enable multiple web properties to share collaborative metadata while gaining insight from the broader social activities of the community. Simply by participating, sites are able to cross promote people and information without "owning" all the information. Users are the connection engine. ETS takes collaborative filtering and begins to knit a central view of individuals and content.

Collaborative Information Organization

The Internet is formed by a series of competing web destinations. Advertising is likely the only common service that ties multiple web properties – even competing web properties – together.

There is little motivation to cooperate as each site is motivated to attract and keep a customer. On an intranet, a closed network isolated from the Internet. Businesses have more freedom and incentive to make sense of web destinations. One of the key activities that can be facilitated in a controlled or cooperative environment is collaborative information organization.

On the Internet, the Web 2.0 properties that support collaboration, communities and fingerprint interactions are isolated. People tie these sites together through the consistency of their online identities. Content is often posted multiple times manually or automatically to simulate integration. Moreover, integration is "on the glass" so individuals feel like Flickr and Facebook are integrated, while they run separate. Each site has a honey pot of collaborative data around people and information, with little interest or ability to link to the other participation on the net.

Intranets are managed by organizations that want a private network. They support all the standards and interactions of the Internet, but are closed from public view. This offers a level of security, privacy and isolation from a larger community. Intranets, like the Internet, have multiple destinations competing for attention. Often, intranets have web applications and tooling that mimic the external equivalents. IBM, for example, has the IBM Media Library, which is like the company YouTube. Part of Lotus Connections delivers similar capabilities to that of Delicious. There are many examples of this and inside an intranet, a major advantage exists – there is no barrier to knitting a person's collaborative activities together. All the contributions and fingerprints for a given user can be leveraged to understand their interests, the communities that are participating in and how the company as a whole is focused. While it sounds big brother, the motivation is pure, deliver and empower people with highly filtered content and a single identity. Relieve the individual from having to manage their fragments and assemble and use them to increase their productivity.

To illustrate this radical evolution in collaborative organization and filtering, consider four of the many web properties that compete for employee attention at IBM: On Demand Workplace, IBM Media Library, Lotus Connections Dogear and ThinkPlace.

The primary launch point and information aggregation point for an employee is the On Demand Workplace portal. Employees have role-based access to the tools and information that help them execute their job. When employees read news articles the ETS widget displays enabling collaborative tagging.

The IBM Media Library houses a variety of multimedia, from podcasts to videos to documents and images. Associated with each item or series are a set of tags and ratings. These fingerprints are private to the IBM Media Library, but are made available to ETS via feeds, allowing rich content to be recommended and people surfaced on ETS widgets.

Lotus Connections Dogear is the social bookmarking system that employees use to manage web links. Again, tags and people are associated with these bookmarks and are made available to ETS via a feed. ThinkPlace is IBM's idea management system, allowing employees to suggest new ideas from helping make the company be more energy efficient to new business ideas.

ThinkPlace uses tags to help the community organize ideas and surface related ideas and people to employees. ThinkPlace leverages the ETS widgets to facilitate tagging as well as pulling related content and people from ETS using feeds.

Each of these four web applications captures contributions and fingerprints. Employees are able to participate in many places, while having their contributions impact the entirety of the intranet. Content and people are knitted together through the collaborative participation of the employee base. The efforts of a relative few deliver benefits to the many.

Collaborative Recommendations via Ad hoc Communities

The broad adoption of ETS is facilitated by delivering on both immediate and delayed satisfaction. Participation with the common rating and tagging widget allows people to identify and collaborative classify content and people. In addition, by default, the widget displays related people and related content. The better the tagging, the more accurate the recommendations are. All the collaborative activity occurring on the intranet informs related people and content. The actions of engaged employees create relationships and ad hoc communities helping the rest of the company find the right information. The delayed benefit of collaborative filtering in the context of any specific web experience is the integration of these fingerprints into the enterprise wide search experience. As people use traditional mechanisms for finding content, the social activities of employees are used to boost relevancy of information and people results. Additional processing of these collaborative social artifacts allows for dashboards that are even more sophisticated.

Filtering through the Eyes of Few

A subtle important aspect of collaborative organization and filtering is that it takes only a relative few to be extremely valuable. By leveraging the collaboration of the core community to alter search results or provide more recommendations that are intelligent. (Mehta et al., 2007) The challenge is that the relatively small community does not always accurately reflect the larger community. Recommendations can be narrow or even inaccurate based on low participation. (Bischoff et al., 2008) The items on Amazon with high ratings but a low number of ratings has less impact. (Sundar et al, 2008) Similarly, systems like ETS gain considerable ground by leveraging diverse participation.

CHALLENGES WITH MEDIATION

"The mediated world is capacious. Its middle names are Diverse and Inclusive. There's room for everybody and everything. But remember. The issue is no longer representation versus reality, phony versus authentic, artificial versus natural. That was for nineteenth-century Romantics to worry about. A few existentialists and a bunch of hippies tried to revive those concerns in the twentieth century, but we know what happened to them. We've read the books, heard the music, seen the movies—and the remakes. But there is no going back to reality just as there is no going back to virginity. We have been consigned to a new plane of being engendered by mediating representations of fabulous quality an inescapable ubiquity, a place where everything is addresses to us, everything is for us, and nothing is beyond us anymore." Page 11, Thomas De Zengotita, 2007

De Zengotita says a lot in his book, Mediated. His focus is on how all the multitude of media (TV, radio, magazines, celebrities, the Internet games, etc.) shapes the world around you in the most profound ways. The notion that what you consume is increasing tailored for you often by people like you and as part of some activity you did is frighteningly cyclical. In a world where we are at the center, and everything is presented neatly to us for our consumption, rework and expression, the diversity and inclusiveness that De Zengotita becomes critical. Not in the way he presents it, which simply describes the vastness of who is engaged, but the need to ensure that not every Top 10 list is created by the 1%.

A study by Berkovsky et al. looked at collaborative filtering and the effects of domain specialization. (Berkovsky et al., 2007) When filtering is done with a domain focus, quality increases. This also means quality encourages islands of knowledge. Often overlooked, the user experience is not just about the interaction with tools, but includes the emotions and dialogue of users and these have been shown to alter user perceptions of what success means in the process of information seeking. (Arapakis et al., 2008) Pachet explores the closed loop of consciously partaking in a self-referencing experience where users "boost individual realization" and "develop inner dialogues through which personal content can emerge." (Pachet, 2008) Up until this point we have been covering smaller forms of expression and interaction – web based collaboration enabled by social spaces. With the propensity and need to leverage such artifacts (generated by the populous) to re-frame user experience, emotions, inner dialogues, the need to broaden the mediation is critical. At a much larger anthropological level, De Zengotita is presenting us with a world we cannot or have will to escape. In the world of technical social and collaborative creation, filtering and association, we must strive for mediation that improves our view not limits it. Left naturally, the information we consume and collaborate with will be no more diverse than those found in countries with censoring governments.

Collaborative social filtering mediates the content people experience. The power of the collaborative filtering is also its challenge. The fragmentation and massive diversity of content on the Internet delays these effects to some degree. On an intranet, the knitting together of the fragmented self actually accelerates this effect. The lack of massive content diversity, that only the global nature of the Internet can provide, makes intranets particularly susceptible to mediated messaging. Therefore, while it is easier to create rich identities from the numerous fingerprints left by employees, there is an inherent need to focus on participation diversity.

Diversity is required to ensure collaborative interactions do not create isolated communities. Zhang et al. published the requirement to diversify related content to ensure the same content is presented with less frequency. (Zhang et al., 2008) This is particularly noticed when top ten lists are used to present related content. The top content or experts stabilize and is usually the same. How-

Figure 4. The cycle of using fingerprints to mediate experiences

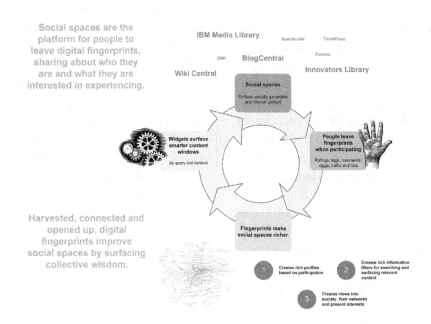

ever, the next ten results may be just as relevant, but statistically hidden. The mediation of content and experience is something that exists and is the desired effect to encapsulate the communal point of view. Broader participation is the key to ensure higher diversity in the collaborative web overlay. If you drive experiences or filter content based on past collaboration activity, then both the volume and diversity of these events matters (illustrated in Figure 4).

CONCLUSION

This chapter explored social spaces as a platform, supporting the often-overlooked micro-interactions referred to as digital fingerprints. Collaborative interactions are the basis for connecting people to other people and content. These connections embody the interest of individuals and the ad hoc communities they create. A verity of examples illustrates these collaborative interactions and specifically, IBM's Enterprise Tagging

Service is explored discussing one solution to the fundamental problems of the proliferation of siloed experiences. In addition, the end-to-end experience of interaction to fingerprint to self-mediated experience is explored through the employment of ETS. Finally, the need for diversity in participation is posited as the most critical factor in limiting the mediation of related content. Future work should focus on how various collaborative overlays can be combined to increase intelligence of recommendations, while ensuring diversity and volume of participation.

REFERENCES

Amazon. (2011). *Amazon.com: Help > Amazon.com site features > your content > recommendations.* Retrieved May 6, 2011, from http://www.amazon.com /gp/help/customer/display.html?ie =UTF8&nodeId=13316081&qid=1236889341 &sr=1-2#rate

Arapakis, I., Jose, J. M., & Gray, P. D. (2008). Affective feedback: an investigation into the role of emotions in the information seeking process. In *Proceedings of the 31st Annual International ACM SIGIR Conference on Research and Development in Information Retrieval* (Singapore, Singapore, July 20 - 24, 2008), SIGIR '08, (pp. 395-402). New York, NY: ACM.

Arrington, M. (2009). *Social networking: Will Facebook overtake MySpace in the U.S. in 2009?* Retrieved May 6, 2011, from http://www. techcrunch.com /2009/01/13/ social-networking-will-facebook-overtake-myspace-in-the-us-in-2009/

Arrington, M. (2009). *Facebook now nearly twice the size of MySpace worldwide.* Retrieved May 6, 2011, from http://www.techcrunch.com /2009/01/22/facebook-now-nearly-twice-the-size-of-myspace-worldwide/

Berkovsky, S., Kuflik, T., & Ricci, F. (2007). Distributed collaborative filtering with domain specialization. In *Proceedings of the 2007 ACM Conference on Recommender Systems* (Minneapolis, MN, USA, October 19 - 20, 2007), RecSys '07, (pp. 33-40). New York, NY: ACM.

Bischoff, K., Firan, C. S., Nejdl, W., & Paiu, R. (2008). Can all tags be used for search? In *Proceeding of the 17th ACM Conference on Information and Knowledge Management* (Napa Valley, California, USA, October 26 - 30, 2008), CIKM '08 (pp. 193-202). New York, NY: ACM.

Brin, S., & Page, L. (1998). The anatomy of a large-scale hypertextual Web search engine. *Computer Networks and ISDN Systems, 30,* 107–117. doi:10.1016/S0169-7552(98)00110-X

Chow, A., Goodman, B. D., Rooney, J., & Wyble, C. D. (2007). Engaging a corporate community to manage technology and embrace innovation. *IBM Systems Journal.* Retrieved from http://www.research.ibm.com /journal/abstracts/sj/464/chow.html

CXO Media Inc. (2008). *CIO 100 2008: Winner detail.* Retrieved May 6, 2011, from http://www.cio.com /cio100/detail/1840

de Zengotita, T. (2004). *Mediated: How the media shapes your world and the way you live in it.* New York, NY: Bloomsbury Publishing.

Delicious. (2011). *Delicious.* Retrieved May 6, 2011, from http://www.delicious.com/

Digg. (2011). *Digg – All news, videos & images.* Retrieved May 6, 2011, from http://www.digg.com/

Facebook. (2007). *Facebook | statistics.* Retrieved from http://www.facebook.com /press/info.php?statistics

Facebook. (2011). *Facebook | home.* Retrieved May 6, 2011, from http://www.facebook.com/

Florida, R. L. (2002). *The rise of the creative class: And how it's transforming work, leisure, community and everyday life.* New York, NY: Basic Books.

Fuxman, A., Tsaparas, P., Achan, K., & Agrawal, R. (2008). Using the wisdom of the crowds for keyword generation. In *Proceeding of the 17th International Conference on World Wide Web* (Beijing, China, April 21 - 25, 2008), WWW '08, (pp. 61-70). New York, NY: ACM.

Google. (2011). *YouTube | Broadcast yourself.* Retrieved May 6, 2011, from http://www.you-tube.com/

Guy, I., Jacovi, M., Shahar, E., Meshulam, N., Soroka, V., & Farrell, S. (2008). Harvesting with SONAR: The value of aggregating social network information. In *Proceeding of the Twenty-Sixth Annual SIGCHI Conference on Human Factors in Computing Systems* (Florence, Italy, April 05 - 10, 2008), CHI '08, (pp. 1017-1026). New York, NY: ACM.

Heckner, M., Neubauer, T., & Wolff, C. (2008). Tree, funny, to read, Google: What are tags supposed to achieve? A comparative analysis of user keywords for different digital resource types. In *Proceeding of the 2008 ACM Workshop on Search in Social Media* (Napa Valley, California, USA, October 30 - 30, 2008), SSM '08, (pp. 3-10). New York, NY: ACM.

Horowitz, B. (2006, February 17). Creators, synthesizers, and consumers. *Elatable: Thoughts on technology (and not) from Bradley Horowitz of Yahoo.* Retrieved from http://www.elatable.com /blog/?p=5

Howe, N., Strauss, W., & Matson, R. (2000). *Millennials rising: The next great generation.* New York, NY: Vintage Books/Random House, Inc.

IBM. (2009). *Lotus connections - Dogear.* Retrieved from http://www-01.ibm.com /software/ lotus/products/ connections/dogear.html

Keller, P. (2005). *Delicious statistics.* Retrieved on December 1, 2007, from http://www.pui.ch / phred/archives/ 2005/12/delicious-statistics.html

Keller, P. (2007). *Del.icio.us stats.* Retrieved on December 1, 2007, from http://deli.ckoma.net/ stats

Krishnan, V., Narayanashetty, P. K., Nathan, M., Davies, R. T., & Konstan, J. A. (2008). Who predicts better? Results from an online study comparing humans and an online recommender system. In *Proceedings of the 2008 ACM Conference on Recommender Systems* (Lausanne, Switzerland, October 23 - 25, 2008), RecSys '08, (pp. 211-218). New York, NY: ACM.

Lee, J., & Hwang, S. (2008). Ranking with tagging as quality indicators. In *Proceedings of the 2008 ACM Symposium on Applied Computing* (Fortaleza, Ceara, Brazil, March 16 - 20, 2008), SAC '08, (pp. 2432-2436). New York, NY: ACM.

Morello, D., & Burton, B. (2006). *Future worker 2015: Extreme individualization.* Gartner, Inc. Publication.

MySpace. (2009). *MySpace | A place for friends.* Retrieved from http://www.myspace.com/

O'Reilly, T. (2005). *What is Web 2.0: Design patterns and business models for the next generation of software.* Retrieved May 6, 2011, from http://www.oreillynet.com /pub/a/oreilly/tim/ news/2005/09/30/ what-is-web-20.html

Orlov, L. (2005). *IBM's technology adoption program taps ideas.* IT's Role. In *Innovation series, (Sept. 2005).* Forrester Research.

Pachet, F. (2008). The future of content is in ourselves. *Computers in Entertainment, 6,* 1–20. doi:10.1145/1394021.1394024

Rader, E., & Wash, R. (2008). Influences on tag choices in del.icio.us. In *Proceedings of the ACM 2008 Conference on Computer Supported Cooperative Work* (San Diego, CA, USA, November 08 - 12, 2008), CSCW '08, (pp. 239-248).

Raman, T. V. (2009). Toward 2^W, beyond web 2.0. *Communications of the ACM, 52,* 52–59. doi:10.1145/1461928.1461945

Saleem, M. (2007, July 19). *The power of Digg top users (one year later).* Pronet Advertising. Retrieved May 6, 2011, from http://www.pronetadvertising.com /articles/the-power-of-digg-top-users-one-year-later34409.html

Seomoz. (2006). *Top 100 Digg users control 56% of Digg's home page content.* Retrieved May 6, 2011, from http://www.seomoz.org /blog/top-100-digg-users-control-56-of-diggs-homepage-content

Stelter, B., & Arango, T. (2009, May 4). Losing popularity contest, MySpace tries a makeover. *New York Times*. Retrieved May 6, 2011, from http://www.nytimes.com /2009/05/04/technology/ companies/04myspace.html

Sundar, S. S., Oeldorf-Hirsch, A., & Xu, Q. (2008). The bandwagon effect of collaborative filtering technology. In *CHI '08 Extended Abstracts on Human Factors in Computing Systems* (Florence, Italy, April 05 - 10, 2008), CHI '08, (pp. 3453-3458). New York, NY: ACM.

Technorati. (2011). *Technorati: About us*. Retrieved May 6, 2011, from http://technorati.com/about/

Weiss, A. (2005). The power of collective intelligence. *Networker, 9*, 16–23. doi:10.1145/1086762.1086763

Wikipedia. (2011). *Wikipedia: About*. Retrieved May 6, 2011, from http://en.wikipedia.org /wiki/ Wikipedia:About

Yahoo. (2011). *Flickr: Explore / tags / New York / clusters*. Retrieved May 6, 2011, from http://www.flickr.com /photos/tags/newyork/clusters/

Yahoo. (2011). *Welcome to Flickr*. Retrieved May 6, 2011, from http://www.flickr.com/

Zhang, M., & Hurley, N. (2008). Avoiding monotony: Improving the diversity of recommendation lists. In *Proceedings of the 2008 ACM Conference on Recommender Systems* (Lausanne, Switzerland, October 23 - 25, 2008), RecSys '08, (pp. 123-130). New York, NY: ACM.

ADDITIONAL READING

Agichtein, E., Castillo, C., Donato, D., Gionis, A., & Mishne, G. (2008). Finding high-quality content in social media. In *Proceedings of the International Conference on Web Search and Web Data Mining* (Palo Alto, California, USA, February 11 - 12, 2008), WSDM '08, (pp. 183-194).

Agrahri, A. K., Manickam, D. T., & Riedl, J. (2008). Can people collaborate to improve the relevance of search results? In *Proceedings of the 2008 ACM Conference on Recommender Systems* (Lausanne, Switzerland, October 23 - 25, 2008), RecSys '08, (pp. 283-286).

Bian, J., Liu, Y., Agichtein, E., & Zha, H. (2008). A few bad votes too many? Towards robust ranking in social media. In C. Castillo, K. Chellapilla, & D. Fetterly (Eds.), *Proceedings of the 4th International Workshop on Adversarial Information Retrieval on the Web* (Beijing, China, April 22 - 22, 2008), AIRWeb '08, ACM (pp. 53-60).

Bryan, L., & Joyce, C. (2005). The 21st-century organization. *The McKinsey Quarterly, 3*, 25–33.

Chen, L., & Pu, P. (2008). A cross-cultural user evaluation of product recommender interfaces. In *Proceedings of the 2008 ACM Conference on Recommender Systems* (Lausanne, Switzerland, October 23 - 25, 2008), RecSys '08, (pp. 75-82).

de Gemmis, M., Lops, P., Semeraro, G., & Basile, P. (2008). Integrating tags in a semantic content-based recommender. In *Proceedings of the 2008 ACM Conference on Recommender Systems* (Lausanne, Switzerland, October 23 - 25, 2008), RecSys '08, (pp. 163-170).

Hardt, D. (2005). *Identity 2.0*. OSCON 2005 Keynote, August 1-5, 2005. Retrieved on December 1, 2007, from http://identity20.com /media/ OSCON2005/

Heymann, P., Koutrika, G., & Garcia-Molina, H. (2008). Can social bookmarking improve web search? In *Proceedings of the international Conference on Web Search and Web Data Mining* (Palo Alto, California, USA, February 11 - 12, 2008), WSDM '08, (pp. 195-206). New York, NY: ACM.

Hütter, C., Kühne, C., & Böhm, K. (2008). Peer production of structured knowledge: An empirical study of ratings and incentive mechanisms. In *Proceeding of the 17th ACM Conference on Information and Knowledge Management* (Napa Valley, California, USA, October 26 - 30, 2008), CIKM '08, (pp. 827-842).

Klaisubun, P., Kajondecha, P., & Ishikawa, T. (2007). Behavior patterns of information discovery in social bookmarking service. In *Proceedings of the IEEE/WIC/ACM international Conference on Web Intelligence* (November 02 - 05, 2007), (pp. 784-787). Washington, DC: IEEE Computer Society.

Lerman, K., & Galstyan, A. (2008). Analysis of social voting patterns on Digg. In *Proceedings of the First Workshop on online Social Networks* (Seattle, WA, USA, August 18 - 18, 2008), WOSP '08, (pp. 7-12).

Li, X., Guo, L., & Zhao, Y. E. (2008). Tag-based social interest discovery. In *Proceeding of the 17th International Conference on World Wide Web* (Beijing, China, April 21 - 25, 2008), WWW '08, (pp. 675-684).

Mehta, B., Hofmann, T., & Nejdl, W. (2007). Robust collaborative filtering. In *Proceedings of the 2007 ACM Conference on Recommender Systems* (Minneapolis, MN, USA, October 19 - 20, 2007), RecSys '07, (pp. 49-56). New York, NY: ACM.

Nakamoto, R. Y., Nakajima, S., Miyazaki, J., Uemura, S., Kato, H., & Inagaki, Y. (2008). Reasonable tag-based collaborative filtering for social tagging systems. In *Proceeding of the 2nd ACM Workshop on Information Credibility on the Web* (Napa Valley, California, USA, October 30 - 30, 2008), WICOW '08, (pp. 11-18). New York, NY: ACM.

Sen, S., Harper, F. M., LaPitz, A., & Riedl, J. (2007). The quest for quality tags. In *Proceedings of the 2007 international ACM Conference on Supporting Group Work* (Sanibel Island, Florida, USA, November 04 - 07, 2007) 361–370.

Shirky, C. (2006, January 25). Ontology is overrated: Categories, links, and tags. *Clay Shirky's writings about the Internet*. Retrieved May 6, 2011, from http://www.shirky.com /writings/ ontology_overrated.html

Sinha, R. (2006, January 18). A social analysis of tagging. *Rashmi Sinha: thoughts on technology design and cognition*. Retrieved May 6, 2011, from http://www.rashmisinha.com /archives/06_01/ social-tagging.html

Sunstein, C. R. (2004). Democracy and filtering. *Communications of the ACM, 47,* 57–59. doi:10.1145/1035134.1035166

Terdiman, D. (2005, February 2). Folksonomies tap people power. *Wired: Science: Discoveries*. Retrieved on December 1, 2007 from http://www.wired.com /science/discoveries/ news/2005/02/66456

Thom-Santelli, J., Muller, M. J., & Millen, D. R. (2008). Social tagging roles: Publishers, evangelists, leaders. In *Proceeding of the Twenty-Sixth Annual SIGCHI Conference on Human Factors in Computing Systems* (Florence, Italy, April 05 - 10, 2008), CHI '08, (pp. 1041-1044). New York, NY: ACM.

Xu, S., Bao, S., Fei, B., Su, Z., & Yu, Y. (2008). Exploring folksonomy for personalized search. In *Proceedings of the 31st Annual International ACM SIGIR Conference on Research and Development in Information Retrieval* (Singapore, Singapore, July 20 - 24, 2008), SIGIR '08, (pp. 155-162).

Yanbe, Y., Jatowt, A., Nakamura, S., & Tanaka, K. (2007). Can social bookmarking enhance search in the web? In *Proceedings of the 7th ACM/IEEE-CS Joint Conference on Digital Libraries* (Vancouver, BC, Canada, June 18 - 23, 2007), JCDL '07, (pp. 107-116). New York, NY: ACM.

Zanardi, V., & Capra, L. (2008). Social ranking: uncovering relevant content using tag-based recommender systems. In *Proceedings of the 2008 ACM Conference on Recommender Systems* (Lausanne, Switzerland, October 23 - 25, 2008), RecSys '08, (pp. 51-58). New York, NY: ACM.

KEY TERMS AND DEFINITIONS

Collaboration: People working together for a common outcome

Community: A group of people joined by common attribute

Content: Information; often made up of text, media and metadata

Filtering: Removing information in order to focus on a specific portion

Mediation: People or systems connecting information that could alter intent

People: Human often the source of implicit connections and the actors in creating explicit connections

Social: People interacting with each other physically or virtually

Tag: A non-hierarchical text label associated with information often thought of as descriptive metadata

Chapter 3
SpotTheLink:
A Game–Based Approach to the Alignment of Ontologies

Stefan Thaler
STI-Innsbruck, University of Innsbruck Austria

Elena Simperl
AIFB, Karlsruhe Institute of Technology, Germany

Katharina Siorpaes
STI-Innsbruck, University of Innsbruck, Austria

Stephan Wölger
STI-Innsbruck, University of Innsbruck, Austria

ABSTRACT

A multitude of approaches to match, merge, and integrate ontologies, and more recently, to interlink RDF data sets, have been proposed over the past years, making ontology alignment one of the most active and at the same time mature area of research and development in semantic technologies. While advances in the area cannot be contested, it is equally true that full automation of the ontology-alignment process is far from being feasible; human input is often indispensable for the bootstrapping of the underlying methods, and for the validation of the results. The question of acquiring and leveraging such human input remains largely unaddressed, in particular when it comes to the incentives and motivators that are likely to make users invest their valuable time and effort in alignment tasks such as entity interlinking and schema matching, which can be domain-knowledge-intensive, technical, or both. In this chapter, the authors present SpotTheLink, a game whose purpose addresses this challenge, demonstrating how knowledge-intensive tasks in the area of the Semantic Web can be collaboratively solved by a community of non-experts in an entertaining fashion.

DOI: 10.4018/978-1-4666-0894-8.ch003

1. INTRODUCTION

A large share of tasks in knowledge engineering crucially rely on human input (Siorpaes and Simperl 2010). This applies in particular to those tasks which are acknowledged to be hardly approachable in a systematic, engineering-driven fashion; and also, though to a lesser extent, to the wide array of (semi-) automatic methods and techniques that have been proposed as an attempt to reduce the costs of knowledge-engineering projects by minimizing the need for human involvement in these projects. In this second case, despite constant progress in improving the performance of the corresponding algorithms and the quality of their results, experiences show that human input is nevertheless required, even if it just for the configuration of the algorithms, the creation of knowledge corpora the algorithms can be trained on, or the validation of (intermediary) algorithm outputs. Examples of such knowledge engineering tasks are numerous, including machine translation, information extraction, text summarization, data integration, multimedia analysis, and conceptual modeling.

One novel approach which proved successful to resolve technical tasks via human computation is based on 'games with a purpose' (Van Ahn 2006). The idea behind games with a purpose is simple, but effective; tasks which remain difficult to handle by computers, but which humans seem to tackle easily are hidden behind entertaining, collaborative games targeting not experts, but casual Internet users. By playing a game with a purpose, users are indirectly generating data that can be capitalized to build knowledge corpora required for the training of algorithms, thus providing a powerful example of how human and computational intelligence can be combined to address important, challenging problems. Since the original proposal by Van Ahn in 2006 games with a purpose have been applied to tasks as diverse as image and video annotation,[1] genetics,[2] natural language processing,[3] and knowledge engineering.[4]

In our work we have applied the idea of games with a purpose in the area of semantic technologies. Semantic technologies exploit machine-understandable representations of data, processes and computational resources in order to create IT systems and applications that are able to better interpret and process the information needs of their users, and to interact with other systems in an interoperable way. A fundamental building block of this approach are ontologies, which are used to capture and structure knowledge in a given domain in terms of classes, instances, relationships and axioms, as a baseline for the implementation of the functionality just mentioned. OntoGame[5] is the framework for the implementation casual games which we designed for this purpose. OntoGame capitalizes on fun and competition as two key motivators for people to willingly invest their valuable time and effort in executing specific knowledge-engineering related tasks, whose technicalities are hidden behind the game experience (Siorpaes and Hepp 2008). Compared to other similar games targeting the same or related tasks, OntoGame's distinctive feature lies in the fact that the input of the players is translated into Semantic Web content, for instance ontologies and metadata encoded in RDFS and OWL,[6] which are W3C standards for the representation of data on the Semantic Web. In this chapter we present one of the latest releases of the OntoGame series, called SpotTheLink, which is dedicated to the task of ontology alignment. The design principles, enabling technology and evaluation methodology we relied upon to develop SpotTheLink can be applied in a variety of human computation scenarios targeting different other knowledge-engineering tasks. We have done so ourselves with games such as OntoPronto, which classifies entities from the English Wikipedia according to an upper-level ontology;

SeaFish, which clusters images on the Web according to pre-defined categories; and TubeLink, which tags videos according to tags suggested by an automatic algorithm. Nevertheless, designing a game that is both entertaining or even addictive for people to play, and useful with respect to the output it produces remains an art more than an engineering exercise; from our experiences with the OntoGame series, complemented by literature in the area of human computation and collective intelligence, we were able to identify a number of features of tasks which increase the likelihood of a successful game-inspired user interaction design, and summarizes the insights we gained in a number of guidelines. These guidelines provide IT developers with a baseline to create knowledge engineering games that are not just functional and purposeful with respect to the data they create, but also engaging for users to play.

The remainder of this chapter is organized as follows. We start with an introduction of ontology alignment as a knowledge engineering task in the context of the Semantic Web which by its very nature calls for technology and tools combining human and computational intelligence (Section 2). Once we have established the types of human input that are required in this context, we introduce the game by which these inputs can be collaboratively generated in Section 3. In Section 4 we focus on the evaluation of the game in terms of the user experience and the quality of the outputs from a knowledge engineering point of view. Sections 5 and 6 target the realization of similar games. Section 5 introduces the OntoGame platform, which provides the basic technical building blocks for the implementation of the games, including user management, scoring and rewards, and the conversion of user inputs into machine-understandable data; Section 6 focuses on principles and guidelines for game design. We conclude the paper with a summary of the work presented and an outline of future games in the area of alignment.

2. ONTOLOGY ALIGNMENT AND THE ROLE OF HUMAN CONTRIBUTIONS

In a nutshell, ontology alignment is concerned with finding and establishing correspondences and connections among a set of ontologies and the associated instance data (Euzenat and Shvaiko 2007). Technically it is typically conceived as an operation that takes as input two or more ontologies with

Similar or overlapping domains and an alignment schema, and delivers a set of alignments (Figure 1). Alignments refer to ontological classes and instances, and are discovered according to various criteria, as discussed in more detail in this section. Most of ontology alignment systems focus on detecting equivalences between ontological elements, while some can also express nuances such as broader match, narrower match, and incompatibility. Once correspondences have been found, merging algorithms generate a unified target ontology, obtained by aggregating elements from the source ontologies which have been assigned a similarity score above a given threshold. By contrast, mapping algorithms restrict to explicitly defining the relationships between these elements. In many cases, it is required that ontology alignment results are validated and enhanced manually (Shvaiko and Euzenat 2008).

Usually one distinguishes between individual matching algorithms (e.g., FCA- MERGE (Stumme and Maedche 2001) or S-Match (Giunchiglia, Yatskevich et al. 2007))—applying only a single method of matching items e.g., linguistic or taxonomical matchers—and combinations of the former, which intend to overcome their limitations by proposing hybrid solutions. A hybrid approach (e.g., Cupid (Madhavan, Berstein et al. 2001)) follows a black-box paradigm, in which various individual matchers are melt together to a new algorithm, while the so-called composite matchers allow an increased user interaction (e.g.,

Figure 1. Ontology alignment process

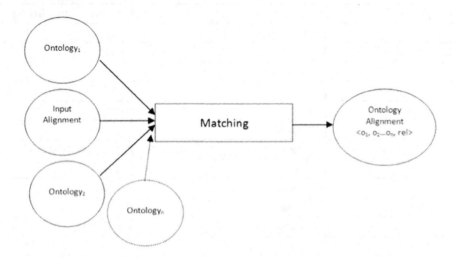

GLUE (Doan, Madhavan et al. 2004),COMA (Do and Rahm 2002), CMC (Tu and Yu 2005)). In open environments such as the World Wide Web, in which the emergence of a unique ontology for a given application domain is considered both unrealistic and unintended, application interoperability is greatly dependent on the availability of consistent mappings between ontologies adopted by inter-communicating systems and applications. Approaches coping with this problem propose a (formal) specification of the semantic overlap between ontologies and integrate matching techniques to automatically discover mapping candidates (Doan, Madhavan et al. 2002), (Ehrig and Sure 2004), (Kalfoglou and Schorlemmer 2003), (Maedche, Motik et al. 2002), (Maedche, Motik et al. 2002).

With respect to the techniques used, one distinguishes between

- Syntactic techniques interpreting the form and the structure of the input;
- External techniques resorting to auxiliary resources such as linguistic thesauri, upper-level ontologies, but also existing alignments; and
- Semantic techniques which investigate the formal semantics of the input.

Independently of the classifications discussed so far, most approaches are semi- automatic and rely on user intervention at various stages of the alignment process (Euzenat and Shvaiko 2007),(Falconer and Storey 2007),(Noy, Griffith et al. 2008),(Shi, Li et al. 2009),(Shvaiko and Euzenat 2008),(Siorpaes and Simperl 2010),(Zhdanova and Shvaiko 2006) in order to:

- Provide initial alignments for training purposes;
- Develop and maintain the background knowledge base that is required in external and semantic techniques;
- Tune thresholds and specify configurations; as well as
- Validate the results and provide feedback.

In the following we consider a selection of the most relevant methods and techniques in this area. We focus on the tools described in the book by Euzenat and Shvaiko in 2007. We would like to point our readers to the Ontology Alignment Evaluation Initiative[7] that evaluates alignment approaches from a more technical perspective rather than for the required human contribution.

Our findings are summarized in Table 1.

Table 1. Classification of approaches to ontology alignment

Approach	Nature	Required input
HOVY	semi-automatic	validation
TransSCM	semi-automatic	rules
SKAT / ONION	semi-automatic	rules
H-Match	automatic	-
Anchor-Prompt	semi-automatic	feedback
OntoBuilder	semi-automatic	feedback
MapOnto	semi-automatic	user-provided alignment, validation
OntoMerge	semi-automatic	rules
CtxMatch	semi-automatic	user input
S-Match	automatic	-
HCONE	automatic/semi-automatic	user-provided alignment, validation
Moa	automatic	-
ASCO	automatic	-
OMEN	automatic	user-provided alignment
T-Tree	automatic	instances
CAIMAN	semi-automatic	instances, validation
FCA-Merge	semi-automatic	instances, feedback (lattice)
GLUE	automatic	instances, feedback
IF-MAP	automatic	instances, user input
QOM	automatic	instances
OMAP	automatic	instances, training
Xu and Embley's	automatic	instances, training
OLA	automatic	instances
Falcon-AO	automatic	instances
RIMOM	automatic	instances

Only four of the surveyed approaches are fully automatic. For evidence of the nature of each approach we refer to the authors themselves or to the evaluation by Euzenat and Shvaiko (Euzenat and Shvaiko 2007). In the summary column we give an assessment of the types of inputs of the corresponding algorithms. When user inputs or training are required, the manual effort associated with the algorithm is naturally higher than when the algorithm relies solely on ontology instances, which are either available or can be generated using machine learning techniques.

While the importance of human contributions is largely acknowledged in the ontology alignment community, the question of how to optimally collect and harvest these contributions during the operation of an alignment system leaves room for further research (Shi, Li et al. 2009). In (Falconer and Storey 2007) the authors describe the results of an observational study of the problems users experience by ontology matching, emphasizing the difficulties experienced by laymen in understanding and following the individual steps of an alignment algorithm; their tool CogZ provides graphical enhancements and informative measures for ontologies that support the user throughout the execution of the algorithm, abstracting from specific technicalities. A second approach to user involvement resorts to Web 2.0 technologies and principles to engage a community of users in defining the alignment, thus increasing the acceptance of the results and distributing the associated labor costs (McCann, Shen et al. 2008), (Siorpaes, Hepp et al. 2008), (Noy, Griffith et al. 2008). In an early work on collaborative alignment Zhdanova and Shvaiko developed a community-driven ontology matching service (Zhdanova and Shvaiko 2006). This service facilitated the sharing of alignments in a publicly available repository. Another collaborative system for matching ontologies in a biomedical domain is described in (Noy, Griffith et al. 2008). (McCann, Shen et al. 2008) propose payment and volunteering schemes to encourage people to participate in this task, reducing the barrier of entry for non-expert users for the verification of automatically generated alignments by asking simple questions.

SpotTheLink exploits many of the ideas discussed above. It relies on crowdsourcing as well as on intrinsic motivators such as fun and competition which are supported by design in 'games with a purpose' to involve users in providing alignments and improve the quality and acceptance of automatically generated alignment results. In doing so SpotTheLink turns the knowledge-intensive, but also technical, abstract and even boring ontology alignment process into an enjoyable, interactive game, which addresses a much broader audience that the wide array of expert tools available. Additionally, the game interface addresses the problems that users experienced by solving alignment issues raised in (Falconer and Storey 2007), which concern the design of the algorithms in terms of the steps to be followed and the ways users are expected to intervene in their execution.

3. THE SPOTTHELINK GAME

In this section, we outline the SpotTheLink game, a collaborative casual game for the alignment of ontologies. The game is built on top of the Onto-Game platform and is designed according to the generic game infrastructure proposed in (Siorpaes and Hepp 2008) We introduce the main goal of the game, explain the most important design decisions and give an overview of the basic design.

The Goal of the Game

The goal of the game is to relate concepts of two ontologies to each other. In our example, the objective of the game is to match two generic ontologies, DBpedia and PROTON[8]. DBpedia is a community-driven effort aiming to create a machine-understandable knowledge base containing a selection of some of the most important entities described in Wikipedia. The knowledge base is structured with the help of an ontology containing 272 classes and 1300 properties, according to which millions of Wikipedia articles are classified.[9] PROTON was designed as a so-called upper-level ontology that captures generic concepts and their features and is used as a knowledge backbone for information extraction and semantic annotation purposes (Terziev et al 2005). It has a similar size as the DBpedia ontology; its main concepts are depicted in Figure 2.

Note that these ontologies are only used as examples to illustrate the concept of the game for ontology alignment. Through the OntoGame platform (Section 5), one can configure the game for arbitrary ontologies, and trigger specific user behavior by changing the scoring and rewards mechanisms (see below). The output generated by playing the game enables applications to query and process data sets referring to two different ontologies in an integrated fashion. In addition, the game can be used just as well for

Figure 2. Representative excerpt of PROTON (Terziev at al 2005)

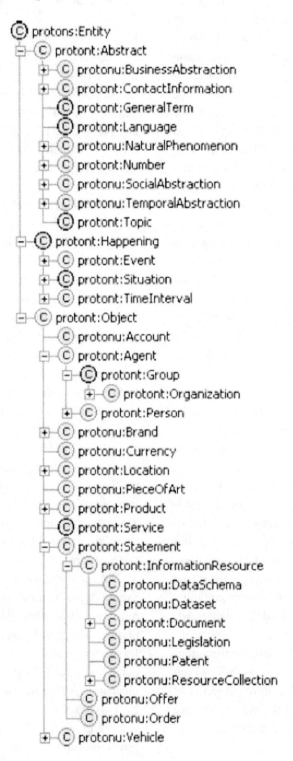

other ontology alignment problems, such as creating training sets in order to enable automatic algorithms to autonomously continue the matching process.

Starting the Game

Users have three means to start a SpotTheLink game. Firstly, they may play the game as a guest. To do so they visit the OntoGame homepage.[10] There, after clicking on the "Play" logo they may start the game. They obtain a temporary account that enables people to peek into the games. Secondly, players may register if they plan to return and have their scores recorded in the game and shared within the network of players. In this case players choose a username and password which they may use later on for authentication. Thirdly the game may also be started via the OntoGame Facebook app.[11] The process resembles to the one from the OntoGame homepage, but users are identified via their Facebook profile.

Game Screens

Apart from the loading teaser there are two main screens in SpotTheLink: the high-score screen and the game screen, both depicted Figure 3.

The high-score screen is displayed directly after the SpotTheLink client was started and after a game round has finished or has been aborted. It displays the top seven players as well as the personal rank of the given player with one better and one worse player. If the player clicks the "Play" button from this screen the partner negotiation process is initiated. It either results in a matching partner, or the player has to try again later. In case two matching partners have been found the interface switches to the game screen for both players.

The game screen is shown during a game round. It contains a display for the remaining time as well as one for the player's current score. Furthermore, there is an area for a concept with description on the left as well as a hierarchical tree of concepts to map to on the right. Apart from that there is a label which advices the player what to do next and an option box for choosing the relationship between two concepts. Next, there is a status line that indicates the status of the game partner, i.e., whether they have chosen or been disconnected. Finally, there are two buttons located at the bottom of the game screen, the "Ok" button and the "Skip" button. Clicking the former indicates that a player has made a choice, while clicking the latter leads to a continuation of the game with

Figure 3. SpotTheLink game screens

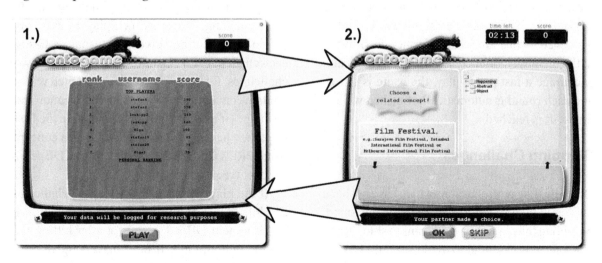

a new concept. From the game screen one can return to the high-score screen in one of the following three scenarios: the game runs out of time and ends, the game partner quits the game, or the server stops running.

Scoring and Rewards

When dealing with unknown data and player one has very limited means to verify whether the provided input is correct or not. To encourage the intended user behavior we use specific scoring scheme. Points in games are a simple tool to motivate people to keep playing. It allows them to easily compare their performance to others and nurtures competition. Not doing anything or skipping game rounds all the time does not result in any points, thus any player who wants to gain points is incentivized to interact with the game in the intended fashion. Agreement between alignment choices is rewarded by points. Due to the fact that players are randomly paired and (in theory) do not have any means to communicate outside the game, there are low chances for a cheating strategy to yield any positive scoring results across multiple game steps and rounds. In addition, we reward players' commitment to advance in a game; the deeper players advance in class hierarchy, i.e., the stronger the consensus on one concept, the higher their gain. This should motivate players to think about their choices more thoroughly, as the score is significantly higher for concepts that are located further downwards in the hierarchy. To increase the competition and encourage a fast paced play, the game is timed, and each round is automatically finished when a time-out is reached.

Skipping Challenges

When dealing with questions which have not been answered in the course of an earlier game round, providing the players with a means to skip certain challenges is essential to avoid players' frustra-

tion and keep the game flow smoothly. The fact that the challenges are generated randomly from a given knowledge corpus, and that their answers are not known in advance has the advantage that the game designer does not have to invest any resources in providing golden standards to evaluate the inputs of the players. In fact, generating this data would mean that the main purpose of the game would disappear, as the only meaningful use for the knowledge acquired via the game would be to validate the existing answers, a task which is slightly easier to address than open-scale questions. See, for instance, similar considerations on the performance of crowdsourcing approaches such as Amazon's Mechanical Turk on closed versus open-scale problems. A similar trade-off exists between the representativeness of the knowledge corpus from which challenges are selected for the task to be solved and the resources to be invested in creating this corpus.

Players can vote to proceed to the next concept to be aligned, and the current round is skipped if both players agree on this. In case one player gives and answer and the other one intends to skip they have to revise their decision.

Playing the Game

When a player starts a new game round she is assigned a random partner who is logged in to the game in the same time. The team has to solve challenges together, i.e., players will only get points when they give consensual replies to each challenge. Each game round consists of two challenges. First, the players are presented with a random concept along with a short description and an image (if available) from DBpedia. In the first step, they have to choose and agree on a concept from PROTON that is related to the DBpedia concept (see Figure 4).

If the player intends to answer the challenge she hits "OK" button, otherwise she continues with the next DBpedia concept after hitting the "Skip" button. Only if both players agree on a

Figure 4. SpotTheLink - Step 1

decision, that is, answer or skip, the game is resumed. Otherwise, players have to answer again. In the second step, they have to agree on the type of relationship among these concepts. The process of answer negotiation remains the same.

In the example shown in Figure 4, players have to choose whether the "Film Festival" concept (presented on the left-hand side) is a "Happening," an "Abstract" or an "Object" (all concepts from PROTON displayed in tree form on the right-hand side of the screen, see also Figure 5). If their answers are identical they earn points and the next step is to agree on a relationship for this match, i.e., whether the concepts they just matched are more specific or the same. This is depicted in Figure 6. For the relationships we have chosen SKOS mapping relations (skos:exactMatch and skos:narrowMatch),[12] however, we renamed them for a clearer understanding for a broad audience of players. SKOS (Simple Knowledge Organization System) provides a vocabulary for the description of concepts from different types of knowledge organization structures, not just ontologies, but also related structures such as taxonomies and

classification systems, and their relationships. If both players choose to skip or if they disagree they continue playing on a new concept. Otherwise, if they agree on both concepts and the associated relationship and the game is resumed with one of the sub-concepts of the agreed concept in the PROTON ontology. In the example just discussed,

Figure 5. SpotTheLink – Proceed in the hierarchy

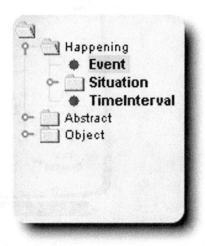

players may try and match "Film Festival" to "Event," "Situation" or "TimeInterval," all specific types of "Happening"s (see Figure 4).

A game round ends in the following cases: players disagree on either a concept or a relationship, players agree to skip, or the deepest level of the hierarchy has been reached. This is indicated in the hierarchy by a black-dot symbol, whereas the folder-symbol hints that there is another level of more specific concepts to be explored. The overall game ends in the following three situations: a player closes the game, a partner is disconnected from the server or the game time is up. Afterwards player may start a new game round in which they are paired with a new random partner. According to the guidelines we discussed earlier, we use the simple methods in game design to prevent cheating: The players are paired randomly and anonymously and they have no possibility to interact with each other.

Deriving Semantic Content

In our example scenario we aim to match the DBpedia and PROTON ontologies, and encode the alignments via SKOS. The game output includes selection of concepts as well as the type of relationship defining the level of similarity between the concepts: narrow matches, for a pair of concepts in which one concept is more specific than the other one, and exact matches for pairs of concepts that are perceived to be the same or equivalent. An example of the SKOS data export is available in Section 4 (see Figure 7).

Game input is converted into ontology alignments according to the following procedure:

- First the program checks whether the concept has been played at least six times by different players.
- If that is the case, it calculates the percentage for each unique answer combination, i.e., other concepts and relationships. Answer combinations that include concepts from a deeper hierarchy level are

Figure 6. SpotTheLink – Step 2

Figure 7. Game export

```
<!-- SpotTheLink SKOS concept scheme -->
<skos:ConceptScheme rdf:about="http://ontogame.sti2.at/spotthelink">
    <dc:description>Alignment of Proton and DBpedia</dc:description>
    <dc:title>SpotTheLink alignment</dc:title>
    <dc:creator>INSEMTIVES team</dc:creator>
    <dc:date>20100608</dc:date>
</skos:ConceptScheme>
<!-- instances -->
<skos:Concept rdf:about="http://dbpedia.org/ontology/LunarCrater">
    <skos:inScheme rdf:resource="http://ontogame.sti2.at/spotthelink"/>
    <skos:narrowMatch rdf:resource="http://proton.semanticweb.org/2005/04/protont#Location"/>
</skos:Concept>
<skos:Concept rdf:about="http://dbpedia.org/ontology/RecordLabel">
    <skos:inScheme rdf:resource="http://ontogame.sti2.at/spotthelink"/>
    <skos:narrowMatch rdf:resource="http://proton.semanticweb.org/2005/04/protont#Abstract"/>
</skos:Concept>
<skos:Concept rdf:about="http://dbpedia.org/ontology/City">
    <skos:inScheme rdf:resource="http://ontogame.sti2.at/spotthelink"/>
    <skos:narrowMatch rdf:resource="http://proton.semanticweb.org/2005/04/protont#Location"/>
</skos:Concept>
    <skos:Concept rdf:about="http://dbpedia.org/ontology/MixedMartialArtsEvent">
    <skos:inScheme rdf:resource="http://ontogame.sti2.at/spotthelink"/>
<skos:narrowMatch rdf:resource="http://proton.semanticweb.org/2005/04/protont#Event"/>
</skos:Concept>
    <skos:Concept rdf:about="http://dbpedia.org/ontology/Actor">
    <skos:inScheme rdf:resource="http://ontogame.sti2.at/spotthelink"/>
    <skos:narrowMatch rdf:resource="http://proton.semanticweb.org/2005/04/protont#Person"/>
</skos:Concept>
<skos:Concept rdf:about="http://dbpedia.org/ontology/Canal">
    <skos:inScheme rdf:resource="http://ontogame.sti2.at/spotthelink"/>
    <skos:narrowMatch rdf:resource="http://proton.semanticweb.org/2005/04/protont#Location"/>
</skos:Concept>
```

weighted higher because they implicitly state that concepts that are located upwards on the path to the root of the hierarchy tree have been agreed upon as well.

- If the percentage of an answer combination exceeds 50 percent the concept match will be marked for export.

With the help of the OntoGame platform each of these steps can be adjusted according to the specific behavior the game designer intends to encourage.

4. EVALUATION

Evaluation Methodology

The evaluation was performed in a controlled experiment with 16 users who played the game in parallel on the average around 20 minutes each. The evaluation included both an assessment of the quality of the alignments from a content and ontological point of view, and a user satisfaction survey following the questions listed in Table 2. In the experiment, the majority of the participants had a Computer Science background, but only few of them were proficient in semantic technologies, thus being familiar with the actual task that the game attempts to solve.

After the game session was concluded we have analyzed the collected data and conducted face-to-face interviews with the players. For the analysis of the data, we investigated the level of consensus, i.e., how often were player teams able to reach an agreement on the alignments, and we asked two ontology engineering experts to judge the correctness of the alignments. For the user experience analysis we were primarily interested in the fun factor of the game design, the clarity of the rules, and the role of the human partner as a motivator for playing the game.

Table 2. SpotTheLink user satisfaction survey

Question	Possible Answers
What is your gender?	Male, Female
How old are you?	<20, 21-30, 31-40, 41-50, 51-60, >60
What is your background? (Multiple answers possible)	Background in Computer Science, Background in Semantic Web, Other technical background, No technical background
How many concepts did you match?	0-10, 11-20, 21-30, 31-50, 51+
Assess the games comprehensibility (Multiple answers possible)	It's easy to grasp the games goal, It's easy to match corresponding concepts, It's easy to relate corresponding concepts.
Assess the overall gaming fun. The game is:	Addictive, Great Fun, Average, Fairly Boring, Boring
Assess the interface. It is: (Multiple answers possible):	Well-designed, Self-explanatory, Readable, Easy to use, Responsive
How often would you play SpotTheLink again?	Daily, More than once a week, More than once a month, Hardly ever, Never
Other feedback, remarks, suggestions?	Free text

Evaluation Results

As mentioned earlier the experiment involved 16 players playing the game on average 20 minutes each, equaling 5 hours of ontology alignment effort. This resulted in 190 game rounds involving 246 DBpedia concepts with two players each. Participants matched 32 of the 246 DBpedia concepts to the PROTON ontology. 6 of these matches were consensual. On average, each player produced 23.5 matches during 20 minutes she interacted with the game. 146 of all game rounds were logged as consensual, which means that in more three of four cases players were able to find consensus on challenges, match concept and the relationship (see Table 3). This confirms findings from previous evaluations of our work (Siorpaes and Hepp 2008) that a collaborative game-based approach to knowledge engineering tasks yields to consensual results among anonymous players.

The following concepts that were matched were found "correct" by the ontology experts (see Figure 7). We use "dbp:" as abbreviation for http://dbpedia.org/ontology/ and "pt:" as abbreviation for http://proton.semanticweb.org/2005/04/protont.

- dbp:LunarCrater is a more specific pt#Location.
- dbp:City is a more specific pt#Location.
- dbp:MixedMartialArtsEvent is a more specific pt#Event.
- dbp:Actor is a more specific pt#Person.
- dbp:Canal is a more specific pt#Location.

The dbp:LunarCrater, dbp:City and dbp:Canal are correct because they are sub-classes of dbp:Place which is described as location. dbp:MixedMartialArtsEvent is correct because it is a sub class of dbp:Event. Finally, dbp:Actor is also a sub concept of dbp:Person. The following alignment was found "wrong" by the ontology experts: – dbp:RecordLabel is a more specific pt#Abstract.

After playing the game the participants filled out the online survey about SpotTheLink (see Table 4). Most of our contributors (94.1%) were male, had background in Computer Science (94.1%) as well as a background in the Semantic Web (88.2%). All of our evaluation participants are aged between 21 and 40.

Table 3. Game statistics

Number of concepts played	32
Game rounds in total	190
Players	16
Average game rounds per player	23.5
Number of inputs recorded	882
Consensual game rounds	77.84%
Exported matchings	6
Correct matchings	5

- **Challenge and Understanding:** A majority of the attendants stated that playing SpotTheLink poses some intellectual challenge (52,9%) or has just the right intellectual challenge (23.5%), whereas about 24,6% of the players stated that it was difficult or too challenging. Nobody considered the game any challenge at all. Almost two third of the participants found it easy to grasp the game's goal as well as to find a corresponding concept (58.8%) and less than the half found it easy to select an appropriate relationship between the two concepts (47.1%).
- **The Game Interface:** A majority of the participants (57.1%) considered the interface comprehensible, however less than half of them (42.9%) found it easy to used and liked the design. Only slightly more than one third (35.7%) thought of the interface as responsive and less than one third experienced it as self-explanatory (28.6%). This resulted in a re-design of the OntoGame interface concept, whose core was developed for the OntoPronto game as the first release of the series. Our most recent developments are using different paradigms and graphic styles to increase the appeal of the interfaces to casual gamers.
- **Game Fun:** Almost all participants would rather not (64.7%) or not (29.4%) play

SpotTheLink again. Accordingly, most of the players considered the game boring (11.8%) or boring (52,9%). About a third of the people found the game fun (35,3%). In Sections 6 and 7 we will discuss the implications of these findings in more detail (refer to Table 5).

Free Text Feedback

We also asked players to free-text feedback. The responses included the following comments:

- Provide a clear definition of what to do. The game challenge is not immediately clear.
- Emphasize on the purpose of the game, because people are more likely to contribute if they understand that they are doing something with a purpose.
- It is quite difficult to navigate top-level categories of the PROTON ontology. Provide examples and or clear definitions.
- The sound of the game was perceived as annoying.

From the results of the user experience analysis, we can conclude that tasks (concept selection and relationship selection) must be even further simplified: fast paced casual games require repetitive and extremely simple tasks - this still needs improvement for SpotTheLink. Furthermore, the way in which concepts and ontology hierarchies

Table 4. Replay factor

Would you play SpotTheLink again?	
Daily	0,0%
More than once a week	5,9%
More than once a month	0,0%
Hardly ever	64,7%
Never	29, 4%

Table 5. Game fun

Assess the overall gaming fun. The game is:	
Addictive	0,0%
Great fun	0,0%
Average	35,3%
Fairly boring	52,9%
Boring	11,8%

are represented should be improved to foster immediate understanding of players. The results on the correctness of ontology matches confirm previous findings: the output of the games for general knowledge problems is generally of high-quality. The greatest challenge is nevertheless to find the sweet spot between an appealing game design and the usefulness of the data it generates.

5. ENABLING TECHNOLOGY: THE ONTOGAME PLATFORM

SpotTheLink has been developed using the OntoGame API and the associated Generic Gaming Toolkit.[13] The API offers a set of Java classes that abstract common processes and workflows that are used to derivate semantic data from game inputs. The toolkit consists of a J2EE API and several J2EE components developed based on this API. It has been developed for the open Apache Geronimo implementations of the J2EE specification. In addition, the Generic Gaming Toolkit uses Sesame's RDF repository as well the AliBaba Object Repository extension for managing the RDF data produced through the games, together with a series of services for generic semantic content management, semantic search and tag recommendations for images.

Components

In the Generic Gaming Toolkit there are four main conceptual entities: challenges, inputs, resources, and play records. A *challenge* abstracts from the actual task players carry out while playing the game. Each challenge can be split into several sub-challenges, which are structured hierarchically. In SpotTheLink the main task is to align two concepts from two given ontologies, and is sub-divided into two atomic tasks: finding related concepts, and defining the relationship between these concepts. A *resource* abstracts from the topic a challenge is about, for example, a YouTube video, an ontology concept or a Wikipedia article. A resource may also refer to the answer provided by a player, which in the SpotTheLink case, are either related concepts or relationships between concept pairs. An *input* represents an answer of a player to a certain challenge. It is always related to a resource, deals with a specific challenge and may contain a resource as answer. A *play record* behaves like a container for player inputs about a specific resource. It is used for all subsequent background computations by which player inputs are translated into semantic content, including the evaluation of the inputs, and the actual encoding to SKOS.

Agreement Negotiation

Figure 8 provides a high-level overview of the agreement negotiation process within a game model. The process starts with collecting inputs from of all players. These can be: "Disagreed" in case it is not clear whether or not to skip a given challenge, "Skipped" if both players decided to skip, and "Agreed" if they declared that they want to provide an answer to the question raised in the game round at hand. Once the inputs of all players have been collected, the game is resumed according to a pre-defined negotiation strategy. In the games implemented so far as part of the OntoGame series, we ask players to reach an agreement on whether to skip or accept a challenge; however, the toolkit can be easily extended to support variations of this simple model, for instance, for multi-player scenarios in which the majority of players decide upon the questions to be answered.

Partner Matching

Another important feature of the Generic Gaming Toolkit is the matching of the players. When a users logs to a game the system selects a game partner according to criteria such as IP-addresses, location, age, and gender, all of which may influence the quality of the inputs collected. The selection of players within the game ensures that players remain anonymous while consensually resolving challenges, thus increasing the probability that they behave as intended by the game designer. In other games of the OntoGame family we have also used recorded game rounds, for which answers are already available from previous players, in order to realize a single-player mode in addition to the two-players mode deployed in SpotTheLink.

Reliability

A player's reliability, that is a rough indicator of their trustworthiness, is a very important aspect of the process of semantic content creation in the Generic Gaming Toolkit, since the game mechanics are always about questions where the answer is actually unknown to the game designer. It has to be assumed that there are at least some players that want to trick the system and behave in an irrational and unfavorable way. As the very

purpose of the games is to derive useful, structured knowledge from game inputs, each game needs to implement functionality to verify whether an input comes from a trustworthy player or a cheater. Permitting cheating would decrease the gaming fun as well as the quality of the generated data.

Consensus Finding

One of the most important features of the Generic Gaming Toolkit is the abstract projection of the process to find consensus for the set of answers provided for each question. Finding consensus can be achieved in many different ways such as plainly by a simple majority. However, there are also more sophisticated ways of identifying a consensual set of answers, e.g., by weighting each answer by their player's reliability, considering only answers that have been answered similarly by all players of a certain game round. Additionally restrictions such as a minimum number of different players or a minimal number of answers on a challenge can be imposed on the process of consensus finding.

Ranking

Ranking is used to give an indication of the importance of a play record. The importance defines which record is most suited to be played next. Ranking metrics can be implemented in various ways, depending on the needs of the game, i.e., one could rank the records that are closest to produce output highest, or records that have not yet been played very frequently. In the Generic Gaming Toolkit we have implemented two different strategies: one that does not rank at all, which is required when ranking is not to be considered during the record selecting procedure; and a second one considering the number of required answers, the number of different players, and the number of questions that have been answered.

Figure 8. N-player agreement

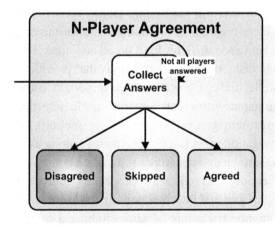

Matching

The last relevant conceptual feature of the Generic Gaming Toolkit is the process of defining whether or not a set of answers coincide. Note that this is different from assessing consensus, as matching answers is used to compute an equality between answers. An example of doing so is comparing two players' answers and evaluating their similarity. Another implemented matching algorithm checks whether a player's answer equals the majority of all previous collected answers about this resource.

6. GUIDELINES FOR THE DESIGN OF GAMES FOR COLLABORATIVE KNOWLEDGE ENGINEERING

The evaluation of SpotTheLink adds to our experiences from previous games: in this section, we provide a number of guidelines for designing games for collaborative knowledge engineering that emerged from these experiences.

Task Selection

The identification of those tasks that are suitable to be carried out as a game is a crucial and basic step. Hiding tasks behind games is not trivial and will not work out when the task is not suitable for this purpose in terms of the level of difficulty - neither too difficult, nor too easy – the audience targeted, allowing to realistically find a consensus, and sufficiently structured to be broken down into separate game challenges. Breaking down tasks into smaller chunks that can be eventually mapped into the different steps a game round consists of bears additional challenges. In particular, our experiences show that the resulting workflows have to be not just constrained in their structure – basically sequences of atomic tasks which are approached and solved consensually by players – but also in size. As a rule of thumb, a sequence of more than 3 to 4 interrelated tasks is likely to

lead to challenges that are too complicated for players to learn and keep track of at the fast pace the game is expected to be played. This makes the game less appealing for players, thus diminishing their willingness to play and reducing the amount of data produced from their inputs. Each atomic task results in a question – to which the correct answer is not known in advance to the game designer – which needs to be answered by the pair of players competing against each other at a certain point in time in the game. This includes open-scale questions, whose answers are typed in by users in a dedicated field, or closed-scale ones, for which the system provides a set of possible answers from which the players have to choose one viable option. In the first scenario one needs to make use of specific matching algorithms to cope with potential variations in the form of the answers – for instance, different spellings – in order to ensure that consensus finding is feasible in most cases. Nevertheless, if the set of potentially correct answers is too broad for a consensus to be likely to emerge in most cases, the task is probably less appropriate for a game-based approach and additional knowledge has to be taken into account to reduce the space of possible solutions.

Game Fun

The greatest challenge when designing a game with a purpose is that the game is designed in such a way that the targeted goal is achieved and the game is still fun to play. Games for semantic content creation are in many cases on the edge of being too difficult for a broad audience. They hide tasks behind online games that provide an intellectual challenge, which is important to keep the games sufficiently interesting. In selection-agreement games (see following section), the navigation must force users to move along existing knowledge structures and make a consensual selection. This requires appropriate visualization techniques and interface paradigms. Moreover, it is in the very nature of games to have a colorful and pretty interface. Therefore, the user interface of the games must be especially usable as well as attractive. This includes employing well-established techniques from user-experience design and usability engineering, but in the same time bears some distinctive challenges related to the very nature of games for knowledge engineering. One important aspect is the representation of the underlying knowledge corpus to the players. Most games with a purpose expect users to describe or answer questions referring to one or more digital resources, for instance, text documents, images or videos; the way these resources are presented and explained to the user is crucial for the extent to which the user is able to provide the right answers and requires additional techniques by which the meaning and content of a resource is disclosed unambiguously. This includes text summarization techniques to show the most representative information conveyed in a text document – as the users will not spend their time during the game to comprehend lengthy portions of text, as well as natural language representations of formal structures such as ontologies.

Massive user participation and generation of output is crucial for the games and the methods they incorporate: they require a critical amount of contribution. Even though the games are designed such that the task is an intellectual challenge and the interface is usable and attractive, we cannot expect massive user involvement per se. Thus, we aim at providing additional incentives to make users start playing and continue playing. This can involve the following measures:

- Competition and reputation: The ranking is an important feature of every game. Players have an interest to improve their reputation within the player community. Competition can also be a strong motivation: being better than the rest. A measure could be to inform users when they are about to lose a rank or when they improved.

- Social component: the social component is extremely important in the games. Knowing that they are playing with a real partner is motivating for many players. As the games are cooperative in their very nature, players might want to know more about their partner. Allowing communication after the games (if they achieve a certain amount of points) can be such a measure. Moreover, players should be able to indicate preferences for the choice of their partners.

Rewarding Mechanism

Rewarding mechanisms serve two different purposes: first, they keep people playing as they enable comparability and therefore competition, e.g., via high-score tables. Furthermore, they stir up ambition and people sticking with repetitive tasks, like in badge systems. Second, they influence players behaviors to a certain extend. This can be used to improve the desired output. For example, rewarding remaining time disproportionally high will cause players to finish as fast as possible.

Knowledge Corpora

The games usually need a corpus of knowledge to start from and that is an integral part of the game challenges. An important characteristic of the games is that challenges are not repeatedly shown to the same players. This requires a large repository of knowledge in the background that can be used as input. Naturally, the choice of such a corpus depends on the task to be solved through the game. Examples for this are Wikipedia articles and YouTube videos, however, one question which still requires additional thinking is the actual topic or the domain of the resources presented, to which the expected audience has to be familiar.

From this discussion and the requirements for game design outlined in earlier work of ours

(Siorpaes and Hepp 2008) we derive the following, simplified rules for building games for collaborative knowledge construction:

1. Challenges should be timed.
2. Score keeping should be facilitated.
3. High score lists and rankings should be visible.
4. Challenges should be selected in an unpredictable way for the players.
5. Players should be matched randomly and play anonymously.
6. Repetition should be an underlying feature.
7. The interaction with the human partner should be obvious.
8. Knowledge corpora should be large.
9. Knowledge corpora should be chosen with the audience in mind.
10. Tasks should be simplistic and easy to understand.
11. User interface should be well-designed.
12. Purpose and semantic content creation task should be carefully selected.

7. CONCLUSION AND FUTURE WORK

Ontology alignment is without doubt one of the most active and mature area of research and development in semantic technologies. A multitude of approaches to match, merge and integrate ontologies, both at the schema and instance levels have been proposed and successfully applied to resolve heterogeneity issues, and, more recently, to interlink RDF data sets exposed over the Web as part of the Linked Open Data Cloud.[14] The strengths and weaknesses of existing systems, as well as their natural limitations and principles combinations have been intensively studied, not least through community projects such as the Ontology Alignment Evaluation Initiative.[15] Human input remains a key ingredient of ontology alignment, either as a source of domain knowledge used to train matching algorithms and to build the underlying knowledge base, or to validate automatically computed results. SpotTheLink provides a means to systematically harvest this input as a side-product of an entertaining collaborative online game.

In a nutshell, in SpotTheLink pairs of players interact with each other to identify correspondences between concepts and instances of two Semantic Web ontologies. Correspondences have to be defined consensually. This offers an effective mechanism to validate the data collected, and to discourage unwanted behavior - as players are randomly selected and cannot communicate to each other through other channels than the game, in the long run their best-bet strategy is to attempt to answer the questions and challenges defined throughout each round of the game truthfully. SpotTheLink can be used for arbitrary pairs of ontologies, though our user trials showed that for certain categories of ontologies - in terms of the captured knowledge, the structure of the inheritance graph, and the type of ontologies (as in upper-level, core, domain, or task ontologies, see (Guarino 1998)) - the game is likely to be more successful than for others. The particular instance used in this paper is based on DBpedia and the upper-level ontology PROTON, which was also at the core of one of our previous games, OntoPronto.

Following a similar approach as in SpotTheLink for the task of interlinking multimedia fragments we are currently working on TubeLink, a game for video interlinking (Hausenblas, Troncy et al. 2009). In short, the gameplay can be explained as follows: Before a game round starts, mini instructions help players to quickly grasp the basic idea of the game. When the game starts, a YouTube video is streamed within a crystal ball and tags start floating around (see Figure 9). The player is expected to choose tags describing what she sees in the video by clicking, dragging and

Figure 9. TubeLink interface

releasing these tags on the crystal ball within a specific time interval. Points are earned if the tags are assessed as relevant by a pre-defined number of players. The reward is higher the closer the match to the average time is, e.g. if most of the players have tagged a given video at 1':23" with "Fire," choosing this tag at 1':20" in the video is worth more points than the same with a certain delay, say at 1':28". Whenever the player matches a tag the orb charges with energy. After a sufficient number of matching tags have been provided the crystal sphere dramatically explodes, and the game round ends.

TubeLink translates players' inputs – timed descriptions of the content of a video - into machine-understandable semantic content as follows. The tags that the player can choose from for each video are labels of concepts and entities from the DBpedia ontology, which we also used in Spot-TheLink. They are generated automatically in an iterative process, bootstrapped by the YouTube tags available; this initial set of descriptors are matched (linguistically) against the DBpedia ontology. The game is used also to validate this matching process, as players can mark irrelevant tags in the course of the game; in addition, a tag is considered correct if it is used in a number of game rounds to the description of the same content. Validated tags are then used to identify further related tags. Just as in the case of SpotTheLink, the scenario just presented is only one of the many possible instances of the game concept for video interlinking. Through the OntoGame platform the game designer can easily configure the game to use a different collection of videos, or different algorithms for tag recommendation.

ACKNOWLEDGMENT

The work presented has been funded by the FP7 project INSEMTIVES under EU Objective 4.3 (grant number FP7-231181).

REFERENCES

Berners-Lee, T. (2006). *Linked data, design issues*. Retrieved May 8, 2011, from http://www.w3.org /DesignIssues/LinkedData.html

Chamberlain, J., Massimo, P., & Kruschwitz, U. (2009). A demonstration of human computation using the Phrase Detectives annotation game. *Proceedings of the ACM SIGKDD Workshop on Human Computation* (pp. 23-24). ACM

Do, H.-H., & Rahm, E. (2002). COMA: A system for flexible combination of schema matching approaches. *Proceedings of the 28th International Conference on Very large Data Bases* (pp. 610-621). VLDB Endowment

Doan, A., Madhavan, J., Domingos, P., & Halevy, A. (2002). Learning to map between ontologies on the Semantic Web. *Proceedings of the 11th International World Wide Web Conference* (pp. 662-673). ACM

Doan, A., Madhavan, J., Domingos, P., & Halevy, A. (2004). Ontology matching: A machine learning approach. In Staab, S. (Ed.), *Handbook on ontologies* (pp. 385–516). Springer.

Ehrig, M., & Sure, Y. (2004). Ontology mapping - An integrated approach. *Proceedings of the 1st European Semantic Web Symposium* (pp. 76-91). Springer.

Euzenat, J., & Shvaiko, P. (2007). *Ontology matching*. Berlin, Germany: Springer.

Falconer, S. M., & Storey, M.-A. (2007). A cognitive support framework for ontology mapping. *Proceedings of the 6th International The Semantic Web and 2nd Asian Conference on Asia* (pp. 114-127). ACM.

Giunchiglia, F., Yatskevich, M., & Shvaiko, P. (2007). Semantic matching: Algorithms and implementation. *Journal on Data Semantics, 9*, 1–38.

Guarino, N. (1998). Formal ontology and information systems. *Proceedings of the 1ˢᵗ International Conference on Formal Ontologies in Information Systems* (pp. 3–15). IOS-Press.

Hausenblas, M., Troncy, R., Raimond, Y., & Bürger, T. (2009). *Interlinking multimedia: How to apply linked data principles to multimedia fragments*. Paper presented at the Linked Data on the Web Workshop, Amsterdam, Netherlands.

Kalfoglou, Y., & Schorlemmer, M. (2003). IF-Map: An ontology mapping method based on information flow theory. *Journal on Data Semantics, 1*(1), 98–127. doi:10.1007/978-3-540-39733-5_5

Ma, H., Chandrasekar, R., Quirk, C., & Gupta, A. (2009). Page hunt: Improving search engines using human computation games. *Proceedings of the 32nd International ACM SIGIR Conference on Research and Development in Information Retrieval* (pp. 746-747). ACM.

Madhavan, J., Berstein, P., & Rahm, E. (2001). Generic schema matching with Cupid. *Proceeedings of the 27th International Conference on Very larged Data Bases* (pp. 48-58). VLDB Endowment.

Maedche, A., Motik, B., Silva, N., & Volz, R. (2002). MAFRA: A mapping framework for distributed ontologies. *Proceedings of the 13th European Conference on Knowledge Engineering and Knowledge Management* (pp. 235-250). Springer.

McCann, R., Shen, W., & Doan, A. (2008). Matching schemas in online communities: A Web 2.0 approach. *Proceedings of the 18th International Conference on Data Engineering* (pp 110-119). IEEE.

Noy, N. F., Griffith, N., & Musen, M. A. (2008). Collecting community-based mappings in an ontology repository. *International Semantic Web Conference* (pp. 371-386). Springer.

Shi, F., Li, J., Tang, L., Xie, G. T., & Li, H. (2009). Actively learning ontology matching via user interaction. *International Semantic Web Conference ISWC2009* (pp. 585-600). Springer.

Shvaiko, P., & Euzenat, J. (2008). *Ten challenges for ontology matching. OTM Conferences* (pp. 1164–1182). Springer.

Siorpaes, K., & Hepp, M. (2008). OntoGame: Weaving the Semantic Web by online games. *Proceedings of the European Semantic Web Conference* (pp. 751-766). Springer.

Siorpaes, K., Hepp, M., Klotz, A., & Hackl, M. (2008). *myOntology: Tapping the wisdom of crowds for building ontologies.* Unpublished technical report, STI Innsbruck, Austria.

Siorpaes, K., & Simperl, E. (2010). Human intelligence in the process of semantic content creation. *World Wide Web Journal, 13*(1), 33–59. doi:10.1007/s11280-009-0078-0

Siorpaes, K., & Simperl, E. (2010). *Incentives, motivation, participation, games: Human computation for linked data,* (p. 700). Retrieved May 8, 2011, from http://linkeddata.future-internet. eu /images/9/91/FIA2010_Human_Computation_for_Linked_Data.pdf.

Stumme, G., & Maedche, A. (2001). FCA-Merge: Bottom-up merging of ontologies. *Proceedings of the Seventeenth International Joint Conference on Artificial Intelligence* (pp. 225–234). Morgan Kaufmann.

Terziev, I., Kiryakov, A., & Manov, D. (2005). Base-upper-level ontology guidance. *Deliverable D1.8.1 of the EU-IST Project IST-2003-506826 SEKT.* Retrieved May 8, 2011, from http://proton. semanticweb.org /D1_8_1.pdf

Tu, K., & Yu, Y. (2005). CMC: Combining multiple schema-matching strategies based on credibility prediction. *Proceedings of the 10th International Conference on Database Systems for Advanced Applications* (pp. 888-893). Springer.

Von Ahn, L. (2006). Games with a purpose. *IEEE Computer, 29*(6), 92–94. doi:10.1109/MC.2006.196

Von Ahn, L., & Dabbish, L. (2004). Labeling images with a computer game. *Proceedings of the 2004 Conference on Human Factors in Computing Systems* (pp. 319-326). ACM.

Von Ahn, L., Dannenberg, R. B., & Crawford, M. (2007). *Tagatune: A game for music and sound annotation.* Paper presented at the International Conference on Music Information Retrieval, Vienna, Austria.

Von Ahn, L., Liu, R., & Blum, M. (2006). Peekaboom: A game for locating objects in images. *Proceedings of the SIGCHI Conference on Human Factors in Computing Systems* (pp. 55-64). ACM.

Wölger, S., Siorpaes, K., Bürger, T., Simperl, E., Thaler, S., & Hofer, C. (2011). *Interlinking data - approaches and tools.* Unpublished technical report, STI Innsbruck, Austria.

Zhdanova, A., & Shvaiko, P. (2006). *Community-driven ontology matching.*

ADDITIONAL READING

Barua, A., Sophie Lee, C. H., & Whinston, A. B. (1995). Incentives and computing systems for team-based organizations. *Organization Science, 6,* 487–504. doi:10.1287/orsc.6.4.487

Batson, C. D., Ahmad, N., & Tsang, J. (2002). Four motives for community involvement. *The Journal of Social Issues, 58*(3), 429–445. doi:10.1111/1540-4560.00269

Bernstein, M., Tan, D., Smith, G., Czerwinski, M., & Horvitz, E. (2008). Collabio: A game for annotating people within social networks. *Proceedings of the 22nd Annual ACM Symposium on User Interface Software and Technology* (pp. 97-100). ACM. Auer, S., Dietzold, S., & Riechert, T. (2006). OntoWiki – A Tool for Social, Semantic Collaboration. *In the Proceedings of the 5th International Semantic Web Conference* (pp. 736-749), Springer

Braun, S., Schmidt, A., & Walter, A. (2007). Ontology maturing: A collaborative Web 2.0 approach to ontology engineering. *Proceedings of the Workshop on Social and Collaborative Construction of Structured Knowledge at the 16th International World Wide Web Conference.* CEUR-WS.org.

Cheng, R., & Vassilieva, J. (2006). Design and evaluation of an adaptive incentive mechanism for sustained educational online communities. *User Modeling and User-Adapted Interaction, 16*(3/4), 321–348. doi:10.1007/s11257-006-9013-6

Hemetsberger, A. (2002). Fostering cooperation on the Internet: Social exchange processes in innovative virtual consumer communities. *Advances in Consumer Research. Association for Consumer Research (U. S.), 29*, 354–356.

Hudso, J., & Bruckman, A. (2004). The bystander effect: A lens for understanding patterns of participation. *Journal of the Learning Sciences, 13*(2), 165–195. doi:10.1207/s15327809jls1302_2

Kotis, K., & Vouros, G. (2006). Human-centered ontology engineering: The HCOME methodology. *International Journal of Knowledge and Information Systems, 10*(1), 109–131. doi:10.1007/s10115-005-0227-4

Kuo, Y., Lee, J., Chiang, K., Wang, R., Shen, E., Chan, C., & Hsu, J. Y. (2009). Community-based game design: Experiments on social games for commonsense data collection. In *Proceedings of the ACM SIGKDD Workshop on Human Computation* (pp. 15-22). ACM.

Ling, K., Beenen, G., Ludford, P., Wang, X., Chang, K., & Li, X. (2005). Using social psychology to motivate contributions to online communities. *Journal of Computer-Mediated Communication, 10*(4).

Moore, T. D., & Serva, M. A. (2007). Understanding member motivation for contributing to different types of virtual communities: A proposed framework. *Proceedings of the 2007 ACM SIG-MIS CPR Conference on Computer Personnel Research: The Global Information Technology Workforce,* (pp. 153-158). ACM.

Riechert, T., & Lohmann, S. (2007). Mapping cognitive models to social semantic spaces-collaborative development of project ontologies. *The Social Semantic Web 2007, Proceedings of the 1st Conference on Social Semantic Web* (pp. 91 – 98). GI. Hacker, S., & Von Ahn, L., (2009). Matchin - Eliciting user preferences with an online game. In *Proceedings of the 27th International Conference on Human Factors in Computing Systems* (pp. 1207-1216). ACM.

Solachidis, V., Mylonas, P., Geyer-Schulz, A., Hoser, B., Chapman, S., & Ciravegna, F. … Avrithis Y. (2008). *Generating collective intelligence.* Presented at the 32nd Annual Conference-Advances in Data Analysis, Data Handling and Business Intelligence, Hamburg, DE.

Von Ahn, L. Ginosar, S., Kedia, M., Liu, R.,& Blum, M. (2006). Improving accessibility of the Web with a computer game. In *the Proceedings of the 2006 Conference on Human Factors in Computing Systems* (pp. 79-82). ACM.

Von Ahn, L., Kedia, M., & Blum, M. (2006). Verbosity: A game for collecting commonsense facts. In *the Proceedings of the 2006 Conference on Human Factors in Computing Systems* (pp. 75-78). ACM.

KEY TERMS AND DEFINITIONS

Alignment: The process of defining correspondences between two classes and instances in an ontology.

Casual Games: Simple games used by a mass audience.

Incentive: Reward assigned by an external 'judge' to a performer for a certain task.

Interlinking: The process of identifying equivalences between entities denoted by URIs in Linked Data.

Linked Data: A collection of principles and best practices for publishing and accessing structured data on the Web according to standard Web technologies and protocols (HTTP, RDF, SPARQL).

OntoGame: A platform for games for knowledge acquisition producing data encoded according to Semantic Web principles.

Ontology: Conceptualization of domain knowledge in terms of classes, instances, properties and axioms, in the context of the Semantic Web represented using specific W3C standards.

ENDNOTES

[1] http://www.gwap.com/
[2] http://fold.it
[3] http://galoap.codeplex.com/
[4] http://apps.facebook.com/conceptgame/
[5] http://ontogame.sti2.at/
[6] http://www.w3.org/TR/rdf-schema/, http://www.w3.org/2004/OWL/
[7] http://oaei.ontologymatching.org/2008/results/
[8] http://dbpedia.org/, http://proton.semantic-web.org/
[9] http://www4.wiwiss.fu-berlin.de/dbpedia/dev/ontology.htm
[10] http:///www.ontogame.org/games
[11] http://apps.facebook.com/ontogame
[12] http://www.w3.org/2004/02/skos/
[13] http://insemtives.svn.sourceforge.net/viewvc/insemtives/generic-gaming-toolkit/trunk/
[14] http://linkeddata.org/
[15] http://oaei.ontologymatching.org/

Chapter 4
Knowledge Management

Salman Iqbal
Massey University, Manawatu Campus, New Zealand

Hayati Abdul Jalal
Massey University, Manawatu Campus, New Zealand

Paul Toulson
Massey University, Manawatu Campus, New Zealand

David Tweed
Massey University, Manawatu Campus, New Zealand

ABSTRACT

Organisational culture plays an important role for enabling the process of knowledge sharing. Organisational culture is not only reflected in the visible aspects of organization such as structure, mission, and objectives, it is also embedded in the behaviour of people. The purpose of this chapter is to close research gaps present in knowledge sharing success by examining the linkages between employees' knowledge-sharing through collaboration, perceived values of involvement, trustworthiness, and formal recognition. The research data was collected by using simple random sampling techniques from a population of knowledge workers in Malaysian IT organisations. The findings highlight the importance of organisational culture for successful knowledge sharing within organisations. The results of factor analysis show the emergence of four new cultural values extant in the Malaysian context. These values are involvement, trustworthiness, formal recognition, and independence. Successful knowledge sharing is significantly related to the perceived value of involvement, trustworthiness, and formal recognition. This chapter will be beneficial for researchers, practitioners, scholars, and organisations (leaders and employees); it will also be helpful for those interested in organisational structure and relationships across organisations in knowledge contexts.

DOI: 10.4018/978-1-4666-0894-8.ch004

INTRODUCTION

One of the most basic concerns in organisations is the regeneration and development of scarce resources through which organisations can secure competitive advantage. The shift from an industrial to knowledge economy implies that people's knowledge becomes the main source of production. From an organisation's view, it is the employees' competence (human capital) that needs to be captured through knowledge sharing behavior.

Individual employees play an important role in organisational performance because the knowledge embedded in an individual can act as a profit lever in the organisation. Profit levers act to enhance or, if not used fully, inhibit the effectiveness of an organisation in a competitive and dynamic business environment. All forms of knowledge are rooted in individuals' personal experience known as tacit knowledge, which cannot be imitated as easily as other productive resources in the organisation (Pathirage, Amaratunga, & Haigh, 2007). Organisations manage to retain the flow of knowledge through various means. We suggest that organisational culture, in terms of employees' collaboration, can positively influence innovativeness. We also suggest that management practices, especially those employed by senior managers, help to motivate individuals to use their knowledge effectively for innovation.

The purpose of this chapter is to give the reader a better understanding of employees' knowledge sharing behaviour in organisations. We first review the literature from several fields of inquiry, such as the information and decision sciences, management theory, human resource management, strategic management, organisational communication and organisational behavior. Although knowledge exists at many levels in organisations, our focus in this chapter is the knowledge that exists within individuals and how the main organisational culture influences knowledge sharing practices.

LITERATURE REVIEW

An individual employee's knowledge plays an important role in organisational performance. For instance, it has been suggested that individual skills and abilities have long been known as essential for maintaining an organisation's economic competitiveness (Coffield, 2002). The world economy has shifted from being industrial to knowledge based, where information has become the primary output and people's knowledge has become the main means of production (Davis, 2004). In this knowledge era, it is important to understand that the main profit lever becomes employee knowledge. Further, all the assets in a firm except employee knowledge are lifeless and passive until they become subject to human application which generates value (Fitz-enz, 2000).

Knowledge

Knowledge is information, and managing this information helps organisations to function effectively. Barnard (2005) suggests that knowledge itself, then, becomes the real asset of organisations. Knowledge is intangible, as opposed to other traditional tangible resources. Leaders of effective organisations realise that employee knowledge (human capital) is part of an organisation's intellectual capital including relationship capital and structural capital (Fitz-enz, 2000). Yang and Guo (2007) conclude that knowledge is an important source to help organisations to achieve competitive advantage. The concept of knowledge as a means of competitive advantage in organisations has become popular in the literature (Alvesson & Karreman, 2001).

De Long & Fahey (2000) argue that knowledge resides at three levels in organisations, known as the individual, the group, and the organizational levels. Roos and Krogh (1992) further subdivide the organisational level into departments and divisions. This chapter focuses on the most basic of these levels, the knowledge that is possessed by individuals (employees). Furthermore the sharing of individual knowledge with other individuals is essential for the transfer, distribution and further creation of knowledge at all the other levels within an organisation. For instance, employees of IT sector can learn new developments from peers, and managers to enhance their own knowledge.

Employees' Knowledge (Tacit Knowledge)

People develop personal knowledge through their personal experience which cannot be expressed or documented easily. Kikoski and Kikoski (2004) suggest that personal knowledge is soft knowledge developed through experience and intelligence which cannot be codified or documented. All forms of knowledge are derived from tacit knowledge (Pathirage, et al., 2007). Baumard (1999) suggests that tacit knowledge is really the knowledge that exists only in our minds, and this is far greater than any information that is passed on. Tacit knowledge, as a critical resource, can provide competitive advantage to the organisation (Al-Alawi, Al-Marzooqi, & Mohammed, 2007; Aulawi, Sudirman, Suryadi, & Govindaraju, 2008). Employees' tacit knowledge can make an organisation different from its competitors by sharing, transferring and implementing employees' knowledge. For example, employees' of higher education institutes, IT industries and other knowledge intensive organisations, which have a pool of skilled knowledge workers, can perform better through knowledge sharing in open discussion, forums, seminars or colloquiums.

Knowledge Sharing in Organisations

Knowledge management through sharing and transferring employee's knowledge can help to increase competitive advantage and organisational performance (Earl, 2001; Nonaka, 1994; Sveiby, 1997; Tuomi, 2003). Knowledge residing in an individual's brain is unproductive and

fruitless if it is not transferred, shared and used in an organisation (Aulawi, et al., 2008; Nonaka & Takeuchi, 1995). Interpersonal trust and management support helps to build an environment of knowledge sharing, which encourages other employees to participate in knowledge sharing activities such as informal collaboration to enhance the possibility of creativity (Hsu, 2008; Ipe, 2003). Knowledge sharing thus gives us a linkage among individuals and their organisation, which improves organisational capability to innovate (Cohen and Levinthal, (1990).

Knowledge Sharing Enablers

There is little empirical research specifically in the field of knowledge sharing among the individuals in organisations, however, some researchers have begun to discover some of the multifaceted dynamics that are present in knowledge sharing processes. Employees leave traces of their knowledge during everyday assignments in knowledge organisations through discussions, networks, formal meetings and informal chats. This chapter focuses on the how specific knowledge sharing enablers such as organisational culture (collaboration) formalisation, employees' autonomy and trust influence knowledge sharing between individuals in organisations to use the traces of knowledge for organisational effectiveness. However, we also acknowledge, and understand that other knowledge sharing enablers discussed in the literature such as IT support, hiring practices, the nature of knowledge, motivation to share, opportunities to share and rewards also affect employees' knowledge sharing behaviour.

What is Organisational Culture?

Organisational culture refers to the perceived desirable values that guide organisational members to act appropriately and share knowledge within the interaction context (Alavi, Kayworth, Timothy, & Leidner, 2005). It is recognised as an important factor in promoting knowledge sharing practices. For instance, Davenport and Prusak (1998) note that organisational culture creates an environment which motivates employees to share knowledge throughout the organisation. De Long & Fahey (2000) describe four ways in which organisational culture encourages knowledge sharing practices: First, the culture identifies the type of knowledge that is valuable in a particular organisation. Second, it describes the relationship between individual and organisational knowledge. Third, it develops social integration among employees within organisation. Fourth, it determines how new knowledge should be distributed in the organisation. Moreover, "organisational culture orients the mindset and action of every employee" (1995, p. 167).

Organisational culture helps to distinguish between knowledge that can be shared and knowledge to hold and use within organisations (T. H. Davenport, 1997). Studies investigating the relationship of organisational culture to knowledge management identify several attempts to model the organisational culture of knowledge management processes, as well as a number of identifiable organisational variables believed to influence the performance of knowledge management processes (Alavi et al., 2005; Lee & Choi, 2003; Ruppel & Harrington, 2001). Subsequently, Alavi et al.'s (2005) cultural model with the additional value of trust was adapted for our research into this question. These values include collaboration, innovativeness, formalisation, autonomy, expertise and trust.

A collaborative culture facilitates knowledge creation by increasing the exchange of knowledge by reducing fear due to loss of value and knowledge if shared through collaboration (Lee and Choi 2003). Additionally, the involvement of people from several departments or communities may encourage the development of an innovative culture through cross pollination of ideas or insights across departments or communities (Alavi et al 2005). This learning emphasises open communication flows and reasoned risk-taking, thus encouraging reward change and creativity, which reveals innovativeness (Bock, Zmud, Kim and Lee 2005). Nevertheless, to some extent, the individual's degree of freedom to be innovative will be restricted by management through policies and procedures that require adherence. Alavi et al. (2005), however, suggest that formalisation engenders an appropriate way of doing things. As such, Hall (2001) suggests that autonomy must be provided for and people should be able to step out of their designated roles in order to cultivate an innovative culture. Autonomy may be critical to knowledge workers as knowledge work calls for the exercise of professional judgment in the effort to solve complex and unique problems (Alavi et al 2005; Robertson and Hammersley 2000). Expertise, as part of tacit knowledge, gives specific individuals status and recognition within an organisation as other staff seek answers from them. However, this status does not necessarily relate to their position in the organisation (Alavi et al 2005).

Knowledge sharing, through collaboration, can be facilitated by different means. Employees learn when they meet with experts in their own fields. Sahin (2007), Noorderhaven and Harzing (2009) suggest that organisations manage tacit knowledge sharing through communities of practice (face to face interactions), where a space is provided and employees interact formally in their work time or informally in meal breaks. Face-to-face interaction is one of the best means to collaborate with others, because of its capability for effective knowledge sharing. Davenport (1994) emphasises that a manager gets information mostly through interpersonal contact. McDermott (2000) suggests that employees prefer to get information and knowledge through face to face interaction with other employees because this increases clarity and understanding. Furthermore, face to face interaction develops a sense of reciprocity and trust, which is a key feature of the effective transfer of tacit knowledge (Gray, 2001). According to empirical research, the knowledge received by an employee from others encourages a reciprocal flow of knowledge towards the direction of the knowledge source both up and down in organisations. Further, reciprocity is one of the main motivators of knowledge sharing in communities of practice (Bartol, Liu, Zeng, & Wu, 2009). However, some employees fear exploitation of their knowledge during interactions, which can badly damage the knowledge sharing process (Empson, 2001). For example, Knowledge workers in the IT field might feel that if they share their knowledge they may become worthless, due to rapid growth in software knowledge. Thus, investment in sharing tacit knowledge through collaboration has dual benefits: it improves organisational performance by engaging employees in a learning environment; and, it also allows employees to validate their knowledge through expert and peer feedback.

The Importance of Trust

Trust is included in this chapter because there is general agreement that trust between co-workers and trust towards management are both believed to have a strong influence on the achievement of knowledge sharing (Abrams, Cross, Lesser and Levin 2003; Al-Alawi et al 2007; Renzl 2008). Trust among employees and the extent to which organisational members identify themselves with the organisation influences employee motivation to share knowledge (Adler and Kwon 2002). Employees' interpersonal trust promotes effective knowledge creation and sharing in organizations (Tsai & Ghoshal, 1998). According to Penley and Hawkins (1985) building trust among employees helps them to share and transfer knowledge quickly, smoothly and effectively. Cross, Rice, and Parker (2001) suggest that trust removes knowledge sharing barriers and ensures that the knowledge is well understood, absorbed and can be used effectively. On the other hand, the lack of trust leads to poor knowledge integration and imperfect information (M. Alavi & Tiwana, 2002).

Kristiina, Hanna, and Rebecca (2007) suggest that interpersonal trust improves through similarities among employees. Renzl (2008) suggests that promoting vertical interpersonal trust between managers (line and senior managers) and employees is a strategy that reduces the fear of losing unique value while allowing the discovery of synergies. Further, Moreland (2006) suggests that joint problem solving techniques facilitated by managers enhance interpersonal trust on both the horizontal and vertical levels. Little is known, however, about how trust can foster similar groups and behaviours. Employees can mingle easily in similar networks on and off the job, which can boost the knowledge sharing process. However, an empirical study is needed to find out the extent that trust between employees undergirds knowledge sharing practices in knowledge–intensive organisations.

The Importance of Innovativeness

Organisations acquire basic and traditional knowledge for their survival. However, some organisations always try to be innovative to maintain a competitive advantage over others. For instance, Harrison & Samaon (2002) suggest that most organisations are trying to increase their innovation capability in order to achieve an advantage over their competitors. Organisations' innovative capabilities are caught up in knowledge sharing behaviour (Aulawi, et al., 2008; Birchall & Tovstiga, 2006; Carillo & Zazzaro, 2000; Clegg, Unsworth, Epitropaki, & Parker, 2002; Ellonen, Blomqvist, & Puumalainen, 2008). Tacit knowledge sharing will often result in the creation of innovative ideas and is considered critical to innovative capabilities in organisations (Armbrecht, et al., 2001). Earl (2001) suggests that innovative capabilities help organisations to modify and review their products and services according to customer needs. Thus, by drawing primarily on the literature, a conceptual framework was proposed and presented in Figure 1.

Figure 1. Organisational culture and knowledge sharing success

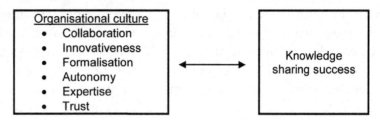

Research Questions

Several possible linkages have been identified which can now be taken forward for empirical testing. Research questions that need to be explored include:

1. Do organizational cultural values relate to knowledge sharing success?
2. Does knowledge sharing success relate to employees' involvement?

METHODOLOGY

Sample and Research Process

For this research the population of interest was employees identified as "knowledge workers" in Malaysian-owned Information Technology (IT) companies. These IT companies are characterised as software developers and are IT solutions providers to government agencies situated in Wilayah Persekutuan and Selangor. IT companies with over 100 employees of multiracial composition and multimedia super corridor (MSC) status were selected. Companies with over 100 employees are more likely to have formally established HRM systems (Collins and Smith 2006). A list of eligible companies was obtained from the MSC and PIKOM databases. Twenty companies fulfilled the characteristics outlined for this research and of these, seven initially agreed to participate in the study. Unfortunately, due to the economic crisis, three companies were no longer suitable for the current study as they were in the midst of merger and acquisition (M&A) activities during the data collection period. In the end employees from four companies made up the final sample.

A simple random sampling technique was applied to the database to select a suitable number of respondents identified by management as knowledge workers. Knowledge workers were defined as employees "critical for creating new knowledge or developing innovations within the organisation" (Collins and Smith, 2006:549). They were of Malaysian nationality, having been employed by the company for at least a year, and were involved in creating new knowledge or developing innovations. It was assumed that Malaysian employees working in those participating organisations for more than one year had become familiar with the culture of organisations in the Malaysian context.

The number of knowledge workers identified by each participating company was in the range of 175 – 285 persons, making a total number of 810 accessible employees as the population for this research. According to guidelines provided by Krejcie and Morgan (1970), the minimum desirable sample size is $n = 260$ to obtain a known precision ±5% and a confidence level of 95%. The sample size, however, may be increased to support further analysis in order to answer research objectives using correlation and multiple regression analysis (Chuan, 2006). Therefore, from the list of names provided by each organisation, a final sample of 500 respondents was selected using random number tables. From these, 270 completed surveys were received and were considered usable, representing a 54% response rate. Pair-wise deletion was used to deal with missing cases, that is, while missing cases were omitted, cases with valid values for other variables were included in the statistical analyses.

The Questionnaire

All constructs, in the questionnaire, except for expertise, were measured using existing and tested scales. Collaboration and formalization were operationalised using a measure developed by Lee and Choi (2003). The former describes the degree of cooperation, support and help among employees in the organisation and the latter refers to the degree of formal rules, procedures and standard policies in the organisation (Alavi et al 2005; Lee and Choi 2003). Innovativeness, explains the degree of tolerance to failure by allowing a free flow of information for organisational improvement (Alavi et al 2005; Bock et al 2005). This measure was based on Bock et al's (2005) innovativeness scale. Autonomy was operationalised using an instrument developed by Hackman and Oldham (1976). This measure describes the extent to which employees exploit their self-direction in scheduling work and determining the procedures to be used in undertaking tasks (Alavi et al 2005; Hackman and Oldham, 1976). Trust is defined as "faith in the trustworthy intentions of others and confidence in the ability of others" (Cook and Walls 1980:40). It was operationalised using a combination set of measures developed by Cook and Wall (1980), and Staples and Webster (2008). Employee know-how and skills denote expertise that can eventually become symbolised through a change of status and recognition as an expert for facilitation of information flow within an organisation (Alavi et al 2005). However, no extant measures were available while conducting this research. Therefore, the instrument for measuring expertise was developed based on a review of the findings of Alavi et al (2005). Finally one construct measuring knowledge sharing success (KSS), which explains the extent to which recipients obtain ownership of, commitment to, and satisfaction with shared knowledge, was measured using items developed by Cummings and Teng (2003). (Details of the questionnaire can be obtained from the principal author).

RESULTS

In this study, the 40 items in the two sections of the questionnaires that formed the dataset are factor analysed to verify that they clustered into the 7 constructs in the conceptual framework shown in Figure 1. The initial principle components factor analysis is run with eigenvalues set at > 1 and a maximum of 25 iterations. This resulted in the identification of 8 components with many multiple loading items, which accounted for 61.17% of total variance. A second factor analysis is then undertaken with 7 factor solution and a maximum of 25 iterations. The resulting varimax rotated component for both analyses are not as expected. Only the items in the knowledge sharing success section are clustered as expected, but the distribution patterns for organisational culture is not consistent with previous studies utilising the similar items measuring these constructs. An attempt is also made to verify whether the measurement items in the questionnaire clustered into the two main concepts of the study. Therefore, the 40 Likert items are subjected to two factor solution with maximum of 25 iterations. The resulting varimax rotated component matrix except knowledge sharing success is also not as expected. The analyses' direction utilising EFA are then changed. Each section of the questionnaire is then subjected to individual factor analysis.

The 22 items of organisational culture (OC) scale were analysed using principle components analysis and varimax rotation used to increase the interpretability of the factor solution (Hair, Black,

Babin and Anderson 2006). The suitability of the data for factor analysis was also assessed following the guidelines recommended by Pett, Lackey and Sullivan (2003). Bartlett's Test of Sphericity was statistically significant and the Kaiser-Meyer-Olkin (KMO) value was 0.801. All MSA values for individual items exceeded the recommended value of 0.60, thus supporting the factorability of the correlation matrix.

Principle component analysis reveals the presence of six components with eigenvalues exceeding 1, explaining 23.52%, 10.36%, 9.25%, 6.45%, 5.13% and 4.55% of the variance respectively. However, the resulting distribution pattern is not as expected. To further confirm the distribution pattern of the organisational culture, the 22 items are subjected to another factor analysis with eigenvalues set at > 1 and a three, four, five and seven factor solution at a time. However, these varimax rotated component matrix do not result in any differences from the previous results.

An inspection of the scree plot (see Appendix A) revealed a clear break in the trend for eigenvalues after the fourth component. Using Catell's scree test (Pallant 2005), it was decided to retain four components for further investigation. This was further supported by the result of a parallel analysis, which showed only four components had eigenvalues exceeding the corresponding criterion values for a randomly generated data matrix of the same size. Furthermore, a four factor solution was preferred due to an insufficient number of primary loadings and the difficulty of interpreting factor loadings for less than or more than four factors. The rotated solution revealed the presence of a simple structure with all components showing a number of strong loadings and all variables loading substantially on only one component (DeVellis 2003; Hair et al 2006; Pallant 2005). The four component solution explains 49.56% of the variance, with Component 1 contributing 19.34%, Component 2 contributing 10.35%, Component 3 contributing 10.33% and Component 4 contributing 9.54%. Table 1

presents the rotated factor structure for the four factor solution.

In this research, the items measuring organisational culture did not cluster as expected. New components with a combination of multiple dimensions were established and revealed the presence of several cross loading factors. Hair et al. (2006) suggest that items with moderate–sized loadings on multiple factors should not be dropped even though they note that the presence of these items makes the interpretation of factors more difficult. In this research, the reassigning of a place for multiple loading items was assessed by including and excluding the items through examination of each component's inter-item reliability (Pett et al 2003). As such, item "15" was placed on Factor 2 (see Table 1); items "11" and "29" were placed on Component 3 and item "27" was place on Factor 4. The alpha coefficients for all components show that the majority are highly reliable and acceptable with alpha scores exceeding 0.6, the threshold recommended by Hair et al (2006) for exploratory research. The value of the alphas indicates that each of the scales possesses a moderate to high level of internal consistency. The overall alpha for the organisational culture measures was found to be 0.784.

Component 1 (Table 1) incorporated those items which addressed the perceived value of innovativeness, collaboration, trust, expertise and formalisation. It is labeled as '*Involvement*', which describes the ability of organisations to improve successful knowledge sharing by encouraging employees to actively participate in organisational activities, and to develop a sense of 'collaboration' amongst organisational members through responsive management strategies. When analysing items comprising Component 2, it was clear that this component incorporated all questions posed in regard to trust and autonomy. Reviewing the wording and interpretation of Component 2 enabled the identification of the importance of trust in knowledge sharing. Component 2 was then labelled as '*Trustworthiness*' defined as "faith in

Table 1. Rotated factor structure matrix for organisational culture

Cronbach's alpha, α =	Component			
	1 .777	2 .704	3 .709	4 .671
Q20 Employees encouraged to find new methods	.714			
Q17 Willingness to collaborate across organisational units	.702			
Q16 Employees encouraged to suggest ideas	.676			
Q14 Willingness to accept future responsibility	.636			
Q21 Employees satisfied by the degree of collaboration	.633			
Q18 Management sincere to understand employees' opinion	.627			
Q19 Employees motivated to share knowledge and be known expert	.591			
Q12 Rules and procedures are written	.468			
Q11 Employees supportive	.453		*.403*	
Q23 Expertise expedites flow information	.379			
Q22 Employees feel they will not able to count on co-workers to help		.788		
Q30 Job denies employees any chance to use personal initiative		.726		
Q33 If possible employees would not give co-worker any influence		.680		
Q15 Employees wish to oversee work of co-workers	.460	.552		
Q24 Contacts occur on a planned or formal basis			.624	
Q29 Employees confident organisation will treat them fairly	.446		.563	
Q32 Employees want to share knowledge to gain recognition			.509	
Q26 Employees can ignore rules and reach informal agreement				.791
Q28 Prefer activities not covered by formal procedures				.730
Q25 Job permits employees to decide on their own				.531
Q13 Employees make own rules on the job				.531
Q27 Employees put much value on taking risks			-.518	.526

the trustworthy intentions of others and confidence in the ability of others" (Cook and Wall 1980:40). Items comprising Component 3 incorporated items of those which addressed formalisation, trust and expertise. Component 3 is named '*Formal recognition*' which demonstrates that employees stress the importance of well developed procedures as a means of receiving fair treatment from management and recognition as supportive employees for successful knowledge sharing. When analysing those items comprising Component 4, it was clear that this component incorporated items of those which addressed formalisation and autonomy. Component 4, labeled '*Independence*', portrays

concerns with openness, nonconformity and risk taking (if decisions fail).

A similar procedure as reported above was followed to assess the factorability of the correlation matrix for knowledge sharing success. Bartlett's Test of Sphericity reached statistical significance, with a KMO value of 0.950, the factor solution accounting for 55.433% of total variance and the overall alpha was 0.933. The varimax rotated component matrix failed to converge in 25 iterations because only one component was extracted. The 18 items of knowledge sharing success were then subjected to a further factor analysis with Eigen values set at > 1 for separate ethnic variables. The varimax rotated component matrix did not result in any differences from the previous result. Therefore, only one component of knowledge sharing success was used for further investigation.

The Relationship of Organisational Cultural Values to Knowledge Sharing Success (KSS)

Pearson product moment correlation coefficients were computed to determine the relationships between the independent variables, organisational culture and the dependent variable, knowledge sharing success. Table 2 shows the resultant correlations.

There are significant and positive correlations between each of the cultural value variables, except independence and knowledge sharing success at $p < 0.01$. Moderate relationships are indicated between involvement and formal recognition and knowledge sharing success. Although there is a significant relationship between trustworthiness and KSS, the correlation strength is small. Additionally, multiple regression analysis was also conducted to determine which among the three cultural variables makes the strongest unique contribution to explaining the dependent variable, when the variance explained by all other variables in the model are controlled for. Table 3 summarises the results of the regression analysis.

The findings reveal that *involvement* ($\beta = 0.473$) was the respondents' most preferred value for successful knowledge sharing, followed by *formal recognition* ($\beta = 0.425$) and *trustworthiness* ($\beta =$

0.189). The β value for *trustworthiness* is slightly lower than those for *involvement* and *formal recognition*, indicating that *trustworthiness* made a smaller significant contribution to the success of knowledge sharing.

CONCLUSION

Based on the results of this survey of 270 employees identified as knowledge workers of four knowledge based organisations in two states of Malaysia, a modified conceptual framework was constructed (see Figure 2).

The emergence (by cluster) of four new labels for organisational culture reflects indigenous Malaysian values that emphasis's extended family and collectives where everyone takes responsibility for fellow members of their group (Abdullah 1992; Kennedy 2002). These values emphasis close ties between individuals, a respect for authority, being tolerant of errors, generosity, friendliness, collectivity and care for others. The identification of cultural values specific to other societies may also emerge if the research is conducted in other settings. Further, these results show significant relationships between organisational culture and knowledge sharing success through the values of involvement, trustworthiness and formal recognition.

Therefore, these results suggest that increasing acceptability and desirability for organisational culture is associated with increasing knowledge

Table 2. Correlations of organisational culture and KSS

	Knowledge sharing success
Involvement	0.474**
Trustworthiness	0.185**
Formal recognition	0.429**
Independence **indicates a significant result	-0.015

Table 3. Results of regression analyses of knowledge sharing success on independent variables

Variables	β	Std error	Std. β	t	ρ
Involvement	0.479	0.048	0.473	9.972	0.000
Trustworthiness	0.192	0.048	0.189	4.119	0.000
Formal recognition	0.432	0.048	0.425	8.971	0.000
Independence	-0.015	0.048	-0.015	-0.320	ns

Figure 2. The resultant framework

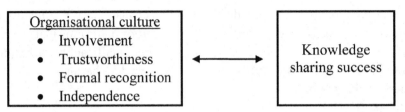

sharing success. This indicates that by ranking the values preferred, organisations can identify knowledge management outcome deficiencies as well as actions for overcoming any gaps. Research indicates that HRM departments may support knowledge management by nurturing the right culture (Bollinger and Smith 2001; Greengard 1998; Soliman and Spooner 2000). This can be achieved by emphasising the "must have" values that will close gaps, thus assisting organisations to increase knowledge sharing through re-orientation of their practices. These findings have implications for HRM in the Malaysian context.

The emergence of new cultural labels indicates that many of the Western values that underlie HRM practices in relation to knowledge sharing may not effectively transfer into workplaces in non-Western cultures. Local HRM practitioners should have an understanding of what constitutes acceptable and desirable values that align with the establishment of practices at the workplace to be considered effective managers. As such, for HRM to effectively support KM initiatives, the design of its practices should therefore be culturally translated to align with acceptable values of the local workforce. One possible approach in this direction is to have managers evaluate employees' preferred values and find the best possible way to incorporate them in the design of practices at the workplace for KM initiatives and thus increase knowledge sharing success. Organisational stakeholders and especially management should explore and develop individual and collectively based reward systems to encourage and promote these managerial practices, as

well as reinforce these values in the design of organisational practices that have become part of the Malaysian IT work culture. This resonates with Roberston and Hammersley's (2000:251) view that "cultural fit implied a willingness and ability to share knowledge and skills" as well as increased employee loyalty due to the ability of organisations to nourish a unique working environment. HR practices, such as collaboration through informal activities, provide individual employees with an opportunity to discuss their past successes and failures and it improves professional relationships in the organisation. Collaboration also helps to undermine the myths and misperceptions about contextual knowledge which exist in organisations. Furthermore, collaboration through informal face-to-face meetings increases respect, pride and trust, resulting in gains for all participants. Trust, between employees, helps foster productive knowledge transfer. Building an environment based on trust through collaboration, especially face-to-face meetings, should extend vertically from the top of the organisation to the grass roots.

FUTURE RESEARCH

The greatest potential for successful knowledge sharing can be realised by focusing on the design of HRM practices. HRM practices, especially hiring practices, improve absorption capacity both at the individual and organisation levels. However, recruiting groups of experienced, and talented individuals cannot guarantee competitive advantage until these individual employees work together to achieve improved organisational capability for better organisational performance. HR managers should design systems and processes to recruit, develop, retain and motivate knowledge workers. However, if organisations only focus their HR practices on retrieving and storing individual personal knowledge rather than retaining individuals, then individuals may hoard their tacit knowledge. Organisations should actively support individuals to encourage their own learning in a mutual knowledge sharing environment. Proper organisational support in terms of relevant HR practices will reduce the barriers to individual employees' knowledge sharing.

While the findings of this study are based on data collected from Malaysian setting, one must apply caution when generalising the findings beyond Malaysia. It is suggested that future research should be conducted in other cultural setting using the same questionnaire. A comparative study should also be undertaken to see the difference of perceptions of organisational culture and knowledge sharing success between Malaysia and other countries, particularly "western values" countries. This knowledge is vital in explaining the potential contributions of HRM practices from both perceptions of cultural context in facilitating employees' knowledge sharing behaviours. For example, while the importance of autonomy has been emphasised within western HRM practices (e.g. Cabrera et al., 2006; Roberston & Hammersley, 2000), hierarchical differences and status conscious within eastern context delineate the significant role of autonomy in explaining employees' knowledge sharing success. Depending on specific situation, some cultural values that important in particular context may appear least significant to be nourished in other setting. Thus, balancing the gaps by identifying, evaluating, combining and recombining the cultural values that work well within own context is appropriate

in facilitating knowledge sharing success among employees.

In future, questions that need to be asked include: to what extent do each of the HRM practices impact on knowledge sharing; and, to what extent do employees' knowledge sharing practices impact on organisational absorption, innovation, learning and storage capability? Finally, this chapter can provide help to senior managers (especially human resource managers); to better understand how HRM practices can enable the establishment of a knowledge sharing culture. Further, we conclude that the incorporation of such HR practices can lead to superior and sustainable performance.

Potential Benefits and Uses

These findings will assist knowledge based organisations, especially those in South East Asia, as well as international investors gain a competitive advantage through knowledge sharing. The results can also be used to assist stakeholders and management in the design of HRM practices that not only advance employees' know-how, but create successful knowledge sharing, a valued workforce, and increase the return on investment from such knowledge management initiatives. There is no doubt that such local preferred values are useful in trying to help IT organisations create a unique working environment for successful knowledge sharing. Whether the results from fostering these values and the re-orientation of such practices provide the basis for predicting knowledge sharing success in IT organisations needs further study and will require further empirical confirmation. Finally, this chapter can provide help to senior managers, especially human resource managers, to better understand how HRM practices can enable the establishment of a knowledge sharing culture. Further, we argue that the incorporation of such HR practices can lead to superior and sustainable performance.

Significance of the Chapter

The research can help top level managers, especially human resource managers to better understand the importance of knowledge sharing behaviour and the way organisational culture can enable it effectively. Further, the incorporation of such practices leads to superior and sustainable performance in knowledge-intensive organisations.

Prospective Audience

The prospective audience of this chapter is students (both undergrad and post grade levels), knowledge workers, managers, research scholars and professionals. This book can be utilised as a text book for undergraduate and post graduate courses in the field of Knowledge management, Human capital and Human resource management.

REFERENCES

Abdullah, A. (1992). The influence of ethnic values on managerial practices in Malaysia. *Malaysian Management Review, 27*(1), 3–18.

Abrams, L. C., Cross, R., Lesser, E., & Levin, D. Z. (2003). Nurturing interpersonal trust in knowledge-sharing networks. *The Academy of Management Executive, 17*(4), 64–77. doi:10.5465/AME.2003.11851845

Al-Alawi, A. I., Al-Marzooqi, N. Y., & Mohammed, Y. F. (2007). Organizational culture and knowledge sharing: Critical success factors. *Journal of Knowledge Management, 11*(2), 22–42. doi:10.1108/13673270710738898

Alavi, M., Kayworth, T. R., & Leidner, D. E. (2005). An empirical examination of the influence of organizational culture on knowledge management practices. *Journal of Management Information Systems, 22*(3), 191–224. doi:10.2753/MIS0742-1222220307

Alavi, M., & Tiwana, A. (2002). Knowledge integration in virtual teams: The potential role of KMS. *Journal of the American Society for Information Science and Technology, 53*(12), 1029–1037. doi:10.1002/asi.10107

Alvesson, M. (2004). *Knowledge work and knowledge-intensive firms*. Oxford, UK: Oxford University Press.

Alvesson, M., & Karreman, D. (2001). Odd couple: Making sense of the curious concept of knowledge management. *Journal of Management Studies, 38*(7), 995–1018. doi:10.1111/1467-6486.00269

Armbrecht, F., Chapas, R., Chappelow, C., Farris, G., Friga, P., & Hartz, C. (2001). Knowledge management in research and development. *Research-Technology Management, 44*(4), 28–48.

Aulawi, H., Sudirman, I., Suryadi, K., & Govindaraju, R. (2008). *Knowledge sharing behavior, antecedent and its influence towards the company's innovation capability*. Paper presented at the 2008 IEEE International Conference on Industrial Engineering and Engineering Management, IEEM 2008.

Barnard, Y. F. (2005). *Developing industrial knowledge managment: Knowledge sharing over boundaries*. Paper presented at the International Conference on Advances in the Internet: System and Interdesciplinary Research.

Bartol, K., Liu, W., Zeng, X., & Wu, K. (2009). Social exchange and knowledge sharing among knowledge workers: The moderating role of perceived job security. *Management and Organization Review, 5*(2). doi:10.1111/j.1740-8784.2009.00146.x

Baumard, P. (1999). *Tacit knowledge in organizations*. Sage Publications Ltd.

Birchall, D. W., & Tovstiga, G. (2006). *Innovation performance measurement: Expert vs. practitioner views.* Paper presented at the Portland International Conference on Management of Engineering and Technology.

Bock, G.-W., Zmud, R. W., Kim, Y.-G., & Lee, J.-N. (2005). Behavioral intention formation in knowledge sharing: Examining the roles of extrinsic motivators, social-psychological forces, and organizational climate. *Management Information Systems Quarterly, 29*(1), 87–111.

Cabrera, Ã. n., Collins, W. C., & Salgado, J. F. (2006). Determinants of individual engagement in knowledge sharing. *International Journal of Human Resource Management, 17*(2), 245–264. doi:10.1080/09585190500404614

Carillo, M. R., & Zazzaro, A. (2000). Innovation, human capital destruction and firms' investment in training. *Manchester School, 68*(3), 331–348. doi:10.1111/1467-9957.00197

Chuan, C. L. (2006). Sample size estimation using Krejcie and Morgan and Cohen statistical power analysis: A comparison. *Jurnal Penyelidikan IPBL, 7*, 78–86.

Clegg, C., Unsworth, K., Epitropaki, O., & Parker, G. (2002). Implicating trust in the innovation process. *Journal of Occupational and Organizational Psychology, 75*, 409–422. doi:10.1348/096317902321119574

Coffield, F. (2002). Britain's continuing failure to train: The birth pangs of a new policy. *Journal of Education Policy, 17*(4), 483–497. doi:10.1080/02680930210140275

Cohen, W., & Levinthal, D. (1990). Absorptive capacity: A new perspective on learning and innovation. *Administrative Science Quarterly, 35*(1), 128–152. doi:10.2307/2393553

Collins, C. J., & Smith, K. G. (2006). Knowledge exchange and combination: The role of human resource practices in the performance of high-technology firms. *Academy of Management Journal, 49*(3), 544–560. doi:10.5465/AMJ.2006.21794671

Cook, J., & Wall, T. (1980). New work attitude measures of trust, organizational commitment and personal need non-fulfillment. *Journal of Occupational Psychology, 53*(1), 39–52. doi:10.1111/j.2044-8325.1980.tb00005.x

Cross, R., Rice, R., & Parker, A. (2001). Information seeking in social context: Structural influences and receipt of informational benefits. *IEEE Transactions, 31*(4), 438–448.

Davenport, T. (1994). Saving IT's soul: Human-centered information management. *Harvard Business Review, 72*, 119–119.

Davenport, T. H. (1997). *Information ecology.* Oxford, UK: Oxford University Press.

Davenport, T. H., & Prusak, L. (1998). *Working knowledge.* Boston, MA: Harvard Business School Press.

Davis, F.D. (2004). Improving computer skill training: behavior modeling, symbolic mental rehearsal, and the role of knowledge structures. *The Journal of Applied Psychology, 89*, 509–523. doi:10.1037/0021-9010.89.3.509

De Long, D., & Fahey, L. (2000). Diagnosing cultural barriers to knowledge management. *The Academy of Management Executive, 14*(4), 113–127. doi:10.5465/AME.2000.3979820

DeVellis, R. F. (2003). *Scale development: Theory and applications* (2nd ed.). Thousand Oaks, CA: Sage Publications, Inc.

Earl, M. (2001). Knowledge management strategies: Toward a taxonomy. *Journal of Management Information Systems, 18*(1), 215–233.

Ellonen, R., Blomqvist, K., & Puumalain-en, K. (2008). The role of trust in organisational innovativeness. *European Journal of Innovation Management, 11*(2), 160. doi:10.1108/14601060810869848

Empson, L. (2001). Fear of exploitation and fear of contamination: Impediments to knowledge transfer in mergers between professional service firms. *Human Relations, 54*(7), 839. doi:10.1177/0018726701547003

Fitz-enz, J. (2000). *The ROI of human capital: Measuring the economic value of employee performance.* New York, NY: AMACOM.

Gray, P. (2001). The impact of knowledge repositories on power and control in the workplace. *Information Technology & People, 14*(4), 368–384. doi:10.1108/09593840110411167

Hackman, J. R., & Oldham, G. R. (1975). Development of the job diagnostic survey. *The Journal of Applied Psychology, 60*, 159–170. doi:10.1037/h0076546

Hall, H. (2001). Input-friendliness: Motivating knowledge sharing across intranets. *Journal of Information Science, 27*(3), 139–146. doi:10.1177/016555150102700303

Harrison, N., & Samaon, D. (2002). *Technology management: Text and international cases.* New York, NY: McGraw-Hill.

Hsu, I. C. (2008). Knowledge sharing practices as a facilitating factor for improving organizational performance through human capital: A preliminary test. *Expert Systems with Applications, 35*(3), 1316–1326. doi:10.1016/j.eswa.2007.08.012

Ipe, M. (2003). Knowledge sharing in organizations: A conceptual framework. *Human Resource Development Review, 2*(4), 337–359. doi:10.1177/1534484303257985

Janz, B. D., Colquitt, J. A., & Noe, R. A. (1997). Knowledge worker team effectiveness: The role of autonomy, interdependence, team development, and contextual support variables. *Personnel Psychology, 50*(4), 877–904. doi:10.1111/j.1744-6570.1997.tb01486.x

Janz, B. D., & Prasarnphanich, P. (2003). Understanding the antecedents of effective knowledge management: The importance of a knowledge-centered culture. *Decision Sciences, 34*(2), 351–384. doi:10.1111/1540-5915.02328

Kennedy, J. C. (2002). Leadership in Malaysia: Traditional values, international outlook. *The Academy of Management Executive (1993), 16*(3), 15-26.

Kikoski, K., & Kikoski, F. (2004). *The inquiring organization: Tacit knowledge, Conversation and knowledge creation, skills for 21st-century organizations.* Praeger.

Kristiina, M., Hanna, K., & Rebecca, P. (2007). Interpersonal similarity as a driver of knowledge sharing within multinational corporations. *International Business Review, 16*, 1–22. doi:10.1016/j.ibusrev.2006.11.002

Lee, H., & Choi, B. (2003). Knowledge management enablers, processes, and organizational performance: An integrative view and empirical examination. *Journal of Management Information Systems, 20*(1), 179–228.

McDermott, R. (1999). Why information technology inspired but cannot deliver knowledge management. *California Management Review, 4*, 103–117.

Moreland, R. (2006). Transactive memory: Learning who knows what io word groups and organizations. *Small groups: Key readings*, 327.

Nonaka, I. (1994). A dynamic theory of organizational knowledge creation. *Organization Science, 5*(1), 14–37. doi:10.1287/orsc.5.1.14

Nonaka, I., & Takeuchi, H. (1995). *The knowledge creating company: How Japanese companies create the dynamics of innovation.* New York, NY: Oxford University Press.

Noorderhaven, N., & Harzing, A. W. (2009). Knowledge-sharing and social interaction within MNEs. *Journal of International Business Studies, 40*(5), 719–741. doi:10.1057/jibs.2008.106

Pallant, J. (2007). *SPSS Survival Manual: A step-by-step guide to data analysis using SPSS for Windows (Version 15)* (3rd ed.). NSW, Australia: Allen Unwin.

Pathirage, P. C., Amaratunga, G. D., & Haigh, R. P. (2007). Tacit knowledge and organisational performance: construction industry perspective. *Journal of Knowledge Management, 11*(1), 115–126. doi:10.1108/13673270710728277

Penley, L. E., & Hawkins, B. (1985). Studying interpersonal communication in organizations: A leadership application. *Academy of Management Journal, 28*, 309–326. doi:10.2307/256203

Pett, M. A., Lackey, N. R., & Sullivan, J. J. (2003). *Making sense of factor analysis: The use of factor analysis for instrument developmet in health care research.* Thousand Oaks, CA: Sage Publications.

Renzl, B. (2008). Trust in management and knowledge sharing: The mediating effects of fear and knowledge documentation. *Omega, 36*(2), 206–220. doi:10.1016/j.omega.2006.06.005

Renzl, B. (2008). Trust in management and knowledge sharing: The mediating effects of fear and knowledge documentation. *OMEGA - The International Journal of Management Science, 36*(2), 206-220.

Roos, J., & Von Krogh, G. (1992). Figuring out your competence configuration. *European Management Journal, 10*, 422–422. doi:10.1016/0263-2373(92)90006-P

Sahin, A. (2007). *A case in effective knowledge management.* Paper presented at the Portland International Conference on Management of Engineering and Technology.

Staples, D. S., & Webster, J. (2008). Exploring the effects of trust, task interdependence and virtualness on knowledge sharing in teams. *Information Systems Journal, 18*(6), 617–640. doi:10.1111/j.1365-2575.2007.00244.x

Sveiby, K.-E. (1997). *The new organizational wealth: Managing and measuring intangible assets.* San Francisco, CA: Berret-Koehler.

Tsai, W., & Ghoshal, S. (1998). Social capital and value creation: The role of intrafirm networks. *Academy of Management Journal, 41*, 464–476. doi:10.2307/257085

Tuomi, D. (2003). The future of knowledge management. *Lifelong Learning in Europe, 7*(2), 69–79.

Yang, Y. F., & Guo, P. (2007). *The estimation of enterprise's human capital operation.* Paper presented at the 2006 International Conference on Management Science and Engineering, ICMSE'06 (13th).

KEY TERMS AND DEFINITIONS

Employees' Knowledge (Tacit Knowledge): People develop personal knowledge through their personal experience which cannot be expressed or documented easily

Innovativeness: Organisations are trying to increase their innovation capability in order to achieve an advantage over their competitors. Organisations' innovative capabilities are caught up in knowledge sharing behaviour

Knowledge: Knowledge is information, and managing this information helps organisations to function effectively

Organisational culture: Organisational culture refers to the perceived desirable values that guide organisational members to act appropriately and share knowledge within the interaction context

Trust: Trust among employees and the extent to which organisational members identify themselves with the organisation influences employee motivation to share knowledge

APPENDIX A

Scree Plot for Organisation Culture variables

Figure 3. Scree Plot

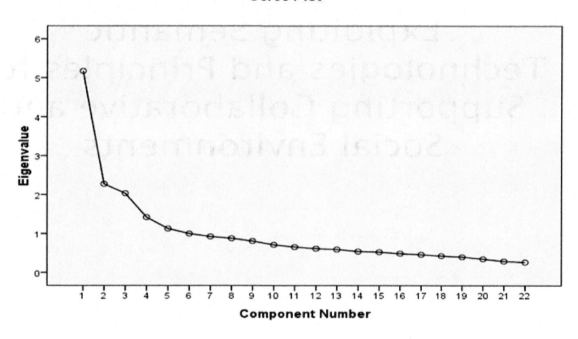

Section 2
Exploiting Semantic Technologies and Principles for Supporting Collaborative and Social Environments

Chapter 5
Enhancing Social Networks with Agent and Semantic Web Technologies

Federico Bergenti
Università degli Studi di Parma, Italy

Enrico Franchi
Università degli Studi di Parma, Italy

Agostino Poggi
Università degli Studi di Parma, Italy

ABSTRACT

In this chapter, the authors describe the relationships between multi-agent systems, social networks, and the Semantic Web within collaborative work; they also review how the integration of multi-agent systems and Semantic Web technologies and techniques can be used to enhance social networks at all scales. The chapter first provides a review of relevant work on the application of agent-based models and abstractions to the key ingredients of our work: collaborative systems, the Semantic Web, and social networks. Then, the chapter discusses the reasons current multi-agent systems and their foreseen evolution might be a fundamental means for the realization of the future Semantic Social Networks. Finally, some conclusions are drawn.

INTRODUCTION

In recent years we have witnessed a huge diffusion of social networking Web sites that have quickly become an unprecedented cultural phenomenon (Boyd & Ellison, 2008). Such Web sites have attracted users with very weak interests in tech-

nology and some of the largest ones constitute a separate, closed and parallel Internet-scale network.

Social Networking Sites (SNSs) allow members to publish personal information in a semi-structured form and to define links to other members with whom they have relationships of various kinds. These relationships are usually suggested by the system that governs the SNS. In order

DOI: 10.4018/978-1-4666-0894-8.ch005

to suggest possible acquaintances, the system analyses every piece of information provided by the users, e.g., their posts, their profiles and the queries they made. The information is used to infer real-life acquaintances and possible new friendships taking into account shared features like common interests and friends.

The huge amount of extremely sparse and heterogeneous users' data requires an integrated, aggregated and fused approach to the realization of SNSs capable of simplifying users' interactions. The Semantic Web indeed provides a conceptual framework, which is definitely ideal to fulfill such needs. The evolution of SNSs is therefore expected to heavily rely on the use of Semantic Web technologies, like ontologies, to publish members' information and to manage social connections (Mika, 2005; Breslin & Decker, 2007). Moreover, there is a trend of integration among different SNSs (Blue, 2009; Grossberg, 2007; Osterloh, 2010), which makes imperative the adoption of technologies capable of lifting such complex integrations from purely syntactic to fully semantic. Such technologies would then enable richer forms of integration among SNSs that would go far beyond the simple match of profiles and that would provide a truly integrated view of different profiles in different networks.

Needless to say, we are already experiencing the introduction of Semantic Web technologies in existing SNSs. For example, some of the most important social networking platforms already adopted RDF (Manola, Miller & Mc Bride, 2004) and we expect more to follow (Facebook, 2010). However, the very strict privacy and trust concerns that naturally arise in relation to the increased automatic processing features that Semantic Web technologies provide should also be taken into serious account. Private companies own most actual SNSs and the main revenue of such companies comes from advertisements, which can be far more effective if precisely targeting well-identified groups of users. The identification of such groups requires the automatic process-

ing of sensitive data and therefore it is subject to local government laws and regulations that call for specific and well-defined treatment methods (Bergenti, 2008).

In previous works we have already studied how Agent and Semantic Web technologies may become a key factor of future SNSs mainly from an implementation point of view (Franchi, 2010; Bergenti, Franchi & Poggi, 2010; Franchi & Poggi, 2011). On the contrary, in the present work, we focus on how social networks are important for the adoption and evolution of the Semantic Web research itself.

The models and abstractions of social networks are applicable every time a system manages a collection of individuals with some relationships. The systems implementing SNSs can be used to perform and optimize queries and to associate a level of trust to the answers, considering the referrals that led to the answering agent. For example, SNSs are crucial for the realization of a web of trust that enables the estimation of information credibility and trustworthiness (Sabater & Sierra, 2002). This is the case of systems where agents often interact with unknown parties and need to establish the trustworthiness of the parties themselves. The use of a SNS increases the capability to compute the reputation of the parties considering also the past experiences of his/her acquaintances. The judgment is likely to be unbiased since the short length of paths makes manipulation very hard, and it also increases the likelihood to find a possible known trustworthy party that would ground the judgment.

Another possible use of the abstractions at the heart of social networks is in the construction of ontologies and folksonomies (Van Damme, Hepp & Siorpaes, 2007). The analysis of the social connections among the members of a community can be helpful in finding relationships among concepts of an ontology, or tags of a folksonomy, that model the information shared in the community.

Social networks have a very close relationship also with *Multi-Agent Systems (MASs)*. MASs are based on the very idea of autonomous agents cooperating or competing to pursue individual or common goals (Wooldridge, 2002): every MAS implicitly defines a social network. From this point of view, a MAS and a human social network share structure and scope since both: *(i)* are composed of agents (either human or not) connected with some relationship; and *(ii)* are realized for accomplishing individual and/or common goals, even though the goals of human societies are usually not formally specified (and not easily identifiable).

Finally, it is worth noting that social networks play also a crucial role in supporting collaborative work. In general, a collaborative activity is supported by a group communication, i.e., by an exchange of information among a group of participants, called *collaborators*, in a session (Bergenti & Poggi, 2000). Collaborators may play different roles in a session and the roles can be changed dynamically; moreover collaborators may also join and leave dynamically a running session. A collaborative platform is required to provide all the facilities needed to support the dynamic nature of the collaboration while guaranteeing the availability of suitable media for information exchange. We already studied how agent technology can be effectively used to support the development of collaborative platforms (Bergenti, Poggi & Somacher, 2002) and we now propose to jointly exploit the novel ideas of social networks to enhance our previous results.

It is natural to think about synergies between social networks and MASs research, and applications in the scope of collaborative work easily follow. First, MAS models, techniques and technologies have been used and have important potentialities for the study and for the development of social networks. Then, the results stemming from the experimentation on the most widespread SNSs could be used for the improvement of MAS models, techniques and technologies. Moreover, MASs are considered important components for building Semantic Web applications and they have all the potentialities for becoming one of the most

important means for the realization of the new generation of social networks. Finally, the crucial role of MASs in the realization of collaborative work platforms and in the conceptualization of collaborative work itself is well known and understood.

In the next section we separately describe the relationships between: *(i)* Multi-Agent Systems and Collaborative Systems, providing a review on how MASs have been used to support Collaborative Systems; *(ii)* Multi-Agent Systems and Semantic Web, emphasizing the widespread adoption of MAS models and abstractions in the context of the Semantic Web; *(iii)* Multi-Agent Systems and Social Networks, drawing connections between two apparently distant research areas.

In the section after that we discuss the reasons why current MASs and their foreseen evolution might be a fundamental means for the realization of the future Semantic Social Networks (Jung & Euzenat, 2007), which are bridging the Social Networks with Semantic Web. Finally, a few conclusions are drawn.

MULTI-AGENT SYSTEMS IN INNOVATIVE SCENARIOS OF COLLABORATION

Agents and MASs are among the most interesting areas in software research and they have been significantly contributing to the development of the theory and the practice of complex distributed systems (Jennings, Corera & Laresgoiti, 1995; Muller, 1998; Bordini, Dastani, Dix & Fallah-Seghrouchni, 2005).

Although there is no single definition of an agent (Genesereth & Ketchpel, 1994; Wooldridge & Jennings, 1995; Russel & Norvig, 2003) all definitions agree that an agent is essentially a special software component that: *(i)* has autonomy; *(ii)* provides an interoperable interface to an arbitrary system and *(iii)* behaves like a human agent, working for some clients in pursuit of its own agenda. In particular, an agent is: *(i)* autonomous, because it operates without the direct intervention of humans or others and it has full control over its actions and internal state; *(ii)* reactive, because it perceives its environment, and responds in a timely fashion to changes that occur in the environment; *(iii)* pro-active, because it does not simply act in response to its environment and it is able to exhibit goal-directed behaviour by taking the initiative. Moreover, if necessary, an agent can be: *(i)* mobile, showing the ability to move between different nodes in a computer network; *(ii)* truthful, providing the assurance that it will not deliberately communicate false information; *(iii)* benevolent, always trying to perform what is required; *(iv)* rational, always acting in order to achieve its goals, and never to prevent its goals from being achieved; and *(v)* capable of learning and adapting to fit its environment and to the desires of its users.

Even if a complex system can be based on a solitary agent working within its environment – that may or may not comprise users – usually agent-based systems are realized in terms of multiple, interacting agents, i.e., agent-based systems are normally MASs. MASs are generally considered appropriate for modelling complex, distributed systems, even if such a multiplicity naturally introduces the possibility of having different agents with potentially conflicting goals. Agents may decide to cooperate for mutual benefit, or they may compete to serve their own interests. Agents take advantage of their social ability to exhibit flexible coordination behaviours that make them able to both cooperate in the achievement of shared goals and to compete on the acquisition of resources and tasks. Agents have the ability of coordinating their behaviours into coherent global actions.

Coordination among agents can be handled by a variety of approaches including, negotiation, multi-agent planning and organizational structuring. Negotiation is the communication process of a group of agents in order to reach a mutually accepted agreement on some matter (Jennings, Faratin & Lomuscio, 2001). Negotiation can be competitive or cooperative depending on the behaviour of the agents involved. Competitive negotiation is used in situations where agents have independent goals that interfere. Agents are always somehow competitive and never a-priori cooperative, e.g., sharing information or willing to back down for the greater good. On the other hand, cooperative negotiation is used in situations where agents have a common goal to achieve or a shared task to execute. Multi-agent planning techniques enable agents to build plans intended to move agents towards their common/individual goal, preventing possible interferences among the actions of the different agents (Tonino, Boss, de Weerdt & Wittevee, 2002). In order to avoid inconsistent or conflicting actions and interactions, agents build a multi-agent plan that details all the future actions and interactions required to achieve their goals, and they interleave execution with incremental planning and re-planning. Multi-agent planning can be either centralized or distributed (Rosenschein, 1982; Durfee, 1999). In centralized multi-agent planning, there is usually a coordinating agent that either provides the plans to other agents or modifies the plans of other agents to avoid potential inconsistencies and conflicting interactions. Finally, organizational structuring techniques allow the definition of the most appropriate organization of a MAS for managing and monitoring the distributed execution of the tasks needed to implement the desired functionalities (Horley & Lesser, 2004).

A MAS is a suitable means for modelling and simulating complex systems: a model consists of a set of agents that encapsulate the behaviours of the various individuals that make up the system, and whose execution emulates these behaviours (Parunak, Savit & Riolo, 1998). The use of MASs is especially appropriate for the modelling of systems that are characterized by a high degree of localization and distribution and dominated by discrete decisions.

Multi-Agent Systems and Collaborative Systems

The Web is assuming a central role in the way people share the information in local and geographic networks, mainly because Web browsers are available everywhere and because they offer an integrated view of different services into a common, easily accessible, platform-independent user interface. For these reasons, the Web has already been adopted as the principal medium capable of supporting the collaboration between people in nearly all scenarios (Bentley et al., 1997). Unfortunately, the basic communication patterns traditionally offered by the Web are not sufficient to support an interactive approach to collaboration. The communication needs for which the Web was designed were about consulting structured documents and did not involve supporting an interactive discussion among a *virtual team*. Nevertheless, the widespread availability of high-bandwidth in fixed and mobile infrastructures allows people sharing information with heterogeneous hardware (desktop, laptop, tablet computers and smart phones), using different operating systems and different communication media, and therefore there is high potential for the adoption of the Web in support of very dynamic virtual teams (Bergenti et al., 2002).

In order to understand the peculiarities of collaborative systems, we need to briefly consider the founding ideas behind them. In general, a *collaborative session* is the activity of a communication group in which the participants exchange information (Gall & Hauck, 1997). Collaborators may play different roles in a session and the roles can be changed dynamically; moreover collaborators may also join and leave a running session. A *collaborative platform* is required to provide all the facilities needed to support the dynamic nature of the collaboration while guaranteeing the availability of suitable media for information exchange. In fact, the exchanged information essentially depends on the media provided by the collaboration support. Collaborative platforms can

be roughly classified as *centralized* or *replicated* (Minenko, 1995). In a centralized platform, the shared information is maintained in a single physical location and participants to the virtual team are supplied only with a view of the information. In a replicated platform, each user owns a copy of the shared information and the platform provides the mechanisms to synchronize the copies.

Collaborative activities, i.e., the joint activities occurring within a virtual team, can be roughly classified into two categories, depending on the information exchange dynamics: *synchronous* or *asynchronous* (Gall & Hauck, 1997). Synchronous collaboration is characterised by a high level of interaction within the group: all collaborators share a single view of the discussion and the information is exchanged when it becomes available. Conversely, in an asynchronous collaboration the information is transferred only when requested, thus lowering the degree of interaction in the group. The classic Web communication facility supports only an asynchronous collaboration mainly because HTTP protocols rely on a communication model in which the browser always needs to request fresh information from the server. We need to extend the classic Web communication facility towards *push technology*, that many Web frameworks today provide in very different ways, to support synchronous collaboration effectively (Bozdag, Mesbah & van Deursen, 2007; Mesbah & van Deursen, 2008, Hickson, 2011).

Any collaboration support needs to provide *consistency-guarantee mechanisms* (Dourish, 1996) to correctly manage the shared information. In synchronous collaborative environment, where collaborators share a single view of the shared information, consistency is typically managed by a floor-control policy (Poggi & Golinelli, 1998). This policy guarantees that when a collaborator is free of modifying shared data, no other collaborator has the same ability. This modification privilege is commonly described in terms of possessing the modification token, and the floor-control policies can be roughly classified into explicit and implicit depending on how the collaboration support assign the modification token. Explicit floor control states that the collaboration support explicitly assigns the modification token; while in implicit policies the token is assigned without the collaborators being aware of this.

In the second half of the nineties, the new paradigm of agent-oriented software development received an ever-growing interest for application in various scenarios, as previously briefly discussed. The synergy between Web-based and agent-based approaches has been dominant during the last fifteen years for the implementation of collaborative systems. An earlier review of multi-agent collaborative systems can be found in (Lander, 1997). Shen, Norrie & Barthès (2001) discuss in detail the issues in developing agent-oriented collaborative systems and give a review of significant, related projects.

Generally speaking, agents have been applied in the context of collaborative systems and platforms for several purposes, such as: *(i)* entity modelling, where users, teams, and resources are represented by agents; *(ii)* distribution handling, where the distributed nature of the collaborative platform requires mechanisms for information transport from one network node to another; *(iii)* remote execution, especially to negotiate communication parameters, when parameters not only need to be transported, but also code to be executed remotely; and *(iv)* autonomy, because agents autonomously decide how to contact their respective real-world counterpart.

Among the most notable cross-fertilization between agents and collaborative systems we can mention projects SHARE (Toye, Cutkosky, Leifer, Tenenbaum & Glicksman, 1993), SiFAs (Brown, Dunskus, Grecu & Berker, 1995), DIDE (Shen & Barthès, 1997), Co-Designer (Hague & Taleb-Bendiab, 1998), A-Design (Campbell, Cagan & Kotovsky, 1999) and the more recent Collaborator (Bergenti, Costicoglou & Poggi, 2003), UNITE (Zapf, Reinema, Wolf & Türpe, 2002) and Co-Cad (Liu, Cui & Hu, 2008).

SHARE (Toye et al. 1993) is concerned with developing open, heterogeneous, network-oriented environments for concurrent engineering, particularly for sharing through asynchronous collaboration and design information and data capturing.

SiFAs (Brown et al., 1995) is intended to address the issues of patterns of interaction, communication, and conflict resolution using single function agents.

DIDE (Shen & Barthès, 1997) is a typical MAS and is developed to study system openness, legacy systems integration, and geographically distributed collaboration.

Co-Designer (Hague & Taleb-Bendiab, 1998) is a system that can support localized design agents in the generation and management of conceptual design variants.

A-Design (Campbell et al. 1999) presents a new design generation methodology, which combines aspects of multi-objective optimization, MAS, and automated design synthesis. It provides designers with a new search strategy for the conceptual stages of product design, which incorporates agent collaboration with an adaptive selection of designs.

The major goal of the Collaborator project (Bergenti et al., 2003) is the realization of an agent-based, decentralized software environment to provide a shared workspace supporting the activities of virtual teams in heterogeneous fixed and mobile environments. Based on a novel approach, Collaborator integrates standard Web technologies with agent technologies, enhancing the classic Web communication mechanisms to support synchronous sharing of applications.

UNITE (Zapf, 2002) aims to do research and development on cooperative workplaces and their implementation based on an agent-oriented cooperative platform. Such a platform is the key system component that provides the facilities for devices, components and networks to fully interact, despite the possible original inherent heterogeneity and which takes care that a uniform and ubiquitous view is presented to all team members regardless of their physical location.

Adopting the JADE (Bellifemine, Poggi & Rimassa, 2001) platform as the underlying multi-agent environment, the Co-Cad (Liu et al., 2008) platform is an intelligent collaborative design software in which every user, design software, management software, equipment and resource is regarded as an agent, while the legacy design process is abstracted to be a structured interaction between agents.

Multi-Agent Systems and the Semantic Web

The synergy of MASs with Semantic Web techniques and technologies was already considered in the first works that introduced the idea of Semantic Web (Hendler, 2001). In fact, the distributed nature of the Web requires that a network of intelligent and autonomous software agents supports both the retrieval of information (Shah, Finin, Joshi, Cost & Matfield, 2002) and the provision of services (Paolucci & Sycara, 2003; Huhns et al., 2005).

Chenggang, Wenpin & Qijia (2001) proposed an information retrieval service based on ontologies and on a MAS, which integrates several kind of agents, e.g., interface agents, pre-processing agents, management agents, information processing agents and information searching agents. The system also uses ontologies to classify the domains of documents and to assist users to normalize their queries. Using this system, dynamic changes of information on the Internet can be reflected timely, and the navigational ability of the process of information retrieval is highly improved.

CoMMA (Gandon, Poggi, Rimassa & Turci, 2002) is a MAS designed to manage a corporate memory in the form of a local, semantic network of knowledge. This system aims at helping users in the management of a corporate memory, facilitating the creation, dissemination, transmission and reuse of knowledge in an organization. The implementation provided integration for several

emerging technologies: MAS technology, using the FIPA-compliant platform JADE (Bellifemine et al., 2001), knowledge modelling and XML technology for information retrieval, using the CORESE semantic search engine (Corby, Dieng-Kuntz, Faron-Zucke & Gandon, 2006), and machine learning techniques.

Zou, Finin, Ding, Chen & Pan (2003) extended and enhanced Trading Agent Competition (Wellman, Greenwald, Stone & Wurman, 2002) scenario to work in Agentcities (Dale, Willmot & Burg, 2002), an open multi-agent environment, using semantic web tools (i.e., RDF and OWL) as a unifying concept: (*i*) to specify and publish the underlying ontologies; (*ii*) as a content language within the FIPA ACL messages; (*iii*) as the basis for agent knowledge bases.

Küngas, Rao & Matskin (2004) propose a symbolic negotiation framework, based on the MAS AGORA (Matskin, Kirkeluten, Krossnes & Sæle, 2001), where service providers and requesters can meet taking advantages of an AI planner for symbolic reasoning and automated composition of Web services, whose descriptions are given in DAML-S.

Seagent (Dikenelli, Erdur & Gumus, 2005) is an agent development framework and platform that supports the development of MASs taking advantage of semantic techniques and technologies. In particular, all agents and services in the platform use Semantic Web standards to represent their internal knowledge and Semantic Web query languages are used to question them. Moreover, agents have the ability to discover and dynamically invoke Semantic Web services.

Chen et. al (2004) introduced EasyMeeting, a smart meeting room system built around multi-agent systems ideas, that uses semantic web ontologies, reasoning and declarative policies for security and privacy. Middleware support is provided by Context Broker Architecture (Chen, Finin & Joshi, 2004), which also uses ontologies.

SEMMAS (García-Sánchez, Fernándes-Breis, Valencia-García, Gomes & Martínes-Béjar, 2006) is an ontology-based, domain-independent framework for seamlessly integrating intelligent agents and Semantic Web services. SEMMAS has been built by using JADE (Bellifemine et al., 2001) and OWL for the representation of ontologies, and it is independent from both the domain and the actual application in which it is to be applied. In order to develop a specific application for a concrete domain, developers only need to set the appropriate domain ontologies and to decide on what agents to instantiate and which services to access. SEMMAS is suitable for the development of applications in several business scenarios and complex, dynamic and open environments: it has been used for developing eGovernment, eScience, eBusiness and Supply Chain Management applications.

S-APL (Katasonov & Terziyan, 2008) is a language for the Semantic Web that integrates the semantic description of the domain resources, based on RDF, with the semantic description of the agents' behaviours, based on semantic predicates. S-APL can be used as the content language in the communications between agents, both in querying for data and in requesting for action. In particular, an agent can exchange with another agent commitments, plans or other belief structures or it can query another agent for behaviour rules either to understand how it will react if a certain situation occurs or how to achieve a certain goal.

Ma et. al (2009) used semantic approximation technologies for implementing better multi-agent communication based on partial shared distributed ontologies; Through approximate semantic coordination among multiple agents, the authors obtained effective semantic query results and achieved information sharing across distributed ontologies. The system they developed to test their hypotheses is OntoQ.

Luo and Xue (2010) proposed an information retrieval system that integrates Semantic Web with MAS techniques to retrieve relevant documents or information by analyzing semantics contained in the queries and documents. In particular, the agents

of such a system can adapt users' own interests and hobbies, collect information based on users' behaviour, dig up semantics in the Internet and feedback and share information between different users, so the search results will be more in line with users' needs and will help users to complete complex tasks. Therefore, this system provides a set of features that it is suitable for knowledge management, document management, search engines and other applications that require searching through large bases of information to achieve the purpose of reusing and sharing knowledge.

Multi-Agent Systems and Social Networks

As we already pointed out, social networks and MASs share both the structure and the scope, since they are composed of entities connected with some kind of relationship and they are meant to accomplish individual and/or common goals. Essentially, there are some different aspects: *(i)* how can social networks enhance MASs; *(ii)* how can MASs support social networks as a technological tool; and *(iii)* how can MAS techniques help the research on social networks.

If we consider how social networks can improve MASs, we notice how social networks can be used as a source of information, so that the (local) knowledge of the network constitutes an important part of the reasoning behind the agents' actions. For example in (Kalogeraki, Gunopulos & Zeinalipour-Yazti, 2002) the nodes of a P2P network are enhanced using knowledge about their social network in order to handle queries in more efficient ways. The authors prove that using a social network built from previous contacts with other nodes, the system is far more efficient than using standard search algorithms. Although the system is not, strictly speaking, multi-agent, its nodes have been enhanced with sufficient reasoning capabilities to call them autonomous, thus making the distinction blurred.

A similar point of view is the one taking into account the intrinsic computational properties of social networks themselves: indeed, without these properties, social networks would not be effective structures for MASs and MASs could not be used to build software systems supporting social networking.

The first insights on these properties came from Milgram's experiment (Milgram, 1967), which led to the investigation of the *small world phenomenon*. In Milgram's experiment, a group of randomly chosen people were given the name and whereabouts of a person from a city in a different state; then, they were asked to route a mail message toward the target person being limited to only forward to friends or close acquaintances. The experiment made clear two facts: *(i)* people are connected through very short chains of acquaintances (in average 5-6 links); and *(ii)* people is able to route the messages to the target person using mostly local information and only performing local actions.

In Milgram's experiment people behaviour was not dissimilar from the behaviour of rational autonomous agents: examining his/her list of acquaintances, every person chose the successor in the chain leading to the target using essentially only local and elementary information to pursue a global, complex goal, which is something machines could do as well. This is especially relevant from our point of view, because it is about one of the key properties of MASs, i.e., the emergence of global behaviour from local strategies.

Such a property of a social network is usually called *navigability*. We say that a network is navigable if a simple decentralised algorithm exists that is able to deliver a message to any node, starting from any other node, in polylogarithmic number of steps. With *simple* we mean that each node passes the message to a single neighbour using some ranking function to decide which one. The ranking function must not encompass global knowledge of the long-range links. The delivery time of an algorithm is the expected number of steps required to reach the target, randomly choosing the start and the end node.

Social network analysis gives precise results on whether a network is navigable or not. In (Kleinberg, 2000; Kleinberg, 2002) artificial network structures have been enhanced in order to make them navigable. In fact, it has been proved (Duchon, Hanusse, Lebhar & Shabanel, 2006; Kleinberg, 2002; Kleinberg, 2006; Nguyen & Martel, 2005) that a wide category of graphs can be made navigable. Specifically, if it is possible to impose a bi-dimensional grid structure on the network, then the network is navigable if the probability that two distant nodes are connected is proportional to inverse of the square of their distance on the grid.

In (Liben-Nowell, Novak, Kumar, Raghavan & Tomkins, 2005) an interesting experiment has been carried out. The authors proved that the Live-Journal social network (LiveJournal, 2010) is navigable using simulation; then they superimposed a bi-dimensional lattice on the social network using geographical coordinates. The researchers found out that the probability of two distant nodes u and v to be connected was proportional to the inverse of a ranking function proportional to the number of people nearer to u than v. This probability is the same as the one predicted by Kleinberg, if the network is complete and regular.

The navigability of social networks has been implicitly used by many research projects in the last 20 years, e.g., expert finders or recommendation networks (Adamic & Adar, 2005; Kautz & Selman, 1997; Yu & Singh, 2003). Expert finders provide their users with the ability to search their SN to a (remote) contact with a given expertise, while in recommendation networks the focus is also on the chain of people leading to expert; the trustworthiness of people in the chain is used to determine the trustworthiness of the expert himself. A comparison of these systems can be found in (Franchi & Poggi, 2011).

MASs have also been used to support a social network. That is to say, SNSs have been created using multi-agent technologies. Some of the earliest examples of this are (Mika, 2005; Yoshida, Kamei, Ohgur & Kuwabara, 2003), more recently the topic has been dealt in (Franchi, 2010).

Another important area of application of MASs in social network research is simulation. MAS simulation is indeed a very important topic in its own right in social sciences (Axtell, 1999; Epstein, 1999), and although network analysis traditionally uses analytical tools to analyse the networks, MASs are a suitable means for developing simulations, since the agents can embed enough intelligence to closely simulate human behaviour in social networks (Bergenti, Franchi, & Poggi, 2011).

There are already interesting applications showing how MASs can be used to gain a better understanding of social network formation. For example, the original utility model for social and economics network formation described in (Jackson & Wolinsky, 1996) could only be analytically studied near the equilibrium. On the other hand, in (Doreian, 2006; Hummon, 2000) the system was studied during the whole process and additional equilibriums were discovered.

TOWARD AGENT-BASED SEMANTIC SOCIAL NETWORKS

The usual definitions of social networks, i.e., social structures of individuals connected by one or more types of relationships (Newman, 2010), are not specific with respect to the actual kind of relationship taken into account. There are good reasons for such a generality: *(i)* different kinds of relationship may be of interest depending on the context; *(ii)* sometimes researchers are concerned with real life acquaintance, while sometimes with weaker forms of acquaintance (e.g., a telephonic contact). In other contexts, stronger relationships

are examined, such as actual relations of trust, professional collaborations or family bonds.

These relationships are not always presented explicitly (e.g., a phone call log) and have to be discovered from secondary data. Archetypal examples are collaboration and co-authorship networks (Barabasi et. al, 2002): these networks have to be extracted from secondary data sources, such as the actual papers. In this case the relationship is very easy to discover: simple queries on bibliographic databases provide all the information that is needed. This is not the case in other examples, e.g., the relationship "having an interest in a given topic." Understanding that someone is interested in a topic is not easy to do automatically, and if such relationships have to be discovered in extremely large context (e.g., the blogosphere), the only possible solution is automatic processing.

Word co-occurrence and other statistical means may be adequate for the task of matching the interests of two authors and they can also be distributed in a MAS (Foner, 2007); however, it would be unsuitable for collaboration or automatic information sharing between users. In this situation, semantic understanding by the involved agents becomes a necessity.

All in all, if different agents have to understand that their respective users are actually interested in the same topics and that they want to share information, agents essentially have to figure out that the potentially different ontologies are similar and that can be merged.

Considering a similar scenario, where interest in the same topic is used as a ground for collaboration, (Jung & Euzenat, 2007) have proposed the concept of *Semantic Social Network* (*SSN*). A SSN is a structure made of three different networks:

1. A regular social network, where the relationship is something such as "common interest";
2. An *ontology network*, which links ontologies using explicit import relationships or implicit similarity; and

3. A *concept network*, which relates concepts on the basis of explicit ontological relationships or implicit similarity.

The layers constituted by the three networks have inter-layer relationships as well. People are linked to the ontologies they use, and ontologies are linked to the concepts they define. As clearly described in (Jung & Euzenat, 2007), the identified three-layer structure of a SSN allows using the structure of the knowledge to infer relationships between people. For example, if we can assume that similar people use similar ontologies (or the same ontology), we can use such a piece of information to infer other relationships. Consequently, such inferred relationships are emerging from the conceptual network under such ontologies and we can explore them using standard reasoning techniques.

The idea is that once relationships and similarities between people are discovered, they are used to standardise the ontologies they use, taking into account social network metrics to assess the relative influence people have. For example, ontologies of more authoritative people – in the sense of HITS, (Kleinberg et al., 1999), or other similar ranking algorithms – are better suited to merge ontologies.

Essentially, analysing SSN has two main purposes: *(i)* helping people to find peers with similar profiles (e.g., interests); and *(ii)* helping peers to find the best peers for starting designing consensus ontologies.

The first of the two purposes is typical of social networking systems, and consequently we believe that SSN analysis could improve such systems. The second purpose, although more specific, is even more interesting, considering that a typical problem in knowledge representation is defining the common concepts to ground the work.

Having adequately framed the scope about the idea of SSN, it is quite straightforward to note that the MAS and the Semantic Web are obvious ingredients of this idea. The Semantic Web is es-

sential to provide concrete means for describing ontologies and for reasoning about them. The whole literature on the Semantic Web provides notable results that cover most needs of SSN. In particular, the standard languages for describing ontologies provide concrete tools to model needed ontologies and to support reconciliation tasks. Moreover, such languages are meant to support open-world reasoning on ontologies, which is inherently capable of supporting reasoning with implicit knowledge. Finally, recent research on synergic combination of ontologies and folksonomies is indeed meant to enable structure digging into folksonomies so to explicate hidden ontologies (Cattuto, Loreto & Pietronero, 2006).

A rather different situation holds for MAS: the characteristic autonomy of agents is not a key part of the idea of SSN, but it becomes compulsory when using SSNs to support collaboration between people. The autonomy of agents that makes them able to express pro-active behaviours can largely improve the effectiveness of a SSN. Actually, the discovery of implicit relationships and the need of shared ontologies is normally associated with an explicit initial query from a user of the network. On the contrary, the pro-activity of agents makes any initial query irrelevant and it may prompt users with unforeseen relationships and unexpected needs for common ontologies. This is much the same of having a social networking system supporting only friendship queries and another social networking system with also a friendship proposal service.

Finally, from the specific point of view of the relationship between MASs and social networks, it is worth noting that SSNs provide the common ground for the agents to communicate. One of the typical problems is about having to decide the ontologies beforehand. In some cases this can be easily done as there are standard or near standard ontologies (e.g., FOAF). However, in general, two agents in an open system may be required to communicate because their users need to collaborate. In this situation, SSNs may at least help to shape a common ontology for the communication to occur. This problem may be relatively small if the two collaborators have been chosen because of similarity of interests suggested by the SSN itself; in such a case they would probably have a similar ontology as well. However, collaboration needs may also arise for external reasons.

CONCLUSION

This chapter dealt with the inherent relationships between social networks, MASs and the Semantic Web in the support of new forms of collaboration. The topic is extremely relevant and we think that the effective utilization of such technologies would be the solid ground for next generation collaborative systems and services. This is also witnessed by some research initiatives that started grouping worldwide researchers around this theme, e.g., the yearly ACEC (Agent-based Computing for Enterprise Collaboration) workshop within the IEEE WETICE (Workshops on Enabling Technologies: Infrastructures for Collaborative Enterprises) container and the recent Social Networks and Multiagent Systems Symposium within the convention of the UK Society for the Study of Artificial Intelligence and Simulation of Behaviour (AISB).

This paper began with an introduction to the research theme that motivates the rest of the work: the strict relationships between social networks, MASs and the Semantic Web are obviously present but the research have not yet found a coherent framework to captures all these models and abstractions. Then the paper briefly reviewed recent developments in the context of MAS-mediated collaboration and outlooked future directions also taking into account the recent hype on social networks. Finally, the paper considered the idea of SSNs as a first draft of a coherent view of

mentioned technologies. Unfortunately SSNs do not really use the full power of agent technology and we still need much work to finally grasp the full power of this research area.

REFERENCES

Adamic, L., & Adar, E. (2005). How to search a social network. *Social Networks, 27*(3), 187–203. doi:10.1016/j.socnet.2005.01.007

Axtell, R. (1999). Why agents? On the varied motivations for agent computing in the social sciences. *Proceedings of Agent Simulation: Applications, Models, and Tools.*

Barabási, A.L., Jeong, H., Neda, Z., Ravasz, E., Schubert, A., and Vicsek, T. (2002). Evolution of the social network of scientific collaborations. *Physica A: Statistical Mechanics and its Applications, 311*, 590-614.

Bellifemine, F., Poggi, A., & Rimassa, G. (2001). Developing multi agent systems with a FIPA-compliant agent framework. *Software, Practice & Experience, 31*, 103–128. doi:10.1002/1097-024X(200102)31:2<103::AID-SPE358>3.0.CO;2-O

Bentley, R., Busbach, U., Hinrichs, E., Kerr, D., Sikkel, K., Trevor, J., & Woetzel, G. (1997). Basic support for cooperative work on the World Wide Web. *International Journal of Human-Computer Studies, 46*(6), 827–846. doi:10.1006/ijhc.1996.0108

Bergenti, F. (2008). Toward a probabilistic model of trust in agent societies. In Artikis, A., O'Hare, G. M. P., Stathis, K., & Vouros, G. A. (Eds.), *Engineering Societies in the Agents World VIII, Lecture Notes in Artificial Intelligence, 4995* (pp. 270–283). Springer-Verlag. doi:10.1007/978-3-540-87654-0_15

Bergenti, F., Costicoglou, S., & Poggi, A. (2003). A portal for ubiquitous collaboration. In *Proceedings of the 15th Conference on Advanced Information Systems Engineering (CAiSE 2003)*, volume 75 of CEUR Workshop Proceedings.

Bergenti, F., Franchi, E., & Poggi, A. (2010). *Using HDS for realizing multi-agent applications*. Presented at the Third International Workshop on Languages, Methodologies and Development Tools for Multi-Agent Systems (LADS'010), Lyon, France.

Bergenti, F., Franchi, E., & Poggi, A. (2011). Selected models for agent-based simulation of social networks. In *Proceedings from 3rd Symposium on Social Networks and Multiagent Systems (SNAMAS '11)*, York.

Bergenti, F., & Poggi, A. (2000). CollAge: A replicated-instances platform for collaborative applications. *The Journal of Applied Systems Studies, 1*(3), 421–435.

Bergenti, F., Poggi, A., & Somacher, M. (2002). A collaborative platform for fixed and mobile networks. *Communications of the ACM, 45*(11), 39–44. doi:10.1145/581571.581591

Blue, A. (2009). *LinkedIn works with Twitter, and vice versa*. Retrieved from http://blog.linkedin.com/2009/11/09/allen-blue-twitter-and-linkedin-go-together-like-peanut-butter-and-chocolate/

Bordini, R., Dastani, M., Dix, J., & Fallah-Seghrouchni, A. (Eds.). (2005). *Multi-agent programming: Languages, platforms and applications. Multiagent Systems, Artificial Societies, and Simulated Organizations* (*Vol. 15*). Berlin, Germany: Springer Verlag.

Boyd, D. M., & Ellison, N. B. (2008). Social network sites: Definition, history, and scholarship. *Journal of Computer-Mediated Communication, 13*(1).

Bozdag, E., Mesbah, A., & van Deursen, A. (2007). A comparison of push and pull techniques for AJAX. In *Proceedings of the 2007 9th IEEE International Workshop on Web Site Evolution (WSE '07)*, Washington, DC, USA, (pp. 15-22).

Breslin, J., & Decker, S. (2007). The future of social networks on the Internet: The need for semantics. *IEEE Internet Computing, 11*(6), 86–90. doi:10.1109/MIC.2007.138

Brown, D. C., Dunskus, B., Grecu, D. L., & Berker, I. (1995). Support for single function agents. In *Proceedings of Applications of Artificial Intelligence in Engineering*. Udine, Italy: SINE.

Campbell, M. I., Cagan, J., & Kotovsky, K. (1999). A-Design: An agent-based approach to conceptual design in a dynamic environment. *Research in Engineering Design, 11*, 172–192. doi:10.1007/s001630050013

Cattuto, C., Loreto, V., & Pietronero, L. (2006, May 4). Collaborative tagging and semiotic dynamics. *Proceedings of the National Academy of Sciences of the United States of America, 104*, 1461–1469. doi:10.1073/pnas.0610487104

Chen, H., Finin, T., & Joshi, A. (2004). Semantic Web in the context broker architecture. In *Proceedings of the 2nd IEEE Conference on Pervasive Computing and Communications Workshops (PerCom 2004)*, (pp. 277-286). Orlando, FL, IEEE Press.

Chen, H., Finin, T., Joshi, A., Perich, F., & Chakraborty, D. (2004). Intelligent agents meet the Semantic Web in smart spaces. *IEEE Internet Computing, 8*(6), 69–79. doi:10.1109/MIC.2004.66

Chenggang, W., Wenpin, J., & Qijia, T. (2001). An information retrieval server based on ontology and multiagent. *Journal of Computer Research & Development, 38*(6), 641–647.

Corby, O., Dieng-Kuntz, R., Faron-Zucker, C., & Gandon, F. (2006). Searching the Semantic Web: Approximate query processing based on ontologies. *IEEE Intelligent Systems, 21*(1), 20–27. doi:10.1109/MIS.2006.16

Dale, J., Willmot, S., & Burg, B. (2002). Challenges and deployment of next-generation service environments. In *Proceedings of Pacific Rim Intelligent Multi-Agent Systems*. Tokyo, Japan: Agentcities.

Dikenelli, O., Erdur, R. C., & Gumus, O. (2005). SEAGENT: A platform for developing Semantic Web based multi agent systems. In *Proceedings of the Fourth International Joint Conference on Autonomous Agents and Multiagent Systems (AAMAS '05)*, (pp. 1271-1272). New York, NY.

Doreian, P. (2006). Actor network utilities and network evolution. *Social Networks, 28*(2), 137–164. doi:10.1016/j.socnet.2005.05.002

Dourish, P. (1996). Consistency guarantees: Exploiting application semantics for consistency management in a collaboration toolkit. In *Proceedings of the ACM, Conference on Computer-Supported Collaborative Work*.

Duchon, P., Hanusse, N., Lebhar, E., & Schabanel, N. (2006). Could any graph be turned into a small-world? *Theoretical Computer Science, 355*(1), 96–103. doi:10.1016/j.tcs.2005.12.008

Durfee, E. (1999). Distributed problem solving and planning. In Weiss, G. (Ed.), *Multiagent systems: A modern approach to distributed artificial intelligence* (pp. 121–164). Cambridge, MA: MIT Press.

Epstein, J. M. (1999). Agent-based computational models and generative social science. *Complexity, 4*(5), 41–60. doi:10.1002/(SICI)1099-0526(199905/06)4:5<41::AID-CPLX9>3.0.CO;2-F

Facebook. (2010). Open graph protocol. Retrieved from http://developers.facebook.com /docs/opengraph

Foner, L. (1996). A multi-agent referral system for matchmaking. *Proceedings the First International Conference on the Practical Application of Intelligent Agents and Multi-Agent Technology (PAAM '96)*, (pp. 22-24).

Franchi, E. (2010). A multi-agent implementation of social networks. *Proceedings of WOA 2010 Undicesimo Workshop Nazionale "Dagli Oggetti agli Agenti"*, Rimini.

Franchi, E., & Poggi, A. (2011). Multi-agent systems and social networks. In Cruz-Cunha, M., Putnik, G. D., Lopes, N., Patrícia, G., & Miranda, E. (Eds.), *Business social networking: Organizational, managerial, and technological dimensions*. Hershey, PA: IGI Global. doi:10.4018/978-1-61350-168-9.ch005

Gall, U., & Hauck, F. J. (1997). Promondia: A Java-based framework for real-time group communication in the Web. In *Proceedings of the 6th International WWW Conference*.

Gandon, F., Poggi, A., Rimassa, G., & Turci, P. (2002). Multi-agents corporate memory management system. *Applied Artificial Intelligence Journal, 16*(9-10), 699–720. doi:10.1080/08839510290030453

García-Sánchez, F., Fernández-Breis, J. T., Valencia-García, R., Gómez, J. M., & Martínez-Béjar, R. (2006). Combining Semantic Web technologies with multi-agent systems for integrated access to biological resources. *Journal of Biomedical Informatics, 41*(5), 848–859. doi:10.1016/j.jbi.2008.05.007

Genesereth, M., & Ketchpel, S. (1994). Software agents. *Communications of the ACM, 37*(7), 47–53. doi:10.1145/176789.176794

Grossberg, J. (2007). *Integration between Twitter and Facebook status*. Retrieved from http://www.twittersweet.com /2007/9/30/integration-between-twitter-and-facebook-status

Hague, M. J., & Taleb-Bendiab, A. (1998). Tool for management of concurrent conceptual engineering design. *Concurrent Engineering: Research and Applications*, 6(2), 111–129. doi:10.1177/1063293X9800600203

Hendler, J. (2001). Agents and the Semantic Web. *IEEE Intelligent Systems*, 16(2), 30–37. doi:10.1109/5254.920597

Hickson, I. (2011). *Server-sent events*. W3C Working Draft. Retrieved from http://www.w3.org / TR/eventsource/

Horley, B., & Lesser, V. (2004). A survey of multi-agent organizational paradigms. *The Knowledge Engineering Review*, 19, 281–316.

Huhns, M. N., Singh, M. P., Burstein, M., Decker, K., Durfee, E., & Finin, T. (2005). Research directions for service-oriented multiagent systems. *IEEE Internet Computing*, 9(6), 65–70. doi:10.1109/MIC.2005.132

Hummon, N. (2000). Utility and dynamic social networks. *Social Networks*, 22(3), 221-249. Elsevier. Jackson, M. O., & Wolinsky, A. (1996). A strategic model of social and economic networks. *Journal of Economic Theory*, 71, 44–74.

Jennings, N., Corera, J., & Laresgoiti, I. (1995). Developing industrial multi-agent systems. In *Proceedings of the First International Conference on Multi-Agent Systems (ICMAS-95)*, (pp. 423–430).

Jennings, N., Faratin, P., & Lomuscio, A. (2001). Automated negotiation: Prospects, methods and challenges. *Group Decision and Negotiation*, 10(2), 199–215. doi:10.1023/A:1008746126376

Jung, J. J., & Euzenat, J. (2007). Towards semantic social networks. In Franconi, E., Kifer, M., & May, W. (Eds.), *The Semantic Web: Research and Applications* (*Vol. 4519*, pp. 267–280). Lecture Notes in Computer Science Springer-Verlag. doi:10.1007/978-3-540-72667-8_20

Kalogeraki, V., Gunopulos, D., & Zeinalipour-Yazti, D. (2002). A local search mechanism for peer-to-peer networks. *Proceedings of the Eleventh International Conference on Information and Knowledge Management* (*CIKM '02*), 300-307.

Katasonov, A., & Terziyan, V. (2008). Semantic agent programming language (S-APL): A middleware platform for the Semantic Web. In *Proceedings of the 2008 IEEE International Conference on Semantic Computing (ICSC '08)* (pp. 504-511).

Kautz, H., & Selman, B. (1997). Referral Web: Combining social networks and collaborative filtering. *Communications of the ACM*, 40(3), 63–65. doi:10.1145/245108.245123

Kleinberg, J. (2000). The small-world phenomenon: An algorithm perspective. *Proceedings of the 32nd ACM Symposium on Theory of Computing* (pp. 163-170).

Kleinberg, J. (2002). Small-world phenomena and the dynamics of information. *Advances in Neural Information Processing Systems*, •••, 14.

Kleinberg, J. (2006). Complex networks and decentralized search algorithms. *Proceedings of the International Congress of Mathematicians (ICM)* (Vol. 3, pp. 1-26). Madrid, Spain.

Kleinberg, J., Kumar, R., Raghavan, P., Rajagopalan, S., & Tomkins, A. S. (1999). The web as a graph: Measurements, models, and methods. *Proceedings of the 5th Annual International Conference on Computing and Combinatorics*, (pp. 1-17). Springer-Verlag.

Küngas, P., Rao, J., & Matskin, M. (2004). Symbolic agent negotiation for Semantic Web service exploitation. In Li, Q., Wang, G., & Feng, L. (Eds.), *Advances in Web-Age Imformation Management* (*Vol. 3129*, pp. 458–467). Lecture Notes in Computer Science Springer-Verlag. doi:10.1007/978-3-540-27772-9_46

Lander, S. E. (1997). Issues in multi-agent design systems. *IEEE Expert, 12*(2), 18–26. doi:10.1109/64.585100

Liben-Nowell, D., Novak, J., Kumar, R., Raghavan, P., & Tomkins, A. (2005). Geographic routing in social networks. *Proceedings of the National Academy of Sciences of the United States of America, 102*(33), 11623–11628. doi:10.1073/pnas.0503018102

Liu, Q., Cui, X., & Hu, X. (2008). An agent-based multimedia intelligent platform for collaborative design. *International Journal of Communications. Network and System Sciences, 3*, 207–283.

LiveJournal. (2010). Retrieved from http://www.livejournal.com

Luo, J., & Xue, X. (2010). Research on information retrieval system based on Semantic Web and multi-agent. In *Proceedings of 2010 International Conference on Intelligent Computing and Cognitive Informatics*, (pp. 207-209). Kuala Lumpur, Malaysia.

Ma, Y., Zhang, S., Li, Y., Yi, Z., & Liu, S. (2009). An approach for multi-agent coordination based on semantic approximation. *International Journal of Intelligent Information Database Systems, 3*(2), 163–179. doi:10.1504/IJIIDS.2009.025161

Manola, F., Miller, E., & McBride, B. (2004). RDF primer. *W3C recommendation.*

Matskin, M. Kirkeluten, O.J., Krossnes, S. B., & Sæle, O. (2001). Agora: An infrastructure for cooperative work support in multi-agent systems. In T. Wagner & O. F. Rana, (Eds.), *Proceedings of the International Workshop on Infrastructure for Multi-Agent Systems, Lecture Notes in Computer Science, Volume 1887,* (pp. 28-40). Springer-Verlag.

Mesbah, A., & van Deursen, A. (2008). A component- and push-based architectural style for Ajax applications. *Journal of Systems and Software, 81*(12), 2194–2209. doi:10.1016/j.jss.2008.04.005

Mika, P. (2005). Flink: Semantic Web technology for the extraction and analysis of social networks. In *Web Semantics: Science, Services and Agents on the World Wide Web, 3*(2-3), 211-223, Elsevier B. V.

Milgram, S. (1967). The small world problem. *Psychology Today, 1*(1), 61-67.

Minenko, W. (1995). *The application sharing technology*. The X Advisor.

Muller, J. (1998). Architectures and applications of intelligent agents: A survey. *The Knowledge Engineering Review, 13*(4), 353–380. doi:10.1017/S0269888998004020

Newman, M. E. J. (2010). *Networks: An introduction*. Oxford University Press, 2010.

Nguyen, V., & Martel, C. (2005). Analyzing and characterizing small-world graphs. *Proceedings of the 16th Annual ACM-SIAM Symposium on Discrete Algorithms* (pp. 311–320). Society for Industrial and Applied Mathematics.

Osterloh, R. (2010). *Skype with Facebook integration and group video calling*. Retrieved from http://blogs.skype.com /en/2010/10/new_skype.html

Paolucci, M., & Sycara, K. (2003). Autonomous Semantic Web services. *IEEE Internet Computing, 7*(5), 34–41. doi:10.1109/MIC.2003.1232516

Parunak, V. D., Savit, R., & Riolo, R. L. (1998). Lecture Notes in Computer Science: *Vol. 1534. Agent-based modeling vs. equation-based modeling: A case study and users' guide. Multi-Agent Systems and Agent-Based Simulation* (pp. 10–15). Berlin, Germany: Springer Verlag.

Poggi, A., & Golinelli, G. (1998). Automatic storing and retrieval of large collections of images. In *Proceedings of the 11ᵗʰ International Conference on Industrial & Engineering Applications of Artificial Intelligence & Expert Systems* (IEA/AIE-98), Spain.

Rosenschein, J. (1982). Synchronization of multi-agent plans. *Proceedings of the National Conference on Artificial Intelligence*, (pp. 115-119).

Russel, S. J., & Norvig, P. (2003). *Artificial intelligence: A modern approach*. Upper Saddle River, NJ: Pearson Education.

Sabater, J., & Sierra, C. (2002). Reputation and social network analysis in multi-agent systems. *Proceedings 1ˢᵗ International Joint Conference on Autonomous Agents and Multiagent Systems (AAMAS '02)*, 1, (pp. 475-482). ACM Press.

Shah, U., Finin, T., Joshi, A., Cost, R. S., & Matfield, J. (2002). Information retrieval on the Semantic Web. In *Proceedings of the 11ᵗʰ International Conference on Information and Knowledge Management (CIKM '02)*, (pp. 461-468). New York, NY.

Shen, W., & Barthès, J. P. (1997). An experimental environment for exchanging engineering design knowledge by cognitive agents. In *Knowledge Intensive CAD-2* (pp. 19–38). Chapman & Hall.

Shen, W., Norrie, D. H., & Barthès, J. P. (2001). *Multi-agent systems for concurrent intelligent design and manufacturing*. London, UK: Taylor and Francis.

Tonino, H., Boss, A., de Weerdt, M., & Wittevee, C. (2002). Plan coordination by revision in collective agent based systems. *Artificial Intelligence*, *142*(2), 121–145. doi:10.1016/S0004-3702(02)00273-4

Toye, G., Cutkosky, M. R., Leifer, L., Tenenbaum, J., & Glicksman, J. (1993). SHARE: A methodology and environment for collaborative product development. In *Proceedings of 2ⁿᵈ Workshop on Enabling Technologies: Infrastructure for Collaborative Enterprises*, (pp. 33–47).

Van Damme, C., Hepp, M., & Siorpaes, K. (2007). FolksOntology: An integrated approach for turning folksonomies into ontologies. In *Proceedings of ESWC 2007 Workshop "Bridging the Gap between Semantic Web and Web 2.0"*, Innsbruck, Austria, (pp. 71-84).

Wellman, M. P., Greenwald, A., Stone, P., & Wurman, P. R. (2002) The 2001 trading agent competition. In *Proceedings of the 14ᵗʰ Innovative Applications of Artificial Intelligence Conference (IAAI-2002)*, (pp. 935-941). Edmonton.

Wooldridge, M., & Jennings, N. (1995). Intelligent agents: Theory and practice. *The Knowledge Engineering Review*, *10*(2), 115–152. doi:10.1017/S0269888900008122

Wooldridge, M. J. (2002). *An introduction to multi-agent systems*. John Wiley and Sons.

Yoshida, S., Kamei, K., Ohguro, T., & Kuwabara, K. (2003). Shine: A peer-to-peer based framework of network community support systems. *Computer Communications*, *26*(11), 1199–1209. doi:10.1016/S0140-3664(02)00254-2

Yu, B., & Singh, M. (2003). Searching social networks. *Proceedings of the Second International Joint Conference on Autonomous Agents and Multiagent Systems*, (pp. 65-72).

Zapf, M., Reinema, R., Wolf, R., & Türpe, S. (2002). UNITE - An agent-oriented teamwork environment. *Lecture Notes in Computer Science*, (n.d)., 2521.

Zou, Y., Finin, T., Ding, L., Chen, H., & Pan, R. (2003). Using Semantic Web technology in Multi-Agent systems: A case study in the TAGA Trading agent environment. In *Proceeding of the 5th International Conference on Electronic Commerce (ICEC 2003)*, Pittsburgh, PA.

KEY TERMS AND DEFINITIONS

Agent-based model: A class of computational models for simulating interacting agents.

Collaboration platform: A collaboration platform is a software platform that adds broad social networking capabilities to work processes.

Coordination: A process in which a group of agents engages in order to ensure that each of them acts in a coherent manner.

Expert finding: The problem of searching, in a distributed way, someone with a given set of skills and a given level of trust using a social network.

Groupware: A category of computer software designed to help people involved in a common task achieve their goals.

Multi-agent system: A loosely coupled network of software agents that interact to solve problems that are beyond the individual capacities or knowledge of each software agent.

Semantic social network: A semantic social network is the result of the use of Semantic Web technologies in social networks and online social media.

Social network: Social structure made of agents (individuals) which are connected by one or more different relationships

Software agent: A computer program that is situated in some environment and capable of autonomous action in order to meet its design objectives.

Utility: Measure of the agent satisfaction mapping possible outcomes on elements of a totally ordered set (e.g., the set of real numbers with the < relation).

Chapter 6
Exploiting Social Media Features for Automated Tag Recommendation

Rabeeh Ayaz Abbasi
Quaid-i-Azam University, Pakistan

ABSTRACT

In today's social media platforms, when users upload or share their media (photos, videos, bookmarks, etc.), they often annotate it with keywords (called tags). Annotating the media helps in retrieving and browsing resources, and also allows the users to search and browse annotated media. In many social media platforms like Flickr or YouTube, users have to manually annotate their resources, which is inconvenient and time consuming. Tag recommendation is the process of suggesting relevant tags for a given resource, and a tag recommender is a system that recommends the tags. A tag recommender system is important for social media platforms to help users in annotating their resources. Many of the existing tag recommendation methods exploit only the tagging information (Jaschke et al., 2007, Marinho & Schmidt-Thieme, 2008, Sigurbjornsson & van Zwol, 2008). However, many social media platforms support other media features like geographical coordinates. These features can be exploited for improving tag recommendation. In this chapter, a comparison of three types of social media features for tag recommendation is presented and evaluated. The features presented in this chapter include geographical-coordinates, low-level image descriptors, and tags.

DOI: 10.4018/978-1-4666-0894-8.ch006

1. RELATED WORK

A tag recommendation system is used to assist users in tagging resources. These systems have been discussed in various research works over the last few years. Researchers have come up with frameworks which allow the comparison of different tag recommendation methods. (Jaschke et al., 2009) presents a tag recommendation framework for their system Bibsonomy. The framework allows the evaluation of different tag recommendation algorithms. The framework is though limited to the tag recommender systems which only use the tagging information.

(Jaschke et al., 2007) compared two algorithms, FolkRank and Collaborative Filtering (Goldberg et al., 1992) for tag recommendation. FolkRank is based on PageRank (Brin and Page, 1998). It uses random walk techniques on the graph of users, tags, and resources and assumes that popular users, tags, and resources can reinforce each other. In collaborative filtering, similarity between users and tags and between users and resources is used to recommend tags. Their experiments based on the datasets from delicious (http://www.delicious.com/), last.fm (http://www.last.fm/), and Bibsonomy (http://www.bibsonomy.org/) show that the FolkRank algorithm outperforms other methods. The tag recommendation methods as proposed by (Jaschke et al., 2007) depend mainly on the tagging information and do not consider the features (like geographical coordinates or low-level image features) available in rich media (like photos or videos). The tag recommendation methods proposed by (Jaschke et al., 2007) suggest tags for already partially tagged resources.

(Sigurbjornsson and van Zwol, 2008) presents a tag recommendation system which evaluates different similarity measures, tag aggregation methods and ranking strategies. Given a photo and some initial tags, candidate tags are derived for each of the given tag. The candidate tags are retrieved based on the tag co-occurrence information. All of the candidate tags are then merged and

ranked. A final list of tags is then presented to the user. As in the work presented by (Jaschke et al., 2007), the methods proposed by (Sigurbjornsson and van Zwol, 2008) lack a tag recommendation strategy for newly uploaded resources. Although the experiments were performed on Flickr (photos) dataset, the methods do not consider the available rich media features.

Nowadays, the state-of-the-art imaging devices provide photos together with the geographical coordinates (*geo-tags*) stating precisely where they have been acquired. Therefore, more and more researchers make use of this additional information. (Cristani et al., 2008) exploits geographical coordinates for improving visualization of images on a map. (Kennedy et al., 2007) and (Kennedy and Naaman, 2008) use low-level image features and geographical coordinates to identify the landmarks of a city. (Moellic et al., 2008) presents a system which combines tags and low-level image features for clustering images. They suggest that clustering images can enhance the browsing and visualization of the images.

In addition to the features available in rich media, some researchers have used external data sources for recommending tags. (Heymann et al., 2008) predicts tags by using information available in the resource content, anchor text, and already available tags. Given a set of objects, and a set of tags applied to those objects by users, their approach predicts whether a given tag could/should be applied to a particular object. (Heymann et al., 2008) formulates the problem of tag recommendation into a supervised learning problem. For each tag to be recommended, they train a binary Support Vector Machine (SVM) classifier which predicts the association of a resource with the tag. Their approach is limited to a set of tags that can be recommended and may not be applied in a generic large scale scenario. Resource features like titles of webpages have also been exploited by other researchers (Lipczak, 2008). (Lipczak, 2008) suggests a tag recommendation system which extracts the tags from the resource title. The tag co-occurrence information available within the resource's posts in form of a personomy is used for recommending tags. In addition to exploiting external data sources and resource contents, some researchers have also used formal ontologies in the process of tag recommendation. (Adrian et al., 2007) presents a system called ConTag. It generates semantic tag recommendations for documents based on Semantic Web ontologies and Web 2.0 services.

Other recent research work related to tag recommendation includes (Illig et al., 2009, Rae et al., 2010, Krestel et al., 2009, Jin et al., 2010). (Illig et al., 2009) presents an algorithm for tag recommendation based on the contents of the resources. They train different classifiers like *SVM* and *Multinomial Nave Bayes* etc. on the training data for recommending tags for newly upload resources. (Rae et al., 2010) proposes a method of tag recommendation for partially annotated media. Their method exploits different contexts of the users. It achieves best results using the *Social Group* context. (Krestel et al., 2009) and (Jin et al., 2010) have used probabilistic methods like *Latent Dirichlet Allocation* (LDA) for tag recommendation. The method proposed by (Krestel et al., 2009) discovers latent topics using tagging information and these topics are then used to recommend tags for the new resources relevant to the same topic. (Jin et al., 2010) combines *Language Model* and *Latent Dirichlet Allocation* to recommend tags.

Finally some of the tag recommendation methods exploit rich media features like geographical coordinates and low-level image features. (Moxley et al., 2008) presents a tag recommendation tool called *SpiritTagger* which uses the geographical coordinates of the images available at Flickr. Their approach weights geographically relevant annotations for tag recommendation for an image database. Experimental results on two cities show that their approach outperforms the geographical and visual baselines for smaller cities, but the

geographical coordinates give the best results for larger cities. The tag recommendation framework presented in this chapter also focuses on different rich media features and compare the performance of each of these features.

2. SYSTEM OVERVIEW

The tag recommendation framework presented in this chapter is split into two parts: training and classification. During the training phase, a classification model is learned which is later used for tag recommendation. Depending upon the training data, the training phase can become computationally expensive, but as it is a onetime process it is done offline. The system is trained based on the image features available in social media, once the system is trained, it is used for recommending tags for new images. Figure 1 shows the tag recommendation process. The training phase is shown in the bottom (shaded region) of the figure. The tag recommendation process is shown in the top (non-shaded region) of the figure. During the classification phase a new image is mapped to one of the clusters learned during the training phase and the representative tags of that cluster are assigned to the image. Following is the brief description of the training and the classification phases:

Training

In the training phase images are clustered (see Section 4.1) based on their features. A cluster contains homogeneous images depending upon the types of features used for clustering. In this chapter geographical coordinates, low-level image features and tags are explored for tag recommendation. As an example, a cluster based on geographical coordinates represents the images taken in a particular location. A cluster based on low-level image features contains images sharing

Figure 1. Overview of the tag recommendation system

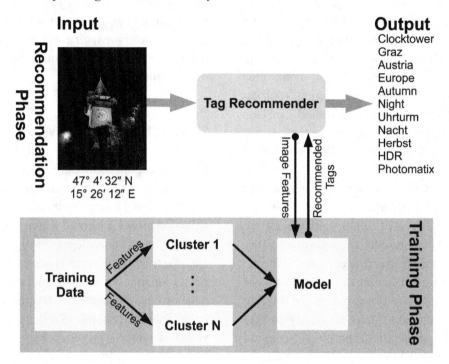

a particular texture or a color like the images of a sea or a forest. A cluster based on tagging data represents resources related to high level concepts like concert or river. The clustering process used is described in Section 4.1. Representative tags of a set of homogeneous images are used to annotate new images. The method of identifying representative tags is described in Section 4.2.

Classification

Clusters learned in the training phase are used as a model for tag recommendation. A new image is classified into its closest cluster of images and the representative tags (see Section 4.2) of that cluster are assigned to the new image. The method of classifying an image to its closest cluster and recommending tags are described in Section 4.3. Some of the features available in social media and explored in this chapter are described in the following section.

3. FEATURES IN SOCIAL MEDIA

Three different social media features are explored in this chapter to analyze their effect on the performance of a tag recommendation system. The three features are detailed below.

Geographical Coordinates

With the advancement in camera and mobile technologies, nowadays many devices are available in the market that are able to capture the location of the image using a built-in or an external GPS (global positioning system) device. In addition to the possibility of capturing the location of an image using a GPS device, some social media platforms like Flickr facilitate the users to add geographical coordinates to their images by providing a map interface where users can place their images on the map as shown in Figure 2. Due to the ease in associating geographical location to an image, there are many images in Flickr which are enriched with geographical information. In the CoPhIR dataset (Bolettieri et al., 2009), around 4 million out of 54 million images are annotated with geographical coordinates. The number of geographically annotated images is supposed to increase in future as more devices will be able to capture the geographical coordinates. Formally, geographical coordinates of images are represented in a two dimensional vector space $G \in \Re^2$. Each row vector $\vec{g}_i$ of the feature space G represents the geographical coordinates of the image i.

Low-Level Image Features

An image can be represented in a variety of low-level image features. Some of these features use MPEG-7 multimedia content description standard (Manjunath et al., 2002). There are five different types of low-level MPEG-7 features available in the CoPhIR dataset for 54 million images. Table 1 shows the properties and dimensions of the low-level features available in the CoPhIR dataset. Based on initial experimental results, two low-level image features are explored in this chapter due to their overall better performance, the MPEG-7 *Edge Histogram Descriptor* (EHD) and *Color Layout* (CL). EHD represents the local edge distribution. Each image is divided into 4×4 non-overlapping blocks (resulting into 16 equal partitions). Edges in each block are categorized into five directions: vertical, horizontal, 45 diagonal, 135 diagonal and non-directional edges. The information about these edges is stored in a vector of 80 coefficients (Bolettieri et al., 2009). The Color Layout descriptor captures both color and spatial information. It is obtained by applying the discrete cosine transformation (DCT) on a 2-dimensional array of local representative colors in Y or Cb or Cr color space. The information is stored in 12 co-efficients (Bolettieri et al., 2009). The low-level image features based on EHD and CL are represented in 80 and 12-dimensional

feature spaces $L_E \in \Re^{80}$ and $L_C \in \Re^{12}$ respectively. A row vector $\vec{\ell}_i$ of the feature space L_E or L_C represents the edge histograms or color layout of the image i respectively.

Tags

Tags are freely chosen keywords associated with the images. There is no restriction in selecting a tag for an image. A tag might represent a concept in an image, describe the image itself or it might also represent the context of the image (e.g. location, event, time etc.). On average there are only few tags associated with the images. In 54 million images of the CoPhIR dataset, each image has on average 3.1 tags. The tags are represented by a tag by resource matrix T. A row vector $\vec{t}_{i,*}$ of the matrix T represents a resource. The non-zero values of the row vector $\vec{t}_{i,*}$ represent the tags associated with the resource i. A column vector $\vec{t}_{*,j}$ represents a tag vector whose non-zero values represent the resources associated with the tag j. A non-zero value of the matrix $T_{i,j}$ represents that the resource i is associated with the tag j.

To reduce the bias towards resources with many tags and very common tags, the tags of the resources are normalized by their Term Frequency

Table 1. Properties and dimensions of low-level features available in the CoPhIR dataset

Low-level Feature	Properties	Dims
Scalable Color	Color histogram	64
Color Structure	Localized color distributions	64
Color Layout	Color and spatial information	12
Edge Histogram	Local-edge distribution	80
Homogeneous Texture	Texture	62

Figure 2. Screenshot of Flickr interface where users can add geographical coordinates to their images using a map

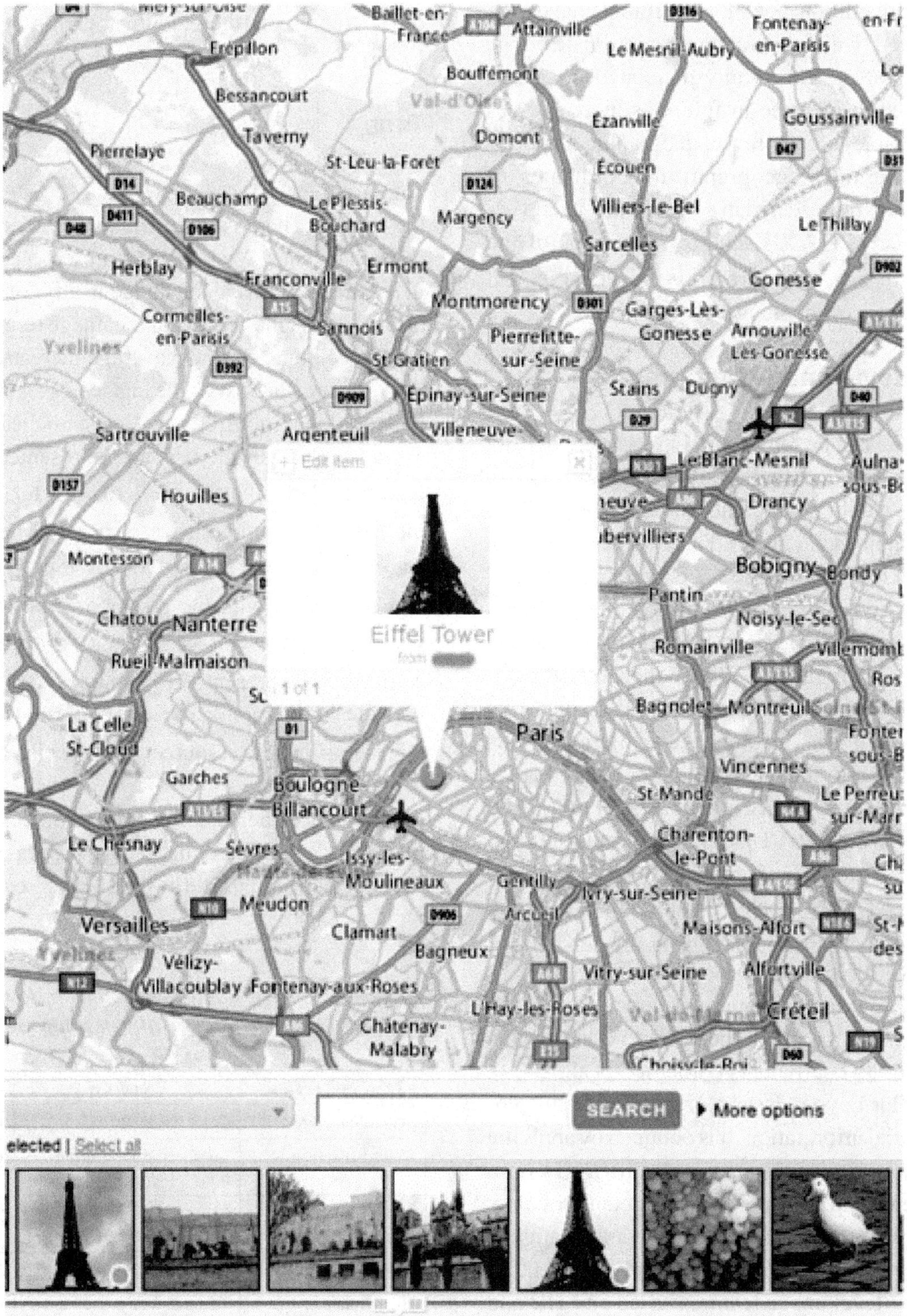

(TF) and Inverse Document Frequency (IDF) respectively. TF and IDF are computed as follows:

$$TF_{i,j} = \frac{n_{i,j}}{\sum_{k} n_{k,j}} \tag{1}$$

where $n_{i,j}$ is the number of times the tag t_i appears in the resource j, and the denominator is the sum of number of occurrences of all tags in the resource j.

$$IDF_i = \log \frac{N}{N_i} \tag{2}$$

where N is the number of resources in the dataset and N_i is the number of resources in which the tag t_i appears.

4. TAG RECOMMENDATION

This section explains the proposed tag recommendation system in detail. In the training phase of tag recommendation, the resources are first clustered (see Section 4.1), then for each cluster, its representative tags are identified (see Section 4.2). In the tag recommendation phase, a new resource is classified to its closest cluster and the representative tags of the closest cluster are recommended for the new image (see Section 4.3).

4.1 Clustering

The images are grouped (clustered) to build a model which is used for tag recommendation. There are many algorithms for clustering resources, each of these algorithms could affect the final quality of the recommended tags. The tag recommender system evaluated in this chapter uses a well-known clustering technique called *K-Means* (MacQueen, 1967). K-Means is capable of clus-

tering very large and high dimensional datasets. Of course, other clustering methods can also be employed in the framework, when one desires to fine tune the performances or improve the results. The K-Means algorithm is described in Figure 3. Different parameters used in K-Means algorithm are described as follows:

Number of Clusters

There is no generally accepted rule for setting the number of clusters for using K-Means. The number of clusters used in the evaluation is defined as following (Mardia et al., 1979, page 365):

$$k = \sqrt{\frac{n}{2}} \tag{3}$$

By using k as defined in the above equation for n images, the number of clusters for different feature spaces is always the same.

Initial Cluster Centroids

In K-Means clustering, the quality of clustering also depends on the selection of initial cluster centroids. In the evaluation, k images are randomly selected as initial cluster centroids. The same set of randomly selected images is used as cluster centroids for each feature space.

Computing Distance/Similarity between Resources

During the clustering process, each image is grouped with its closest centroid (see Figure 3, step 4). A distance measure is needed to compute the distance between an image and its closest centroid. The most popular distance measure used is *Euclidean Distance* (Han and Kamber, 2006, page 388). Euclidean Distance between two m

Figure 3. K-Means clustering algorithm

```
Input: Feature space F ∈ {G, L, T, D}, Number of clusters k
Output: A set of k clusters
Method:
 1:  Randomly select k vectors from the feature space F as initial cluster
     centroids
 2:  while values of cluster centroids are updated do
 3:      for each resource r do
 4:          find the cluster c whose centroid is closest to the resource r
 5:          assign r to the cluster c
 6:      end for
 7:      for each cluster c do
 8:          recompute the centroid of the cluster c based on the document
             assigned to it
 9:      end for
10:  end while
```

-dimensional vectors $\vec{f}$ and $\vec{c}$ is defined as follows:

$$euclidean(\vec{f}, \vec{c}) = \sqrt{\sum_{i=1}^{m}(\vec{f}_i - \vec{c}_i)^2} \qquad (4)$$

In this chapter, Euclidean distance is used for non-text feature spaces (i.e. geographical, and low-level feature spaces). For text (or tag) based feature spaces it is common to use *Cosine Similarity* (Han and Kamber, 2006, page 397). The cosine similarity between two m dimensional vectors $\vec{f}$ and $\vec{c}$ can be computed as:

$$cosine(\vec{f}, \vec{c}) = \frac{\vec{f} \cdot \vec{c}}{\|\vec{f}\| \cdot \|\vec{c}\|} \qquad (5)$$

Experimental results show that Cosine similarity for tag/text based features performs significantly better than Euclidean distance. In addition to cosine similarity and Euclidean distance, other distance/similarity measures like Manhattan distance can also be used during the clustering

process. Manhattan distance between two vectors $\vec{f}$ and $\vec{c}$ is defined as follows:

$$manhattan(\vec{f}, \vec{c}) = \sum_{i=1}^{m} |\vec{f}_i - \vec{c}_i| \qquad (6)$$

In addition to generic similarity/distance measures, there are specific distance/similarity measures which are used for finding similarity/distance between images. One of such measures is *Histogram Intersection* (Smith, 1997). Histogram Intersection between two images is computed as follows:

$$HI(\vec{f}, \vec{c}) = \frac{\sum_{i=1}^{m} min(\vec{f}_i, \vec{c}_i)}{min(|f|, |c|)} \qquad (7)$$

4.2 Identifying Representative Tags

After grouping the images into k clusters, the representative tags for each cluster are identified. One possible method of identifying the representative tags is to sort the tags by their frequency in a cluster. The tag which appears most frequently in the resources of a cluster is ranked the highest followed by other frequent tags. This method of ranking tags is affected by the tags assigned by a single user to the resources present in a cluster. To avoid the bias towards the tags assigned by a single user, the tags can be ranked by their user frequency. A tag which is used by most users is ranked the highest followed by the other frequent tags. Let's assume that Figure 4 represents the tags in a cluster. The tags which are used by more users are ranked higher in the cluster, e.g., the tags *Clocktower* and *Graz*. The tags which are used by fewer users are ranked lower, e.g., the tags *HDR* and *Photomatix*. Ranking by user frequency instead of resource frequency avoids the situation where many resources in a cluster are tagged by a single user. The ranked tags of a cluster are recommended for the new image. Section 5.4 discusses about the number of tags that should be recommended.

4.3 Classification and Tag Recommendation

The training for the proposed tag recommender system is completed after identifying the representative tags for each cluster. The tag recommendation system can be trained off-line using a large dataset. After the completion of the training phase, given a new image, it has to be mapped to the closest cluster, whose representative tags are assigned to the image. As in the case of clustering, many choices of classification algorithms exist for training a classifier which learns its model based on the clusters identified in Section 4.1. One can train a one-class classifier (Manevitz and Yousef, 2002) considering images in a cluster as positive training examples. It is also possible to use a two class classifier (Baeza-Yates and Ribeiro-Neto, 1999), where images in one cluster are used as positive training examples, and images in other clusters are used as negative training examples. A much simpler classification method is Rocchio

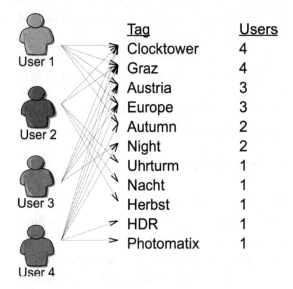

Figure 4. Example showing the ranking of the tags. The tags used by more users are ranked higher than other tags

Tag	Users
Clocktower	4
Graz	4
Austria	3
Europe	3
Autumn	2
Night	2
Uhrturm	1
Nacht	1
Herbst	1
HDR	1
Photomatix	1

classification (Rocchio, 1971). Using Rocchio classification, a new image is mapped to a cluster whose centroid is at minimum distance from the image. The most representative tags associated with the mapped cluster are assigned to the new image.

For clusters based on geographical coordinates, the new image is classified into one of the clusters whose centroid is at minimum geographical distance from the new image. For low-level clusters, the new image is classified based on the distance between its low-level features and the cluster centroids. For tag based clusters, as there are no tags for the new image, the new image is classified based on the distance between its geographical coordinates and the mean of geographical coordinates of the tag based clusters. The mismatch between feature spaces used for tag based clustering and the new image negatively affects the results of tags based clustering.

5. EXPERIMENTS AND RESULTS

The tag recommendation system described in the previous sections is evaluated on a large dataset. The image dataset is briefly described in Section 5.1, the distinction between the training and the test data comes in Section 5.2, which is followed by the evaluation method in Section 5.3. Section 5.4 presents the comprehensive results achieved during evaluation.

5.1 Image Dataset

The CoPhIR dataset (Bolettieri et al., 2009) consists of images uploaded to Flickr by hundreds of thousands of different users, which makes the dataset very heterogeneous. One can find images of very different types like portraits, landscapes, people, architecture, screen shots etc. To perform an evaluation on different types of features (geographical coordinates, tags, low-level) on a reasonably large scale, a subset of the original CoPhIR dataset is created as follows.

The images taken in national capitals (http://en.wikipedia.org/wiki/National_capitals) of all the world countries are selected in the evaluation dataset. For this purpose, all the images at a geographical distance of less than 0.1 Euclidean units from the center of the capital cities are considered. The capital cities which had less than $1,000$ images are ignored; this resulted into a set of 58 cities. To keep the experiments scalable, $30,000$ images for cities which had more than $30,000$ images are randomly selected. There were only three such cities Paris, London, and Washington DC. In the end, the evaluation dataset contains images of 58 capital cities, ranging from $1,000$ to $30,000$ images with an average of $8,000$ images per city. Total number of images in the evaluation dataset is $413,848$. Images are trained and evaluated separately for each city.

Base Line

In order to compare the effectiveness of different image features, a random feature space for the images is also created. A random value between 0 and 1 is assigned to each image in the dataset as its random feature. The random feature is considered as the baseline for the comparison of different image features. Same clustering methods are applied on the random features as on the other features. Random feature space is uni-dimensional and is represented as $D \in \Re$.

5.2 Training and Test Data

It is important to carefully select the training and test datasets, because when a user uploads images to Flickr, he or she can perform batch operations on the set of images. For example, he or she can assign the same tags or geographical coordinates to all the images in a batch. It is also possible that the images have very similar low-level features. Now if the images are randomly split into training and test datasets, there is a chance that the images belonging to one user are used in both of the training and the test dataset. Such a random split may affect the final evaluation. Test images from one user might be mapped to a cluster which is trained on the images from the same user. It is very likely that the test image is annotated with the perfect tags, as the tags of both the test and the training images were provided by the same user.

To make the evaluation transparent, instead of randomly splitting the resources into training and test dataset, the resources are split based on users. For each city, resources belonging to 75% of the users are used for training and resources belonging to 25% of the users are used for testing. No image in the test dataset is annotated by a user who has also annotated images in the training dataset. After splitting the users into training and test datasets, $310,590$ images are used for training the system and $103,258$ images are used as ground truth for evaluating the system.

Another aspect of fair evaluation is the quality of the tags. There are some tags which are very common in both test and training datasets. These tags mostly represent city or country names, which can be suggested by looking into a geographical database. Some common tags might not be very specific, e. g., the tags *geo-tagged, 2007, travel* etc. Very common tags also affect the evaluation results, as they are abundant in both test and training datasets, and are almost always recommended for every test image. This results in higher precision and recall values.

To make the evaluation more transparent, the ten most frequent tags for each city are not considered and the frequent tags *geo-tagged* and *geotag* are also ignored, because all the images in the evaluation dataset are geo-tagged and most of the images have these two tags. For each city, the rare tags are also removed. These tags might be incorrectly spelled tags or tags specific to a particular user. For this reason, for each city, tags which are used by less than three users are ignored.

5.3 Evaluation

Tags associated with the $103,258$ test images are considered as ground truth. The images in the ground truth are tagged by different users and as there is no restriction on the selection of tags for a resource, therefore the tags in the ground truth are very noisy. The noise in the data leads to inferior results, but the overall results show the comparative analysis of different feature spaces. The methods are evaluated using standard evaluation methods used in information retrieval: Precision P, Recall R, and F-Measure F. The evaluation measures are defined as follows:

$$P = \frac{\text{Number of correctly recommended tags}}{\text{Number of tag recommended}}$$

(8)

$$R = \frac{\text{Number of correctly recommended tags}}{\text{Number of Expected Tags}}$$

(9)

$$F = \frac{2 \times P \times R}{P + R}$$

(10)

5.4 Results

The results presented in this section give a comparative view of tag recommendation based on different types of features. The automated evaluation on one hand provides the possibility to do evaluation on a large scale, but on the other hand the ground truth (test data) contains many invalid tags, which results into inferior results. The evaluation is made transparent and more meaningful by filtering certain types of tags (see Section 5.2).

By removing very common tags, there is a certain decrease in the performance of recommender system, but it is an important step towards a fair evaluation. The results obtained through the evaluation done without filtering the dataset produce better results in terms of precision and recall. For example, the random feature space in non-filtered datasets results into an F-Measure value of 0.42. This is because very common tags are being recommended for the test images and there is always a major overlap between common tags of the training and the test data.

The precision, recall, and F-Measure values presented in this section might appear to be low for the reader, but one should consider that the dataset was filtered to make the evaluation more transparent.

The Figure 5, Figure 6, and Figure 7 depict the so called micro average evaluation and were generated in accordance to the evaluation criteria (see Equation 8), (see Equation 9), and (see Equation 10) respectively. As one can see, in all three cases the results are significantly better when using geographical coordinates for image description.

The performance of the tag recommendation using low-level features and textual tags differs only slightly from the results based on random clustering. For exactly one tag being recommended, the precision amounts to: 0.1385 for geographical coordinates, 0.0502 for low-level features, 0.0512 for textual tags, and 0.0338 for random clustering. Besides the fact that low-level image features perform worse than the geographical coordinates, one possible reason could be the sparsity of tagging data in the training dataset. The training dataset consisted of the images from Flickr where users might not have added a sufficient amount of tags to their resources. When observing the results of different clustering methods, it is noticed that though the low-level image features resulted into meaningful clusters, the images in the clusters were not properly tagged. For example, a cluster based on low-level image features depicting a football ground in all of its images did not contain the tag *ground*. Similarly a cluster of images having

close-ups of crowd in the stadium did not contain the tag *crowd*. Such kind of sparsity in the training data could have affected the results of tag recommendation using low-level image features.

In addition to the problem of data sparsity, the worse results of tag recommendation based on the tag feature could be a result of the feature mismatch problem (see Section 4.3). The proposed framework recommends the tags for new images, and as the new images are not already tagged, their feature space cannot be used to map them on existing clusters. In the evaluation, the geographical coordinates of a new image are used to map it on the existing clusters (based on tag feature). This mismatch of different feature spaces of the new image and the existing clusters (in case of tag clustering) could have affected the results of tag recommendation for tag feature.

For more than 10 tag recommendations, random feature performs slightly better than the tag features, this is due to the micro evaluation measures (see Equations 8, 9, 10). In random

Figure 5. Micro precision for geographical, low-level (edge histogram descriptor), tag, and random image features. Precision for geographical coordinates is higher than all other image representations.

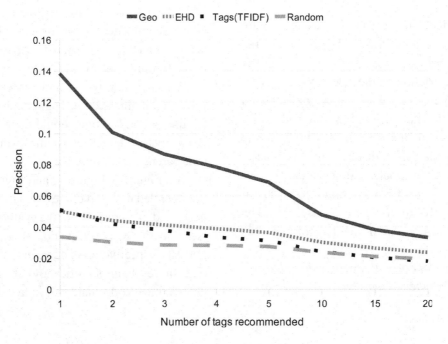

feature, tags are equally distributed among different clusters, and because some of the common tags like *night* or *sky* are correct for many images, therefore overall performance of the random feature remains comparable to the tag based features or low-level image features.

The results also suggest the threshold for the number of tags that should be recommended for a new resource. For a tag recommender whose focus is more on the correctness of the tags, only the top few tags should be recommended, as obvious from Figure 5, when more tags are recommended, the precision of the recommendation gets lower. In the case of a tag recommender system which does not require the tag recommendations with higher precision, four to five tags can be recommended. As shown in Figure 7, the best results (in terms of F-Measure) are achieved when four tags are recommended, this is the best compromise between the precision and the recall for the tag recommendations.

Although the fine tuning of experiments is avoided for most of the cases, experiments to compare effectiveness of different alternative methods related to the features of the resources are performed. In the Figures from 8 to 12 results of further evaluations are presented. The Figure 8 explains why using the simple Euclidean distance has appeared to be sufficient. The results remain almost the same when using Manhattan distance.

Using different low-level features did not significantly affect the performance of the tag recommender system. As one can see in the Figure 9, that the Edge Histogram Descriptor (EHD) performs almost the same as the Color Layout (CL) feature in terms of micro F-Measure.

When measuring similarity between resources based on low-level features, a variety of options are available, similarity between images using histogram intersection (see Equation 7) is also evaluated. Figure 10 shows the micro F-Measure applied the two different distance measures.

Figure 6. Micro recall for geographical, low-level (edge histogram descriptor), tag, and random image features. Recall for geographical coordinates is higher than all other image representations. For more than 5 tag recommendations, random feature performs slightly better than the tag feature due to the micro recall evaluation measure.

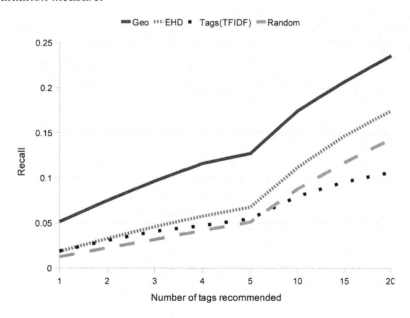

Figure 7. Micro F-measure for geographical, low-level (edge histogram descriptor), tag, and random image features. Geographical feature performs better than all the other image representations.

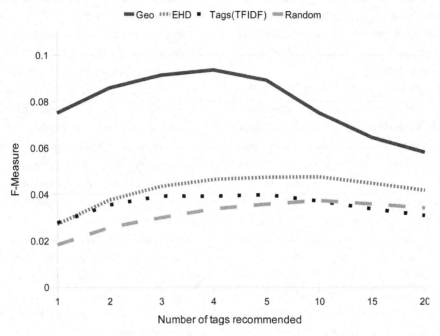

Figure 8. Micro F-Measure comparison of Manhattan (Manh) and Euclidean (Eucl) distances for non-text based features. Dark lines show the results obtained using Euclidean distance and gray lines show results obtained using Manhattan distance. Performance for both distances is almost same for all the image features.

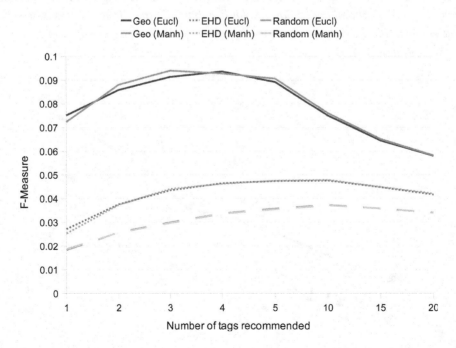

Figure 9. Micro F-Measure comparing results of two different low-level features edge histogram descriptor (EHD) and color layout (CL). Both of the low-level image features performs almost the same.

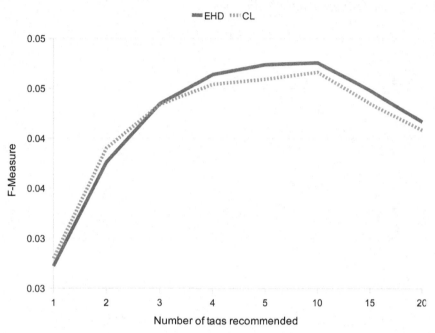

Euclidean distance for tag recommendation performs significantly better than the histogram intersection. The performance of tag recommendation using Euclidean distance starts to decline when more than 10 tags are recommended, however, in case of histogram intersection the performance continues to improve for 15 and 20 tag recommendations.

Cosine similarity was used for tag based feature space and Figure 11 shows a clear advantage of the Cosine distance over the Euclidean distance for tag based features.

To investigate the effect of different weight schemes for the tag features, the results using two different normalization strategies are evaluated, which are, term frequency (TF), and term frequency-inverse document frequency (TF-IDF). Although the overall effect of normalization is not significant, but applying TF-IDF normalization on simple tag feature slightly improves the tag recommendation process as shown in Figure 12.

6. CONCLUSION

The methods discussed in this chapter exploit three kinds of image features, namely geographical coordinates, tags, and low-level features, to recommend tags for the new resources uploaded to a social tagging system. In order to compare the benefits each of these features brings to a tag recommender system on its own, these features are investigated independently of each other.

First, the existing data collection was clustered separately for the geographical coordinates, tags, and low-level features. Additionally, random clustering was performed in order to provide a baseline for experimental results. Once a new image was uploaded to the system, it was assigned to one of the clusters using either its geographical or low-level representation. Finally, the most representative tags for the resulting cluster were recommended to the user for annotation of the new image. Section 5 evaluated tag recommender systems of the architecture proposed.

Figure 10. Micro F-Measure comparison of Euclidean (Eucl) and Histogram Intersection (HI) metrics for MPEG-7 edge histogram descriptor. Recommendations based on Euclidean distance perform significantly better than the histogram intersection measure.

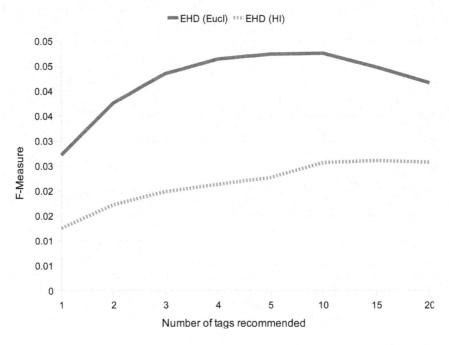

Figure 11. Micro F-Measure comparison of Cosine (Cos) and Euclidean (Eucl) distances for tag/text based features. Cosine distance performs significantly better than the Euclidean distance when using tag feature for recommendation.

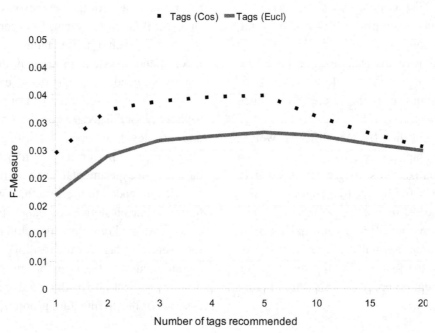

Figure 12. Micro F-Measure comparison of tags features with different normalization strategies (tag frequency-TF, tag frequency inverse document frequency-TF-IDF). TF-IDF normalized tag features perform better than no normalization and TF based normalization.

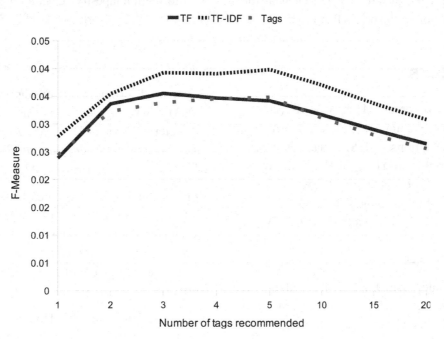

Large-scale experiments performed for more than $400,000$ images compared the different image representation techniques in terms of precision and recall in tag recommendation. A tag recommender system of the architecture proposed benefits the most from geographical information associated with the images.

One of the important contributions of this chapter is the evaluation on a large-scale image database. For evaluation, the CoPhIR dataset (Bolettieri et al., 2009) is used. It includes images uploaded to Flickr by hundreds of thousands of different users. The total number of images in the evaluation dataset was $413,848$.

Another significant contribution was considering the tag recommendation problem separately for images described with tags, geographical coordinates, and low-level features, as well as comparing the results to a baseline achieved based on random clustering.

The results presented in Section 5 showed that geographical coordinates are the most helpful image descriptors for tag recommendation, while textual tags and low-level features provide only a slightly better performance than the random baseline. It might sound disappointing, but low-level features and textual tags do not seem to be suitable for tag recommender systems connected to large-scale heterogeneous image databases. However, textual tags and low-level features might be very helpful for small image databases with a clearly defined domain (e.g., medical domain (Muller et al., 2003)) and also in a situation where geographical coordinates are not available.

ACKNOWLEDGMENT

This chapter is an extension of the research work published in (Abbasi et al., 2009) co-authored by

Prof. Dr. Marcin Grzegorzek and Prof. Dr. Steffen Staab. I would like to acknowledge both Prof. Dr. Marcin Grzegorzek and Prof. Dr. Steffen Staab for their contribution to the original research work.

REFERENCES

Abbasi, R., Grzegorzek, M., & Staab, S. (2009). Large scale tag recommendation using different image representations. In T. S. Chua, Y. Kompatsiaris, B. Mérialdo, W. Haas, G. Thallinger, & W. Bailer (Eds.), *Proceedings of 4th International Conference on Semantic and Digital Media Technologies, Semantic Multimedia, Lecture Notes in Computer Science 5887*, (pp. 65-76). Berlin, Germany: Springer.

Adrian, B., Sauermann, L., & Roth-Berghofer, T. (2007). ConTag: A semantic tag recommendation system. In T. Pellegrini & S. Schaffert (Eds.), *Proceedings of I-Semantics*, (pp. 297-304). JUCS.

Baeza-Yates, R., & Ribeiro-Neto, B. (1999). *Modern information retrieval*. Addison Wesley.

Bolettieri, P., Esuli, A., Falchi, F., Lucchese, C., Perego, R., Piccioli, T., & Rabitti, F. (2009). CoPhIR: A test collection for content-based image retrieval. *CoRR*, abs/0905.4627v2.

Brin, S., & Page, L. (1998). The anatomy of a large-scale hypertextual Web search engine. *Proceedings of the Seventh International World Wide Web Conference Computer Networks and ISDN Systems, 30*(1-7), 107-117.

Cristani, M., Perina, A., Castellani, U., & Murino, V. (2008). Content visualization and management of geo-located image databases. In *Proceedings of Extended Abstracts on Human factors in Computing Systems* (pp. 2823–2828). New York, NY: ACM. doi:10.1145/1358628.1358768

Goldberg, D., Nichols, D., Oki, B. M., & Terry, D. (1992). Using collaborative filtering to weave an information tapestry. *Communications of the ACM, 35*(12), 61–70. doi:10.1145/138859.138867

Han, J., & Kamber, M. (2006). *Data mining: Concepts and techniques* (2nd ed.). Morgan Kaufmann.

Heymann, P., Ramage, D., & Garcia-Molina, H. (2008). Social tag prediction. In *Proceedings of 31st International ACM Conference on Research and Development in Information Retrieval*, (pp. 531-538). New York, NY: ACM.

Illig, J., Hotho, A., Jäschke, R., & Stumme, G. (2009). A comparison of content-based tag recommendations in folksonomy systems. In *Postproceedings of the International Conference on Knowledge Processing in Practice*, (pp. 1-14). Springer.

Jäschke, R., Eisterlehner, F., Hotho, A., & Stumme, G. (2009). Testing and evaluating tag recommenders in a live system. In D. Benz & F. Janssen (Eds.), *Workshop on Knowledge Discovery, Data Mining, and Machine Learning*, (pp. 44 -51).

Jäschke, R., Marinho, L., Hotho, A., Schmidt-Thieme, L., & Stumme, G. (2007). Tag recommendations in folksonomies. In J. Kok, J. Koronacki, R. Lopez de Mantaras, S. Matwin, D. Mladenic, & A. Skowron, (Eds.), *Proceedings of Knowledge Discovery in Databases*, volume 4702 of *Lecture Notes in Computer Science*, (pp. 506-514). Berlin, Germany: Springer.

Jin, Y., Li, R., Cai, Y., Li, Q., Daud, A., & Li, Y. (2010). Semantic grounding of hybridization for tag recommendation. In Chen, L., Tang, C., Yang, J., & Gao, Y. (Eds.), *Web-Age Information Management* (*Vol. 6184*, pp. 139–150). Lecture Notes in Computer Science Berlin, Germany: Springer. doi:10.1007/978-3-642-14246-8_16

Kennedy, L., Naaman, M., Ahern, S., Nair, R., & Rattenbury, T. (2007). How flickr helps us make sense of the world: context and content in community-contributed media collections. In *Proceedings of 15th International Conference on Multimedia*, (pp. 631-640). New York, NY: ACM.

Kennedy, L. S., & Naaman, M. (2008). Generating diverse and representative image search results for landmarks. In *Proceedings of the 17th International Conference on World Wide Web*, (pp. 297-306). New York, NY: ACM.

Krestel, R., Fankhauser, P., & Nejdl, W. (2009). Latent dirichlet allocation for tag recommendation. In *Proceedings of the Third ACM Conference on Recommender Systems*, (pp. 61-68). New York, NY: ACM.

Lipczak, M. (2008). Tag recommendation for folksonomies oriented towards individual users. In *Proceedings of the ECML/PKDD Discovery Challenge Workshop*.

MacQueen, J. (1967). Some methods for classification and analysis of multivariate observations. In L. M. Le Cam, & J. Neyman (Eds.), *Proceedings of 5th Berkeley Symposium on Mathematical Statistics and Probability*, (pp. 281-297). Berkeley, CA: University of California Press.

Manevitz, L. M., & Yousef, M. (2002). One-class SVMs for document classification. *Journal of Machine Learning Research*, *2*, 139–154.

Manjunath, B. S., Salembier, P., & Sikora, T. (2002). *Introduction to MPEG-7 - Multimedia content description interface*. Chichester, UK: John Wiley & Sons Ltd.

Mardia, K., Kent, J., & Bibby, J. (1979). *Multivariate analysis*. Academic Press.

Marinho, L. B., & Schmidt-Thieme, L. (2008). Collaborative tag recommendations. In Bock, H. H. (Eds.), *Data analysis, machine learning and applications, studies in classification, data analysis, and knowledge organization* (pp. 533–540). Berlin, Germany: Springer.

Moëllic, P.-A., Haugeard, J.-E., & Pitel, G. (2008). Image clustering based on a shared nearest neighbors approach for tagged collections. In *Proceedings of the International Conference on Content-Based Image and Video Retrieval*, (pp. 269-278). New York, NY: ACM.

Moxley, E., Kleban, J., & Manjunath, B. S. (2008). Spirittagger: A geo-aware tag suggestion tool mined from Flickr. In *Proceedings of the 1st ACM International Conference on Multimedia Information Retrieval*, (pp. 24-30). New York, NY: ACM.

Müller, H., Michoux, N., Bandon, D., & Geissbuhler, A. (2004). A review of content-based image retrieval systems in medical applications - Clinical benefits and future directions. *International Journal of Medical Informatics*, *73*(1), 1–23. doi:10.1016/j.ijmedinf.2003.11.024

Rae, A., Sigurbjörnsson, B., & van Zwol, R. (2010). Improving tag recommendation using social networks. In *Proceedings of 9th International Conference on Adaptivity, Personalization and Fusion of Heterogeneous Information*. Paris, France: CID.

Rocchio, J. J. (1971). Relevance feedback in information retrieval. In Salton, G. (Ed.), *The SMART Retrieval System: Experiments in Automatic Document Processing* (pp. 313–323). Englewood Cliffs, NJ: Prentice-Hall Series in Automatic Computation.

Sigurbjörnsson, B., & van Zwol, R. (2008). Flickr tag recommendation based on collective knowledge. In *Proceedings of the 17th International Conference on World Wide Web*, (pp. 327-336). New York, NY: ACM.

Smith, J. (1997). *Integrated spatial and feature image systems: Retrieval, analysis and compression*. PhD thesis, Graduate School of Arts and Sciences, Columbia University, New York, NY.

Chapter 7
Semantic Technology for Improved Email Collaboration

Simon Scerri
DERI, National University of Ireland, Galway

ABSTRACT

Digital means of communications such as email and IM have become a crucial tool for collaboration. Taking advantage of the fact that information exchanged over these media can be made persistent, a lot of research has strived to make sense of the ongoing communication processes in order to support the participants with their management. In this chapter, a workflow-oriented approach is pursued to demonstrate how, coupled with appropriate information extraction techniques, robust knowledge models, and intuitive user interfaces, semantic technology can provide support for email-based collaborative work. While eliciting as much knowledge as possible, the design concept in this chapter imposes little to no changes and/or restrictions to the conventional use of email.

INTRODUCTION

Despite the rise of competing technologies, email remains a crucial business communication tool and an important source of enterprise information. Email's successes are attributed to a very simple, effective protocol, whose asynchronousity frees the participants from the constraints of time and space. However, email also has many disadvantages, the majority of which are attributed to the many ways in which people use email, which are beyond its intended design. The use of email for these functions results in email overload, and it

DOI: 10.4018/978-1-4666-0894-8.ch007

induces widespread (inter)personal information management problems, especially affecting users that thoroughly depend on email to carry out their daily work.

Email serves as a virtual extension to the user's workplace, within which they collaborate, generating and sharing new personal information in the process. From this perspective, email overload can be considered as a workflow management problem where, users become overwhelmed with the increasing amount and complexity of co-executing workflows. Although ad-hoc in nature, these workflows are conceptually well-formed. This approach considers the source of email overload to lie partly in the lack of structure imposed by the email model, and partly in the fragmented way in which these workflows are represented on the user's desktop. Thus, it was necessary to investigate whether by providing automated support for structured email workflows, email overload and the ensuing information management hardships can be reduced.

BACKGROUND

Many related research efforts have targeted the email overload problem (Whittaker & Sidner, 1996) by enabling machines to support the users with better managing their email data. Some have taken a direct approach, e.g., through automatic email classification, enhanced search and retrieval; whereas others have taken less direct approaches to solving the problem, e.g., by facilitating email visualization. Most of these efforts however, offer only a somewhat superficial solution that does not target the source of the problem -- which lies in email technology being utilised not only as a simple communication means, but also to effectively perform collaborative work. From this perspective, the email overload problem can be projected as a workflow management problem where, users become overwhelmed with the increasing amount (and complexity) of co-executing workflows, re-

sulting in a loss of control over their email-based collaborative work. The source of this problem lies partly in the lack of structure imposed by the email model, and partly in the fragmented way in which these workflows are 'represented' on the user's conventional desktop. This 'representation' amounts to nothing but a number of physically-unrelated, albeit workflow-related, resources such as messages, contacts, documents, events, tasks, etc. At one stage or another, all these different types of data abstractions participate in the execution of the workflow, and can thus be considered as workflow artefacts. Unfortunately for the user, these artefacts are stored separately in different desktop data silos such as email folders, system folders, contact lists, calendars, task managers, etc., with no links or associations being retained in between.

TOWARDS A SEMANTIC COMMUNICATION SUPPORT SYSTEM

Research Challenges

Our approach to easing email overload addresses the following problems:

1. How can one model and represent email workflows?

Given the ad-hoc nature of email workflows, each conversational move – or update to the workflow – is largely unpredictable. However, analogously to spoken conversations, it also manifests repeated patterns of communication. Therefore, the modelling pursued needs to investigate whether, and to which extent, can email conversational moves be predicted. Nevertheless, email's flexibility must at all times be considered as an intrinsic characteristic, as despite its obvious modelling disadvantages, it remains email's most favourable feature.

2. Can machines be enabled to work with workflow representations?

In order to provide automated workflow support, the envisaged modelling needs to be exposed to machines. The engineering of a dedicated (set of) ontology(ies) can sufficiently represent the necessary concepts and their relationships. However, in order to allow machines to work directly with email workflows, the conceptualisation must favour a workflow concept and support the representation of workflows independently to the representation of email messages through which they execute, although semantic relations must be retained.

3. To what extent can new email workflows be automatically elicited?

Before providing workflow support, a semantic email client needs to first become aware of their initiation. This makes for a knowledge-acquisition bottleneck problem, especially since to ensure usability, the users cannot be burdened with this task. Therefore, techniques for the (semi)automatic recognition of executing workflows must be investigated.

4. Can the envisaged semantic email and workflow representations provide non-intrusive support to conventional email-based collaboration?

An answer to this question can only be provided following the implementation and evaluation, of a semantic, workflow-oriented, communication support system. Here, an important design criterion is that additional workflow support is provided alongside conventional emailing practices, which must change minimally, if at all. This calls for a seamless integration of semantic technology within the existing technical landscape. Here, an intelligent user interface can play a major role in mediating between the introduced semantic technology and the conventional email user, who must never be directly exposed the former.

Approach

Our approach focuses on Speech Acts as the basic units of email workflows. Speech Act Theory (Searle, 1969) states that every utterance (or, in this context, written text) has one or more associated explicit or implicit acts. The theory has been applied to email on a number of occasions, in particular to classify email based on the sender's intent (Goldstein & Sabin, 2006) and ease task management arising through email (Khoussainov & Kushmerick, 2005). The described approach has a broader scope, and attempts to structure email, or more specifically email workflows. A speech act-based approach to email workflow structuring requires an appropriate system of categorisation. From a number of existing speech act taxonomies, the one designed by Carvalho & Cohen (2006) was deemed the most appropriate. This taxonomy however was still not satisfactory as it was not designed around a workflow concept, i.e. speech act sequencing was not the design's focus. A number of ways to improve the flexibility of speech acts in the model were identified, resulting in a custom speech act model that is more expressive yet more concise. The model and the results of its evaluation, are introduced in the first subsection below.

The next step was to investigate the nature and strength of relationships between successive speech act instances in email threads. A study in email speech act sequentiality led to the design of a speech act-based workflow model, introduced in the second subsection. Through a semantic email ontology, the knowledge models are put into practice in Semanta – a semantic extension to existing email clients. To enable the recognition of action items (a user-friendly term for speech acts) and the consecutive workflows in email, an

Figure 1. The speech act action, object and subject

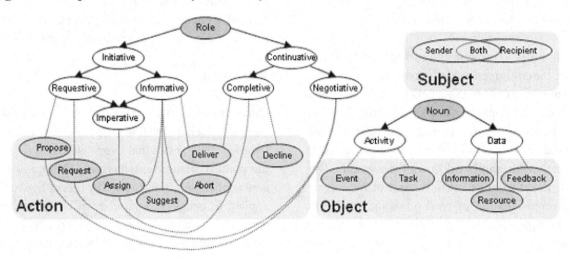

Ontology-based Information Extraction (OBIE) technique was implemented, overviewed in the third subsection. The final subsection will then demonstrate how the theoretical complexity of the models was abstracted and hidden from the user beneath and intuitive and intelligent user interface in Semanta.

A Speech Act Model

A Speech Act is defined as the triple (a,o,s), where a denotes an Action i.e., what is being performed e.g. a request, delivery or assignment; o the Object of the action e.g. a request for a meeting; and s the Subject or agent of the action e.g. meeting participant(s). Actions can have varying Roles (Figure1), e.g. Initiative for actions used to initiate discourse and Continuative otherwise. Actions may serve particular roles in different situations (e.g. Deliver can be Responsive as a response to a request, and Informative otherwise). The speech act object represents instances of Nouns, categorised under Data nouns - representing something which can be represented within email (Information, Resource, Feedback); and Activities - representing external actions occurring outside of email (Task, Event). The speech act subject is applicable to speech acts with an activity as their

object, and it represents who is involved in that activity – e.g. for a meeting, the subject can be the Sender ("Can I attend?"), the Recipient ("You have to write the document") or Both ("Let's meet tomorrow").

The model enables speech act instances, e.g. a request for permission to attend an event is represented as (Request, Event, Sender), a notification of a joint task as (Assign, Task, Both), and a request for information as (Request, Information, Ø). An experiment to measure the human inter-annotator agreement was carried out to evaluate the model's adequacy (Scerri et al., 2008b). The two annotators had the task of identifying instances of 22 valid combinations of speech act parameters in 174 messages from the Enron email corpus. The resulting agreement - 0.811, fares better than the 0.756 observed for the earlier model (Carvalho & Cohen, 2006).

Each speech act is assigned a semantics, in the form of two properties – the sender's expected action (SEA) on sending a speech act and the recipient(s)'s expected reaction (RER) on receiving it. The available re/actions are: Await (a reply from recipient), Do Nothing, Acknowledge (on receipt), Reply (to sender) and Attend (e.g. attend to a task or to a joint event after committing or approving it). These two characteristics define a speech act's conditions of satisfaction and determine the state of an exchanged speech act, which can theoretically be either pending, or completed, e.g. a speech act with an SEA of await will remain pending until a reply is sent back. The speech act state is a crucial property in view of our approach – which considers an exchanged speech act as either the initiation, or the resumption of an executing workflow.

A Behavioural Model for Semantic Email

Related sequences of speech acts in email threads can be interpreted as independent but concurrently executing e-mail workflows. By breaking down email into speech acts, each of which executes within a formal workflow, the email process can be given a semantics. The inter-annotator experiment was extended to study speech act sequencing in email threads. Confirming the view withheld by some linguists, it was observed that although unpredictable by nature, a "significant percentage of conversational language is highly routinised into prefabricated utterances" (Stubbs, 1983), or in this case, speech act sequences which carry out e-mail ad-hoc workflows. To illustrate this concept, Figure 2 provides a graphical example of a meeting

scheduling workflow. It is initiated by a Meeting Proposal speech act sent by Martin to Claudia and Dirk (Propose, Event, {Martin,Claudia,Dirk}), over email m1. Claudia and Dirk both reply to this proposal via emails m2 and m3, in which they state their availability (represented as a Deliver Feedback). Once Martin receives and acknowledges both replies, he announces a meeting, via a Meeting Announcement (Assign, Event, {Martin,Claudia,Dirk,Ambrosia}) over email m4. Martin also addresses the announcement to Ambrosia, with whom he discussed the meeting offline. When all three recipients receive and acknowledge the announcement, a meeting has been scheduled for all participants, and the workflow terminates.

The Semantic E-mail Workflow (SEW) model is a behavioural model for ad-hoc e-mail workflows, explicitly modelled using standardised patterns provided by the Workflow Patterns Initiative (Voorhoeve & van der Aalst, 1997). Each speech act in the first message of an email thread generates a new workflow, which can be modelled using a distinguishable SEW. The SEW models frequently occurring email workflows, e.g. the one in Figure2, while simultaneously providing support for their ad-hoc nature. Spontaneous courses of action in the workflows are not con-

Figure 2. Email ad-hoc workflow example – scheduling a meeting over email

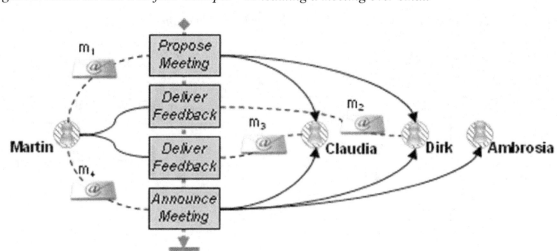

sidered as deviances, but as an intrinsic part of the workflow model. To show its flexibility, the earlier workflow example is revisited, this time represented by a relevant snapshot (Figure 3) from the entire workflow model (Scerri et al., 2008a), which is expressed using UML 2.0 Activity Diagram notations. A vertical swimlane distinguishes between the workflow initiator (Martin, left-hand side) and each other workflow participant (right-hand side). The workflow initiates when Martin sends a proposal for an activity (an event, i.e. the meeting) to the two participants. Activity Proposals are just one of seven categories of speech acts which Martin can initiate a workflow with. When each participant (right-hand side) receives the proposal, the only default option provided by the SEW is to send a Feedback Delivery back to provide their time/date preferences. However, just as at any other point in a workflow, all participants can pursue any other option, e.g. send a related Information Request (e.g. 'Why are you proposing this meeting?') before providing their availability. These possibilities are represented by a "[…]", and would result in the initiation of a subworkflow of the executing workflow.

The 'Collect Feedback' component is a special component which features a persistant trigger workflow pattern that continuously checks whether all participants have provided their feedback (refer to corresponding publication for details). When all participants have provided their availability, back on the initiator's side the SEW provides Martin with two default options for resuming the workflow. On the event that there is no common availability, Martin can amend and resend the proposal. In the example, this is not necessary and instead, Martin replies to all participants (including Ambrosia) with a meeting announcement at the chosen date and time, represented as an Assign Activity (event) speech act. As shown in Figure 3, since Martin is also implied in this event (as one of the speech act subjects) the parallel split requires him to manage the activity. Similarly, on acknowledgment of the meeting announcement on the right-hand side, all participants are expected to do the same, as shown with the equivalent parallel split. Typically this requires exporting the generated activity to an appropriate manager, e.g. a calendar in this case. The participants however, have the option of delegating the meeting to their subordinates via the Delegate path, which splits in two: first to notify Martin of the delegation via a Deliver Data (Information) speech act, and second to perform the actual delegation to a chosen 3rd party.

The speech act and workflow models are exposed to machines by the semantic e-mail

Figure 3. Email ad-hoc workflow model – A snapshot for the given example

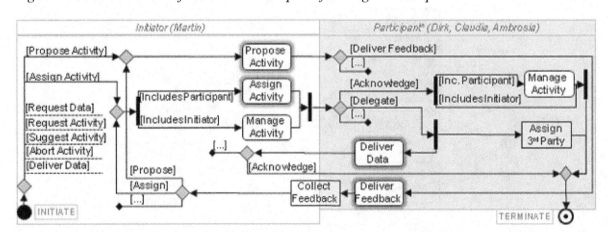

Figure 4. The semantic email ontology: speech acts, email, workflows

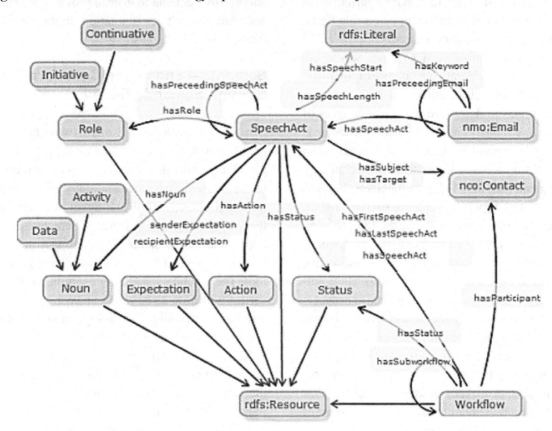

ontology (Scerri, 2008) (Figure 4), which provides vocabulary for the representation of e-mail (nmo:Email), its 'standard' properties (e.g. sender, recipient, date, etc.), instances for various kinds of speech acts (smail:SpeechAct) embedded within e-mail, and email workflows (smail:Workflow). The ontology itself derives some conceptualisation from other ontologies developed for the Social Semantic Desktop (SSD) (Reif et al., 2008), e.g. the NMO Messaging Ontology and the NCO Contact Ontology. Thus, aside from providing extensible semantic email conceptualisation standards, the ontology also enables integration of desktop data from the email to other domains, e.g. calendaring, task management, etc. The design of the ontology echoes the conceptualisation requirements set out in the second challenge targeted by this Chapter, i.e., although at the instance level both email and

workflow instances point to speech acts (unlinked and unordered in the former case, and linked and ordered in the latter), at the ontology level there is a strict separation between email and workflow representations. Therefore, as demonstrated shortly, workflows can be managed and visualised separately to email messages, or threads.

Eliciting Email Workflows

The SEW enables Semanta to support on-the-fly workflow knowledge elicitation through user interaction, but only if the semantic email client is aware of the workflows in the first place. This requires the recognition of speech acts that are not already bound to an existent workflow (i.e. an existing sequence of speech acts). However, Semanta cannot rely on the user to manually perform this task. Therefore, at least partial, automation is required. For the purpose, a rule-based classification model for the classification of email textual clauses into speech acts, was developed. It takes into consideration a number of linguistic features (Scerri et al, 2010a), such as sentence form, tense, modality and the semantic roles of verbs. Based on this model, an OBIE technique is employed to elicit instances of speech acts from the ontology from email content. The technology is implemented in GATE (Cunningham, 2002) as an ANNIE IE Pipeline, which consists of standard GATE components (e.g. tokeniser, POS tagger), a gazetteer lookup augmented with customised keywords/phrases, and an own set of handcoded JAPE grammars (Cunningham, 1999). The grammars constitute a cascade of finite state transducers over patterns of annotations, such that the output of one transducer becomes the input of the next. Each transducer consists of a collection of phases containing pattern/action rules. The most important is the Speech Act Transducer, which matches combinations of intermediate annotations to one of the speech act instances in the ontology. It alone consists of 58 rules within 14 different phases, such that textual clauses matched in the initial phases are excluded from later ones.

In an evaluation of this technology, 12 people were employed to review annotations generated for over 100 emails. Positive ratings, representing correct classifications, amounted to 41%, negative ratings (representing false positives) to 31%, and 28% were missing speech acts manually highlighted by the evaluators. The resulting F-measure of 0.58 needs to be interpreted in the light of the result obtained earlier for the inter-annotator agreement experiment (0.81), which indicated the difficulty of the classification task even when performed by humans. Also, both results are well within the reasonable performance range described in related literature for IE tasks of a similar complexity (Cunningham, 2005). However, a reliability of 58% is not suitable for full automation. Thus, the technology was adopted by Semanta to instead provide for semi-automatic speech act annotation, in the form of user-reviewable suggestions.

Semanta – Enhancing Collaboration through Semantic E-mail

Semanta is provided as add-ons to two of the most popular email clients in use: Microsoft Outlook and Mozilla Thunderbird. This section will show how, based on the models and technology presented so far, and equipped with an intelligent user interface that provides innovative features, Semanta serves both as a semantic communication support system, as well as an email-based workflow management tool. The meeting scheduling example provided earlier will now serve as a use-case will show how Semanta provides on-the-fly support to email communication, and on-request email workflow visualisations to improve their management.

To start with, before Martin sends the email, the results of automatic classification are highlighted in the content and presented for review (for UI details, refer to Scerri et al., (2010b)). If required, an intuitive annotation wizard supports Martin with adjusting the classified speech acts. The resulting action items (a user-friendly term for speech acts) are then encoded with other harvested email metadata within the email headers (in RDF) and transported alongside the email. When the email reaches Claudia and Dirk's inbox, Semanta displays the number of pending action items alongside other conventional information in the inbox (e.g. sender, date). This adjusts dynamically as action items are taken care of. Specific action items are highlighted when displaying email messages, such that the users can interact with them. Depending on the semantics of each (workflow model), a number of relevant options are provided. Some of these will result in the generation of a reply item. For example, whereas upon receiving the Meeting Announcement at the end of the example, the Claudia, Dirk and Ambrosia are required to simply acknowledge it, the semantics of the initial Meeting Proposal require some form of reply, be this an approval, rejection or amendment. However action items can also be ignored (and later unignored) indefinitely. More importantly, apart from the case-based options provided by the workflow model, users are allowed to react in additional ways, via an 'Other..' option. Here, the user can type in free text which is again automatically classified into a speech act for review. Whenever the user's interaction results in a new speech act to be sent in an email reply, e.g. the Deliver Feedback in reply to the above meeting proposal, Semanta notes this as the next workflow update. All workflow metadata is stored on the local user's RDF store.

The metadata generated/transported for an email in the example above is shown in Figure. 5 as within emailGraph. Beside an RDF representation of conventional email properties (e.g., from, to), it also refers to the Deliver Feedback speech act within (claudia:EMA3644F2000SA0) and its properties. Below emailGraph, workflowGraph contains metadata for the workflow to which that speech act belongs. Although represented separately, both workflow and email metadata refer to the same speech acts instance above. The relation is as follows: the speech act, delivered over the email represented by emailGraph, is the last in the speech act sequence for workflowGraph. Workflow metadata includes references to its participants (smail:hasParticipant) and status (smail:hasStatus). The latter is affected by, but is not equivalent, to the status of the last exchanged speech act. In fact, the semantics of a Deliver Feedback mean that although the speech act's status is completed on sending/receipt, the status of the workflow requires further action (and emails) from Martin to change to smail:Completed.

The workflow metadata enables Semanta to detect events/tasks generated over email. For example, on approving a task, the user is prompted to export it directly to the associated Tasklist.

Figure 6 shows how the stored links between three workflow artefacts are exploited. Since the Task Request in email 1 (Figure 6) was answered with a Task Approval in email 2, the two are linked via the 'Previous/Next Email' buttons. The task generated at the end of the workflow (Figure 5-3) is also linked by the 'Related Activity' button. Furthermore, Semanta extends the display of task/calendar items by a 'Conversation' panel which shows the workflow history leading to that item, in terms of text associated with the underlying speech acts. The user can also jump from these items to the email messages wherein they were generated, i.e. Figure 6-1, 2.

Semanta also exploits the gathered workflow knowledge to visualise them, thus enabling users to navigate from a workflow to the individual messages over which it executes. A 'Workflow Treeview' (Figure6-S) is available alongside Thunderbird's default email treeview (Figure 7-T), providing three views, each of which enables the UI components on the right-hand side. The main view ('All') displays a list of workflows that have taken place or are still running/pending (displayed in bold) in the 'Workflow List' (Figure7-1). When one is selected (e.g. the Meeting Proposal underlying "Can we have a meeting tomorrow") the speech acts constituting it, in order of succession, are shown in the 'Workflow Details' below (Figure 7-2). In turn, when one of these is selected Semanta retrieves the email within which it has been exchanged and displays it in the 'Email Message' component below (Figure7-3).

This workflow visualisation is more akin to Martin's mental recollection of workflows, such as that shown in Figure 2. Alongside the main view, the workflow treeview provides two other useful views: 'Pending Incoming' shows all incoming speech acts (e.g. requests, assignments, suggestions) which the user still needs to address; 'Pending Outgoing' shows all outgoing action items (e.g. requests) for which the user is still

Figure 5. Email and workflow metadata, stored in respective named graphs

```
:emailGraph{
   claudia:EMA3644F2000 a nmo:Email;
      nmo:from :ClaudiaStern;
      smail:hasSpeechAct claudia:EMA3644F2000SA0;
      nmo:messageId "0000000094A633229025F385F0";
      nmo:sentDate "2010-09-24T13:33:53";
      nmo:to claudia:MartinWilliams .

   claudia:EMA3644F2000SA0 a smail:SpeechAct;
      smail:hasAction smail:Deliver;
      smail:hasNoun smail:Feedback;
      smail:hasRole smail:Completive;
      smail:hasSpeechLength "16";
      smail:hasSpeechStart "53";
      smail:hasStatus smail:Completed;
      smail:hasTarget claudia:MartinWilliams;
      smail:recipientExpectation smail:Acknowledge;
      smail:senderExpectation smail:None .

   claudia:MartinWilliams a nco:PersonContact;
      nco:hasEmailAddress claudia:MartinWilliamsEmail;
      rdfs:label "Martin Williams" .

   claudia:MartinWilliamsEmail a nco:EmailAddress;
      nco:emailAddress "martin.williams@deri.org". }

:workflowGraph{
   claudia:EMA3644F2000WF0 a smail:Workflow;
      smail:hasParticipant  claudia:ClaudiaStern,
                            claudia:DirkHageman,
                            claudia:MartinWilliams;
      smail:hasFirstSpeechAct claudia:EMA3656F2121SA0;
      smail:hasLastSpeechAct claudia:EMA3644F2000SA0;
      smail:hasSpeechAct claudia:EMA3644F2000SA0,
                         claudia:EMA3656F2121SA0;
      smail:hasStatus smail:Pending . }
```

awaiting a reply. These enable the user to keep track of email action items, resume stalled workflows, or send reminders to urge others to do so.

The results of a summative evaluation of Semanta, which compared it to the standard Thunderbird client, suggest that the use of Semanta does improve the email experience for the user, helping them with keeping track of email action items, retrieving additional workflow information from previously physically unrelated items, and aggregating content and messages to visualise entire workflows. However, an increase in the email writing time was also reported, mainly due to the required annotation reviewing stage. Although in a summative question most users felt that this added stage was to an extent or another worth the subsequent support (69%) some seemed less enthusiastic (25% voted 'No', with 5% having 'No Opinion').

FUTURE RESEARCH DIRECTIONS

Machine-learning and case-based reasoning techniques are being considered to further reduce the reliance on the user to review speech act annotations. The semantic technology underlying Semanta is rather doman-independent, and besides other email clients (web-based included) it can also, with little effort beyond an effective UI, be applied to other text-based digital communication media such as IM, text messaging, customer services or online fora. In the spirit of the Linked Open Data initiative (Bizer et al., 2007), which focuses on linking useful semantic data, the generated semantic data could be semantically linked to other Semantic Web data. A step in this direction has already been taken within the personal desktop, by integrating the ontology with others engineered for the SSD. In fact, metadata generated by Semanta can easily

Figure 6. Linking e-mail workflow artefacts: Speech acts, messages, events, et cetera

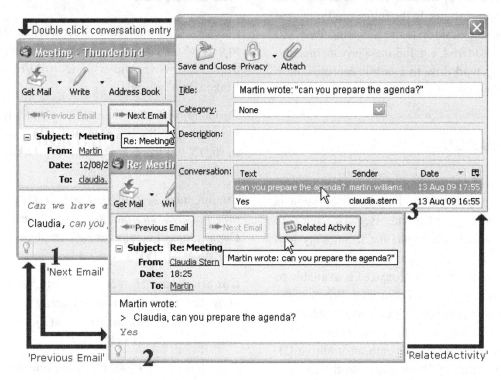

Figure 7. Semanta's alternative workflow-based e-mail visualisation

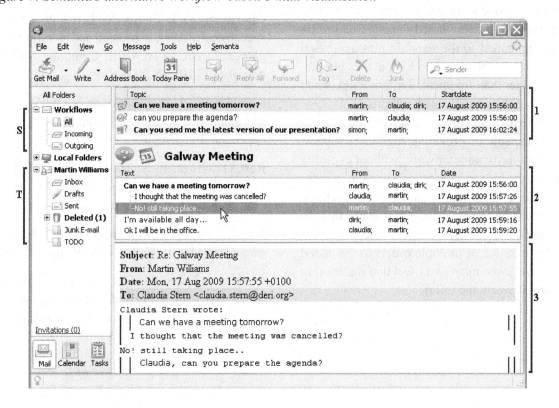

be retrieved and operated upon by other semantic desktop applications. In the future unidirectional links from the desktop to the Semantic Web will also be considered, e.g. linking a private meeting scheduling workflow to a public representation of a conference in the LOD cloud.

CONCLUSION

Our vision of a semantic communication support system to support email-based collaboration is realised through Semanta. Because Semanta seamlessly integrates semantic technology into the existing technical landscape (i.e. email clients and transport technology), it is available to anyone using a personal computer. Whereas the introduced functionalities are clearly visible to the user, the complex modelling and theory behind is successfully hidden beneath an intuitive UI. The latter successfully provides on-the-fly support to email collaboration, without demanding significant changes to conventional email use. The most innovative feature is the introduction of an alternative workflow-based email visualization as a supplement to the standard message-based view. This enables users to look at the 'big picture', rather than fragmented information, when managing their email collaborations.

This experience affirms that semantic technology is capable of providing high-level support to day-to-day computer work, without exposing users to the hidden semantics. Although in order to provide reliable support, users are still required to oversee the semantic annotation stage, this can be significantly reduced. Also, provided the resulting benefits are of multiple orders to the added cognitive costs, most users feel that the ensuing support is worth the effort.

REFERENCES

Bizer, C., Cyganiak, R., & Heath, T. (2007). *How to publish linked data on the web*. Retrieved from http://sites.wiwiss.fuberlin.de /suhl/bizer/pub/ LinkedDataTutorial/

Carvalho, V. R., & Cohen, W. W. (2006). Improving email speech acts analysis via n-gram selection. In *ACTS '09 Workshop* (pp. 35-41). Association for Computational Linguistics.

Cunningham, H. (1999). *JAPE: A Java annotation patterns engine. Research memorandum.* Department of Computer Science, University of Sheffield.

Cunningham, H. (2002). Gate, a general architecture for text engineering. *Computers and the Humanities, 36*(2), 223–254. doi:10.1023/A:1014348124664

Cunningham, H. (2005). Information extraction, automatic. In Brown, K. (Ed.), *Encyclopedia of language and linguistics.*

Goldstein, J., & Sabin, R. E. (2006). Using speech acts to categorize email and identify email genres. In *HICSS'06*. IEEE Computer Society. doi:10.1109/HICSS.2006.528

Khoussainov, R., & Kushmerick, N. (2005). *Email task management: An iterative relational learning approach*. In CEAS'05.

Reif, G., Groza, T., Scerri, S., & Handschuh, S. (2008). *Final NEPOMUK architecture deliverable D6.2.B*. NEPOMUK Consortium.

Scerri, S. (2008b). *Semantic email ontology*. Retrieved from http://ontologies.smile.deri.ie /smail

Scerri, S., Gossen, G., Davis, B., & Handschuh, S. (2010a). *Classifying action items for semantic email*. In LREC'10, European Language Resources Association (ELRA).

Scerri, S., Gossen, G., & Handschuh, S. (2010b). *Supporting digital collaborative work through semantic technology*. In KMIS'10, Valencia, Spain.

Scerri, S., Handschuh, S., & Decker, S. (2008b). Semantic email as a communication medium for the Social Semantic Desktop. In *ESWC'08* (pp. 124-138).

Scerri, S., Mencke, M., Davis, B., & Handschuh, S. (2008c). *Evaluating the ontology powering smail - A conceptual framework for semantic email*. In LREC'08.

Searle, J. R. (1969). *Speech acts: An essay in the philosophy of language*. Cambridge, UK: Cambridge University Press.

Stubbs, M. (1983). *Discourse analysis*. Blackwell.

Voorhoeve, M., & van der Aalst, W. M. P. (1997). Ad-hoc workflow: Problems and solutions. In *DEXA'97 Workshop* (pp. 36-40).

Whittaker, S., & Sidner, C. (1996). Email overload: Exploring personal information management of email. In *CHI '96* (pp. 276–283). New York, NY: ACM. doi:10.1145/238386.238530

Winograd, T. (1986). A language/action perspective on the design of cooperative work. In *CSWC'86* (pp. 203–220). New York, NY: ACM Press. doi:10.1145/637095.637096

KEY TERMS AND DEFINITIONS

Ad-hoc Workflow: Workflows having a non-traditional flexibility, which means that they cannot be completely and/or precisely modeled before runtime, due to the unpredictable nature of the underlying business processes.

Digital Communication Media: Technological media that support the digital exchange of messages between communicators. Examples of text-based forms are email and instant messages.

Email Collaboration: Teamwork that takes place electronically through the exchange of email messages.

Email Speech Act: A written-form of the more traditional linguistic concept, whereby an explicit utterance by a speaker (in this case a textual communicative exchange initiated by the sender) is associated with one or more explicit or implicit acts expected on the part of the speaker, the hearer(s), or a combination of. A user-friendly alternative terms is Email Action Item. A string of sequential, related speech acts is considered as unique and independent email workflow.

Email Workflow: Email collaboration with specific, albeit possibly dynamic, goal and objectives, where the collaborators, exchanged resources, resulting tasks/events and the exchanged email messages themselves are treated as workflow artefacts. Email workflows are ad-hoc by nature.

Semantic Technology: Technology that operates on the semantically-rich knowledge representation formats, and data, originally modelled for the Semantic Web.

Social Semantic Desktop: A desktop that is enriched with rich metadata about its contents, based on a Semantic Web language like RDF. In turn, the standard representation language enables metadata to be shared across a (social) network of Semantic Desktops.

Section 3
Acquiring, Querying, and Discovering Knowledge from Collaborative and Social Environments

Chapter 8
The Reflexive Practitioner:
Knowledge Discovery through Action Research

Stephen Dobson
Sheffield Hallam University, UK

ABSTRACT

This chapter aims to set out relevant discourse and approaches to consider when planning strategies for acquiring and building knowledge for formal ontology construction. Action Research (AR) is offered as a key means to help structure the necessary reflexivity required to enrich the researcher's understanding of how they know what they know, particularly within a collaborative research setting. This is especially necessary when revealing tacit domain knowledge through participation with actors and stakeholders: "In this kind of research it is permissible to be openly normative and to strive for change, but not to neglect critical reflection" (Elfors & Svane 2008, 1).

INTRODUCTION

Ontologies are becoming increasingly valued in research and practice; both to help organise information within a domain and to facilitate it being shared between domains.

"Ontologies encode knowledge in a domain and also knowledge that spans domains...Ontologies include computer-useable definitions of basic concepts in the domain and the relationships among them and are increasingly valued because of the ever-increasing need for knowledge interchange." (Mounce et al 2010, 40)

Whilst much discussion concerning formal domain ontologies has focussed on the technical issues or semantic structures of the conceptualisation - perhaps less focus has been placed on epistemology in this setting. Semantic relationships or 'links' between concepts are a critical part of the formal ontology. However, the means for unpacking the assumptions which ultimately inform these links are not always fully surfaced.

DOI: 10.4018/978-1-4666-0894-8.ch008

BACKGROUND

In discussing the process of formal ontology construction Roussey (2005) refers to both Gruber (1993) and Studer *et al* (1998) in outlining that ontologies are explicitly defined and shared specifications of concepts. The formal ontology may be considered as a framework of understanding about the world enabling more effective data sharing, retrieval, reuse and ultimately leading to increased communication between domains. It is therefore seen as: "a unifying framework to solve problems…an ontology necessarily entails or embodies some sort of world view with respect to a given domain" (Uschold and Gruninger 1996, 5).

The "reach" of this formalised view of the world is often defined by its intended application and/or by the concerns of a particular subject domain (e.g. the Art and Architecture Thesaurus[1]). In practice these 'worlds views', as expressed by those in a given domain, may often be tacit prior to formal specification. Teller underlines the role of the formal ontology as helping to clarify the semantic structures which reside in tacit understanding:

"Ontologies have also an important role to play in revealing the logical structure of existing conceptualizations. Conceptualizations are often tacit. They are often not thematized in a systematic way. But tools can be developed to specify and to clarify the concepts involved and to establish their logical structure, and thus to render explicit the underlying taxonomy" (Teller 2007, 2)

Depending upon the intended nature of communication (from natural dialogue to machine-understandable code) four classifications of ontology are offered by Uschold and Gruninger (1996) based on levels of required formality. These range from, the highly informal and expressed loosely in natural language; the semi-informal which may result in restricted use of terms to aid communication; the semi-formal involving "artificial formally defined language"; and rigorously-formal, employing "meticulously defined terms with formal semantics" (Uschold and Gruninger 1996, 6). However, regardless of the level of formality of the ontology, a key concern underpinning the process of construction is the means by which knowledge is acquired and the epistemological basis relating to this. How do we know what we know? Uschold and Gruninger refer to the explicit ontology as being "an agreement about shared conceptualizations" and so the means by which this agreement is formed is obviously an area of key importance.

Guarino (1995) outlines key debates concerning epistemology and *formal* ontology in knowledge representation and relates to Nutter (1987) in defining Epistemology as being; "the field of philosophy which deals with the nature and sources of knowledge" (Guarino 1995, 628). Whilst Guarino describes ontology as being the nature of the world - independent of our knowledge about it, the definition of a *formal* ontology is acknowledged as still a matter for debate. Here, Guarino asserts that, potentially, the act of formalising knowledge for domain or local application may conflate philosophical approaches of analytical 'descriptive metaphysics' (Strawson 1959) and phenomenology (summarised in Burkhardt and Smith 1991). In, for example, the following passage from *Ontology Development 101: A guide to creating your first ontology* we can see the philosophical status of the formal ontology is, as Guarino suggests, 'still a matter for debate':

"…one of the most important things to remember is the following: there is no single correct ontology for any domain. Ontology design is a creative process and no two ontologies designed by different people would be the same. The potential applications of the ontology and the designer's

understanding and view of the domain will undoubtedly affect ontology design choices (Noy and McGuiness 2001, 23).

In relating to the nature of subjectivity, as is alluded to in the above passage, Guarino highlights academic debate between Woods (1975) and Brachman (1979). Here the fundamental question is whether links within a formal ontology are conceptual or epistemological - i.e. based on reasoning or representation. Rotondo (2010) suggests that: "A domain ontology…is expected to express the viewpoints and satisfy the informational needs of multiple stakeholders and interest groups". (Rotondo 2010, 53) However, we might consider whether these viewpoints are based upon ontology, epistemology or more likely a conflation of the two. A practical way forward is recommended toward a 'commonsense metaphysics' (Guarino 1995, 630).

Fernandez *et al* (1997) (see Roussay 2005) outline the practical stages and activities involved in formal ontology development and describe these as being underpinned by an evolving and iterative process; a point which is also underlined by Noy and McGuinness (2001). Knowledge acquisition, documentation and evaluation are considered as 'support activities' which feed into the 'planning stage' of the 'ontology lifecycle' (Fernandez *et al* 1997). The planning stage comprises of; 'specification', 'conceptualisation', 'formalisation', 'integration', 'implementation' and 'maintenance' and is arguably where much methodological literature concerning ontology development is focussed. A 'common sense' approach - as called for by Guarino - is recommended by Fernandez *et al,* (also Roussay 2005; Gandon 2002) in that, ideally, this process should remain highly flexible; enabling the ontologist to add, remove or modify definitions at any time. The ontology lifecycle offered by Fernandez *et al* illustrates the potential for knowledge acquisition to inform all planning

stages, but does not make explicit the potential for the relationship between knowledge acquisition and the planning stage to be an *iterative* cycle. Whilst knowledge is gained through interaction with the real world the model does not define this as an ongoing *two way* dialogue between the main planning process and the acquisition process. Particularly with participatory ontology construction, an iterative cycle between planning and practice may be considered essential and is outlined by Akkermans *et al* (2004) in their description of the Obelix project (Ontology-Based Electronic Integration of Complex Products and Value Chains).

Here, a formal ontology approach is used to help design service elements of a real world service bundle; in this case, concerning electricity supply and broadband internet provision. A multidisciplinary approach is adopted to help build a rich understanding from the perspectives of both supplier and customer in order to help design the service process. Success in this case is measured in pragmatic terms:

"We consider an ontology to be 'good' if it's used in and validated against independent business scenarios and industrial use cases…Consequently, the Obelix ontologies have undergone significant refinement over the past years as a result of their industrial application" (Akkermans et al 2004, 63)

A case-study approach was adopted for the project and was considered important for refinement and application testing, but also as a means to: "convince practitioners about the added value of semantics-based methods" (Akkermans *et al* 2004, 63). Triangulation is acknowledged here as being important throughout the reasoning process illustrating the need for ongoing testing and refinement through continual collaboration with users and practitioners. Knowledge therefore has the potential to be both acquired and tested in these real world scenarios to ensure a robust ontology which is 'fit for purpose'. The role of the researcher in this case may then be considered a highly active and 'critical' one because of the underlying goal of, in this instance, service improvement through intervention. The period of time required is demonstrated to be extensive in order for the necessary depth of understanding to be revealed, interpreted, and formalised.

The need to convince practitioners is also referred to above and so outlines a championing role for the researcher through the act of building collaboration. Akkermans *et al* observe that ontologies are often best informed by the domain specialists themselves and recommend that the ontologist adopt a facilitating and participatory role. Real world testing therefore offers an ongoing opportunity for refinement; i.e. "…'the proof is in the pudding' - we can assess the quality of our ontology only by using it in applications for which we designed it" (Noy and McGuinness 2001, 23). Since there is potential for a collaborative relationship to extend over years and for tacit understanding to be both revealed and tested in practice (through the critical intervention of the ontologist-researcher) action research (AR) is explored here as a potentially beneficial approach to adopt; in order to embrace the potentially highly social context of what is often perceived to be as a singularly technical pursuit.

ACTION RESEARCH AND 'EPISTEMOLOGY OF PRACTICE'

Action Research (AR) is a critical approach particularly applied in organisational development and popular in the fields of business management, educational research and work science (Elfors and Svane 2008, 3; Ladkin 2004). Initially pioneered by Kurt Lewin (1946), AR incorporates many qualitative methods which are highly applicable for ontology development (such as brain-storming,

critical reflection, group discussion and interviews etc.) but is particularly characterised by the active nature of the researcher and their participatory role with a partner organisation. Bradbury and Lichenstein (2000) refer to AR as a means to actively test knowledge in research-practice collaboration with the 'sense-making' of the organisation or domain in question. Therefore, an AR (also referred to as an 'action-oriented') approach offers a reflexive means of 'idea-testing' by the constant shifting between theory and practice. Since not all ontologies have business/industrial application or a market place/customer base for validity testing it is important for the researcher to underpin assumptions made about the world with robust reflexivity; i.e. an 'epistemology of practice' (Baskerville and Wood-Harper 1998). AR may be defined as:

"…research that is shared by researchers and stakeholders. It involves the researcher acting as a change agent with community participants functioning as co-researchers… its goal is to produce new visions and approaches to realize those visions by means of collective, participatory and multiple stakeholder investments of learning" (Corey and Wilson 2006, 189)

The researcher therefore becomes intrinsically part of an organisational/community process of collaborative learning. The key benefit is that the researcher is able to help define, rather than solely observe, the change process and so is afforded a privileged perspective on the various motives and structures of change: "action research is a means to investigate changes and their effects while overcoming researchers' "self-imposed distance from the world of action" (Dash, 1999, 479)" (Blichfeldt and Andersen 2006, 2). In this case the researcher's actions can be described as 'critical research' in that they are not only "interested in the value positions and beliefs of the group, but the researcher abandons any pretence of neutrality and often evokes specialist knowledge to stimulate the group into examining the ethics, morality and politics of their situation." (Melrose 1996, 52). It is also assumed that this form of research: "is directed towards a greater understanding and improvement of practice over *a period of time*" (Bell 1997, 8).

AR is presented here therefore as an effective strategy for supporting formal ontology development; particularly since an ongoing concern within AR research activities relates to success criteria, that is; "how will you make professional judgements about your work?" (McNiff *et al* 2005). AR therefore requires the researcher to be active in:

"sharing initial results with participants, to test whether the researcher's ideas are congruent with the sensemaking within the organizational context (see Argyris et al 1985)...this interpersonal process is seen to increase the validity and reliability of the research, and bring the researcher in closer contact to the organization s/he is studying." (Bradbury and Lichtenstein (2000, 561).

Key characteristics of AR are that it encourages an *active* role for the researcher within the practice-based scenario. For this reason, a research diary becomes a key source of data and acts as a reflexive 'log' tracking the researcher's own journey of learning. Since the AR researcher is seeking to help bring about improvements in practice another characteristic of this approach is that the researcher adopts the role of a change agent. Improvements are sought through an iterative process involving the 'planning', 'carrying out' and 'assessment' of actions. This process of assessment or validation in practice may be considered particularly relevant to the ontology development - particularly in domains which may not have direct industrial or commercial application. In such cases assessment of quality may be necessarily subjective and therefore much more likely to be achieved through consensus. A third

characteristic is the potential, which AR affords the researcher, to adopt the role of 'knowledge broker'. Since the ontologist working in a collaborative practice-setting is aiming to reveal and define tacit domain knowledge the role of knowledge-broker may be both a beneficial and natural one to assume. In this sense, the role of knowledge-broker, especially between disciplinary domains, can offer key opportunities to explore shared conceptualisations. The researcher as knowledge broker therefore plays a key role in "rendering implicit knowledge explicit" and "creating, mixing, spreading and using different kinds of knowledge" (Selman 2006, 100). In aiming to improve practice through active collaboration the AR researcher therefore does not try to achieve impartiality but instead aims to be, as Ladkin (2004) suggests; 'critically subjective'. McNiff *et al* (2005) provide a valuable starting point for planning and initiating AR fieldwork and consists of three key areas for consideration before setting out:

Stage 1: Identifying a concern: What questions and issues are to be addressed? "as well as seeking answers to this question you will be exploring the underlying meaning of the question itself".

Stage 2: Action Planning: What strategies will help to address these questions, what do you plan to do? It is important to identify opportunities to 'step back' from the research in the planning stage.

Stage 3: Involving others: How will others be involved? Who will contribute and benefit from the collaborative research? What will be the researcher's relationship to them?

Specifically AR may be considered to be concerned with three predominant project foci for intervention; these are outlined both by Zuber-Skerritt (1996) and Elfors and Svane (2008) as 'technical, 'practical' and 'emancipatory'. Each form may be considered to be differentiated by the level of impact upon the 'social life' of the participatory environment (Kemmi 1993). For example, a 'technical' AR project focus may be described as primarily concerned with examination of tools, functions and innovation of procedures. It refers to knowledge which is: "…oriented essentially towards functional improvement measured in terms of its success in changing particular outcomes of practices " (Elfors and Svane 2008, 3; see also Kemmis 2001). The evaluation of research impact will tend to focus on whether a process or tool has been functionally improved and is perhaps less directly concerned with exploring the wider social impacts which may have resulted from such an intervention. 'Practical' AR, (as advocated by Schön 1983 for example) places greater emphasis upon the understanding of social context of AR. This form of AR leads the researcher toward a greater level of ethnographic enquiry since it is the impact of intervention on the wider participant group that is of interest here. Research within in a 'practical' AR context therefore is not solely concerned within an individual learning model; as would tend to characterise 'technical' enquiry. The third form of involvement is described as 'critical' or 'emancipatory' AR:

"This form of action research aims not only at improving outcomes, and improving the self-understanding of practitioners, but also at assisting practitioners to arrive at a critique of their social or educational work and work setting" (Elfors and Svane 2008, 3-4; see also Kemmis 2001).

Zuber-Skerritt suggests that emancipatory AR is aimed at empowering participants to question the boundaries of their organisation or condition. "More precisely, action research is *emancipatory* when it aims not only at technical and practical improvement, the participant's transformed consciousness…but when it also aims at changing the system itself" (Zuber-Skerritt 1996, 84-5). An emanipatory focus within the context of ontology development would see the research programme evaluating, not just the functional success of a formal ontology i.e. does it do what we wanted it to do? But also the wider societal or domain impacts i.e. how has this transformed the thinking of others? How has this ultimately changed the world of the participants? Establishing the research focus, whether 'technical', 'practical' or 'emancipatory' will therefore be critical stage when planning AR since data collection and analysis strategies will vary depending upon the fundamental nature of the questions being posed.

All forms of AR however require the researcher to be reflexive and aware of their subjectivity within the study environment. All actions in practice therefore have a 'motive', the 'action' itself, and some form of assessment of 'outcome'. The recording of these interactive 'action cycles' provide the basic dynamic of researcher activity in an AR setting. McNiff (2005), recommends this form of reflective loop in documenting fieldwork activity and can essentially be summarised by the questions: What do I wish to do and why? What did I do? What happened and what did I learn? This is referred to by Elfors and Svane (2008) as a cycle or spiral of steps which is an ongoing, rather than a distinct process - involving the planning of action, acting and then subsequent evaluation of the results.

Such an iterative 'action orientated' approach is suggested here as greatly beneficial where qualitative approaches are required at the knowledge acquisition stage of the ontology lifecycle process. However if we are to aim for this to both inform and be informed by the planning stage of ontology construction (Fernandez *et al* 1997) then the action cycle of 'motive', 'action' and 'outcome' must refer to both the theoretical processes of ontology specification as well as the activities in real-world practice scenarios which both help generate and test conceptualisations.

Figure 1. Argyris and Schön's double loop learning process

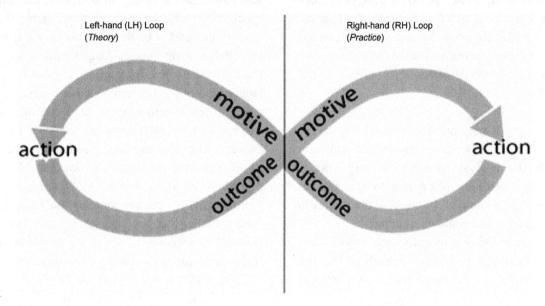

This form of double-loop learning (Figure 1) was initially introduced by Argyris and Schön (1978) and Schön (1983). In this case, the motives for action in practice may be considered as being the result of outcomes relating to theoretical and conceptual development. Additionally, the outcomes and observations of such practical action may subsequently feed into the motives for further theoretical consideration ('action'). This constant oscillation between practice and theory may be applied to many different contexts however here, we might consider that this model articulates the iterative movement between practice-based knowledge acquisition and lab-based ontology development in the ontology lifecycle illustrated by Fernandez *et al* (1997) and Roussey (2005).

The benefits of this form of structured thinking in complex AR environments are outlined by Blichfeldt and Andersen (2006). Here they refer to McKay and Marshall (2001), Morton (1999) and Dash (1999) in suggesting that the process of thinking in both 'action' and 'research cycles offers a useful means to clearly differentiate the roles of the practice-based researcher. Bradbury and Lichtenstein (2000) reflect that in a participatory research setting the oscillation between an 'insider/outsider approach' is not only beneficial, but essential. This process is also emphasised by a double loop approach to reflexive research since it encourages the researcher to shift their field of vision between detail and big picture; between local and global conceptualisations. Recording these phases in a study diary is an essential means for contextualising day-to-day activities and discussions, especially when revealing and building relational knowledge with participants over time. This is an inductive approach and helps build both knowledge 'in' practice and knowledge 'about' practice. Potential problems of working with ontologies in practice were raised by Teller, Tweed and Rabino (2008) whilst introducing the proceedingfs of the 2nd worshop of the COST Action C21 – 'Towntology'[2]:

"The absence of a large number of papers addressing particular problems of using ontologies in practice could be taken as a good sign. Perhaps there is little to say, because ontology developers are getting it right and users have nothing to complain about. Maybe ontologies are not as

problematic in practice as we might imagine. More likely, however, is that the very idea of ontologies in practice is so novel that many people are unaware of the terminology and so fail to recognise ontological issues when they arise" (Teller, Tweed and Rabino 2008, 3).

Whilst AR may provide a useful framework to structure collaborative knowledge acquisition – inductive analysis of reflexive diary work is also suggested here as a means to help address this potentially 'novel' problem of ontologies in practice by contextualising practice.

The retrospective inductive analysis of diary material can be a useful means to help understand the processes which have led up to relational knowledge and understanding between the researcher and the participant. The diary may be seen in this case as providing an essential record for tracking the trajectories of actions over long periods of engagement and is an essential resource for recognising causality between actions/outcomes and subsequent actions/outcomes. By adopting a degree of ethnographic observation and reflection in the diary work (rather than purely technical accounts) there is much greater potential for the researcher to be able to establish a participant's tacit assumptions, values and beliefs. Inductive 'grounded research' (Corbin and Strauss 2008) provides a valuable means to both dis- and re-organise observations and actions recorded in the research diary.

Grounded research is extensively outlined in the literature; for example see Corbin and Strauss (2008); Strauss and Corbin (1990); Glaser (1978) and was originally developed by Glaser and Strauss (1967). A principal aim of grounded theory is to reveal variables and categories through the fragmentation of data and its subsequent and multiple rebuilding through the assignment of thematic codes. Coding of texts, such as diary work and talk, may be considered to focus upon either 'emic' and 'etic' terms. 'Emic' (or *in vivo*) terms represent participant defined categories i.e. language specific to a particular community or organisation. Such terms tend to be the most obvious and immediately evident 'themes' for qualitative analysis and are usually directly expressed in participant's language or organisational documentation. 'Etic' codes however are more theoretically defined and explore underlying themes and subjects which the researcher may establish through the process of analysis and interpretation. Jackson (2001), describes this as long process of grouping and regrouping (i.e. 'constant comparision') to enable the researcher to assess specific content in relation to wider themes. Crang (1997) suggests that 'grounded' transcript reading is about both what is being said and what it means, this helping to reveal beliefs and assumptions which: "may not be apparent to the informants themselves" (Crang 1997). In this case, the deconstruction and fragmentation of a research diary may help to reveal tacit knowledge and provide context within which the formal ontology is being assessed.

To achieve this, firstly superficial emic codes relating to stakeholder terminology, followed by etic (researcher defined) codes, are freely assigned after one or more readings of the text. This is referred to as the process of *open* or *free coding*:

"Concepts are the building blocks of theory. Open coding in grounded theory method is the analytical process by which concepts are identified and developed in terms of their properties and dimensions" (Strauss and Corbin 1990, 74).

These are then cross-referenced for inconsistencies and/or similarities and then reorganised, through a process of *axial coding*, into more generalised concepts which may link terms. Data is therefore conceptualised and placed in researcher conceived categories. This is a process of deconstruction as sentences, paragraphs or observations are taken out of context and grouped:

"Open coding fractures the data and allows one to identify categories, their properties and dimensional locations…Axial coding puts those data back together in new ways by making connections between a category and its subcategories" (Strauss and Corbin 1990, 97).

"Grounded" inductive analysis of qualitative material has proven a popular and important means for building conceptual models and theories about the field of study and in this sense offers an approach which has many parallels with the semantic reasoning and data linking intrinsic to formal ontology development. However such long term reflexive accounts, as described through diary work, may also form a broader epistemological context within which the ontologist-research may evaluate, 1) their underlying assumptions about the local and/or domain ontology. 2) the very social environment they are part of. In the example offered below - two case organisations, which the author has conducted AR interventions with, are described. Referred to here simply as 'A' and 'B' these two cases represent UK public sectors bodies whereby AR participatory research was aimed at providing support for strategy development within urban spatial planning contexts. The focus of the research was 'technical' in the sense that its primary aim was to evaluate the relevance of a Geographic dataset in order to help refine its structure through practical application. The research was conducted with numerous domain stakeholders such as urban planners, ecologists, forward planners, transport specialists, housing officers, heritage/conservation officers and parks/green space planners. In this case the research also provided a wider 'practical' focus incorporating the social dynamic of the workplace since tacit domain assumptions about the world were surfaced through the process of refining a dataset to suit all stakeholder needs. The potential for communication problems between such actors, especially in an urban ontology context, is acknowledged by Ban and Ahlqvist (2010) This resulted in the potential for both the data structure to be refined but also for participant assumptions and 'world views' to be questioned by exploring how they responded to the conceptual model/structure underpinning the data set. Obviously the active researcher therefore is influencing more than just a technical development and has the potential to change and influence the working practices and communication between participants in the workplace. This also provides an important epistemological context for the researcher to assess their own assumptions as these become influenced by the practice setting within which they are being formed. This is captured by the research diary being used both for recording technical progress and also the social nature and context of the workplace. The diaries relating to organisation A and also organisation B which spanned a 12 month period were then inductively analysed using grounded methods.

Whilst many codes were formed throughout the free and axial stages of data analysis relating to specific technical activities, broader themes were able to be developed characterising the very context and nature of the research environment. This becomes a valuable reflexive record to help the researcher gauge the epistemological 'robustness' of their findings. This is particularly important when the intervention takes place over a long period of time and therefore potentially difficult to critically 'stand back' from the field of work. Whilst many hundreds of passages of text were originally coded (using NVivo 8) Table 1 simply outlines those which, in retrospect, seemed to describe the more 'significant' actions within the period of research.

Firstly the numerous codes relating to diary passages were aggregated within an axial phase of analysis until they either described a 'thinking' or 'doing' stage of the double loop AR cycle. It is evident that whilst the two case organisations contained broadly similar amounts of 'doing' (A=41, B=50), Case 'B' seemed to offer many more opportunities for significant actions relating to 'thinking' (A=17, B=45). It is interesting to note in this context that although the research diary for Case 'A' was coded as having fewer significant opportunities for 'thinking', it displays more opportunities for significant 'technical' development (A=22, B=17). Whereas Case B was deemed to have afforded more time to 'developing concepts' than Case A (A=10, B=30). Both AR cases contained opportunities for 'championing beliefs' however these are more prevalent in Case A (A=17, B=12). Presumably, because of the greater emphasis on technical activities, rather than conceptual development, resulting in the author feeling a greater need to persuade participants in Case A of the virtues of the research!

This means for contextualising the research workplace provides a simple illustration how a wider focus (from the purely 'technical' toward the 'practical' and 'emancipatory' characteristics of action-orientated research) helps to build a critical picture of the way that participatory intervention, and therefore the researcher's own agency, may have evolved. We might interpret for example that the greater perceived focus of Case 'B' on 'Developing concepts' might be more conducive

Table 1. Summarising key significant actions within the placements

CODES	CASE 'A' Refs(Coverage)	CASE 'B' Refs(Coverage)
Doing(RH loop)	**41**(77.39%)	**50**(67.07%)
Championing Beliefs	**17**(20.40%)	**12**(11.37%)
Technical	**22**(19.78%)	**17**(11.38%)
Relational-	**02**(01.83%)	**13**(18.19%)
Thinking (LH loop)	**17**(36.85%)	**45**(37.30%)
Developing Concepts	**10**(18.04%)	**30**(25.18%)

for collaborative ontology development through *reasoning*; whereas for Case 'A' this may suggest that conceptual models were formed predominantly through *representation*.

FUTURE RESEARCH DIRECTIONS

The potential to support and develop these approaches for critical reflexivity in social knowledge acquisition are offered by Trausan-Matu and Rebedea (2010). Here, social interaction as evidenced through chat and discussion forums, blogs, wikis and instant messaging are processed through the use of a chat analysis system ConcertChat (Homer, Kienle and Wessner 2006). The concept of 'polyphony' (Bakhtin 1973) as being an analysis of communities of voices are employed by Trausan-Matu and Rebedea to help build ontologies based upon conversation topics and so reveal the underpinning conceptual structures hidden in 'chat'. This work would appear to bridge the areas outlined in this chapter by acknowledging the need to inductively build linked concepts within real-world social interaction. This would, for example, provide a significant means for the action-orientated researcher to use social media as a research diary and for participatory chat and discussion, relating to the collaborative research, to be automatically and semantically analysed; thus helping to construct the conceptual links which are formed through the grounded research processes of free and axial coding. It is not my intention to suggest that such automation should replace the need for manual analysis; however, it would certainly appear to have great potential to support it.

CONCLUSION

Whilst AR is a well established approach to researching in practice we might consider that discussion around formal ontology development has traditionally considered the mechanics of defining the ontology and perhaps focussed less on the dynamics of the knowledge acquisition stage in practice (Teller, Tweed and Rabino 2008). Whilst Fernandez *et al* have illustrated that a practical approach to formal ontology development must include knowledge acquisition input throughout all formal stages it is argued here that the act of researching in practice provides opportunities to also test assumptions in practice. AR also provides a key approach to reflexively acknowledge the wider role of the researcher. Whilst the technical task of ontology development may provide the primary focus a much greater level of awareness of the social context of the participatory scenario enables the researcher to be sensitive to the wider impacts the intervention might make. Additionally, inductive analysis through grounded research methods allow the researcher to reveal tacit knowledge to help in ontology development, but more significantly will also illustrate much wider contextual dimensions of the research experience over time. It is often impossible to fully 'stand back' from a practice scenario however reflexivity of action and reflexivity in analysis provide two means to help distance the researcher from the field of work. In retrospect, and through analysis of working diaries, it may also be possible to acknowledge to what extent the conceptual links developed in formal ontology work could be considered to be based upon reasoning or reflection – ontology or epistemology.

REFERENCES

Akkermans, H., Baida, Z., & Gordijn, J. (2004). Value Webs: Using ontologies to bundle real-world services. *IEEE Intelligent Systems*, (4): 57–66. doi:10.1109/MIS.2004.35

Argyris, C., Putman, R., & Smith, D. (1985). *Action science*. San Francisco, CA: Jossey Bass.

Argyris, C., & Schön, D. (1978). *Organisational Learning: A theory of action perspective*. Reading, MA: Addison-Wesley.

Bakhtin, M. M. (1973). *Problems of Dostoevsky's poetics*. Ardis.

Ban, H., & Ahlqvist, O. (2010). User evaluation of a software interface for communication in urban ontologies. In Teller, J., Cutting-Decelle, A.-F., & Billen, R. (Eds.), *COST Action C21 - Future of urban ontologies*. Universite de Liege.

Baskerville, R., & Wood-Harper, A. T. (1998). Diversity in information systems action research methods. *European Journal of Information Systems*, *7*(2), 90–107. doi:10.1057/palgrave.ejis.3000298

Bell, J. (1997). *Doing your research project*. Buckingham, UK: Open University Press.

Blichfeldt, B. S., & Andersen, J. R. (2006). Creating a wider audience for action research: Learning from case-study research. *Journal of Research Practice*, *2*(1), 1–12.

Brachman, R. J. (1979). On the epistemological status of semantic networks. In Findler, N. V. (Ed.), *Associative networks: Representation and use of knowledge by computers*. London, UK: Academic Press.

Bradbury, H., & Lichtenstein, B. M. B. (2000). Relationality in organizational research: Exploring the space between. *Organization Science*, *11*(5), 551–564. doi:10.1287/orsc.11.5.551.15203

Burkhardt, H., & Smith, B. (Eds.). (1991). *Handbook or metaphysics and ontology*. Munich, Germany: Philadelphia Verlag.

Corbin, J., & Strauss, A. (2008). *Basics of qualitative research: Techniques and procedures for developing grounded theory* (3rd ed.). London, UK: Sage Publications.

Corey, K. E., & Wilson, M. (2006). *Urban and regional technology planning: Planning practice in the global knowledge economy*. London, UK: Routledge.

Crang, M. (1997). Analyzing qualitative materials. In Flowerdew, R., & Martin, D. (Eds.), *Methods in human geography: A guide for students doing research projects*. Harlow, MA: Longman.

Dash, D. P. (1999). Current debates in action research. *Systemic Practice and Action Research, 12*(5), 457–492. doi:10.1023/A:1022465506555

Elfors, S., & Svane, Ö. (2008). Action research for sustainable housing: Theoretical and methodological implications of striving for research as a tool for change. *The Journal of Transdisciplinary Environmental Studies, 7*(2), 1–12.

Fernandéz, M., Gómez-Pérez, A., & Juristo, N. (1997). *Methontology: From ontological art towards ontological engineering*. Spring Symposium Series, AAAI97 Stanford.

Gandon, F. (2002). *Distributed artificial intelligence and knowledge management: Ontologies and multi-agent systems for a corporate semantic web*. Scientific Philosopher Doctorate Thesis in Informatics, 7th November 2002, INRIA and University of Nice - Sophia Antipolis

Glaser, B. (1978). *Theoretical sensitivity*. Mill Valley, CA: Sociology Press.

Glaser, B., & Strauss, A. (1967). *The discovery of grounded theory*. Chicago, UK: Aldine.

Gruber, T. R. (1993). A translation approach to portable ontologies. *Knowledge Acquisition, 5*(2), 199–220. doi:10.1006/knac.1993.1008

Guarino, N. (1995). Formal ontology, conceptual analysis and knowledge representation. *International Journal of Human-Computer Studies, 43*, 625–640. doi:10.1006/ijhc.1995.1066

Holmer, T., Kienle, A., & Wessner, M. (2006). Explicit referencing in learning chats: Needs and acceptance. In W. Nejdl & K. Tochtermann, (Eds.), *Innovative approaches for learning and knowledge sharing*. First European Conference on Technology Enhanced Learning, Springer.

Jackson, P. (2001). Making sense of qualitative data. In M. Limb & C. Dwyer, (Eds.), *Qualitative methodologies for geographers*. London, UK: Arnold.

Kemmis, S. (1993). Action research and social movement: A challenge for policy research. *Education Policy Analysis, 1*(1).

Kemmis, S. (2001). Exploring the relevance of critical theory for action research: Emancipatory action research in the footsteps of Jürgen Habermas. In Reason, P., & Bradbury, H. (Eds.), *Handbook of action research: Participative inquiry and practice*. Thousand Oaks, CA: Sage.

Ladkin, D. (2004). Action research. In Seale, C., Gobo, G., Gubrium, J. F., & Silverman, D. (Eds.), *Qualitative research practice*. London, UK: Sage. doi:10.4135/9781848608191.d39

Lewin, K. (1946). Action research and minority problems. *The Journal of Social Issues, 2*, 34–46. doi:10.1111/j.1540-4560.1946.tb02295.x

McKay, J., & Marshall, P. (2001). The dual imperatives of action research. *Information Technology & People, 14*(1), 46–53. doi:10.1108/09593840110384771

McNiff, J., Lomax, P., & Whitehead, J. (2005). *You and your action research project*. London, UK: Routledge Falmer.

Melrose, M. J. (1996). Got a philosophical match? Does it matter? In Zuber-Skerritt, O. (Ed.), *New directions in action research*. London, UK: Falmer Press. doi:10.4324/9780203392935_chapter_4

Morton, A. (1999). Ethics in action research. *Systemic Practice and Action Research, 12*(2), 219–222. doi:10.1023/A:1022430231458

Mounce, S., Brewster, C., Ashley, R., & Hurley, L. (2010). Knowledge management for more sustainable water systems. In Teller, J., Cutting-Decelle, A.-F., & Billen, R. (Eds.), *COST action C21 - Future of urban ontologies*. Universite de Liege.

Noy, N. F., & McGuinness, D. L. (2001). *Ontology development 101: A guide to creating your first ontology*. Stanford University Knowledge Systems Laboratory Technical Report KSL-01-05, March 2001.

Nutter, J. T. (1987). Epistemology. In Shapiro, S. (Ed.), *Encyclopedia of artificial intelligence*. London, UK: John Wiley.

Rotondo, F. (2010). Future perspectives in ontologies for urban regeneration. In Teller, J., Cutting-Decelle, A.-F., & Billen, R. (Eds.), *COST action C21 - Future of urban ontologies*. Universite de Liege.

Roussey, C. (2005). *Technical report n°1 guidelines to build ontologies: A bibliographic study*. COST Action C21 "Urban Ontologies for an improved communication in urban civil engineering projects" - TOWNTOLOGY Project. Retrieved from http://www.towntology.net/

Schön, D. (1983). *The reflective practitioner: How professionals think in action*. New York, NY: Basic Books.

Selman, P. (2006). *Planning at the landscape scale*. Oxon, UK: Routledge.

Strauss, A., & Corbin, J. (1990). *Basics of qualitative research: Techniques and procedures for developing grounded theory*. London, UK: Sage Publications.

Strawson, P. F. (1959). *Individuals: An essay in descriptive metaphysics*. London, UK: Routledge. doi:10.4324/9780203221303

Studer, R., Benjamins, V. R., & Fensel, D. (1998). Knowledge engineering: Principles and methods. *Data & Knowledge Engineering, 25*(1-2), 161–197. doi:10.1016/S0169-023X(97)00056-6

Teller, J. (2007). Ontologies for improved communication in urban development projects. *Studies in Computational Intelligence, 61*, 1–14. doi:10.1007/978-3-540-71976-2_1

Teller, J., Tweed, C., & Rabino, G. (Eds.). (2008). *Conceptual models for urban practitioners*. Bologna, Italy: Societa Editrice Esculapio.

Trausan-Matu, S., & Rebedea, T. (2010). Ontology-based analysis of chat conversations: An urban development case. In Teller, J., Cutting-Decelle, A.-F., & Billen, R. (Eds.), *COST action C21 - Future of urban ontologies*. Universite de Liege.

Uschold, M., & Gruninger, M. (1996). Ontologies: Principles, methods and applications. *The Knowledge Engineering Review, 11*(2), 1–63. doi:10.1017/S0269888900007797

Woods, W. A. (1975). What's in a link: Foundations for semantic networks. In Bobrow, D. G., & Collins, A. M. (Eds.), *Representation and understanding: Studies in cognitive science*. London, UK: Academic Press.

Zuber-Skerritt, O. (1996). Emancipatory action research for organisational change. In Zuber-Skerritt, O. (Ed.), *New directions in action research*. London, UK: Falmer Press.

ENDNOTES

[1]   http://www.getty.edu/research/tools/vocabularies/aat/index.html

[2]   http://www.towntology.net

Chapter 9
Data Mining, Validation, and Collaborative Knowledge Capture

Martin Atzmueller
University of Kassel, Germany

Stephanie Beer
University Clinic of Wuerzburg, Germany

Frank Puppe
University of Wuerzburg, Germany

ABSTRACT

For large-scale data mining, utilizing data from ubiquitous and mixed-structured data sources, the extraction and integration into a comprehensive data-warehouse is usually of prime importance. Then, appropriate methods for validation and potential refinement are essential. This chapter describes an approach for integrating data mining, information extraction, and validation with collaborative knowledge management and capture in order to improve the data acquisition processes. For collaboration, a semantic wiki-enabled system for knowledge and experience management is presented. The proposed approach applies information extraction techniques together with pattern mining methods for initial data validation and is applicable for heterogeneous sources, i.e., capable of integrating structured and unstructured data. The methods are integrated into an incremental process providing for continuous validation options. The approach has been developed in a health informatics context: The results of a medical application demonstrate that pattern mining and the applied rule-based information extraction methods are well suited for discovering, extracting and validating clinically relevant knowledge, as well as the applicability of the knowledge capture approach. The chapter presents experiences using a case-study in the medical domain of sonography.

DOI: 10.4018/978-1-4666-0894-8.ch009

INTRODUCTION

Whenever data is continuously collected, for example, using intelligent documentation systems in a medical context, data mining and data analysis provide a broad range of options. The mining and analysis step is often implemented using a data-warehouse, e.g., Kimball & Ross (2002). For the data preprocessing and integration of several heterogeneous sources, there exist standardized extract-transform-load (ETL) procedures that need to incorporate suitable data schemas, and integration rules. Additionally, for unstructured or semi-structured textual data sources, the integration requires effective information extraction methods. For clinical discharge letters, for example, the structure of the letter is usually non-standardized, and thus dependent on different writing styles of different authors.

However, a prerequisite of data mining is the validation and the quality assurance of the integrated data. Especially concerning unreliable extraction and integration methods, the quality of the obtained data can vary significantly. If the data has been successfully validated, then the trust in the data mining results and their acceptance can be increased. After that, the comprehensive data set can be used for quality and knowledge management.

This chapter describes a system for integrated data mining and collaborative knowledge management, capture and refinement in a health informatics context. It presents its application using a case-study in the medical domain of sonography.

The approach applies information extraction techniques together with data mining methods for initial data validation and is applicable for heterogeneous sources integrating structured and unstructured data. We focus on an incremental level-wise approach, such that both methods can complement each other in the validation and refinement setting. Validation knowledge can also be formalized in a knowledge base, for assessing known and expected relations. After that, the con-

solidated data set can be applied for comprehensive quality and knowledge management.

The approach has been implemented in a clinical application context for knowledge management and data mining with data from clinical information systems, documentation systems, and clinical discharge letters. Its workflow features the integration of data mining, information extraction, data validation, and collaborative knowledge management and refinement.

The clinical application is targeted at extended quality control, profiling, and knowledge and experience management in the medical domain of sonography. This application context concerns the data integration from heterogeneous databases and the information extraction from textual documents. After that, the data can be checked with respect to deviations concerning expected relations, relations modeled in the background knowledge as well as by applying statistical validation techniques. For collaborative knowledge management tagging provides helpful techniques: It enables the flexible collection, annotation, organization, and distribution of resources and information. A combination with a wiki then provides powerful but easy to use approaches for a broad range of applications. The presented approach is thus implemented using a system for collaborative knowledge management and refinement, backed by a semantic wiki extension. For this purpose, sonographic images are collected, annotated and commented in order to serve as instructive examples for typical but also exceptional features of certain disorders. In this way, effective tutoring and discussion between the examiners can be initiated and the social collaboration can facilitate incremental knowledge capture and refinement concerning the data collected in the collaborative training system.

The rest of this chapter is structured as follows: We first briefly outline the application context given by the SONOCONSULT knowledge system. Furthermore, we present the mining and validation approach in detail. Next, we describe the social application for collaborative knowledge capture and refinement. Both sections are illustrated by examples from the SONOCONSULT system. After that, we conclude with a summary.

BACKGROUND: SONOCONSULT

SONOCONSULT (SC), cf. Huettig et al. (2004), Puppe et al. (2008), is a multifunctional knowledge system for sonography, which has been in routine use since 2002 documenting more than 12000 patients in two clinics. The system covers the entire field of abdominal ultrasound (liver, portal tract, gallbladder, spleen, kidneys, adrenal glands, pancreas, stomach, intestine, lymph nodes, abdominal aorta, cava inferior, prostate, and urinary bladder). It was developed with the knowledge system d3web (www.d3web.de), e.g., Puppe (1998). The system interacts with the user via dynamic questionnaires for all organs and generates two outputs: a structured report in a

standard word processing system for the hospital information system and a data base of all cases for statistical analysis and data mining. An example of a screenshot of the SONOCONSULT dialog is shown in Figure 1. While the middle part shows the questionnaire, the right part shows inferences made by the diagnostic component.

The terminology of SONOCONSULT is descriptive and follows that of standard textbooks and publications. Based on the completed questionnaires a textual report (see Figure 2) is generated using a rule based template. The knowledge base makes use of medical heuristics as knowledge source, cf. Clement & McDonald (1996), and was built according to the principles applied for the construction of HepatoConsult, see Buscher et al. (2002). SC uses five main concepts: symptoms (input data), symptom classes (questionnaires grouping the input questions), symptom abstractions, diagnoses (output), and rules. Symptoms consist of a pair (attribute, value), e.g. "liver size"

Figure 1. Screenshot (in German) of a section of an SC-questionaire with part of the hierarchy of questionnaires (partially opened, left panel) and the currently generated probable system diagnoses (right panel)

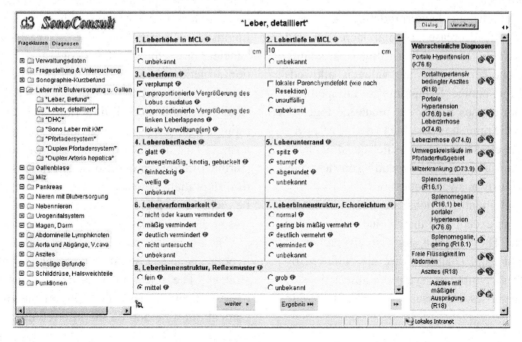

Figure 2. Part of a generated SC-report

Age: 75; female
Clinical problem: uncertain abdominal complaint; gallstone disease

Findings: date 01/07/06; good condition of examination

Liver: height in medio-clavicular axis 10 cm; depth in MCA 11 cm; regular shape; smooth sur-
face; caudal margin in shape of an acute angle; elasticity not or almost not reduced; structure of
slightly to moderately elevated echogenity; intermediate reflex pattern; regular vessel structure of
the liver
Common bile duct: diameter 8.5 mm; regular
Gallbladder: normal size
Spleen: longitudinal size 8.5 cm; dephth 3 cm; regular size, shape and structure
Portal system: diameter of portal vein 8 mm, regular
Pancreas: head and body visible; body diameter 1.3 cm; general structure of homogenously increased echogenity; duct system regular
Kidney: *right kidney:* orthotopic position; length 9 cm; thickness of parenchyma 1 cm; normal
echogenity of parenchyma; scarred retraction; pyelon not dilated, not measured; regular calices
left kidney: orthotopic position; length 9.5 cm; thickness of parenchyma 1.4 cm; normal echogen-
ity of parenchyma; regular renal structure; scarred retraction; pyelon not dilated, not measured;
regular calices
Abdominal aorta: partly visible; diameter 1.6 cm; regular
Vena cava: regular
Lymph nodes: in visible regions not detectable or not enlarged
Urinary bladder: not judgeable (insufficiently filled)
Gynecological tract: *Uterus:* not examined

(symptom name) and e.g., "increased" (symptom value). In interactive settings, the attributes are questions and the values are the answers by the user. There are two main types of attributes: choice and numerical.

Choice attributes have a predefined range (e.g. for liver size: decreased, normal, increased) and are differentiated according to their cardinality as one-choice (exactly one value is allowed) or multiple choice. Symptoms are grouped into symptom classes if they are requested together most of the time. It is possible to define rules in a symptom class that specify which questions have to be asked in which order depending on the values of previously answered questions.

Symptom abstractions are very similar to symptoms except that their values are inferred by rules. They allow a stepwise abstraction of the input data. Diagnoses are also inferred by rules from symptoms, symptom abstractions or other diagnoses. They usually aggregate uncertain evidence.

While d3web allows different reasoning mechanisms for inferring diagnoses, in SC a score-based (fuzzy) reasoning scheme is used, i.e. the rules are assumed to be independent and add or subtract points to the score of a diagnosis, which is rated by thresholds in one of the linguistic categories "probable", "possible" and "unclear or excluded". Rules consist of a condition, an action and exceptions. The condition may be a nested logical combination of criteria, e.g., "and", "or" and "not". Rule actions include, e.g., rating diagnoses, computing values for symptom abstractions, indicating symptom classes and (further) follow-up questions. Exceptions allow to differentiate between two types of negation, i.e., whether a fact is yet unknown or definitely wrong. For more details, see Puppe (1998).

The diagnostic procedure of SC follows the hypothesis-and- test- and the establish-refine-strategy. The selection of a specific question-naire (symptom class) depends on the overall clinical question and on the inferred diagnoses. Data gathering stops when (a) the user jumps to the conclusions or (b) all suspected diagnoses (category "possible") are either "probable" or "unclear or excluded" by means of the program's expertise or (c) there are no useful questionnaires left for clarification.

Concerning the evaluation and validation of a system and its collected data, the use of test cases for system is probably the method for the validation of intelligent systems, e.g., Preece (1998). Since the acquisition of test cases is usually time-consuming and costly, a number of methods have been proposed to decrease the acquisition costs of the test knowledge by automatically generating test cases, e.g., Knauf, Gonzalez & Abel (2002), Gupta & Biegel (1990): These approaches rely on an existing knowledge base, and they generate test cases based on the available set of derivation knowledge.

However, such a methodology can only cope with the first of our evaluation objectives, i.e., with the evaluation and analysis of potential errors within the intelligent system, i.e., contained in the applied knowledge base. Further analysis for detecting external explanations is then rather difficult, in contrast to our approach. Using data mining, we can identify factors (e.g., diagnoses, findings, other parameters), e.g., Atzmueller & Puppe (2009), that are associated with the occurrence of system errors. Additionally, the second application, that is, quality profiling and management, is usually not supported by the existing evaluation approaches. It is possible to use the test cases for system evaluation but not for "evaluation" of the profiling of the users, that is, for building profiles of their behavior, e.g., Atzmueller et al. (2005).

DATA MINING, VALIDATION, AND KNOWLEDGE REFINEMENT

In the following, we first describe how the collected data can be applied for system evaluation and validation. After that, we summarize the gen-

eral mining and validation process, and discuss validation options. The following sections contain illustrative examples from the SONOCONSULT system described above. The next section presents the collaborative application for incremental knowledge capture and refinement.

System Evaluation and Validation

The input and output relations for a given set of cases can be transparently evaluated by domain specialists that provide a gold standard for the solutions of the system. Then, the acquired cases are compared by a before-after strategy that needs to be done manually by the domain specialists. Such a procedure usually works relatively well, e.g., Puppe et al. (2008). However, providing the gold-standard takes a lot of time and is thus very cost-intensive. Therefore, other options that do not need to rely on a domain specialist are promising. Additionally, a continuous monitoring of all the possible test cases would potentially require an unlimited set of expert rated solutions, which is rather unfeasible. We provide a data mining method that relies on external data from other data sources (examinations). If all the available data has been integrated into a data warehouse, then the evaluation of the input – output relations is straight-forward using complementary data sources given by laboratory and/or other examinations, for example, magnetic resonance imaging or CT tomography. Using these and special examinations, e.g., histology results, data close to a gold-standard can be collected. This is then automatically compared to the solutions of the system in order to identify potentially incorrect solutions that were documented using the intelligent system.

We can perform a rather simple evaluation just by comparing the accumulated solutions to the respective system solution. In this way, we can acquire initial statistics that can already indicate problems with the intelligent system. For a more sophisticated approach we need to apply pattern

Figure 3. Validation of mixed-structured data using pattern mining and information extraction

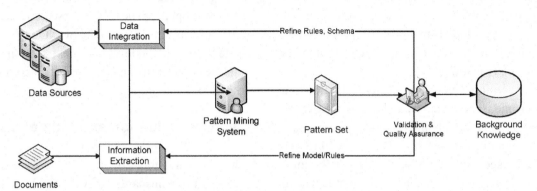

mining in order to implement more advanced analysis goals: Using the applied subgroup mining approach we can also consider the gold-standard solution as the target variable, and identify system solutions that are associated with this target, that is, other correct and incorrect solutions. Another analysis option is given by constructing a binary target variable that is true, if the gold-standard and the system solution match, and false otherwise. In this way, we obtain a set of subgroup patterns indicating situations or combinations of factors that indicate potential causes for the observed discrepancies. Then, using explaining variables from the remaining data, we can try to identify explaining factors for the mismatch between the correct and the system solution. However, the system solutions may be incorrect due to two different reasons. First, the solution of the system may be wrong, and secondly, the provided input findings may be wrong and/or inconsistent with respect to the true input description. In the first case, we need to refine the knowledge system, whereas in the second case we need to make sure, that the input findings are entered in the correct way, for example, by initiating tutoring sessions or by special training of the users. In order to clarify such situations, we therefore also need to consider the performance of the users that provide the input to the system, as discussed in the next section. Using the approach discussed above, that is, the analysis of the system solutions with respect

to a gold-standard, we can only detect situation of the first kind; therefore both analysis options complement each other.

Overview on the Mining and Validation Process

Figure 3 provides a bird eye's view on the process of validation and refinement of mixed-structured data using pattern mining and information extraction methods. The input of the process is given by data from heterogeneous data sources, and by textual documents. The former are processed by appropriate data integration methods adapted to the different sources. The latter are handled by information extraction techniques, e.g., rule-based methods that utilize appropriate extraction rules for the extraction of concepts and relations from the documents. In general, a variety of methods can be applied.

The process supports arbitrary information extraction methods, e.g., automatic techniques like support vector machines or conditional random fields as implemented in the ClearTK toolkit, cf. Ogren et al. (2008), for statistical natural language processing. However, the refinement capabilies vary for the different extraction approaches: While black-box methods like support vector machines or conditional random fields only allow an indirect refinement and adaptation of the model, i.e., based on adapting the input data and/or the method parameters for constructing the model, a white-box approach implemented using rules provides for a direct modification of its model, i.e., the provided rules.

Therefore, we especially focus on rule-based methods due to their rich refinement capabilities. After the integration and extraction of the data, the result is provided to the pattern mining system which obtains a set of validation patterns as output. This set is then checked both for internal consistency and compared to the formalized background knowledge. In the case of discrepancies and/or errors, refinements are proposed for the data integration and/or the information extraction steps. After the rules have been refined, the process iterates with the updated schemas and models.

In the medical domain, for example, patterns are usually first assessed on the abstract level, before they are checked and verified on concrete patient records, i.e., on a very detailed level of abstraction. Then, discrepancies are modeled in the background knowledge, for example, certain exception conditions for certain subgroups of patients. The validation phase is performed on several levels: On the first level, we can use a (partial) gold-standard both for checking the data integration and information extraction tasks. We only require a partial gold-standard, i.e., a sample of the correct relations, because we need to test the functional requirements of the data integration and extraction phases. On the next level, we can incrementally validate the integrated data using the extracted information, or vice versa, using the mined patterns. In the case of discrepancies, we can rely on the partial gold-standard data for verification, or we can identify potential causes and verify these on concrete cases. Therefore, the final decision for the refinements relies on the user, which reviews all proposed refinements in a semi-automatic approach.

For the refinement steps, we can either extend the (partial) gold-standard, or we perform a boot-strapping approach, using a small gold-standard sample of target concepts for validation, e.g., for validating and refining the information extraction approach, which is in turn used for the validation of the data sources. In the next step, the validation targets can be extended and the process for refinement is applied inversely. The boot-strapping approach for validation and refinement is thus similar to the idea of co-training, e.g., Blum & Mitchel (1998) in machine learning that also starts with a small labeled (correct) dataset and iteratively adapts the models using another co-trained dataset.

Subgroup Mining Using VIKAMINE

Subgroup mining (or subgroup discovery) is a flexible data mining method for discovering local patterns that can be utilized for global modeling in the context of exploratory data analysis, description, characterization and classification. Subgroup mining is applied for identifying relations between a (dependent) target concept and a set of explaining (independent) variables. Then, the goal is to describe subsets of the data that have the most unusual characteristics with respect to the concept of interest given by the target variable, cf. Wrobel (1997). For example, the risk of coronary heart disease (target variable) is significantly higher in the subgroup of smokers with a positive family history than in the general population. In the context of the proposed validation approach, we consider certain diagnostic concepts as targets, as well as target concepts that are true, if and only if equivalent concepts from two different sources match. Then, we can identify combinations of factors that cause a mismatch between the concepts. These combinations can then indicate candidates for refinement.

Furthermore, for identifying profiles of the diagnostic patterns of examiners, subgroups specified by specific sonographic diagnoses or diagnoses documented more (or less) frequently by a certain examiner (target concept) compared to the means of all examiners are potential subgroups of interest. The subgroups correspond to documentation patterns, i.e. the occurrence of certain diagnoses and findings (and their interactions) by specific examiners is significantly more (or less) frequently than would be expected by chance.

Subgroup mining is especially suited for the sketched analytical tasks in the medical domain, since it does not necessarily rely on finding complete relationships between the specific target concept (dependent variable, i.e., *examiner*) and the explanatory variables (set of *findings* and/or d*iagnoses*). In contrast, subgroup mining is focused on identifying unexpected and conspicuous relations, as local patterns specific for a subset of the data. Due to this criterion the discovered patterns do not necessarily fulfill high support criteria, which are rather common for other prominent data mining approaches, e.g., methods for the discovery of association rules.

For data mining, we apply the subgroup mining tool VIKAMINE, cf. Atzmueller & Puppe (2005), for knowledge discovery and quality control. VIKAMINE provides an integrated subgroup mining environment and facilitates efficient and effective knowledge discovery and visualization methods.

Rule-Based Information Extraction

Information extraction methods aim at extracting a set of concepts, entities and relations from a set of documents. TEXTMARKER, e.g., Kluegl, Atzmueller & Puppe (2009) is a robust system for rule-based information extraction. It can be applied very intuitively, since the used rules are especially easy to acquire and to comprehend. Structured data can then be extracted from unstructured and semi-structured data, and data sets be easily created in a post-processing step of TEXTMARKER, cf. Atzmueller, Kluegl & Puppe (2008).

Humans often apply a strategy according to a highlighter metaphor that is often performed during 'manual' information extraction: First, top-level text blocks are considered and classified according to their content by coloring them with different highlighters. The contained elements of the annotated texts segments are then considered

further. The TEXTMARKER system tries to imitate this manual extraction method by formalizing the appropriate actions using matching rules: The rules mark sequences of words, extract text segments to modify the input document depending on textual features. TEXTMARKER aims at supporting the knowledge engineer in the rapid prototyping of information extraction applications. The default input for the system is semi-structured text, but it can also process structured or free text. Technically, HTML is often the input format, since most word processing documents can be obtained in HTML format, or converted appropriately.

In addition to its rule-based features, TEXT-MARKER can also be complemented by other standard information extraction approaches, for example, ClearTK, cf. Ogren et al. (2008). Its extensibility makes it a viable tool for supporting a broad range of data mining methods in the applied natural language processing context, e.g., Atzmueller (2011) for an overview.

EXEMPLARY SONOCONSULT RESULTS

In the following we discuss exemplary results obtained from the SONOCONSULT system described above. A data warehouse typically contains data from different heterogeneous sources (Kerkri et al. 2001) that need to be accumulated, standardized, and finally imported into the data warehouse (Han and Kamber 2000). For the presented approach, we integrated several heterogeneous data sources ranging from structured data records containing the examination data from the sonographic records, various laboratory parameters, the final diagnoses from the hospital information system SAP i.s.h.med, but also unstructured data given by the textual discharge letters. From these, several additional data about further examinations is extracted. The implementation of the data warehouse required a lot of data cleaning efforts, since all the data neglecting the SONOCONSULT data needed to be extracted from legacy database systems.

The data warehouse was completed after an initial design and several incremental refinement cycles for which the data sources and the selected data needed to be adapted and tuned. The data was integrated with the SAP-based i.s.h.med system, and the information extraction techniques were applied for textual discharge letters from the respective patients; SONOCONSULT was used for documentation. By integrating different data sources into the warehouse it is possible to measure the conformity of sonographic results with other methods or inputs. In our evaluations, we applied computer-tomography diagnoses and additional diagnoses (from the hospital information system).

As outlined above, we distinguish two objectives for the evaluation and quality analysis of intelligent systems:

1. System evaluation and analysis: Comparing and evaluating the input–output behavior of the system using external data for assessing the system solutions.
2. Quality management: Assessing the input quality; in the medical domain this corresponds to the documentation quality of the users (examiners).

System Evaluation and Analysis

Table 1 shows the correlation of SONOCONSULT based diagnosis with CT/MR, diagnoses listed in the discharge letter and diagnoses contained in the hospital information system for a selection of cases from a certain examiner. It was quite interesting that the conformity between SONO-CONSULT based diagnoses with the diagnoses contained in the hospital information system was relatively low. Evaluating this issue it was obvious that various diagnoses were not listed in the hospital information system because they were not revenue enhancing and not relevant for all clinical situations. Therefore, we looked at

the accordance with the discharge letters which were found to be highly concordant at least for the diagnosis of liver metastasis. Liver cirrhosis is more awkward to detect using ultrasound and has to be in a more advanced stage. Therefore, some of the discharge diagnoses "liver cirrhosis" were only detected using histology or other methods. In some cases, there are discrepancies with respect to the expected relations that still persist after refinement of the rules and checking the data sources. In such cases, explanation-aware mining and analysis components provide appropriate solutions for resolving conflicts and inconsistencies. By supporting the user with appropriate justifications and explanations, misleading patterns can be identified, and the background knowledge can be adapted. The decision whether the background knowledge needs to be adapted is performed by the domain specialist.

Quality Management

For the task of quality management or quality control we consider all the users individually that can enter findings for generating cases with a specific solution. In the context of the medical documentation system SONOCONSULT, the users are sonographic examiners that document the case by entering the specific findings they identify on the sonographic images. Since sonographic examination is highly subjective and dependent on the experience of the examiner, the quality management is essential in order to identify examiners that deviate from the norm, if we assume a "similar" share of patients for each examiner. Ultrasound is a method which is strongly dependent on the examiner's degree of knowledge. Therefore, it is interesting to know how well the results of the examination agree between different examiners and with the results of other methods.

Essentially, we can first discover circumstances under which examiners show a significantly different performance. Second, we can then try to

Table 1. Conformity of system diagnoses with various sources of diagnosis input. The columns indicate the relative degree of correlation of the different sources with SONOCONSULT diagnoses measured by the number of covered cases. It is easy to see, that the conformity for certain diagnoses is relatively high (liver metastasis), while the conformity for liver cirrhosis is lower. This indicates the potential for the training of the sonographic examiners and provides the motivation for the collaborative application discussed below.

Total Case Number	SONO CONSULT Diagnoses	SAP Diagnoses	%Conformity with SONO CONSULT	CT/MR Diagnonses	%Conformity with SONO CONSULT	Discharge Letter Diagnoses	%Conformity with SONO CONSULT
Liver cirrhosis							
16	12	6	20	1	33	9	50
Liver metastasis							
28	16	11	65	15	87	17	94

identify explanations from these in order to train examiners, for example, beginners that are not very experienced. For the quality management step we build user profiles statistically and test for all solutions, for which examiners there is a significantly different distribution: Essentially, we compare the frequency of documented diagnoses depending on the examiner. This method is easily implemented using subgroup mining by regarding the examiner as the target variable, and considering all diagnoses and/or findings as independent (explaining) variables. Figure 4 shows the results of this analysis as an overview statistic for several clinically important diagnoses. For testing the significance of the subgroups, we applied the standard chi-square-test for independence. Values of $p < 0.001$ were considered significant.

The results show that there are some major differences in the frequency of diagnosing a specific disease for the different examiners. For example, several examiners do not document certain diagnoses at all ("aorta sclerosis, not calcified" or "portal hypertension") – in contrast to the assumption that all examiners should encounter a "similar" share of patients (and diseases). The principal cause for this discrepancy may be due to the fact that the different examiners work in different departments and therefore the patients stock of each sonographic examiner has a different distribution of diseases. Since the data ware-

house is continuously being extended, we plan to investigate these issues in more detail given a larger number of cases. Additionally, we can then also control the analysis for this situation and profile different departments individually.

First results of the application of the presented approach demonstrate its effectiveness and applicability in the presented context. The validation of solutions for system evaluation already shows a high share of correct diagnoses. However, due to the highly subjective documentation procedure of the input diagnoses, we also suspect a dependency on the experience of the examiner. If the results of the examiner profiling study are only attributable to this specific issue, or if they depend on other confounding factors, for example, different patient distributions due to different departments needs to be clarified using a larger number of cases. The main advantage of the data warehouse-based approach using data mining techniques compared to the manual validation approach is its cost-effectiveness, ease of use, and potentially continuous application throughout the lifecycle of the intelligent system. Ultimately, it can be automated and can provide important feedback to certain types of user, for example, inexperienced examiners. Then, the quality of the documentation and of the input findings can be significantly increased.

Figure 4. Diagnostic profiles for several examiners. The rows denote the frequencies of several different diagnoses, for which the column F specifies the absolute and % the relative frequency.

Diagnoses	All F	All %	Examiner 1 F	Examiner 1 %	Examiner 2 F	Examiner 2 %	Examiner 3 F	Examiner 3 %	Examiner 4 F	Examiner 4 %
All	2498	100	757	34	104	4,7	392	17,6	359	16,1
fatty liver	683	27,3	212	33,3	20	3,1	136	21,4	117	18,4
liver cirrhosis	42	1,7	22	52,4	0	0	15	35,7	0	0
aortic sclerosis, non calcified	29	1,2	3	10,7	0	0	0	0	18	64,3
aortic sclerosis, calcified	510	20,4	96	19,7	27	5,5	126	25,8	82	16,8
ascites	160	6,4	60	41,1	4	2,7	27	18,5	16	11
cholezystolithiasis	345	13,8	107	35,7	13	4,3	41	13,7	47	15,7
chron. deg. kidny disease	219	8,8	66	30,3	9	4,1	50	22,9	45	20,6
gut disease	35	1,4	10	28,6	2	5,7	18	51,4	1	2,9
mass/liver	119	4,8	39	33,9	3	2,6	21	18,3	25	21,7
obstructive cholestasis	15	0,6	3	23,1	0	0	6	46,2	3	23,1
lymphnode intraabdominal	33	1,3	16	59,3	2	7,4	3	11,1	1	3,7
pleural effusion	128	5,1	31	27	3	2,6	31	27	24	20,9
portal hypertension	35	1,4	16	45,7	0	0	11	31,4	1	2,9
prostata disease	334	13,4	55	18,1	4	1,3	50	16,4	79	26
liver size = very enlarged	178	7,1	25	15,8	3	1,9	26	16,5	35	22,2

COLLABORATIVE KNOWLEDGE CAPTURE AND REFINEMENT

Both Web 2.0 and semantic technologies enable the creation of powerful tools for knowledge management. While social tagging systems e.g., Golder & Huberman (2006), provide for versatile approaches for the distributed collection, annotation, organization, and distribution of resources that are especially easy to use, wiki-based systems allow the collaboration of a community of users in a simple way. Therefore, combining both approaches seems to be an attractive solution since they complement each other well: The wiki-based system provides the tools for accessing and managing the content, while the tagging application takes care of the annotation, and categorization of the resources. In this way, a community-driven knowledge management approach can be well supported. Additionally, by embedding semantic web technology, cf. Antoniou & Harmelen (2004), e.g., for accessing the tagged resources or modeling the tag relations, a flexible and powerful user experience can be implemented. The KNOWTA (Knowledge Tagging) system, cf. Atzmueller & Hörnlein (2009), combines tagging and wiki-editing in a social system for knowledge and experience management. KNOWTA is well suited for handling multi-modal knowledge, e.g., containing text and images. The system supports a variety of resource types that can be embedded into a wiki page, in addition to the rich textual edit actions. Specifically, the system enables the management of image data with corresponding texts for knowledge management. Then, image and textual data, i.e., multi-modal information, can both be tagged and semantically annotated using the functionality of the social tagging system and/or the wiki-features, respectively.

As an extension, the system can be configured for closed-communities such that controlled vocabularies for the tags, i.e., the tag ontology of the system can be defined. This is especially useful for specific application projects with a fixed specific set of contributing users.

Semantic Representation

KNOWTA utilizes the semantic core component of the knowledge wiki system d3web.KnowWE, e.g., Reutelshoefer et al. (2007), Baumeister, Reutelshoefer & Puppe (2010), which was extended as needed. The included semantic core relies on Sesame as RDF-Triple storage and OWLIM as reasoning engine integrated in the d3web.KnowWE system, a basic semantic wiki system featuring an extensible annotation syntax and the possibility of SPARQL-query embedding. As the tagging of a resource is a specialized case of a semantic annotation, the tagging functionality is merely a convenient way to introduce this annotation into the backend ontology. Due to the fact, that the tags are stored in the ontology of the wiki, it is possible to integrate arbitrary SPARQL-queries for tags or pages tagged with specific tags everywhere in the wiki, for example, within any page or even the menu structure. This approach allows for powerful semantic browsing options for accessing the stored resources and content. For semantic browsing and querying users, resources, tags, links, and the content itself can be considered.

Connections between resources/tags are then either established using (explicit) links between the resources, implicit relations/links given by the matching set of tags of different resources, or by considering the relations between the tags defined in a domain ontology (for closed communities). The general knowledge and experience management functions are supported by the wiki-enabled information handling – using unstructured, semi-structured, and structured information. Since the knowledge can be collaboratively extended, the system provides for a knowledge-rich collaborative environment for a broad range of applications (refer to Figure 5).

Clinical Application

For a sonography (ultrasound) examination, the examiners need to closely inspect the ultrasound images, for example, see Figure 6 in order to document the correct findings. Since this process is highly subjective and also significantly dependent on the experience of the examiner, there are often discrepancies between beginners and more senior examiners concerning the correct findings, cf., Puppe et al. (2008). Therefore, a system for the collection and annotation of interesting, i.e., exceptional or typical images for certain medical phenomena with associated textual descriptions provides for a powerful tool. In this context, KNOWTA thus provides an ideal framework for implementing an image pool for tutoring, targeted training and general knowledge management. Special cases of ultrasound phenomena can be uploaded to the system. Figure 6 shows an example for a set of liver-related phenomena.

The resources can be easily described, tagged and annotated, and junior examiners can search for specific (difficult) situations using the tag cloud and/or the search functionality. Additionally, hints can be easily communicated using the annotation and/or comment function of the system.

So far, the collected working set comprehensively covers the problem domain of sonography and provides for an experience base for supporting medical training and consultation by knowledge and experience management.

Additionally, the system features the capability to semi-automatically export the collected data to the CaseTrain training system, see Hoernlein et al. (2009): After the resources have been collected in the KNOWTA system, they are readily available for further processing. In order to apply the system for knowledge capture for designing and building tutoring cases, a semi-automatic export to the CaseTrain system is provided. Furthermore, an automatic option is given by exporting all images with their associated 'main' tag (the page title) and storing the complete list as 'long menu' questions for all images. However, for creating the cases this list can of course be edited in a semi-automatic fashion in order to increase the didactic quality of the case.

Figure 5. KNOWTA: Exemplary resource/image with annotation and tags (in German)

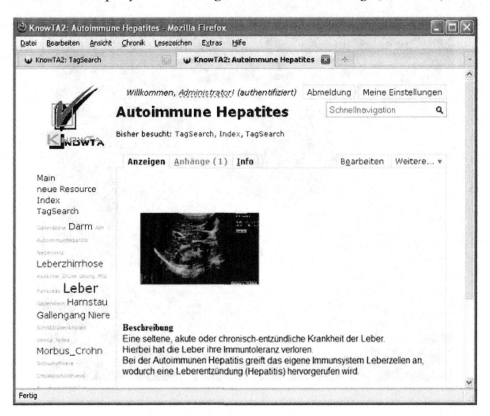

In the simplest case a (potentially randomly selected) subset of tagged images is obtained; for tutoring, the user needs to select a specific tag from the *long menu* that describes the image best. In this way, the images, the annotations and tags can be utilized for creating new quizzes for tutoring and teaching purposes.

Using links to KNOWTA articles, CaseTrain users can also get background information about the case. An exemplary CaseTrain screenshot is given in Figure 7.

CONCLUSION

This chapter presented an approach for integrated data mining, validation and collaborative refinement using information extraction and pattern mining methods. In an incremental approach,

data can both be validated and refined with an increasing level of accuracy, then being applied for system evaluation and profiling.

The presented approach has been successfully implemented in a medical project targeted at integrating data from clinical information systems, documentation systems, and textual discharge letters. The context of this work was given by SONOCONSULT, a documentation and consultation system in the medical domain that provides a good example for a typical intelligent system to be evaluated. The approach is based on the availability of a data warehouse containing the system solutions and external data for validation.

The experiences and results so far demonstrate the flexibility and effectiveness of the pattern mining and information extraction methods for the presented validation and refinement approach. For a broader application, further experiences in a

Figure 6. Exemplary image from an ultrasound examination

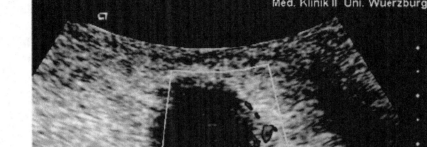

Figure 7. Exemplary CaseTrain case (in German)

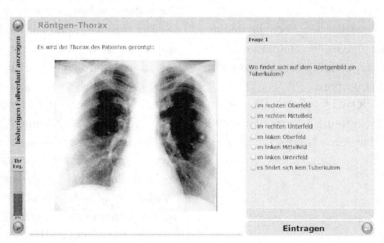

comprehensive clinical context are envisioned for improving and extending the presented approach further. However, first results and experiences of the implemented project application already show the potential of its continuous application in clinical routine.

Concerning the collaborative approach, we have introduced the KNOWTA system for tutoring and general knowledge management. We discussed the different components and features of the system, and we have described its integration into the presented real-world clinical context.

In summary, the presented data mining, validation, and collaborative knowledge refinement approach facilitates an incremental and cost-effective process. It is not limited to the medical domain as described above, but provides for a broad range of applications in various domains.

REFERENCES

Antoniou, G., & Harmelen, F. v. (2004). *A Semantic Web primer*. Cambridge, MA: MIT Press.

Atzmueller, M. (2011). Data mining. In McCartney, P., & Boonthum-Denecke, C. (Eds.), *Applied natural language processing and content analysis: Advances in identification, investigation and resolution*. Hershey, PA: IGI Global.

Atzmueller, M., Beer, S., & Puppe, F. (2009). A data warehouse-based approach for quality management, evaluation and analysis of intelligent systems using subgroup mining. In *Proceedings of 22nd International Florida Artificial Intelligence Research Society Conference*, (pp. 372–377). AAAI Press.

Atzmueller, M., Haupt, F., Beer, S., & Puppe, F. (2009). Knowta: Wiki-enabled social tagging for collaborative knowledge and experience management. *Proceedings International Workshop on Design, Evaluation, and Refinement of Intelligent Systems*, Krakow, Poland

Atzmueller, M., Kluegl, P., & Puppe, F. (2008). Rule-based information extraction for structured data acquisition using TextMarker. In *Proceedings of LWA 2008 (Knowledge Discovery and Machine Learning Track)*, University of Wuerzburg

Atzmueller, M., & Puppe, F. (2009). A knowledge-intensive approach for semi-automatic causal subgroup discovery. In Berendt, B. (Eds.), *Knowledge discovery enhanced with semantic and social information*. Springer. doi:10.1007/978-3-642-01891-6_2

Atzmueller, M., Puppe, F., & Buscher, H. P. (2005). Profiling examiners using intelligent subgroup mining. In *Proceedings 10th International Workshop on Intelligent Data Analysis in Medicine and Pharmacology*, (pp. 46–51). Aberdeen, Scotland

Baumeister, J., Reutelshoefer, J., & Puppe, F. (2010). KnowWE: A semantic Wiki for knowledge engineering. In *Applied intelligence*. Springer. doi:10.1007/s10489-010-0224-5

Blum, A., & Mitchel, T. (1998). Combining labeled and unlabeled data with co-training. In *COLT: Proceedings of the Workshop on Computational Learning Theory*, (pp. 92–100). Morgan Kaufmann.

Buscher, H.-P., Engler, C., Führer, A., Kirschke, S., & Puppe, F. (2002). HepatoConsult: A knowledge-based second opinion and documentation system. *Journal Artificial Intelligence in Medicine, 24*(3), 205–216. doi:10.1016/S0933-3657(01)00104-X

Clement, J., & McDonald. (1996). Medical heuristics: The silent adjudicators of clinical practice. *Annals of Internal Medicine, 124,* 56–62.

Golder, S., & Huberman, B. A. (2006). Usage patterns of collaborative tagging systems. *Journal of Information Science, 32*(2), 198–208. doi:10.1177/0165551506062337

Gupta, U. G., & Biegel, J. (1990). A rule–based intelligent test case generator. In *Proceedings of AAAI–90 Workshop on Knowledge–Based System Verification, Validation and Testing.* AAAI Press.

Hoernlein, A., Ifland, M., Kluegl, P., & Puppe, F. (2009). CaseTrain: Design and evaluation of a case-based training-system and its comprehensive application in university (Konzeption und Evaluation eines fallbasierten Trainingssystems im universitätsweiten Einsatz (CaseTrain)). *GMS Medizinische Informatik, Biometrie und Epidemiologie, 5*(1).

Huettig, M., Buscher, G., Menzel, T., Scheppach, W., Puppe, F., & Buscher, H. P. (2004). A diagnostic expert system for structured reports, quality assessment, and training of residents in sonography. *Medizinische Klinik, 99*(3), 117–122. doi:10.1007/s00063-004-1020-y

Kerkri, E. M., Quantin, C., Allaert, F. A., Cottin, Y., Charve, P., Jouanot, F., & Yetongnon, K. M. (2001). An approach for integrating heterogeneous information sources in a medical data warehouse. *Journal of Medical Systems, 25*(3), 167–176. doi:10.1023/A:1010728915998

Kimball, R., & Ross, M. (2002). *The data warehouse toolkit: The complete guide to dimensional modeling.* New York, NY: John Wiley & Sons, Inc.

Kluegl, P., Atzmueller, M., & Puppe, F. (2009). TextMarker: A tool for rule-based information extraction. In *Proceedings of the Biennial GSCL Conference 2009, 2nd UIMA@GSCL Workshop,* (pp. 233-240). Gunter Narr Verlag.

Knauf, R., Gonzalez, A. J., & Abel, T. (2002). A framework for validation of rule-based systems. *IEEE Transactions on Systems, Man, and Cybernetics. Part B, Cybernetics, 32*(3), 281–295. doi:10.1109/TSMCB.2002.999805

Ogren, P. V., Wetzler, P. G., & Bethard, S. (2008). *ClearTK: A UIMA toolkit for statistical natural language processing.* In UIMA for NLP workshop at Language Resources and Evaluation Conference (LREC).

Preece, A. (1998). Building the right system right. In *Proceedings KAW'98, 11th Workshop on Knowledge Acquisition, Modeling and Management.*

Puppe, F. (1998). Knowledge reuse among diagnostic problem-solving methods in the shell-kit D3. *International Journal of Human-Computer Studies, 49,* 627–649. doi:10.1006/ijhc.1998.0221

Puppe, F., Atzmueller, M., Buscher, G., Huettig, M., Lührs, H., & Buscher, H. P. (2008). Application and evaluation of a medical knowledge-system in sonography (SonoConsult). In *Proceedings 18th European Conference on Artificial Intelligence,* (pp. 683–687). Patras, Greece.

Reutelshoefer, J., Haupt, F., Lemmerich, F., & Baumeister, J. (2009). *An extensible semantic wiki architecture.* In SemWiki'09: 4th Workshop on Semantic Wikis.

Wrobel, S. (1997). An algorithm for multi-relational discovery of subgroups. In *Proceedings of 1st European Symposium on Principles of Data Mining and Knowledge Discovery,* (pp. 78–87). Berlin, Germany: Springer.

ADDITIONAL READING

In the following, we briefly discuss related approaches and additional material that discusses selected topics in greater depths.

Prather et al. (1997) present a conceptual approach for knowledge discovery in clinical data warehouses, and discuss the implications. For general questions related to data mining, Han & Kamber (2008) provide a comprehensive overview on the topic. Atzmueller (2007) presents an extensive introduction and discussion of knowledge-intensive subgroup mining with comprehensive tools and techniques. Furthermore, the VIKAMINE system is described with several case studies, in medical and technical domains. Klösgen (1996) provides a statistical view on subgroup mining (or subgroup discovery) as one of the first articles on this topic. Further information on subgroup discovery can be found, for example, in Lavrac et al. (2004) and Atzmueller, Puppe & Buscher (2005) also present a comprehensive case study of applying background knowledge for subgroup discovery and the different knowledge elements and types.

A general reference for including data validation and quality issues in data mining is given by Hipp et al. (2001). Luebbers, Grimme & Jarke describe a systematic approach for developing such tools. Dasu et al. (2002) describe a more user-oriented interactive approach for mining structural dependencies and applying these for improving data quality. Pipino, Lee & Wang (2002) consider the development of usable data quality metrics for data quality assessment.

Atzmueller & Nalepa (2009) describe an approach for textual subgroup mining, i.e., text mining using subgroup discovery, and discuss its application for the initial learning of knowledge bases.

Ferucci & Lally (2004) describe the UIMA software, i.e., the Unstructured Information Management Architecture, for applications in natural language and text mining systems: UIMA components can also be embedded in the TEXT-MARKER system providing modular extension capabilities. Concerning the information extraction techniques, Schuhmann et al. (2007) provide an expectation-driven approach for information extraction related to the TEXTMARKER system. Furthermore, Kluegl, Atzmueller & Puppe (2009) describe a framework for Meta-Level Information Extraction providing a comprehensive evaluation on a medical case study. The approach shows good performance compared to automatic methods and is especially suitable for difficult domains, e.g., for the medical domain. As described in Atzmueller & Roth-Berghofer (2010) there are several continuous explanation dimensions in the context of data/text mining and analysis that can be utilized for improving the explanation capabilities. Foundational issues can be found in Roth-Berghofer & Cassens (2005) for case-based reasoning.

Brickley & Miles (2005) present the SKOS core format, i.e., the Simple Knowledge Organization system that can also be utilized for the KNOWTA system.

Hammond et al. (2005) provide a comprehensive overview on social bookmarking tools. For tag recommendations, Jaeschke et al. (2007) give a comprehensive overview on available approaches. A discussion of Folksonomies can be found, e.g., in Guy & Tonkin (2006) or Specia & Motta (2007). Nalepa (2010) discusses several aspects of semantic wiki based systems, and provides an overview on collective knowledge engineering in this context.

Atzmueller, M. (2007). Knowledge-intensive subgroup mining. *Diski, 307.*

Atzmueller, M., & Nalepa, G. J. (2009). A textual subgroup mining approach for rapid ARD+ model capture. In *Proceedings of 22nd International Florida Artificial Intelligence Research Society Conference*, (pp. 414–419). AAAI Press

Atzmueller, M., Puppe, F., & Buscher, H.-P. (2005). Exploiting background knowledge for knowledge-intensive subgroup discovery. In *Proceedings of 19th International Joint Conference on Artificial Intelligence*, (pp. 647–652). Edinburgh, Scotland.

Atzmueller, M., & Roth-Berghofer, T. (2010). *Ready for the MACE? The mining and analysis continuum of explaining uncovered*. In AI-2010: 30th SGAI International Conference on Artificial Intelligence, Cambridge, UK.

Brickley, D., & Miles, A. (2005). *SKOS core vocabulary specification 2005-11-02*. W3C working draft. Retrieved from http://www.w3.org /TR/swbp-skos-core-spec

Dasu, T., Johnson, T., Muthukrishnan, S., & Shkapenyuk, V. (2002). Mining database structure; or, How to build a data quality browser. In *Proceedings of the 2002 ACM SIGMOD International Conference on Management of Data* (SIGMOD '02), (pp. 240-251). New York, NY: ACM.

Ferrucci, D., & Lally, A. (2004). UIMA: An architectural approach to unstructured information processing in the corporate research environment. *Natural Language Engineering, 10*(3-4), 327–348. doi:10.1017/S1351324904003523

Guy, M., & Tonkin, E. (2006). Folksonomies: Tidying up tags? *D-Lib Magazine, 12*(1).

Hammond, T., Hannay, T., Lund, B., & Scott, J. (2005). Social bookmarking tools (I) - A general review. *D-Lib Magazine, 11*(4). doi:10.1045/april2005-hammond

Han, J., & Kamber, M. (2006). *Data mining: Concepts and techniques* (2nd ed.). San Francisco, CA: Morgan Kaufmann.

Hipp, J., Güntzer, U., & Grimmer, U. (2001). Data quality mining – Making a virtue of necessity. In *6th ACM SIGMOD Workshop on Research Issues in Data Mining and Knowledge Discovery (DMKD 2001)*, (pp. 52–57). Santa Barbara, California.

Jäschke, R., Marinho, L. B., Hotho, A., Schmidt-Thieme, L., & Stumme, G. (2007). Tag recommendations in folksonomies. In *Proceedings of PKDD '07, LNCS 4702*, (pp. 506–514). Berlin, Germany: Springer Verlag.

Klösgen, W. (1996). Explora: A multipattern and multistrategy discovery assistant. In U. M. Fayyad, G. Piatetsky- Shapiro, P. Smyth, & R. Uthurusamy (Eds.), *Advances in knowledge discovery and data mining* (pp. 249–271). AAAI Press.

Kluegl, P., Atzmueller, M., & Puppe, F. (2009). Meta-level information extraction. In *Proceedings of 32nd Annual Conference on Artificial Intelligence*, Springer, Berlin, 2009

Lavrac, N., Kavsek, B., Flach, P., & Todorovski, L. (2004). Subgroup discovery with CN2-SD. *Journal of Machine Learning Research, 5*, 153–188.

Luebbers, D., Grimmer, U., & Jarke, M. (2003). Systematic development of data mining-based data quality tools. In *International Conference on Very Large Data Bases (VLDB)*. Orlando, Florida. Morgan Kaufman.

Nalepa, G. (2010). Collective knowledge engineering with semantic wikis. *Journal of Universal Computer Science, 16*(7), 1006–1023.

Pipino, L., Lee, Y., & Wang, R. (2002). Data quality assessment. *Communications of the ACM, 45*(4), 211–218. doi:10.1145/505248.506010

Prather, J., David, C., Lobach, F., Goodwin, L. K., Hales, J. W., Hage, M. L., & Hammond, W. E. (1997). Medical data mining: Knowledge discovery in a clinical data warehouse (pp. 101.-105). In *Proceedings of AMIA Annual Fall Symposium (AIMA-1997)*.

Roth-Berghofer, T., & Cassens, J. (2005). Mapping goals and kinds of explanations to the knowledge containers of case-based reasoning systems. In H. Munoz-Avila & F. Ricci (Eds.), *Case-Based Reasoning Research and Development, 6th International Conference on Case-Based Reasoning, ICCBR 2005*, (pp. 451-464). Heidelberg, Germany: Springer

Schuhmann, M., Puppe, F., Buscher, H.-P., & Klügl, P. (2007). Expectation-driven information extraction in incomplete sentences. In *Proceedings of LWA, 2007*, 237–243.

Specia, L., & Motta, E. (2007). Integrating folksonomies with the Semantic Web. In *ESCW '07, Proceedings of the 4th European Conference on The Semantic Web: Research and Applications* (pp. 624-639). Berlin, Germany: Springer.

KEY TERMS AND DEFINITIONS

Data Mining: The term data mining is either used as a synonym for the knowledge discovery process as a whole, or as the core step of this process, that is, employing data mining methods for the modeling step for obtaining descriptive patterns or predictive models.

Data Validation: In the data mining context, data validation describes the process for assessing whether input and/or output data conform to the expected (correct) data, or benchmark data, if available.

Information Extraction: The term information extraction describes methods and techniques that aim at extracting structured information (data) from unstructured and/or semi-structured documents that are available in electronic form.

Knowledge Capture: Aims at capturing explicit or implicit knowledge into formal knowledge by various methods; can include incremental elements for knowledge elicitation and refinement.

Pattern Mining: Aims at the discovery of interesting patterns in the data according to a given quality measure. Pattern mining can be applied both for descriptive and predictive approaches.

Social Tagging: A form of user-driven indexing enabled by social software, in which tags are assigned freely to resources.

Subgroup Mining: As a method for local pattern detection, subgroup mining or subgroup discovery aims to detect statistically interesting subgroups with respect to a certain property of interest, for example, comparing shares or means of a specific target variable in a subgroup and the general database.

Chapter 10
Hidden Markov Models for Context–Aware Tag Query Prediction in Folksonomies

Chiraz Trabelsi
University Tunis El-Manar, Tunisia

Bilel Moulahi
University Tunis El-Manar, Tunisia

Sadok Ben Yahia
University Tunis El-Manar, Tunisia

ABSTRACT

Recently, social bookmarking systems have received surging attention in academic and industrial communities. In fact, social bookmarking systems share with the Semantic Web vision the idea of facilitating the collaborative organization and sharing of knowledge on the web. The reason for the apparent success of the upcoming tools for resource sharing (social bookmarking systems, photo sharing systems, etc.) lies mainly in the fact that no specific skills are needed for publishing and editing, and an immediate benefit is yielded to each individual user, e.g., organizing one's bookmarks in a browser-independent, persistent fashion, without too much overhead. As these systems grow larger, however, the users address the need of enhanced search facilities. Today, full-text search is supported, but the results are usually simply listed decreasingly by their upload date. The challenging research issue is, therefore, the development of a suitable prediction framework to support users in effectively retrieving the resources matching their real search intents. The primary focus of this chapter is to propose a new, context aware tag query prediction approach. Specifically, the authors adopted Hidden Markov Models and formal concept analysis to predict users' search intentions based on a real folksonomy. Carried out experiments emphasize the relevance of the proposal and open many issues.

DOI: 10.4018/978-1-4666-0894-8.ch010

INTRODUCTION

Complementing the Semantic Web effort, a new breed of so-called Web2.0 applications recently emerged on the Web. Indeed, social bookmarking systems, such as *e.g., Del.icio.us*[1], *Bibsonomy*[2] or *Flickr*[3] have become the predominant form of content categorization of the Web2.0 age. The main thrust of these Web2.0 systems is their easy use that relies on simple, straightforward structures (folksonomies) by allowing their users to label diverse resources with freely chosen keywords *aka* tags. Social bookmarking systems share with the Semantic Web vision, the idea of facilitating the collaborative organization and sharing of knowledge on the web.

However, a main difference lies in the fundamentally opposite approach: the Semantic Web aims at a formal knowledge representation in form of ontologies (written in XML, RDF, or OWL), whereas social bookmark tools follow a grass-root approach: there are no limitations on the kind of tags users may select. In contrast to ontologies (Gruber, 1993), the resulting structures are called folksonomies, that is, *"taxonomies"* created by the *"folk."*

Considered as a tripartite hyper-graph (Mika, 2005) of tags, users and resources, the new data of folksonomy systems provides a rich resource for data analysis, information retrieval, and knowledge discovery applications. In fact, the success of folksonomies originated from members' ability to centrally collect and manage content collections on the web, overcoming local storage policies. Users of folksonomies are granted ubiquitous access to their collections of photos, web sites, or publications regardless their current location or the currently used device. These personal advantages came in conjunction with a social component. This derives from the fact that most folksonomies allow the sharing of content with other users, the discovery of content other users considered interesting, or the communication with other users through various channels.

Hence, aggregating the interests of up to millions of users, folksonomies reflect the dynamics of the underlying domains. High traffic websites will, then, likely reappear among the popular resources in a community such like *Del.icio.us* (Heymann *et al.*, 2008). Furthermore, external trends, *e.g.*, the advent of a new web site or a new influential blog entry, were found to reappear in folksonomies almost without any delay (Heymann *et al.*, 2008). Combining these characteristics with the existence of user-generated annotations, folksonomies have become an invaluable source for information retrieval (IR) (Pan *et al.*, 2009). These benefits come at a low cost, since all information is centrally available, and no continuous, distributed crawling process as for web indexing is required. Indeed, one of the main services provided by social tagging systems is searching. Searching occurs when the user enters a tag as a query and a, ranked by relevance, list of related resources are yielded to the user. Even though collaborative tagging applications have many benefits, they also present some thriving challenges for Information Retrieval (IR). Actually, the core of many search engines is the ranking algorithm. However, the most currently used ranking algorithms are not straightforwardly adaptable to folksonomies. Furthermore, these traditional tools for web information retrieval constitute a hindrance, since they do not consider neither social nor behavioral facts into account in the retrieval task of resources nor help understanding user's information needs.

In addition, one significant problem arising from such free-formedness stands in the tag ambiguity: tags that have several meanings, *e.g., "Java"* as coffee or a programming language or an island in Indonesia. Moreover, folksonomy tags are unstructured as assigned tags to a given resource are simply enumerated in a list and finally, no special organization or categorization of the tags is made (by the folksonomy site). As per Golder and Huberman (2005), the main problems of social tagging systems include ambiguity, lack of synonymy and discrepancies in granularity. Specifically, when a user tries to retrieve information using a certain tag, *e.g.*, *"mackintosh,"* he can receive restrictive results since the system retrieves resources tagged with that particular tag regardless of the eventual vocabulary derivations or synonyms of this later, *e.g.*, *"mac,"* *"macintosh"* or *"mack."* Hence, if it is possible to clean such tags and render somewhat more standardized, this could be helpful to improve the efficiency of folksonomies from an information retrieval point of view.

Therefore, as a folksonomy pre-processing step, we firstly present, in this chapter, a methodology, inspired from a previous work (Trabelsi, Ben Jrad, & Ben Yahia, 2010), for tackling tag vocabulary derivations, morphological similarity and meaning similarity problems. Furthermore, assuming that capturing the tag query context given by the users who have used the tag query as well as the resources being retrieved may help understanding the user's information need, thus, a context-aware approach to resource recommendation and tag query suggestion may improve users' search experience substantially. However, the existing methods (Fonseca et *al.*, 2005) for web search engine, which may suggest good queries in some cases, are not context-aware since they do not consider the preceding queries as context in query suggestion.

Challenging research issue is then the development of suitable framework to support folksonomy users in effectively retrieving the resources matching their real search intents.

Example 1: *(SEARCH INTENT AND CONTEXT)* Suppose that a user submits a query *"java,"* then it seems to be hard to determine the user's search intent, *i.e.*, whether the user is interested in the java island, java programming language, or the java song.

Hence, without looking at the context of search, the existing methods often suggest many queries for various possible intents, and thus may have a low accuracy in query suggestion. Therefore, if we find that a community of users has submitted a query *"beautiful island"* before *"java,"* then

it is very likely that the user is interested in the *"java island."* Moreover, we can predict, the most-probable next queries of the current user. Therefore, the query context which consists of the recent queries issued by a community of users, sharing the same interest for a particular topic as the current user, can help to better understand the user's search intent and enable us to make more accurate queries suggestions.

Hence, in this chapter, we also introduce a novel context-aware tag query prediction model to address two major challenges facing information retrieval in folksonomies: *(i)* Discovering and modeling users' search intents in a folksonomy; and *(ii)* Predicting users' next queries by suggesting alternatives queries and recommending a set of resources that fulfills users' information needs concisely and accurately.

Therefore, to tackle the challenging task, we firstly propose, to define a user' search intent as a subset of folksonomy users who implicitly agree (on subset of resources) on a common conceptualization. From a data mining perspective, the discovery of shared conceptualizations opens a new research field which may prove interesting also outside the folksonomy domain: *"Closed itemset mining in triadic data,"* which is located on the confluence of the research areas of *Association Rule Mining and Formal Concept Analysis* (Jaschke et *al.*, 2008). Indeed, in folksonomies, the usage of tags of users with similar interests tends to converge to a shared vocabulary. To this end, we use an algorithm, called Trias, to unveil these users' search intents that are hidden in a folksonomy. On the other hand, as well recognized by many previous studies, a user often raises multiple queries and conducts multiple rounds of interaction with a search engine to fulfill an information need. For instance, a user u plans to buy a computer; he may decompose his general search task, comparing various computers, into several specification sub-tasks, such as searching the Dell's computers. In each sub-task, u may bear particular search intent in mind and formulate a query q to describe the intent. Furthers, u may selectively choose some related resources to consult. Actually, a Hidden Markov Models (HMM for short) naturally describe the search process. Hence, we propose to model each search intent as a state of the HMM, and consider the query and accessed resources as observations generated by the state. The whole search process can be then modeled as a sequence of (auto)-transitions between states.

Therefore, our intention is to discover hidden users' search intents as subsets of folksonomy users who implicitly agree (on subsets of resources) on a common conceptualization. Indeed, in folksonomies, the usage of tags of users with similar interests tends to converge to a shared vocabulary. To this end, we use an algorithm, called Trias, to unveil these shared conceptualizations that are hidden in a folksonomy.

The remainder of the chapter is organized as follows. Section 1 thoroughly scrutinizes the related work. We describe later in Section 3 our probabilistic approach for users' search intents prediction composed of two major steps, namely, the model learning step and Matching & prediction step. We dedicate Section 4 for underpinning, through an illustrative example based on a sample taken from a real dataset, the guidelines of our approach. The experimental study of our approach is illustrated in Section 5. Finally, we conclude this chapter and sketches avenues for future work.

1. SCRUTINY OF THE RELATED WORK

Recent years witnessed an overwhelming number of publications on different aspects of folksonomies. The respective publications of Golder and Huberman (2006) constituted so far a cornerstone in the study of the structure as well as the dynamics of collaborative tagging systems and advocated modeling them formally as s tripartite hypergraphs (Mika, 2005).

Folksonomies have recently been studied for their potential with respect to information retrieval. The most complete analysis of the *Del.icio.us* bookmarking system is provided by Heymann et *al.,* (2008). In this respect, the authors investigated the potential benefits of collaborative bookmarking for web search. Among other results, the authors showed that there exists a reasonably high overlap between search query terms and tags found in the *Del.icio.us* system. Furthermore, they report that social bookmarking systems reflect changes within the underlying web structure, such as newly appearing or recently modified web pages, earlier than search engines or web directory services, such as the Open Directory Project. The authors concluded that social bookmarking services can provide additional information about items not available in content-based settings.

The distributional similarity between query terms and tags is also reported by Carman et *al.*, (2009). The authors further propose the use of tags for smoothing document content models in order to improve document retrieval performance. Krause et *al.*, (2008), compared the distributions of *Del.icio.us* tags and search terms and discover power-laws in both cases. They also found that tag-based item rankings and query results show high correlations in some settings. This correlation is especially high for topics related to information technology, which are well covered by *Del.icio.us*. This lets the authors assume that *Del.icio.us* users rely on search engines to find interesting content, which in turn is reflected in the bookmarked resources. These evaluations are complemented by the work of Bischoff et *al.*, (2008). In accordance with our own observations, the authors pointed out that some tags are more valuable for search than others, more personal tags. However, Bischof et *al.*, (2008), assumed that this concerns only a small percentage of overall tags. Instead, our own studies show that the majority of tags serve individual tasks. This heterogeneity may be ignored in cases where cumulative effects create stable item vocabularies. However, these peculiarities are of crucial importance for user-centric retrieval scenarios. Furthermore, we believe that the information about who assigned which tag will help to design better retrieval models.

Other research studies have attempted to exploit folksonomy data structure in order to recommend resources, tags or even other users. Hence, Hotho et *al.*, (2006) proposed an adaptation of link analysis to the folksonomy data structure for resource recommendation. This technique was baptized FolkRank, since it computes a PageRank (Brin & Page, 1998) vector from the tripartite graph. In (Jaschke et *al.*, 2007), the authors made use of the FolkRank for tag recommendation.

In (Lipczak, 2008), the authors use the title of a resource, the posts of a resource and the user's vocabulary to recommend tags. The obtained results showed that the retrieved tags from the own user's vocabulary outperform recommendations driven by resource information. However, it is worth of mention that experiments were carried out on a very special dataset; called *Bibsonomy*, *i.e.*, a Folksonomy focused on scientific publications, and thus might not be applicable on other datasets. In the context of user's search intents, a wealthy number of works highlighted that such intents are in snugness connection of the context of the submitted queries. Hence for identifying groups of related tags, approaches using clustering or statistical similarity metrics techniques for the organization of related tags into clusters are widely used. In (Mika, 2005), the author use co-occurrence information to build graphs relating tags with users and tags with resources, and applies techniques of network analysis to discover sets of clusters of semantically related tags. Later, Begelman et *al.*, (2006) organize the tag space as an undirected graph, representing co-occurring tags as vertices, weighting the edges between them according to their co-occurrence frequency, and applying a spectral clustering algorithm to refine the resulting groups. However, in such approaches, correlation between tags, users and resources are often lost. Indeed, a semantically relation between

tags is usually discovered if they had been assigned by users with similar interests. Moreover, related resources are usually tagged many times by semantically related tags and finally users may have similar interests if they share many resources in their assignments.

Similarly, in our proposed approach, we make use of the semantic relatedness embodied in the different frequencies of co-occurrences among users, resources and tags in the folksonomy. However, instead of using probabilistic models or network analysis techniques for grouping related tags, we mine frequent triadic concepts (Jaschke, Hotho, Schmitz, Ganter, & Stumme, 2008). Indeed, the triadic concept structure describes three types of sets: *(i)* the set T of related tags; *(ii)* the set U of the associated users, *i.e.*, users whose have tagged by T and; *(iii)* the set of related resources, *i.e.*, which were assigned with *T* by users *U*. Hence, triadic concepts allow grouping semantically related tags taking into account the Users' tagging behavior in a folksonomy. In fact, in (Jaschke et *al.*, 2008) and (Jaschke et *al.*, 2006), the authors have considered a folksonomy as a triadic context and proposed an algorithm called Trias to get out implicit shared conceptualizations formally sketched by triadic concepts In the following, we introduce a novel approach for predicting users' search intents in a folksonomy with the following salient features:

- **Folksonomy Pre-Processing:** Only few attentions were paid to tackling tag synonyms or tag ambiguity problems within folksonomy context. Thus, we adopted a pre-processing methodology, inspired from a previous work (Trabelsi et *al.*, 2010), where processed tags are not discarded after each filtering stage, but added to a set of tagsets delineated by cleaned ones, *i.e.*, representative tags.

- **Use of the semantic relatedness embodied in the different frequencies of co-occurrences among users, resources and tags in the folksonomy**: instead of using probabilistic models or network analysis techniques for grouping related tags, we mine frequent triadic concepts (Jaschke et al., 2008). Indeed, the triadic concept structure describes three types of sets: *(i)* the set *T* of related tags; *(ii)* the set *U* of the associated users, *i.e.*, users whose have tagged by *T* and; *(iii)* the set of related resources, *i.e.*, which were assigned with *T* by users *U*. Hence, triadic concepts allow grouping semantically related tags taking into account the Users' tagging behavior in a folksonomy

- **A Hidden Markov Model (HMM) for learning and then predicting users' search intents in a folksonomy**: On the contrary of the surveyed approaches which split the 3-dimensional space into 2-dimensional pair relations {*user, item*}, {*user, tag*} and {*tag, item*} missing by the way a part of the total interaction between the three dimensions, we introduce a unified framework to concurrently model the three dimensions handled by a HMM (Rabiner, 1989).

2. FOLKSONOMY PRE-PROCESSING

Most existing approaches dedicated to folksonomy searching, handle in a brute force manner the contained tags and the underlying folksonomy network. This intuitive approach neglects many fundamental properties of tags. Indeed, tagging information can be noisy and inconsistent (Mathes, 2004). Indeed, ambiguity is a well known problem in information retrieval and has been identified as a hindrance in folksonomies search (Mathes, 2004). Thus, in (Lee et al., 2009), WordNet has been used to identify ambiguous tags and disambiguate them by using synonyms. Pan et al., (2009) have proposed to expand folksonomy with ontologies to solve the ambiguity in tagging systems. Moreover, Specia and Motta (2007) have

proposed a pre-processing strategy for cleaning and filtering tags to make explicit the semantics behind the tag in social tagging systems. Similarly, in (Szomszor, Alani, OHara, & Shadbolt, 2008), a tag filtering architecture has been proposed to clean and reduce generated tag-clouds. Since, whenever manual tags are introduced with a non-controlled tagging mechanism, people often make grammatical mistakes (*e.g.* "*webdesgn*" instead of "*webdesign*"), tag concepts indistinctly in singular, plural or derived forms ("*start*," "*starts*," "*starting*"). Sometimes, adjectives, adverbs, prepositions or pronouns are added to the main concept of the tag ("*beautiful car*," "*to read*"), or use synonyms and acronyms that could be converted into a single tag ("*Web*" and "*WWW*," "*hk*" and "*hong kong*"). As a result, important correlations between resources and users are sometimes lost simply because of the syntactic mismatches in the tags they have used. Hence, to tackle these fundamental properties of tags which highly affect folksonomy searching, we adopted a pre-processing methodology inspired from a previous work (Trabelsi et al., 2010) that cleans and filters user generated tag-clouds.

At first, let us start by presenting a simplified definition of a folksonomy (Hotho, Jaschke, Schmitz, & Stumme, 2006) that will be of use throughout the paper:

Definition 1 *(FOLKSONOMY)* A folksonomy is a set of tuples $F = (ID, T, RS, G)$, where $G \subseteq ID \times RS \times T$ denoting a ternary relation and each $g \subseteq G$ can be represented as a triple: $g = \{(id, rs, t) \mid id \in ID, rs \in RS, t \in T\}$ which describes the assignment of the tag *t* by the user *id* to the resource *rs*.

The folksonomy pre-processing step is a sequential execution where the input stands in the set of tags T retrieved from the folksonomy. The output from one pre-processing step is used as input to the next one. The resulting structure of the whole pre-processing stage is referred as a representative folksonomy where the set of tags *T*

Figure 1. The framework of the approach

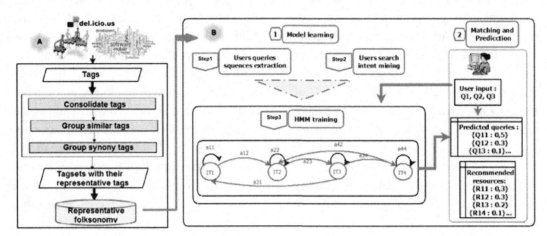

is replaced by the set of the representative tags Q. Hence, in order to correctly perform this step, we have considered three external resources:

1. **WordNet[4]:** A lexical database and thesaurus that group English words into sets of cognitive synonyms called *synsets*, providing definitions of terms, and modeling various semantic relations between concepts: synonym, hypernym, hyponym, among others.
2. **Wikipedia[5]:** A multilingual, open-access, free-content encyclopedia on the Internet. Wikipedia contains collaboratively generated categories that classify and relate entries, and also supports term disambiguation and dereferencing of acronyms.
3. **Google "*did you mean*" mechanism[6]:** When a searched term is entered, the Google engine checks whether more relevant search results are found with an alternative spelling. Since Google's spell check is based on occurrences of all words on the Internet, it is able to suggest common spellings for proper nouns that would not appear in a standard dictionary.

As it will be explained below, we have additionally used a number of software components such as syntactic filters and semantic filters. Deck *A* in Figure 1 provides a visual representation of

the pre-processing process where a set of tags is generated from a folksonomy tags and transformed into a set *tagsets*. Each step in the pre-processing deck corresponds to a step outlined below.

Step 1: Consolidate Tags

The goal of this step is to clean and enrich the user's generated tag. Hence, for each tag, different filtering stages are performed to retrieve a related set of cleaned and enriched tags. However, contrarily to both (Specia & Motta, 2007) and (Szomszor et al., 2008), a selected tag t is not discarded after each stage but added to a set of *tagsets* called *Setagset*, where each *tagset* contains the user's tag t and *SNewtags*, *i.e.*, the set of new tags generated in each stage. Hence, we have: *Setagset* = {*SNewtags*}.

Moreover, in order to facilitate the folksonomy data analysis and integration, the vocabularies used in the folksonomy are shaped into following four categories (Lin et al., 2009):

- **Standard tags**: Which can be found in traditional dictionaries,
- **Compound tags**: A non-standard expression, *e.g.*, "*web design*,"

- **Jargon tags**: Another non-standard expression frequently used to quickly express user's ideas, *e.g.*, "*hk*" and "*folksonomy*,"
- **Other nonsense tags**: Such as misspelling tags, *e.g.*, "*desgn*."

1. **Tag transformation:** The selected tag t_i is set to the lower case and special characters, such as accents, dieresis and caret symbol, are converted to their base form. For example, the tag "*Zürich*" is converted to "*Zurich*." Additionally, common stop-words, such as pronouns, articles, prepositions and conjunctions are discarded. The transformed tag t_j is added to the set of *SNewtags*. Hence, the set *Setagset* is updated as follows:

   Example 2: Let us consider that The selected tag t_i correspond to the tag "*to web-disïgn*" then *Setagset* will contain the set {*to webdesïgn*, {*webdesign*}}.

2. **Syntactic filtering:** It aims to check whether the transformed tag t_j, *e.g.*, "*webde-sign*," is a standard one, *i.e.*, it has an exact matching with an entry in WordNet. In this case, we return back to the stage *(1)* and select the next tag from *T*. Otherwise, we skip to the next step, *e.g.*, the tag "*webdesign*" has not an entry in WordNet.

3. **Wikipedia correlation:** In order to provide an agreed representation of t_j, we check whether this tag is a jargon one. In such case, we correlate it to its appropriate Wikipedia entry. For example, when searching the tag "*webdesign*" in Wikipedia, the entry with the title "*web design*" is retrieved. Hence, this title is added to the set *SNewtags* and the next tag from *T* is selected. For instance, by considering the *Example 2*, *Setagset* will contain {*to webdesïgn*, {*webdesign*, *web design*}}. The rationale behind the use of Wikipedia to agree on folksonomy tags is that Wikipedia constitutes a community-driven knowledge base, much like folksonomies are, so that it rapidly adapts to accommodate new terminology.

4. **Tag correction**: If the transformed tag is not a standard tag or a jargon one, *i.e.*, nonsense tag, *e.g.*, "*honkong*," we consider possible misspellings and/or compound nouns. Hence, inspired from the work of Specia and Motta (2007) to solve these problems, we make use of Google which suggests a common spelling, *e.g.*, for the tag "*honkong*," Google suggests "*hong kong*." Therefore, the suggested term is added to the set *SNewtags* and the next tag from *T* is selected. Note that the consolidate tags step comes to end after handling all the tags of *T*.

Step 2: Group Similar Tags

Another issue to be considered during the tag's pre-processing step is that users often use morphologically similar terms to refer to the same idea. Hence, in this step we are interested in discovering the set of similar *tagsets* among the previously retrieved set of *tagsets*, *i.e.*, *Setagset*. Indeed, one very common example of this is the no discrepancy between singular and plural terms, such as "*cloths*," and other morphological deviations, *e.g.*, "*clothing*." In this step, we use a stemming algorithm provided by Lucene[7], which reduces morphologically similar tags, *e.g.*, "*clothing*" and "*cloths*" are reduced to the root tag "*cloth*." Hence, for each set of similar *tagsets*, the shortest term found in WordNet is used as the representative tag, *i.e.*, "*cloth*."

Step 3: Group Synonym Tags

The goal of this step is to handle the problem of synonymy control of representative tags, previously obtained. For this purpose, we use Wikipedia repository as knowledge base to detect synonym tags. In fact, the basic unit of information in Wikipedia is the article where each article describes a single concept. Moreover, there is a single article for each concept (Medelyan et *al.*, 2009). Thus, our aim is to associate each representative tag to a particular article. More precisely, we want to shrink the folksonomy's vocabulary *T* by merging representative tags with a very similar meaning, *i.e.*, which are described by a same article, into a single representative tag. For this end, the redirect and disambiguation pages are used. For instance, let us consider that tags[8] t_1, $t_2 \in T$, t_1 = *textile* and t_2 = *cloth* are present. They both refer to the same semantic concept of textile in Wikipedia.

Then we would create a *synset*[9] by merging the *tagsets* represented by t_1 and t_2.

Example 3: Let us consider two sets of similar *tagsets* discovered in the previous step:

- {*cloth*, {*cloeth;*, *cloeth*}}
- {*textile*, {*textil*}}

Note that the first element of both sets, respectively "*cloth*" and "*textile*," are representative tags. Thus, by performing the group synonym tags step, we obtain the *synset s* = {*textile*, {*cloeth;*, *cloeth*, *textil*}} where the two representative tags, "*cloth*" and "*textile*," are replaced by the same referenced concept in Wikipedia, *i.e.*, the concept textile. We will refer to the resulting folksonomy as the representative folksonomy.

3. HIDDEN MARKOV MODELS FOR CONTEXT-AWARE TAG QUERY PREDICTION IN FOLKSONOMIES

As we previously mentioned, predicting user search intent is a compelling issue for effectively retrieving resources that fulfills user information need concisely and accurately.

Thus, the most salient features of our approach are as follows: *(i)* It is a completely unsupervised one during the folksonomy analysis and user's queries sequences extraction; *(ii)* It is a domain independent solution, since no domain assumptions are formulated and no predefined knowledge is needed and; *(iii)* It performs a triadic concept analysis to mine users' search intents. The triadic concepts can be used as an access structure for providing important hidden correlations between tags, resources and users. The general approach, as depicted in Figure 1, consists of two main steps: Model Learning and User search Intent Prediction.

a.   The Model-Learning Step

The goal of this step is to learn users' search behavior by identifying users' search intents behind queries. However, recent works (Fonseca et *al.*, 2005; Baeza-Yates & Tiberi, 2007) have argued that mining search engine log data for query recommendation enjoy many advantages such as providing rich user behavior information; they are not adaptable for folksonomy based systems, since the availability of search log is limited due to the privacy concern. Indeed, in the search log approach, the researchers make an assumption that the user clicks reflect their relevance judgment. Thus they can collect a lot of experiment data without any extra user efforts. As for conducting our approach, we make use of the duality hypothesis of search and tagging, two important behaviors of web users.

DUALITY HYPOTHESIS: The users bookmarking and tagging actions reflect their personal relevance judgment.

For example, if a user assigned the tag "*java*" to the Apache Lucene homepage (http://lucene.apache.org) we assume that the user will consider this web page as relevant if he issues "*java*" as a query.

The duality hypothesis immediately suggests that the query log data and the tagging data can be equally valuable for inferring a user's information preferences, thus improving many information management tasks such as search and information recommendation. Although query log data has so far proven extremely useful for learning user behavior and improving search engine accuracy, the availability of search log data is unfortunately limited because of serious privacy concerns. Fortunately, tag data by nature is all publicly available, and the amount of data is increasing rapidly. Thus the duality hypothesis and related probabilistic models potentially open up a highly promising new direction for using tagging data to approximate query log data to analyze user behavior and improve search accuracy (Begelman et al., 2006; Bischoff et al., 2008; Krause et al., 2008). The duality hypothesis has already been exploited in some recent work where tagging data has been exploited to improve retrieval accuracy. In (Heymann et al., 2008), the authors uses empirical statistics to shows that tagging data can be used to enhance search. But our formulation of the duality hypothesis explicitly reveals a more fundamental connection between search and tagging, and its potential impact goes far beyond these previous studies as will be discussed later.

Therefore, taking into account the folksonomy pre-processing stage, we define the resulting folksonomy as following:

Definition 2. (REPRESENTATIVE FOLKSON-OMY)

A representative folksonomy is a set of tuples $F_\nabla = (ID, Q, RS, G)$, where:

- *ID, Q, RS* respectively define, all user *IDs*, the submitted queries and the accessed resources,
- $G \subseteq ID \times Q \times RS$ represents a triadic relation, where each $g \subseteq G$ can be represented by a triplet: $g = \{(id, q, rs) \mid id \in ID, q \in Q, rs \in RS\}$. Roughly speaking, a user identified by *id*, retrieved the resource *rs* queried by the query *q*.

Note that, submitted queries Q, correspond actually to representative tags obtained after the folksonomy pre-processing step.

Hence, regarded as a tripartite graph of users identifiers, submitted queries and accessed resources, the folksonomy can be, formally, represented as a triadic context (Lehmann & Wille, 1995).

Example 4. Figure 2 illustrates an example of a folksonomy F_∇ where $ID = \{id_1, id_2, id_3, id_4\}$, Q= $\{q_1, q_2, q_3, q_4, q_5\}$ and $RS = \{rs_1, rs_2, rs_3\}$.

Note that each $\times$ is a triadic relationship between a user identifier belonging to *ID*, a query from Q and the resource accessed belonging to *RS*.

The model-learning step proceeds concurrently by retrieving user's queries sequences from a folksonomy and then mining users' search intents. Thereafter, the results of the previously stages, will be used for the HMM training. *Deck* 1 in Figure 1 provides a visual representation of the model-learning step. Each step in model-learning deck is outlined below.

Stage 1: User's queries sequences extraction: In this step we are interested in discovering the queries sequences SL_i of each user idu_i. Hence, we must firstly collect user's sessions S_i from the folksonomy. Lets us, at first, give the definition of a user session.

Definition 3. (USER SESSION)

A user session S_i, related to a user idu_i, is defined as: $S_i := \{\{$User queries $q_{Si,p}\}, rs_{Si,j}\}$, with $rs_{Si,j} :=$ The resource j accessed by the user idu_i in the session S_i, $q_{Si,p} :=$ The p ordered submitted query in S_i.

Table 2 illustrates an example of users' sessions. For example, the user session S_2, highlights that the user idu_2 has retrieved the resource $rs_{2,3}$ after submitting the two queries $q_{2,3}$ and $q_{2,4}$.

Figure 2. An example of the proposed approach on a sample of a real dataset

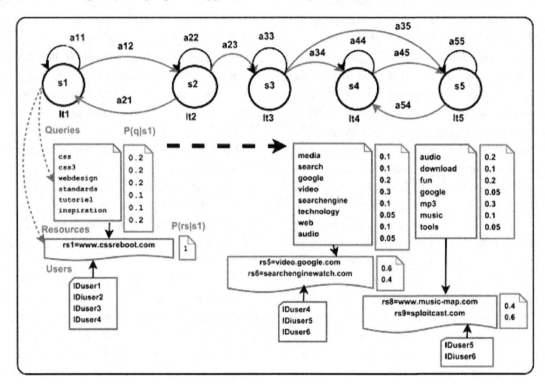

Once the users' sessions are collected, we derive user's queries sequences by keeping, for each user, the sequences of queries related to his session and discard useless information. An example of user's queries sequences associated to the Table 1 is given in the following:

SL_1: $((q_{1,1} \Rightarrow q_{1,2} \Rightarrow q_{1,3}); (q_{1,1} \Rightarrow q_{1,4}))$, SL_2: $(q2,3 \Rightarrow q_{2,4})$, SL_3: $((q_{3,2} \Rightarrow q_{3,3}); (q_{3,4} \Rightarrow q_{3,5}))$ where SL_i, describes query sequences of the user idu_i.

Stage 2: User search intent mining: The second step of the model-learning step is to mine users' search intents from the folksonomy. Hence, since, at one hand, different users may submit different queries to describe the same search intent and on the other hand, different users sharing the same interest for a specific topic, may retrieve different resources even if they submit exactly

the same query, therefore we define a user search intent in a folksonomy as the common interest shared by a community of users U for a retrieved set of resources R' queried by a certain set of queries Q'.

Let us firstly recall in the following the main definitions related to a tri-set and a triadic concept (Jaschke *et al.*, 2008) that will be used in the remainder.

Definition 4: *(A (FREQUENT) TRI-SET)* Let F_∇ = *(ID, Q, RS, G)* be a folksonomy.

A tri-set of F_∇ is a triple *(A, B, C)* with $A \subseteq ID$, $B \subseteq Q$, $C \subseteq RS$ such that $A \times B \times C \subseteq G$. A tri-set *(A, B, C)* of L is said frequent whenever $|A| \geq$ *id-minsupp*, $|B| \geq$ *q-minsupp* and $|C| \geq$ *rs-minsupp* with *id-minsupp*, *q-minsupp* and *rs-minsupp* are user-defined thresholds.

Table 1. An example of a folksonomy

ID / RS – Q	rs$_1$					rs$_2$					rs$_3$				
	q$_1$	q$_2$	q$_3$	q$_4$	q$_5$	q$_1$	q$_2$	q$_3$	q$_4$	q$_5$	q$_1$	q$_2$	q$_3$	q$_4$	q$_5$
id$_1$		×	×	×			×	×	×			×	×	×	
id$_2$		×	×	×		×	×	×	×		×	×	×	×	
id$_3$		×	×	×		×	×	×	×		×	×	×	×	
id$_4$	×					×			×		×			×	

Table 2. User's sessions example

$S_1 := \{\{q_{1,1}, q_{1,2}, q_{1,3}\}, rs_{1,1}\}; \{\{q_{1,1}, q_{1,4}\}, rs_{1,2}\}$
$S_2 := \{q_{2,3}, q_{2,4}, rs_{2,3}\}$
$S_3 := \{\{q_{3,2}, q_{3,3}\}, rs_{3,4}\}; \{q_{3,4}, q_{3,5}, rs_{3,6}\}$

Definition 5: *(TRIADIC CONCEPT) A* triadic concept (tri-concept for short) of a folksonomy $F_\nabla = (ID, Q, RS, G)$ is a triple *(ID, Q, RS)* with $ID \subseteq ID$, $Q \subseteq Q$, and $RS \subseteq RS$ with $ID \times Q \times RS \subseteq G$ such that the triple *(ID, Q, RS)* is maximal, *i.e.*, for $ID_1 \subseteq ID$, $Q_1 \subseteq Q$ and $RS_1 \subseteq RS$ with $ID_1 \times Q_1 \times RS_1 \subseteq G$, the containments $ID \subseteq ID_1$, $Q \subseteq Q_1$, and $RS \subseteq RS_1$ always imply *(ID, Q, RS)* = (ID_1, Q_1, RS_1).

Consequently, a search intent can be, formally, represented, in a folksonomy $L = (ID, Q, RS, G)$, as a triadic concept $IT = (U', T', R')$ where $U' \subseteq ID$, $T' \subseteq Q$, and $R' \subseteq RS$ with $U' \times T' \times R' \subseteq G$. Indeed, mining tri-concepts to discover and model users' search intents, allows addressing the sparseness of queries and interpreting users' information needs more accurately. The users' search intents are therefore obtained by applying the TRIAS algorithm (Jaschke et *al.*, 2006) on the folksonomy L. TRIAS takes as input the folksonomy L as well as three user-defined thresholds: *id–minsupp*, *q–minsupp* and *rs–minsupp* and outputs the set of all frequent tri-concepts, *i.e.*, search intents, that fulfill these aforementioned thresholds. For example, the search intent $IT_1 =$

$\{(id_1, id_3, id_4), (q_4, q_5), (rs_1, rs_2)\}$ is obtained by applying TRIAS algorithm on the folksonomy depicted by Figure 2, with *id–minsupp = q–min-supp = rs–minsupp = 2*. Roughly speaking, the search intent IT_1, highlights that the community of users *(id$_1$, id$_3$, id$_4$)* share the same interest in the resources *(rs$_1$, rs$_2$)* queried by q_4 and q_5. Given the user's queries sequences and the users' search intents, previously extracted, we proceed in the next section with the HMM training.

Stage 3: HMM training: For the last step of our approach, we are interested in training HMM. In fact, in a HMM, there are two types of states: the observable states and the hidden ones. Thereby, we define user's queries sequences as the observable states in the HMM, whereas the hidden states are modeled by the users' search intents. Note that, if we model individual queries and resources directly as states in the HMM, then we not only increase the number of states and thus the complexity of the model, but also lose the faithful preservation of the semantic relationship among the queries and the accessed resources within the same search intent. Therefore, given the set of hidden states $S = \{s_1, ..., s_{ns}\}$, we denote the set of distinct queries as $Q = \{q_1, ..., q_{nq}\}$, the set of accessed resources $RSs = \{rs_1, ..., rs_{nrs}\}$ and a set of user *ID*; $IDus = \{idu_1, ..., idu_{nidu}\}$, where *ns* is the number of states of the model, *nq* is the total number of queries, *nrs* is the total number of resources, *nidu* is number of users, and SL_i is a state sequence. Our HMM noted $\lambda = (A, B, B', \pi)$, is a probabilistic model defined as follows:

- $\pi = [...\ \pi_i\ ...]$, the initial state probability, where $\pi_i = P(s_i)$ is the probability that a state s_i occurs as the first element of a state sequence SL_i.
- $B = [...\ b_j(q)...]$, the query emission probability distribution, where $b_j(q) = P(q|s_j)$, denotes the probability that a user, currently at a state s_j, submits a query q.
- $B' = [...\ b_k(rs)...]$, the resource emission probability distribution, where $b_k(rs) = P(rs|s_k)$, denotes the probability that a user, currently at a state s_j, accesses the resource rs.
- $A = [...\ a_{ij}\ ...]$, the transition probability, where $a_{ij} = P(s_j|s_i)$ that represents the transition probability from a state s_i to another one s_j.

Once the HMM is formalized, we proceed with learning its parameters (A, B, B', π) from a folksonomy. This is done by performing two distinct stages namely: *(i)* the initial HMM parameters values assignment; and *(ii)* HMM parameters values re-estimation.

In the following, we present each stage.

The initial HMM parameters values assignment.

The goal of this stage is to compute the four sets of the HMM parameters: the initial state probabilities $\{P(s_i)\}$, the query emission probabilities $\{P(q_i|s)\}$, the resource emission probabilities $\{P(rs|s_k)\}$, and the transition probabilities $\{P(s_j|s_i)\}$.

1. $\pi_i = P(s_1) =$ with:
    a. $SL_c = \cup_{i \in 1...t} \{E_i\} =$ total set of candidate states sequences to which could be matched a sequence of queries where E_i denotes the set of candidate states that could match a query from a given sequence of queries.

b. $\varphi(s_j)=$ set of states sequences in SL_c starting from s_j.

2. $bj(q) = P(q|s_j) = \dfrac{\sum_{rs \in RS_j} Count(rs,q)}{\sum_{q \in Q_j} \sum_{rs \in RS_j} Count(rs,q)}$

3. $b_k(rs) = P(rs|s_k) = \dfrac{\sum_{q \in Q_k} Count(rs,q)}{\sum_{q \in Q_k} \sum_{rs \in RS_k} Count(rs,q)}$ where $Count(rs,q) =$ number of times the resource rs is accessed as an answer to the query q in the folksonomy.

4. $a_{i,j} = P(s_j|s_i) = \dfrac{CS(s_i,\ s_j)}{NC}$ with:
    a. $NC =$ the number of occurrences of s_j in SL_c.
    b. $CS(si,\ sj) =$ the number of times the state s_i is followed by the state s_j in SL_c.

For more accurate predictions results, we are interested, in the next stage, in reestimating the HMM initial values parameters to yield more accurate predictions.

The HMM parameters values re-estimation:

We mainly give a brief presentation of the used algorithm namely, the Baum-Welch algorithm (Dempster et *al.*, 1977). In fact, Baum-Welch algorithm aims to find the maximum-likelihood estimate of the parameters of a HMM given a set of observed feature vectors.

Hence, considering the initial set $\lambda = (A, B, B', \pi)$. The Baum-Welch algorithm updates the parameters of λ iteratively until convergence. Thus, given the total set of observations O, *i.e.*, the set of all query sequences, the Baum-Welch algorithm finds:

$\lambda^* = argmax_{\lambda}\ ln\ P(O|\lambda)$ - that is, the HMM λ^*, that maximizes the probability of the observation O. Based on the Baum-Welch algorithm, we get out λ^* that relieves the set of observation sequences with the highest probability of occurrence.

4.2. Matching and Prediction Step

Once the model-learning step is performed, we proceed with the matching and prediction step for identifying the query context and then predict the next user query according to the next HMM state. Indeed, when a user submits a query q, two consecutive stages are carried out: *(i)* Matching the current user query q to its corresponding context according to HMM states; and then *(ii)* Predicting the next HMM state which represents the user's search intent. Hence, the prediction process starts by looking for the most likely HMM state s_{MS} to which q could better belong. This is done by computing, for each HMM state, the value of the quantity $Mat_i = \pi_i \times b_i(q)$, where π_i is the initial probability of the state s_i and $b_i(q)$ is the emission probability of q at s_i. Therefore, the state with the highest value, *i.e.*, s_{MS}, of Mat_i will define the context of q. Thereafter, the prediction of the user's search intent is then performed, by looking for the next state s_{NextMS} of s_{MS}. This is obtained by computing the index value *NextMS* as follows: $NextMS = argmax_j \{a_{\{MS,j\}} \times b_j(q)\}$, where q denotes a query belonging to the state s_j, successor of s_{MS} in the HMM.

Thus, the state s_{NextMS} represents the most probably search intent to which the user may transit after submitting the query q.

5. ILLUSTRATIVE EXAMPLE OF THE PROPOSED APPROACH ON A REAL DATASET

Figure 3 represents a HMM with five states $\{s_1, s_2, s_3, s_4, s_5\}$ where each state denotes a user search intent, *i.e.*, It_1, It_2, It_3, It_4 and It_5, extracted by the algorithm TRIAS from a sample taken from the real test data collected from Del.icio.us.

Each search intent is represented by a triplet, *i.e.*, the set of all queries frequently used by a set of users looking for a set of resources. The corresponding transition matrix A, and the distribu-

tions of the different probabilities of observation (of resources and queries) are obtained by computing probabilities as described in Section 3. The corresponding HMM with five states is shown in Figure 2. Suppose that the generated HMM with five states $\{s_1, s_2, s_3, s_4, s_5\}$ has a transition probability matrix as follows:

$$A = \begin{pmatrix} 0,40,6000000 \\ 0,20,50,30000 \\ 00000,30,20,5 \\ 0000000,30,7 \\ 0000000,60,4 \end{pmatrix}$$

And let us assume that $\pi = (0,2\ 0,2\ 0,2\ 0,2\ 0,2)$. Hence, considering the search intent represented by the state s_1, users have a probability of *0.4* to keep the same search intent and a probability of *0.6* to skip for a new search intent represented by the state s_2. For example, if a user submits the query *"audio,"* then the prediction process starts by looking for the most likely HMM state to which the query *"audio"* could better belong. This is obtained by computing for each of the five states, the quantity $Mat_i = \pi_i \times b_i(audio)$ including:

- $Mat_1 = \pi_1 \times b_1(audio) = 0,2 \times 0 = 0$; $Mat_2 = Mat_3 = 0$; $Mat_4 = \pi_4 \times b_4(audio) = 0,2 \times 0,05 = 0,01$ and $Mat_5 = \pi_5 \times b_5(audio) = 0,2 \times 0,2 = \mathbf{0,04}$.

Consequently, s_5 is the state which has the highest probability to represent the user's search intent for the query *"audio."* Thus, the candidate resources (*rs8:www.music-map.com/*) and (*rs9:www.sploitcast.com/*), with the respective probabilities *0.6* and *0.4*, are recommended to the user.

Furthermore, possible states transitions from s_5 are either s_4 or s_5 (*i.e.*, a user may keep the same search intent). Thus, the corresponding candidate queries to be predicted, after the *"audio'"*'s query submission, are computed by the following for-

Figure 3. Number of tri-concepts (search intents) vs. that of tri-sets

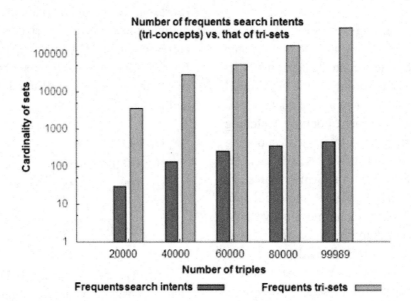

mula, $argmax_j \{a_{5,j} \times b_j(q)\}$ with $j \in \{4, 5\}$ (i.e., possible state transition from s_5) and q is a query belonging to the search intents represented by s_4 or s_5 states.

Otherwise, given that in the one hand: $Max(b_5(q)) = 0,3$ and $Max(b_4(q)) = 0,3$ for all queries q in the fifth and the fourth state respectively, and on the other hand $argmax_j \{a_{5,5} \times b_5(q), a_{5,4} \times b_4(q)\} = argmax_j \{0,12; 0,36\} = 4$, then the search intent to be predicted is represented by the state of index 4 (i.e., s_4). Thus, queries { *"video," "media," "google"* etc.} belonging to the search intent represented by s_4 will be suggested to the user in an increasing ranked list of probability. Likewise, the corresponding resources of the considered search intent could be recommended in the same way.

6. EXPERIMENTAL EVALUATION

The evaluation of all folksonomies' recommender systems, in general, is still an open challenge. In fact, results of different systems have been evaluated using different datasets and following different evaluation strategies. As an evidence of the lack of social bookmarking systems that exploit search intents prediction, as far as we know, there is no work with topic published via the scholarly literature. Hence, the evaluation of our approach is a complex task. The evaluation of our system is considered on two complementary aspects: *(i)* we analyze the accuracy of our approach by adopting two popular parameters borrowed from the Information Retrieval field, namely Precision and Recall (Baeza-Yates & Berthier, 1999); *(ii)* through an anthropocentric evaluation, we assessed users' judgments on the ease and friendliness of the prediction system.

6.1. The Dataset Description and Preparation

To fully evaluate our approach, we carried out experiments on a dataset collected from a real-world social bookmarking system, *i.e.*, *Del.icio. us*[10]. *Del.icio.us* is a fast growing social bookmarking service. It offers hosts to its users to centrally collect and share their bookmarks, which can refer to any resource on the web as long as this resource can be identified by an *URL*. *Del.icio. us* went online in *September 2003* and is still constantly growing. The folksonomy used to conduct our experiments is around *10MB* in size (compressed) and are freely downloadable[11] where tags represent queries, users identifiers correspond to session *IDs*, and resources that users tagged with the query words are considered as accessed resources. Hence, the folksonomy data set contains *99989* triples sessions, *i.e.*, assignments, *18066* queries, *53397* resources and *43419* users. From the considered folksonomy, we first extract user's queries sequences as described in Section 3.1. Since we are interested in training our HMM to model users' search behavior for search intents prediction, infrequent queries sequences were Withdrawn. Therefore, we record the frequencies of queries in user's queries sequences. To be specific, we remove a user query sequence SL_i if its frequency is less than the *minsupp* threshold. In our experiments, *minsupp* is set to *3*, *i.e.*, at least, *3* queries sequences are commonly used by a community of users.

6.2. Baselines Models

To the best of our knowledge, search intent prediction (using hidden markov models) in such social bookmarking systems has never been modeled before. Thus, for enhancing the effectiveness of our approach, we have selected two baselines models for query prediction, i.e., the most popular queries recommender which predicts queries according to their global occurrence in the training data. On the other hand, the most popular query aware recommender, which ranks queries according to their global co-occurrence in the training set, with the query tag in the test set. For each of the algorithms of our evaluation, we briefly describe in the following the specific settings used to run them.

- **Most popular queries recommender**: For each query tag we counted in how many user sessions it occurs and used the top queries (ranked by occurrence count) as recommendations.
- **Most popular query aware recommender**: These recommenders weight query tags by their co-occurrence with a given query. We then used the most co-occurrent tag queries as a suggestion.

6.3. Efficiency of Modeling the HMM

As mentioned above, to determine the HMM hidden states representing the users' search intents, we applied the Trias algorithm. Hence, we set minimum support values of *id-minsupp = 2*, *q-minsupp = 2* and *rs-minsupp = 1*, *i.e.*, at least, *2* users have formulated the same queries (*2* at least) for looking for a same resource.

Figure 3 illustrates the number of frequent tri-concepts, *i.e.*, search intents, *vs.* that of frequent tri-sets on the *y-axis*, whereas the *x-axis* depicts the number of triples in *Y* which grows from *20000* to *99989*. The obtained results comfort our hypothesis.

Indeed, directly modeling the hidden states by tri-concepts instead of individual tri-sets of queries, users and resources allows a drop around *98.26%* of the number of states and hence the complexity of the model.

6.4. Effectiveness of the Approach

We assess the performance of the proposed approach on query prediction using a supervised learning method. From each dataset, *i.e.*, the original and the pre-processed one, we build two test sets. Specifically, we randomly split each dataset into two parts, a training part and a test part. The training parts are used to estimate the model while the test parts are used to for evaluating. Hence, for a given sequence of queries, the first *n* queries are used for generating predictions, whereas, the

Figure 4. Left: Averages of Recall on the original Del.icio.us dataset; Right: Averages of Recall on the pre-processed Del.icio.us dataset.

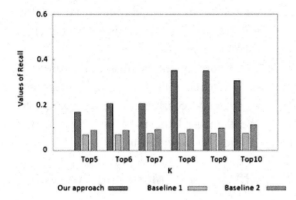
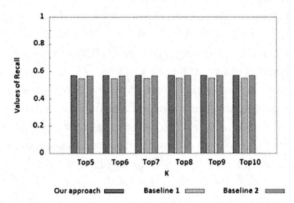

remaining part Q_T of the queries is considered as the set of queries actually formulated by the user, as the ground truth. The performance is then assessed by precision, recall and the corresponding F-Measure at different ranks K.

Suppose that for a user query q_T, the proposed approach predicts a list of queries Q_R, thus, the measures of *Recall, Precision* are given as follows:

$$\text{Recall} = \frac{\left|Q_R \cap \{Q_T \setminus q_T\}\right|}{\left|Q_T \setminus q_T\right|},$$

$$\text{Precision} = \frac{\left|Q_R \cap \{Q_T \setminus q_T\}\right|}{\left|Q_R\right|}$$

We report in the following results averaged over all user sessions and *6* test runs.

Figure 4 (Left), depicts averages of recall for different values of K, *i.e.*, the number of predicted queries, ranging from *5* to *10*. Thus, according to the sketched histograms, we can point out that our approach outperforms the two baselines, for both, the original and the pre-processed datasets. In fact, as expected, the Recall values of the individual baselines are much lower than those achieved by our approach. Furthermore, the average Recall on the original folksonomy achieves high percentage for higher value of K. Indeed, for $K = 9$, the average Recall is equal to *0,351*, showing an increase of *51,85%* compared to the average Recall for K

= *5*. In this case, for a higher value of K, *i.e.*, $K = 9$, by matching current user's queries with their corresponding contexts, the proposed approach can produce all of the queries that are likely to be formulated by the user.

However, according to Figure 5 (Right), the percentage of Precision for the proposed model outperforms the two baselines over the two datasets. Our approach achieves the best results when we choose the value of K around *8*. In fact, for $K = 5$, the mean precision, is equal to *12, 3%*. Whereas, for $K = 8$, it has an average of *24, 5%* showing a drop of the query prediction accuracy of *49,79% vs.* an exceeding about *19,6%* against the first baseline and around *17,4%* against the second one. These results highlight that the proposed approach can better improve query prediction accuracy even for a high number of predicted queries regardless the handled dataset. Moreover, our approach achieves a good coverage, since it produces predictions for *76%* of queries contained in the test set Q_T.

6.5. Online Evaluation

We present in figure 6 the runtime of our system. Since it is hard to measure the exact runtime of the model, we simulated an online execution of our system among the *Del.icio.us* dataset with

Figure 5. Left: Averages of precision on the original Del.icio.us dataset; Right: Averages of precision on the pre-processed Del.icio.us dataset

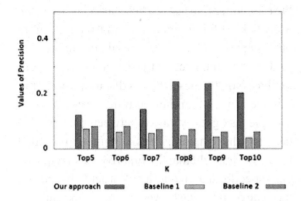 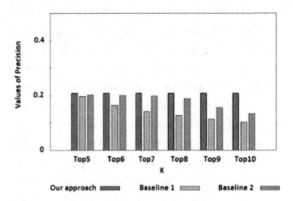

different values of K, *i.e.*, the number of predicted queries, ranging from *5* to *10*.

Hence, for each tag query on the dataset, we report the average runtime of the related top K result. Figure 6 describes the online execution of our system. In fact, the maximum value of run time is about *0.025(s)*, whereas the minimum value is around *0.013(s)* which is efficient and satisfactory.

6.6. Anthropocentric Evaluation

In order to evaluate on the one hand the effectiveness of search intent prediction in standard folksonomies, when compared to preprocessed ones and on the other hand, the impact of the HMM-based query prediction tool as a support to existing techniques for search in social bookmarking systems, we carry out an additional series of experiments based on users judgments. Hence, considering both the pre-processed folksonomy and the original ones, we describe in the following, our anthropocentric evaluation methodology and discuss the obtained results.

Methodology: Our evaluation had ten participants in total (all Computer Science undergraduate students). Five of the participants reported themselves as experienced web searchers, two said they were average, and the remaining three noted that they were inexperienced in searching for web. All

Figure 6. The run time of the system online on the Del.icio.us dataset with different values of K

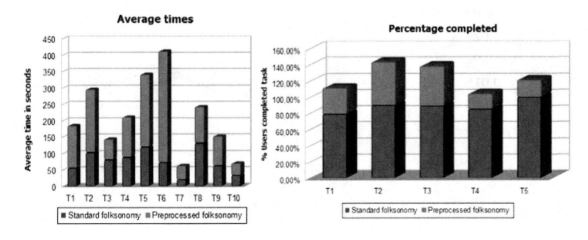

participants were surveyed at various stages of the experiment in order to allow them to describe what they liked/disliked about the system in use. Each user was given ten tasks to perform. The first five tasks asked the user to search for specific *Web2.0* resources. The second five tasks asked the user to find resources that meet a specification (*e.g.*, find a *URL* that the user thinks that it matches its intention for searching resources relative to *web design*). Each user performed two of each type of tasks on the preprocessed folksonomy and two using the original one, and no user performed the same task on both datasets (in order to avoid learning bias in their searching process).

By examining how users completed these tasks, we gained an understanding of the users experience with each of the two datasets. Users were timed for each task and the number of times they redefine their search query was recorded. This information as well as information provided by the user about their experience allowed us to draw conclusions on the effectiveness of search intent prediction in standard folksonomies when compared to preprocessed ones.

Evaluation results: Using both search types, users found the first five tasks much harder than the remaining five tasks. These tasks involved the user looking for an intention and trying to figure out what search terms they should use in order to find it. The final second tasks involved searching based on the descriptions discussed earlier in this section. The amount of time a user spent on a single task greatly varied between the first five tasks and the remaining ones. Comments provided by users highlight that the first five tasks required very specific search queries in order to be carried out. The final five tasks were more ambiguous and allowed them to rely on their own description of what they were looking for rather than what the contributor of the resource tagged it as.

Users spent out much less time on three out of the first five tasks when using a preprocessed dataset (as illustrated in the leftmost chart in Figure 7). The right-most chart in Figure 8 illustrates that users were more successful completing the first five tasks with a preprocessed dataset than standard one (all users successfully completed tasks *6 – 10* with both types of search). User comments suggest that this was due to the suggestions provided by

Figure 7. Left: Bar charts showing the average time taken to complete tasks; Right: The percentage of users whom completed each of the first five tasks

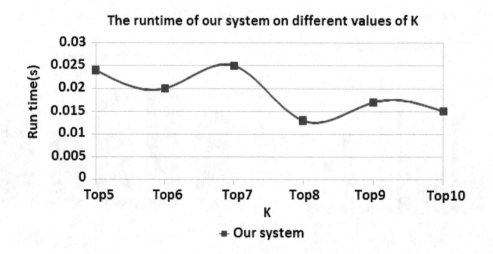

our system when the folksonomy used in training phase of the HMM is preprocessed. One user commented that search intent prediction provided *"options that you wouldn't think of."* Another user stated that the preprocessing step *"help to filter potentially a lot of queries and resources which saves time."*

These results and these generally supportive user comments allow us to conclude that the additional queries provided by our system aided the users in choosing appropriate tags to find the resource they were searching for.

CONCLUSION AND FUTURE WORK

In this paper, we have introduced a novel approach for users' search intents prediction in a folksonomy. We have applied probabilistic models to this problem and developed a powerful coupling model, which is based on effective use of HMM and triadic concept analysis. We tackle the challenge of learning a large HMM from hundreds of thousands of user's sessions by summarizing individual queries, resources and users into search intents, formally, represented as triadic concepts which can greatly lower the number of the HMM states and allow to interpret users' information needs more accurately.

Finally, we extensively evaluated our proposed approach on a large dataset, carried out from a real world folksonomy, through common metrics and anthropocentric evaluation. We have also highlighted that tackling tag synonymy and polysemy problems boosts the query prediction relevance and accuracy.

To the best of our knowledge, search intent prediction (using HMMs) in such social bookmarking systems has never been modeled before. Our research should provide numerous useful insights toward the next generation of queries prediction in folksonomies search.

Our future avenues for future work mainly address the focus on other more sophisticated Markov models such as variable length HMM in a folksonomy search. This includes modeling hidden states that represent users' search intents, which could be an underlying semantic concept, especially with the help of domain knowledge such as the online ontologies. Indeed, the use of online ontologies may allow prediction systems to find out how specific the user interest is, and use this information to fine predictions. It remains to be seen whether more sophisticated models can further raise the performance bar for the query prediction in folksonomies. Moreover, *Del.icio. us* now allows users to form links with other, *e.g.*, friends, groups. Such social links could be explored for further interest and search intent analysis.

Finally, for deploying the work on an online system, the analysis on the frequency of re-preprocessing the dataset to adapt to new tag assignments trends would be also an important issue to tackle.

ACKNOWLEDGMENT

This work is partially supported by the French-Tunisian project PAI-CMCU 11G 1417. We thank the anonymous reviewers for helpful remarks on previous drafts of this paper.

REFERENCES

Baeza-Yates, R., & Berthier, R.-N. (1999). *Modern information retrieval*. Boston, MA: Addison-Wesley Longman Publishing Co., Inc.

Baeza-Yates, R., & Tiberi, A. (2007). Extracting semantic relations from query logs. *Proceedings of the 13th International Conference on Knowledge Discovery and Data mining, KDD 2007* (pp. 76-85). New York, NY: ACM.

Begelman, G., Keller, P., & Smadja, F. (2006). Automated tag clustering: Improving search and exploration in the tag space. *Proceedings of the the Collaborative Web Tagging Workshop, WWW 2006.*

Bischoff, K., Firan, C., Nejdl, W., & Paiu, R. (2008). Can all tags be used for search? *Proceedings of the 17th ACM Conference on Information and Knowledge Management, CIKM 2008* (pp. 193-202). Napa Valley, CA: ACM Press.

Brin, S., & Page, L. (1998). The anatomy of a large-scale hypertextual Web search engine. *Proc. of the Seventh International Conference on World Wide Web*, (Vol. 7, pp. 107-117).

Carman, M., Baillie, M., Gwadera, R., & Crestani, F. (2009). A statistical comparison of tag and query logs. *Proceedings of the 32nd Annual International Conference on Research and Development in Information Retrieval, SIGIR 2009* (pp. 123-130). Boston, MA: ACM.

Dempster, A., Laird, N., & Rubin, D. (1977). Maximum likelihood from incomplete data via the EM algorithm. *Journal of the Royal Statistical Society. Series B. Methodological, 39*, 1–38.

Fonseca, B., Golgher, P., Pôssas, B., Ribeiro-Neto, B., & Ziviani, N. (2005). Concept-based interactive query expansion. *Proceedings of the 14th ACM International Conference on Information and Knowledge Management, CIKM 2005* (pp. 696-703). Bremen, Germany: ACM.

Golder, S., & Huberman, B. (2006). Usage pattern of collaborative tagging systems. *Journal of Information Systems, 32*(2), 198–208.

Golder, S., & Huberman, B. A. (2005). *The structure of collaborative tagging systems. Technical report.* HP Labs.

Gruber, T. R. (1995). Towards principles for the design of ontologies used for knowledge sharing. *International Journal of Human-Computer Studies, 43*(5-6), 907–928. doi:10.1006/ijhc.1995.1081

Heymann, P., Koutrika, G., & Garcia-Molina, H. (2008). Can social bookmarking improve web search? *Proceedings of the First ACM International Conference on Web Search and Data Mining, WSDM 2008* (pp. 195-206). New York, NY: ACM.

Hotho, A., Jaschke, R., Schmitz, C., & Stumme, G. (2006). *Information retrieval in folksonomies: Search and ranking. The Semantic Web: Research and Applications, LNCS 4011* (pp. 411–426). Heidelberg, Germany: Springer.

Jaschke, R., Hotho, A., Schmitz, C., Ganter, B., & Stumme, G. (2006). Trias - An algorithm for mining iceberg tri-lattices. *Proceedings of the 6th IEEE International Conference on Data Mining, ICDM 2006* (pp. 907-911). Hong Kong: IEEE Computer Society.

Jaschke, R., Hotho, A., Schmitz, C., Ganter, B., & Stumme, G. (2008). Discovering shared conceptualizations in folksonomies. *Web Semantics: Science, Services and Agents on the World Wide Web, 6*, 38–53.

Jaschke, R., Marinho, L., Hotho, A., Schmidt-Thieme, L., & Stumme, G. (2007). Tag recommendations in folksonomies. *Proceedings of 11th European Conference on Principles and Practice of Knowledge Discovery in Databases, PKDD 2007* (pp. 506-514). Warsaw, Poland: Springer.

Krause, B., Hotho, A., & Stumme, G. (2008). A comparison of social bookmarking with traditional search. *Proceedings of the 30th European Conf. on IR Research, Advances in Information Retrieval, ECIR 2008, LNCS 4956*, (pp. 101-113). Springer.

Lee, K., Kim, H., Shin, H., & Kim, H. (2009). Tag sense disambiguation for clarifying the vocabulary of social tags. *Proceedings of IEEE International Conference on Computational Science and Engineering* (pp. 729-734). Los Alamitos, CA: IEEE.

Lehmann, F., & Wille, R. (1995). A triadic approach to formal concept analysis. *Proceedings of the 3rd International Conference on Conceptual Structures: Applications, Implementation and Theory* (pp. 32-43). Springer.

Lin, H., Davis, J., & Zhou, Y. (2009). An integrated approach to extracting ontological structures from folksonomies. *Proceedings of the 6th European Semantic Web Conference, ESWC 2009, LNCS 5545*, (pp. 654-668). Heidelberg, Germany: Springer.

Lipczak, M. (2008). Tag recommendation for folksonomies oriented towards individual users. *Proceedings of ECML PKDD Discovery Challenge, RSDC 2008*, (pp. 84-95).

Mathes, A. (2004). *Folksonomies - Cooperative classification and communication through shared metadata*. Graduate School of Library and Information Science, University of Illinois Urbana-Champaign.

Medelyan, O., Milne, D., Legg, C., & Witten, I. (2009). Mining meaning from Wikipedia. *International Journal of Human-Computer Studies, 67*, 716–754. doi:10.1016/j.ijhcs.2009.05.004

Mika, P. (2005). Ontologies are us: A unified model of social networks and semantics. *Proceedings of the 4th International Semantic Web Conference, ISWC 2005, LNCS 3729*, (pp. 522-536). Galway, Ireland: Springer.

Miller, G. (1995). WordNet: A lexical database for English. *Communications of the ACM, 38*, 39–41. doi:10.1145/219717.219748

Pan, J., Taylor, S., & Thomas, E. (2009). Reducing ambiguity in tagging systems with folksonomy search expansion. *Proceedings of the 6th Annual European Semantic Web Conference, ESWC 2009* (pp. 669-683). Springer.

Rabiner, L. (1989). *A tutorial on hidden Markov models and selected applications in speech recognition* (pp. 257–286).

Specia, L., & Motta, E. (2007). Integrating folksonomies with the Semantic Web. *Proceedings of the 4th European Semantic Web Conference, ESWC 2007, LNCS 4519*, (pp. 624-639). Innsbruck, Austria: Springer.

Szomszor, M., & Alani, H. OHara, K., & Shadbolt, N. (2008). Semantic modelling of user interests based on cross-folksonomy. *Proceedings of the 7th International Semantic Web Conference, ISWC 2008*, Karlsruhe, Germany.

Trabelsi, C., Ben Jrad, A., & Ben Yahia, S. (2010). Bridging folksonomies and domain ontologies: Getting out non-taxonomic relations. *Proceedings of the 10th IEEE International Conference on Data Mining Workshops, ICDM Workshops 2010* (pp. 369-379). Sydney, Australia: IEEE Computer Society.

ENDNOTES

1. www.delicious.com
2. www.bibsonomy.org
3. www.flickr.com
4. http://wordnet.princeton.edu/
5. http://en.wikipedia.org/
6. http://www.google.com/

[7] An open-source search engine that provides full text indexing and searching capabilities, http://lucene.apache.org/.

[8] The representative tags which identified in the previous step.

[9] We use the term "synset" in the same way it is used in WordNet (Miller, 1995): a synset is a set of words with a semantically equivalent meaning.

[10] http://www.delicious.com

[11] http://data.dai-labor.de/corpus/delicious/

Chapter 11
Techniques for Named Entity Recognition:
A Survey

Girish Keshav Palshikar
Tata Research Development and Design Centre, India

ABSTRACT

While building and using a fully semantic understanding of Web contents is a distant goal, named entities (NEs) provide a small, tractable set of elements carrying a well-defined semantics. Generic named entities are names of persons, locations, organizations, phone numbers, and dates, while domain-specific named entities includes names of for example, proteins, enzymes, organisms, genes, cells, et cetera, in the biological domain. An ability to automatically perform named entity recognition (NER) – i.e., identify occurrences of NE in Web contents – can have multiple benefits, such as improving the expressiveness of queries and also improving the quality of the search results. A number of factors make building highly accurate NER a challenging task. Given the importance of NER in semantic processing of text, this chapter presents a detailed survey of NER techniques for English text.

INTRODUCTION

Given the vast amounts of text available on the Web, it is becoming increasingly clear that Internet based tools (e.g., search engines, content creation and management) and applications (e.g., Wikipedia, social networking, blogs) need to understand at least rudimentary semantics of the contents of the Web, which is of course the fundamental motivation for Semantic Web (Shadbolt et al 2006). While semantics is a complex subject and understanding (and using) the complete meaning of a piece of text may well be impossible, it is easy to identify limited types of semantic elements in a text.

DOI: 10.4018/978-1-4666-0894-8.ch011

Named entities (NE) – like names of persons, organizations, locations and dates, times, phone numbers, amounts, zip codes – are just such basic semantic elements of a text that carry a specific and limited kind of meaning. An ability to automatically perform *named entity recognition (NER)* – i.e., identify occurrences of NE in Web contents – can have multiple benefits, such as improving the expressiveness of queries and also improving the quality of the search results. Examples where processing queries containing NE as keywords requires NER: Kawasaki the person and Kawasaki the manufacturing company, Jackson the scientist and Jackson the musician, dates in different formats, identifying that Robert Feynman and Dick Feynman are the same persons, Jobs as a person versus jobs as a common noun, high blood pressure and hypertension as synonymous medical terms. As another example, identifying two successive dates in a text can help compute the duration of some event (e.g., of a project). Lack of NER abilities make representation and execution of queries such as *"Find all European physicists who lived for at least 70 years"* difficult for many of today's search engines. Given the frequent use and relatively well-defined semantics of NE, it is possible to use NER to automatically annotate the occurrences of NE in web contents, which can then be used for improving search and other functions. NE are frequently used as sources (origins) of hyperlinks. Further, since NE occur frequently as part of annotations, notes, comments, bookmarks, hyperlinks etc., NE play an important role in collaborative semantic web applications.

Given the importance of NER in semantic processing of text, this paper presents a detailed (but not necessarily exhaustive) survey of NER techniques. We focus on NER in English text, though there is a considerable work for other languages, which presents complex challenges. We focus mainly on NER for generic NE. However, there is a large amount of work on NER for extracting domain-specific NE. NE in the bio-medical domain are the most well-explored, among the various possible domains.

NER is an important sub-problem in text processing – particularly in *information extraction (IE)* – and is useful in many practical applications in the Semantic Web context. The goal of NER is to identify all occurrences of specific types of *named entities* in the given document collection. NE may be divided into several categories.

- **Generic NE** consist of names of persons (PERSON), organizations (ORG), locations (LOCATION), amounts, dates, times, email addresses, URLs, phone numbers etc. Other generic NE include: film title, book title etc. In a richer problem setting (called *fine-gained NER*), the problem is to identify generic NE which are hierarchically organized; e.g., PERSON may be sub-divided into politicians, sports persons, film stars, musicians etc.
- **Domain-specific NE (DSNE)** consist of, for example, names of proteins, enzymes, organisms, genes, cells etc., in the biological domain. As another example, DSNE in the manufacturing domain are: names of manufacturer, product, brand and attributes of the product (Fig. 1).

Often the NER needs to be performed on a fixed type of input text; e.g., news items or research paper abstracts. NER in speech is a much more difficult problem, since information such as capitalization, punctuation etc. is not available in speech data (though some other kinds of information, such as emphasis, may be available). In this paper, we focus on the NER for English text.

Challenges in NER

Several factors make NER a challenging task. First, there is the open nature of the vocabulary; e.g., it is obviously not feasible to maintain a list of all known person names. Clues such as capitalization

Figure 1. Example sentences containing occurrences of generic NE

```
[J. P. Morgan]ORG strengthens domestic treasury management offering in
[Malasia]LOCATION.

In a strategic reshuffle at [Bank of America-Merrill Lynch]ORG, [Atul Singh]PERSON
has taken over as managing director of Global Wealth and Investment Management in
[India]LOCATION.
```

are error-prone; words may be wrongly capitalized and capitalization of first words in a sentence may lead to some confusion as in **Jobs said** ... or **Jobs are harder to find** .... Complex techniques such as co-reference resolution are needed to detect indirect occurrences of NE; e.g., through the use of pronouns. In **Prospects of ABC Corp. are looking bright. It has declared a dividend** ..., the pronoun **It** stands for **ABC Corp**. and may need to be identified as an occurrence of ORG. Another problem is the overlap between NE types; e.g., **Washington** can be used both as a PERSON or a LOCATION; **White House** can be used as both a LOCATION and an ORG. Many NE are multi-word (e.g., **Bank of America**). In such cases, identifying the boundary (i.e., the exact sequence of words) of a NE occurrence can be tricky; e.g., is **Boston Gas and Light Company** a single organization or a conjunction of two organizations? Also, NER is (at least partly) a language-specific task. For example, capitalization may be used in English to indicate a PERSON name but such a method is not available in many languages (like Hindi) which do not have capital letters. Alternatively, the form of a verb in a sentence indicates the gender of the subject in many languages (not English), which can help in NER (e.g., to detect PERSON names).

Another difficulty arises due to the different ways of referring to the same NE in the same document: abbreviations (**IBM** versus **International Business Machines**) and shortened names (**Mitsubishi Motor Company** versus **Mitsubishi**). It requires some reasoning to decide that **Boston Gas**

and Light Company is a single ORG and does not denote a conjunction of two ORG here, unlike in **Microsoft and Google**). While most NER can be done when processing each individual sentence, sometimes *long distance* clues from other sentences may be helpful. For example, we can decide that **MURDOCH** is a PERSON (though it is in all capitals) in **MURDOCH SATELLITE EXPLODES ON TAKE OFF** if we were able to determine when processing ... **Rupert Murdoch's ambition** ... later in the document that **Murdoch** is a PERSON. Thus a lazy approach to NER – where local decisions or evidences are effectively combined - might be useful, where some NE occurrences may initially be left untagged and which are tagged after sufficient evidence is available later. A one use per document principle might be useful to decide that all occurrences of **Philip Morris** (or **Morris**) are an ORG throughout a document, if even one sentence in the document provides a strong clue that **Philip Morris** is an ORG (... **president of Philip Morris said** ...). An effective NER system would require the use of use of a large amount of prior common-sense knowledge. For example, occurrence of a phrase like **Mitsubishi** and **Nissan** suggests that both these words should be assigned the same NE type. The task of assigning the correct NE type to a group of words in a sentence becomes quite subtle due to the complex nature of interdependencies among various parts of sentences. Overall, it is quite a technical challenge to build NER systems that rival human performance.

Desirable Characteristics of an NER System

Some desirable properties that a good NER system should possess are as follows. First, the system should obviously be highly accurate in its output. Next, it should be as efficient as possible; e.g., in terms of the time taken to tag a set of documents. The system should be robust in the presence of noise such as spelling and grammatical errors, wrong capitalization, incorrect sentence boundaries (e.g., missing periods) etc. The NER system should be as much corpus independent as possible i.e., it should be possible to reuse it on documents in different corpora, such as news items, emails, reports or blogs. Sometimes it is desirable to design an NER system which is portable or language independent and can identify NE in documents written a variety of (related) languages. Further, ideally an NER system should be designed to be largely domain independent, which can be adapted with little or no effort to identify new types of NE, possibly from different domains such as banking or manufacturing. Another aspect of an NER system is extendibility, which is the ability of the expert users to extend the knowledge sources used by the system (e.g., rules and gazetteers of known examples of a NE). Clearly, meeting all (or even most) of these goals is difficult and hence building a good NER system is a challenging task. Evaluation of the accuracy of an NER system is critical for enabling comparison between systems.

Techniques for NER

Approaches to build an NER system can be broadly divided into 4 groups. It should be emphasized that while this grouping helps in understanding the broad category of techniques, many NER systems reported in the literature contain two or more techniques.

1. **Rule-based Approaches**: Here, a set of rules is manually crafted by experts to recognize a particular NE type. The rules are based on syntactic, linguistic and domain knowledge.

2. **Supervised Learning Approaches**: Here, a large hand-tagged corpus is manually created by human experts, where instances of the given NE type are explicitly identified. Supervised learning algorithms from machine learning are used to generalize and discover NER rules from this labeled training dataset.

3. **Unsupervised Approaches**: Here, usually the system is provided a small set of seed instances (or examples) of the NE type; e.g., cities {'New York', Boston, London, Seoul}. The system then examines the given document collection and learns some rules from the sentences in which the seed NE examples occur. These rules are applied to identify new examples of NE and then learn a new set of rules. The system continues to learn in this way and stops when no new rules can be discovered.

4. **NE Extraction (NEX)**: The NEX task is quite similar to the unsupervised approaches, except that the goal is not to learn rules for NER but to create a *gazette* (*list* or *gazetteer*) of examples of the NE. Also, NEX is often applied to learn from web pages rather than documents. The idea is that once a comprehensive list of NE examples is created, NER in a given document corresponds to simple look up in this list.

In this paper, we discuss representative work from each of these approaches; see (Nadeau and Sekine 2007) for an excellent survey of NER literature. Detailed guidelines, issues and examples for NER are discussed in (Chinchor 1998), (Sang et al 2003). (Ratinov and Roth 2009) discuss some interesting issues and challenges in NER - particularly, the choice of an inference mechanism and representation of text chunks. Inclusion of the NER task in MUC and coNLL conferences as well as

Table 1. Some Tagged corpora for English NER

Corpus	URL
MUC-7 corpus	http://www.itl.nist.gov/iaui/894.02/relatedprojects/muc/proceedings/muc 7 proceedings
coNLL 2002 shared task corpora	http://cnts.uia.ac.be/conll2002/ner/
coNLL 2003 shared task corpora	http://cnts.uia.ac.be/conll2003/ner/
ACE corpora	http://www.ldc.upenn.edu/Projects/ACE/
GENIA	http://www-tsujii.is.s.u-tokyo.ac.jp/GENIA/home/wiki.cgi

availability of several corpora tagged with named entities has given a boost to the research in NER.

This chapter is organized as follows. First, the tagged datasets available for evaluating accuracy of an NER system are surveyed. Then methods to compute the accuracy of an NER system are presented. Next, specific types of NER techniques are reviewed. Lastly, the techniques are compared and some open problems are discussed.

TAGGED DATASETS FOR NER

Table 1 shows a list of some tagged corpora for NER tasks; see (Fort *et al* 2009) for guiding principles and a methodology for creating effective tagged NE datasets (tagging is also called *NE annotation*); see similar guidelines from LDC (http://projects.ldc.upenn.edu/ace/docs/English-Entities-Guidelinesv6.1.pdf). The Message Understanding Conferences MUC-6 and MUC-7 had a special track for NER tasks. There were a few broad classes of NE. The class Enamex consisted of 3 types of generic NE: PERSON (name of a person), LOCATION (name of a physical location such as city, state, country etc.) and ORG (name of an organization). The class Timex consisted of types of NE such as DATE and TIME. The class Numex consisted of various expressions used to state numeric quantities like state amounts, rates, numbers etc. MUC-7 provided a tagged corpus for these NE. This corpus contains 100 news items containing 4091 Enamex occurrences: 1880 ORG (46%), 1324 LOCATION (32%) and 887 PERSON

(22%). The corpus was tagged by several experts and there was substantial (97%) agreement among them. See Fig. 2 for an example.

The CoNLL-2003 shared task corpus for English contains a collection of news wire articles (there is a German corpus as well). The data files contain four columns separated by a single space. Each word is put on a separate line and there is an empty line after each sentence. The first item on each line is a word, the second a POS tag, the third a syntactic chunk tag and the fourth the NE tag. The chunk tags and the NE tags have the format I-TYPE which means that the word is inside a phrase of type TYPE. Only if two phrases of the same type immediately follow each other, the first word of the second phrase will have tag B-TYPE to show that it starts a new phrase. A word with tag O is not part of a phrase. The sentence **U.N. official Ekeus heads for Baghdad.** is tagged as follows:

U.N. NNP I-NP I-ORG
official NN I-NP O
Ekeus NNP I-NP I-PER
heads VBZ I-VP O
for IN I-PP O
Baghdad NNP I-NP I-LOC
. . O O

EVALUATION OF NER ALGORITHMS

The steps for evaluating any NER system are fairly standardized:

Figure 2. A sample news item in MUC-7 corpus: original and tagged text

```
CAPE CANAVERAL, Fla. &MD; Working in chilly temperatures Wednesday night, NASA
ground crews readied the space shuttle Endeavour for launch on a Japanese
satellite retrieval mission. Endeavour, with an international crew of six, was
set to blast off from the Kennedy Space Center on Thursday at 4:18 a.m. EST, the
start of a 49-minute launching period. The nine day shuttle flight was to be the
12th launched in darkness. <ENAMEX TYPE=''LOCATION''>CAPE CANAVERAL</ENAMEX>,
<ENAMEX TYPE=''LOCATION''>Fla.</ENAMEX> &MD; Working in chilly temperatures
<TIMEX TYPE=''DATE''>Wednesday</TIMEX> <TIMEX TYPE=''TIME''>night</TIMEX>,
<ENAMEX TYPE=''ORGANIZATION''>NASA</ENAMEX> ground crews readied the space
shuttle Endeavour for launch on a Japanese satellite retrieval mission. <p>
Endeavour, with an international crew of six, was set to blast off from the
<ENAMEX TYPE=''ORGANIZATION|LOCATION''>Kennedy Space Center</ENAMEX> on <TIMEX
TYPE=''DATE''>Thursday</TIMEX> at <TIMEX TYPE=''TIME''>4:18 a.m. EST</TIMEX>,
the start of a 49-minute launching period. The <TIMEX  TYPE=''DATE''>nine
```

1. Select a gold standard (or key) tagged corpus containing documents, each of which contains annotated instances of the given types of named entities. This corpus is often tagged manually. Randomly divide the documents in the corpus into training and testing sets (often in 80% − 20% proportion).

2. Use the training set to learn and to tune the NER knowledge base. Usually 10-fold cross validation is used to estimate the training error. No further changes should be made to the knowledge base after the training step is declared complete. Care should be taken to avoid any manual knowledge engineering specifically for improving the accuracy of the proposed algorithm over the given corpus.

3. Use the learned and tuned knowledge base to extract entities from the documents in the test set.

4. For each NE type, compute the precision, recall and an overall accuracy measure such as the F-measure.

Let $A = \{a_1, a_2, \ldots, a_N\}$ denote (multi)set of N occurrences of the chosen type of NE in the test corpus. Let $B = \{b_1, b_2, \ldots, b_M\}$ denote the (multi)set of the M occurrences of the chosen type of NE identified by the algorithm in the test corpus. An occurrence $b_i \in B$ is classified as a *true positive* (*TP*) (as *false positive* (*FP*)) if $b_i \in A$ ($b_i \notin A$ respectively). Thus the number of true positives identified by the algorithm is the number of occurrences which are in both B and A i.e., $\#TP = |A \cap B|$. The number of occurrences which are in B but not in A is the number of false positives: $\#FP = |B - A|$. An occurrence a_i in A is classified as a *false negative* (*FN*) if $a_i \notin B$. The number of occurrences which are in A but not in B is the number of false negatives: $\#FN = |A - B|$. Then the precision P, recall R and F-measure accuracy of the algorithm are:

$$P = \frac{\#TP}{|B|} = \frac{\#TP}{\#TP + \#FP}$$

$$R = \frac{\#TP}{|A|} = \frac{\#TP}{\#TP + \#FN}$$

$$F = \frac{2PR}{P + R}$$

Precision P indicates the fraction of the extracted entities that are correct. Recall R indicates the fraction of the correct entities that are extracted. Low precision indicates high value of #*FP* i.e., lot of noise in extraction. Low recall indicates high value of #*FN* i.e., lots of misses in extraction. The *F*-measure computes an overall accuracy by combining precision and recall. There are other ways of measuring the performance of NER algorithms, though *P*, *R* and *F* are most commonly used.

A delicate issue is how to compare the extracted occurrence and the occurrence in the *gold copy*. For example, suppose the gold copy marks **Bill Clinton** as a PERSON in a sentence and an NER algorithm extracts only **Clinton** as a PERSON in that sentence. Is this a correct match? An exact matching scheme treats such extraction as a mismatch i.e., FP. But often a more forgiving scheme is employed, which accepts partial matches; e.g., left match or right match; see (Tsai *et al* 2006).

RULE-BASED NER

While one can often use lexical (word-level) and syntactic cues for recognizing an NE type (e.g., a person name often begins with a capital letter), these rules are not sufficient; there are many special cases and most rules have exceptions. Following are some example rules to identify the occurrence of a PERSON in a sentence.

- Often consists of a sequence of words each of which begins with a capital letter followed by all lowercase letters (**John Ryder**); the first word is often a known first name (**John**) and the next word is unknown (**Ryder**).
- May contain a prefix title such as **Mr., Dr.** or **Prof. (Dr. Enrico Fermi)**
- May contain an initial in the middle or beginning (**Winston S. Churchil, A. John Northrop**)
- May contain a suffix such as **Jr.** or **III** (as in **George Bush Sr.**)

- May contain a designation indicator prefix such as **President, Justice, Sen., Colonel** or **CEO (President Clinton)**
- May be followed by an appositive NP suffix whose head word is singular and indicates a profession or a relation (**Malviya, a retired analyst, said ...;** or **Nielson, whose stepfather ...**)
- Does *not* include special characters such as **$, &** or **% (Johnson & Johnson)**
- Does *not* include prepositions (**Castle Of Windsor**)

Clearly, the rules are not sufficient to identify all occurrences of PERSON in a document. For one, the rules use many hand-crafted lists (e.g., titles, suffixes, designation or profession indicators etc.), which are likely to be incomplete. Also, the rules themselves are incomplete; e.g., they do not cover many examples: **White, 33, was arrested** ... and **Murdoch himself arrived** ... etc. In fact, many more rules can be defined based on a much deeper syntactic or semantic knowledge; e.g., a copula-based rule can be defined to cover examples like **Ryder is a popular juggler**. Another set of rules can be used to identify **Spasky** as a PERSON in **Spasky alighted quickly from the train** ... but this will require deep knowledge of what verbs (e.g., alight) can take only a PERSON as subject and under what situations. Rule-based approaches usually lack robustness and portability. Each new source of text requires significant tweaking of rules to maintain optimal performance and the maintenance efforts tend to be quite steep.

Some well-known rule-based NER systems are Univ. of Sheffield's LaSIEII (Humphreys *et al* 1998), ISOQuest's NetOwl (Krupka and Hausman 1998), Facile (Black *et al* 1998), SRA (Aone *et al* 1998) and Univ. of Edinburgh's LTG system (Mikheev *et al* 1999) and FASTUS (Appelt 1998) for English NER. These systems are mainly based on a set of hand-crafted syntactic and semantic rules for identifying NE instances.

LaSIE-II system (Humphreys *et al* 1998) is a modular IE system and uses a combination of NLP techniques for NER, including word sense disambiguation, co-reference resolution, a shallow semantic representation of the text in quasi-logical form and representation of the domain of discourse as a semantic net. Nodes represent concepts (along with properties) and edges represent hierarchy and support property inheritance; e.g., node *launch_event* has sub-nodes like *vehicle, payload, astronaut* and has properties such as *launch_date, launch_site, launch_org* etc. NER is posed essentially as a co-reference task. When processing a sentence, a set of presupposition rules may detect a new instance of a node (e.g., rule if *launch of X* then *X is-a vehicle*) and a set of consequence rules may fill up properties of an already detected instance of a node (e.g., if *launch ... from Y* then *Y is-a launch_site* property).

The FACILE system (Black *et al* 1998) consists of a set of hand-crafted patterns for NER in a regular expression like rule notation. The rules include a co-reference mechanism that detects and uses common text from previous occurrence of the same NE (**foreign secretary Robin Cook** and **Mr. Cook**). Interestingly, each rule predicts a NE type, with a certainty factor, if a condition is satisfied. An evidence combination mechanism is used to combine the certainty values of two matched rules for the same NE type.

The LTG system (Mikheev *et al* 1999) uses a lazy approach to NER where the rules are applied in phases, starting with the "sure fire" rules and proceeding to rules which are more "relaxed" and tag the NE occurrences left untagged by the previous phases, by making use of the already tagged occurrences of NEs. A grammar-like formalism is used for defining the rules. (Fukuda *et al* 1998) discussed a rule-based NER system for identifying protein names (e.g., p53, interleukin 1 (IL-1)-responsive kinase, insulin) in biomedical documents. (Bellot *et al* 2002) describes an NER system based on hand-crafted patterns (regular expression transducers) and its application to a question-answering system.

SUPERVISED LEARNING APPROACHES

In supervised learning approaches, NER is essentially posed as a classification problem. A set of labeled training dataset is given as input, where instances of the named entities in these documents are identified by human experts. A classification algorithm is used to generalize from these examples and discover a set of rules that can be applied to a new document to identify any instances of the named entities in it. Several distinct approaches to classification algorithms are developed in the machine learning, pattern recognition and statistics literature. Figure. 3 shows the conceptual architecture of an NER system based on supervised learning approach.

Hidden Markov Model Based Approaches

Several authors have used Hidden Markov Models (HMM) for NER; e.g., (Bikel *et al* 1999), (Seymore *et al* 1999), (Collier et al 2000), (Miller et al 1998), (Klein *et al* 2003). HMM approach has also been used for NER in languages other than English. HMM approach has also been used for DSNE; e.g., biomedical domain (Shen et al 2003), (Zhang et al 2002), (Zhao 2004); see also (Liu *et al* 2005) who used HMM for identifying NE such as product names. HMM models the sequence dependencies well and hence are useful for NER because the NE type of a particular word intuitively depends on previous words. The approaches using HMM differ mainly in the structure of the model and in the methods used to compute the associated probabilities.

See (Rabiner 1989) for an overview of the HMM formalism. Briefly, an HMM is like a finite-state automaton, except that each transition

Figure 3. Conceptual architecture of an NER system based on supervised learning

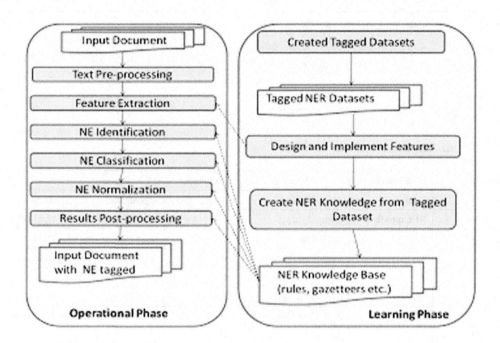

has a probability and transitions are not labeled with any symbol. The HMM also has a set of emission symbols. Each state emits a symbol with a particular probability. Given an observed sequence σ of emitted symbols, the decoding problem for HMM is efficiently solved by the Viterbi algorithm, which identifies a most probable sequence of states through which the HMM may have passed so as to generate σ. Typically, emission symbols are words and σ is the observed sequence of words. The corresponding state sequence obtained by decoding σ is the sequence of NE types, one for each word in σ.

We describe the approach of (Collier *et al* 2000), who used an HMM to detect NEs in the biomedical domain: PROTEIN, DNA, RNA, VIRUS, TISSUE, CELLLINE, CELLTYPE etc. Each state in the HMM represents an NE type. There are special states for start and end of a sentence. Each state emits a word W. Each word is represented as a tuple (W, F) where W is an actual word and F is a vector of features of that word. Features used include DigitNumber (15), Single-

Cap (M), GreekLetter (alpha), CapsAndDigits (I2), TwoCaps (RalGDS), InitCap (Interleukin), LowCaps (kappaB), lowercase (kinases), Hyphen (-), Fullstop (.) etc. (see Table 2 for more lexical word features). The probability $P(C_i|C_{i-1})$ of transition from the current state (i.e., NE type) C_{i-1} to next state C_i depends on the current and previous word and their features and the current state. It is computed as follows in Exhibit 1.

The λ_i's are constants such that $\sum_{i=1}^{5} \lambda_i = 1$. The authors manually set the values of λ_i's; but techniques such as Baum re-estimation algorithm could be used to estimate them. $f(X|Y)$ denotes the maximum likelihood estimate of the corresponding probability $P(X|Y)$; e.g., $f(X|Y) = \#(X \wedge Y)/\#Y$, where $\#(X \wedge Y)$ and $\#Y$ denote the number of occurrences of event (X and Y) and Y respectively. The above formula employs a progressive back-off to lesser details. For example, suppose $C_{i-1} =$ PERSON, $W_{i-1} =$ **Thomas**, $W_i =$ **Alva**. Suppose we use only 2 word features: InitCap and Lowercase; thus $F_{i-1} = (1, 0)$, $F_i = (1, 0)$. If the sequence

Exhibit 1.

$$P(C_i \mid C_{i-1}) = P(C_i \mid < W_i, F_i >, < W_{i-1}, F_{i-1} >, C_{i-1})$$
$$= \lambda_0 f(C_i \mid < W_i, F_i >, < W_{i-1}, F_{i-1} >, C_{i-1}) + \lambda_1 f(C_i \mid < \_, F_i >, < W_{i-1}, F_{i-1} >, C_{i-1})$$
$$+ \lambda_2 f(C_i \mid < W_i, F_i >, < \_, F_{i-1} >, C_{i-1}) + \lambda_3 f(C_i \mid < \_, F_i >, < \_, F_{i-1} >, C_{i-1}) + \lambda_4 f(C_i \mid C_{i-1})$$
$$+ \lambda_4 f(C_i)$$

Table 2. Orthographic features useful for NER

Feature	Example	Feature	Example	Feature	Example
CapAllLower	**John**	AlphaDigits	**pm50**	AlphaDash	**Hayes-Roth**
CapMixedAlpha	**NFCappaB**	DigitsAlpha	**22A**	DigitsComma	**12,000,000**
AllCaps	**IBM**	SingleCap	**P**	DigitsDot	**12.34**
SingleDigit	**9**	SingleCapDot	**P.**	ContainsAt	**x.y@z.com**
TwoDigits	**99**	LowMixedAlpha	**mRNA**	ContainsDot	**x.y@z.com**
FourDigits	**1999**	DigitAlphaDigit	**32Dc13**	ContainsDash	**12-Dec-1999**
AllDigits	**12345**	AlphaDigitAlpha	**IL23R**	ContainsGreek	**NFkappaB**
RomanNumeral	**IV,xi**	AllCapsDot	**I.B.M.**	AllCapsAnd	**AT&T**

of words **Thomas** followed by **Alva** has not occurred in the corpus, then the transition probability is estimated using only F_i without using the word **Alva**. If the corpus does not contain **Thomas** followed by a word with features (1, 0) then the probability is estimated using only the F_{i-1} and F_i and so on. The probability that the first word in a sentence will belong to some NE type C_j is computed using a similar but separate formula and depends only on the first word and its features, since there is no previous state and previous word.

(Zhou and Su 2002) is also an HMM-based NER system. One distinguishing feature of this system is the use of an HMM-based chunk tagger to identify chunks (i.e., sequences of words) which are candidates for NE. A separate HMM is then used to assign an NE type to each chunk. Another interesting aspect of this work is the use of a feature which checks whether any of the words in the current chunk are part of an NE already identified in the text. The system also integrates various gazetteers (e.g., holidays, cities) and uses match of the current chunk with any of the gazetteers as a feature.

In a different HMM-based approach to NER, called *character-level HMM*, characters (rather than words and phrases) are taken as the primary representation of the text. The idea is to use character-level features to perform NER; e.g., PERSON names often begin with a capital letter, have a mixed case and are preceded by character sequences such as **Mr.**

We describe the model of (Klein *et al* 2003). States encode an NE type and observations are characters (a character is emitted one at a time). Each state is a pair (t, k), where t is an NE type (such as PERSON, LOCATION, ORG etc. including OTHER) and k is the length of the time the model has been in state t; e.g., the state (PERSON, 2) indicates the state reached after processing the second letter in a person's name. The final letter of a word is followed by a space (inserted, if not present in the text) and the model transitions to a special state like (PERSON, F). Also, when k reaches n (the n-gram history order), it is not incremented any further. The transitions are defined in such a way that a state like (PERSON, 2) can transition to (PERSON, 3) or (PERSON, F) only. A final state like (PERSON, F) can only transition a beginning state like (OTHER, 1).

Probability of emitting a particular character in state s depends on the last $n-1$ observed characters: $P(c_0|c_{-5}c_{-4}c_{-3}c_{-2}c_{-1}, s)$, where c_0 is the current character, c_{-1} is the previous character and so on. Empirically, $n = 6$ is recommended. For example, $P(s|\textbf{Thoma}, PERSON, 6)$ is the probability of emitting character **s** in state (PERSON, 6) when the last 5 observed characters were Thoma. This probability is estimated from the corpus and smoothed using the method of deleted interpolation. The state transition probabilities (e.g., probabilities of going from (PERSON, 2) to either (PERSON, 3) or (PERSON, F)) are also estimated from the corpus. The Viterbi decoding is done in a standard way. For example, given the observed character sequence **I flew from Washington to Denver** the most likely sequence of states can now be found using the Viterbi algorithm.

Maximum Entropy Models

Several authors have used a *maximum entropy* (*ME*) based approach for NER; e.g., (Bender *et al* 2003), (Curran and Clark 2003), (Chieu and Ng 2003). ME based approaches have also been used for languages other than English, such as German, Spanish and Dutch. ME based approaches have been used for detecting DSNE in biological domain; e.g., (Lin *et al* 2004), (Raychaudhuri *et al* 2002). ME approach (which is a supervised approach) is used for NER because of its superior method of estimating a most uniform PDF from training data i.e., one which makes the least additional assumptions. This PDF is then used for predicting the NE type for given sequence of words. The ME approach is often used in conjunction with an HMM approach. The specific works of

various authors differ mainly in the features used. See (Berger *et al* 1996) for a good introduction to ME methods for natural language applications.

Given a labeled training dataset (e.g., a corpus containing tagged occurrences of NE), many features (or summary statistics) can be defined, each of which characterizes a particular aspect of the phenomenon (rules used for NE tagging, in our case). Often each feature is modeled as a binary-valued function f_j of arity more than 1, where the first argument denotes the NE type for the ith word in a sentence and the rest of the arguments denote the context of that word. A feature can be thought of as a black box that takes some context of the current word as input and produces the NE tag for the current word as output. Let W_i and C_i denote the *random variables* (*RV*) which take on values as words and NE types respectively (W_i is the ith word in a sentence and C_i is its NE type). Then some examples of features are as follows:

$f_1(C_i, W_i) = 1$ if W_i begins with a capital letter and C_i = PERSON; 0 otherwise

$f_2(C_i, W_{i-1}) = 1$ if POS tag of W_{i-1} is verb and C_i = PERSON; 0 otherwise

$f_3(C_i, W_{i-1}) = 1$ if POS tag of W_{i-1} is preposition and C_i = OTHER; 0 otherwise

Expected value of each feature may be considered as a summary statistic of the training dataset. For example, in a particular corpus, one may find that 37% words that begin with a capital letter were tagged as PERSON; 19% words that follow a verb may be found to be tagged as PERSON; and 88% words that follow a preposition may be found to be tagged as OTHER. The empirically observed expected values of f_1, f_2 and f_3 are $\textbf{E}_{OBS}(f_1) = 0.37$, $\textbf{E}_{OBS}(f_2) = 0.19$ and $\textbf{E}_{OBS}(f_3) = 0.88$ respectively. The expected value of feature f_1 in the training dataset is defined as follows:

$$E_{OBS}(f_1) = \sum_{c \in C,\ words\ w} P_{OBS}(c, w) f_1(c, w)$$

where $P_{OBS}(c, w)$ is the probability of observing the word w tagged with NE type c in the training dataset; this probability is estimated as relative frequency.

Suppose that we want to identify a *probability distribution function* (*PDF*) $P(C_i|W_i, W_{i-1})$ that predicts the NE type of the current word given its previous word. The observed statistics impose three constraints on the desired PDF: the expected values of features f_1, f_2 and f_3 as computed using P should be the same as those empirically observed in the training dataset.

$\mathbf{E}(f_1) = \mathbf{E}_{OBS}(f_1)$ i.e., $\mathbf{E}(f_1) = 0.37$ and
$\mathbf{E}(f_2) = \mathbf{E}_{OBS}(f_2)$ i.e., $\mathbf{E}(f_2) = 0.19$ and
$\mathbf{E}(f_3) = \mathbf{E}_{OBS}(f_3)$ i.e., $\mathbf{E}(f_3) = 0.88$

In general, an infinite number of PDFs may be consistent with the given constraints. The ancient *principle of insufficient reason* says that one should choose that hypothesis which is consistent with the given facts and which makes the fewest possible additional assumptions. A mathematical formalization of this principle is the *principle of maximum entropy* (*ME*): choose that PDF (among those consistent with the given constraints) which is as uniform as possible i.e., one which has the maximum entropy. It can be shown that such a PDF always exists and is unique. *Entropy* of a PDF $P(X)$ is the expected number of bits required to specify values of RV X drawn according to P.

$$H(P(X)) = \mathbf{E}\left(\frac{1}{\log_2(P(x))}\right) = -\sum_x P(x)\log_2(P(x))$$

Here, x varies over all values of the discrete RV X. Analogously, the entropy of a conditional PDF $P(Y|X)$ is defined as:

$$H(P(Y|X)) = -\sum_x P(x)\sum_y P(y|x)\log_2(P(y|x))$$

In our case, the principle of ME has suggested to identify a conditional PDF (e.g., $P(C_i|W_{i-1}, W_i)$)

which satisfies the given constraints and which has the maximum conditional entropy. This is a problem in constrained optimization: maximize a function having the form of conditional entropy under given constraints having the form $\mathbf{E}_{OBS}(f_j)$ = $\mathbf{E}P(f_j)$. The method of Lagrangian multipliers can be applied to find the optimal solution to this constrained optimization problem. It can be shown that the required conditional CDF (which is consistent with the given constraints and has the maximum entropy) has a particular form. In our example, the required conditional PDF $P(C_i|W_{i-1}, W_i)$ has the following form:

$$P(C_i = c \mid W_{i-1} = u, W_i = v) = \frac{e^{\lambda_1 f_1(c,v)+\lambda_2 f_2(c,v)+\lambda_3 f_3(c,v)}}{\sum_{d \in C} e^{\lambda_1 f_1(d,v)+\lambda_2 f_2(d,v)+\lambda_3 f_3(d,v)}}$$

$\lambda_1, \lambda_2, \lambda_3$ are unknown Lagrangian multipliers, one for each constraint. Once their values are determined, we can compute the required probability for any situation; e.g., the probability that the NE type for **John** given its previous word is **to** is computed as:

$$P(C_i = PERSON \mid W_{i-1} = \text{to}, W_i = \text{John}) = \frac{e^{\lambda_1 1+\lambda_2 0+\lambda_3 0}}{e^{\lambda_1 1+\lambda_2 0+\lambda_3 0} + e^{\lambda_1 0+\lambda_2 0+\lambda_3 1}} = \frac{e^{\lambda_1}}{e^{\lambda_1}+e^{\lambda_3}}$$

Assuming that the predicted NE type for **John**, given its previous word is **to** is PERSON, we have $f_1(\text{PERSON, John}) = 1$, $f_2(\text{PERSON, to}) = 0$, $f_3(\text{PERSON, to}) = 0$ and $f_3(\text{OTHER, to}) = 1$. In the testing phase, the NE type for **John** would be unknown. The above probability computation can be made for all NE types (e.g., LOCATION, OTHER etc.) and the one having the maximum value is output as the prediction. The optimal values for the Lagrangian multipliers can be found using algorithms such as the Generalized Iterative Scaling.

To summarize, given a labeled training dataset, the principle of ME can be used to estimate a PDF that assigns a NE label to any word in a given sentence, given its context. This is a supervised learning approach, since the constraints are based on a labeled training dataset. The ME approach crucially depends on the feature functions used as summary statistics for the training dataset. The chosen features must be relevant and sufficient for NER. Hundreds of different features can be defined, based on orthographic, lexical and syntactic analysis of the given word and its context. Hence, selection of appropriate features is an important task in the ME approach. Feature selection is a large research area in itself; see (Berger *et al* 1996) for a discussion relevant to the ME approach.

The ME approach has been extended in several ways when used for NER. A common approach (Barthowick 1999) simultaneously assigns NE types to all words in a sentence, rather than one word at a time. Given a sequence of words w_1, ..., w_n in a sentence, the corresponding sequence of NE types c_1, ..., c_n is one which has the highest posterior probability among all possible NE type sequences:

$$c_1, \ldots c_n = \arg\max_{d_1, \ldots, d_n} P(d_1, \ldots, d_n \mid w_1, \ldots, w_n)$$

Such a maximum posterior probability sequence is computed using the Viterbi algorithm. Basically, one defines a Hidden Markov Model, where each state corresponds to an NE type. Transition probability matrix (probability p_{ij} that an NE type i is followed by NE type j) is estimated from the training dataset.

Each state has a probability distribution for emitting a word (or its corresponding feature vector). The Viterbi algorithm efficiently estimates the most likely sequence of states traversed by the HMM in order to generate the given word sequence.

(Chieu and Ng 2003) have proposed the use of global features, based on the entire corpus, in addition to features based on only the local context of a word in a sentence. For example, they compile various lists from the corpus: UNI is a list of words that frequently precede the occur-rence of a given NE type; UBI is a list of bigrams that frequently precede the occurrence of a given NE type (e.g., **city of** for LOCATION); SUF is a list of 3-letter suffixes that frequently terminate words in a given NE type (e.g., **inc** for ORG); FUN is a list of function words that frequently occur in occurrences NE type (e.g., **van der** for PERSON). They defined features based on these lists; e.g., whether a word contained a suffix from SUF. They also include features that detect use of acronyms. For example, if **Federal Communications Commission** is detected to be an ORG in a document then the word **FCC** in that document should get tagged as an ORG, since it matches with the sequence of first letters in a known ORG.

(Park *et al* 2006) has used a 2-step approach – *NE identification* (also called *NE boundary detection*) followed by NE classification – for biomedical NER, where they used a separate ME classifier for each step. Mostly lexical features were used in each step and they were divided into groups such as salient words, morphological patterns and collocations.

(Chen and Rosenfeld 1999) proposed a smoothing method to compute the ME model parameters (i.e., the Lagrange multipliers) by assuming a Gaussian prior distribution on their values; all Langrage multipliers have the same Gaussian distribution. This method avoids very large values and also eliminates features that "fire" rarely. (Bender et al 2003) and (Curran and Clark 2003) used this method for their ME-based NER.

Support Vector Machines

Consider a labeled training dataset $\{(\mathbf{x}_1, y_1), (\mathbf{x}_2, y_2), \ldots, (\mathbf{x}_N, y_N)\}$ where each $\mathbf{x}_i$ is a point in n-dimensional real space (value of every feature is a real number) and each class label y_i is either $+1$ or -1. A *support vector machine* (*SVM*) (Vapnik 1998) is a binary classifier that learns the equation $\mathbf{w} \cdot \mathbf{x} + b = 0$ of a separating hyperplane that has the maximum margin. Here, $\mathbf{w}$ is the vector of feature weights and b is the offset of the hyperplane from the origin. Both **w** and *b* are learned from the training dataset. Given a query point $\mathbf{q} \in \mathbf{R}^n$, the classification decision is made as follows: if $\mathbf{w} \cdot \mathbf{x} + b > 0$ then predict class label $+1$ else predict class label -1. *Margin* is defined as the distance between the hyperplane and the *support vectors* (i.e., points from the training dataset which are nearest to the hyperplane). Hyperplane with the maximum margin tends to be more accurate for classifying unseen data i.e., it has a better generalization. Identifying the maximum margin hyperplane can be formulated as a quadratic optimization problem. Its solution (i.e., formulas to compute the values for w and b) requires only computations of the inner products $\mathbf{x}_i \cdot \mathbf{x}_j$ of the feature vectors in the training dataset. Note that a hyperplane is a linear separator for the training dataset.

If the training dataset is not linearly separable, then SVM employs the so-called *kernel trick*. Each n-dimensional point $\mathbf{x}_i$ in the training dataset is transformed into a (usually higher dimensional) point $\Phi(\mathbf{x}_i)$ such that the inner product in the transformed space is computed efficiently using the *kernel function K* i.e., $\Phi(\mathbf{x}_i) \cdot \Phi(\mathbf{x}_j) = K(\mathbf{x}_i, \mathbf{x}_j)$. Hopefully, the training dataset in the transformed space is linearly separable and then the hyperplane in the transformed space can be used to classify query points. A linear separator in the transformed space corresponds to a non-linear separator in the original space. The kernel function K is required to satisfy certain conditions (e.g., K should be positive definite). For example, the transformation

$$\Phi(x_1, x_2) = \left(x_1^2, x_2^2, \sqrt{2}x_1, \sqrt{2}x_2, 1 \right)$$

maps a 2-dimensional point (x_1, x_2) to a 5 dimensional point. The polynomial kernel function $K(\mathbf{u}, \mathbf{v}) = (\mathbf{u} \cdot \mathbf{v} + 1)^m$ ($m = 2$ here) satisfies the required property that $\Phi(\mathbf{u}) \cdot \Phi(\mathbf{v}) = K(\mathbf{u}, \mathbf{v})$, as can be checked.

SVM is a binary classifier i.e., it handles only 2 classes. But in general, the number of NE types M is more than 1 (e.g., PERSON, LOCATION,

ORG). For this reason, several methods have been proposed to extend SVM for multi-class classification. In *one-vs-rest* method, *M* SVMs are constructed where the ith SVM predicts class $+1$ for i^{th} class (NE type) and -1 for the rest of the classes together. The query point **q** is given to all *M* SVMs and the predicted class for **q** is the one which has the maximum value of $\mathbf{w} \cdot \mathbf{q} + b$. In the *pair-wise* method (Krebel 1999), $M(M-1)/2$ SVMs are constructed, where a particular SVM predicts whether the given point belongs to class *i* or class *j*. Treating the decision of each SVM as a *vote*, the predicted class for a given query point **q** is the one that gets the maximum votes. (Isozaki and Kazawa 2002) uses a one-vs-rest approach for multi-class NER using SVM for Japanese; they also propose a feature selection method as well as a method for reducing the dot product computations of the given sample with all support vectors in all the SVMs.

In the training phase, each word in the labeled input text is represented as a vector of numeric features and a class label (NE type). Features for a word can be lexical (AllCap, AllCapDot, InitCap, AllLowerCase, CapDot, ContainsDash, ContainsGreek etc.), POS tag, syntactic tag (NP, VP etc.). Other features can also be used such as whether the word contains a specific prefix, suffix (e.g., **enese**) or substring. Some features for a word may refer to properties of previous or next words.

Several implementations of SVM are available in the public domain such as LIBSVM and SVM^{light}. Several approaches have been developed for using SVM for NER (Yamamoto et al 2003), (Lee et al 2004), (Kazama *et al* 2002), (Song et al 2005), (Takeuchi and Collier 2002) which have more or less followed the above approach, with some modifications for efficiency improvements.

(Lee et al 2004) split the NER task into two parts: *identification* or *boundary detection* (identifying the contiguous sequence of words called region that forms a NE) and *classification* (assigning an NE type such as PERSON to an identified region). Identification is itself a binary classification task: T (current word is part of a NE) or O (current word not part of an NE). One SVM is created for identification and M SVMs are created for classification (M = number of NE types). They correct the errors made by the SVM in identifying the boundary using an entity-word dictionary.

Since NE occurrences are relatively less frequent, there is severe class imbalance in the training dataset; e.g., PERSON occurs much less frequently than OTHER NE type. One solution to handle such class imbalance (Kazama *et al* 2002) is to split the OTHER NE type into several sub-types (e.g., one sub-type for each of the 45 POS tags in Penn TreeBank). Other problem is related to data sparseness: creating a large and high quality tagged corpus is difficult. One approach to handle data sparseness is to use more general features (e.g., disjunctions) which apply to more instances. Another approach has used the state of an HMM trained on an untagged corpus as a word feature.

Since a tagged corpus is difficult to create, (Yi *et al* 2004) and (Sasano 2003) have developed techniques to expand the corpus by adding virtual examples using domain knowledge. (Yi *et al* 2004) also proposed the use of M edit distances as word features: average edit distance of a given word from each entry in a dictionary for a specific NE type. Edit distance captures structural similarity between two words; if a word is similar (less edit distance) to a known example of an NE type, then it is likely to have the same NE type. *Edit* (or *Levenshtein*) *distance* between two strings X and Y is defined as the minimum number insert, delete, substitute operations required to transform X into Y. For example, the edit distance between **kitten** and **sitting** is 3.

Other Approaches

Other supervised learning approaches have been used for NER; e.g., decision trees (Sekine 1998), conditional random fields (CRF) (Lafferty 2001),

(Watanabe 2002), (McCallum and Li 2003) and so on. Since the Web is a vast knowledge source, (Kazama and Torisawa 2007) uses category labels from Wikipedia definition of a word as a feature when learning a CRF-based NE classifier. (Settles 2004) uses CRF for biomedical NER, which used, apart from standard features, a number of gazetteers containing semantic knowledge (such as known genes, chromosome locations, viruses, amino acids, proteins and cell-lines etc.). (Gliozzo *et al* 2005) describes some pre-processing techniques that helps in improving classifier performance and accuracy. (Meulder and Daelemans 2003) uses a feature-weighted nearest neighbour classifier: all training examples, along with their features and NE type are stored and when given a new candidate word (and its features), the NE type for it is decided from the NE types of the k nearest examples to it. (Krishnan and Manning 2006) uses two coupled CRF classifiers that use non-local (i.e., long-range dependency) features; e.g., *label consistency* or *one use per document* (all occurrences of **New York** should get the same NE type in a document).

(Sun *et al* 2002) used the *n-gram statistical language models* (*LM*) for performing NER in Chinese. Each NE type is a class and class OTHER indicates a non-NE word. In a LM, the probability of nth word is estimated using probabilities of the occurrences of previous $n-1$ words. The context model computes the probability $P(c_3|c_2, c_1)$ for a sequence w_1, w_2, w_3 of words; these probabilities are estimated using a corpus where NE are labeled. The entity model (separate for each NE type) computes the probability of seeing the given sequence of words assuming that each word is labeled with the given NE type; e.g., probability of seeing the sequence of words Air China Corporation assuming that all three words are labeled as ORG. These probabilities are estimated using a corpus and lists. *Deep Belief Net* (*DBN*) have also been used for NER. A DBN is a multi-layer neural network that consists of one or more Restricted Boltzmann Machine layers and a Back Propagation layer. DBN is claimed to have both an efficient learning mechanism and good expressive power.

UNSUPERVISED LEARNING APPROACHES

A basic problem with supervised learning approaches to classification is their crucial dependence on the availability of large, representative and high-quality labeled training datasets. Typically, such labeled datasets are created manually by experts. This makes creation of labeled datasets an expensive, time-consuming and error-prone task. Further, sometimes even the experts disagree among themselves, and this needs to be handled. *Unsupervised learning* approaches work on an unlabeled set of documents to automatically infer occurrences of NE. One typically starts with a small given *seed list* of known NE of a specific NE type (e.g., a small list of known person names) and attempts to discover additions to this list. This is done by detecting common patterns in the usage of given examples and conjecturing that any words that fit into these patterns are candidate NE occurrences. For example, examining the sentences in which cities from the seed list occur, one may find that in several sentences they were preceded by words **city of**. Generalizing this pattern, in another sentence the word following **city of** is a candidate occurrence of NE type CITY. The main question then is: how to discover common patterns in the usage of a given instances of an NE type? We discuss two prominent unsupervised approaches to NER. Such approaches are also called *bootstrapping* or *weakly supervised*.

Unsupervised approaches are somewhat different from *semi-supervised* approaches typically used in classification tasks. Here, in addition to the seed list, a large set of unlabeled examples is also available; e.g., in NER, occurrences of proper nouns may be considered as unlabeled examples and each NE type corresponds to a class. The classifier design takes into account this unlabeled examples.

(Collins and Singer 1999) start with a given list of simple *decision rules*; e.g., contains(*Incorporated*) → ORG and *full_string* = *Microsoft* → ORG. An untagged corpus is then examined (using syntactic rules) to identify candidate proper names (sequence of consecutive proper nouns). For example, one syntactic rule extracts a proper name if it occurs within an NP and its last word is the head of the NP (e.g., **Al Gore** is extracted from the NP **vice president Al Gore**). Another rule extracts a proper name in an NP *X* if *X* has an appositive modifier NP whose head is a singular noun; e.g., proper name **Maury Cooper** in ..., **says Maury Cooper, a vice president at S&P**. is extracted because the head of the appositive modifier NP is a singular noun (**president**). In each iteration of their DL-coTrain algorithm, first context rules and then spelling rules are discovered as follows. The unlabeled text is labeled using current rules. Then context rules (e.g., *context* = president or *context_type* = *appos*) having precision above a given threshold are extracted. Next, using these new and old rules, new spelling rules (of the form *AllCap1* → ORG or *nonalpha* = .) having high precision are extracted in a similar manner. The iterations stop when a limit on the maximum number of new rules is exceeded.

Clearly, a look up approach to NER would be very efficient. It would also be accurate, provided the lists (*gazetteers*) of known NE are guaranteed to be complete. *Named Entity Extraction* (*NEX*) also called *automatic gazetteer construction* consists of a system that automatically constructs a list of the instances of entities of a given type (e.g., CITY) from a given source such as a set of Web pages. The system is typically weakly unsupervised, in the sense that it does not use a large hand-tagged corpus where instances of the given NE type are explicitly identified. It may, however, start with a small set of seed instances of the NE type; e.g., an NEX system to identify all CITY names may start with a seed set of 4 cities {'**New York**', **Berlin**, **London**, **Seoul**}. The NEX task is somewhat different from the NER task because of ambiguity. For example, even if **Jobs** is present in the previously created list of PERSON instances, it still remains a challenge to recognize whether the word **Jobs** in a given document is used as a person name or as a common noun.

KNOWITALL (Etzioni *et al* 2005) is an unsupervised NEX system that uses the Web as a corpus to create a list of instances of the given NE type (e.g., CITY or FILM). It starts with a set of domain independent patterns instantiated for the given NE type. One such pattern is that if one entry in a list is of the given NE type then all others in the list must also be of the same NE type. This pattern is specified as: NP1 such as ListOfNP2, where head of NP1 is a plural form of the NE label (**cities**) and head of each NP2 is a proper noun (**cities such as London, Paris and Tokyo**). There are additional constraints such as NP1 and each of NP2 must be simple noun phrases and the NE label should be the head of NP1 (which avoids pitfalls such as **city clubs such as** ... where city is not the head of the NP. The proper noun test of NP2 is important to avoid examples such as **Detailed maps for several cities such as street maps, railway maps** .... Whenever an occurrence of an extractor rule is detected in the given text, an assessor module checks whether there is high *point-wise mutual information* (*PMI*) between the occurrence and some automatically generated discriminator phrases. For example, to check whether **Liege** is a CITY, the assessor module computes the PMI between **Liege** and phrases such as **Liege is a city**. PMI between an instance *I* and a discriminator phrase *D* is computed as the ratio of the number of times *I* and *D* occur together (e.g., in the same sentence) to the number of times *I* occurs alone:

$$PMI(I, D) = \frac{\#(D \wedge I)}{\# I}$$

If there are *m* discriminator phrases, then we have *m* PMI values for the given instance. These *m* PMI values are converted to a Boolean feature vector $F_I = (f_1, f_2, \ldots, f_m)$ for *I* where $f_i = 1$ if the ith PMI value is above its threshold and 0 otherwise. KNOWITALL then uses a *Naive Bayes Classifier* (*NBC*) to classify F_I as belonging to the given NE type or not. To estimate the conditional probabilities needed by the NBC, KNOWITALL uses a labeled training dataset of $k = 10$ positive and $k = 10$ negative seed examples for each NE type. KNOWITALL has a simple bootstrapping algorithm to automatically select these $2k$ seed examples (based on their hit counts and PMI scores). Some examples of the discriminator phrases automatically identified by the bootstrapping method are: <I> **is a city**, <I> **and other towns**, **cities** <I> and **cities including**. The threshold for each discriminator phrase is also automatically determined using a separate labeled training dataset of $k = 10$ positive and $k = 10$ negative seed examples for each NE type. KNOWITALL also contains a learning algorithm to automatically discover additional extractor patterns (which are very different from the given "built-in" patterns like NP1 **such as** NP2List discussed above); e.g., **headquartered in** <CITY>. Essentially, this algorithm finds phrases that co-occur frequently with known examples of the given NE type and evaluates them using a metric based on a modified notion of precision and recall.

Among other work on unsupervised NER, (Watanabe et al 2003) uses CRF to create gazetteers from Wikipedia. (Jimeno *et al* 2008) compares various NER methods for automatically creating a gazetteer as well as an annotated NER corpus for disease names in medicine. Given a seed list of NE type examples, (Talukdar *et al* 2006) learns a pattern (as an automaton) from their contexts (*k* words before and after). The contexts are pruned using the IDF measure and then an automaton is induced from the contexts using a grammatical induction algorithm. Each transition in the induced automaton is given a probability and transitions with weak probability are pruned. (Meulder and Daelemans 2003) use a simple conjunction-based generalization to construct a gazetteer from a seed list (if a word in a conjunction is a known NE type then the other words in the conjunction also have the same NE type). (Liao and Veeramachaneni 2009) is an iterative unsupervised algorithm that starts by learning a CRF NE classifier from seed examples, and then identifies NE occurrences from the text that the classifier classifies with low confidence but for which strong independent evidence is available; e.g., if **Safeway Inc.** is known to be ORG then **Safeway** in **Safeway has recently opened** ... is also likely to be ORG with high confidence, even though the classifier may have low confidence on it. The CRF classifier is retrained after adding such examples to the training dataset. The process stops when no new examples are found. (Kim *et al* 2002) use a similar iterative approach (seed examples, train classifier, add new examples re-train) for NER in Korean text, except that they used an ensemble of 3 machine learning methods (nearest-neighbour, network of Winnows and ME). Final NE type is selected by a voting mechanism based on the probability of correct decision for each of the 3 classifiers. (Shinyama and Sekine2004) propose an interesting method to identify NE from a set of comparable news articles (e.g., news articles reporting the same events but from different newspapers and on different days). The idea is that a general word like **killed** will have a very different distribution (in the corpus of comparable articles) than a NE word such as **Yitzhak** (e.g., diffuse versus spiky).

Unsupervised approaches have also been applied to the task of *fine-grained NER*, where the goal is to assign an appropriate sub-class from a given ontology *T* to each occurrence of a NE; e.g., each PERSON may be assigned a sub-class such as *politician, scientist, sports-person, film-star* or *musician*. The ontology *T* is generally organized as a hierarchy; e.g., a *scientist* may be *physicist,*

chemist or *biologist*. Due to the large and changing nature of the ontology, it is very effort-intensive to create a manually tagged corpus with sufficient examples of each class. Hence, unsupervised approaches are attractive for fine-grained NER. Fine-grained NER is likely to be more useful for tasks related to semantic web.

(Fleischman and Hovy 2002) use supervised classification methods (decision trees, neural network, nearest neighbour, SVM and Naive Bayes) to classify PERSON NE into 8 subclasses (*athlete, politician, clergy, businessperson, artist, lawyer, scientist, police*) based on local context, topic-specific terms and as WordNet hypernyms for the context words. (Tanev and Magnini 2008) combines dependency-analysis results obtained from all the contexts in which a given seed example occurs into a single graph. Context of a candidate NE is then compared (for similarity) with each of these syntactic models (graphs) to decide its class. In a similar manner, (Ganti *et al* 2008) take the union of the words present around each occurrence of the given NEs and use frequently occurring *n*-grams in these aggregated contexts as features. For example, **painted** by may frequently occur around a given NE **Picasso**. They also use memberships of the context words in given lists of known NEs as features; e.g., if **NBA** is known to be a sport ORG then **Ming is drafted by NBA** gives a clue that **Ming** may be a sports-person. A separate classifier is then built for each subclass using this training data. (Ekbal et al 2010) develop an unsupervised method for acquiring a comprehensive dataset for fine-grained NER (for PERSON) by applying linguistic patterns (and filtering rules) to a corpus acquired from the Web; e.g., a pattern like [the|The]? [JJ|NN]* [NN] [NP] matches ... **writings of the abstract painter Kandinsky frequently explored similarities between** ... and can extract NE **Kandinsky** with fine-grained class label *painter*. They also develop an ME classifier for fine-grained NER.

NER IN OTHER LANGUAGES

Along with English, NER techniques have been developed for many other languages. These techniques can be broadly understood as either (i) language-specific NER techniques designed to use characteristics and linguistic knowledge of a particular language; or (ii) application of a language-independent NER technique across a class of related languages. Conferences CoNLL-2002 and coNLL2003 included a shared task for language independent NER. Here, we review only a scattering of the work in this area, as a more complete review of NER in other languages needs a separate paper. NER techniques have been applied to European languages (French, German, Spanish, Greek etc.), Asian languages (Arabic, Chinese, Japanese, Korean, Vietnamese) and Indic languages (Hindi, Urdu, Bengali, Tamil, Marathi, Oriya etc.). Several differences - such as richer morphology, gender sensitive word-forms, different word ordering and lack of capitalization - between English and many of the other languages make the NER task different (and sometimes harder). As an example, detecting whether a word (e.g., **Ganga**) is a proper or a common noun (POS tag is an important feature for NER) is difficult in Indic languages, because there is no capitalization - a problem that may also occur in noisy English texts such as blogs. One may have to refer to a lexicon to make such a decision (proper nouns are generally not present in a lexicon). Word segmentation itself is a major problem in many languages including Chinese and Japanese.

CONCLUSION AND FUTURE RESEARCH DIRECTIONS

We have reviewed (in a far from exhaustive manner) some major approaches to English NER. We now discuss some open areas in NER research.

One critical issue that has received less attention is that of post-processing of results produced by an NER system. NER is often accompanied by some post-processing to correct classification errors that may have occurred. (Lin *et al* 2004) propose a simple method to correct classification errors. They also propose a method for correcting NE boundary errors when only part of the NE has been detected correctly (e.g., rules for extending the detected NE to right or left). Combining the outputs of several NER systems, in the spirit of classifier ensembles, also has not received as much attention as it should have. Such classifier

ensemble methods have shown promise in that the overall accuracy is better than that of the constituent classifiers, in standard statistical classification tasks (not necessarily NER). (Florian *et al* 2003) uses a class-error based voting scheme to combine the outputs of NER classifiers based on ME, HMM, Robust risk minimization and transformation-based learning. (Thao *et al* 2007) compares 3 voting mechanisms (majority, total accuracy, class-wise accuracy) to combine CRF, SVM, Naive Bayes and decision tree based NER classifiers for Vietnamese (see also (Tsai *et al* 2006)). (Wang and Patrick 2009) reports a combination scheme to combine SVM, ME and CRF classifiers and its application to perform NER from clinical notes. (Ekbal and Bandyopadhyay 2010) use a majority voting approach to combine NER classifiers for Bengali based on ME, CRF and SVM and demonstrate an increase of about 11% over the best performing SVM classifier for this task.

Systematic comparison of various NER techniques, particularly for different languages, over different domains and across varied and unseen corpora, is an important issue. (Krishnarao *et al* 2009) compare CRF and SVM based NER systems for Hindi. (Petasis et al 2004) compares the performance of different NER systems on English, French, Greek and Italian web-pages. (Sekine and Eriguchi 2000) compare various techniques (ME, Decision Tree, HMM as well as hand-crafted patterns) for Japanese NER. NER from sources other than plain text (e.g., news articles) has received less attention, except possibly for HTML web-pages.

Building an NER system that works smoothly (with little or no tuning) on multiple types of text sources is a difficult task. It is often observed that an NER system trained on one type of text source (e.g., news articles) does not work well on other text sources (e.g., Web pages). (Maynard *et al* 2001) describes a system called Muse (based on the open GATE architecture framework for NLP systems), which is capable of NER from diverse types of text sources. A separate set of resources (patterns, gazetteers etc.) are developed for each text type (like emails, spoken text, scientific text, religious text). (Balasuriya *et al* 2009) evaluate an NER system trained on manually tagged Wikipedia pages.

We have barely mentioned in this paper other important problems in NER. First, there is *NE disambiguation*, where the task is to identify correct NE type for an identified NE instance; (e.g., does **Washington went ahead** mention a PERSON, a LOCATION, or an ORG?). Among much work done for NE disambiguation, we mention (Cucerzan 2007), (Bunescu and Pasca 2006) and (Han and Zhao 2009) which use Wikipedia as a knowledge source to perform NE disambiguation. Most pages in Wikipedia are associated with an entity or concept, along with NE type (PERSON, LOCATION, ORG etc.) and category/topic tags. In addition, much knowledge can be derived about the entity by analyzing the content of the associated page. For example, a document that contains the surface forms **Columbia** and **Discovery** is likely to refer to the Space Shuttle Columbia and the Space Shuttle Discovery because these candidate entities share the category tags *LIST_astronomical_topics*, *CAT_Manned_spacecraft*, *CAT_Space_Shuttles*, while alternative entity disambiguations, such as **Columbia Pictures** and **Space Shuttle Discovery**, do not share any common category tags.

(Nadeau *et al* 2006) uses the web as a source for NE disambiguation. (Mikheev 1999) proposes heuristics for NE-noun disambiguity (**Jobs** as a PERSON or noun). For example, in a given document, assume that a word or phrase with initial capitals (e.g., **Jobs**) is a NE unless (1) it sometimes appears in the document without initial capitals (e.g., **jobs**), (2) it only appears at the start of a sentence or at the start of a quotation (e.g., "**Jobs that pay well** ..." or (3) it only appears inside a sentence in which all words with more than three characters start with a capital letter (e.g., a title or section heading).

NE-NE ambiguity is harder to resolve; e.g., is **France** a LOCATION or PERSON? (Nguyen and Cao 2008) proposes a hybrid methodology for NE disambiguation that uses a both statistical and rule-based steps in an iterative manner. Knowledge from WordNet ontologies can also be used for NER; e.g., see (Negri and Magnini 2004). For example, WordNet hypernym tree for **Mississippi** includes location. Further, WordNet gloss and relations can provide trigger words that can be used for NER.

In *NE boundary detection*, the task is to identify the correct NE boundary (e.g., does the **Alliance for Democracy in Mali** mention one, two, or three entities?). (Palmer and Day 2006) and (Nadeau *et al* 2006) prescribe heuristics; e.g., merge all consecutive words of the same NE type and every NE type occurrence with any adjacent capitalized words. As an example, if **Jean** and **Smith** are both marked as PERSON then mark Jean Smith as PERSON and if **Red Sox** is an ORG then tag **Boston Red Sox** also as ORG.

In many domains (e.g., biomedical), there are several names for the same conceptual entity. In that case, a normalization step is required, where two different NE occurrences are mapped to a unique conceptual NE; e.g., (Cohen 2005) uses techniques such as removing noise words and identifying orthographic variants (e.g., **IL-10** and **IL 10**) to perform normalization.

With steady progress in NER, it has now become possible to look at another important problem, which may be called *NE Relation Rec-*

ognition (*NERR*): that of identifying a semantic relation (if any) that connects NE instances; e.g., an occurrence of a PERSON and an ORG may be connected through relations such as JOINED, LEFT and HOLDS-POSITION. Similarly, several relations are possible between PERSON and PERSON (PARENT, SIBLING, GRANDPARENT, ASSOCIATE, BOSS etc.). Conversely, detection of a particular relation among candidate NE instances may itself help in NER. Note that relation extraction is a more general problem than NERR in the sense that relations may exist between non-NE words as well; e.g., **car** and **wheel** have a relation PART-OF. Special kinds of relation features can be devised to perform NERR, either in a supervised or unsupervised manner. A good starting point for this work is the collection of papers in the special shared task track on NERR in ACE04 conference (Doddington *et al* 2004). Kernel-based approaches are being explored for NERR in particular and relation extraction in general; see, for example, (Zhao and Grishman 2005) and (Culotta and Sorensen 2004).

While the output of an NER system over a given set of documents is useful in itself, other uses for NER have not been widely explored; see (Bellot et al 2002) for question-answering, (Montalvo et al 2006) for document clustering and (Aramaki *et al* 2009) for document summarization. In particular, the use of NER in semantic web tools and applications needs to be explored more extensively.

It is quite clear from the literature that there is a need for a systematic linguistic theory of named entities, both generic and domain-specific. While we have a number of operational features, rules etc. to identify named entities, we need a more linguistic (or more semantic) theory, which we can use to answer basic questions like the following. What is a named entity, really? What are the characteristics of a NE? What are the relationships between NE? For example, what is the semantic difference between a domain-specific NE and a generic NE? It is clear that for outperforming human experts, the next generation NER system would need to incorporate a considerable amount of linguistic, domain and common sense knowledge. Automatically creating such NER-related knowledge (particularly, linguistic knowledge) in a form that can be reused, edited and understood by human experts, is a challenging task. Many researchers have proposed a "look up" approach to NER based on large gazetteers of known NE. Hence, creating such gazetteers for each type of NE is an important task. We have already discussed various NEX systems for the purpose of automatically creating gazetteers or annotated NER corpus.

Designing techniques for automatically discovering the features relevant for NER, particularly in a language independent manner, is also helpful, since identifying the right features required a lot of linguistic knowledge. (Li and McCallum 2003) use CRF for performing NER in Hindi, where the features are not hard-coded into the system but are induced from the labeled training data using an automatic feature induction technique. CRFs are undirected graphical models used to calculate the conditional probability of values on designated output nodes given values on other designated input nodes. Features are arbitrary (typically Boolean) functions about the two consecutive states, any part of the observation sequence and the current position; e.g., a conjunctive feature may ask whether a word is a known ORG and is followed by the word **spokesman**.

REFERENCES

Aone, C., Halverson, L., Hampton, T., & Ramos-Santacruz, M. (1998). SRA: Description of the IE2 system used for MUC-7. In *Proceedings of the 7th Message Understanding Conference*.

Appelt, D., Hobbs, J., Bear, J., Israel, D., Kameyama, M., & Martin, D. … Tyson M. (1995). SRI international FASTUS system: MUC-6 test results and analysis. In *Proceedings of the 6th Message Understanding Conference*, (pp. 237–248).

Aramaki, E., Miura, Y., Tonoike, M., Ohkuma, T., Mashuichi, H., & Ohe, K. (2009). Text2table: Medical text summarization system based on named entity recognition and modality identification. In *Proceedings of the BioNLP-2009 Workshop*, (pp. 185–192).

Balasuriya, D., Ringland, N., Nothman, J., Murphy, T., & Curran, J. (2009). Named entity recognition in wikipedia. In *Proceedings of the 2009 Workshop on the Peoples Web Meets NLP (ACL IJCNLP 2009)*, (pp. 10–18).

Barthowick, A. (1999). *A maximum entropy approach to named entity recognition*. Unpublished doctoral dissertation, New York University.

Bellot, P., Crestan, E., El-Beze, M., Gillard, L., & de Loupy, C. (2002). Coupling named entity recognition, vector-space model and knowledge bases for TREC 11 question answering track. In *Proceedings of 11th Text Retrieval Conference (TREC-2002)*.

Bender, O., Och, F. J., & Ney, H. (2003). Maximum entropy models for named entity recognition. In *Proceedings of Conference on Computational Natural Language Learning (CoNLL-2003)*, (pp. 148–151).

Berger, L., Pietra, S. A. D., & Pietra, V. J. D. (1996). A maximum entropy approach to natural language processing. *Computational Linguistics, 22*(1), 39–72.

Bikel, D. M., Schwartz, R., & Weischedel, R. M. (1999). An algorithm that learns what's in a name. *Machine Learning, 34*, 211–231. doi:10.1023/A:1007558221122

Black, W., Rinaldi, F., & Mowatt, D. (1998). FACILE: Description of the NE system used for MUC-7. In *Proceedings of the 7th Message Understanding Conference*.

Bunescu, R., & Pasca, M. (2006). Using encyclopedic knowledge for named entity disambiguation. In *Proceedings of the 11th Conference of the European Chapter of the Association for Computational Linguistics (EACL-2006)*, (pp. 9–16).

Chen, S., & Rosenfeld, R. (1999). *A Gaussian prior for smoothing maximum entropy models*. Unpublished technical report CMUCS-99-108, Carnegie Mellon University.

Chieu, H., & Ng, H. (2003). Named entity recognition with a maximum entropy approach. In *Proceedings of Conference on Computational Natural Language Learning (CoNLL-2003)*, (pp. 160–163).

Chinchor, N. (1998). MUC-7 named entity task definition, v3.5. In *Proceedings of the 7th Message Understanding Conference*.

Cohen, A. (2005). Unsupervised gene/protein named entity normalization using automatically extracted dictionaries. In *Proceedings of the ACL-ISMB Workshop on Linking Biological Literature, Ontologies and Databases: Mining Biological Semantics*, (pp. 17–24).

Collier, N., Nobata, C., & Tsujii, J. (2000). Extracting the names of genes and gene products with a hidden Markov model. In *Proceedings of the Conference on Computational Linguistics (COLING-2000)*, (pp. 201–207).

Collins, M., & Singer, Y. (1999). Unsupervised models for named entity classification. In *Proceedings of Joint SIGDAT Conference on Empirical Methods in Natural Language Processing and Very Large Corpora (EMNLP-1999)*.

Cucerzan, S. (2007). Large-scale named entity disambiguation based on Wikipedia data. In *Proceedings of the 2007 Joint Conference on Empirical Methods in Natural Language Processing and Computational Natural Language Learning (EMNLP-CoNLL-2007)*, (pp. 708–716).

212

Culotta, A., & Sorensen, J. (2004). Dependency tree kernels for relation extraction. In *Proceedings of the 42nd Annual Meeting on Association for Computational Linguistics* (*ACL-2004*), (pp. 423–429).

Curran, J., & Clark, S. (2003). Language independent NER using a maximum entropy tagger. In *Proceedings of Conference on Computational Natural Language Learning* (*CoNLL-2003*), (pp. 164–167).

Doddington, G., Mitchell, A., Przybocki, M., Ramshaw, L., Strassel, S., & Weischedel, R. (2004). The automatic content extraction (ace) program: Tasks, data and evaluation. In *Proceedings of the Fourth International Conference on Language Resources and Evaluation* (*LREC-2004*), (pp. 837–840).

Ekbal, A., & Bandyopadhyay, S. (2010). Improving the performance of a NER system by postprocessing and voting. In *Structural, Syntactic, and Statistical Pattern Recognition, LNCS 5342* (pp. 831–841). Springer.

Ekbal, A., Sourjikova, E., Frank, A., & Ponzetto, S. P. (2010). Assessing the challenge of fine-grained named entity recognition and classification. In *Proceedings of the 2010 Named Entities Workshop*, (pp. 93–101).

Etzioni, O., Cafarella, M., Downey, D., Popescu, A.-M., Shaked, T., Soderland, S., & Weld, D. (2005). Unsupervised named-entity extraction from the web: an experimental study. *Artificial Intelligence, 165*, 91–134. doi:10.1016/j.artint.2005.03.001

Fleischman, M., & Hovy, E. (2002). Fine grained classification of named entities. In *Proceedings of Conference on Computational Linguistics* (*COLING-2002*).

Florian, R., Ittycheriah, A., Jing, H., & Zhang, T. (2003). Named entity recognition through classifier combination. In *Proceedings of 7th Conference on Natural Language Learning at HLT-NAACL 2003*, (pp. 168–171).

Fort, K., Ehrmann, M., & Nazarenko, A. (2009). Towards a methodology for named entities annotation. In *Proceedings of the Third Linguistic Annotation Workshop*, (pp. 142–145).

Fukuda, K., Tsunoda, T., Tamura, A., & Takagi, T. (1998). Towards information extraction: identifying protein names from biological papers. In *Proceedings of the Pacific Symposium on Biocomputing* (*PSB-98*).

Funayama, H., Shibata, T., & Kurohashi, S. (2009). Bottom-up named entity recognition using a two-stage machine learning method. In *Proceedings of the 2009 Workshop on Multiword Expressions* (*ACL-IJCNLP-2009*), (pp. 55–62).

Ganti, V., Konig, A., & Vernica, R. (2008). Entity categorization over large document collections. In *Proceeding of the 14th ACM SIGKDD International Conference on Knowledge Discovery and Data Mining* (*KDD-2008*), (pp. 274–282).

Gliozzo, A., Giuliano, C., & Rinaldi, R. (2005). Instance filtering for entity recognition. *SIGKDD Explorations Newsletter, 7*, 11–18. doi:10.1145/1089815.1089818

Han, X., & Zhao, J. (2009). Named entity disambiguation by leveraging Wikipedia semantic knowledge. In *Proceeding of the 18th ACM Conference on Information and Knowledge Management* (*CIKM-2009*), (pp. 215–224).

Humphreys, K., Gaizauskas, R., Azzam, S., Huyck, C., Mitchell, B., Cunningham, H., & Wilks, Y. (1998). Univ. of Sheffield: Description of the LaSIE-II system as used for MUC-7. In *Proceedings of the 7th Message Understanding Conference*.

Isozaki, H., & Kazawa, H. (2002). Efficient support vector classifiers for named entity recognition. In *Proceedings of the Conference on Computational Linguistics (COLING-2002)*.

Jimeno, A., Jimenez-Ruiz, E., Lee, V., Gaudan, S., Berlanga, R., & Rebholz-Schuhmann, D. (2008). Assessment of disease named entity recognition on a corpus of annotated sentences. *BMC Bioinformatics*, *9*(3), 1–10. doi:10.1186/1471-2105-9-S3-S3

Kazama, J., Makino, T., Ohta, Y., & Tsujii, J. (2002). Tuning support vector machines for biomedical named entity recognition. In *Proceedings of ACL 2003 Workshop on Natural Language Processing in the Biomedical Domain*, (pp. 1–8).

Kazama, J., & Torisawa, K. (2007). Exploiting Wikipedia as external knowledge for named entity recognition. In *Proceedings of the 2007 Joint Conference on Empirical Methods in Natural Language Processing and Computational Natural Language Learning (EMNLP-CoNLL-2007)*, (pp. 698–707).

Kim, J.-H., Kang, I.-H., & Choi, K.-S. (2002). Unsupervised named entity classification models and their ensembles. In *Proceedings of the Conference on Computational Linguistics (COLING-2002)*.

Klein, D., Smarr, J., Nguyen, H., & Manning, C. (2003). Named entity recognition with character-level models. In *Proceedings of 7th Conference on Natural Language Learning (HLT-NAACL-2003)*, (pp. 180–183).

Krebel, U. H.-G. (1999). Pairwise classification and support vector machines. In Scholkopf, B., Burges, C., & Smola, A. (Eds.), *Advances in kernel methods - Support vector learning. MIT Press, 1999*.

Krishnan, V., & Manning, C. (2006). An effective two-stage model for exploiting non-local dependencies in named entity recognition. In *Proceedings of the 21st International Conference on Computational Linguistics and 44th Annual Meeting of the Association for Computational Linguistics*, (pp. 1121–1128).

Krishnarao, A., Gahlot, H., Srinet, A., & Kushwaha, D. (2009). A comparison of performance of sequential learning algorithms on the task of named entity recognition for Indian languages. In *Proceedings of the International Conference on Computational Science (ICCS 2009)*, *LNCS 5544*, (pp. 123–132). Springer.

Krupka, G. R., & Hausman, K. (1998). IsoQuest Inc.: Description of the NetOwl™ extractor system as used for MUC-7. In *Proceedings of the 7th Message Understanding Conference*.

Lafferty, J., McCallum, A., & Pereira, F. (2001). Conditional random fields: Probabilistic models for segmenting and labeling sequence data. In *Proceedings of the International Conference Machine Learning (ICML-2001)*.

Lee, K.-J., Hwang, Y.-S., Kim, S., & Rim, H.-C. (2004). Biomedical named entity recognition using two-phase model based on SVMs. *Journal of Biomedical Informatics*, *37*(6), 393–428. doi:10.1016/j.jbi.2004.08.012

Li, W., & McCallum, A. (2003). Rapid development of Hindi named entity recognition using conditional random fields and feature induction. *ACM Transactions on Asian Language Information Processing*, *2*(3), 290–294. doi:10.1145/979872.979879

Liao, W., & Veeramachaneni, S. (2009). A simple semi-supervised algorithm for named entity recognition. In *Proceedings of the NAACL HLT-2009 Workshop on Semi-Supervised Learning for Natural Language Processing*, (pp. 58–65).

Lin, Y.-F., Tsai, T.-H., Chou, W.-C., Wu, K.-P., Sung, T.-Y., & Hsu, W.-L. (2004). A maximum entropy approach to biomedical named entity recognition. In *Proceedings of Workshop on Data Mining in Bioinformatics (BIOKDD04)*, (pp. 56–61).

Liu, F., Zhao, J., Lv, B., Xu, B., & Yu, H. (2005). Product named entity recognition based on hierarchical hidden Markov model. In *Proceedings of the Fourth SIGHAN Workshop on Chinese Language Processing*, (pp. 40–47).

Maynard, D., Tablan, V., Ursu, C., Cunningham, H., & Wilks, Y. (2001). Named entity recognition from diverse text types. In *Proceedings of the Conference on Recent Advances in Natural Language Processing (RANLP-2001)*.

McCallum, A., & Li, W. (2003). Early results for named entity recognition with conditional random fields, feature induction and web-enhanced lexicons. In *Proceedings of the Seventh Conference on Natural language learning at HLT-NAACL 2003 - Volume 4*, (pp. 188–191).

Meulder, F., & Daelemans, W. (2003). Memory-based named entity recognition using unannotated data. In *Proceedings of the Seventh Conference on Natural language learning at HLT-NAACL-2003 - Volume 4*, (pp. 208–211).

Mikheev, A. (1999). A knowledge-free method for capitalized word disambiguation. In *Proceedings of the Conference of Association for Computational Linguistics (ACL-1999)*.

Mikheev, A., Moens, M., & Grover, C. (1999). Named entity recognition without gazetteers. In *Proceedings of 9th Conference of the European Chapter of the Association for Computational Linguistics (EACL-1999)*, (pp. 1–8).

Miller, S., Crystal, M., Fox, H., Ramshaw, L., Schwartz, R., Stone, R., & Weischedel, R., & the Annotation Group. (1998). BBN: Description of the SIFT system as used for MUC-7. In *Proceedings of the 7th Message Understanding Conference*.

Montalvo, S., Martinez, R., Casillas, A., & Fresno, V. (2006). Multilingual document clustering: An heuristic approach based on cognate named entities. In *Proceedings of the 21st International Conference on Computational Linguistics and 44th Annual Meeting of the Association for Computational Linguistics*, (pp. 1145–1152).

Nadeau, D., & Sekine, S. (2007). A survey of named entity recognition and classification. *Lingvisticae Investigationes, 30*, 3–26. doi:10.1075/li.30.1.03nad

Nadeau, D., Turney, P., & Matwin, S. (2006). Unsupervised named-entity recognition: Generating gazetteers and resolving ambiguity. In *Proceedings of the 19th Canadian Conference on Artificial Intelligence*.

Negri, M., & Magnini, B. (2004). Using WordNet predicates for multilingual named entity recognition. In *Proceedings of Global WordNet Conference* (pp. 169–174). GWC.

Nguyen, H., & Cao, T. (2008). Named entity disambiguation: A hybrid statistical and rule-based incremental approach. In *Proceedings of the 3rd Asian Semantic Web Conference on The Semantic Web (ASWC-2008), LNCS 5367*, (pp. 420–433). Springer-Verlag.

Palmer, D., & Day, D. (2006). A statistical profile of the named entity task. In *Proceedings of ACL Conference for Applied Natural Language Processing (ANLP-1997)*.

Park, K.-M., Kim, S.-H., Rim, H.-C., & Hwang, Y.-S. (2006). ME-based biomedical named entity recognition using lexical knowledge. *ACM Transactions on Asian Language Information Processing, 5*(1), 4–21. doi:10.1145/1131348.1131350

Petasis, G., Karkaletsis, V., Grover, C., Hachey, B., Pazienza, M.-T., Vindigni, M., & Coch, J. (2004). Adaptive, multilingual named entity recognition in web pages. In *Proceedings of 2004 European Conference on Artificial Intelligence (ECAI-2004)*, (pp. 1073–1074).

Rabiner, L. (1989). A tutorial on hidden Markov models and selected applications in speech recognition. *Proceedings of the IEEE, 77*(2), 257–286. doi:10.1109/5.18626

Ratinov, L., & Roth, D. (2009). Design challenges and misconceptions in named entity recognition. In *Proceedings of the 13th Conference on Computational Natural Language Learning (CoNLL-2009)*, (pp. 147–155).

Raychaudhuri, S., Chang, J., Sutphin, P., & Altman, R. (2002). Associating genes with gene ontology codes using a maximum entropy analysis of biomedical literature. *Genome Research.* (n.d)., 37.

Sang, T. K., Erik, F., & de Meulder, F. (2003). Introduction to the CoNLL-2003 shared task: Language-independent named entity recognition. In *Proceedings of the Conference on Computational Natural Language Learning (coNLL-2003)*, (pp. 142–147.

Sasano, M. (2003). Virtual examples for text classification with support vector machines. In *Proceedings of Conference on Empirical Methods in Natural Language Processing (EMNLP-2003)*.

Sekine, S. (1998). Description of the Japanese NE system used for MET-2. In *Proceedings of the 7th Message Understanding Conference*.

Sekine, S., & Eriguchi, Y. (2000). Japanese named entity extraction evaluation - Analysis of results. In *Proceedings of the Conference on Computational Linguistics (COLING-2000)*, (pp. 1106–1110).

Settles, B. (2004). Biomedical named entity recognition using conditional random fields and novel feature sets. In *Proceedings of Joint Workshop on Natural Language Processing in Biomedicine and its Applications (JNLPBA-2004)*, (pp. 104–107).

Seymore, K., McCallum, A., & Rosenfeld, R. (1999). Learning hidden Markov structure for information extraction. In *Proceedings of AAAI'99 Workshop on Machine Learning for Information Extraction*.

Shadbolt, N., Hall, W., & Berners-Lee, T. (2006). The Semantic Web revisited. *IEEE Intelligent Systems*, (May/June): 96–101. doi:10.1109/MIS.2006.62

Shen, D., Zhang, J., Zhou, G., Su, J., & Tan, C.-L. (2003). Effective adaptation of a hidden Markov model-based named entity recognizer for biomedical domain. In *Proceedings of the Meeting of Association for Computational Linguistics (ACL-2003)*.

Shinyama, Y., & Sekine, S. (2004). Named entity discovery using comparable news articles. In *Proceedings of the Conference on Computational Linguistics (COLING-2004)*, (pp. 848–853).

Song, Y., Yi, E., Kim, E., & Lee, G. (2005). POSBIOTM-NER: A machine learning approach for bio-named entity recognition. *Bioinformatics (Oxford, England), 21*(11), 2784–2796.

Sun, J., Gao, J., Zhang, L., Zhou, M., & Huang, C. (2002). Chinese named entity identification using class-based language model. In *Proceedings of the Conference on Computational Linguistics (COLING-2002)*.

Takeuchi, K., & Collier, N. (2002). Use of support vector machines in extended named entity recognition. In *Proceedings of 2002 Conference on Natural Language Learning (coNLL-2002)*, (pp. 119–125).

Talukdar, P., Brants, T., Liberman, M., & Pereira, F. (2006). A context pattern induction method for named entity extraction. In *Proceedings of the 10th Conference on Computational Natural Language Learning (CoNLL-2006)*, (pp. 141–148).

Tanev, H., & Magnini, B. (2008). Weakly supervised approaches for ontology population. In *Proceeding of the 2008 Conference on Ontology Learning and Population: Bridging the Gap between Text and Knowledge*, (pp. 129–143).

Thao, P., Tri, T., Dien, D., & Collier, N. (2007). Named entity recognition in Vietnamese using classifier voting. *ACM Transactions on Asian Language Information Processing, 6*(4), 1–18. doi:10.1145/1316457.1316460

Tsai, R., Wu, S., Chou, W., Lin, Y., He, D., & Hsiang, J. (2006). Various criteria in the evaluation of biomedical named entity recognition. *BMC Bioinformatics, 7*(92).

Vapnik, V. (1998). *Statistical learning theory*. Wiley Interscience.

Wang, Y., & Patrick, J. (2009). Cascading classifiers for named entity recognition in clinical notes. In *Proceedings of the Workshop on Biomedical Information Extraction*, (pp. 42–49).

Watanabe, Y., Asahara, M., & Matsumoto, Y. (2007). A graph-based approach to named entity categorization in Wikipedia using conditional random fields. In *Proceedings of the 2007 Joint Conference on Empirical Methods in Natural Language Processing and Computational Natural Language Learning (EMNLP-CoNLL-2007)*, (pp. 649–657).

Yamamoto, K., Kudo, T., Konagaya, A., & Matusmoto, Y. (2003). Protein name tagging for biomedical annotation in text. In *Proceedings of ACL 2003 Workshop on Natural Language Processing in Biomedicine*.

Yi, E., Lee, G. G., Song, Y., & Park, S.-J. (2004). SVM-based biological named entity recognition using minimum edit-distance feature boosted by virtual examples. In *Proceedings of International Joint Conference on Natural Language Processing (IJCNLP-2004), LNCS 3248*, (pp. 807–814).

Zhang, J., Shen, D., Zhou, G., Su, J., & Tan, C.-L. (2002). Enhancing HMM-based biomedical named entity recognition by studying special phenomena. *Journal of Biomedical Informatics, 12*(6), 411–422.

Zhao, S. (2004). Named entity recognition in biomedical texts using an HMM model. In *Proceedings of the International Joint Workshop on Natural Language Processing in Biomedicine and Its Applications*, (pp. 84–87).

Zhao, S., & Grishman, R. (2005). Extracting relations with integrated information using kernel methods. In *Proceedings of the 43rd Annual Meeting on Association for Computational Linguistics (ACL-2005)*, (pp. 419–426).

Zhou, G., & Su, J. (2002). Named entity recognition using an HMM-based chunk tagger. In *Proceedings of 40th Meeting of Association of Computational Linguistics (ACL-2002)*, (pp. 473–480).

Section 4
Applications

Chapter 12
Ontological Collaboration Engineering

Stefan Werner Knoll
Delft University of Technology, The Netherlands

Till Plumbaum
Berlin Institute of Technology, Germany

Ernesto William De Luca
University of Applied Sciences Potsdam, Germany

Livia Predoiu
University of Magdeburg, Germany

ABSTRACT

This chapter gives a comprehensive overview of ongoing research about semantic approaches for Collaboration Engineering. The authors present a new ontology-based approach, where each concept of the ontology corresponds to a specific collaboration step or a resource, to collect, manage, and share collaborative knowledge. The chapter discusses the utility of the proposed ontology in the context of a real-world example where the authors explain how collaboration can be modelled and applied using their ontology in order to improve the collaboration process. Furthermore, they discuss how well-known ontologies, such as FOAF, can be linked to their ontology and extend it. While the focus of the chapter is on semantic Collaboration Engineering, the authors additionally present methods of reasoning and machine learning to derive new knowledge about the collaboration process as a further research direction.

INTRODUCTION AND MOTIVATION

Collaboration is very important in many aspects of our lives. When we work together, we can reach goals faster, yield better results and inspire each other during our collaboration activities. The synergy effects can boost all kinds of endeavours tremendously. However, there are also collaboration efforts that do not work well. Thus, it is very important to be able to assist, analyse and support collaboration with technological means. Despite its iniquitousness, we introduce into the topic by considering collaboration in organizations.

DOI: 10.4018/978-1-4666-0894-8.ch012

Nowadays, both profit and non-profit organizations have to be innovative to maintain their competitive position. This is due to a number of factors, including globalization and liberalization of markets, geographical development and an ever growing number of new technologies. To be innovative, organizations may implement a multi-stage process that combines a variety of techniques and methods to analyse the market situation, define strategic goals, and generate and implement ideas, yielding new products and market strategies. In order to obtain synergy effects, collaboration is used during these processes to combine the expertise and knowledge of employees with complementary skills.

Terveen (Terveen, 1995) defines collaboration as the process of a group where participants work together to achieve a shared goal. Over the years, the research focus on collaboration has changed from groups whose members work in a same place to geographically distributed virtual groups. This results to the fact that virtual groups which use temporary technical support for collaboration comprise an important structural component of many multinational organizations (Nunamaker Jr., Reinig, & Briggs, 2009), who use virtual groups to lower travel and facility costs.

The collaboration process and its outcomes are affected by different internal and external factors like the characteristics of the individuals, the task, the context, and the technology used (Dennis, George, Jessup, Nunamaker, & Vogel, 1988; Nunamaker, Dennis, Valacich, Vogel, & George, 1991). Different theories exist that describe and predict the influence of these factors on group behaviours and performances in relation to group communication (Poole & Hollingshead, 2005), group participation (Diehl & Stroebe, 1991; Karau & Williams, 1993; Csikszentmihalyi, 1997) and group cohesiveness (Janis, 1982; Edmondson, 1999). However, most of the influencing factors cannot be generalized for collaboration in general. Depending on the given process characteristics,

need for support can be necessary for organizations to handle negative group behaviours and support group performance.

Collaboration support can consist of tools, processes and services that support groups during the design and execution of collaboration. Technical support is given by groupware technologies which offer a variety of local and web-based applications to structure collaborative activities and improve group communication (DeSanctis & Gallupe, 1987; Dennis, Haley, & Vandenberg, 1996; Nunamaker et al., 1991; Vreede, Vogel, Kolfschoten, & Wien, 2003). Today, a huge amount of web-based applications exist that can be adapted in different ways to implement different collaboration processes (Mittleman, Briggs, Murphy, & Davis, 2008).

Considering the possible complexity of a collaboration process, the faithful appropriation of a groupware technology is fundamental to design predictable and efficient collaboration (DeSanctis & Poole, 1994; Dennis, Wixom, & Vandenberg, 2001). With regard to the Technology Transition Model (Briggs et al., 1999), using technological support for collaboration can lead to a high conceptual and perceptual load if the practitioners misunderstand the use of groupware technology for collaboration. To ensure faithful appropriation of groupware technology, organizations can use professional facilitators who have expertise in design and execution of collaboration involving technological support. However, economic and political factors can prevent organizations to hire external skilled facilitators. As a result, existing collaboration knowledge cannot be used and the efficiency of collaboration is not guaranteed. This situation leads to challenges in collaboration research:

- How can a faithful appropriation of groupware technology be supported?
- How can collaboration knowledge be transferred to reduce needed experience?

Beside professional facilitators, knowledge about collaboration can be captured and shared in different ways: by handbooks for group facilitation, by methods databases or by pattern approaches. In this chapter, we will analyse the use of Collaboration Engineering (Briggs, Vreede, & Nunamaker, 2003) as a pattern approach that formalize collaboration work practices and will explore the combination of this pattern approach with an ontological approach to capture and share knowledge about collaboration. We believe that this knowledge can be used to obtain a deeper and better understanding of collaboration. It can further be used to develop a generic groupware technology that is capable to perform a higher level of automatic introspection about the collaboration processes.

STATE OF THE ART IN COLLABORATION ENGINEERING

Briggs et al. (Briggs et al., 2003) assume that the expertise needed for design and execution of collaboration can be reduced by packing and transferring knowledge about collaboration. They introduce Collaboration Engineering as a facilitation, design and training approach for collaboration work practices that can be executed by practitioners without ongoing support from collaboration professionals such as facilitators. To reach this goal, Collaboration Engineering classifies collaboration into six key patterns of collaboration:

- **Generate:** Move from having fewer to having more concepts in the pool of concepts shared by the group;
- **Reduce:** Move from having many concepts to a focus on fewer concepts that the group deems worthy of further attention;
- **Clarify:** Move from having less to having more shared understanding of concepts and of the words and phrases used to express them;

- **Organize:** Move from less to more understanding of the relationships among concepts the group is considering;
- **Evaluate:** Move from less to more understanding of the relative value of the concepts under consideration;
- **Build Consensus:** Move from having fewer to having more group members who are willing to commit to a proposal.

ThinkLets were introduced as design patterns for best facilitation practice (Briggs et al., 2003; Briggs, Kolfschoten, Vreede, & Dean, 2006) and form a pattern language for collaboration. They are defined as named, scripted, reusable, and transferable collaborative activities for creating specific known variations of the six patterns of collaboration among people working together toward a goal (Briggs et al., 2006). The initial conceptualization of a thinkLet tied a thinkLet closely to a specific technology in a specific configuration (Kolfschoten, Briggs, Vreede, Jacobs, & Appelman, 2006). It based on the concept of design pattern introduced by Alexander (Alexander, Ishikawa, & Silverstein, 1977) and comprises the components (Vreede, Kolfschoten, & Briggs, 2006):

- **Identification:** Contains a name attribute, which is intended to emphasize the specific group dynamics the thinkLet invokes;
- **Script:** Defines how to create the required pattern of collaboration by using a technology in defined configuration;
- **Selection Guide:** Contains different attributes such as patterns of collaboration to support the practitioner in the selection of a thinkLet.

A more formal specification of a thinkLet as a technology-independent logical design element is given by the thinkLet class diagram (Kolfschoten et al., 2006). This specification uses the unified modelling language (UML) notation to illustrate and define the key concepts and relations of a thinkLet script. An essential component is the concept rule, whose instances define the script of a thinkLet. A rule defines the actions a participant must do individually in a given role, the constraints under which the actions must be executed, and the capabilities that will be required (Briggs et al., 2006).

According to the given design approach for collaboration processes, collaboration engineering decomposes a collaboration process into a sequence of design pattern thinkLet (Kolfschoten & Vreede, 2009). Each thinkLet contains knowledge about the used setting and its configuration for a given task as well as a script for each activity in the process that is needed to engender the pattern of collaboration. A designed collaboration process will be documented as a paper-based handbook. A transition approach is used to transfer tacit knowledge and skills to practitioners with less expertise (Kolfschoten, Vreede, & Pietron, 2010). Research indicates that a practitioner who is trained in using thinkLets can repeatedly engender the patterns of collaboration for a designed collaboration process by following the description of the handbook (Vreede & Briggs, 2005).

Our research analyses the possibility to design a generic groupware technology for collaboration based on the existing theories and methods of Collaboration Engineering. The goal is to improve technological support for collaboration by formalizing the workflow of a collaboration process into a machine-readable process description. We think that a generic groupware technology could use the underlying process logic of the workflow to provide functionalities for the design and execution of a collaboration process.

A GROUP PROCESS MODELING LANGUAGE

In earlier work, we analysed the applicability of the Collaboration Engineering approach to logical process descriptions similar to the concept workflow of Business Process Engineering (Hol-

lingshead, 1995). The resulting logical model for collaboration, called Group Process Modelling Language (GPML), illustrates different pieces of process information to define the workflow of a collaboration process (Knoll, Hörning, & Horton, 2008; Knoll & Horton, 2011):

- **Process Activity:** Defines the order and type of the activities of a participant with a defined role in a collaborative process;
- **Process Data:** Defines the type and value of the data elements that will be used or developed during the collaboration process;
- **Process Event:** Defines the influence of internal or external events on the collaborative process.

The GPML adopts the design pattern thinkLet as a process template that creates one known collaboration pattern. ThinkLets can be combined to different collaboration processes which can be adapted to a group goal by the configuration of their parameters and activities. The thinkLet script defines a sequence of abstract actions a group of participant must do to achieve an intended collaboration pattern. However, these actions only provide abstract guidelines for facilitation, details facilitation skills must be transferred by the training approach. Research indicates that the quality of facilitation is vital for collaboration success (Niederman, Beise, & Beranek, 1993; Wong & Aiken, 2003). As a result, we think that a rule of a thinkLet script should include information about facilitation as a formal instruction entity.

Based on the Shannon-Weaver Model for communication (Shannon, 1948), we introduced a design approach for a reusable formal instruction element called thinXel, which represents an instance of a thinkLet rule. The concept thinXel is originally defined as an atomic facilitator instruction, leading to a response of the participants that has a well-defined function in the context of the group goal (Knoll, Chelvier, & Horton, 2007). Experimental results have shown that by using thinXel during a collaboration process, misunderstanding of facilitation instructions by the participants can be reduced (Knoll et al., 2007). Further the attention of the participants can be hold to the intended collaboration process.

We combined the concepts thinkLet and thinXel in the GPML to define personalized processes for the participants of a group (Knoll et al., 2008). To illustrate concurrent processes of participants with different roles, we distinguish between an individual participant and a group of participants. Currently the GPML can be expressed in a graphical form or in a formal language notation. The graphical representation combines well proven modelling constructs with new abstract representations for the concepts of a thinkLet and thinXel to improve the understanding of a collaboration process design (Knoll et al., 2008; Knoll & Horton, 2011). Rules for the composition of these primitive modelling constructs were defined by adapting given workflow patterns (Aalst, Hofstede, Kiepuszewski, & Barros, 2003). The semantically representation use the extensible markup language (XML) to describe objects for each elements of the graphical GPML similar to the XML Process Definition Language (XPDL) (Workflow Process Definition Interface – XML Process Definition Language, 2008).

Our first application of GPML was a prototype of a generic groupware technology that links a group via the Internet and implements the activities of a collaboration process via a website (Knoll, Hörning, & Horton, 2009). We have used the properties of GPML to design a method called Participant Flow Algorithm (Knoll et al., 2009), which uses the logical design of a collaboration process to compute the active activity and the next step of the participants. Currently, the prototype provides no support to secure the efficient combination of thinkLets as well as no functionalities for the design of guidelines for the configuration of the logical model by other practitioner. Equally important, the prototype provides no functionality to capture and share knowledge that results

in context with the execution of a collaborative process. We think that this knowledge is necessary to obtain a deeper and better understanding of collaboration. Further, knowledge about collaboration can be used to develop new design guidelines for the efficient design and execution of collaboration. For this reason, we analysed the applicability of an ontology to capture knowledge about collaboration.

RESEARCH ON ONTOLOGICAL COLLABORATION

By definition, an ontology is a formal specification of a conceptualization of a domain of interest (Gruber, 1993) that specifies a set of constraints that declare what should necessarily hold in any possible world. Ontologies are used to identify what "is" or "can be" in the world. It is the intention to build a complete world model for describing the semantics of information exchange, which nicely fits the needs of the GPML defined collaboration processes, where ontologies could be used to facilitate knowledge sharing and reuse.

To reach the long-term goal of this work, enabling groupware technologies to serve as libraries of reusable knowledge that can be triggered by other applications, an ontology is the perfect basis. By building a common vocabulary for collaboration and defining relations and dependencies between them, we enable information exchange between agents. Those agents, sharing the ontology, do not need to have the same knowledge base; each agent knows facts the others do not know. This is in our opinion a great strength of an ontology approach for collaboration systems; each agent can query other agents for collaboration information and therefore enhance his own collaboration process.

From the literature review, we found different ontological approaches to capture knowledge about collaboration. For example, Oliveira et al. (Oliveira, Antunes, & Guizzardi, 2007) present domain ontology for collaboration in the context of collaborative web browsing. According to the 3C collaboration model, they divide the ontology into the sub-ontologies cooperation, communication and coordination. With regard to the Collaboration Engineering approach, the ontological approach can be used to model design patterns for collaboration but provides no concept to identify a collaboration pattern. Further we found no concepts to define conditions for the participant flow, which are needed to define sequences of intended activities in relation to the resulting behaviours of the participants.

Another approach for an ontology-based process definition is given by Rajsiri et al. (Rajsiri, Lorré, Bénaben, & Pingaud, 2008). They define a collaboration network ontology that is composed of a collaboration ontology and a collaboration process ontology. The collaboration ontology regards the characterization of collaborative network, details and abstract services of participants. The collaborative process ontology defines the task of the participants at a functional level, which has input and output resources.

A design pattern approach is also used by Pattberg and Fluegge (Pattberg & Fluegge, 2007), who capture knowledge about collaboration by creating an ontological approach that uses a structure of various levels of abstraction. These levels clarify the relation of a collaboration pattern (proven solution for a collaboration problem) to collaboration services (reusable implementation services) to the underlying communication technology of a collaboration process.

In summary, the given ontologies fulfil our requirement to model collaboration by using design patterns. However, collaboration is always a dynamic process that base on human behaviours. As a result, it is difficult to prescribe these processes by a predefined sequence of design pattern. We found restrictions for all ontologies for modelling a participant flow that can be adapted in relation to the resulting behaviours or generated resources. However, different ontological approaches exist

to model participant dynamics (Vivacqua, Garcia, & Gomes, 2011) or human interaction (Lee, Seo, Kim, & Kim, 2010), but we found no common collaboration ontology that can be used to model collaboration patterns in relation to the resulting behaviours.

THE COLLABORATION ONTOLOGY

In this section we present our approach for a collaboration ontology. First, we introduce the research methodology used for the collaboration engineering process and then outline goals and the scope of the collaboration ontology. The main part of this section presents the structure of the collaboration ontology to give a deeper understanding of how one can used. At the end of this section, the readers know how we defined the goals and scope of the ontology and captured and formalized it. In the following section, we show a real world example and how we utilized the ontology for a given collaboration process.

RESEARCH METHODOLOGY FOR ONTOLOGY ENGINEERING

Ontology engineering aims at building a formal representation of domain knowledge (concepts in a domain) and creating a common understanding of the structure of information in the domain (relations between the concepts) among people or software agents (Predoiu & Zhdanova, 2007; Studer, Benjamins, & Fensel, 1998; Gruber, 1995). Today, several methods and methodologies for developing ontologies exist (Corcho, Fernández-López, & Gómez- Pérez, 2003). Uschold and Gruninger (Uschold & Gruninger, 1996) present a methodology for ontology engineering. We adopted these methodologies for ontology building (Grüninger & Fox, 1995; Pinto & Martins, 2004) for our collaboration engineering process. Our ontology creation process considered four steps (Knoll, Plumbaum, Hoffmann, & De Luca, 2010):

1. **Defining The Goals And The Scope Of The Ontology:** To define scope of the ontology we conducted a literature research on collaboration, examined current collaboration support systems and evaluated existing collaboration processes. We also defined a set of questions that our ontology should be able to answer, called competency questions, to determine the exact situations, goals, we want to handle with the ontology.

2. **Defining And Formalizing The Ontology:** We organized a brainstorming session with experts with different computer science and collaboration science backgrounds to identify all potentially relevant tasks and terms the ontology has to cover. We structured the terms and used the resulting groups to capture key concepts and relationships. A graphical representation was used to build a conceptual model. We analysed the integration of other existing ontologies to use previously established conceptualizations. The conceptual model was then transformed into a formal model, and implemented using a formal representation language.

3. **Practical Usage Of The Ontology:** We evaluated the ontology in respect to the purpose and its intended use. In doing so, we used the competency questions to verify the ontology regarding to its consistency and completeness.

4. **Ontology Documentation:** We documented the concepts and relationships in a data dictionary, where each concept is describes by its name, description, cardinality, etc.

We used this approach to develop our collaboration ontology. The steps one, two and four are presented in this section. Step three is presented in the following section where we apply our ontology to a real world example.

GOALS AND SCOPE OF THE COLLABORATION ONTOLOGY

The scope of an ontology depends on the kind of user and the scenario it should support. Hence, we determined potential user groups of such a collaboration ontology. According to Collaboration Engineering (CE) (Kolfschoten & Vreede, 2009), we identified three user group levels that we want to support that have different knowledge bases (Knoll et al., 2010). First, there is the

- **Collaboration Engineer:** Who designs collaboration processes and has knowledge about theories on collaboration and resulting factors that affect the outcome of a collaboration process;

Second, there is the

- **Practitioner:** A domain expert who has knowledge about the allocated resources, the client goal and the stakes of a collaboration process. Here, additional semantic modelling might need to be done in order to gather the full benefit of using ontologies and semantics;

Third, there is the

- **Participant:** Who participates in a collaboration process and has knowledge about what is necessary to reach the client goal.

Any of these user group levels should utilize our collaboration ontology to their advantage and share its individual knowledge and therefore provide knowledge that enhances the design, adaption and execution of collaboration. For example, collaboration engineers can describe existing and new design pattern, thinkLets, and use the experience of other practitioners and participants with these thinkLets to define rules for the use of such thinkLets.

Another group of users consists of professional facilitators that do not use CE to design collaboration processes but have own knowledge about group work and facilitation. A professional facilitator can use the ontology to model common facilitation techniques and therefore share these techniques. This knowledge can lead to new design patterns.

From a computer science point of view, there is another user group that consists of software engineers. Software Engineers could use the ontology to develop different applications that use the ontology to share and reuse knowledge. An example for these applications is a Computer Aided Process Engineering technology, a tool for designing a collaboration process to convert a designed process into a hand-out version for facilitation (Kolfschoten, de Vreede, & Briggs, 2008). Additionally, knowledge engineers could use the ontology to deduce or even learn new relations between the concepts of the ontology.

To straighten the scope of the ontology besides supporting the identified groups of users, we developed competency questions to identify areas of knowledge and collaboration the ontology should cover. Therefore, we conducted a literature research on collaboration and group facilitation (VanGundy, 1988; Schumann, 2005; Briggs & Vreede, 2003) and analysed case scenarios of collaboration workshop of a consulting company (Zephram, 2011). These face-to-face workshops are booked from different organizations to generate new product ideas, improve customer value or find new business areas. Each process represents a combination of different collaboration techniques involving participants with different roles like facilitators, experts, freelancers or an organizational staff in the background that prepares the workshop and executes follow-up tasks.

We inspected the facilitator script (agenda, cue cards) and the activities of the organizational staff. Further, we participated as freelancers in some of these workshops. We came up with a set of competency questions that our collaboration ontology

should be able to answer (Knoll et al., 2010). We classified the questions into different topics, which are listed in Table 1. For each topic, we ask a question like "What are the patterns of collaboration" as introducing question (this example belongs to topic 1, patterns). Since the questions just touch the surface, we defined follow-up questions to identify details. This chapter discusses only some of these questions in-depth.

Our design approach for a collaboration ontology based on existing methods and concepts of CE and GPML. Thus, the defined competency questions particularly considering the design patterns thinkLet and thinXel. To model the workflow of a participant, we asked what the next collaboration pattern or atomic activity of a participant in the collaboration process is.

In contrast to the collaboration ontology by Oliveira et al. (Oliveira et al., 2007), we looked at the participants of a collaboration process in more detail. Also, we adopted the design pattern thinkLet that defines the actions of a participant in relation to its skills, a defined role and the capabilities (Vreede et al., 2006). Each activity of a participant will be executed in a defined location and generate different kind of artefacts. To further define the actions of a participant we asked what kind of equipment or technology is needed. The case scenarios showed us that the activities of

Table 1. Topics of competency questions

	Topic
1	Patterns
2	Styles
3	Participants
4	Objectives
5	Results
6	Artefacts
7	Resources
8	Communication Channels
9	Sections of a process
10	Sections of a pattern

participants are also related to the elements money and time. Further, we focused on organizational elements like food and logistics.

Similar to Rajsiri et al. (Rajsiri et al., 2008), we looked at collaboration from different points of views. Therefore we asked for the objectives of a client, a collaboration process, a collaboration pattern (thinkLets) and an atomic activity (thinXels). To measure the achievement of these objectives, we asked how results are represented and how they would compare to previously defined objectives.

DEFINING AND FORMALIZING THE ONTOLOGY

Defining the collaboration ontology demands to identify key concepts, naming important properties and defining relationships between the entities. These entities are based on the given concepts of CE and GPML. In a first step, a brainstorming session was organized to explore all potentially relevant terms. We structured the terms to get a better overview and reduced and abstracted them to get the key concepts of collaboration (Knoll et al., 2010).

After the identification of key concepts we depicted the entities to create a graphical conceptual model. Like Rajsiri et al. (Rajsiri et al., 2008) we divided the key concepts into different ontologies: One named collaboration ontology (co) that describes the external point of view on collaboration of a client, and another one named collaboration process ontology (cpo) that contains the concepts belonging to the internal description of collaboration processes. The interface between these two is the concept cpo:CollaborationProcess, which is present in both ontologies.

Iteratively, we added unique relationship descriptors between entities and properties like names or descriptions. While creating, we verified it. We took the competency questions that we defined in the beginning and tried to answer them abstractly by use of the ontologies. We observed

that in some cases we were not able to do so. In those cases we refined the ontologies. After this step, our created ontologies held all the knowledge we wanted them to hold. Each key concept, property and relationship is unambiguously described in a dictionary.

In the next section, we will present the ontology containing all identified concepts and relationship in more detail. We discuss only the key concepts of the ontologies in-depth. Please note that in the following subsections names of concepts are capitalized.

THE ONTOLOGY

Based on the work of the previous sections we created a combined ontology that consists of two parts or two sub-ontologies (Knoll et al., 2010): One is called collaboration ontology (CO) that describes the external point of view on collaboration of a client, and the other one called collaboration process ontology (CPO) that comprises structural information about the collaboration process in a pattern paradigm. This section will give a compact overview of the used concepts and their relations to the collaboration engineering approach. Our website (Collaboration Ontology, 2011) presents a current snapshot of our ontology engineering efforts. This ontology provides a framework of modelling primitives for collaboration engineering in general. When a specific collaboration topic is chosen, additional modelling might be necessary. However, due to the linked open data trend towards reusable ontological modelling in different domains, we might also be able to use freely available knowledge modelled in RDF and OWL available in the linked open data cloud. However, we need mappings between our concepts and relations and some of the ones in the linked open data cloud in order to enable a first connection which can be deepened with machine learning algorithms. One example of a very important Semantic Web vocabulary we need to provide mappings to clearly is FOAF (FOAF, 2010).

Figure 1. Concepts and relations of the collaboration ontology (CO)

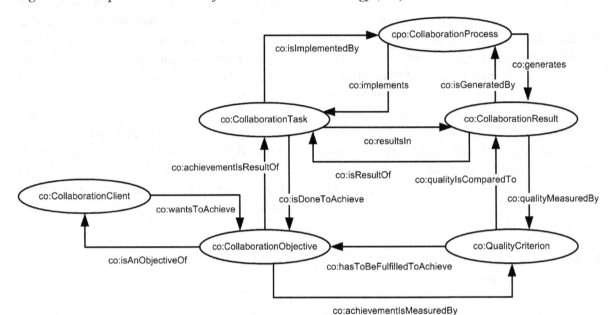

THE COLLABORATION ONTOLOGY

The purpose of the collaboration ontology is to describe collaboration from an external point of view. We define the following key concepts (Knoll et al., 2010): co:CollaborationClient, co:CollaborationObjective, co:CollaborationTask, co:CollaborationProcess, co:CollaborationResult and co:QualityCriterion. You can see the concepts and relations in Figure 1; meta information connected to the concepts is not displayed. Table 2 describes the concepts and their purpose.

The concept co:CollaborationClient denotes a possible client of a collaboration process, e.g. a company, an organization or a single person. A client has one or more objectives (co:CollaborationObjective) which should be achieved by usage of a collaboration process. According to the objectives, one or more tasks (co:CollaborationTask) can be instantiated by the client or a collaboration engineer. The concept co:CollaborationProcess is a designed process description with the goal to implement such a task and achieve a defined objective. A

Table 2. Conceptual dictionary of the collaboration ontology (CO)

Concept	Description
CollaborationClient	Denotes a person or a group of people that has the need for collaboration
CollaborationObjective	Denotes a goal set by the CollaborationClient to describe a desired result; motivation for the CollaborationProcess
CollaborationTask	Denotes a step to achieve the CollaborationObjective in a collaborative manner
CollaborationProcess	Denotes the part in which participants interact for the purpose of collaboration; the implementation of a given CollaborationTask
CollaborationResult	Denotes the actual outcome of a CollaborationProcess
QualityCriterion	Denotes a criterion that results from the CollaborationObjective and against which the CollaborationResult is evaluated

cpo:CollaborationProcess represents the collaboration process ontology (abbreviated cpo) which will be defined in the next subsection. The outcome of the collaboration process is stored in the concept co:CollaborationResult. To make a statement regarding the quality or fitness of the results we have defined the concept co:QualityCriterion, which can be measured against the co:CollaborationObjective.

THE COLLABORATION PROCESS ONTOLOGY

The second ontology is called collaboration process ontology (cpo) and describes the inner setup of a collaboration process (Knoll et al., 2010). It comprises agents (persons or process-supporting machines like computers), structural information about the collaboration process in a pattern paradigm and artefacts that are produced or consumed by the process.

First, we describe the concepts concerning the concept Agent (Table 3). An cpo:Agent is either a cpo:System or a cpo:Participant. It is the entity that executes an activity that is related to the collaboration process. The participant concept is shown in more detail in Figure 2. A cpo:Participant, on the other hand, is a human being taking part in a collaboration process. This entity has certain cpo:Skill that can be a prerequisite of a cpo:Role in a process. A cpo:Role is defined by the process description

and denotes abstractly a set of behaviours, rights and obligations. Furthermore, cpo:Participant can be assigned to a cpo:Group for collaboration work. The concepts cpo:Role and cpo:Skill are important to distinguish different participants and thus to be able to define requirements for the participants of a collaboration process. A cpo:System is a place-holder for some entity doing background work, for example sorting lists of ideas. This can be done by a machine or a human being; the difference is not important to the collaboration process. Note that cpo:agentDescriptions, cpo:skillNames and cpo:roleNames are here modelled as being strings. However, when we intend to use the full potential of the Semantic Web, we need to plug in other ontologies modelling the relevant domains of interest of the specific collaboration process at hand.

Second, we take a look at the collaboration process, depicted in Figure 3 (Table 4 and Table 5). We use a pattern approach that is based on CE and the GPML and therefore define the key concepts cpo:ThinkLet (see Figure 4) and cpo:ThinXel. A cpo:ThinkLet denotes the concept of a scripted and reusable collaborative activity for creating a known pattern of collaboration (Briggs et al., 2006) by a cpo:Group. We implement the pattern of collaboration by the concept cpo:CollaborationPattern. By using cpo:CollaborationPattern, the six key pattern of collaboration can be described. Further it is possible to add new collaboration pattern, if the resulting knowledge indicates it. Based on our

Table 3. Conceptual dictionary of the collaboration process ontology (CPO), excerpt concerning agents

Concept	Description
Agent	Denotes a person, system, software, etc.
System	Denotes an agent that is not a participant; a machine, e.g. a computer, software
Participant	Denotes a person that participates at a collaboration process
Skill	Denotes an ability of a certain level that is a requirement or property of a role or participant to fulfil a task
Role	Denotes a set of behaviours, rights and obligations
Group	Denotes some participants that work together as a group in a collaboration process

Figure 2. Participant concept and related concepts

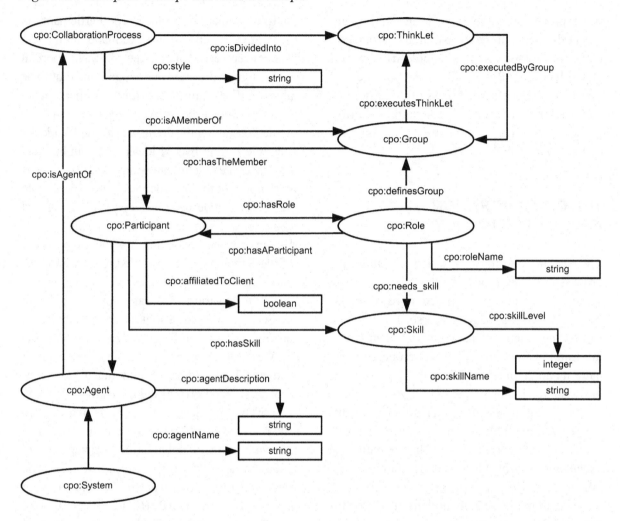

experience with collaboration workshops, we suggest adding a social collaboration pattern that can be used to introduce the participants to each other or to level social behaviours in a group. To measure the achievement of a collaboration pattern, we defined the concept cpo:ThinkLetObjective and cpo:ThinkLetQualityCriterion. A collaboration process can be divided into a sequence of different cpo:ThinkLet. To model a defined order of cpo:ThinkLet we implement a precondition called cpo:ThinkLetCondition which must be fulfilled in order that it is executed.

According to GPML, a cpo:ThinkLet consists of different cpo:ThinXel, which is shown in Fig-

ure 5, which is defined as an atomic facilitator instruction leading to an activity of a participant (Knoll et al., 2009). Furthermore, in the context of the ontology, the concept cpo:ThinXel defines the relation between an agent, an intended activity, and Table 4: Conceptual Dictionary of the Collaboration Process Ontology (cpo), excerpt concerning the cpo:CollaborationProcess an intended result under use of certain cpo:Artifact. We use the concept cpo:ThinXelObjective to represent the intended activity. The result of a cpo:ThinXel is denoted by the concept cpo:ActivityResult. The concept cpo:ActivityResult changes cpo:Artifact. However, a cpo:ThinXel

Figure 3. Process concept

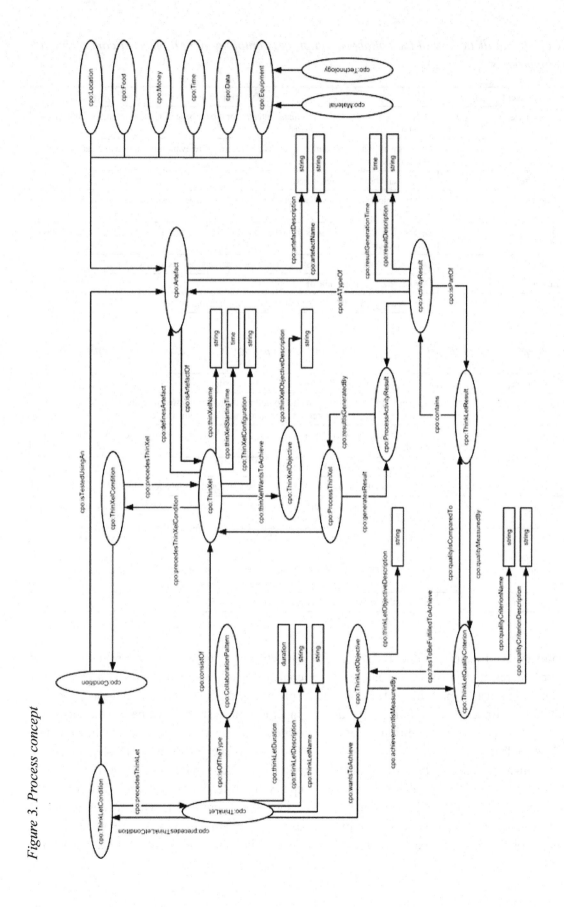

Table 4. Conceptual dictionary of the collaboration process ontology (CPO), excerpt concerning the collaborationprocess

Concept	Description
CollaborationProcess	Denotes the part in which participants interact for the purpose of collaboration; the implementation of a given CollaborationTask
ThinkLet	Denotes a design pattern for collaborative work, i.e. all relevant information to create a pattern of collaboration
CollaborationPattern	Denotes an abstract design pattern for collaboration
ThinkLetObjective	Denotes a goal set by the collaboration engineer to describe a desired result; motivation for the ThinkLet
ThinkLetQualityCriterion	Denotes a criterion that results from the ThinkLetObjective and against which the ThinkLetResult is evaluated
ThinkLetCondition	Denotes a condition of a ThinkLet that can be tested and results a logical value
ThinkLetResult	Denotes the actual outcome of a ThinkLet
Condition	Denotes a condition that can be tested and results in a logical value

Table 5. Conceptual dictionary of the collaboration process ontology (CPO), excerpt concerning ThinXel

Concept	Description
ThinXel	Denotes a single step in a ThinkLet. It defines the relation between an agent, an instruction, an intended activity, and an intended result under use of certain artefacts
ThinXelObjective	Denotes a goal set by the collaboration engineer to describe a desired result; motivation for the ThinXel
ActivityResult	Denotes a result of a thinXel activity
ThinXelCondition	Denotes a condition of a ThinXel that can be tested and results a logical value
ConfigThinXel	Denotes a ThinXel that is specified for an agent that leads to a context change. Its intended use is to instruct the system or facilitator.
ConfigActivityResult	Denotes a ActivityResult of a ConfigThinXel; changes the setting of a context (agents, artefacts)
ProcessThinXel	Denotes a ThinXel that is specified for a participant with a predefined role and creates or changes artefacts in a specific context. It leads to a thinking step
ProcessActivityResult	Denotes the ActivityResult gained by a ProcessThinXel

has no quality criteria because one does not check the quality of the result of an activity as part of a thinXel but as dedicated part of a thinkLet. Similar to the concepts cpo:ThinkLet, a cpo:ThinXel can have a precondition called cpo:ThinXelCondition.

We distinguish the concept cpo:ThinXel into the subclasses cpo:ConfigThinXel and cpo:ProcessThinXel. A cpo:ConfigThinXel inherits from ThinXel and represents an activity with the intention to change the existing context.

This change can be necessary to provide a required context for follow-up activities of a participant. For example, the activity to provide pen and paper is required to be done before the activity to write an idea on a sheet of paper can be executed. The result of a cpo:ConfigThinXel is defined by cpo:ConfigActivityResult which inherit from cpo:ActivityResult. A cpo:ConfigThinXel is executed by a cpo:Agent, what means it can be executed by any participant or external person, but also, in some cases, by a computer or machine.

Figure 4. ThinkLet concept

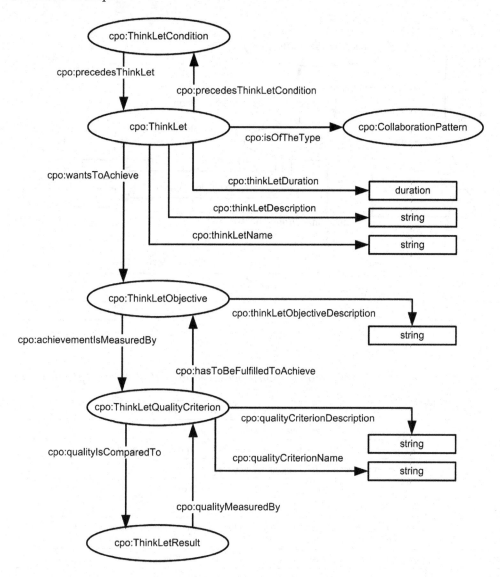

A cpo:ProcessThinXel inherits from ThinXel and represents an activity for a defined role with the intention to change the actual outcome of a thinkLet. It results in a cpo:ProcessActivityResult inheriting from cpo:ActivityResult. A cpo:ProcessThinXel requires a cpo:Role. Because of this it can only be executed by a participant, ergo a human being.

Third, we describe the Artefacts and concepts inheriting from it (Table 6). A cpo:Artefacts denote products consumed or produced by the process. They are specialized by the concepts cpo:Data, cpo:Time, cpo:Money, cpo:Location, cpo:Food and cpo:Equipment. A cpo:Equipment for itself can be divided in cpo:Technology (like a video projector) and cpo:Material (like pens or paper). A cpo:Artefacts describe most of the relevant context of cpo:ThinXel and therefore of cpo:ThinkLet and the whole collaboration process.

Note again that the elements which are defined to be strings, like e.g. cpo:thinkLetDescription, cpo:qualityCriterionDescription, cpo:thinXelConfiguration, cpo:thinkLetObjectiv

Figure 5. ThinXel concept

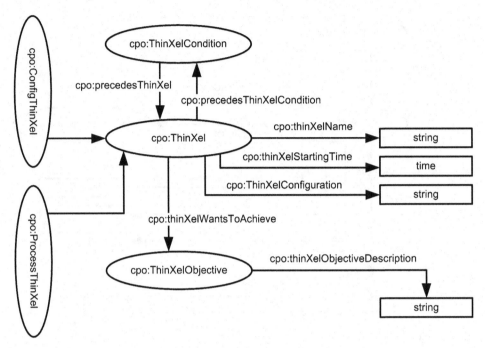

Table 6. Conceptual dictionary of the collaboration process ontology (CPO), excerpt concerning artefact

Concept	Description
Artefact	Denotes any kind of resource used in the collaboration process
Data	Denotes an artefact that describes a single piece of information, e.g. an idea
Time	Denotes an artefact that describes a time duration
Location	Denotes an artefact that describes where a collaboration process or parts of it take place
Equipment	Denotes an artefact that describes a single piece of equipment, i.e. material or technology
Material	Denotes a piece of equipment that describes the material used in the collaboration process, e.g. pens, paper, post-it etc.
Technology	Denotes a piece of equipment based on technology, e.g. a watch, video projector, etc.
Money	Denotes an artefact that describes the monetary demands of certain steps in the collaboration process
Food	Denotes an artefact that describes food, e.g. coffee or snacks

eDescription, cpo:thinXelObjectiveDescription, cpo:artefactDescription, cpo:resultDescription. can and should be replaced by appropriate domain ontologies which might either be modelled by the domain expert or taken from the linked open data cloud or maybe even a combination of both.

Currently we use OWL (the Web Ontology Language) to represent the collaboration ontology in a formal language. We leave it up to the collaboration engineer and the domain expert to decide for the proper OWL variant for the modelling task at hand. The modelling experts need also decide whether they want model the modelling primitives as instances or sub concepts of our basic collaboration ontological primitives. We provide an XML syntax for our ontology and a huge part of the core ontology is based on RDF schema which allows basically all kinds of ontology languages to be used for any specific collaboration engineering task.

In contrast to the GPML, the ontology allows us to capture and share more information about the collaboration process and its context. The GPML adopts the design pattern thinkLet as a process template and provide different process information to define the workflow of a collaboration process. However, besides information about the activities of a participant, the used and developed data elements and possible internal or external events, the GPML provides no information about group characteristic and collaboration context. As a result, defined collaboration processes provide no guidelines for the group composition and still leave open the question which criteria should be used to assign a participant to a defined workflow. By using the ontology, we can increase process information about collaboration. Information about the group characteristics, like the skills of the participants can be used to define formalized rules for group composition. Context information further provides the possibility to adopt the design pattern approach also for the whole collaboration process. Thereby the objective and the description of the client can be used to define selection guides for a generic collaboration process.

USING THE COLLABORATION ONTOLOGY

In this section, we present an example and show how specific collaborations can be modelled in our ontology. Furthermore, with our example, we show how recommendations and analysis of the collaboration process can be done by means of reasoning and machine learning. The difference between reasoning and machine learning is that with reasoning we use the explicitly available information represented by means of an ontology to deduce new implicitly available information with the reasoning processes available in the logic underlying the ontology language. With machine learning, we might use explicitly available information represented by means of an ontology for deriving new knowledge, but the new knowledge is not available implicitly in the knowledge base when we just consider the logic underlying the ontology language. This means that with machine learning, we can derive completely new information and knowledge beyond deduction within the underlying knowledge representation formalism of the ontology language.

Our example is depicted in Figure 6 and deals with a collaborated book chapter writing process. In Figure 6, the node in the lower left corner represents the starting point of the collaborative book chapter writing process. This process is divided into three ThinkLets: planning the project (PlanProject as an instance of cpo:ThinkLet), writing the chapter (WriteChapter as an instance of cpo:ThinkLet) and revising the chapter (ReviseChapter as an instance of cpo:ThinkLet). Note that here, we could have also decided to model PlanProject, WriteChapter and ReviseChapter as sub concepts of the corresponding concepts they are instances of now. This is a modelling decision the Collaboration Engineer has to take depending on the OWL variant he or she wants to use and the reasoning tasks he or she wants to provide access and support to the participants.

For our example, we confined ourselves to describe only the cpo:ThinkLet WriteChapter in more detail. The cpo:ThinkLet WriteChapter is of the cpo:CollaborationPattern type Generate which is one of the 6 main collaboration patterns we found within our literature research. Basically, the writing of a chapter consists of three ThinXels which can be considered as the script for the cpo:ThinkLet WriteChapter. The three ThinXels are doing literature research (cpo:ThinXel DoLiteratureResearch), writing content (cpo:ThinXel WriteContent) and drawing figures (cpo:ThinXel DrawFigure). For doing literature research, the artefact literature database (cpo:Artefact LiteratureDatabase) has to be used. The result of doing literature research is a

Figure 6. Collaborative book chapter writing

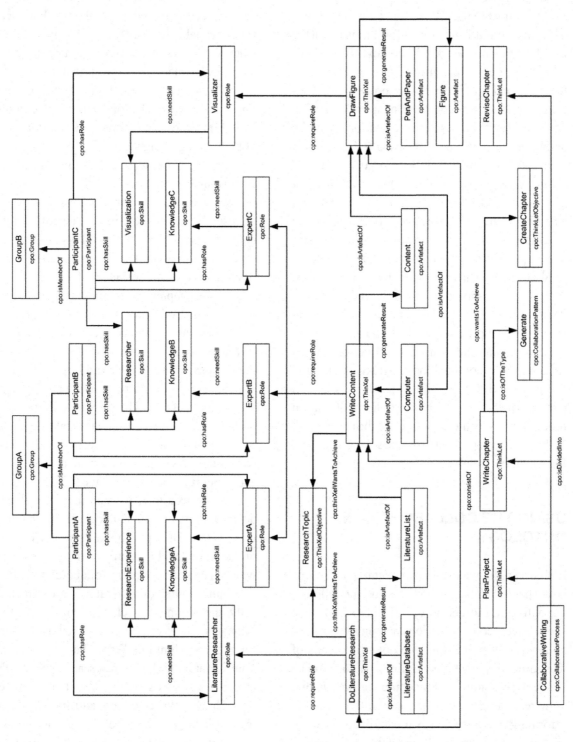

(cpo:Artifact LiteratureList) which also is an artefact used by the writing content activity. Both activities DoLiteratureResearch and WriteContent aim at providing results in a specific research topic (cpo:ThinXelObjective ResearchTopic). Both activities WriteContent and DrawFigure use the cpo:Artefact computer. WriteContent generates the cpo:Artefact Content which is used by the activity DrawFigure. DrawFigure uses also the cpo:Artefact PenAndPaper and generate the cpo:Artefact Figure.

All three ThinXels DoLiteratureResearch, WriteContent and DrawFigure require a specific cpo:Role or cpo:Skill. E.g. for being able to do literature research one has to be able to fulfil the cpo:Role LiteratureResearcher and have the corresponding skill. For drawing figures, one needs to be able to fulfil the cpo:Role Visualizer and have the corresponding skill. For writing content, one has to be expert in the areas A, B, C and needs to have knowledge about the aforementioned areas provided the book chapter shall deal with these three areas.

In our example, two groups work together, e.g. a cpo:Group GroupA somewhere in Germany consisting of two group members ParticipantA and ParticipantB. The second cpo:Group GroupB consists of one group member ParticipantC and might be located somewhere in the UK. ParticipantA has the role of the literature researcher (cpo:Role LiteratureResearcher) but he also provides content with his role as expert in area A in this collaboration project (cpo:Role ExpertA). Furthermore, ParticipantA is also an expert in area A since he has knowledge in area A (cpo:Skill KnowledgeA) and also research experience (cpo:Skill ResearchExperience) which both are required for the cpo:Role LiteratureResearcher. The other two participants are either a research or a visualization expert and are also experts in either cpo:Skill KnowledgeB or cpo:Skill KnowledgeC. Similar to ParticipantA, ParticipantC fulfils two roles, namely the role of a Visualizer (cpo:Skill Visualization) and the role of an expert in area C (cpo:Skill ExpertC).

In the following sections, we describe how collaboration engineering can profit by means of using an ontology and making use of the Semantic Web and the Linked (Open) Data cloud (see also http://linkeddata.org/). First we will describe how to analyse and provide recommendations with reasoning and afterwards, we discuss the potential of using machine learning.

REASONING

As mentioned above, we have first to decide whether to model the modelling primitives of the collaboration process at hand as instances or sub concepts. E.g. ParticipantA could be modelled as a specific person and thus as an instance. When modelling the artefact computer, however, we should not model it as an instance since the content writing and the figure drawing would not be done on the same computer. As mentioned above, PlanProject, WriteChapter, ReviseChapter are modelled as an instance of cpo:ThinkLet.

By means of a proper formalization in an OWL variant, the collaboration engineer and the domain expert can benefit in many ways. One very important benefit is in using the reasoning task satisfiability. I.e. the modelling experts can verify whether their modelling does not contain inconsistencies and thus the modelling has not been done properly. Another important reasoning task is whether the modelling is meaningful, i.e. whether all classes of the ontology can have instances. Or the modeling experts can check with reasoning support whether their ontology including the domain specifications is correct, i.e. the modelling captures the intended intuitions of the domain experts. The modellers can by means of reasoning also check whether the ontology including the domain specifications is minimally redundant, i.e. does not contain unintended synonyms. Thus, reasoning provides the modelers a lot of help in modelling their ontology and domain knowledge properly.

As soon as the ontology and the domain knowledge has been modelled properly and/or important knowledge from the linked open data cloud has been linked via mappings between collaboration ontology primitives and important vocabulary from the linked open data cloud, reasoning can support the recommendation process and help in deducing answers for different kinds of queries important to either the collaboration of domain experts or even the users. E.g. when a specific knowledge area of e.g. ParticipantA is given and also an ontology in the linked open data cloud with a taxonomy of areas of expertise (possibly with the proliferation of synonyms and additional relation declarations between the areas of expertise) and persons who are experts for certain areas of expertise, different reasoning and recommendation procedures are conceivable, e.g.

- If it is not clear who might be a good candidate for ParticipantA, a recommendation can be generated with the additional information from the linked open data cloud.
- Recommendations for collaborators for ParticipantA could be generated. ParticipantA will be able to read the papers written by the recommended experts, i.e. can get recommendations for her literature research. Or ParticipantA can ask the recommended experts questions or even collaborate with them in writing the chapter.
- Recommendations for related areas of expertise can be generated. E.g. via the sub concepts of the area of expertise mentioned in KnowledgeA, but also via specific relations between areas of expertise that indicate special kinds of relatedness.

Imagine a Facebook FOAF export and the possibilities for recommendations when considering the experts of certain areas of expertise and their connections. It is possible that the connections of the experts are also experts in similar areas and thus provide even further recommendations for the literature research.

A GRAPH-BASED APPROACH TO INFER NEW KNOWLEDGE

In this section, we give an introduction on how to leverage information about collaboration processes modelled with our ontology to improve preparation and execution of such a collaboration process. In Figure 6, the presented example describes a collaborated book chapter writing process. On the basis of this example, we show how to compute recommendations and thus support users or managers of such a collaboration process. We present two scenarios where we discuss how we can apply graph-based methods. The first scenario supports the participant by recommending the next collaboration step or material needed for the process. The second scenario focuses on the manager of the collaboration process and how our ontology can support the process of creating a collaboration process. Before we start with the scenarios we give some theoretical background about our machine learning approach.

GRAPH-BASED RECOMMENDATIONS

The collaboration information in the ontology consists of nodes and connections between theses nodes. That means we have a graph of information where information is connected. The computational model on which we compute recommendations must reflect this structure. Therefore, we define a model for combining the edge of a path between two nodes. The model must consider the case of parallel edges and the case of a sequence of edges. Figure 7 shows different approaches for defining edge algebras. In most applications, for simplicity we applied the model of weighted paths. Another

Figure 7. Different edge algebras

	Weighted Path	Resistance Path	Shortest Path
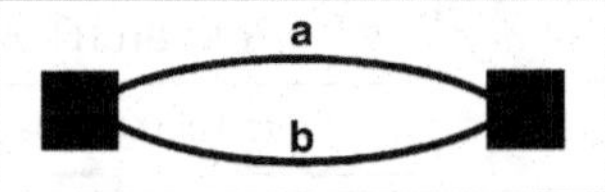	a+b	(a*b)/(a+b)	min(a,b)
	a*b	a+b	a+b

important step for computing recommendations is to specify a prediction model that defines which properties an entity must fulfil to be relevant for a query. The most commonly used recommender model is the semantic similarity of an entity with the input entities. This model follows the idea that entities connected with short paths (having a high weight) to the input entities and entities for that several parallel paths exist are most relevant to the input entities. Alternative recommender models are triangle closing or number of common neighbours.

For computing recommendations, we calculate and weight paths in the model starting from a set of given input entities (e.g. the participants or existing material). Entities reachable from the input entities are ranked according to their semantic similarity rating. This rating is calculated based on the edge weights of the respective paths. For parallel edges/paths the ratings are summed up; for a sequence of edges the weights are multiplied and weighted by a discount factor (dependent on the path length).

SUPPORT PARTICIPANTS

The participant of a collaboration process has to fulfil different tasks (ThinkLets) and subtasks (ThinXels) to contribute to the overall goal of the collaboration process. In our scenario, the book writing chapter, cpo:Participant ParticipantA has the cpo:Role LiteratureResearcher, see Figure

6. The task is to find relevant literature for the section State of the Art. The task and all related entities are visualized in Figure 8. To support the participant, one can recommend a selection of related literature. This helps to speed up the literature task as the participant only has to look through recommended papers. The recommendation process, using our path based recommendation approach, would take into account the cpo:ThinXel DoLiteratureResearch and the related nodes cpo:ThinXelObjective ResearchTopic, cpo:Artefact LiteratureDatabase and cpo:Artefact LiteratureList. The cpo:ThinXelObjective ResearchTopic describes one or more research topics the chapter should cover, thus, it is the starting point for our recommendation service. The cpo:Artefact LiteratureDatabase describes a resource containing information about research papers (which could come from another source like the Semantic Web Conference Corpus (*Semantic Web Conference Corpus,* 2011)). Our graph based approach now traverse through the connected information and selects all data related to the ResearchTopic. This condensed list is then presented to the user which then can select the papers to be included in the book chapter

SUPPORT THE MANAGER OF THE COLLABORATION PROCESS

A manager of a collaboration process has to select the right participants and resources needed for the

Figure 8. Supporting participants: Recommending material

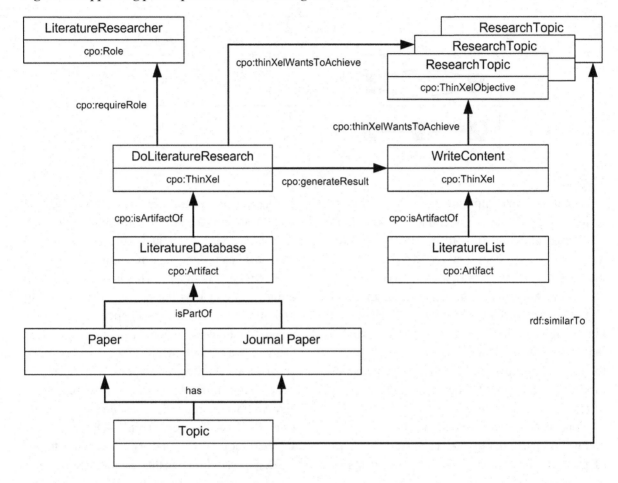

success of the whole process. This selection process can be well supported with our graph-based approach. Taking the cpo:ThinXel WriteContent as the starting point for our graph based algorithm, we see it needs a cpo:Artefact LiteratureList which can be achieved by the cpo:ThinXel DoLiteratureResearch which presupposes the cpo:Skill ResearchExperience. Our graph-based method would recommend cpo:Participant ParticipantA to take part in the collaboration process with the cpo:Role LiteratureResearcher. This recommendation helps the manager to automatically preselect the participants which should take part in the process and which Role they should occupy.

CONCLUSION

In this chapter, we presented an ontology as the basis for supporting groups in designing and executing collaboration work and discussed a possible integration of Semantic Web technologies with Collaboration Engineering. The presented work fills a gap as currently general technical standards to formalize the collaboration process are missing. We believe that an ontological approach can be used to define a common vocabulary for collaboration. The presented Collaboration Ontology is a first step to capture, share and reuse knowledge about collaboration in general. However, the ontology allows adding additional knowledge about the task either by domain experts or by means of the linked open data cloud. We have shown that the ontology can be used to model collaboration process and we presented further research and application areas like reasoning to generate recommendations and providing means for analysing the model. We have also shown how reasoning and machine learning algorithms can profit from such an ontology-based representation.

Based on this version of the ontology, further work on the ontology is needed. In the current form, the ontology lacks of some semantics. The representation of information as strings, like cpo:thinkLetDescription, cpo:qualityCriterion Description, cpo:thinkLetObjectiveDescription , should be reduced to a minimum and should also be modelled as semantic concepts. This can be done by either linking existing ontologies to our ontology covering the domain or to develop a new ontology for the domain.

Additionally, the integration of Social Web functionalities must be considered in the collaboration process and the corresponding modelling. For instance, a group could use feedback or competition tools to reduce social loafing. By connecting these technologies as applications for groupware technology and defining rules for their use adapted to the collaboration pattern, the participants could be supported in creating and sharing information and ideas for collaboration work. These rules could consider parameters like the time estimation, the conceptual ideas and the related results of a thinkLet. These properties could be retrieved from already existing ontologies, browsed by all participants and integrated in the collaborative work, so that a real dynamic collaboration process could take place.

REFERENCES

Alexander, C., Ishikawa, S., & Silverstein, M. (1977). *A pattern language, towns, buildings, construction*. New York, NY: Oxford University.

Briggs, R. O., Adkins, M., Mittlemann, D. D., Kruse, J., Miller, S., & Nunamaker, J. F. Jr. (1999). A technology transition model derived from qualitative field investigation of gss use aboard the U.S.S. Coronado. *Journal of Management Information Systems*, *15*(3), 151–195.

Briggs, R. O., de Vreede, G.-J., & Nunamaker, J. F. Jr. (2003). Collaboration engineering with thinklets to pursue sustained success with group support systems. *Journal of Management Information Systems*, *19*(4), 31–64.

Briggs, R. O., Kolfschoten, G. L., de Vreede, G.-J., & Dean, D. L. (2006). Defining key concepts for collaboration engineering. In *Americas Conference on Information Systems* (AMCIS) (Vol. 12, p. 121-128).

Briggs, R. O., & Vreede, G.-J. de. (2003). *Thinklets: Building blocks for concerted collaboration*.

Collaboration Ontology. (2011). Retrieved from http://www.collaborationontology.com

Corcho, O., Fernández-López, M., & Gómez-Pérez, A. (2003). Methodologies, tools and languages for building ontologies. Where is their meeting point? *Data & Knowledge Engineering*, *46*(1), 41–64. doi:10.1016/S0169-023X(02)00195-7

Csikszentmihalyi, M. (1997). *Creativity: Flow and the psychology of discovery and invention*. New York, NY: HarperCollins Publishers.

de Vreede, G.-J., & Briggs, R. O. (2005). Collaboration engineering: Designing repeatable processes for high-value collaborative tasks. In *Proceedings of the 38th Hawaii International Conference on System Sciences (HICSS)*.

de Vreede, G.-J., Kolfschoten, G. L., & Briggs, R. O. (2006). Thinklets: A collaboration engineering pattern language. *International Journal of Computer Applications of Technology*, *25*(2/3), 140–154. doi:10.1504/IJCAT.2006.009064 de Vreede, G.-J., Vogel, D., Kolfschoten, G. L., & Wien, J. (2003). Fifteen years of gss in the field: a comparison across time and national boundaries. In *Proceedings of the 36th Annual Hawaii International Conference on System Sciences (HICSS)*.

Dennis, A. R., George, J. F., Jessup, L. M., Nunamaker, J. F. Jr, & Vogel, D. R. (1988, December). Information technology to support electronic meetings. *Management Information Systems Quarterly, 12*(4), 591–624. doi:10.2307/249135

Dennis, A. R., Haley, B., & Vandenberg, R. J. (1996). A meta-analysis of effectiveness, efficiency, and participant satisfaction in group support systems research. In *Proceedings of the 17th International Conference on Information System*.

Dennis, A. R., Wixom, B. H., & Vandenberg, R. J. (2001, June). Understanding fit and appropriation effects in group support systems via meta-analysis. *Management Information Systems, 25*(2), 167–193. doi:10.2307/3250928

DeSanctis, G., & Gallupe, R. B. (1987). A foundation for the study of group decision support systems. *Management Science, 33*(5), 589–609. doi:10.1287/mnsc.33.5.589

DeSanctis, G., & Poole, M. S. (1994, May). Capturing the complexity in advanced technology use: Adaptive structuration theory. *Organization Science, 5*(2), 121–147. doi:10.1287/orsc.5.2.121

Diehl, M., & Stroebe, W. (1991). Productivity loss in idea-generating groups: Tracking down the blocking effect. *Journal of Personality and Social Psychology, 61*(3), 392–403. doi:10.1037/0022-3514.61.3.392

Edmondson, A. (1999, June). Psychological safety and learning behavior in work teams. *Administrative Science Quarterly, 44*(2), 350–383. doi:10.2307/2666999

FOAF. (2011, January). Retrieved from http://www.foaf-project.org/

Gruber, T. R. (1993, June). A translation approach to portable ontology specifications. *Knowledge Acquisition, 5*, 199–220. doi:10.1006/knac.1993.1008

Gruber, T. R. (1995). Toward principles of the design of ontologies used for knowledge sharing. *International Journal of Human-Computer Studies, 43*, 907–928. doi:10.1006/ijhc.1995.1081

Grüninger, M., & Fox, M. (1995). Methodology for the design and evaluation of ontologies. In *ijcai'95, Workshop on Basic Ontological Issues in Knowledge Sharing*, April 13, 1995.

Hollingshead, A. B. (1995, January). *The workflow reference model* (Tech. Rep.). Workflow Management Coalition.

Janis, I. (1982). *Groupthink* (2nd ed.). Boston, MA: Houghton-Mifflin.

Karau, S. J., & Williams, K. D. (1993, October). Social loafing: A meta analytic review and theoretical integration. *Journal of Personality and Social Psychology, 65*(4), 681–706. doi:10.1037/0022-3514.65.4.681

Knoll, S. W., Chelvier, R., & Horton, G. (2007). Formalised online creativity using thinxels. In *Proccedings of the 10th European Conference on Creativity and Innovation (ECCI)*.

Knoll, S. W., Hörning, M., & Horton, G. (2008). A design approach for a universal group support system using thinklets and thinxels. In *Proceedings of the Group Decision and Negotiation Meeting 2008 (GDN)*.

Knoll, S. W., Hörning, M., & Horton, G. (2009). Applying a thinklet and thinxel-based group process modeling language: A prototype of a universal group support system. In *Proceedings of the 42nd Hawaii International Conference on System Sciences (HICSS)*.

Knoll, S. W., & Horton, G. (2011). (in press). Formalized collaboration using collaboration engineering: How to improve collaboration with a universal gss. *Group Decision and Negotiation*.

Knoll, S. W., Plumbaum, T., Hoffmann, J. L., & De Luca, E. W. (2010). Collaboration ontology: Applying collaboration knowledge to a generic group support system. In *Proceeding of the Group Decision and Negotiation Meeting 2010 (GDN)*.

Kolfschoten, G. L., Briggs, R. O., de Vreede, G.-J., Jacobs, P. H. M., & Appelman, J. H. (2006). A conceptual foundation of the thinklet concept for collaboration engineering. *International Journal of Human-Computer Studies, 64*(7), 611–621. doi:10.1016/j.ijhcs.2006.02.002

Kolfschoten, G. L., & de Vreede, G.-J. (2009). A design approach for collaboration processes: A multimethod design science study in collaboration engineering. *Journal of Management Information Systems, 26*(1), 225–256. doi:10.2753/MIS0742-1222260109

Kolfschoten, G. L., de Vreede, G.-J., & Pietron, L. (2010). A training approach for the transition of repeatable collaboration processes to practitioners. *Group Decision and Negotiation, 20*(3), 1–25.

Kolfschoten, G. L., Vreede, G.-J. de., & Briggs, R. O. (2008) Computer aided pattern-based collaboration process design: A computer aided collaboration engineering tool. In *Proceedings of the 14th International Workshop on Groupware 2008 (CRIWG)*.

Lee, J., Seo, W., Kim, K., & Kim, C.-H. (2010). An owl-based ontological approach to rad modeling of human interactions for business collaboration. *Expert Systems with Applications, 37*(6), 4128–4138. doi:10.1016/j.eswa.2009.11.011

Mittleman, D. D., Briggs, R. O., Murphy, J., & Davis, A. (2008, September). Toward a taxonomy of groupware technologies. In Groupware: Design, Implementation, and Use, LNCS 5411 (pp. 305–317). Berlin, Germany: Springer-Verlag. doi:10.1007/978-3-540-92831-7_25doi:10.1007/978-3-540-92831-7_25

Niederman, F., Beise, C. M., & Beranek, P. M. (1993). Facilitation issues in distributed group support systems. In *Proceedings of the 1993 Conference on Computer Personnel Research* (pp. 299–312). New York, NY: ACM.

Nunamaker, J. F. Jr, Dennis, A. R., Valacich, J. S., Vogel, D., & George, J. F. (1991). Electronic meeting systems to support group work. *Communications of the ACM, 34*(7), 40–61. doi:10.1145/105783.105793

Nunamaker, J. F. Jr, Reinig, B. A., & Briggs, R. O. (2009). Principles for effective virtual teamwork. *Communications of the ACM, 52*(4), 113–117. doi:10.1145/1498765.1498797

Oliveira, F. F., Antunes, J. C. P., & Guizzardi, R. S. S. (2007). *Towards a collaboration ontology*. 2nd Workshop on Ontologies and Metamodels in Software and Data Engineering.

Pattberg, J., & Fluegge, M. (2007). Towards an ontology of collaboration patterns. In *Proceedings of Challenges in Collaborative Engineering 07*.

Pinto, H. S., & Martins, J. P. (2004, July). Ontologies: How can they be built? *Knowledge and Information Systems, 6*(4), 441–464. doi:10.1007/s10115-003-0138-1

Poole, M. S., & Hollingshead, A. B. (2005). *Theories of small groups*. Thousand Oaks, CA: Sage Publications.

Predoiu, L., & Zhdanova, A. V. (2007). Semantic web languages and ontologies. In Freire, M., & Pereira, M. (Eds.), *Encyclopedia of internet technologies and applications* (pp. 512–518). Hershey, PA: IGI Global. doi:10.4018/978-1-59140-993-9.ch072

Rajsiri, V., Lorré, J.-P., Bénaben, F., & Pingaud, H. (2008). Collaborative process definition using an ontology-based approach. *Pervasive Collaborative Networks, 283,* 205–212. doi:10.1007/978-0-387-84837-2_21

Schumann, S. (2005). *The IAF handbook of group facilitation: Best practices from the leading organization in facilitation.* San Francisco, CA: Jossey-Bass.

Semantic Web Conference Corpus. (2011). Retrieved from http://data.semanticweb.org/

Shannon, C. E. (1948, July). October). A mathematical theory of communication. *The Bell System Technical Journal, 27,* 379–423, 623–656.

Studer, R., Benjamins, V., & Fensel, D. (1998). Knowledge engineering: Principles and methods. *IEEE Transactions on Data and Knowledge Engineering, 25*(1-2), 161–197.

Terveen, L. G. (1995). Overview of human-computer collaboration. *Knowledge-Based Systems, 8*(2-3), 67–81. doi:10.1016/0950-7051(95)98369-H

Uschold, M., & Gruninger, M. (1996). Ontologies: Principles, methods and applications. *The Knowledge Engineering Review, 11,* 93–136. doi:10.1017/S0269888900007797

van der Aalst, W. M. P., ter Hofstede, A. H. M., Kiepuszewski, B., & Barros, A. P. (2003). Workflow patterns. *Distributed and Parallel Databases, 14,* 5–51. doi:10.1023/A:1022883727209

VanGundy, A. B. (1988). *Techniques of structured problem solving.* New York, NY: Van Nostrant Reinhold.

Vivacqua, A. S., Garcia, A. C. B., & Gomes, A. (2011). BOO: Behavior oriented ontology to describe participant dynamics in collocated design meetings. *Expert Systems with Applications, 38*(2), 1139–1147. doi:10.1016/j.eswa.2010.05.007

Wong, Z., & Aiken, M. (2003). Automated facilitation of electronic meetings. *Information & Management, 41*(2), 125–134. doi:10.1016/S0378-7206(03)00042-9

Workflow Management Coalition. (2008, October). *Workflow process definition interface – XML process definition language* (Tech. Rep. No. WFMC-TC-1025).

Zephram. (2011, January). Retrieved from http://www.zephram.de /?lang=en

ADDITIONAL READING

Enderton, H. B. (2002). *A mathematical introduction to logic* (2nd ed.). Academic Press.

Gómez-Pérez, A., Fernández-López, M., & Corcho, O. (2004). *Ontological engineering.* Heidelberg, Germany: Springer Verlag.

Heath, T., & Bizer, C. (2011). *Linked data: Evolving the web into a global data space.* Morgan & Claypool Publishers.

Hitzler, P., Krötzsch, M., & Rudolph, S. (2009). *Foundations of Semantic Web technologies.* Chapman & Hall/CRC.

Kunegis, J., Lommatzsch, A., Bauckhage, C., & Albayrak, S. (2008). On the scalability of graph kernels applied to collaborative recommenders. In *Proceedings ECAI 2008 Workshop on Recommender Systems* (pp. 35–38).

De Lathauwer, L. D., Moor, B. D., & Vandewalle, J. (2000). A multilinear singular value decomposition. *Matrix Analysis and Applications, 21*(4), 1253–1278. doi:10.1137/S0895479896305696

Mitchell, T. M. (1997). *Machine learning.* McGraw-Hill.

Robinson, A., & Voronkov, A. (2001). *Handbook of automated reasoning* (*Vol. 1-2*). Elsevier.

Saul, L. K., Weinberger, K. Q., Sha, F., Ham, J., & Lee, D. D. (2006). Semisupervised learning. In Chapelle, O., Schölkop, B., & Zien, A. (Eds.), *Spectral methods for dimensionality reduction.* MIT Press.

Staab, S., & Studer, R. (Eds.). (2004). *Handbook on ontologies.* Springer.

KEY TERMS AND DEFINITIONS

Collaboration Engineering: A facilitation, design and training approach for recurring high-value tasks that provide benefits of professional facilitation to groups without access to professional facilitators

Collaboration Pattern: A description of the nature of the group's collaborative activities when observed over a period of time as they move from a starting state to some end state

Collaboration Support: Tools, processes and services that support groups during the design and execution of collaboration

Collaboration: A process in which participants joint effort toward a goal

Machine Learning: A scientific discipline concerned with the design and development of algorithms that allow computers to evolve behaviours based on empirical data, such as from sensor data or databases

Ontology: A formal specification of a conceptualization of a domain of interest that specifies a set of constraints that declare what should necessarily hold in any possible world

Reasoning: The process of rewriting logical formulae based on rules belonging to the underlying logic of the knowledge representation formalism and, in this way, inferring new knowledge, i.e. new symbolic formulae, which did not exist in the knowledge base before

Semantic Web: The World Wide Web enhanced with Semantics yielding the "Web of Data" or "Linked Data" that enables machines to understand the semantics, or meaning of information on the World Wide Web

ThinkLet: A named, scripted collaborative activity that gives rise to a known pattern of collaboration among people working together toward a goal

ThinXel: An atomic facilitator instruction leading to a response of the participants that has a well-defined function in the context of the group goal

Chapter 13

Developing a Web-Based Cooperative Environment to Software Project Development

Seyed Morteza Babamir
University of Kashan, Iran

ABSTRACT

A software project is developed by collaboration of some expert people. However, the collaboration puts obstacles in the way of software development when the involved people in the project are scattered over the world. Although Internet has provided a collection of scattered islands in which the denizens of the islands are able to communicate with each other, it lacks full requisite qualifications for the collaboration among the denizens. The emerging idea is that a supportive environment should be developed on the Web for providing full requisite qualifications and facilitating collaboration. Towards providing such an environment, this chapter aims to present a framework exploiting Open Hypermedia System (OHS) and a Web-based collaboration protocol. OHS assists in saving and restoring artifacts constructed by the scattered people, and the protocol provides channels to concurrent communication and distributed authoring among the people.

INTRODUCTION

Software intensive systems such as airspace, telecommunication and stock systems are the systems where software is their main part. In other words, daily efforts of present-day people increasingly depended on the systems in which software plays the main role. Development of such systems without collaborative effort is a difficult task. However, bringing together the scattered collaborators under a same roof is an obstacle to collaborate. Distance between collaborates, acclimatization of collaborators to their environment

DOI: 10.4018/978-1-4666-0894-8.ch013

and their familiarities with own tools are some restrictions of physical gathering. World Wide Web has brought down the restrictions by providing a distance communication among the people.

Although Web has facilitated distance and virtual collaboration among the people, it wants more capabilities. This chapter aims to present a framework to furnish the capabilities on the Web. To this end we should: (1) Create a social network among people is distributed through the Web and (2) Manage artifacts created by collaborators. The framework aims to provide an environment to support software product from idea to the production maintenance on the Web. The environment: (1) obviates organizational hindrances existing in the way of collaboration, (2) enables the end user to participate in analyzing requirements, (3) enables the involved expert people to examine, recognize and document problem and to present recommendations for production, (4) enables distribution of software and reduces costs needed to complete the production.

In fact, Web-based collaborative software development is a new kind of social effort in a virtual organization that is not limited to certain geographical locations and membership. However, the present-day Web is used to read and review information and so has no enough qualifications to fulfill the aim of social network of software development. Synthesis and production of software intensive systems, design of industrial products, authoring books and technical documents are typical teamwork include a *common purpose*, a *common data space*, *collaboration tool* and involved people.

Consider Figure 1. The first part is responsible for supporting: (1) users' activity consisting of

Figure 1. Web-based collaboration

| Web-based social network |
| Artifacts management system |

constructing and modifying their documents using tools like Web browsers and (2) some mechanism to simultaneous access to the documents. The second part: (1) is responsible for supporting the communication between Web users and artifacts management system (AMS) and (2) includes the artifacts management system. The system including a repository for users' documents, manages relation among them. Figure 2 shows more detail of the proposed framework and Table 1 shows tasks of each part.

Artifact management system which is in fact the main part of the model will process users' request, support non-concurrency collaboration between them, and appropriately maintain compatible links and contents of repository and cope with users request through reacting with repository to store, access or editing components. The parts tasks are shown by Table 1.

Repository management is not solely a management for component maintenance, because in this model we try to make component to possible support of consistency between components and its proper reservations. Therefore it should be noted that though the management of components the users' construction and consistency between them is the task of management layer, i.e. the forth layer, there are some relations, between components, which are not solely structural relations but they are conceptual relations, the consistency of which should be provided by repository management.

For example, the programmer wishes to construct the compiled program file or an executable program file and tries to establish link between these constructions and also their links to their required data which are conceptual relations. Support of development environment without developer's request and establishment of such links automatically, will be effective in implementation phase of system both for construction and production of programs in view of:

- Releasing developer's power and energy considered to environment problems and

Figure 2. The proposed framework

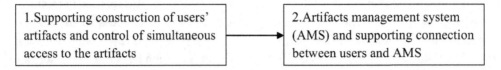

helping him to concentrate on problem solution,

- Integrating components. When developer changes some program, the program change should be applied without programmer interference in compiled and executable forms of the program to reach compatibility between different forms of the program. Another important role of repository management is related to the implementation of users' programs. The programs are implemented in the main memory through reacting with repository and its management. Since a part of software development environment backup relates to implementation environment and repository management should support this back up, this environment should provide two kinds of supports for users and its constructions (1) compatibility and integrity between different types of a program and between programs and data (2) providing implementation environment within software development environment. It means that users' program implementation environment should not be separate from construction environment in which the users construct components. Thus, the programmer who constructs a program and then implements it should not enter an environment separated from his/her development environment.

Inconsistency among software components and also among software and data can be resulted because of the following reasons: (1) the lack of referred components, (2) the existence of unusual components and (3) repeated components. The inconsistency producing in major errors during the implementation of program makes the programmer return to program development environment which is a separate one to make it ready for implementation after error handling.

LAYER-1: SUPPORTING CONSTRUCTION OF USER ARTIFACTS

In this layer technologies *persistent environment* and *open hypermedia system* are used to support construction of users' artifacts. Sections "Per-

Table 1. The framework tasks

Part	Layer	Task	Task
1	1	Supporting construction of users' artifacts	Authoring and versioning artifacts and announcing sensitivity to the change of some artifacts
	2	Control of simultaneous access to artifacts	Prevention of unwanted rewriting artifacts and missing artifact updates
2	3	Supporting connection between users and artifact management system	Passing requests and artifacts from users to the system and passing replies from the system to the users
	4	Artifact management system	Repository management, Search and user notification services

sistent Environment" and "Open Hypermedia System" address these technologies.

Persistent Environment

In a persistent programming environment, the difference between program and data will be omitted and programs are considered as data. This allows using the new methods of software production and maintenance. The concept of persistency was introduced by Atkinson and Morrison (1990, 2000). The aim of persistent programming languages is to generate a programming environment to present all aspects of software development process within a unit and consistent framework. An independent internal review by IBM identifies that in some non-persistent programs, up to 30% of source is used only in exchanging data between program and file or database (IBM, 1978). Many researches have been underway to examine the persistency and its use in the integration of database systems and programming languages. Most products of object-oriented databases provide some interface forms of persistent language. The SUN Company and the others have used their experiences in adding persistency to Java while many systems may not use persistency thoroughly but clearly borrow its necessary concepts. By introducing persistence abstraction concept on data properties such as store place, saved time and format, a basic technology for systems with high volume and long-term has been created.

Figure 3 shows data access in non-persistent programs. The link between program and existing data is established only at run time, i.e. programs have no pre-defined link with data. The links between existing programs are established by copying library programs into main program during linking and loading phase (a phase before running phase). In non-persistent environment, programs and data are provided and stored independently Figure 4 shows programs access to data in a persistent data environment. This environment differs from non-persistent environments in 2 aspects: (1)

the entities inside the persistent environment, in spite of persistent environment, jointly together in a graph form, and there is no entity outside the graph. In non-persistent environment there is no similar relation between entities and the programmer should create relations in the required form. (2) The entities inside the persistent environment include executable data and programs.

Open Hypermedia System

Nowadays open systems and data integrity are two important factors in information systems. Operation environments include programs, systems and variable tools which are used to support different tasks like software development, authoring, design and communication. Each of these tools has a certain method to store and retrieve information. Therefore data are stored in different forms and are reserved in heterogeneous data repositories distributively. The lack of integrity between tools and data is presented as a major problem. Open hypermedia linking like Microcosm (Hall, Davis & Hutchings, 1996) and Chimera (Anderson, Taylor & Whitehead, 1999) has presented a proper solution to integrate measurement environments.

Hypermedia System Architecture

Microcosm was one of the first hypermedia systems which allowed other applied systems to use linking facilities provided by this system (Hall et al., 1996). This method is called link service. Microcosm was accompanied by several pre-constructed text browser and some methods to inform external applications of existence of a link server in the environment. By development of open hypermedia systems, they tried to provide an environment for collaborative efforts to develop huge engineering projects.

The second generation of open hypermedia systems is distributed systems. ABC (Smith & Smith, 1991) is a construction project of open hypermedia system which was designed to use

Figure 3. Persistent data access in a file-based system

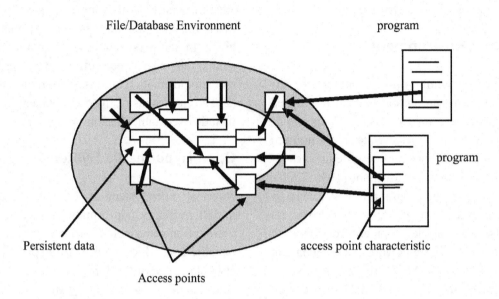

Figure 4. Persistent data access in persistent environment

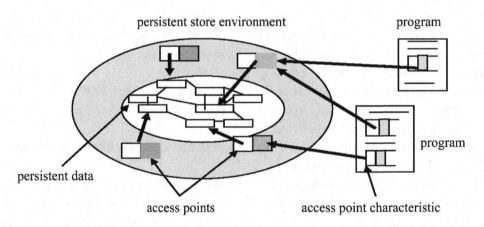

in developed hypermedia. The third generation of open hypermedia systems is designed because of poor efficiency of dynamic structures like Petri nets among preceding generations. The Aquanet System (Marshall, Halaz, Rogres & Janssen, 1991) and its following complement, VIKI (Marshall, Shipman, & Coombs, 1994) are of this kind.

Data Model in Hypermedia

Hypermedia is an environment to support development and presentation of documents of every type, like text, audio, video and link. As a hypermedia supports different types of media, there is a need for using browsers and editors. Such system stores and presents documents different from the method is applied to HTML files. In these systems, links are first class entities in the sense that they have the mentioned type, production time, author and components. In a hypermedia links are presented and stored independent of contents. Regarding the fact that links are first-class objects, a component producer can link constructed components without being obliged to put the links in the components.

Two other important features in hypermedia links are bidirectional and n-way links. In spite of HTML frame in which document browsing is just forwarded by links (from the beginning to the end) and to return (from the end to the beginning) a browser should be used (only in level of the HTML pages). In a hypermedia system links are traversed forward or backward. N-way links, in spite of HTML frame, allow beginning or end of every link to have some entities, rather than only one entity. Both features are required to represent hierarchical structures. Figure 5 shows a general model for data in hypermedia systems (Davis, Millard & Reich, 1998). A link represents a joint between zero or some end points. In many systems, the traverse of a link may cause process running rather than transmission to another point of link, or may cause transmission to another point of link, and also cause a process running. Figure 6 shows a typical example of data general model in a hypermedia system. In this figure, link1 and link2 have "define" and "support" types respectively (Davis et al, 1998).

One endpoint (anchor) is a hypermedia object which keeps the features of a link end. An endpoint from a place in a document to entire document specifies an area in an image, some part of a video etc. Typically an endpoint keeps a traversable direction which can be a source, destination or bidirectional. Consider Figure 6; *link1* may

move from *endpoint1* to *endpoint2* and *link2* from *endpoint4* to *endpoint2* and *endpoint3* and *link2* from *endpoint3* to *endpoint2*. But in *link1* movement may not be from *endpoint2* to *endpoint1* and in *link2* movement may not be from *endpoint2* to *endpoint3* and *endpoint4*. Endpoints and links are reserved outside documents. As endpoints and links are separate, so they can be reserved and maintained independently and can be reviewed and modified independent of the documents interrelated by these links. Nevertheless a combination of link and document should be accessible in form of web pages, if necessary.

A *dataref* defines a general node. A *dataref* includes a *nodespec* and a *locspec* and may depend on zero or some endpoints. Also a *dataref* may refer to more than one endpoint and these endpoints may associate with different links. Consider Figure 6; *dataref2* depends on *endpoint2* and *endpoint3* associates with 2 links.

A *nodespec* will be decomposed into one or more *nodeID* each of which individually specifies a node. A *locspec* keeps information about a chosen place which should be represented. Each of link, endpoint and node objects within a system has an individual *nodeID* and the server managing these objects is called *linkserver*. Figure 7 shows architecture of a multi-user hypermedia system (Gronbak, Hem, Madsen & Sloth, 1993).

Editor and browser processes added to hypermedia, are used by final users and may be text editor, browser, graphic, video and etc. Running processes (RP) which is also called applied layer, provides hypermedia services for a set of editor processes used by a user at the present time. RP is a server relating to editors and is a client for OODB server. RP provides editor's independent

Figure 5. General model of data in hypermedia system

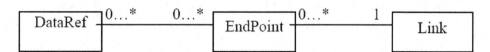

Figure 6. A typical of data model in hypermedia system

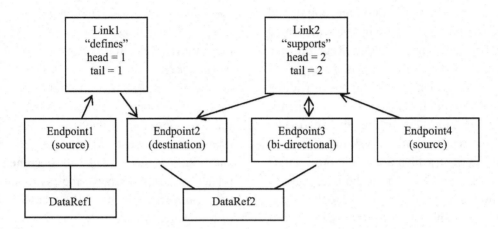

operation to generate and implement component objects and links and distributes information events from OODB to editors. OODB server provides a permanent physical layer for hypermedia objects (links& contents).

OODB server and RPs may be implemented on different computers and in a distributed environment. There is one active RP from hypermedia for every active user. RP is an applicant from OODB server and the two components (RP,OODB) may be implemented on 2 separate computers with different software platforms. Also editors and RPs may be generated on different computers but in practice usually implement on users stations. Distribution of editors on different platforms requires support/backup of hypermedia associate with other environments.

Intractability with Other Environments

In addition to use certain tools for documents, an open hypermedia allows using general tools (the third party) in its environment. Association of hypermedia development with Web led to tools such as Webvise (Gronbak, Sloth & Orbak, 1999) and Chimera. Web is characterized by three features: (a) a well-defined private data section to use by a browser, (b) a URL (Universal Resource Loca-

tor) with its related data transmission protocol (HTTP) and (c) a hypertext writing plan in which exact addresses of link destination are specified as part of source documents. Compared to this network open hypermedia systems have the following features: (a) intractability with different browsers, (b) hypertext authoring approach based on separation of "destination specifier" (links) from source environment and (c) creating non-concurrent collaboration mechanisms.

As an open hypermedia reserves structures (links) separate from contents, in system representation, we can see the structures and component contents are separated or mixed together. So application systems see an open hypermedia as open, when using it, and are not obliged to use some certain data forms or browser tools. Thus, they can link to accessible documents from different sources or give others the possibility of using their sources and services. Figure 8 shows architecture of an open hypermedia system interacting with other environments (Gronbak & Will, 1998). This architecture is used in Chimera and HyperDisco systems. In this figure wrapper is used to allow applications and external repositories to be consistent with OHS protocols. OHS session manager is a tool integrator. This manager provides hypermedia services both for OHS type applications and external applications. An applied OHS system is

Figure 7. Multi-user hypermedia model architecture

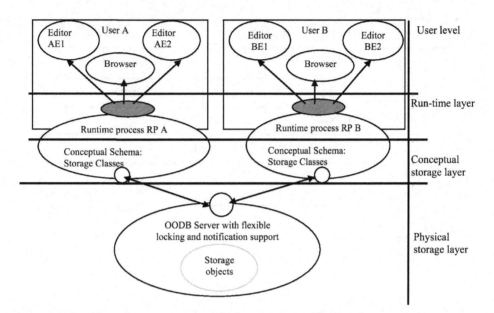

a system which directly backup OHS presentation protocol Similarly an OHS repository directly supports OHS storage protocol. The main power of this general architecture is in using wrapper which is in fact a kind of Application Program Interface (API).

Figure 9 shows this general architecture being specific to Chimera open hypermedia system. In this architecture, browsers A, B, C, D use API to apply a persistent data repository. This repository includes some views that different browsers have created by their request to server and by using raw data and have reserved them when a browser constructs a view, reserves it in view repository to use it when necessary.

Furthermore other browsers can use views produced by other browsers. Each browser, by using API provided, communicates with the server repository to create a browser and reserve it in the related repository. When a view, the browser which not existed in the environment, is requested by client A, the server requests the related browser in client B environment a view construction and after the construction the server

sends the browser to client A to use it or reserves it in the repository. While a browser is involved in an activity, other divisions of client are free. After creating their views the clients don't require to communicate with the server and their other relations are with the repository in which they have reserved their borrowings. Thus distributed-ness has been observed. Figure 10 shows the production of two views made by two browsers and their relations to a link in Chimera. In this figure it can be seen that how different browsers with different definitions of a raw object existed in server repository, construct their views and make access to each other possible.

Users Notification and Collaboration

Basically the relation between client and server in Web is based on client-server model, i.e. the server waits for a request from client to send a response, after processing, to client. In server-client model, the client should consistently monitor the server to be informed of changes in components. This case is not suitable in an environment in which group

Figure 8. Interaction open hypermedia system with users and stores

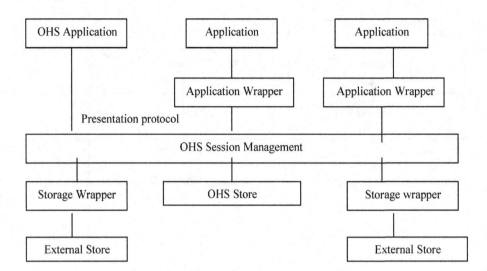

collaboration should be made between members to produce or edit components. Because most of the users are willing to register their wish to change or edit their concerned component, and to notify other users 'desire to change or edit components. As notification mechanism is necessary for group collaboration, open hypermedia systems created based on hyper-base allow event notification. Such servers actively operate (i.e. send message without receiving request) whereas web servers acts passively (i.e. waiting for receiving some request). Thus, a client expresses his desire for changing or editing some components by other users, to be registered by the server; then other users willing to change or edit their concerned component, can be informed.

Designing and authoring in large projects requires collaboration of members who cooperate in a common subject or a general task. This collaboration is done concurrently and non-concurrently. In concurrent collaboration, constructing and editing components is at once and in place so that each user sees other users' work result immediately, after doing it. Thus in every time, there is only one final construction resulted by all members involved (till now). In non concurrency collaboration, each construction and edition of component by every user leads to a new component and final or middle artifact of users are combined and make a general final artifact (a combination of users' final artifacts) or some final artifacts (a combination of some users' middle artifacts in several time).

In a hypermedia based on hyper-base we can exploit non-concurrency collaboration. To this end, users become member of events that happen on their common components through their editors or browsers. A user's running process (i.e. RP) requests OODB server to be notified by changing the components of repository made by RPs related to other users. This user should previously enroll to be notified by the changes in this component. In hypermedia systems, membership in an event is an important subject and when there are many events, components or the users group, individual membership in these events becomes difficult. In this situation, it is necessary that the membership is made automatically i.e. every user, by specifying one or some features of components, events or the group users having these feature(s), can become a member. An event may be starting point of a transaction on a component, locking a

Figure 9. Chimera open hypermedia system architecture

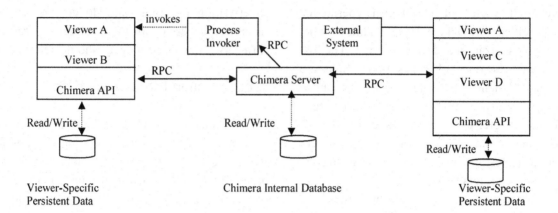

component or leaving a transaction incomplete. The event notification is completely independent of reserved components definition in the server repository. (In other words it isn't a part of component features), for notification is the server task, and the class of repository objects should not be developed for this purpose.

ETHS group authoring system is a typical collaborative system to construct documents which interacts with a hypermedia system based on hyper-base. ETHS uses the events registered in hyper base to lead changes in the common nodes and links network. A client defines a pat-

tern (for instance "notify me whenever every client other than me, wishes to do any operation, other than locking, on components constructed by user *A* before date *D*") and then determines his requirements exactly to be a member of an event or a cluster of events. This applied system was hypermedia system and notification mechanism for real time communications between users. It means that whenever a user determines that he/she wants to edit some part of a component, all readers in real time become notified and get that user s name, immediately communicate with him/her through ETHS internal mechanism.

Figure 10. Two views made by two browsers and their relations to a link in Chimera

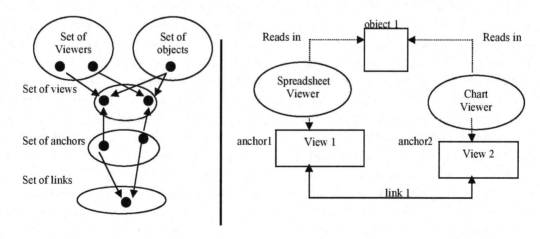

There are two problems for links in Web, which challenge group authoring, but considering the conceptual structure of links in open hypermedia, these problems are tackled. The problems include: (1) link fossilization and (2) link decay. The fossilization is the result of propagation of links as a part of documents. These links cannot be changed without the inspection of documents. Links decay because of refer to destination anchors through certain name and route of document. Thus every change in destination requires some change in every source refers to it.

Two potential risks for accessing hypermedia in huge networks of links are disorientation and cognitive overhead. Disorientation means losing location and direction in non-linear documents, known as lost in space. Cognitive overhead means additional effort and concentration necessary to maintain several tasks or trails in one time. This overhead is because of appearing different ways in every point of route simultaneously and keeping all of them in author's or reader's mind to have more cognition in the next points of the route. Of course, these cases are not specific to hypermedia, but every system which uses large and complex graphs of link, encounters this problem. In Web, hyper-text structure is in the form of open-way link and therefore the possibility of disorientation is less. There is a label for hypermedia links to decrease cognitive overhead problems.

Extension of Web Protocols

The third technology used in the first layer is extension of web protocols. Nowadays, huge and complex software are developed by groups of software engineers which are geographically dispersed. These engineers are in the organizations that are increasingly producing software, are non-centralized and have some divisions dispersed in different places. In addition, there are big companies which are commonly working to produce software products. A key challenge to support distributed groups of software development is the possibility of software development through internet. Thus cases as prevention of undesired overwriting programs and documents, safety, accuracy, access control and reliable operations in a network with great delay, should determined.

Collaboration Structure in Web

The members of distributed groups should collaborate, when they are designing documents, tests, specifications and programs, all of which compose a system to create and complete the project components. This collaboration is required in two forms: (1) non-concurrent parallel collaboration in which every user exerts his changes and editions in separate versions and dependent of other users and, in proper time, combines his artifacts with other's, and creates a new authoring of the main component and (2) concurrent collaboration in which every change or edition on the users' artifacts is carried out in place and finally there is no more than one version of that component in every time.

In concurrent collaboration, exercising concurrency control mechanisms, recovery and locking by supporting environment, for system components are required. Non-concurrent parallel collaboration requires tracking changes in one component which are made by several persons through separate versions. Then the resulted versions are combined and an authoring of that component is produced in proper time. Tracking versions require monitoring history of changes to know that (1) through which changes, (2) when and (3) by who a version of a component has been produced. Also when necessary (for example when an error occurs), it should be possible to return to previous version(s), undo the performed operation and regenerate new versions after renewed changes. This operation, in a system, is done by Configuration Management (Vesperman, 2006). By using Configuration Management, we are able to see previous revisions of a component, difference between revisions, the history of them, and the person responsible for revising, revision date, and comments about every revision.

Architecture of Group Collaboration Systems

The collaboration between distributed members of a group to construct the components of a system requires a distributed Configuration Management as CVS (Concurrent Version System) (Vesperman, 2006) which is currently used by HTTP Apache server (Apache Group) and Mozila explorer (Mozila Project). The background of collaboration among members in CVS is internet in the sense that every user loads one version of program or document on the local memory and makes the required changes on it. During operation, each user is separate from other users; having finished the changes, the user sends his artifacts to the server to combine with other finished artifacts.

Some other Configuration Management systems such as Plush (Albrecht, College, Braud, Dao, Topilski, Tuttle & Snoeren, 2007) use Web environment for distribution and following communicating client with server, attach a helper code to client's explorer to carry out next operations. This code acts as interface between version control system and local environment. In spite of CVS, these types of systems don't rely on their specific protocols to work in Web environment and by using helper code apply Web standards to interact between users.

The other collaboration system which is merely based on Web and better exploit Web standards than Plush is BSCW (Basic Support for Cooperative Works) (OrbitTeam Software, 2005). The system works based on shared workspace. Each group has a workspace to put its artifacts in it. What is necessary is that, in order to do group development and authoring all users should be consistent with each other in using development and authoring tools and use one set of tools. Exploiting one set of tools depends not only on that tool but on the number of people using it, because the more people use this tool, the more exploitation of that tool becomes possible. This fact leads to the result that when a current and standard network protocol assures interaction between authoring tools and group development among the users, the number of servers supporting this protocol for group collaboration increases vise versa when the number of accessible servers increases, the number of authoring and development tools, without more investment on this tool, increases; there would be more people and organizations capable to collaborate in group.

To achieve this aim a group in California university supported by DARPA (Defense Advanced Research Project Agency) which produces complex software, gathered the interested parties from universities and industries in IETF to adopt some development of web standard protocol i.e. HTTP named as WebDAV (web distributed authoring and versioning) (Sanchez & Daboo, 2008 & Mitrix, Davis & Babich, 2008). WebDAV protocol provides some facilities for concurrency control operation needed in workspace, as file omission, addition and copying. Each component has features like name, date of creation, author name, access permission, to be locked, etc. To exploit WebDAV protocol facilities, a WebDAV server and a WebDAV client are required. IIS 5 is a Microsoft Web service for WINDOWS which has promoted file management and locking features of Windows to provide WebDAV facilities to manage features, locking and repository for WebDAV. In the client side, the Office software tool supports WebDAV features (Microsoft).

WebDAV group supports six capabilities in HTTP protocol development, in order to reach authoring support, parallel development and configuration management: (1) prevention of undesired overwriting components, (2) component feature management, (3) namespace management, (4) authoring management, (5) management of clustering components related to each other and (6) control of access to components.

LAYER-2: CONTROLLING SIMULTANEOUS ACCESS TO ARTIFACTS

The collaborative development of the components of software is possible in two ways: concurrent and non-concurrent collaboration. In concurrent collaboration, the operation is supported by concurrency control mechanism and resource locking through a side server existed in the second layer. Each component which should be modified in place is cached in the server's repository cache and its lock feature is activated. If another user decides to modify a cached component, the server will put his request in the queue and announce the situation to this user.

Non-Concurrent Collaboration

The non-concurrent collaboration of component development is possible through two mechanisms: (1) Event notification and (2) component versioning. In the first mechanism, when a user constructs a component and reserves it, asks the system to notify him, whenever another user tries to use that component. Therefore it is necessary that the system registers the first user's URL along with the feature of his favorite component. Generally in every system in which group collaboration is considered, when a certain event occurs in the system, some or all users should be notified to make proper response if required. Then the system should be able to support two characteristics: (1) when an event occurs, the client should be notified without any request from the client and (2) the users favorite events should be registered so that the users are informed of only these events. Considering the fact that the server of an open hypermedia system can send a message to the client, starting from the server, it is enough to generate an event registering server in the fourth layer.

In the second mechanism, i.e. versioning, the scattered members of groups need to collaborate on different components of a project like documents and programs in order to construct and complete them. This collaboration is carried out along with component versioning, so that for every change in document, a separate version is created by hierarchical numbering and a joint to the main document. When several people change one document, for every one, a versioning branch is generated in the versioning tree. If this change occurs in a pre-versioned document, that branch expands. This divergence advances to the final phase of component development and in ending phase of a component, the divergence and combination of branches occur, to have several authoring from several author. In this method, the main purpose is not only the creation of a new versioning but parallel collaboration, in order to generate numerous versioning for a component is also considered. Figure 11 shows versioning process of a component by two users A and B in two separate sites.

Concurrent Collaboration

In concurrent collaboration, because of long-term work on components and therefore their long-term locking, the construction process becomes slow and users wait for releasing components for a long time. In this situation, it is preferred to create a route from resources in two or several branches and then composed as one or some components in the final phase.

Component Versioning

In Sections "Non-Concurrent Collaboration" and "Concurrent Collaboration", content versioning was considered but as the components of a system can be in the form of content, link and a combination of link and content, the possibility of versioning links or combination of link and component should be reviewed, too. In link separation from contents, links are, as contents, first class entities and have production date, author's name, type and other characteristics. So, they should be separated

Figure 11. Distributed authoring and versioning artifact construction

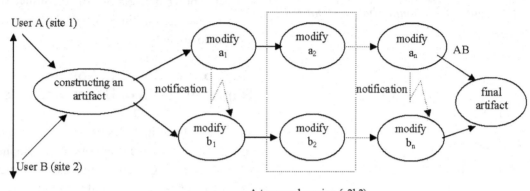

A temporal version (a2b2)

from versioning contents. For example, two users can generate, separately, independent anchors, in different time for one component.

Hypermedia systems, which support link separation from contents and present links as real entities, make component versioning simple. Link versioning is performed, regarding the meta-data in the previous section.

Figure 12 shows three types of versionings. Figure 12-1 shows the versioning components in the form of link and content combination, Figure 12-2 shows content versioning in those components in which content and link are separate, and Figure 12-3 shows link versioning in some components in which link and content are separate.

It should be noticed that in the fourth layer of the model which is established on the basis of an open hypermedia system, links and contents are versioned and reserved separately and there is no combination of links and contents. If: (1) a user requires both coincident content and link and embedded links in content, as HTML pages and (2) just links have been versioned as Figure 12-3, the system has to return all possible compositions (i.e. versions C, D). The third layer is responsible for composing link and content, but if a user wishes to version content along with embedded links, in a general frame as HTML pages, cannot use artifact management system support in the

same way. To provide this support, the development of combined components in repository and their support by artifact management system should be made possible.

LAYER-3: SUPPORTING CONNECTION BETWEEN USERS AND AMS

The server considered in the second layer, for caching components, should be capable of interacting with data repository in the fourth layer. Supporting management of components and repository development, in the fourth layer, has the data transfer protocol specific to itself, which is different from HTTP protocol. But, on the other hand, this server should interact with the web users located in the first layer. So this server should have protocol HTTP to transfer information. As the server cannot interact with the server of the fourth layer, for which there is a separate protocol, protocol exchange should be done between these two servers. To do this, the third layer, a middle and interface layer, is used to protocol exchange between a web server with HTTP protocol and another server with a certain protocol.

Figure 12. 1) Versioning link in combined link and content; 2) Versioning content in separate link and content; 3) Versioning link in separate link and content

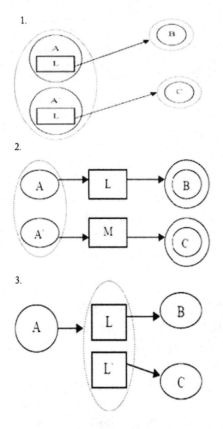

LAYER-4: ARTIFACT MANAGEMENT SYSTEM

The system component and user artifact management are in the fourth layer. This layer gets the users' artifacts by using an interface supposed in the third layer, and delivers them to the store management to maintain. The aims of this layer include:

- To store the components constructed by users in repository,
- To support users for non-concurrent collaboration in developing components,

- To support component versioning,
- To prevent creation of dangling references, i.e. the links which do not refer to a document.

Supporting Construction and Representation of Users' Artifacts

The fourth layer includes three tasks: (1) directing the users toward component development, (2) proper storing components and the structure between them and (3) separate or joint representing them according to the user's need. There are two solutions: (1) Using HTML pages to represent document, HTTP protocol to transfer data and by the web browsers and (2) Providing the environment in which web users are free to choose their applied environment and use their tools, i.e. they are not obliged to use a certain tool.

The first solution cannot be used because of the lack of support for group collaboration in component development. It seems that the solution is using extension of HTTP protocol, i.e. WebDAV protocol which provides group collaboration through added procedures and locating meta-data in documents. Though this protocol has removed two major obstacles on collaborative development of components, the HTML frame cannot be suitable for presenting different structures required in information systems, because in this frame links are embedded in documents and so it is suitable for presenting text structures.

In addition, (1) the WebDAV server is not able to interact with non WebDAV clients and also the servers not familiar with this protocol, i.e. the servers and clients that their environment does not support this protocol. (2) The WebDAV protocol is based on the HTTP protocol, so it is a stateless protocol, i.e. the server-client relation is interrupted after sending an HTML page or a file. Therefore, this protocol is not able to do some cases in which the server should be the initiator (e.g. when a server wants to inform the users). (3) Disconnected collaborations as E-Mail in Web-

DAV are not supported. (4) Dangling references are not prevented.

So, the second solution is selected by using an open hypermedia system. A hypermedia server cannot interact with other hypermedia servers and can be an initiator of message sending. Additionally, it prevents from dangling references. The main privilege of using hyper system is supporting varied media (contents) and users' environments. As a result, the users are not obliged to use a certain frame when they are using an environment. But, despite the existence of an open hypermedia system, there are some deficiencies which need additional preparation and will discuss later.

Event Handler

To generate links such as relation from an executable program to its source program, event occurrence can be considered as a part of an executable component. For example, the user's program compiler is one of the components of persistent environment. An event can be defined for invoking it, so that when this compiler invoked by a user, the defined event happens. Figure 13 shows an event handler located in the fourth layer. If there isn't such a handler, the programmer should directly request this relation between executable program and source program while developing the execut-

able program. If this request is forgotten, there is no relation between different forms of a program.

As Figure 13 shows, having received a request, the event processor sends it to the builder according to the request type, in order to define and create event. If the event has been defined, the request will be sent to the requester of event. The result of operation returns to the event processor to be sent to the event handler.

Another server, located in the fourth layer, is *indent server* (Figure 14) having two tasks: (1) event registration and (2) user notification. To register an event, each user can send its favorite address and component to the indent server, so that the server requests the event registration from the builder. A user's request to modify a component is sent to the ident server and the server delivers the request to the notifier to notify its author in the case he/she has already expressed his interest to the component modification. The user is notified by creating an E-mail and sending it to the client's URL.

Versioning Control Server

As expressed in Section "Component Versioning", one is able to deal with versioning the components. This feature is guided by *versioning control server* (Figure 15). When a user wants to

Figure 13. Proposed event handler

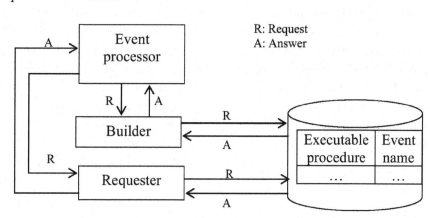

Figure 14. Proposed Ident server

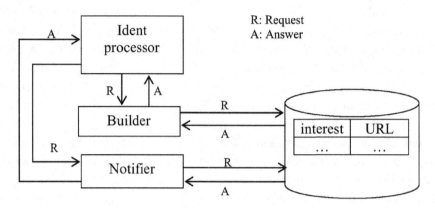

Tasks:
create, remove and modify URL and users' interests
create E-Mail for an interest and send the mail

Figure 15. Proposed version control server

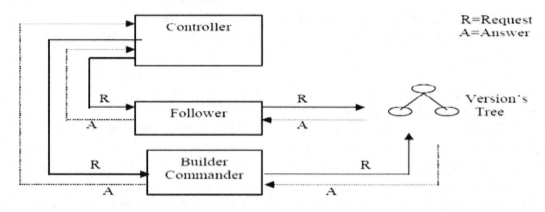

develop or modify a component, his/her request is delivered to the versioning control server so that a version of the new/modified component is located in a proper place on the tree. Consider Figure 13; when the follower receives the user's request from the controller, follows the version tree to find a proper place for the new version of the component. Then, it returns address and specifications of the component to the controller. Consequently, the controller gives the address and specifications to the *builder commander*.

Link and Content Management

In Section "LAYER-4, ARTIFACT MANAGE-MENT SYSTEM", link separation from content and inadequacy of such frames as HTML (which present links as embedded in the contents) to represent some structures as hierarchical structures, were explained. As open hypermedia systems are sufficiently potent and suitable to separate relations from contents and their management, they can properly represent hierarchical form of relations, in applied systems (such as project management system, workflow) between people, tasks and products. In addition, they are good

Figure 16. Proposed Doc server

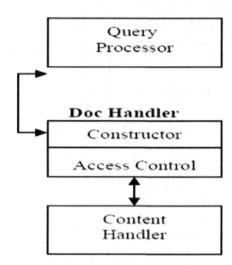

environments to support various media including text, audio and video and they allow using their related tools for interacting with hypermedia management.

In the workflow systems and also some environments as a virtual enterprise, the relations between some individuals and products should be removed or added, by group collaboration, without any need to access themselves and conversely, a product or a task should be changed, removed or added from place to place, without requiring access to their relations. Some individuals should be able to assign only the tasks or present some products, and other people should establish or change the relation between those tasks or products.

Based on the above-mentioned reasons, the independent and separate management of relations from needs can contribute to construct the system abstract model. In the sense that the relations between individuals, tasks and products, should be established or specified before their creation and conversely, the tasks should be assigned firstly and then the relations between them should be created. The relations in hypermedia systems, unlike those in Web, don't have the problem of lacking destination, i.e. if a task, an individual or product should be removed from a project, all of the

relations between this component and other tasks, individuals and products should also be removed in order not to have an invalid relation. For this purpose *Doc Server* (Figure 16) and *Link Server* (Figure 17) are considered in the fourth layer.

In the link handler, the query processor receives the users' request and then sends it to other two processes in the server. The operation link handler implements construction, tracing, traverse and the control of access to the links. The Base handler handles construction, traverse and the control of access to the bases. A Base is a set of related links located in one group. Bases as links may have exclusive, common or general features according to which, access to them is controlled. Bases are useful to categorize subjects, as the links for an authoring or from an author or some links created in a certain date. Other applications of bases are supporting the development of several software systems which should be in an environment, simultaneously.

Doc server (content) as link server includes a query processor to receive requests and send them to their related procedures. Doc handler, constructs and controls access to documents and content handler has the responsibility of managing the content of a component like modifying and changing it.

Coordinator

In the fourth layer, servers are supervised by a *coordinator*. It should be specified that the requests received by the layer are firstly received and processed by servers existed in this layer. In addition, the interaction and collaboration between servers of this layer is required to construct and modify components. The coordinator located in the fourth layer entrance, receives the user's request and sends it to the considered server. Also, when a user's notification is required for non-concurrent collaboration, a message should be produced as E-mail, by *indent server* and then sent to the users. The task of coordinator is to receive E-mail and

Figure 17. Proposed Link server

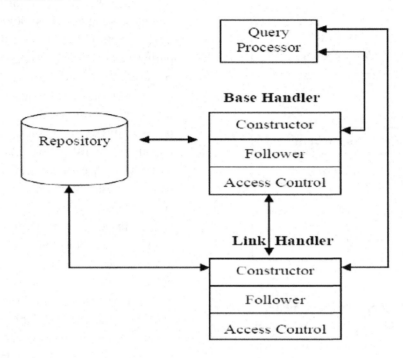

Figure 18. Proposed structure for connection between coordinator and servers in layer 4

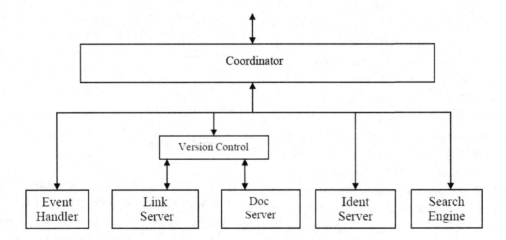

send it to the respective user. Figure 18 shows the relation between coordinator and the respective servers. Figure 19 shows the recommended four-layer model based on the four layer model in Table 1. The interaction between the layers is briefly shown in Figure 20.

IMPLEMENTATION

To implement the four layer model, the existing tools are used in each layer but regarding the interaction between each layer and the next one, some suitable tool to be selected; accordingly, both the certain task is considered for the tool and

Figure 19. Proposed 4-layer model of web-based collaboration of software development in social network

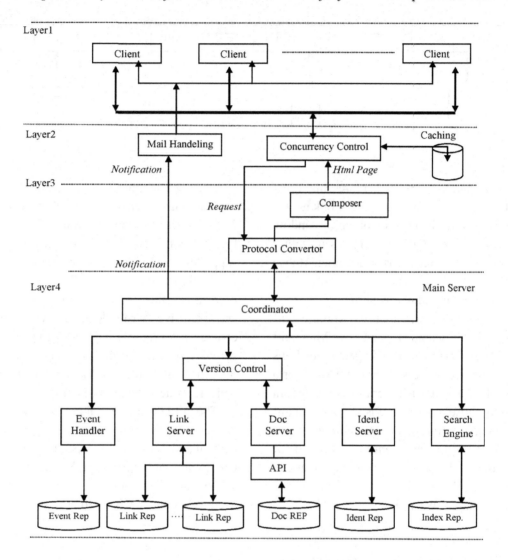

the interaction between layers shall be possible. The tool considered for performing the tasks of layers 1, 2, 3 should be able to have relation with the main server located in layer 4. As the most important task of the main server is to manage and maintain the links and contents components, separate them from each other and support n-ary and multidirectional links, the open hypermedia system is a proper option for the main server. In this case, it is necessary that the components saved in the hypermedia repository consist of meta-data of XML type. Using these meta-data, the possibil-

ity of programming on link, detailed search for components and the use of locking mechanisms for Web network users are provided.

The selection of a server, of an open hypermedia system type, has two other features: support for various media and intractability with the third party applications. WebVise (Gronbak et al, 1999) is a server of open hypermedia system type, which can work with Microsoft word editor and Internet Explorer browser in the user's environment. This server interacts with two windows on the user's screen, which one of them is browser or editor and

Figure 20. Interaction between layers in the 4-layer model in Figure 19

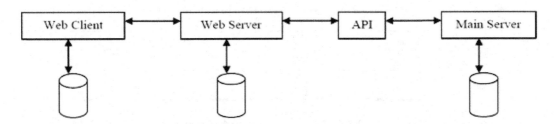

the other one shows hierarchical representation of links. The user can browse both each link generated by himself in the browser or editor window and in the hierarchical structure of links in another window. Also he/she can browse documents those links refer to, by traversing links. Figure 21 shows the client's screen with the windows.

In the first layer, there are users who use general tools of edition and browsing like Microsoft Word. These tools are suitable for generating links and contents. Languages such as VTML (Forta & Weiss, 1999), which is a Markup language, can be used by those users who wish to perform authoring operation through programming. In Microsoft Word, non-concurrent collaboration for constructing and versioning the component can be used by applying sub-folders as "online collaboration" and "Web discussion". Also, this

software can support user notification when it is applied with Microsoft SharePoint (Sampson, 2008 & Mcleod, Childs, Lappin & Siggers, 2010). In the second layer, which requires a server to support the components concurrently, a WebDAV Protocol-aware server like DAV Server can be used. Since this protocol applies shared (read) and exclusive (write) locking mechanisms for concurrency control, one is able to use common software such as word processors (Shen, Xia & Sun, 2007 & Imine, 2008) to collaborative and concurrent development of components.

The third layer undertakes two tasks: (1) converting protocol and (2) making a composite of content and link which are usually performed by using applet and CGI-Script. An open hypermedia server named as Webvise for example, can be used. When a user wishes to browse a destination

Figure 21. Two sample windows of client screen

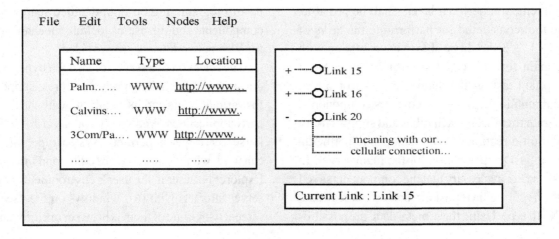

along with its links, he will specify that document by determining its URL in his browser's applet. By inquiring of Webvise, the applet requests the documents and its anchors and then inserts the links in the documents. By choosing each anchor in the constructed combination, the applet is activated again and the previous procedure goes on. Figure 22 shows the relation of the applet and CGI Script with Webvise server and user's browser. In this figure, the applet connects with Web Server on one hand and connects with the main server (Webvise) by CGI, on the other hand.

RELATED WORK AND CONCLUSIONS

A growing trend towards software development is a team work method because increasing developers in the project development brings development life cycle down; however complexities of the team work collaboration make it difficult to manage. Accordingly, methods were proposed to tackle team work collaboration.

A significant method exploited to team work development is pair programming by which programs are constructed by a pair of programmers. The method both increases the rate of program construction and improves its quality (Cockburn & Williams, 2001). In this programming method,

two programmers (1) exchange their ideas to manage complexities of the development, (2) construct same algorithms and programs in collaboration with each other in real-time and (3) check each other's work to take away faults. To pair programming in a network environment, virtual and distributed pair programming was appeared in which programmers may collaborate with each other while they are not in same place (Duque & Bravo, 2008, Winkler, Biffl & Kaltenbach, 2010 & Favela et al, 2004).

Global Software Development (GSD) (Sangwan, Bass, Mullick, Daniel & Juergen, 2006) and Distributed Software Configuration Management (DSCM) (Pond & Roeser, 2004) are other significant methods for teamwork software development. The former is defined as collaborative software development among people scattered at geographical locations real time. It provides: (1) communication among the people for exchanging information, (2) collaboration among teams for involving their activities and artifacts and (3) control of teams to satisfy goals and policies and quality, visibility and management of their artifacts. The latter enables software developers to control the evolution of complex software and provides mechanisms to track the evolution.

However, collaborative software development should provide collaboration for software design and software implementation. While de-

Figure 22. Applet and CGI Script connection with the Webvise server and user's browser

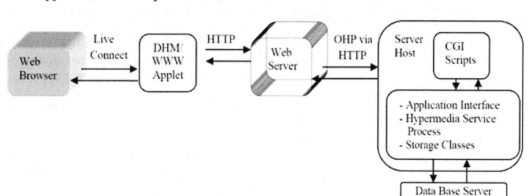

sign is connected with specification of software components, implementation deals with coding, debugging, testing, and documenting the designed components. Having designed and implemented software components, developers should be able to consolidate the components. Therefore, different phases of software development from design to implementation of components and their incorporation is needed. Accordingly, distributed and virtual pair programming and SCM can not fully provide life cycle of software development collaboratively. In other words, each one of methods, pair programming and SCM deals with a phase of software development.

The method proposed in this chapter, aimed to cover life cycle of software development in the collaborative way. Exploiting data models in open hypermedia system perfects software design by allowing media diversity on the one hand and facilitates intractability with browsers to implement software on the other hand. Similar to the work presented in this chapter, Shen and Sun made an effort to put forward a method covering software development collaboratively in all of life cycle phases (Cgan, Cao & Chan, 2005). Also, Cgan, Cao & Chan (2005) used a graph-oriented programming language to design and implement programs collaboratively. Tools used to collaborative development of software have been characterized and classified by Soriano, Fernandez & Jimenez (2009). Service-oriented based method used by Cgan et al (2005) is a customary method in the Web environment for collaboration among service providers and consumers (Arabfard & Babamir, 2011).

REFERENCES

Albrecht, J., College, W., Braud, R., Dao, D., Topilski, N., Tuttle, C., & Snoeren, A. C. (2007). Remote control: Distributed application configuration management, and visualization with Plush, In *Proceedings of the 21ˢᵗ Large Installation System Administration* (pp. 183-201).

Anderson, K., Taylor, R., & Whitehead, E. (1999). Chimera: Hypertext for heterogeneous software development environments. *ACM Transactions on Information Systems*, *18*(3), 211–245. doi:10.1145/352595.352596

Apache Group. (n.d.). Retrieved from http://hadoop.apache.org /zookeeper/

Arabfard, M., & Babamir, S. M. (2011). Resolving impassiveness in service oriented architecture. *Innovative Computing Technology Communications in Computer and Information Science, Lecture Notes in Computer Science*, 241, Part 2, (pp. 48-60). Springer.

Chan, A. T. S., Cao, J., & Chan, C. K. (2005). WEBGOP: Collaborative web services based on graph-oriented programming. *IEEE Transactions on Systems, Man, and Cybernetics. Part A, Systems and Humans*, *35*(6), 811–830. doi:10.1109/TSMCA.2005.851342

Cockburn, A., & Williams, L. (2001). *The costs and benefits of pair programming, Extreme programming examined*. USA: Addison-Wesley.

Davis, H. C., Millard, D. E., & Reich, S. (1998). *OHP-communicating between hypermedia aware applications*. In Towards a New Generation of HTTP, A Workshop on Global Hypermedia Infrastructure, Australia.

Duque, R., & Bravo, C. (2008). Supporting distributed pair programming with the COLLECE Groupware System: An empirical study. In *Proceedings of XP*, (pp. 232-233).

Favela, J., et al. (2004). Empirical evaluation of collaborative support for distributed pair programming. In *Proceedings of CRIWG*, (pp. 215-222).

Forta, B., & Weiss, N. (1999). *Advanced coldFusion 4.0 application development*. QUE.

Gronbæk, K., Hem, J., Madsen, O., & Sloth, L. (1993) Designing dexter-based cooperative hypermedia systems. In *Proceedings of the ACM Conference on Hypertext*, (pp. 25-38). USA.

Grønbak, K., Sloth, L., & Orbak, P. (1999). Webvise: Browser and proxy support for open hypermedia structuring mechanisms on the WWW. In *Proceedings of the 8th International World Wide Web Conference, Elsevier*, (pp. 1331-1345).

Gronbak, K., & Will, U. (1998). Towards a common reference architecture for open hypermedia. *Journal of Digital Information, 1*(2).

Hall, W., Davis, H., & Hutchings, G. (1996). *Rethinking hypermedia: The microcosm approach*. USA: Springer.

IBM. (1978). *Report on the contents of a sample of programs surveyed*. California: IBM.

Imine, A. (2008). Flexible concurrency control for real-time collaborative editors. In *Proceedings of 28th International Conference on Distributed Computing Systems, IEEE Computer*, (pp. 423-428).

Marshall, C., Halaz, F., Rogres, R., & Janssen, W. (1991). Aquanet: A hypertext tool to hold your knowledge in place. In *Proceedings of the 3rd ACM Conference on Hypertext*, (pp. 261-275). USA.

Marshall, C., Shipman, F., & Coombs, J. (1994). VIKI: spatial hypertext supporting emergent structure. In *Proceedings of the 6th ACM Conference on Hypertext*, (pp. 13-23). Scotland.

McLeod, J., Childs, S., Lappin, J., & Siggers, G. (2010). Investigation into the use of Microsoft SharePoint in UK higher education institutions. *Communications in Computer and Information Science, 110*(5), 335–344. doi:10.1007/978-3-642-16419-4_34

Microsoft. (n.d.). Retrieved from http://msdn.microsoft.com/en-us/library/aa923224.aspx

Mitrix, S. R., Davis, J., & Babich, J. (2008). *Web distributed authoring and versioning. RFC 5323*. IETF.

Morrison, R. (2000). Persistent languages: Introduction and overview. In M. P. Atkinson & R. Welland (Eds.), *Fully integrated data environments: Persistent programming languages, object stores, and programming environments*, (pp. 5-8). Springer. *Mozilla Project*. (n.d.). Retrieved from www.Mozila.org

Morrison, R., & Atkinson, M. P. (1990). Persistent languages and architecture. In Rosenberg, J., & Keedy, J. L. (Eds.), *Proceedings of Security and Persistence* (pp. 9–28). Springer. doi:10.1007/978-1-4471-3178-6_2

OrbiTeam Software GmbH. (2005). *Basic support for cooperative work*, Version 4.3 Manual, Retrieved May 2011, from www.orbiteam.de

Pond, J. (2004). *Distributed configuration management reference guide*. Oracle Publication.

Sampson, M. (2008). *Seamless teamwork: Using Microsoft SharePoint technologies to collaborate, innovate, and drive business in new ways (BP-Other)*. Microsoft Press.

Sanchez, W., & Daboo, C. (2008). *WebDAV current principal extension. RFC 5397*. IETF.

Sangwan, R. (2006). *Global software development handbook*. Boston, MA: Auerbach Publications.

Shen, H., & Sun, C. (2000). RECIPE: A prototype for Internet-based real-time collaborative programming. In *Proceedings of the Second International Workshop on Collaborative Editing Systems*, USA.

Shen, H., Xia, S., & Sun, C. (2007). Integrating advanced collaborative capabilities into web-based word processors. *Lecture Notes in Computer Science, 4674*, 1–8. doi:10.1007/978-3-540-74780-2_1

Smith, J., & Smith, F. (1991). ABC: A hypermedia system for artifact-based collaboration. In *Proceedings of the 3rd ACM Conference on Hypertext*, (pp. 179-192).

Soriano, J., Fernandez, R., & Jimenez, M. (2009). Characterization and classification of collaborative tools. In St.Amant, K. (Ed.), *IT outsourcing: Concepts, methodologies, tools, and applications* (pp. 1399–1408). Hershey, PA: IGI Global Publication. doi:10.4018/978-1-60566-770-6.ch087

Vesperman, J. (2006). *Essential CVS*. O'Reilly Media.

Winkler, D., Biffl, S., & Kaltenbach, A. (2010). Evaluating tools that support pair programming in a distributed engineering environment. In *Proceedings of 14th International Conference on Evaluation and Assessment in Software Engineering (EASE)*.

Chapter 14
Knowledge Based Business Intelligence for Business User Information Self–Service

Matthias Mertens
OFFIS – Institute for Information Technology, Germany

Tobias Krahn
OFFIS – Institute for Information Technology, Germany

ABSTRACT

Due to a higher need for healthcare provision, and due to the decreasing number of contributors in the German healthcare system, the market situation has changed over the last years. The resulting competitive and cost pressure forces the executives to tap potentials in a competitive manner. Analytical Information Systems as part of business intelligence can be used to receive information from several integrated data sources that may be used in the decision making process. However, the system's complexity of use can be seen as problematic so that unskilled business users, unlike power users, are not able to execute analyses for their issues in an adequate way. The focus of the presented approach lies on a semantic metadata layer, which is capable to import and manage modeled semantic metadata. Based on this layer, the metadata is supposed to be used for further analyses support functionalities in order to allow a business user information self-service.

1. INTRODUCTION

Against the background of population's increasing awareness of health issues and the demographic change, it can be observed that there is a growing need for healthcare provision in Germany. Soar-

ing costs must be shouldered by ever-decreasing contributors which has financial effects on the German healthcare market. The German hospital market, in particular, is affected (Thoben, 2010). Hospitals are confronted with new financial challenges which derive from the introduction of the German DRG-based (Diagnosis Related Groups) compensation system in 2003, which means that

DOI: 10.4018/978-1-4666-0894-8.ch014

hospitals have to billing their hospitalizations case-related. The increased cost and competitive pressure causes the hospitals to position themselves as commercial enterprises to the market and set themselves apart from their competitors successfully. For ensuring the competitiveness potentials have to be developed target-orientedly.

Therefore, strategic hospital controllers, so called business users, need information on which decisions for the market strategy can be carried out. Here, the actual market and competitive situation - catchment area, market share, market potential, competitors (see Figure 1) - and how this situation will evolve against the backdrop of the demographic change are of particular interest. Accordingly, hospitals have to integrate the datasets of their own hospital information system with other datasets from the National and Federal Office of Statistics (mortality and diagnosis statistics), socio-demographic data (demographic statistics), referring physician data and competition data from the structured quality reports of the hospitals. Based on this integrated dataset, relevant analyses can be carried out. With the aid of geographic and statistical methods, business users can get a comprehensive overview of the actual and long term market situation. Information about changes in the group of patients, the behavior of the referring physician, supply gaps or hidden reserves can be detected (Stibbe, 2011). This information can be used as a basis for strategic decisions such as expanding the performance spectrum of the hospital.

To improve the decision making process and to empower business user concepts and technologies of the area of business intelligence described in the next section 2 can be used. Especially Analytical Information Systems as part of business intelligence allow users to analyze huge integrated datasets in a quality assured and multidimensional manner. However, these systems suffer from several shortcomings that will be explained in section 3. The scientific question and related requirements to an approach are discussed in section 4. Due to the use of ontologies in our approach a general understanding of ontologies and related concepts is discussed in section 5. Our approach to the problem, including the envisioned architecture, concepts and analyses supporting features as well as an example will be presented in section 6. Section 7 shows the corresponding projects to this research and makes statements to the planned evaluation. Section 8 discusses related work in this research area and section 9 summarizes all chapters and points out further work.

2. THE ROLE OF BUSINESS INTELLIGENCE FOR INFORMATION SUPPLY

A key objective of Business Intelligence (BI) is to improve the decision making process and to empower business user, to get all the required information at the right time. The understanding of the concept Business Intelligence may vary from information systems based on multidimensional data structures to system topographies for analysis and information supplying purposes. In Gluchowski, 2006 Business Intelligence is defined as integrated information technology (IT) overall concept that offers viable and interlinked solutions for different requirements of BI-Systems with decision support.

First IT-based Management Support Systems were developed in the 1960 and 1970 years. So called Decision Support Systems (DSS) and Management Information Systems (MIS) allow reporting and decision support in specific application areas. In the 1980 years the term of Management Support Systems (MSS) was introduced, that is used till this date. Through the use of internet technologies in the last fifteen years and the increasing functionality and dynamic as well as the complexity the new term Business Intelligence for MSS has established itself (Gluchowski, 2006).

Figure 1. Market share, market potential, competitors in the catchment area of a hospital

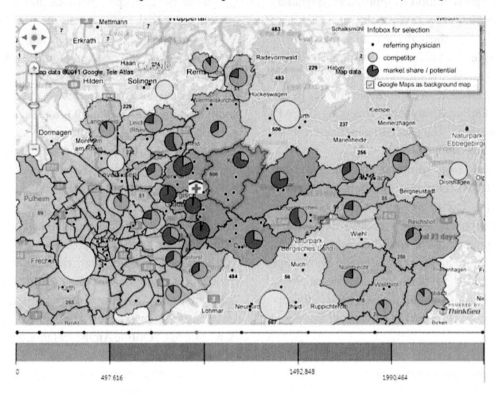

The term was first introduced by the Gartner Group in 1996.

In Gluchowski, 2006 Business Intelligence is composed of all system components that allow collecting and preparing information relevant to the decision making process. Save them in a persistent and application-oriented way and allow these system components to analyse and visualize them in an adequate usage oriented manner. These components interact with each other and can be divided into data provision and data usage.

Typically, the data provision is realized in the BI through a Data Warehouse (DWH). This is defined by Inmon, 1996 as "… a subject oriented, nonvolatile, integrated, time variant collection of data in support of management's decisions". This means that data and information about subjects is integrated from various external information sources or from operational previous systems in a quality-assured manner through an extraction, transformation and load (ETL) process. Nonvola-

tile means that integrated information are never changed again. Therefore, these data can be analyzed over time and management decisions can be thereon based. A DWH has a multidimensional data model (MDM), which structure is broken into Hypercubes that are able to store measures in various dimensions. Each dimension consists of a hierarchy that builds the aggregation layers and different dimension elements on each layer.

The data usage layer consists of tools that are able to prepare and analyse the available integrated data so that these can be provided to the users in a suitable and useful way. In Gluchowski, 2006 these tools are classified as follows:

Generic Basic Systems:

- **Reporting Systems:** These systems allow generating reports for users with the needed information in a periodic way or if a special event appears. As part of this application class and in contrast to the rigid presentation of reports, Management Information Systems enable users a guided navigation through the data space.

- **Ad-Hoc Analyses Systems:** These Systems allow the users to navigate in the data space in an explorative manner by using Online Analytical Processing (OLAP) operations. The user can generate views on the data independently.

- **Model and method based Analyses Systems:** Decision Support Systems as well as Expert Systems are part of this application class. They make extensive use of mathematical and business methods. Therefore analysis and domain knowledge is needed to perform adequate analysis. Data Mining techniques are used in this application class to find patterns in the stored data.

Concept oriented Systems:

- In this application class the containing tools make use of the functions provided by the Generic Basic Systems. In contrast, concept oriented tools implement a business concept or have a specific business focus. Examples are Balanced Scorecard Systems, Risk Management Systems or Customer Relationship Management System.

Presentation and Access Systems:

- In this application class the focus lies on giving the user an adequate access to all the needed information and functionalities from his workstation. This can take place through BI-Portals or Management-Cockpits that integrate the information and functions of the Concept oriented Systems in a consolidated way suitable to the management.

In the BI, concepts, methods and tools were developed with the goal to foster communication, collaboration as well as document and knowledge management on the one side. On the other side, Generic Basic Systems as part of BI came up to enable business users to visualize, use and analyze large amounts of integrated data sets. In Germany Analytical Information Systems (AIS) evolved as synonym for business intelligence and especially for the class of Generic Basic Systems. While the underlying DWH integrates various information sources in a quality-assured and multidimensional manner the analyze-components allow online analytical processing operations (OLAP) and complex statistical or geographic procedures in varying visualizations. In Chamoni, 2006 the term Analytical Information System is defined as logical bracket of the buzzwords "Data Warehouse", "Online Analytical Processing" and "Data Mining".

It can be observed that in the last year's enterprises migrate to a lean management. Decision-making powers are delegated downwards in the organizations hierarchies. Therefore, a sophisticated information logistic is needed to supply the users with information they need (Chamoni, 2006). Analytical Information Systems can be used for this purpose but they suffer from several shortcomings that will be explained in the next section.

3. SHORTCOMINGS OF ANALYTICAL INFORMATION SYSTEMS

AIS allow the analysis of huge integrated datasets to gain answers on questions in different domains. In the Multidimensional Statistical Data Analysis Engine (MUSTANG) (Mertens, 2009), developed at OFFIS – Institute for Information Technology, it is observed that AIS suffer from the following shortcomings:

- Due to their flexibility and powerfulness, AIS are still too complex for business users. They face significant challenges performing adequate ad-hoc analyses, in a self-service manner, for getting answers to their issues. In contrast to power users, business users usually do not have a comprehensive technical understanding of the underlying multidimensional model nor do they have the sufficient analyses and domain knowledge in order to estimate which measures have to be analyzed in which analysis steps for their questions. Also, the usage of the suitable next OLAP operations and visualizations requires corresponding analyses and domain knowledge. Finally, a high interaction with the business user is needed for an adequate analysis which means a huge challenge to users if they are not properly skilled (Mertens, 2011). Especially, small- and medium-sized enterprises which depend on such analyses suffer from this disadvantage because of costs and training periods for their business users.

- Another shortcoming of Analytical Information Systems is the lack of additional supporting metadata associated with the integrated quantitative DWH-data and the DWH structure (measures and dimension elements), like assumptions, definitions, business rules, terminology or background information (ONeil, 2007). Therefore, business users have to exploit the semantics of the data and the structure on their own and they must sustain themselves with additional, external data (Berthold, 2010). Also the usage of external structured linked data for analyses support is not contemplated in AIS at the moment (Bizer, 2008).

- Another problem is that the system is not able to import, process and use explicit analyzes as well as domain knowledge and then make them available for business users analyses support (Mertens, 2011). The main focus lies on expertise like strategies or best practices of getting adequate answers to certain issues regarding special domain analyzes.

In the Meaning of Self-Service Business Intelligence (SSBI) (Imhoff & White, 2011), business users should be empowered to analyze multidimensional quantitative data structures without having all the necessary, above mentioned, knowledge and without being technically skilled. This can be achieved by reducing the perceived system's usage complexity. The system shall be able to support business users in their ad-hoc analysis by using modeled semantic machine readable and reasonable knowledge. This should be provided by a semantic metadata layer. The functions of an advanced assistance for a business user information self-service (Spahn, 2008 and Berthold, 2010) may vary from advanced information for selected data warehouse entities over a navigation support up to a recommendation system.

Therefore, we propose an architecture and thereon based functionalities for an advanced AIS in this chapter. It is intended to use a semantic technology stack as well as modeled domain and analyses knowledge for an ad-hoc analysis support. Thus, it is supposed to enable unskilled business users to provide themselves with necessary information in an efficient and intuitive manner.

4. SCIENTIFIC QUESTION AND REQUIREMENTS

Motivated by the shortcomings, the following scientific question can be derived:

"How can the usage complexity of Analytical Information Systems, with stable amount of flexibility and powerfulness, be reduced in order to empower unskilled business users to perform adequate ad-hoc analysis on their own and provide themselves with all the required information they need in an efficient and intuitive manner."

To encounter this question our envisioned approach to a solution is to provide supporting features for the business user. Especially, these features should be a recommendation, navigation and search service which exploits explicit modeled semantic machine readable and reasonable domain and analyses knowledge. This knowledge will be imported and managed in a semantic metadata layer of the Analytical Information System architecture composed of an extendable semantic metadata model and various concerning services. Based on the depicted observations of section 3, the following functional and non-functional requirements on the approach will be derived:

- **Domain Independent AIS:** The approach is supposed enable domain-independent AIS to support business users in the context of domain specific analytical tasks. Therefore, a generic concept and data model in conjunction with a domain independent Analytical Information System is needed which can be instanced and used for a specific domain.
- **Reduction of Complexity:** A key requirement on the approach is the reduction of the perceived systems usage complexity in conjunction with unchanged flexibility and powerfulness. The system should be more intuitive so that business users with less expertise are also empowered to perform adequate explorative ad-hoc analysis on a DWH in order to find answers to their questions. On the one hand, the approach is supposed to allow the system to compensate users' missing implicit analyses and domain knowledge. On the other hand, the approach is supposed to minimize the number of user-system interactions by reaching the same analyses results. This would also address the effectiveness of the system.

- **Analyses Supporting Function:** For achieving the objectives, reduction of systems complexity and the information self-service of business users, the system should have the following analyses supporting functionalities, based on a modeled, semantic machine - readable and - understandable knowledge. A semantic search should enable the user to find specific metadata to analyses like issues, analyses processes or results based on their semantics. The system is supposed to recommend useful and possible analysis steps in the context of an analysis process. The system should also empower the user to navigate among described semantic relationships in the metadata with a navigation component.
- **Several Kinds of Metadata:** Therefore, the approach is supposed to enable the Analytical Information System to import and handle three different kinds of metadata as well as combine and use these in an intelligent manner for analyses support functionalities. First of all the system should deal with metadata that describes additional information to the DWH structure and especially to the entities of a specific dimension (Network Inference, 2004; Ludwig, 2005; Sell, 2005; Berthold, 2010). This could be another more familiar terminology as well as background information, relationships and business rules. Further metadata describing the analysis process from a conjecture over the analysis steps to the analyses results, should be taken into consideration. This metadata is also known as strategies or best practices describing the expertise, respectively the domain and analyses knowledge of an analyst. Finally, the third kind of metadata describes the quantitative DWH-data and allows describing Analyses Results in terms of an-

notations. This could be recognized trends, correlations or specific relationships.

- **Flexible Metadata Model:** For the use of the described kinds of metadata, there is a need for an appropriate flexible metadata model that provides the entities, their relationships to each other and a domain specific instantiation of the modeled entities. For the description of real world entities and their semantic relations a powerful knowledge representation language on a logical basis is needed, especially to provide transitivity, symmetry, cardinality and uniqueness. Furthermore, the model should be expandable as well as machine readable and reasonable. The instantiated entities will represent concrete analyses and domain knowledge.

- **Support of the Learning Process:** The learning of domain and analyses knowledge is a time and cost consuming process. Therefore, the approach is supposed to support the learning process of knowledge and reduce the initial training and practice effort. Business users should learn from the inherent expertise of the Analytical Information System by using the advanced analyses functions.

- **Domain Specific Instances:** Before using analyses and domain knowledge for specific providing functions in AIS, this knowledge has to be derived, modeled and imported to the AIS. In the domain hospital market, for example, analyses and domain knowledge must be gained from expert interviews and from the literature. Furthermore, original available datasets, integrated datasets and the instantiated multidimensional model must be taken into consideration. For this, it is concluded which issues in Analyses Chains can be analyzed with the available measures of AIS in order to obtain relevant analyses results.

Motivated by the shortcomings of section 2 and the explained requirements for an approach, the next section will present the understanding of ontologies in this research project before a architecture and containing concepts for an semantic metadata layer of an Analytical Information System is explained. Thereon based functions will be discussed.

5. THE UNDERSTANDING OF ONTOLOGIES

In this section, the understanding of ontologies and related semantic web technologies will be presented.

The term ontology originally came from field of philosophy and describes the philosophical study of the nature of being, existence or reality. Entities of the real world and their relationships to each other as well as their attributes are described (Studer, 2007). In information science the concept "ontology" is understood as formal conceptual model that describes the semantics of specific entities of the real world by using knowledge representation languages. These formal structures can be processed and interpreted by machines and represent domain knowledge that can be produced and consumed by multiple interlinked applications.

Gruber, 1993 gave the following definition of the ontology (Studer, 2007): "An ontology is a formal explicit specification of a shared conceptualization":

- **Formal:** The aspect formal means, that the ontology is modeled by using a knowledge representation language such as Resource Description Framework (RDF) or Web Ontology Language (OWL). These are based on logical and formal structures that can be processed and understood by machines.

- **Explicit:** The domain knowledge contained by the ontology must by modeled in an explicit manner to be accessible by the machine. Context knowledge that is natural for humans but not modeled in the ontology can not be recognized by the machine and therefore must be represented in an explicit way.

- **Conceptualization:** The contained domain knowledge is modeled in the form of concepts and their relations to each other. These can be mapped by humans to their mental world view while for machines these concepts are only symbols that need explicit semantics.

- **Shared:** The conceptualization contained in the ontology represents a general understanding formed by a community.

- **Domain specific:** This characteristic additional introduced in Studer, 2007 describes that ontologies represent a specific part of the real world. It has to be taken into consideration that a more limited part of the real world can be modeled in more detail because less relevant areas have to be covered.

Ontologies combine and expand the characteristics of knowledge models like dictionaries, taxonomies, thesauri, and topic maps. It is possible to build classes that can be arranged in taxonomic hierarchical structures as well as graph based structures by using object relations between these classes. Classes may contain several attributes with specific data types and instances can be produced by instantiation of these classes. For the semantic and machine understandable description of ontologies various knowledge representation languages can be used. These can be distinguished by the expressive power and computability. Other aspects are the reusability of basic languages like xml for serialization purposes or the usage of Uniform Resource Identifier (URI) for a global identification possibility. As result of many differ-

ent requirements of various communities several languages had been standardized. According to Studer, 2007 two different classes can be distinguished. On the one side the languages based on the first order predicate logic and the decidable subclass of description logic and on the other side languages of the logic programming. Languages of the first class are DLP, WSML-Core, WSML-DL, SWRL, OWL-lite and OWL-DL. Languages of the second class are Datalog, WSML-Flight, WSML-Rule and F-Logic (LP). The languages RDF(S), OWL-Full and WSML-Full are not assignable to one of these classes. Within the scope of this research especially languages of the semantic web will be considered. These are the RDF(S) and OWL language families standardized by the World Wide Web Consortium (W3C). Additional SPARQL as query language for RDF will be used.

6. ARCHITECTURE AND CONCEPTS

In this section, we will present an architectural sketch which shows the structure of an Analytical Information System extended by a semantic metadata layer. An overview of the included layers and services will be given in subsection 6.1. The following subsection 6.2 will take a closer look at the concepts of the semantic metadata layer. In subsection 6.3 thereon based analyses supported functionalities of the Analytical Information System are presented and in subsection 6.4 an example for the intelligent selection of Dimension Classifications will be shown.

6.1 Architectural Sketch of a Knowledge Based Analytical Information System

In Figure 2, the different layers of an AIS are presented. The "standard" layers are surrounded by black lines while new layers for a semantic metadata layer are surrounded with blue lines referring to the architecture of the Multidimensional

Figure 2. Architectural sketch of an AIS extended with a semantic metadata layer

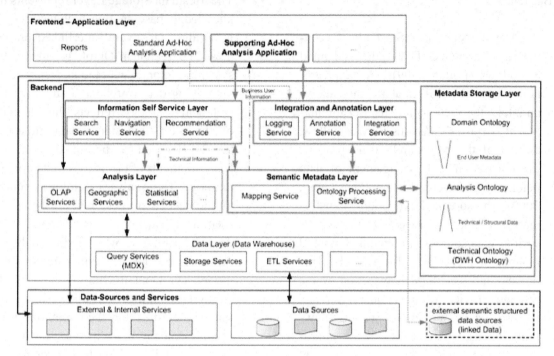

Statistical Data Analysis Engine (MUSTANG) AIS developed by OFFIS (Teiken, 2010). The development of the blue surrounded layers will be reached by establishing a semantic metadata layer that enables the system to import, manage and use analyses and domain knowledge. The presented architecture is designed in a way that the abstraction degree increases from bottom to top.

Data-Sources and Services:

- At the lowest level the data sources can be found which are located outside the system and are integrated in a quality assured manner in the data-warehouse. As described in section 1, data sources of the hospital market domain are German §21 KHEntgG. published by the individual hospitals (as output of their own hospital information systems) as well as the INEK GmbH. Other datasets from the National and Federal

Office of Statistics (mortality and diagnoses statistics), Socio-demographic data (demographic statistics), referring physician data and competition data from the structured quality reports of the hospitals are also integrated in the data-warehouse. Data sources can exist as database-files or as flat-files (xml, csv, xls,…).

- Next to the data sources, external services can be found at the lowest level such as web-services like google maps, local services like geo-servers or statistical software which is used by the AIS for spatial statistical analyses.

- External structured and semantic linked data, for example data from the linked data cloud (Bizer, 2010), can be used as additional external data source. It can be noted that this kind of data in the context of AIS is not considered so far.

Backend:

- The Data Layer of an AIS is build of a central data-warehouse (DWH) that is defined as follows (Bauer, 2009): "A data-warehouse is a physical database that allows an integrated view on any dataset for analytical purposes". Various Services allow, as part of the data-warehousing process, the integration and management of data belonging to different data sources (Jung, 2000). The so-called extraction-, transformation- and load-process (ETL) integrates various data sources in a qualified assured manner in the MDM of the DWH. This process and the MDM is managed by the Storage Service while a Query Service, represented by an OLAP Server, allows multidimensional requests with a standardized query language, the multidimensional expressions (MDX).
- The OLAP Service as part of the Analyses Layer allows querying the Data Layer by using MDX queries. In particular complex measurement calculations with measures from different cubes can be executed by using statistical procedures of a Statistic Service in a statistical Program like R-Project. For a geographic analyses, coordinates of different objects have to be queried with their latitude and longitude, e.g. hospitals, from a geo-server. Related polygons must be marked on a map of the AIS by using a Geographic Service and an external service like google maps.

With the described services a "standard" Analytical Information System can be built that allows analyzing multidimensional data structures. In the following, new parts of AIS will be presented for a knowledge based analyses approach in the context of an Information Self Service for Business Users.

- The Metadata Storage Layer represents the knowledge base in this architecture and is building on several interlinked ontologies. The Technical Ontology enables the system to interact with the elements of the underlying data warehouse. Therefore the technical ontology reflects the elements of the multidimensional data model of the DWH which can be linked by thereon based elements of the analyses and domain ontology. The Analyses Ontology contains all the needed entities, their attributes and relations to each other for modeling metadata describing knowledge for analytical processes on the multidimensional DWH model. The Domain Ontology extends the Analyses Ontology and allows to instantiate the entities and their relations for a specific domain. In the next section 4.2 the ontologies will be described in detail.
- The Information Self Service Layer with its different services builds the core of a knowledge based analyses support. Functionalities like a semantic search, a semantic navigation or a recommender, based on semantic metadata can be used for a supported analyses application. The different functions, described in detail in section 6.3, are realized by different services offering an API for external usage. The services independently use the API of the Semantic Metadata Layer to provide themselves with semantic and technical Metadata from the Metadata Storage layer that imports, manages and provides all kinds of metadata. The access to the Metadata Storage Layer happens only reading. Two kinds of Metadata are used. While the technical information allows interacting with the Analyses Layer, the business user information with a higher abstraction level is given to the business user.

- The Integration and Annotation Layer implies several services that have write access to the Metadata Storage Layer. These services allow a further development of the semantic metadata by enriching these metadata with new contents. The Logging Service is used for logging the analysis steps which are passed during the analysis process. The logging takes place on the OLAP Operations whereby information to relevant steps, to business rules and visualizations can be given. New Analyses Paths can be defined by skilled power users this way. It should be noted that the initial construction of the semantic metadata model is done outside the system and imported by the integration layer. The logging service allows generating further metadata while using the AIS. The Annotation Service enables the system to create semantic annotations on the quantitative DWH-data so that, for example, the data of a specific cube, represented in a specific visualization, can be marked as a "trend", a "cluster", a "relationship" or other annotations if the user interprets the data in this way.

- The Semantic Metadata Layer enables the AIS to access the ontologies of the Metadata Storage Layer by using the Ontology Processing Service. Its function is to manage especially the query and write the metadata of the metadata storage layer. All the metadata is processed by the Ontology Processing Service making it a central component of the architecture. Internally it is used by the Mapping Service. The task of this service is to create and hold a mapping between the entities of the technical ontology and the real entities of the multidimensional model of the DWH. As a mediator this service can use these mappings to query elements of the real DWH by using the entities of the ontology and this service can also rewrite

queries of the Information Self Service Layer based on the semantic metadata so that these can be processed by the Analyses Layer.

Frontend:

- Reporting Application as part of several frontend Applications based on AIS allow generating reports in specific time intervals or by request. These static reports which are delivered to specific business users can be used in order to consider the containing facts in their decision making process.

- A Standard Ad Hoc Analyses Application in contrast to a Reporting Application allows the user to perform explorative ad-hoc analyses on the integrated multidimensional data of the DWH. Rich possibilities can be used to analyze the data in different perspectives to get answers to the issues. Only skilled power users with inherent analyses and domain knowledge are able to use this kind of application in an adequate way.

- Supporting Analyses Application should also allow less skilled users to perform adequate analysis by using analyses supported functionalities based on semantic metadata. For that reason the Information Self Service Layer, the Semantic Metadata Layer and the Metadata Storage Layer must be used in connection with the Analysis Layer and the Data Layer.

To build a Supporting Analysis Application, several layers and services in the backend are necessary. The main focus is on the metadata storage layer which realizes a knowledge base by using several interlinked ontologies. The next section 4.2 will take a closer look at these ontologies.

6.2 Knowledge Base

For the use of semantic metadata in this approach, a flexible metadata model is needed that builds entities, their attributes and relations and allows instantiating them. This metadata model consists of several interlinked ontologies with a generic and domain specific focus. The initialization of included entities allows the modeling of domain specific analyses knowledge.

The task of the Technical Ontology, also called DWH-Ontology, is to describe data warehouse metadata in a semantic rich manner. Thereby this ontology focuses on the areas terminology as well as data structure and meaning (cf. Hartmann, 2008). The DWH-Ontology models on a class level the knowledge over the underlying data warehouse structure of the AIS. Especially entities of the multidimensional model like cubes, measures, dimensions, classification hierarchies, etc. and their semantic relations are taken into consideration. The modeled entities can be identified over a clear identifier. They have an explicit semantic that can be adapted for several real data warehouses. On an instance level the modeled classes can be in instantiated for a real DWH so that instances reflect the multidimensional model of that DWH. These instances can be interlinked with instances of the Analyses and Domain Ontology. The aim of the DWH-Ontology is to provide an access for the Analyses and Domain Ontology to the real underling DWH. Figure 3 shows the entities of the Technical Ontology which is described in the following.

- **Measure:** A Measure describes the quantitative data in the DWH. This data is stored along different Dimensions that can be used in the analysis process. Therefore, measures can by classified or restricted by the associated dimensions. Measures can have different datatypes like string or double values. A Measure can be differentiated in Base Measure and Calculated Measure.

- **Base Measure:** The Base Measure is the quantitative data that is integrated from different data sources in the DWH through an explicit extraction, transformation and load (ETL) process.

- **Calculated Measure:** A Calculated Measure in contrast to a Base Measure is calculated through a calculation rule with utilization of other Base or Calculated Measures.

- **Calculation:** The Calculation represents the calculation rule that is used to create Calculated Measures.

- **Cube:** A Cube or Hypercube is the fundamental data structure for multidimensional analyses that allow different OLAP Operations like pivot, drill down, roll up, slice or dice. Therefore, the Cube is classified in one or more dimensions. Several Base Measures with the same dimensionality can be contained in the same Cube.

- **Dimension:** A Dimension describes a possible view on a measure for analyzing purposes. Therefore, the measure can be classified, restricted or aggregated by a dimension in the analysis process. A Dimension consists of several Dimension Elements.

- **Dimension Element:** A Dimension Element is a collective expression for elements that interact with a Dimension in the way that they belong to this Dimension.

- **Dimension Level:** Dimensions are build of several Dimension levels that are related to each other in parent child relationship and build a hierarchy. As an example of a time dimension, Dimension Levels are all, year, quarter, month and days. A Drill Down or Roll Up OLAP Operation can be performed to split or aggregate the data to other Dimension Levels.

- **Dimension Classification:** Dimension Classifications are the elements located in a Dimension Level. The quantita-

Figure 3. Entities and their relations of a technical ontology

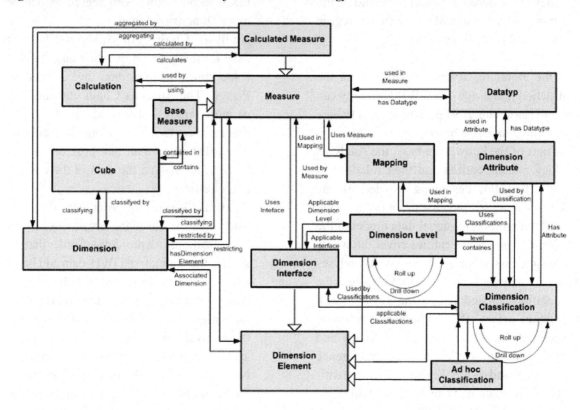

tive DWH-data can be analyzed by using these classifications along one or more Dimensions. As example of a time dimension, Dimension Classifications are 2000, 2001, 2002, ... in the Dimension Level year or Q1/2000, Q2/2000, Q3/2000, Q4/2000 in the Dimension Level quarter. These Elements are also defined in a parent child relationship so that a Drill Down or Roll Up OLAP Operation can be performed.

- **Ad-hoc Classification:** Ad-hoc Classifications are Dimension Classifications that are defined during the analysis process as set of other Dimension Classifications. These Classifications do not have a physical representation in the multidimensional model and are only valid while the analysis is running.

- **Dimension Interface:** A Dimension Interface describes on which Dimension Level the quantitative Data of the DWH is stored. Especially in unbalanced dimension hierarchies in contrast to balanced dimension hierarchies the data can be stored on several Dimension Levels.

- **Dimension Attribute:** A Dimension Attribute allows storing additional Information for a Dimension Classification. If for example a Dimension Classification represents a geographical object latitude and longitude can be defined and saved as Dimension Attribute.

- **Datatype:** Datatypes can be specified for Measures and Dimension Attributes.

- **Mapping:** Mapping means the transformation from one or more Dimension Classifications to one or more others. This Concept can be used for the Transformation of measures if these should be classified and analyzed in other Dimensions ass they were stored. An example could be the transformation of a Measure from a region to postal code dimension.

In the literature, several approaches for the construction and usage of a DWH Ontology can be found (Hartmann, 2008 and Kurze, 2011) where the described model is based on.

As part of the knowledge base, the Analyses Ontology models entities and their relations to each other that allow describing knowledge to the explorative analyses processes in an AIS on the bases of the multidimensional data model of the Data Warehouse. These entities cover the whole analysis process from questions over Analyses Chains to Analyses Results. But they also describe the operations, procedures, business rules as well as different actors. Diverse semantic relations between entities of the Analyses Ontology and the Technical Ontology are defined to reference analysis steps and results. Figure 4 shows the entities and their relations of an Analyses Ontology. These are described in the following:

- **Person:** A Person is an actor in the AIS. He can take over different roles like analyst, business user or administrator. A Person wants answers to his questions. Therefore, the entity Person is linked with the entity Question. To obtain an answer, an Analysis Chain has to be passed.
- **Question:** A Question is a hypothesis that should be answered to base a decision on. An example could be "What is the market share in my catchment area?" Hereby a question should not be viewed detached from others. Rather there could be relations like predecessor, successor and sub question. For example as predecessor question an answer to "What is the catchment area?" must be found and as successor the further question "What are my potentials in catchment area?" could be analyzed. Subquestions analyze the same

measure but refine with regard to one or more Dimension Level.

- **Analysis Chain:** An Analysis Chain is used for analyzing a question and the corresponding subquestions by a specific Person. The Analysis Chain contains one or more Analysis Paths which allow getting answers to the questions. It should be noted that more than one possibility may be right to analyze the data in the context of a question.
- **Analysis Path:** An Analysis Path allows to run through several Analyses Visualizations in a pre-defined order that visualize the quantative DWH-data and build a line of arguments that allows deriving an Analyses Result at the end. Several OLAP Operations have to be executed to change the Analysis Visualizations, whereby these are encapsulated by Domain Operations. Next to the pre-defined Analysis Path they can also be generated by the Domain Operations and their contained Business Rules during runtime.
- **Analyses Visualization:** An Analyses Visualization is the graphical representation of the quantitative DWH-data in the form of pivot tables, diagrams, maps, etc. The fact data is represented along one or more Dimensions, aggregated on specific Dimension Levels and classified or restricted by the chosen Dimension Classifications. Business Rules can be executed if specific constellations of Measures, Dimensions, Dimension Levels, Dimension Classifications and Visualizations occur in the Analyses Visualization. Typically, a set of Analyses Visualizations in a specific order (Analyses Path) have to be analyzed to derive an answer to the investigated question. Hereby, a Start Analyses Visualization and an End Analyses Visualization are defined. While the Start Analyses Visualization is linked

Figure 4. Entities and their relations of an analyses ontology

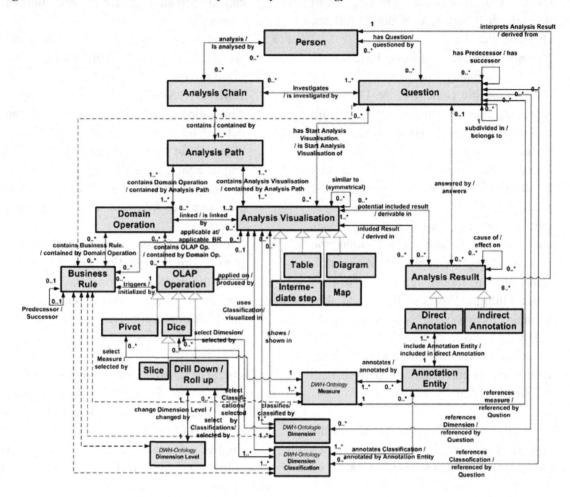

with the Question and serves as entry point to the Analysis, the End Analyses Visualization allows to interpret the represented quantitative DWH-data in the context of the question so that an Analyses Result can be derived.

- **Domain Operation:** Ideally, Business Users want to get from one Analyses Visualization to the next relevant Analyses Visualization without executing all the necessary OLAP Operations like changing the measure (Drill Across), changing the Dimension Level (Drill down / Roll up) or select and remove Dimension Classifications (Slice / Dice). Therefore

Domain Operations encapsulate the OLAP Operations so that the Users have to select one Operation to change the Visualization. In addition to the OLAP Operations also Business Rules are included in the Domain Operations that define the analyses knowledge and the applicability of OLAP Operations on Analyses Visualizations and not visible intermediate steps.

- **OLAP Operations:** As part of the Domain Operations, these Operations are applied on the multidimensional data model of the DWH. They have a direct influence on the visualized quantitative data and they can be used for explorative analyses. Typical

OLAP Operations are pivoting, drill through, drill across, drill down, roll up, slice and dice. [....]

- **Business Rules:** Business Rules were stored as semantic metadata next to the domain specific content of the DWH and represent concrete analyses and domain knowledge. They describe further information and rules and can be part of the Domain Operations. Business Rules can be derived from the Strategies or "best practices" of power users and relate to specific Questions, Analyses Visualizations and Analyses Results or a combination of these. They are applicable if the multidimensional model reaches a defined state. Multiple Business Rules and thus Domain Operations can be applicable in an Analyses Visualization in the context of a Question so that more then one analysis direction can be pursued. New Analysis Path can be created in this way.

If an Analyses Visualization that shows the market share of a hospital in the catchment area a Business Rule can state that as next useful analysis step the market potential should be analyzed. A second rule can state that also the measure should be maintained and the competitors should be analyzed with that measure.

- **Analyses Result:** An Analyses Result describes an interpretation of the quantitative DWH-data. Meaning, a measure that is classified, aggregated and restricted along several Dimensions, Dimension Levels and Dimension Classifications in a specific visualization. Typically, Analyses Results can be seen as answers to questions of business users they can base a decision on. Examples of Analyses Results can be trends, cluster, relationships, geographic agglomerations, etc. Analyses Results

can be divided in Direct and Indirect Annotations.

- **Direct Annotation:** Direct Annotations are Analyses Results that can be recognized directly on the quantitative data.
- **Indirect Annotation:** The indirect Annotations are Analyses Results that are defined on a metalevel and makes statements about direct annotations. As an example, a marketing success can be derived as Analyses Result if a decrease of a specific measure followed by an increase is observed.
- **Annotation Entity:** The Annotation Entity links a Direct Annotation with the instances of the multidimensional data model. It may be possible that different data cells of the multidimensional cubes in combination build the Direct Annotation.

It should be noted that the Analyses Ontology is modeled on an abstract domain independent level. Instances of this ontology will focus on special domain of interest and will, therefore, be initialized in a Domain Ontology. This extends the Analyses Ontology and for this reason all the entities and relations are available. This Domain Ontology holds the analyses and domain knowledge as instances and semantic annotations of the AIS will be stored in this ontology.

Knowledge which is stored in the semantic metadata layer in the form of Domain Ontology instances especially in the German hospital market can be Questions, Analyses Visualizations, Analysis Results, etc. If for Example the Question "What is the market share in my catchment area?" is to be analyzed, the knowledge that a catchment area can be divided in a core market, advanced core market and peripheral market can be modeled (von Schroeders, 2009; Stibbe, 2011). As additional knowledge, the creation of divisions through ad-hoc Classification on a region or postalcode Dimension by taking the number of cases for stationary hospital stays into consideration, may be available. Additional knowledge can describe that further Questions or Sub Questions can be analyzed based on the predecessor Questions and their results. As example the previous question can be refined for the hospital Dimension so that not the hospital itself but the corresponding specialist departments will be analyzed. In that case knowledge about the possible diagnosis and treatments of a specialist department in the form of specific Dimension Classifications of a ICD (International Statistical Classification of Diseases) Dimension should be modeled and exploited in an analysis. Further knowledge that describes how to proceed if special Analyses Results like changes of referring physician or in the scope of patients in the hospital market occur could be modeled.

6.3 Functions for Analysis Support

Assuming that an AIS is enriched with a semantic Meta data layer which imports and manages knowledge that is modeled by a group of analyses experts in a specific domain, new functionalities for analyses support can be developed. These are discussed in the following.

- **Semantic Search:** The goal of this function is to search for and find instances of the metadata model based on their semantics. These are defined by the class membership, the attributes, the named relations to other classes and their instances. In particular this concept allows finding instances of the entity "Question" and linked "Analysis Chains" that are modeled in the systems knowledgebase and that can be adapted for the actual underlying quantitative DWH-data. In addition, also instances of the entity "Analysis Results" that are annotated in the AIS and thereby linked data can be found and visualized again. Analysis results can be understood by viewing the associated Analysis Chain

and Question. These Analyses Results can also be starting points of further analyses.

The semantic search will not be realized as keyword search but as declarative query to the knowledge base. If, for example the question "What is the market share of a specific specialist department of my hospital in the catchment area?" should be found then it can be stated that a instance of the entity question is searched whereby this instance should be linked with the instance "market share" of the entity measure as well as the dimensions "hospital" and "region" and at specific Dimension Levels.

- **Semantic Navigation:** If the entities and the semantic relations between them were initialized for a specific domain in the form of a semantic network one is able to navigate from one instance to the next. In the context of an analyses supported AIS, these functions can be used in several ways. First, a pure navigation through the semantic network, browsing the relations of the entities in the knowledge base, can be performed. This possibility may be used, for example, if someone wants to know the necessary predecessor questions and the feasible successor questions. Or it can be used to specify the declarative query in the semantic search. If a business user wants perform an Analyses Visualization. He can run through a defined Analyses Chain and reach an end Analyses Visualization that allows the interpretation of the visualized quantitative DWH-data in the context of the question. In contrast to the pure navigation browsing the knowledge base, an analyses runs through several Analyses Visualizations which can be represented and linked in the metadata model. Especially the defined domain operations of the metadata model with the included business rules trigger several OLAP Operations that have a direct influence on the quantitative data.

- **Recommender:** A key function of analyses support can be seen in recommendations and tips for the business user in the context of the question while he is performing the analysis. These recommendations and tips are derived from the modeled analyses and domain knowledge. As described in the requirements for this approach. Therefore, several kinds of metadata should be combined in an intelligent manner. These are information to the qualitative DWH-data. In particular, the structure, elements and their relations of the multidimensional data model. Furthermore, information to the analyses processes itself, modeled by the business rules and information to the quantitative DWH-data. Annotations like analyses results for example.

Recommendations suggesting the next possible Analyses Visualizations can be given in a concrete Analyses Visualization in consideration of the question. Here, these Analyses Results do not necessarily have to be part of a predefined Analyses Chain. If the conditions of business rules can fire the rule new Analyses Chains will be created dynamically.

If specific Analyses Results occur further questions should be examined. As a recommendation, the question as well as a start Analyses Visualization may be given. In particular, relevant dimension elements can be preselected. In our hospital example, these may be specific ICD-codes as restriction on the ICD-dimension that are only relevant for a specialist department that should be analyzed in a further analysis step. Next to further questions also previous questions could be recommended if they are marked as necessary and have not been analyzed before. As tips, further information to the calculations and semantics and

terminology of measures and of dimension elements as well as their connections can be given.

Also recommendations that result in a query rewriting to the AIS can be given. If knowledge about mappings over dimensions is modeled then this could be used for rewriting the MDX query to the DWH. These could be mappings through a region and postal code dimension or between identical dimensions in different versions, whereby the last addresses the problem of slowly changing dimensions (Lüpkes, 2011). A query rewriting can also occur, if the system recognizes that the Analyses Visualization is not adequate for analysis of a question. In this case another visualization as well as additional / less measures, dimensions and dimension elements can be selected.

It should be noticed that the supported AIS next to the recommendations and tips also explains these so that Business User can learn from the modeled inherent knowledge of the AIS.

After having explained the functions in theory the next chapter 4.4 shows an example. This focuses on an intelligent selection of Dimension Elements in the context of a specific question using modeled analyses and domain knowledge as well as external structured data.

6.4 Example for the Intelligent Selection of Dimension Classifications

With the intention of securing the own competitive capacity, a hospital pursues the following objective: the competitive orientation of the service spectrum. In order to develop the potential capacity precisely, the controller of this hospital (business user) commissions an external consulting firm (power user) to produce a report. This report is supposed to compare the hospital to its competitors in the following fields: patch, market share, market potential, and demographic change. At this, only competitors with similar logistic emphases shall be taken into account. Assuming that the analyst knows the logistic emphasis of his customer, he is asked to find out which logistic emphases the competitors offer.

Since 2004, in the course of the amendment of the SGB V, German hospitals are imposed to publish a report about the kind of services they are offering and its quality and quantity. This document is called structured quality report (SQB). It serves as a source of information and decision support for patients before a hospital stay (Haeske-Seeberg, 2005). In addition to detailed information about numbers of cases, logistic emphases are documented. Thus, the analyst may consult the quality reports of the competitors in order to select the hospitals for his analysis. A manual scan of the quality reports would be too time-consuming.

Since 2007, the hospitals are supposed to publish their reports in machine-readable form (Roski, 2009). For this reason, it is possible to

make the information of the quality reports available for the AIS. Thus, the quality report in the form of linked data facilitates the analysis notably. By the use of linked data the meaning of data is defined explicitly. Furthermore, via data links other data sources are referenced to gain further information (Hengartner, 2010). In this example, the information of the quality reports can thus be described as metadata in RDF (Resource Description Framework). In such a way, the analyst may put the question of hospitals with similar logistic emphases, for instance via SPARQL. The complete report may contain the Analyses Visualization portrayed in Figure 5.

7. PROJECT CONTEXT AND EVALUATION

As described in section 4 the goal of this research project is to empower the business user

Figure 5. Competitors in catchments area with same logistic emphases (orthopedics)

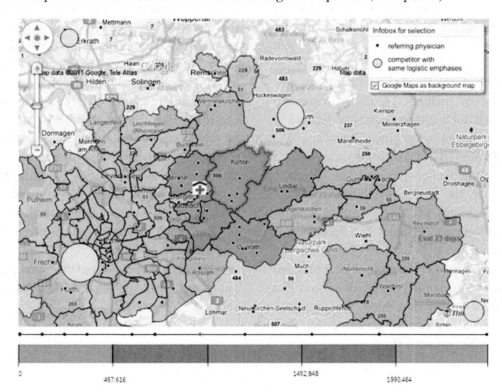

in analyzing multidimensional quantitative data structures by reducing the perceived AIS usage complexity. The system should be able to support business users in their ad-hoc analysis by using modeled semantic machine readable and reasonable knowledge which is provided by a semantic metadata layer. The Figure 2 shows the envisioned architectural sketch that should be implemented in the AIS Multidimensional Statistical Data Analysis Engine (MUSTANG[1]) (Mertens, 2009). Thereby, the presented requirements of section 4 should be complied.

A further development of MUSTANG is currently realized by several parties of the Data Management and Data Analysis (DMA) Group of the OFFIS Division Health and the University of Oldenburg:

- **MUSTANG-Core:** This DMA – Group further develops MUSTANG with its core functionalities. These are the black surrounded Services in Figure 2.
- **Strategy Project Health Services Research:** This DMA Strategy Project focuses on developing various new sources of public healthcare and integrating them in the in multidimensional manner in the DWH of MUSTANG. Furthermore, new statistical methods especially regressive models for socio-demographic data are in development by the project members.
- **PhD KNOBI:** This PhD focuses on the given motivation presented in section 1 and has the goal to tackle the presented shortcomings of AIS. Therefore the requirements of section 4 are developed in conjunction with experts of the AIS and hospital market domain. The presented concepts of section 6 were developed and will be further developed, evaluated and published as part of this ongoing PhD (probably until 2013).

- **Student Project Group KNOBI:** In the summer semester 2011 and winter semester 2011/2012 a project group named KNOBI: Knowledge based Business Intelligence is offered by the University of Oldenburg. Goal of this project is to implement and evaluate KNOBI concepts. Therefore the blue surrounded services of Figure 2 will be developed.
- **Master Thesis Related to KNOBI:** Goal of this Master Thesis is to develop a generic model that is able to link and use data sources that are outside from the AIS and contain additional information about the qualitative DWH data and especially the structure and elements of the multidimensional data model. This data should be used within a MUSTANG analysis to automatic select the dimension elements in the context of the actual question and analysis visualization in an intelligent manner.

All these projects have design science as a common research methodology. In contrast to the research methodology behaviorism which examines the usage and effects on individuals, groups and organizations of existing information systems, design science has the goal to create and evaluate information technology artifacts to solve identified organizational problems. Artifacts can be divided in constructs, models, methods and instances. They reach from mathematical methods over software systems to textual descriptions. It should be noted that behaviorism could be used to identify problems with the used software which result in requirements for a further development of these software tools.

Hevner, 2004 pointed out the following seven guidelines for the research methodology design science:

- **Design as an Artifact:** "Design-science research must produce a viable artifact in the form of a construct, a model, a method, or an instantiation".
- **Problem Relevance:** "The objective of design-science research is to develop technology-based solutions to important and relevant business problems".
- **Rigorous Evaluation Methods:** "The utility, quality, and efficacy of a design artifact must be rigorously demonstrated via well-executed evaluation methods".
- **Contribution to The Academic World:** "Effective design-science research must provide clear and verifiable contributions in the areas of the design artifact, design foundations, and/or design methodologies".
- **Research Rigor:** "Design-science research relies upon the application of rigorous methods in both the construction and evaluation of the design artifact".
- **Design as a Search Process:** "The search for an effective artifact requires utilizing available means to reach desired ends while satisfying laws in the problem environment".
- **Publications:** It is important that the work is published in academic as well as in practitioner's community.

For the various projects especially the mentioned PhD these guidelines should be taken into consideration. As evaluation of the presented approach, the corresponding architecture should be implemented as proof of concept. This should be presented to the users, stakeholders and experts of the BI and hospital market domain. The proof of concept should be evaluated by them with empirical methods, maybe as case study, in order to review the compliance of the requirements presented in section 4. After this a further develop-

ment should be conducted to fulfill the remaining and new requirements of the users.

8. RELATED WORK

There are research issues in the context of Business Intelligence (BI) that focus on capturing analyses knowledge (Baars, 2005) or the adoption of BI tools to new analyses requirements (Sell, 2005; Berthold, 2011). Also integrated queries to different BI tools (Cao, 2006; Spahn, 2008) and annotations of data models with further information for analyses support are of interest (Network Inference, 2004; Ludwig, 2005; Sell, 2005; Berthold, 2010). In many cases the analyst and sometimes the business user should get a higher attention by adapting the BI tools to the individual information needs or by giving analyses support for an information self-service. A lot of papers in the related work address these problems by the use of semantic metadata and related semantic web technologies.

In the area of analyzes process and result documentation (Baars, 2005) describes how to distribute business intelligence knowledge. Reports and analyses templates should be made available through knowledge management systems for organization-wide access. A technical implementation is not mentioned in this article.

In the context of analyses processes the work of Bissantz, 2001 is also relevant. The term of analyses chain is introduced in this article but the focus lays on the human machine interaction. Finding, preparing and visualizing the data could be seen as a technical operational activity. The building of a user centered analysis model, its verification and evolution in contrast is seen as a cognitive task.

During the analysis task, a number of OLAP operations are executed for the exploration of the multidimensional data model and the related quantitative DWH-data. Building queries according to Giacometti, 2008 is a difficult task. Therefore a framework is presented in this paper that allows recommending OLAP operations in the analyses process. This is based on the evaluation of OLAP server query logs.

Another kind of analyses support for a higher user satisfaction in the context of BI is seen in the separation of business and it concerns. Unlike the previously mentioned paper semantic metadata plays an important role. Entities of the underling BI system and their relations to each other can be modeled in Metadata models. These models also allow saving further information like business rules or expert knowledge. In Network Inference 2004 and Ludwig, 2005 the possibilities of these metadata are explained for the extraction, transformation and load process of data warehousing.

A semantic web based architecture for analytical tools that should allow increasing the efficiency in the decision making process is presented in Sell, 2005. A Domain Ontology, modeling the entities and their relations of a domain as well as further information to the structure and relations of qualitative DWH-data should support in the analyses process. On the one hand recommendations to dimension classifications should be given in a pro-active manner. On the other hand a semiautomatic query rewriting based on the semantic metadata should enable the system to enhance the analyses results.

The entities modeled in the domain ontologies were often provided with natural language names as these describe more the business semantics than the corresponding technical names of the multidimensional model. Users can query the system in known terminology. This approach is used in Cao, 2006 and Spahn, 2008 for querying company-wide data integrated from different BI Systems like CRM, ERP, DWH, etc. on an abstract layer.

The support of a technical unskilled business user is especially focussed in Spahn, 2008 and Berthold, 2010. In Berthold, 2010 the emphasis is on a collaborative ad hoc decision-making process. Data of different BI Tools is integrated presented and enriched with further information. Web 2.0 technologies should allow building so called Information Mash-Ups that foster the collaboration of several business users.

Although the own approach focuses on the use of semantic metadata for the support of business users in the analyses process, it can be differentiated from others. The emphasis of the own approach is to model entities and their relations for the analyses processes. Instances of this model should represent analyses and domain knowledge and should be combined with other kinds of metadata especially to the qualitative and quantitative DWH-data. Different functions like a semantic search, navigation and recommendation can use this knowledge to support business users in the context of an Analytical Information System.

9. CONCLUSION

The aim of this work was to show the potentials of a knowledge based Analytical Information System for the information self-service of business users. Actual AIS have a high flexibility and powerfulness that result in a high usage complexity if the users are not properly skilled. Often they do not have the analyses and domain knowledge as well as a deeper technical and conceptual understanding of the AIS so that the execution of an adequate analysis of their issues is a great challenge. Within the context of a changed German hospital market, in which the hospitals must position themselves as economic companies on the market, business users are in the situation that they must analyze their environment. Hospitals must wittingly exploit their potentials by aligning their service offers in a competitive manner.

The need for an information self-service of business users in the context of German hospital market analysis was identified in section 1. The role of Analytical Information Systems in the context of business intelligence as systems for the acquisition of information in the decision process was described in section 2. A high usage complexity and the lack of storing additional metadata to business rules, analyses processes and further information to qualitative and quantitative DWH-data were seen as shortcomings and presented in section 3. In section 4 a scientific question and requirements to an approach that treats these shortcomings were presented. Section 5 described in general the understanding of ontologies. The main focus of this thesis presented in section 6 is an approach for an analyses support of business users in AIS based on semantic metadata. Therefore an architectural sketch with standard AIS layers and especially new layers which build a semantic metadata layer section were explained in subsection 6.1. The subsection 6.2 presents the knowledge base with its different interlinked ontologies. These were explained with their entities and relations that are able to store analyses and domain knowledge. The usages of this knowledge for analyses supporting functionalities were described in subsection 6.3. Especially a semantic search, semantic navigation and recommendation function were presented. An Example for the intelligent selection of dimension elements is shown in subsection 6.4. In Section 7 the project context and the research methodology as well as the planed evaluation of this approach were described. Section 8 gave an overview of the related work, showed the state of the art technologies and pointed out the differences to our approach.

As further steps in this research project, the shown architecture of section 6.1 will be implemented in a proof of concept as part of the MUSTANG. The ontologies of section 6.2 will be instantiated with analyses and domain knowledge in the range of the German hospital market. An evolution of this approach is planned as case study with several partners from the practice.

REFERENCES

Baars, H. (2005). Distribution von Business-Intelligence-Wissen. In Chamoni, P., & Gluchowski, P. (Eds.), *Analytische Informationssysteme* (pp. 409–424). Berlin, Germany: Springer.

Bauer, A., & Günzel, H. (2009). *Data-Warehouse-Systeme - Architektur, Entwicklung, Anwendung*. Heidelberg, Germany: DPunkt Verlag.

Berthold, H., Rösch, P., Zöller, S., Wortmann, F., Carenini, A., & Campbell, S. …Strohmaier, F. (2010). An architecture for ad-hoc and collaborative business intelligence. In *Proceedings of the 2010 EDBT/ICDT Workshops, EDBT '10*. New York, NY: ACM.

Bissantz, N. (2001). DeltaMiner. *Wirtschaftsinformatik, 43*(1), 77–80.

Bizer, C., Haeth, T., & Berners Lee, T. (2008). *Linked data: Principles and state of the art*. Paper presented at the meeting of www2008, Bejing, China

Cao, L., Zhang, C., & Liu, J. (2006). Ontology-based integration of business intelligence. *Web Intelligence and Agent Systems, 4*(3), 313–325.

Chamoni, P., & Gluchowski, P. (2006). *Analytische Informationssysteme*. Berlin, Germany: Springer. doi:10.1007/3-540-33752-0

Giacometti, A., Marcel, P., & Negre, E. (2008). A framework for recommending OLAP queries. In *Proceeding of the ACM 11th International Workshop on Data Warehousing and OLAP, DOLAP '08*. New York, NY: ACM.

Gluchowski, P., & Kemper, H.-G. (2006). Quo vadis business intelligence. *BI Spektrum, 1,* 12–19.

Gruber, T. (1993). *A translation approach to portable ontology specifications*. Stanford University. Retrieved June 13, 2011, from http://ksl-web. stanford.edu /KSL_Abstracts/KSL-92-71.html

Haeske-Seeberg, H. (2005). *Handbuch Qualitätsmanagement im Krankenhaus – Strategien, Analysen, Konzepte*. Stuttgart, Germany: Kohlhammer Verlag.

Hartmann, S. (2008). *Überwindung semantischer Heterogenität bei multiplen Data-Warehouse-Systemen*. Bamberg, Germany: University of Bamberg Press.

Hengartner, U., & Meier, A. (2010). *Web 3.0 & Semantic Web: HMD – Praxis der Wirtschaftsinformatik*. Heidelberg, Germany: DPunkt Verlag.

Hevner, A. R., March, S. T., Park, J., & Ram, S. (2004). Design science in information systems research. *Management Information Systems Quarterly, 28,* 75–105.

Imhoff, C., & White, C. (2011). Self service business intelligence – Empowering users to generate insights. In *TDWI Best Practices Report*. TDWI Research.

Inmon, W. H. (1996). *Building the data warehouse*. New York, NY: Wiley & Sons.

Jung, R., & Winter, R. (2000). Data-Warehousing-Strategie. In *Business-Engineering*. Berlin, Germany: Springer.

Kurze, C., Gluchowski, P., & Bohringer, M. (2010). Towards an ontology of multidimensional data structures for analytical purposes. In *HICSS '10: Proceedings of the 2010, 43rd Hawaii International Conference on System Sciences*. Washington, DC: IEEE Computer Society.

Ludwig, L. (2005). *Business Intelligence und das Semantic Web: ein Traumpaar*. Retrieved June 13, 2011, from http://www.competence-site.de / corporate-performance-management/ Business-Intelligence-und-das-Semantic-Web-39683

Lüpkes, C. (2011). Ad-hoc Datentransformationen für Analytische Informationssysteme. In *Proceedings of the 23rd GI-Workshop on Foundations of Databases*, University of Innsbruck, Obergurgl, Tirol, Austria.

Mertens, M. (2011). Wissensbasiertes business intelligence für die Informations-Selbstversorgung von Entscheidungsträgern. In *Proceedings of the 23. GI-Workshop on Foundations of Databases*, University of Innsbruck, Obergurgl, Tirol, Austria.

Mertens, M., Teiken, Y., & Appelrath, H.-J. (2009). Semantische Anreicherung von strukturierten Daten und Prozessen in analytischen Informationssystemen am Beispiel von MUSTANG. In *Proceedings of Forschungskolloquium Business Intelligence 2009 der GI-Fachgruppe 5.8 - Management Support Systems*. Dortmund, Germany: University of Dortmund.

Network Inference. (2004). *Ontology and data warehousing*. Technology white paper, network Inference, Inc. Retrieved June 13, 2011, from http://me.jtpollock.us /pubs/

ONeil. B. (2007). *Semantics and business metadata*. The Data Administration. Retrieved June 13, 2011, from http://www.tdan.com /view-articles/4934

Roski, R. (2009). *Zielgruppengerechte Gesundheitskommunikation: Akteure – Audience Segmentation – Anwendungsfelder*. Wiesbaden, Germany: VS Verlag.

Sell, D., Cabral, L., Motta, E., Domingue, J., Hakimpour, F., & Pacheco, R. (2005). A Semantic Web based architecture for analytical tools. In *CEC'05: Proceedings of the Seventh IEEE International Conference on E-Commerce Technology*. Washington, DC: IEEE Computer Society.

Spahn, M., Kleb, J., Grimm, S., & Scheidl, S. (2008). Supporting business intelligence by providing ontology-based end-user information self-service. In *OBI '08: Proceedings of the First International Workshop on Ontology-Supported Business Intelligenc*. New York, NY: ACM.

Stibbe, R., Güsgen, J., Dierkes, A., & Tilgen, M. (2011). Geocodierungals Instrument zur Marktanalyse. *KU Gesundheitsmanagement, 1*, 29–31.

Studer, R., Grimm, S., & Becker, A. (2007). *Semantic Web services – Concepts, technologies and applications*. Berlin, Germany: Springer. doi:10.1007/3-540-70894-4

Teiken, Y., Rohde, M., & Mertens, M. (2010). MUSTANG: Realisierung eines Analytischen Informationssystems im Kontext der Gesundheitsberichtserstattung. In *Informatik 2010: Service Science - Neue Perspektiven für die Informatik, CEUR Workshop Proceedings*, Leipzig, Germany.

Thoben, W., Rohde, M., Koch, S., Appelrath, H.-J., & Stuber, R. (2010). Konzepte und Technologien für die strategische Planung im Krankenhausmarkt. *Krankenhaus IT Journal, 5*, 26–27.

von Schroeders, N., & Heller, C. (2009). *Geocoding - Geografische Analyse fürKrankenhäuser*. Kulmbach, Germany: Baumann Fachzeitschriften Verlag.

KEY TERMS AND DEFINITIONS

Analytical Information System: Information system that focuses on analytical issues. These systems include the following concepts and technologies by definition: Data Warehouse, Online Analytical Processing, Data Mining and Business Intelligence-Tools.

Analytical Knowledge: Includes conceptional and technical understanding about the Multidimensional Data Model resp. the Analytical Information System and the applicable analytical options like the Online Analytical operations.

Business User: These people are task oriented Information Consumers who have an information need to base decisions on. These business users generally do not have the time or experience to produce, analyze and combine informations for decision making purposes. In 80% they consume informations presented in role-tailored reports. Typically this group of persons consists of managers, executives or salespeople.

Business User Information Self Service: An approach that enables business users to access and work with an Analytical Information System without assuming broad Analytical Knowledge.

Domain Knowledge: Includes domain specific information about basic analytical questions concerning possible key figures, their semantics and informations about the relations between these key figures.

Linked Data: A subset of the Semantic Web, in which data is explicitly encoded with meaning using technologies like the Resource Description Framework.

MUSTANG: This acronym stands for "Multidimensional Statistical Data Analysis Engine" and describes a Platform for developing Analytical Information Systems. It is part of the research and development activities of the Data Management and Analysis Group of OFFIS – Institute for Information Technology.

Power User: These people are analysis oriented Information Producers who access data sources in ad-hoc and explorative manner and combine them with additional sources as well as their inherent analytical knowledge. Typically this group of persons consist of business analysts, senior managers as well as IT professionals.

Self Service Business Intelligence: This term describes a direction of Business Intelligence where Business Users should be empowered to generate insights without requiring the help of IT.

ENDNOTE

[1] MUSTANG: http://www.offis.de/en/r_d_divisions/health/projects/projects_in_detail/detail/status/mustang.html

Chapter 15
Knowledge Worker Performance in a Cross-Industrial Perspective

Rainer Erne
Leeds Metropolitan University, UK

ABSTRACT

Knowledge workers in specific professional domains form the fastest increasing workforce in OECD countries. Since this fact has been realised by management researchers, they have focussed on the question of how to measure and enhance the productivity of said workforce. According to the author's cross-industrial research undertaken in five different knowledge-intensive organisations, it is, however, not productivity in the traditional meaning of the term which is to be regarded as the crucial performance indicator in knowledge work. There rather exist multiple performance indicators, each of which is, moreover, differently graded as to its importance by different stakeholders. These findings, firstly, indicate the need for an alternative definition of productivity when the term is applied to knowledge work. Secondly, they indicate the need for alternative definitions of the specific challenges that might be involved in making knowledge workers productive. Thirdly, they imply different consequences for the management of knowledge workers. This chapter closes abovementioned research gaps by summarising the indicators employed in five knowledge-intensive organisations from different business sectors for the assessment of knowledge workers' performance, by subsequently deducing the specific challenges involved in the management of knowledge workers and by further delineating consequences for the management of knowledge workers – consequences affecting various knowledge-intensive industries.

DOI: 10.4018/978-1-4666-0894-8.ch015

1 THE CHALLENGE OF KNOWLEDGE WORKER'S PRODUCTIVITY

One of Peter F. Drucker's great achievements is said to have been his ability to anticipate key management challenges decades in advance (Byrne & Gerdes, 2005). In 1969, he defined one such challenge as follows: "To make knowledge work productive will be the great management task of this century, just as to make manual work productive was the great management task of the last century" (Drucker, 1969, p.290).

In one respect, Drucker was unquestionably right: Nearly all surveys of past decades point to a fundamental structural change in the labour markets of the OECD countries:

- There has been, from 1985 onwards, a 10 percentage-points increase in so-called 'derivative services', e.g. consulting, coaching, teaching, researching, development and management work (Weidig et al., 1999; Dostal & Reinberg, 1999; Dostal, 2001; Reinberg & Hummel, 2002).
- The number of occupations of the categories 'manager', 'professional occupation' as well as 'associate professional' and 'technical occupation' has increased by 10 percentage-points over the last two decades (UK National Statistics, 2000; Baldwin & Beckstead, 2003; Beckstead & Gellatly, 2004; UK National Statistics, 2006; Davenport, 2005; US Department of Labor, 2006; Brinkley, 2006).
- The demand for employees with an academic education has increased by 190 percentage-points between 1975 and 2004, whereas the demand for employees with a lower educational background is continually decreasing (Weidig et al., 1999; Kleinert et al., 2000; Dostal, 2001; Reinberg &

Hummel, 2002; Reinberg & Hummel, 2005; OECD, 2006a; OECD, 2006b).
- Levy & Murnane (2006) noted a disproportional increase in the demand for two skill requirements within the US labour force between 1979 and 1999: 'expert thinking' and 'complex communication'. In contrast to this development, they observed that the demand for manual and routine cognitive skills has been continually decreasing within the same time frame (Figure 1).

In regard to Drucker's other thesis, i.e. that the productivity of knowledge workers will be the crucial challenge for 21st century management, it can be stated that he initiated an abundance of research in the description, measurement and enhancement of knowledge workers' productivity (Ray & Sahu, 1989; Sumanth, Omachonu & Beruvides, 1990; Drucker, 1991; Sveiby, 1998; Drucker, 1999; Horibe, 1999; Pfiffner & Stadelmann, 1999; Amar, 2002; Davenport et al., 2002; Hauber, 2002; Newell et al., 2002; Paradi et al., 2002; Ahn & Chang, 2004; Balazova, 2004; Herman, 2004; Ramirez & Nembhard, 2004; Davenport, 2005; Hube, 2005; Suff & Reilly, 2005; Malik, 2006; Stam, 2007; North & Gueldenberg, 2008; Dörhöfer, 2010) – a stream of research that does not seem to come to an end, neither in the near nor in the remote future.

This chapter aims at corroborating three theses:

1. Up to now, there is no such thing as a concept of what knowledge workers' productivity implicates, relating to the business practices of knowledge-intensive companies. Different concepts of knowledge worker productivity have been rather developed from certain academic viewpoints than with a view to daily business practices.
2. Consequently, the challenges involved in making knowledge workers productive have not been stated with a view to the business

Figure 1. Economy-wide measures of routine and non-routine task 1969 -1998 (Levy & Murnane, 2006, p.15)

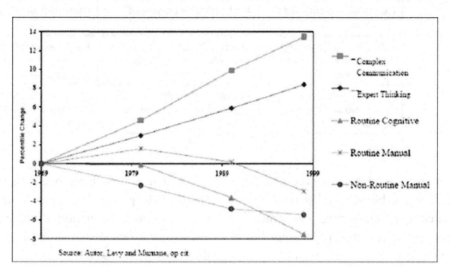

2 CONCEPTS OF KNOWLEDGE WORKER PRODUCTIVITY

needs of knowledge-intensive companies. Therefore, a revised and more specific problem definition is required with a view to the 'management challenges of the 21st century'.

3. Both theses root in a lack of empirical research on this matter in general and on a lack of cross-industrial empirical research into knowledge-intensive businesses in particular. The chapter here presented undertakes to close said research gap.

In order to corroborate these three theses, the chapter starts with a brief review of general concepts of knowledge worker productivity (section 2). Those concepts are being reviewed and, as a consequence, an alternative research design is being proposed (section 3). Section 4 exhibits the major outcomes of the research with respect to concepts of knowledge worker productivity from a cross-industrial point of view on the one hand and involved challenges on the other hand (section 4). Finally, practical management conclusions for rendering knowledge workers productive will be deduced (section 5).

It is evident that 'productivity' in the traditional meaning of 'relation between quantity of output in relation to amount of input' (Gutenberg, 1958; Pedell, 1985) cannot be applied to knowledge work. When summarising the different approaches to knowledge worker productivity, one can distinguish three different concepts which will subsequently be labelled as 'performance concepts' (chapter 2.1), 'authoritative concepts' (chapter 2.2) and 'contribution concepts' (chapter 2.3). These three concepts can be traced back to different academic disciplines: The 'performance concepts' originate in research of cognitive psychology into expert performance, the 'authoritative concepts' have derived from research into the sociology of professions and the 'contribution concepts' stem from approaches to knowledge management (Figure 2).

2.1 Performance Concepts

The first attempt at grasping knowledge worker productivity is based on the fact that in every

Figure 2. Classification of knowledge worker productivity concepts

	Performance concepts	Authoritative concepts	Contribution concepts
Disciplinary origins	• Cognitive psychology: Research into expert performance	• Occupational sociology: Research into professions	• Business management; Research into knowledge management
Major performance indicator	• Celerity and accuracy of the solution of domain specific problems	• Level of authority over a defined knowledge area	• Degree of contribution to the knowledge of an organisation

domain, there are individuals who are able to continually and repeatably accomplish outstanding results, as compared to average performers. Taking this viewpoint, cognitive psychology has tried to describe and explain this phenomenon, investigating experts and their performance in domains such as jurisdiction, physics, engineering, mathematics, education, finance and consulting (Larkin et al., 1980; Chi et al., 1981; Sweller et al., 1983; Posner, 1988; Krems, 1990; Patel & Groen, 1991; Boshuizen & Schmidt, 1992; Gruber & Ziegler, 1996; Sonnentag, 1996; Hron, 2000; Bredl, 2005; Chi 2006; Feltovich et al., 2006). It was found that experts distinguish themselves from average performers by the way in which they represent domain-specific problems as well as in the strategies which they apply in solving such problems: They solve domain-specific problems more efficiently, more effectively and more accurately. This cannot be attributed to general intelligence, but to the way in which they group, store and retrieve domain-specific information. This skill is regarded to be a result of 'deliberate practice' in the respective domain over an extended period of time. Since their performance is measured by the amount of time spent on solving a given domain-specific problem and by the quality of the results (in comparison to novices), the two performance measures here applied can be labelled as measures of 'performance' in the traditional meaning.

Both measures have been assimilated and specified in productivity measurement models such as IBM's 'Function Point Analysis' for software development, which tries to measure development productivity by the amount of business functionality that an information system provides to a user (Garmus & Herron, 2000), Ray & Sahu's (1989) 'Operations-Based Productivity Model', which tries to grasp knowledge worker productivity by indices assigned to categories of job characteristica and work places, or Paradis et al.'s (2002) 'Data Envelopment Analysis', which measures knowledge worker productivity according to 'Decision Making Units' (DMUs).

2.2 Authoritative Concepts

However, since the efficiency and effectiveness of work are frequently difficult to assess, especially when embedded in a social context, there exists an alternative approach to determining whether knowledge work has been successful. It is a simple indicator at work in the daily operations of an organisation: This indicator becomes explicit when an individual has gained more or less exclusive authority over a certain domain, be it hierarchical or a knowledge domain. For authority over a hierarchical domain, i.e. over a group of people on a broader scale, sociology-of-occupations representatives have coined the term 'professions' (Parsons, 1939; Millerson, 1964, Larson, 1977; Abbott, 1988; Hitzler, 1998; Hesse, 1998;

Huber, 1999; Mieg, 2001; Pfadenhauer, 2003a; Pfadenhauer, 2003b). Even though the views of sociologists differ widely with respect to the indicators applied in categorising an occupation as a profession as well as with respect to the reasons offered for the emergence and evolvement of such expert occupations, the tasks ascribed to professionals are viewed as being basically similar by adherents of the psychological perspective: Professional tasks have been defined as 'applying abstract knowledge to particular cases'. The sociological point of view, nevertheless, differs from the psychological one in regard to the features determined which make an expert a professional: not primarily outstanding performance, which would be difficult to observe and measure, but exclusive authority over a particular domain of expertise such as the domain of curing diseases or the domain of jurisdiction. In other words, professionalism can be described as socially institutionalized expertise. In order to maintain this authority on an individual level, the respective professional has to demonstrate expertise (Abbott, 1988; Mieg, 2001; Pfadenhauer, 2003a; Pfadenhauer 2003b).

Therefore, a knowledge worker can also be regarded as being 'productive' if he or she has achieved exclusive authority over a certain domain.

This point of view has been adopted mainly by sociologically inclined management researchers such as Wallace (1995), Blackler (1995), Keuken (1996), Pfadenhauer (2003a, 2003b) and Alvesson (2004), the latter emphasising, above all, the importance of rhetoric management, image and social processes in knowledge-intensive companies.

2.3 Contribution Concepts

A third approach to determining knowledge worker productivity focuses less on individual performance, as cognitive psychologists maintain or on the performance of some occupational groups, as propagated by occupational sociologists, but rather on the contributions an individual or a group make to a certain business.

Since the contribution of knowledge workers does not consist in physical changes resulting from manual work, but in the identification, acquisition, generation, dissemination, application, in the retention and the assessment of knowledge, researchers in knowledge management are looking for approaches in order to identify, acquire, generate, disseminate, apply, detain and assess knowledge in organisations (Nonaka & Takeuchi 1995; North 1999; Willke 2001; Davenport 2005; Hasler Roumois 2007; Probst, Raub & Romhardt 2010).

From this perspective, a knowledge worker's productivity cannot solely be defined by outstanding individual performance or by his attaining an exclusive status. The core of this productivity concept rather lies in the contribution an employee makes to a certain business. This contribution may consist in the acquisition, generation, dissemination, application, retention and / or assessment of knowledge. It is the contribution to an organisation's business that counts, and not the achievements of a single person or a group of persons.

This approach has been adopted by scholars like Sumanth, Omachonu & Beruvides (1990) who proposed a model which adds the 'contribution criterion' to the 'efficiency' and 'effectiveness criteria' of 'white collar worker productivity'. Peter Drucker (1991; 1999) emphasised the importance of regarding knowledge workers as assets, thus enhancing the contribution to an organisation, and Tom Davenport (2005) as well as Pfiffner & Stadelmann (1999) and Francis Horibe (1999) try to distinguish management interventions according to the type of activity a knowledge worker performs, i.e. creating, distributing or applying knowledge.

3 RESEARCH GAPS AND RESEARCH DESIGN

How have above-mentioned concepts been created? In order to answer this question, three types of methodological approaches can be distinguished:

Firstly, purely theoretical approaches, stating general characteristics of 'experts', 'professionals' respectively 'knowledge workers' and corresponding management guidelines on the basis of literature reviewed and of personal experience, however, omitting any systematical empirical foundation (e.g. Horibe, 1999; Pfiffner & Stadelmann, 1999; Davenport, 2005).

Secondly, deductive approaches, testing particular hypotheses in regard of performance, motivation, identification or commitment of engineers, researchers, consultants, physicians or academics in a narrow business segment by usage of quantitative statistical methods and generalising the outcome as attributes of 'experts', 'professionals' resp. 'knowledge workers' on the whole (e.g. Wallace, 1995; Hron, 2000; Baldry et al., 2005).

Thirdly, inductive approaches, generating a theoretical framework for the management of engineers, researchers, consultants, physicians or academics in a narrow business segment by usage of qualitative methods and generalising the outcome as attributes of 'experts', 'professionals' resp. 'knowledge workers' (e.g. Alvesson, 1995; Keuken, 1996; Blackler, 1995).

The first type of studies can be regarded as insufficient in empirical foundation, the last two kinds as too narrow in scope for a generalisation for the management of experts, professionals respectively knowledge workers.

Furthermore, the different disciplines dealing with the same subject matter from different points of view, i.e. cognitive psychology, occupational sociology and knowledge management research, seem not to take much notice of one another (Mieg, 2000).

Hence, despite above-mentioned research results, we still lack certain knowledge on the meaning of knowledge workers' productivity in different industries and on the specific challenges involved in the management of knowledge workers' productivity.

These findings call for a cross-industrial empirical research, aiming at answering two questions:

1. What does 'performance' mean with respect to the notion of the knowledge worker?
2. Which challenges are involved in the management of knowledge workers' performance?

This chapter presents answers to these two questions, based on a cross-industrial empirical research carried out in five different organisations commonly regarded as 'expert', 'professional' or 'knowledge-intensive' organisations in previous treatises (Grossmann, Pellert & Gotwald, 1997; Alvesson, 2004; Davenport, 2005; Brinkley, 2006): a software development company, a hardware development company, a consulting company, a hospital and a university. In these organisations, 42 semi-structured episodic face-to-face interviews (Bortz & Döring, 2003; Lamnek, 2005; Yin, 2009) with experts and their managers from three hierarchical levels were conducted by the author. The data gathered by means of interviews were subsequently coded and interpreted with the aid of Atlas.ti, Version 5.5.4 (Figure 3).

In order to keep the results comparable, the focus of the study was not on the knowledge worker in general, but on that proportion of knowledge workers termed 'experts'. Davenport (2005) provides a useful classification for a differentiation between a specific class of experts and knowledge workers in general (Figure 4).

Following his approach, different types of knowledge workers differ in the way in which they transform knowledge into business value: by carrying out routine or complex tasks, by performing individual or collaborative work etc. (Davenport, 2005). The specific contribution of experts to business value consists in their capabil-

Figure 3. A cross-industrial research design on the productivity of knowledge workers

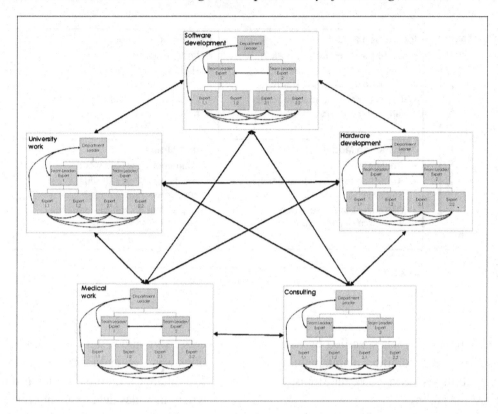

ity of professional discernment, i.e. in applying a comprehensive body of knowledge to individual and rather complex cases. This is the core feature in the work of engineers and consultants as well as of researchers, teachers and physicians.

Owing to confidentiality agreements with all participating organisations the results here presented have been described in an aggregated and abstracted manner. Hence, the original data cannot be disclosed, only referenced.

4 KNOWLEDGE WORKER PRODUCTIVITY REVISED

4.1 Concepts for Knowledge Worker Productivity

Since productivity in its traditional meaning of 'relation between quantity of output in relation to amount of input' (Gutenberg, 1958; Pedell, 1985), as other scholars have already noted, does not reflect any possible indicators for an expert's performance, the question raised by the study and posed to experts as well as to their line managers was: "What is performance in your respective type of expert work?" In this study, only those performance factors are referred to, which have been named by experts and their managers independently. Therefore, it can be concluded that these indicators are shared collectively within the respective organisation, that they may be regarded as collectively motivationally directive and, hence, part of the organisational culture (Sackmann, 1991; Sackmann, 2002).

For the software development company (Erne, 2009a), the predominant performance indicators were:

Figure 4. A classification structure for knowledge workers (Davenport, 2005, p.27)

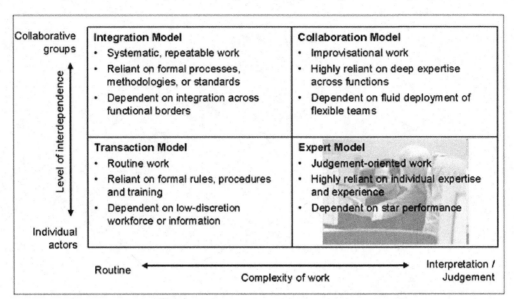

1. Good software, further specified by terms like correctness, stability, maintainability, expandability as well as clarity and transparency of the coding
2. Planning compliance, indicated by achievement of milestones and correctness of resource estimation.
3. Quality of interaction, perceived in the communication and cooperation behaviour of the software developers, in an appropriate broaching of topics towards different stakeholders as well as in the proactive communication of relevant topics to management representatives.
4. Innovation behaviour with respect to the products and processes of the organisation, measured by patent filings, integration of existing solutions, measures to reduce lead times and to detect software bugs earlier in the development process.
5. Personal skill development, which was basically regarded by management representatives to be the ability to move on to other topics according to business demand and development of comprehension for the entire software system beyond single functions was a crucial factor for the experts.
6. Compliance with organisational standards, which includes development processes deployed by the head office - despite criticism from experts as well as line managers - and project-specific agreements.

For the hardware development company (Erne, 2009b) we found a very similar picture:

1. Good hardware quality, which can be measured by static and dynamic hardware tests, by parts per million (PPM) failure rates in the operational area and, moreover, by conformance to specifications.
2. Planning compliance, which is represented by the indicators conformance to specifications, achievement of milestones, compliance with the planned development budget as well as the product target costs and the correctness of resource estimation for a development project.
3. Acquisition rate: Since hardware developers have direct contact to their customers,

the increase of hardware projects is viewed as another success factor of an hardware developers work.

4. Quality of interaction with the relevant stakeholders, which refers to communication and cooperation behaviour with all internal interfaces as well as with different customers, a low escalation rate within the organisation and the appropriate broaching of topics towards different stakeholders.

5. Innovation behaviour, which is indicated by the development of competitive solutions for the future in regard to critical topics, such as power dissipation concepts and electromagnetic compatibility.

6. Personal skill development, which refers to an enhancement in the appreciation of the whole circuit system beyond the particular task as well as to the development of know-how as to specific topics.

7. Compliance with organisational standards, which refers to the observance of development processes which control the cooperation of the different specialists in hardware development.

The experts and managers in the consulting company (Erne, 2009c) mentioned:

1. Accepted solutions and working solutions, which means, above all, functioning systems on the customers side, secondly, re-usable solutions and, thirdly, the number of critical situations.

2. Number of requests for a certain consultant, which is indicated, to describe it quite vividly, by "how often the phone rings" when a client tries to reach a certain consultant.

3. Acquisition rate in customer projects, which can be measured in turnover achieved by the end of the business year.

4. Quality of interaction with relevant stakeholders, which is represented by the quality in which a consultant broaches topics

within and outside of the organisation, by ones visibility within the business sector, by the creation of an image of being a trusted advisor for the customers, by the visibility within the organisation and the professional community as well as by cooperation and communication with customers and other stakeholders in general.

5. Innovation behaviour, which refers to the ability of the consultants to take up new topics on a yearly basis, like Green IT or Service-Oriented Architecture (SOA) which, in turn, can be used for public relations activities, customer projects, development projects and acquisition projects.

6. Number of parallel activities: Any consultant has to handle several activities in parallel, thereby reacting to requirements from within her/his organisation on the one hand and to market demands on the other hand.

7. Personal skill development with respect to the acquisition of knowledge required for actual projects at hand as well as to the acquisition of knowledge which is marketable to customers, colleagues and the expert community.

8. Compliance with organisational standards, which refers to an observance of conformity with common documentation standards, with defined methods as well as with general organisational administrative rules.

The doctors and chief physicians in the hospital (Erne, 2009d) stated the following performance factors:

1. Medical outcome, which can be measured by clinical indicators, like blood loss, mortality rates, post-operative complication rates on the one hand and by more subjective indicators, like patient condition and patient satisfaction, on the other hand.

2. Compliance with professional and organisational standards, which affects transparency

and tidiness when performing a surgery on the one hand as well as compliance with diagnostic and therapeutic methods proven in use.
3. Quality of interaction, which relates, again, to the proactive communication of newsworthy issues to the chief physician, and to the target-group related broaching of topics, e.g. the condition of a patient in ward meetings or the description of treatment and its outcomes in discharge letters.
4. Medical skill development is regarded as one of the crucial indicators for an individual's performance and is being ensured by various measures, such as regular trainings and conferences, individual discussion before and after surgery, personal feedback, joint ward rounds and the controlled delegation of responsibilities.
5. Innovation behaviour, which relates to the institutionalisation of interdisciplinary core areas within the hospital, such as the collaboration between surgeons and internists on certain kinds of cancer treatments, and to the establishment and financing of research activities.

The professors and deans of a university (Erne, 2009e) mentioned the following performance indicators:

1. Quality of research and lectures, which can be assessed by indicators like internationality and topicality of research projects and lectures, academic success of students, the organization of conferences as well as the number and rating of papers published.
2. Acquisition of resources rate, such as third-party funds or internal budgets for research projects, the number of research positions and, especially, professorships in a faculty or team and the attractiveness of an academic activity for scholars.

3. Quality of interaction with relevant stakeholders, in this case, the representation of a faculty or research team to other stakeholders, the ability to bring forth convincing arguments for the acquisition of resources as well as the ability to build up supporting networks within the university.
4. Innovation behaviour, which refers to all activities listed above in order to establish a focal centre of research on a certain topic.

In short: It is neither productivity in the traditional meaning of the term nor one of the different productivity concepts presented in chapter 2 which is regarded to be the key performance factor in the work of experts. Rather, five discrete key factors can be regarded to be the predominant performance indicators for expert work across all investigated business segments. Some of these performance indicators have already been mentioned in previous concepts (e.g. Ray & Sahu, 1989; Drucker, 1999), but never been brought forward as a coherent system based on cross-industrial empirical research.

With respect to the current projects or cases, these performance indicators are (marked in dark grey in Figure 5):

• Quantity and/or quality of daily work results, which differ widely between the different business segments.
• Quality of interaction, which relates to cooperation and communication with different stakeholders, to the quality of representation of specific topics within the respective organisation as well as to varying target groups and the way in which competence and professionalism towards different stakeholder groups are being displayed.
• Compliance with work standards, which can - depending on the individual organisation - be either of a professional kind (and, then, relating to professional methods) or of an organisational nature (and, then, relating to administrative standards).

Figure 5. Performance indicators for experts in different business segments

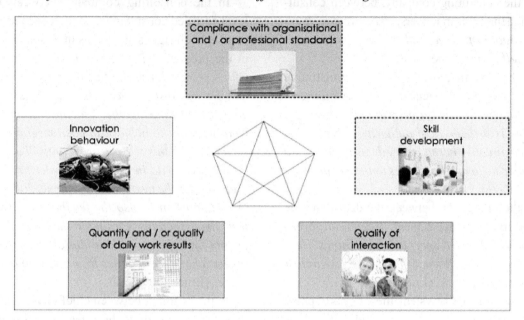

With regard to future developments, the named indicators are (marked in light grey in Figure 4):

- Innovation behaviour with respect to business or professional improvements, which is of varying importance to different individuals and in differing business segments, but has always been named as an important indicator together with the quality of day-to-day work.

- Skill development with respect to either the depths of skills, to the ability to arrive at an overview over a particular topic or to the adaptation of skills to new market demands.

4.2 Challenges in Rendering Knowledge Workers Productive

While performance indicators for experts are widely shared across different business segments - apart from a few exceptions not treated here in depth, differences with respect to the specific challenges faced when attempting to enhance performance in experts within and between organisations can be observed.

The differences observed can be roughly clustered into two strategy categories labelled as 'black box management', on the one hand, and 'white box management', on the other.

The 'black box management' strategy has been followed in all organisations studied. This strategy is best described by the original words of above-mentioned managers themselves:

In the software development company, between software developers and their department heads, *'You have to take care that you do not enter the space of these techies'* (Erne, 2009a, 115). *'Don't interfere'* (Erne, 2009a, 103).

At least partly in the hardware development organisation, between hardware developers and their line managers, *'As a manager I am not the best expert. I think, once, in the past, in this company, there existed the approach that the manager has to be the best hardware developer. Today, this is fortunately no longer required. Moreover, it would no longer be achievable'* (Erne, 2009b, 69).

In the consulting company, between consultants and their line managers, *'What we have here, in this organisation, are nothing but prima donnae. Don't tell them'* (Erne, 2009c, 93).

In the hospital, between the administrative director and the physicians, *'As an administration manager I have a decisional authority. .. But this is a theoretical authority. .. Since, if I issued a directive here, .. every department would demonstrate to me that it does not work this way'* (Erne, 2009d, 90).

In the university, between the deans and the professors in their department, *'A dean can govern a faculty […] with respect to budget topics. He is less able to take influence in issues of research or contents of research'* (Erne, 2009d, 55).

To sum up, in this system, there exists a sphere of professional work, on the one hand, and a sphere of business work, on the other hand, with some overlaps in the area of the definition and prioritisation of topics (not objectives) and in the sphere of performance appraisal. A system a consultant called 'governance' in contrast to 'management' (Erne, 2009c, 63).

The 'white box management' strategy was also identified in all organisations studied:

In the software development company, between software developers and their team leaders, *'The technical team leaders are responsible for controlling the code. .. A few people are reviewing the code, are reviewing the code together. Then, the code is checked with respect to maintainability'* (Erne, 2009a, 101).

In the hardware development organisation, between hardware developers and their group and team managers, *'That is what we expect from a manager, that when he is in a technical business that he does not simply act on an abstract level, but that he has a bit more comprehension of it. Otherwise, he is unable to assess if .. he has been told the truth or if things are going out of track since he cannot assess these things by himself. And that would be bad'* (Erne, 2009b, 93).

In the consulting company, between first-level certified consultants and their second-level certified colleagues as well as their stakeholders in the project, *'[...] Yes, as I worked together with a second-level certified colleague, this colleagues has just defined what meetings we are going to schedule together with the customer and what we want to achieve in each meeting. .. By structuring it this way, it turns out: Okay, what do we have to do in between in order to be well prepared for the next meeting.'* (Erne, 2009c, 71) *'[...] Important is also the feedback I get from, from the associates working in the same project, i.e. not from the consultant himself, but from the others /ehm/ .. colleagues from sales, in the first place'* (Erne, 2009c, 37).

In the hospital, between chief physicians and the doctors as well as the scientific community, *'I always tell my physicians: .. If I observe that one of you becomes sleazy, for example, in stitching up or anything else, .. I will tell them: Please take care that you do it properly. .. Since, if we do not do it properly, then our trainees do not see any necessity to do it properly either'* (Erne, 2009d, 93). *'Since, today, the tumor treatment is no longer unilateral, that means not only a matter of surgery or radiation therapy or internists, but rather an interplay of these three disciplines […], we regularly hold an interdisciplinary meeting on every case. In this meeting, the therapeutical path is being defined by consensus. Certainly, there are different opinions from time to time. Therefore, you have to take care to define it by consensus'* (Erne, 2009d, 77).

In the university, between professors and research assistants as well as the scientific community, *'I told my employee, the first I had hired, I told him: Okay, we are going to do a journal paper together. I have here the preliminary version which I have done. /Eh/ Make something of it. […] Then, we tried, in joint discussions, to make a journal paper. We were lucky that the first one was accepted. /Eh/ For him, this meant a great success. /Eh/ In the first place, for my employee, since he learned what you have to do here: How do I quote properly? How can I define a problem accurately? What are the objectives of my paper?'* (Erne, 2009e, 25). *'I want to experience the success. I think, when I do work in the field of differential equations, when I go to a conference, then I want, when I go to this conference, I want to deliver a great presentation for which I get the feedback: That is great what this guy has done. You see, that is, we want to play in the first league and be competitive on a global scale'* (Erne, 2009e, 33).

Dependent on the strategy employed in order to manage experts, the 'black box management' strategy as well as the 'white box management' strategy are confronted with some challenges which they have in common while two challenges are specific to the 'black box management' strategy. The common challenges are depicted in dark grey boxes in Figure 5 while the challenges which have been named independently of the management strategy are displayed in the light grey boxes (Figure 6).

A.   Assessment of Expert Performance

The first challenge which is typical for the 'black box management' strategy is the difficulty to assess expert performance: In contrast to manual work in which a physical result can be 'touched', compared and measured, it seems difficult to pin down the performance of experts for associates who do not belong to the professional sphere. In this respect, the statement of a business unit head from the software development organisation can be viewed as being paradigmatic for all other statements, *'We try to make the performance of our associates measurable. [...] But we are not in a timbering, we are in a high-technology business segment. [...] Therefore, we have to use auxiliary indicators'* (Erne, 2009c, 53). These auxiliary indicators are, *'positive feedback by two customers, 'peer recognition, .. which refers to the level of recognition a developer obtains from his team*

colleagues .., managers, team members' (Erne, 2009a, 49-53). In other words: For the qualitative part, the scope of performance indicators assessed by the supervisors comprises: quality of interaction, especially a convincing and visible representation of competence and performance to important stakeholders (Pfadenhauer, 2003a; 2003b), visible activities in the field of product and process innovations, and compliance with organisational standards. This observation clarifies why especially these performance indicators are applied by managers of the 'black box management' system, i.e. the line managers of the software and consulting company, the administrative director of the hospital as well as the deans of the university faculties. The following reasons for the challenge of assessing experts' performance have been named: the number of possible indicators, as presented in the previous chapter, the number of independent variables which influence the result of a surgery, of a development result, of a conference or a customer decision, the long time frame during which feedback is available on the results of an expert's action in development or medical work, and the physical and/or intellectual distance a 'black box manager' has to the professional sphere.

B.   Autonomy of Experts

Strongly linked with the difficulty of assessing the performance of experts adequately is the challenge of governing highly autonomous experts. This autonomy can equally be observed in the 'black box management' system where the software developers, consultants, hardware developers, physicians and professors form a kind of an enclosed group in a professional sphere which is clearly distinct from the sphere of administration. This has been clearly stated by a faculty dean, a statement which can be viewed as being exemplary for all other cases, 'In a nutshell, our lecturers are pure 'sole member companies'. ... They perceive me as an administrator. That means, if they need

Figure 6. Challenges in rendering experts productive

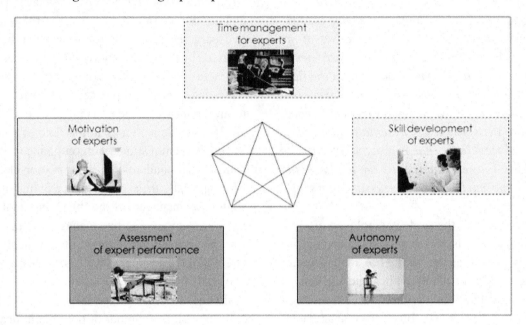

anything, they prefer to come to me, but apart from this case, they want to be left alone. In this perspective, they are a pure *'sole member company' without liability, certainly. A small company, but without liabiliy'* (Erne, 2009e, 59). This mainly applies to the case when administrative tasks are to be performed by experts, as reported by the administrative director of the hospital (Erne, 2009d), the managers of the software company (Erne, 2009a) and the consultants in the consultancy company (Erne, 2009c). As reasons for this challenge, a lack of incentive measures in some organisations (such as the university), the dependency of 'black box managers' on the commitment, cooperation and communication of their experts in order to achieve results and the role behaviour of experts as experts in knowledge-intensive businesses were mentioned.

C. Skill Development in Experts

The skill development of experts has been perceived as a third challenge imposed on the management of experts. This challenge has been broached in three different directions: From the strategic point of view of the department heads, the main challenge is the direction in which the skills of their experts should be developed according to business strategy. The central challenge in the management of experts is, as the department head of the consulting company stated, *'that we recognise in time where the train is heading to and /eh/ that we, consequently, take the right measures in order to guide the associates to the right direction with respect to /eh/ behaviour and mindset as well as skills and technologies. That is /eh/ the biggest challenge'* (Erne, 2009c, 133). Another perspective is being taken by the department heads following the 'black box management' strategy: Here, the focus is clearly on the development of 'soft skills' such as self-presentation and communication, especially for engineers showing a certain degree of 'autism', as was stated by Guenther Dueck (2007) and referred to by some software managers and engineers (Erne, 2009a). A third way in which the skill development of experts has been approached is the formation of professional skills, especially true for 'white box management' systems. In these systems, quality assurance of professional work as well as enhancement of productivity seems to be dependent on one variable: the professional skill of the expert. Hence, everything is focussed on the formation of these skills. In hospital work, for example, this is done by direct instructions, ward rounds, conferences, case studies, coaching, feedback and regular on the job training (Erne, 2009d). Therefore, the challenge of skill development is being viewed differently, but in every perspective as being a crucial one.

D. Motivation of Experts

As a fourth challenge, the interviewees in the different business segments have named the motivation of experts. Similar to skill development, the challenge to motivate experts is elicited by different reasons. A first reason is to retain 'valuable assets' into which extensive endeavours in education have been invested, as especially the software managers, hardware managers and physicians stated (Erne 2009a; Erne 2009b; Erne 2009d), *'I have recently lost my three best surgeons, .. they have been trained to the highest standard, all of them have done more than five thousand surgeries, .. they went to a private clinic. .. Three surgeons. For twelve years, they have been trained here. ... And endowed with five thousand surgeries, and many, many congresses, .. they simply left'* (Erne, 2009d, 267). A second perspective on the motivation topic is the motivation for the accomplishment of specific tasks such as the acquisition of another consultancy project by the end of a year, *'Here we have alternative .. governance measures with respect to remuneration. We are on an, .. on an incentive plan. That means, seventy percentage of our, our .. income is fixed, the rest is variable. In this variable segment, I can identify, selectively, .. small challenges. That are challenges .. I say: Man, .. give it all. If we get that opportunity in the third quarter, then that will make .. a thousand Euros extra for you'* (Erne,

2009c, 061). In contrast to the thesis that payment does not motivate knowledge workers (North & Gueldenberg, 2008), payment for specific tasks is being regarded as being a very effective instrument in motivating experts to undertake specific efforts (Erne, 2009c). A lack of incentives is also being viewed by the deans and professors of the university as one reason why it is so difficult in this organisation to motivate highly autonomous lecturers (Erne, 2009e). Another important factor in keeping experts motivated is the job content, the opportunity of skill development and a sound balance between regulations and autonomy – a balance, however, which could not really be specified in detail by anybody.

E. Time Management for Experts

The fifth specific challenge for rendering experts productive has been named completely independently of the management strategy and the business segment: the aligning of the tasks which an expert has to accomplish with the time disposable. This challenge had been already found by Peter Drucker who emphasised the necessity to organize one's own job, in contrast to the Tayloristic system in which the job organises the employee (Drucker, 1999). The findings of the study, however, do not bring to light many improvements on the individual, team or organisational level. Therefore, one of the main challenges the software engineers perceived was, that, when *'different tasks have to be done at the same time .. /ehm/ .. generating the right ideas on what has to be done in the first place'* (Erne, 2009a, 071). For the hardware developers the biggest challenges are *'the moving targets. Not only internal targets, but the targets which come from outside and punch through everything'* (Erne, 2009b, 047). Similarly, consultants *'permanently work in several streams in parallel. It is not the case that they are faced with one task which they accomplish and, then, they get the next task. But this company, unfortunately, works in the way that unbelievably many work streams are scattered over the day, the week or the month'* (Erne, 2009c, 059). The same is stated by the physicians, *'What imposes the greatest stress on me .. is the acute day ward, since it is permanently crowded. When I want to go and make the ward round, .. you do not get away from it. Yet, I have my plan. When I am on duty, I want to start the ward round at 3 p.m. or 3:30 p.m., in this timeframe, .. that means to look after the in-patients. But this heteronomously directed work, it, it .. annoys me'* (Erne, 2009d, 095). And, finally, the university professors, *'I believe, .. the challenge is to organise one's week in a way not to be diverted by all the different topics'* (Erne, 2009e, 105). Hence, the term 'time management' comprises a couple of different, yet strongly linked challenges: the workload in general and the administrative workload in particular, the parallelity of many topics, multiple stakeholders, task switching and the amount and correctness of input information. With respect to these topics, the perception of the interviewees is that these issues have to be solved on an individual level, not on a team or organisational level.

With the outline of the performance indicators and the challenges named by managers and experts in different business segments and presented in this chapter a scope definition can be outlined of how to enhance productiveness in knowledge workers which goes beyond the scope definition proposed to this day.

5 IMPLICATIONS FOR MANAGING EXPERT PERFORMANCE

The main topics which require further research on the question of how to render experts productive are, according to the study in different business segments here presented, the following:

A. Define Clear Performance Indicators for Expert Work

The study showed clearly that performance indicators for expert work as well as for the stakeholders who are assessing these indicators are multiple and ambiguous. Management systems such as management by objectives, which are in place in all organisations studied, do not solve the problem, but rather exacerbate it. Therefore, the first strategy for rendering experts productive is to establish few, clear, business-specific performance indicators which do not necessarily have to be measured, but which can be assessed according to defined indicators. This practice was followed in the 'white box management' systems, especially in hospital work, *'[With respect to the performance indicators] there is no doubt for me: .. There are two indicators: the first is the medical assessment of the output. This can be measured by objective parameters. […] The second one is, of course, […] the subjective appraisal by the patient if he is content with the performance'* (Erne, 2009d, 47-51).

B. Establish Knowledge Symmetry

In the black box management systems, it became very clear that a stakeholder like a line manager only can gain influence on the performance of experts if he or she is able to compensate for the knowledge asymmetry on a professional level. As the department head of the consulatants stated, *, I have one advantage over the consultants: I work /ehm/ .. /ehm/ on a higher level and know, know some specific details in different, .. different knowledge areas, which they do not know. Yet, they would like to know these details very much, especially if they are related to political discussions. And they use this'* (Erne, 2009c, 121). In this way or in other ways, a line manager has to provide value-adding knowledge or service to the experts, which makes the relationship between the two interdependent and symmetrical. Otherwise, it is nearly impossible to gain influence on an expert's work.

C. Develop Strategies and Measures for Skill Development

The importance which has been assigned to strategic and operative skill development in nearly all organisations studied is in contrast to actual strategies and measures in place. Most interviewees named personal preferences for a skill development, but did so rather randomly and focussed on professional skills in the 'white box management' system. Since the quality and performance of expert work are strongly linked to individual skills – much more so than in manual work -, there have to be additional and new ideas of how to integrate skill development into day-to-day work. In the technical spheres of hardware development, one can find good examples for corresponding measures, *'For this reason I have .. agreed in my team meetings, that we, /ehm/ .. that they, the associates who have all their specific knowledge domain, .. report regularly what they do at the moment, which technical approaches they follow, […] so that they arrive at an understanding of the whole system and not only on that of their own [module]'* (Erne, 2009b, 037). The examples in hospital work have already been depicted in the previous chapter.

D. Find Appropriate Measures for the Motivation of Experts

As the results of the study have shown, the topic of motivation as well as the measures to produce and enhance motivation have to be assessed differently: There is a general task of retaining experts, as Drucker (2009, p.142) stated, as 'assets'. This is being viewed by experts and managers as an issue of payment, balance of regulations and autonomy, work content and the opportunity to

learn. In other words: It is a topic of remuneration and job design, and in contrast to the statements in a broad corpus of literature which only focuses on the last two parameters. A second topic is the motivation for certain tasks by incentives. Here the incentives have not been defined apart from financial ones. In university work professors and deans heavily focussed on another incentive, *'the possibility to gain reputation'* (Erne, 2009d, 61). The different kinds of incentives and their effectivity on different kinds of experts have not been fully explored.

E. Keep Experts Focused

As stated by all interviewees in all business segments, the most common challenge for rendering experts productive is an appropriate handling of the workload in general and the administrative workload in particular as well as multitasking, task switching and, equally, a proper information handling. Since the effects of these working modes have been well explored, it can be viewed as one of the great risks to the productivity of experts, approximately accounting for a 20% to 40% loss in productivity (Rubinstein, Meyer & Evans 2001; Monsell 2003; Spira & Feintuch 2005). Furthermore, it may not be solely solved on an individual level by finding an appropriate personal working mode, as the interviewees have perceived. Since it is a common feature across all business segments, which results, according to the interviewees, in a bulk of uncontrolled tasks building up, one of the management challenges will be to find ways to reduce these 'task cascades', to design jobs and to assign tasks in a way in which all challenges can be addressed: focussing expert work, motivating it, making skill development in the workplace possible, creating a balance between regulations and autonomy and, thus, making expert performance assessable. According to our study, these are the tasks for rendering experts productive.

REFERENCES

Abbott, A. (1988). *The system of professions: An essay on the division of expert labor.* Chicago, IL: University of Chicago Press.

Ahn, J. H., & Chang, S. G. (2004). Assessing the contribution of knowledge to business performance: The KP3 methodology. *Decision Support Systems, 36*(4), 403–416. doi:10.1016/S0167-9236(03)00029-0

Alvesson, M. (1995). *Management of knowledge intensive companies.* Berlin, Germany: De Gruyter.

Alvesson, M. (2004). *Knowledge work and knowledge-intensive firms.* Oxford, UK: University Press.

Amar, A. D. (2002). *Managing knowledge workers: Unleashing innovation and productivity.* Westport, CT: Quorum.

Balazova, M. (2004). *Methode zur Leistungsbewertung und Leistungssteigerung in der Mechatronikentwicklung.* Unveröffentlichte Dissertation, Universität Paderborn.

Baldry, C., et al. (2005). *Knowledge workers, commitment and occupational community.* Paper presented at the International Labour Process Conference 2005, Glasgow.

Baldwin, J. R., & Beckstead, D. (2003). *Knowledge workers in Canada's economy, 1971-2001. Statistics Canada Analytical Paper.* Ottawa, Canada: Statistics Canada.

Beckstead, D., & Gellatly, G. (2004). *Are knowledge workers found only in high-technology industries? Statistics Canada Analytical Paper.* Ottawa, Canada: Statistics Canada.

Blackler, F. (1995). Knowledge, knowledge work and organizations: An overview and interpretation. *Organization Studies, 16*(6), 1021–1046. doi:10.1177/017084069501600605

Bortz, J., & Döring, N. (2003). *Forschungsmethoden und Evaluation für Human- und Sozialwissenschaftler, 3 überarb Aufl.* Berlin, Germany: Springer.

Boshuizen, H. P. A., & Schmidt, H. G. (1992). On the role of biomedical knowledge in clinical reasoning by experts, intermediates and novices. *Cognitive Science, 16,* 153–184. doi:10.1207/s15516709cog1602_1

Bredl, K. (2005). *Kompetenz von Beratern: Analyse des Kompetenzerwerbs bei Unternehmensberatern im Kontext der Expertiseforschung.* Unveröffentlichte Dissertation, Universität Regensburg.

Brinkley, I. (2006). *Defining the knowledge economy: Knowledge economy programme report.* Research Paper. London, UK: The Work Foundation.

Byrne, J. A., & Gerdes, L. (2005, November 28). The man who invented management: why Peter Drucker's ideas still matter. *Businessweek.* Retrieved 13 October, 2009, from http://www.businessweek.com /magazine/content/05_48/b3961001.htm

Chi, M. T. H. (2006). Two approaches to the study of experts' characteristics . In Ericsson, K. A. (Eds.), *The Cambridge handbook of expertise and expert performance* (pp. 24–27). Cambridge, MA: University Press.

Chi, M. T. H. (1981). Categorization and representation of physics problems by experts and novices. *Cognitive Science, 5,* 121–152. doi:10.1207/s15516709cog0502_2

Davenport, T. H. (2005). *Thinking for a living: How to get better performance and results from knowledge workers.* Boston, MA: Harvard Business School Press.

Davenport, T. H., Thomas, R. J., & Cantrell, S. (2002). The mysterious art and science of knowledge-worker performance. *Sloan Management Review, 44*(1), 23–30.

Dörhöfer, S. (2010). *Management und Organisation von Wissensarbeit: Strategie, Arbeitssystem und organisationale Praktiken in wissensbasierten Unternehmen.* Wiesbaden, Germany: VS Verlag für Sozialwissenschaften.

Dostal, W. (2001). *Neue Herausforderungen an Qualifikation und Weiterbildung im Zeitalter der Globalisierung.* Berlin, Germany: Deutscher Bundestag.

Dostal, W., & Reinberg, A. (1999). *Arbeitslandschaft 2010. Teil 2: Ungebrochener Trend in die Wissensgesellschaft. IAB-Kurzbericht, Nr.10.* Nürnberg, Germany: Institut für Arbeitsmarkt- und Berufsforschung.

Drucker, P. F. (1969). *The age of discontinuity: guidelines to our changing society.* New York, NY: Harper & Row.

Drucker, P. F. (1991). The new productivity challenge. *Harvard Business Review, 69*(6), 69–79.

Drucker, P. F. (1999). *Management challenges for the 21st century.* New York, NY: Harper.

Dueck, G. (2007). *Dueck's panopticon: Gesammelte Kultkolumnen.* Berlin, Germany: Springer.

Erne, R. (2009a). *Interview transcripts F&E_SW: Data analysis in Atlas.ti V.5.6.3.* Unpublished Manuscript, Stuttgart.

Erne, R. (2009b). *Interview transcripts F&E_PE: Data analysis in Atlas.ti V.5.6.3.* Unpublished Manuscript, Stuttgart.

Erne, R. (2009c). *Interview transcripts consulting. Data analysis in Atlas.ti V.5.6.3.* Unpublished Manuscript. Stuttgart.

Erne, R. (2009d). *Interview transcripts Medizinische Versorgung KH: Data analysis in Atlas.ti V.5.6.3.* Unpublished Manuscript, Stuttgart.

Erne, R. (2009e). *Interview transcripts Forschung & Lehre Univ.: Data Analysis in Atlas.ti V.5.6.3.* Unpublished Manuscript, Stuttgart.

Feltovich, P. J. (2006). Studies of expertise from psychological perspectives. In Ericsson, K. A. (Eds.), *The Cambridge handbook of expertise and expert performance* (pp. 41–67). Cambridge, MA: University Press.

Garmus, D., & Herron, D. (2000). *Function point analysis: Measurement practices for successful software projects.* Upper Saddle River, NJ: Addison-Weslay.

Grossmann, R., Pellert, A., & Gotwald, V. (1997). Krankenhaus, Schule, Universität: Charakteristika und Optimierungspotentiale. In R. Grossmann, R. (Eds.), *Besser Billiger Mehr: Zur Reform der Expertenorganisation Krankenhaus, Schule, Universität* (pp. 24-35). Wien, Germany: Springer.

Gruber, H., & Ziegler, A. (1996). Expertise als Domäne psychologischer Forschung. In H. Gruber & A. Ziegler (Hrsg.), *Expertiseforschung: Theoretische und methodische Grundlagen* (pp. 7-16). Opladen: Westdeutscher Verlag.

Gutenberg, E. (1958). *Einführung in die Betriebswirtschaftslehre.* Wiesbaden, Germany: Gabler.

Hasler Roumois, U. (2007). *Studienbuch Wissensmanagement: Grundlagen der Wissensarbeit in Wirtschafts-, Non- Profit- und Public- Organisationen.* Zürich, Switzerland: Orell-Füssli.

Hauber, R. (2002). *Performance Measurement in der Forschung und Entwicklung: Konzeption und Methodik.* Wiesbaden, Germany: Deutscher Universitäts Verlag.

Herman, S. (2004). Produktive Wissensarbeit: Eine Herausforderung. In Hermann, S. (Ed.), *Ressourcen strategisch nutzen: Wissen als Basis für den Dienstleistungserfolg* (pp. 207–228). Stuttgart, Germany: Fraunhofer IRB-Verlag.

Hesse, H.-A. (1998). *Experte, Laie, Dilettant: Über Nutzen und Grenzen von Fachwissen.* Opladen, Germany: Westdeutscher Verlag.

Hitzler, R. (1998). Reflexive Kompetenz: Zur Genese und Bedeutung von Expertenwissen jenseits des Professionalismus. In W. K. Schulz (Ed.), *Expertenwissen: Soziologische, psychologische und pädagogische Perspektiven* (pp. 33-47). Opladen, Germany: Leske + Budrich.

Horibe, F. (1999). *Managing knowledge workers: New skills and attitudes to unlock the intellectual capital in your organization.* Toronto, Canada: John Wiley.

Hron, J. (2000). *Motivationale Aspekte von beruflicher Expertise: Welche Ziele und Motive spornen Experten im Rahmen ihrer Arbeit an?* München, Germany: Utz.

Hube, G. (2005). *Beitrag zur Beschreibung und Analyse von Wissensarbeit.* Unveröffentlichte Dissertation, Universität Stuttgart.

Huber, B. (1999). Experts in organizations: The power of expertise. In Academy of Business & Administrative Sciences (Ed.), *Globalization and Emerging Economies: International Conference Proceedings,* July 12-14, 1999, Barcelona, Spain. Retrieved December 12, 2009, from http://www.sba.muohio.edu /abas/1999/huberbe.pdf

Keuken, F. W. (1996). *Management von Akademikerorganisationen.* Hamburg, Germany: Kovac.

Kleinert, J. (2000). *Globalisierung, Strukturwandel und Beschäftigung.* Tübingen, Germany: Mohr Siebeck.

Krems, J. (1990). *Zur Psychologie der Expertenschaft.* Unveröffentlichte Habilitation, Universität Regensburg.

Lamnek, S. (2005). *Qualitative Sozialforschung: Lehrbuch.* Weinheim, Germany: Beltz.

Larkin, J. (1980). Expert and novice performance in solving physics problems. *Science, 208,* 1335–1342. doi:10.1126/science.208.4450.1335

Larson, M. S. (1977). *The rise of professionalism: A sociological analysis.* Berkeley, CA: University of California Press.

Levy, F., & Murnane, R. J. (2006). *How computerized work and globalization shape human skill demands.* MIT IPC Working Paper, 05-006. Retrieved January 09, 2007, from http://web.mit.edu /ipc/publications/ pdf/05-006.pdf

Malik, F. (2006). *Führen, leisten, leben: Wirksames Management für eine neue Zeit. Komplett überarb. Neuaufl.* Frankfurt, Germany: Campus.

Mieg, H. A. (2000). Vom ziemlichen Unvermögen der Psychologie, das Tun der Experten zu begreifen: Ein Plädoyer für Professionalisierung als psychologische Kategorie und einen interaktionsorientierten Expertenbegriff. In Silbereisen, R. K., & Reitzlem, M. (Eds.), *Bericht über den 42. Kongress der Deutschen Gesellschaft für Psychologie 2000* (pp. 635–648). Lengerich, Germany: Pabst.

Mieg, H. A. (2001). *The social psychology of expertise: Case studies in research, professional domains, and expert roles.* Mahwah, NJ: Lawrence Erlbaum.

Millerson, G. (1964). *The qualifying associations: A study in professionalization.* London, UK: Routledge & Kegan Paul.

Monsell, S. (2003). Task switching. *Trends in Cognitive Sciences, 7*(3), 134–140. doi:10.1016/S1364-6613(03)00028-7

Newell, S. (2002). *Managing knowledge work.* Houndmills, UK: Palgrave Macmillan.

Nonaka, I., & Takeuchi, H. (1995). *The knowledge-creating company: How Japanese companies create the dynamics of innovation.* New York, NY: Oxford University Press.

North, K. (1999). *Wissensorientierte Unternehmensführung: Wertschöpfung durch Wissen. 2.* Wiesbaden, Germany: Gabler.

North, K., & Gueldenberg, S. (2008). *Produktive Wissensarbeit(er): Antworten auf die Management-Herausforderung des 21. Jahrhunderts.* Wiesbaden, Germany: Gabler.

OECD. (2006a). *OECD employment outlook. 2006 edition: Boosting jobs and incomes.* Paris, France: Organisation for Economic Co-operation and Development.

OECD. (2006b). *Education at a glance, OECD indicators 2006, indicator A8: Labour force participation by level of educational attainment.* Paris, France: Organisation for Economic Co-operation and Development. Retrieved January 7, 2007, from http://www.oecd.org /document/6/ 0,2340,en_2649_34515_37344774_1_1_1_1,00

Paradi, J. C., Smith, S., & Schaffnit-Chatterjee, C. (2002). Knowledge worker performance analysis using DEA: an application to engineering design teams at Bell Canada. *IEEE Transactions on Engineering Management, 49*(2), 161. doi:10.1109/ TEM.2002.1010884

Parsons, T. (1939). The professions and social structure. *Social Forces, 17*(4), 457–467. doi:10.2307/2570695

Patel, V. L., & Groen, G. J. (1991). The general and specific nature of medical expertise: A critical look. In Ericsson, K. A., & Smith, J. (Eds.), *Towards a general theory of expertise: Prospects and limits* (pp. 93–125). Cambridge, MA: University Press.

Pedell, K. L. (1985). Analyse und Planung von Produktivitätsveränderungen. *Zeitschrift für betriebswirtschaftliche. Forschung, 37*(12), 1078–1097.

Pfadenhauer, M. (2003a). *Professionalität: Eine wissenssoziologische Rekonstruktion institutionalisierter Kompetenzdarstellungskompetenz.* Opladen, Germany: Leske & Budrich.

Pfadenhauer, M. (2003b). Macht – Funktion – Leistung: Zur Korrespondenz von Eliten und Professionstheorien. In Mieg, H. A., & Pfadenhauer, M. (Eds.), *Professionelle Leistung – Professional Performance: Positionen der Professionssoziologie* (pp. 71–87). Konstanz, Germany: UVK.

Pfiffner, M., & Stadelmann, P. (1999). *Wissen wirksam machen: Wie Kopfarbeiter produktiv werden. 2. unveränd.* Bern, Switzerland: Haupt.

Posner, M. I. (1988). Introduction: What is it to be an expert? In Chi, M. T. H., Glaser, R., & Rees, M. J. (Eds.), *The nature of expertise* (pp. xxix–xxxvi). Hillsdale, NJ: Erlbaum.

Probst, G., Raub, S., & Romhardt, K. (2010). *Wissen managen: Wie Unternehmen ihre wertvollste Ressource optimal nutzen.* Wiesbaden, Germany: Gabler.

Ramirez, Y. W., & Nembhard, D. A. (2004). Measuring knowledge worker productivity: A taxonomy. *Journal of Intellectual Capital, 5*(4), 602–628. doi:10.1108/14691930410567040

Ray, P. K., & Sahu, S. (1989). The measurement and evaluation of white-collar productivity. *International Journal of Operations & Production Management, 9*(4), 28–47. doi:10.1108/ EUM0000000001235

Reinberg, A., & Hummel, M. (2002). Zur langfristigen Entwicklung des qualifikationsspezifischen Arbeitskräfteangebots und –bedarfs in Deutschland: Empirische Befunde und aktuelle Projektionsergebnisse. *Mitteilungen aus der Arbeitsmarkt- und Berufsforschung, 35*(4), 580–600.

Reinberg, A., & Hummel, M. (2005). *Höhere Bildung schützt auch in der Krise vor Arbeitslosigkeit. IAB-Kurzbericht Nr. 9*. Nürnberg, Germany: Institut für Arbeitsmarkt- und Berufsforschung.

Rubinstein, J. S., Meyer, D. E., & Evans, J. E. (2001). Executive control of cognitive processes in task switching. *Journal of Experimental Psychology. Human Perception and Performance, 27*(4), 763–797. doi:10.1037/0096-1523.27.4.763

Sackmann, S. A. (1991). *Cultural knowledge in organizations: Exploring the collective mind.* Newsbury Park, CA: Sage.

Sackmann, S. A. (2002). *Unternehmenskultur: Erkennen – Entwickeln – Verändern.* Neuwied, Germany: Luchterhand.

Sonnentag, S. (1996). *Experten in der Software-Entwicklung: Untersuchung hervorragender Leistungen im Kontext intellektueller Teamarbeit.* Unveröffentliche Habilitation, Universität Gießen.

Spira, J. B., & Feintuch, J. B. (2005). *The cost of not paying attention: How interruption impacts knowledge worker productivity.* New York, NY: Basex.

Stam, C. (2007). *Knowledge productivity: Designing and testing a method to diagnose knowledge productivity and plan for enhancement.* Unpublished Ph.D. thesis, Universiteit Twente.

Suff, P., & Reilly, P. (2005). *In the know: Reward and performance management of knowledge workers. HR Network Paper, MP47.* Brighton: Institute for Employment Studies.

Sumanth, D. J., Omachonu, V. K., & Beruvides, M. G. (1990). A review of the state-of-the-art research on white collar / knowledge-worker productivity. *International Journal of Technology Management, 5*(3), 337–355.

Sveiby, K. E. (1998). *Wissenskapital – das unentdeckte Vermögen: Immaterielle Unternehmenswerte aufspüren, messen und steigern.* Landsberg, Germany: Moderne Industrie.

Sweller, J. (1983). Development of expertise in mathematical problem solving. *Journal of Experimental Psychology. General, 112*, 639–661. doi:10.1037/0096-3445.112.4.639

UK National Statistics. (2000). *Standard occupational classification 2000 (SOC 2000): Summary of structure.* London, UK National Statistics. Retrieved January 9, 2007, from www.statistics. gov.uk /methods_quality/ns_sec/ downloads/ SOC2000.doc

UK National Statistics. (2006). *All in employment by socio-economic classification (NS-SEC) (Not seasonally adjusted.* London, UK National Statistics. Retrieved August 20, 2008, from http:// www.statistics.gov.uk /STATBASE/ ssdataset. asp?vlnk=7919 US Department of Labor. (2006). *Occupational outlook handbook.* Washington, DC: Bureau of Labor. Retrieved January 09, 2007, from http://www.bls.gov / oco/home.htm

Wallace, J. E. (1995). Organizational and professional commitment in professional and nonprofessional organizations. *Administrative Science Quarterly, 40*(2), 228–255. doi:10.2307/2393637

Weidig, I. (1999). *Arbeitslandschaft 2010 nach Tätigkeiten und Tätigkeitsniveau. Beiträge zur Arbeitsmarkt- und Berufsforschung, Nr. 227.* Nürnberg, Germany: Institut für Arbeitsmarkt- und Berufsforschung.

Willke, H. (2001). *Systemisches Wissensmanagement. 2. neu bearb.* Stuttgart, Germany: UTB.

Yin, R. K. (2009). *Case study research: Design and methods* (4th ed.). Thousand Oaks, CA: Sage.

ADDITIONAL READING

Antikainen, R., & Lönnqvist, A. (2005). *Knowledge worker productivity assessment*. White Paper. Tampere, Tampere University of Technology. Retrieved March 19, 2010, from http://butler.cc.tut.fi /~mettanen/KWPA-Antikainen-Lonnqvist.pdf

Argyris, C. (1957). *Personality and organization: The conflict between system and the individual.* New York, NY: Harper Collins.

Ashton, R. H., & Ashton, A. H. (1995). Perspectives on judgement and decision making research in accounting and auditing. In *Judgment and decision-making research in accounting and auditing* (pp. 3–28). Cambridge, MA: Cambridge University Press. doi:10.1017/CBO9780511720420.003

Bailyn, L. (1988). Autonomy in the industrial R&D lab. In Katz, R. (Ed.), *Managing professionals in innovative organizations: A collection of readings* (pp. 223–236). New York, NY: Ballinger. doi:10.1002/hrm.3930240204

Barfield, W. (1997). Skilled performance on software as a function of domain-expertise and program organization. *Perceptual and Motor Skills*, *85*(3), 1471–1480. doi:10.2466/pms.1997.85.3f.1471

Benson, J., & Brown, M. (2007). Knowledge workers: What keeps them committed; what turns them away. *Work, Employment and Society*, *21*(1), 121–141. doi:10.1177/0950017007073623

Bosch-Sijtsema, P. M., Ruohomäki, V., & Vartiainen, M. (2009). Knowledge work productivity in distributed teams. *Journal of Knowledge Management*, *13*(6), 533–546. doi:10.1108/13673270910997178

Bucher, R., & Stelling, J. (1969). Characteristics of professional organizations. *Journal of Health and Social Behavior*, *10*(1), 3–15. doi:10.2307/2948501

Chang, L., & Birkett, B. (2004). Managing intellectual capital in a professional service firm: Exploring the creativity-productivity paradox. *Management Accounting Research*, *15*(1), 7–31. doi:10.1016/j.mar.2003.10.004

Charnes, A., Cooper, W., Lewin, A., & Seiford, L. (1994). *Data envelopment analysis: Theory, methodology and application*. Boston, MA: Kluwer Academic Publishers.

Charnes, A., Cooper, W., & Rhodes, E. (1978). Measuring the efficiency of decision-making units. *European Journal of Operational Research*, *2*(6), 429–444. doi:10.1016/0377-2217(78)90138-8

Christopher, W. F. (1984) How to measure and improve the productivity in professional, administrative, and service organizations. In Institute of Industrial Engineers (Ed.), *Issues in White Collar Productivity: Proceedings of the Institute of Industrial Engineers Annual Conference 1984* (pp. 29-37). Norcross, GA: Industrial Engineering and Management Press.

Clark, T. (1995). *Managing consultants: Consultancy as the management of impressions*. Milton Keynes, UK: Open University Press.

Coad, A. F. (1999). Some survey evidence on the learning and performance orientations of management accountants. *Management Accounting Research*, *10*(2), 109–135. doi:10.1006/mare.1998.0083

Coates, J. (1986). Three models for white collar productivity improvement. *Industrial Management (Des Plaines)*, *28*(2), 7–14.

Cortada, J. W. (1998). Where did the knowledge workers come from? In Cortada, J. W. (Ed.), *Rise of the knowledge worker: Resources for the knowledge-based economy* (pp. 3–21). Boston, MA: Butterworth-Heinemann. doi:10.1016/B978-0-7506-7058-6.50005-3

Davenport, T. H. (2002). Making knowledge work productive and effective. *Knowledge Management, 6*(3), 20–23.

Davis, T. (1991). Information technology and white-collar productivity. *The Academy of Management Executive, 5*(1), 55–68.

De Marco, T., & Lister, T. (1999). *Peopleware: Productive projects and teams*, 2nd ed. New York, NY: Dorset.

Ericsson, K. A., & Charness, N. (1994). Expert performance: Its structure and acquisition. *The American Psychologist, 49*(8), 725–747. doi:10.1037/0003-066X.49.8.725

Eschenbach, S., Riedl, D., & Schauer, B. (2006). Knowledge work productivity: Where to start. In Reimer, U., & Karagiannis, D. (Eds.), *Practical Aspects of Knowledge Management* (*Vol. 4333*, pp. 49–60). Lecture Notes in Computer Science Berlin, Germany: Springer. doi:10.1007/11944935_5

Eschenbach, S., & Schauer, B. (2008). More productive knowledge work: A report on a systems theory based approach to identify options for higher knowledge work productivity and its applications in business and public management. In K. Tochtermann, et al. (Eds.) *I-Know '08 and I-Media '08: International Conferences on Knowledge Management and New Media Technology, Conference Proceedings* (pp. 68-75). Graz, Austria: Verlag der Technischen Universität.

Geoff, N. (2006). Expertise in medicine and surgery. In Ericsson, K. A., Charness, N., Feltovich, P. J., & Hoffmann, R. R. (Eds.), *The Cambridge handbook of expertise and expert performance* (pp. 339–353). Cambridge, MA: University Press.

Greenwood, R., Li, S. X., Prakash, R., & Deephouse, D. L. (2005). Reputation, diversification, and organizational explanations of performance in professional service firms. *Organization Science, 16*(6), 661–673. doi:10.1287/orsc.1050.0159

Groysberg, B., & Ashish, N. (2008). Can they take it with them?: The portability of star knowledge workers' performance. *Management Science, 54*(7), 1213–1230. doi:10.1287/mnsc.1070.0809

Jauch, L. R., Glueck, W. F., & Osborn, R. N. (1978). Organizational loyalty, professional commitment, and academic research productivity. *Academy of Management Journal, 21*(1), 84–92. doi:10.2307/255664

Jones, E. C., & Chang, C. A. (2006). A methodology for measuring engineering knowledge worker productivity. *Engineering Management Review IEEE, 34*(3), 71–72. doi:10.1109/EMR.2006.261383

Joseph, R. (2005). The knowledge worker: A metaphor in search of a meaning? In Rooney, D., Hearn, G., & Ninan, A. (Eds.), *Handbook on the knowledge economy* (pp. 245–254). Cheltenham, PA: Edward Elgar Publishing.

Klassen, K. J., Russell, R. M., & Chrisman, J. J. (1998). Efficiency and productivity measures for high contact services. *Service Industries Journal, 18*(4), 1–19. doi:10.1080/02642069800000038

Nomikos, G. E. (1989). Managing knowledge workers for productivity. *National Productivity Review, 8*(2), 165–174. doi:10.1002/npr.4040080209

Picard, R. G. (1998). Measuring and interpreting productivity of journalists. *Newspaper Research Journal, 19*(4), 71–80.

Quinn, R. W. (2005). Flow in knowledge work: high performance experience in the design of national security technology. *Administrative Science Quarterly, 50*, 610–641.

Ray, P. K., & Sahu, S. (1989). The measurement and evaluation of white-collar productivity. *International Journal of Operations & Production Management, 9*(4), 28–48. doi:10.1108/EUM0000000001235

Schroeder, R., Anderson, J., & Scudder, G. (1985). Measurement of white collar productivity. *International Journal of Operations & Production Management, 5*(2), 25–33. doi:10.1108/eb054736

Shapero, A. (1989). *Managing professional people: Understanding creative performance.* New York, NY: Free Press.

Smith, C. (1984). Awareness, analysis and improvement are keys to white collar productivity. *Industrial Engineering (American Institute of Industrial Engineers), 16*(1), 82–86.

Thomas, B. E., & Baron, J. P. (1994). *Evaluating knowledge worker productivity: Literature review.* Interim Report, FF-94/27, USACERL. Retrieved August 15, 2009, from www.cecer.army.mil/kws/tho_lit.htm#abs

Walker, D. L. (2000). Physician compensation: Rewarding productivity of the knowledge worker. *The Journal of Ambulatory Care Management, 23*(4), 48–59.

Yellowlees, R. A. (1986). White collar productivity: The technology challenge. *Industrial Management (Des Plaines), 28*(2), 14–17.

Zigon, J. (1998) *How to measure white collar employee productivity.* ZPG Measurement Resources to Help You Improve Employee Performance. Retrieved April 4, 2009, from http://www.zigonperf.com /store/articles.html

KEY TERMS AND DEFINITIONS

Black Box Management: A management approach which defines and controls goals and resources while leaving the definition and controlling of professional work completely to the experts.

Experts: In cognitive psychology somebody who performs constantly and continually superior in a specific domain when compared to average performers (novices). In sociology an associate who has the role to define and solve ill-defined or complex domain-specific problems.

Knowledge Worker: An employee whose main tasks consists in identifying, creating and/or disseminating knowledge.

Management: The task to bring about results by defining and controlling goals and tasks, methods and tools and/or resources.

Performance: In business management the result of a goal-oriented effort in order to produce an added-value to one or more stakeholders.

Productivity: In the classical production-oriented meaning the quantity of production output in relation to the quantity of production input.

Professional: In occupational sociology a member of a certain occupational group who deals with significant values (like justice or health), who needs a high degree of domain-specific knowledge and who enjoys a high degree of autonomy in carrying out his or her work.

White Box Management: A management approach which, besides defining and controlling goals and resources, also defines and controls the methods and tools of how to achieve the goals and use the resources.

Compilation of References

Abbasi, R., Grzegorzek, M., & Staab, S. (2009). Large scale tag recommendation using different image representations. In T. S. Chua, Y. Kompatsiaris, B. Mérialdo, W. Haas, G. Thallinger, & W. Bailer (Eds.), *Proceedings of 4th International Conference on Semantic and Digital Media Technologies, Semantic Multimedia, Lecture Notes in Computer Science 5887*, (pp. 65-76). Berlin, Germany: Springer.

Abbott, A. (1988). *The system of professions: An essay on the division of expert labor*. Chicago, IL: University of Chicago Press.

Abdullah, A. (1992). The influence of ethnic values on managerial practices in Malaysia. *Malaysian Management Review, 27*(1), 3–18.

Abrams, L. C., Cross, R., Lesser, E., & Levin, D. Z. (2003). Nurturing interpersonal trust in knowledge-sharing networks. *The Academy of Management Executive, 17*(4), 64–77. doi:10.5465/AME.2003.11851845

Adamic, L., & Adar, E. (2005). How to search a social network. *Social Networks, 27*(3), 187–203. doi:10.1016/j.socnet.2005.01.007

Adrian, B., Sauermann, L., & Roth-Berghofer, T. (2007). ConTag: A semantic tag recommendation system. In T. Pellegrini & S. Schaffert (Eds.), *Proceedings of I-Semantics*, (pp. 297-304). JUCS.

Ahn, J. H., & Chang, S. G. (2004). Assessing the contribution of knowledge to business performance: The KP3 methodology. *Decision Support Systems, 36*(4), 403–416. doi:10.1016/S0167-9236(03)00029-0

Akkermans, H., Baida, Z., & Gordijn, J. (2004). Value Webs: Using ontologies to bundle real-world services. *IEEE Intelligent Systems*, (4): 57–66. doi:10.1109/MIS.2004.35

Al-Alawi, A. I., Al-Marzooqi, N. Y., & Mohammed, Y. F. (2007). Organizational culture and knowledge sharing: Critical success factors. *Journal of Knowledge Management, 11*(2), 22–42. doi:10.1108/13673270710738898

Alavi, M., Kayworth, T. R., & Leidner, D. E. (2005). An empirical examination of the influence of organizational culture on knowledge management practices. *Journal of Management Information Systems, 22*(3), 191–224. doi:10.2753/MIS0742-1222220307

Alavi, M., & Tiwana, A. (2002). Knowledge integration in virtual teams: The potential role of KMS. *Journal of the American Society for Information Science and Technology, 53*(12), 1029–1037. doi:10.1002/asi.10107

Albrecht, J., College, W., Braud, R., Dao, D., Topilski, N., Tuttle, C., & Snoeren, A. C. (2007). Remote control: Distributed application configuration management, and visualization with Plush, In *Proceedings of the 21st Large Installation System Administration* (pp. 183-201).

Alexander, C., Ishikawa, S., & Silverstein, M. (1977). *A pattern language, towns, buildings, construction*. New York, NY: Oxford University.

Alvesson, M. (1995). *Management of knowledge intensive companies*. Berlin, Germany: De Gruyter.

Alvesson, M. (2004). *Knowledge work and knowledge-intensive firms*. Oxford, UK: Oxford University Press.

Alvesson, M., & Karreman, D. (2001). Odd couple: Making sense of the curious concept of knowledge management. *Journal of Management Studies, 38*(7), 995–1018. doi:10.1111/1467-6486.00269

Amar, A. D. (2002). *Managing knowledge workers: Unleashing innovation and productivity.* Westport, CT: Quorum.

Amazon. (2011). *Amazon.com: Help > Amazon.com site features > your content > recommendations.* Retrieved May 6, 2011, from http://www.amazon.com /gp/help/customer/display.html?ie=UTF8&nodeId=13316081&qid=1236889341&sr=1-2#rate

Anderson, K., Taylor, R., & Whitehead, E. (1999). Chimera: Hypertext for heterogeneous software development environments. *ACM Transactions on Information Systems, 18*(3), 211–245. doi:10.1145/352595.352596

Antoniou, G., & Harmelen, F. v. (2004). *A Semantic Web primer.* Cambridge, MA: MIT Press.

Aone, C., Halverson, L., Hampton, T., & Ramos-Santacruz, M. (1998). SRA: Description of the IE2 system used for MUC-7. In *Proceedings of the 7th Message Understanding Conference.*

Apache Group. (n.d.). Retrieved from http://hadoop.apache.org /zookeeper/

Appelt, D., Hobbs, J., Bear, J., Israel, D., Kameyama, M., & Martin, D. ... Tyson M. (1995). SRI international FASTUS system: MUC-6 test results and analysis. In *Proceedings of the 6th Message Understanding Conference,* (pp. 237–248).

Arabfard, M., & Babamir, S. M. (2011). Resolving impassiveness in service oriented architecture. *Innovative Computing Technology Communications in Computer and Information Science, Lecture Notes in Computer Science,* 241, Part 2, (pp. 48-60). Springer.

Aramaki, E., Miura, Y., Tonoike, M., Ohkuma, T., Mashuichi, H., & Ohe, K. (2009). Text2table: Medical text summarization system based on named entity recognition and modality identification. In *Proceedings of the BioNLP-2009 Workshop,* (pp. 185–192).

Arapakis, I., Jose, J. M., & Gray, P. D. (2008). Affective feedback: an investigation into the role of emotions in the information seeking process. In *Proceedings of the 31st Annual International ACM SIGIR Conference on Research and Development in Information Retrieval* (Singapore, Singapore, July 20 - 24, 2008), SIGIR '08, (pp. 395-402). New York, NY: ACM.

Argyris, C., Putman, R., & Smith, D. (1985). *Action science.* San Francisco, CA: Jossey Bass.

Argyris, C., & Schön, D. (1978). *Organisational Learning: A theory of action perspective.* Reading, MA: Addison-Wesley.

Armbrecht, F., Chapas, R., Chappelow, C., Farris, G., Friga, P., & Hartz, C. (2001). Knowledge management in research and development. *Research-Technology Management, 44*(4), 28–48.

Arrington, M. (2009). *Social networking: Will Facebook overtake MySpace in the U.S. in 2009?* Retrieved May 6, 2011, from http://www.techcrunch.com /2009/01/13/social-networking-will-facebook-overtake-myspace-in-the-us-in-2009/

Atzmueller, M., Beer, S., & Puppe, F. (2009). A data warehouse-based approach for quality management, evaluation and analysis of intelligent systems using subgroup mining. In *Proceedings of 22nd International Florida Artificial Intelligence Research Society Conference,* (pp. 372–377). AAAI Press.

Atzmueller, M., Haupt, F., Beer, S., & Puppe, F. (2009). Knowta: Wiki-enabled social tagging for collaborative knowledge and experience management. *Proceedings International Workshop on Design, Evaluation, and Refinement of Intelligent Systems,* Krakow, Poland

Atzmueller, M., Kluegl, P., & Puppe, F. (2008). Rule-based information extraction for structured data acquisition using TextMarker. In *Proceedings of LWA 2008 (Knowledge Discovery and Machine Learning Track),* University of Wuerzburg

Atzmueller, M., Puppe, F., & Buscher, H. P. (2005). Profiling examiners using intelligent subgroup mining. In *Proceedings 10th International Workshop on Intelligent Data Analysis in Medicine and Pharmacology,* (pp. 46–51). Aberdeen, Scotland

Atzmueller, M. (2011). Data mining . In McCartney, P., & Boonthum-Denecke, C. (Eds.), *Applied natural language processing and content analysis: Advances in identification, investigation and resolution*. Hershey, PA: IGI Global.

Atzmueller, M., & Puppe, F. (2009). A knowledge-intensive approach for semi-automatic causal subgroup discovery . In Berendt, B. (Eds.), *Knowledge discovery enhanced with semantic and social information*. Springer. doi:10.1007/978-3-642-01891-6_2

Auer, S., Bizer, C., Kobilarov, G., Lehmann, J., Cyganiak, R., & Ives, Z. (2007). Dbpedia: A nucleus for a web of open data. *Proceedings of the 6th International The Semantic Web and 2nd Asian Conference on Asian Semantic Web Conference*, (pp. 722–735). Berlin, Germany: Springer-Verlag.

Aulawi, H., Sudirman, I., Suryadi, K., & Govindaraju, R. (2008). *Knowledge sharing behavior, antecedent and its influence towards the company's innovation capability.* Paper presented at the 2008 IEEE International Conference on Industrial Engineering and Engineering Management, IEEM 2008.

Axtell, R. (1999). Why agents? On the varied motivations for agent computing in the social sciences. *Proceedings of Agent Simulation: Applications, Models, and Tools.*

Baars, H. (2005). Distribution von Business-Intelligence-Wissen . In Chamoni, P., & Gluchowski, P. (Eds.), *Analytische Informationssysteme* (pp. 409–424). Berlin, Germany: Springer.

Baeza-Yates, R., & Tiberi, A. (2007). Extracting semantic relations from query logs. *Proceedings of the 13th International Conference on Knowledge Discovery and Data mining, KDD 2007* (pp. 76-85). New York, NY: ACM.

Baeza-Yates, R., & Berthier, R.-N. (1999). *Modern information retrieval*. Boston, MA: Addison-Wesley Longman Publishing Co., Inc.

Bakhtin, M. M. (1973). *Problems of Dostoevsky's poetics*. Ardis.

Balasuriya, D., Ringland, N., Nothman, J., Murphy, T., & Curran, J. (2009). Named entity recognition in wikipedia. In *Proceedings of the 2009 Workshop on the Peoples Web Meets NLP (ACL IJCNLP 2009)*, (pp. 10–18).

Balazova, M. (2004). *Methode zur Leistungsbewertung und Leistungssteigerung in der Mechatronikentwicklung.* Unveröffentlichte Dissertation, Universität Paderborn.

Baldry, C., et al. (2005). *Knowledge workers, commitment and occupational community.* Paper presented at the International Labour Process Conference 2005, Glasgow.

Baldwin, J. R., & Beckstead, D. (2003). *Knowledge workers in Canada's economy, 1971-2001. Statistics Canada Analytical Paper*. Ottawa, Canada: Statistics Canada.

Ban, H., & Ahlqvist, O. (2010). User evaluation of a software interface for communication in urban ontologies . In Teller, J., Cutting-Decelle, A.-F., & Billen, R. (Eds.), *COST Action C21 - Future of urban ontologies*. Universite de Liege.

Barabási, A.L., Jeong, H., Neda, Z., Ravasz, E., Schubert, A., and Vicsek, T. (2002). Evolution of the social network of scientific collaborations. *Physica A: Statistical Mechanics and its Applications, 311*, 590-614.

Barnard, Y. F. (2005). *Developing industrial knowledge managment: Knowledge sharing over boundaries.* Paper presented at the International Conference on Advances in the Internet: System and Interdesciplinary Research.

Barthowick, A. (1999). *A maximum entropy approach to named entity recognition*. Unpublished doctoral dissertation, New York University.

Bartol, K., Liu, W., Zeng, X., & Wu, K. (2009). Social exchange and knowledge sharing among knowledge workers: The moderating role of perceived job security. *Management and Organization Review, 5*(2). doi:10.1111/j.1740-8784.2009.00146.x

Baskerville, R., & Wood-Harper, A. T. (1998). Diversity in information systems action research methods. *European Journal of Information Systems, 7*(2), 90–107. doi:10.1057/palgrave.ejis.3000298

Bauer, A., & Günzel, H. (2009). *Data-Warehouse-Systeme - Architektur, Entwicklung, Anwendung*. Heidelberg, Germany: DPunkt Verlag.

Baumard, P. (1999). *Tacit knowledge in organizations*. Sage Publications Ltd.

Baumeister, J., Reutelshoefer, J., & Puppe, F. (2010). KnowWE: A semantic Wiki for knowledge engineering . In *Applied intelligence*. Springer. doi:10.1007/s10489-010-0224-5

Beckstead, D., & Gellatly, G. (2004). *Are knowledge workers found only in high-technology industries? Statistics Canada Analytical Paper*. Ottawa, Canada: Statistics Canada.

Begelman, G., Keller, P., & Smadja, F. (2006). Automated tag clustering: Improving search and exploration in the tag space. *Proceedings of the the Collaborative Web Tagging Workshop, WWW 2006*.

Bellifemine, F., Poggi, A., & Rimassa, G. (2001). Developing multi agent systems with a FIPA-compliant agent framework. *Software, Practice & Experience, 31*, 103–128. doi:10.1002/1097-024X(200102)31:2<103::AID-SPE358>3.0.CO;2-O

Bell, J. (1997). *Doing your research project*. Buckingham, UK: Open University Press.

Bellot, P., Crestan, E., El-Beze, M., Gillard, L., & de Loupy, C. (2002). Coupling named entity recognition, vector-space model and knowledge bases for TREC 11 question answering track. In *Proceedings of 11th Text Retrieval Conference (TREC-2002)*.

Bender, O., Och, F. J., & Ney, H. (2003). Maximum entropy models for named entity recognition. In *Proceedings of Conference on Computational Natural Language Learning (CoNLL-2003)*, (pp. 148–151).

Bentley, R., Busbach, U., Hinrichs, E., Kerr, D., Sikkel, K., Trevor, J., & Woetzel, G. (1997). Basic support for cooperative work on the World Wide Web. *International Journal of Human-Computer Studies, 46*(6), 827–846. doi:10.1006/ijhc.1996.0108

Bergenti, F., Costicoglou, S., & Poggi, A. (2003). A portal for ubiquitous collaboration. In *Proceedings of the 15ᵗʰ Conference on Advanced Information Systems Engineering (CAiSE 2003)*, volume 75 of CEUR Workshop Proceedings.

Bergenti, F., Franchi, E., & Poggi, A. (2010). *Using HDS for realizing multi-agent applications*. Presented at the Third International Workshop on Languages, Methodologies and Development Tools for Multi-Agent Systems (LADS'010), Lyon, France.

Bergenti, F., Franchi, E., & Poggi, A. (2011). Selected models for agent-based simulation of social networks. In *Proceedings from 3rd Symposium on Social Networks and Multiagent Systems* (SNAMAS '11), York.

Bergenti, F. (2008). Toward a probabilistic model of trust in agent societies . In Artikis, A., O'Hare, G. M. P., Stathis, K., & Vouros, G. A. (Eds.), *Engineering Societies in the Agents World VIII, Lecture Notes in Artificial Intelligence, 4995* (pp. 270–283). Springer-Verlag. doi:10.1007/978-3-540-87654-0_15

Bergenti, F., & Poggi, A. (2000). CollAge: A replicated-instances platform for collaborative applications. [Cambridge International Science Publishing.]. *The Journal of Applied Systems Studies, 1*(3), 421–435.

Bergenti, F., Poggi, A., & Somacher, M. (2002). A collaborative platform for fixed and mobile networks. *Communications of the ACM, 45*(11), 39–44. doi:10.1145/581571.581591

Berger, L., Pietra, S. A. D., & Pietra, V. J. D. (1996). A maximum entropy approach to natural language processing. *Computational Linguistics, 22*(1), 39–72.

Berkovsky, S., Kuflik, T., & Ricci, F. (2007). Distributed collaborative filtering with domain specialization. In *Proceedings of the 2007 ACM Conference on Recommender Systems* (Minneapolis, MN, USA, October 19 - 20, 2007), RecSys '07, (pp. 33-40). New York, NY: ACM.

Berners-Lee, T. (2006). *Linked data, design issues*. Retrieved May 8, 2011, from http://www.w3.org/DesignIssues/LinkedData.html

Berthold, H., Rösch, P., Zöller, S., Wortmann, F., Carenini, A., & Campbell, S. …Strohmaier, F. (2010). An architecture for ad-hoc and collaborative business intelligence. In *Proceedings of the 2010 EDBT/ICDT Workshops, EDBT '10*. New York, NY: ACM.

Bhalotia, G., Hulgeri, A., Nakhe, C., Chakrabarti, S., & Sudarshan, S. (2002). Keyword searching and browsing in databases using banks. *Proceedings of the 18th International Conference on Data Engineering 2002*, (pp. 431–440).

Bikel, D. M., Schwartz, R., & Weischedel, R. M. (1999). An algorithm that learns what's in a name. *Machine Learning, 34*, 211–231. doi:10.1023/A:1007558221122

Birchall, D. W., & Tovstiga, G. (2006). *Innovation performance measurement: Expert vs. practitioner views.* Paper presented at the Portland International Conference on Management of Engineering and Technology.

Bischoff, K., Firan, C. S., Nejdl, W., & Paiu, R. (2008). Can all tags be used for search? In *Proceeding of the 17th ACM Conference on Information and Knowledge Management* (Napa Valley, California, USA, October 26 - 30, 2008), CIKM '08 (pp. 193-202). New York, NY: ACM.

Bischoff, K., Firan, C., Nejdl, W., & Paiu, R. (2008). Can all tags be used for search? *Proceedings of the 17th ACM Conference on Information and Knowledge Management, CIKM 2008* (pp. 193-202). Napa Valley, CA: ACM Press.

Bissantz, N. (2001). DeltaMiner. *Wirtschaftsinformatik, 43*(1), 77–80.

Bizer, C., Cyganiak, R., & Heath, T. (2007). *How to publish linked data on the web.* Retrieved from http://sites.wiwiss.fuberlin.de /suhl/bizer/pub/ LinkedDataTutorial/

Bizer, C., Haeth, T., & Berners Lee, T. (2008). *Linked data: Principles and state of the art.* Paper presented at the meeting of www2008, Bejing, China

Black, W., Rinaldi, F., & Mowatt, D. (1998). FACILE: Description of the NE system used for MUC-7. In *Proceedings of the 7th Message Understanding Conference.*

Blackler, F. (1995). Knowledge, knowledge work and organizations: An overview and interpretation. *Organization Studies, 16*(6), 1021–1046. doi:10.1177/017084069501600605

Blichfeldt, B. S., & Andersen, J. R. (2006). Creating a wider audience for action research: Learning from case-study research. *Journal of Research Practice, 2*(1), 1–12.

Blue, A. (2009). *LinkedIn works with Twitter, and vice versa.* Retrieved from http://blog.linkedin.com /2009/11/09/ allen-blue-twitter-and-linkedin-go-together-like-peanut-butter-and-chocolate/

Blum, A., & Mitchel, T. (1998). Combining labeled and unlabeled data with co-training. In *COLT: Proceedings of the Workshop on Computational Learning Theory,* (pp. 92–100). Morgan Kaufmann.

Bock, G.-W., Zmud, R. W., Kim, Y.-G., & Lee, J.-N. (2005). Behavioral intention formation in knowledge sharing: Examining the roles of extrinsic motivators, social-psychological forces, and organizational climate. [Article]. *Management Information Systems Quarterly, 29*(1), 87–111.

Bolettieri, P., Esuli, A., Falchi, F., Lucchese, C., Perego, R., Piccioli, T., & Rabitti, F. (2009). CoPhIR: A test collection for content-based image retrieval. *CoRR,* abs/0905.4627v2.

Bordini, R., Dastani, M., Dix, J., & Fallah-Seghrouchni, A. (Eds.). (2005). *Multi-agent programming: Languages, platforms and applications. Multiagent Systems, Artificial Societies, and Simulated Organizations (Vol. 15).* Berlin, Germany: Springer Verlag.

Bortz, J., & Döring, N. (2003). *Forschungsmethoden und Evaluation für Human- und Sozialwissenschaftler, 3 überarb Aufl.* Berlin, Germany: Springer.

Boshuizen, H. P. A., & Schmidt, H. G. (1992). On the role of biomedical knowledge in clinical reasoning by experts, intermediates and novices. *Cognitive Science, 16*, 153–184. doi:10.1207/s15516709cog1602_1

Boyd, D. M., & Ellison, N. B. (2008). Social network sites: Definition, history, and scholarship. *Journal of Computer-Mediated Communication, 13*(1).

Bozdag, E., Mesbah, A., & van Deursen, A. (2007). A comparison of push and pull techniques for AJAX. In *Proceedings of the 2007 9th IEEE International Workshop on Web Site Evolution* (WSE '07), Washington, DC, USA, (pp. 15-22).

Brachman, R. J. (1979). On the epistemological status of semantic networks . In Findler, N. V. (Ed.), *Associative networks: Representation and use of knowledge by computers.* London, UK: Academic Press.

Bradbury, H., & Lichtensein, B. M. B. (2000). Relationality in organizational research: Exploring the space between. *Organization Science*, *11*(5), 551–564. doi:10.1287/orsc.11.5.551.15203

Bredl, K. (2005). *Kompetenz von Beratern: Analyse des Kompetenzerwerbs bei Unternehmensberatern im Kontext der Expertiseforschung*. Unveröffentlichte Dissertation, Universität Regensburg.

Breslin, J., & Decker, S. (2007). The future of social networks on the Internet: The need for semantics. [IEEE Computer Society.]. *IEEE Internet Computing*, *11*(6), 86–90. doi:10.1109/MIC.2007.138

Briggs, R. O., & Vreede, G.-J. de. (2003). *Thinklets: Building blocks for concerted collaboration.*

Briggs, R. O., Kolfschoten, G. L., de Vreede, G.-J., & Dean, D. L. (2006). Defining key concepts for collaboration engineering. In *Americas Conference on Information Systems* (AMCIS) (Vol. 12, p. 121-128).

Briggs, R. O., Adkins, M., Mittlemann, D. D., Kruse, J., Miller, S., & Nunamaker, J. F. Jr. (1999). A technology transition model derived from qualitative field investigation of gss use aboard the U.S.S. Coronado. *Journal of Management Information Systems*, *15*(3), 151–195.

Briggs, R. O., de Vreede, G.-J., & Nunamaker, J. F. Jr. (2003). Collaboration engineering with thinklets to pursue sustained success with group support systems. *Journal of Management Information Systems*, *19*(4), 31–64.

Brin, S., & Page, L. (1998). The anatomy of a large-scale hypertextual Web search engine. *Proc. of the Seventh International Conference on World Wide Web*, (Vol. 7, pp. 107-117).

Brin, S., & Page, L. (1998). The anatomy of a large-scale hypertextual Web search engine. *Proceedings of the Seventh International World Wide Web Conference Computer Networks and ISDN Systems, 30*(1-7), 107-117.

Brinkley, I. (2006). *Defining the knowledge economy: Knowledge economy programme report*. Research Paper. London, UK: The Work Foundation.

Brin, S., & Page, L. (1998). The anatomy of a large-scale hypertextual Web search engine. *Computer Networks and ISDN Systems*, *30*, 107–117. doi:10.1016/S0169-7552(98)00110-X

Brown, D. C., Dunskus, B., Grecu, D. L., & Berker, I. (1995). Support for single function agents. In *Proceedings of Applications of Artificial Intelligence in Engineering*. Udine, Italy: SINE.

Bunescu, R., & Pasca, M. (2006). Using encyclopedic knowledge for named entity disambiguation. In *Proceedings of the 11th Conference of the European Chapter of the Association for Computational Linguistics* (*EACL-2006*), (pp. 9–16).

Burkhardt, H., & Smith, B. (Eds.). (1991). *Handbook or metaphysics and ontology*. Munich, Germany: Philadelphia Verlag.

Buscher, H.-P., Engler, C., Führer, A., Kirschke, S., & Puppe, F. (2002). HepatoConsult: A knowledge-based second opinion and documentation system. *Journal Artificial Intelligence in Medicine*, *24*(3), 205–216. doi:10.1016/S0933-3657(01)00104-X

Byrne, J. A., & Gerdes, L. (2005, November 28). The man who invented management: why Peter Drucker's ideas still matter. *Businessweek* [Internet]. Retrieved 13 October, 2009, from http://www.businessweek.com / magazine/content/05_48/b3961001.htm

Cabrera, Ã. n., Collins, W. C., & Salgado, J. F. (2006). Determinants of individual engagement in knowledge sharing. [Article]. *International Journal of Human Resource Management*, *17*(2), 245–264. doi:10.1080/09585190500404614

Campbell, M. I., Cagan, J., & Kotovsky, K. (1999). A-Design: An agent-based approach to conceptual design in a dynamic environment. *Research in Engineering Design*, *11*, 172–192. doi:10.1007/s001630050013

Cao, L., Zhang, C., & Liu, J. (2006). Ontology-based integration of business intelligence. *Web Intelligence and Agent Systems*, *4*(3), 313–325.

Carillo, M. R., & Zazzaro, A. (2000). Innovation, human capital destruction and firms' investment in training. *Manchester School*, *68*(3), 331–348. doi:10.1111/1467-9957.00197

Carman, M., Baillie, M., Gwadera, R., & Crestani, F. (2009). A statistical comparison of tag and query logs. *Proceedings of the 32nd Annual International Conference on Research and Development in Information Retrieval, SIGIR 2009* (pp. 123-130). Boston, MA: ACM.

Carvalho, V. R., & Cohen, W. W. (2006). Improving email speech acts analysis via n-gram selection. In *ACTS '09 Workshop* (pp. 35-41). Association for Computational Linguistics.

Cattuto, C., Loreto, V., & Pietronero, L. (2006, May 4). Collaborative tagging and semiotic dynamics. *Proceedings of the National Academy of Sciences of the United States of America, 104*, 1461–1469. doi:10.1073/pnas.0610487104

Chamberlain, J., Massimo, P., & Kruschwitz, U. (2009). A demonstration of human computation using the Phrase Detectives annotation game. *Proceedings of the ACM SIGKDD Workshop on Human Computation* (pp. 23-24). ACM

Chamoni, P., & Gluchowski, P. (2006). *Analytische Informationssysteme*. Berlin, Germany: Springer. doi:10.1007/3-540-33752-0

Chan, A. T. S., Cao, J., & Chan, C. K. (2005). WEBGOP: Collaborative web services based on graph-oriented programming. *IEEE Transactions on Systems, Man, and Cybernetics. Part A, Systems and Humans, 35*(6), 811–830. doi:10.1109/TSMCA.2005.851342

Chen, H., Finin, T., & Joshi, A. (2004). Semantic Web in the context broker architecture. In *Proceedings of the 2nd IEEE Conference on Pervasive Computing and Communications Workshops (PerCom 2004)*, (pp. 277-286). Orlando, FL, IEEE Press.

Chen, S., & Rosenfeld, R. (1999). *A Gaussian prior for smoothing maximum entropy models*. Unpublished technical report CMUCS-99-108, Carnegie Mellon University.

Cheng, G., & Qu, Y. (2009). Searching linked objects with falcons: Approach, implementation and evaluation. *International Journal on Semantic Web and Information Systems, 5*(3), 49–70. doi:10.4018/jswis.2009081903

Chenggang, W., Wenpin, J., & Qijia, T. (2001). An information retrieval server based on ontology and multiagent. *Journal of Computer Research & Development, 38*(6), 641–647.

Chen, H., Finin, T., Joshi, A., Perich, F., & Chakraborty, D. (2004). Intelligent agents meet the Semantic Web in smart spaces. *IEEE Internet Computing, 8*(6), 69–79. doi:10.1109/MIC.2004.66

Chieu, H., & Ng, H. (2003). Named entity recognition with a maximum entropy approach. In *Proceedings of Conference on Computational Natural Language Learning (CoNLL-2003)*, (pp. 160–163).

Chi, M. T. H. (1981). Categorization and representation of physics problems by experts and novices. *Cognitive Science, 5*, 121–152. doi:10.1207/s15516709cog0502_2

Chi, M. T. H. (2006). Two approaches to the study of experts' characteristics . In Ericsson, K. A. (Eds.), *The Cambridge handbook of expertise and expert performance* (pp. 24–27). Cambridge, MA: University Press.

Chinchor, N. (1998). MUC-7 named entity task definition, v3.5. In *Proceedings of the 7th Message Understanding Conference*.

Chow, A., Goodman, B. D., Rooney, J., & Wyble, C. D. (2007). Engaging a corporate community to manage technology and embrace innovation. *IBM Systems Journal*. Retrieved from http://www.research.ibm.com /journal/ abstracts/sj/464/chow.html

Chuan, C. L. (2006). Sample size estimation using Krejcie and Morgan and Cohen statistical power analysis: A comparison. *Jurnal Penyelidikan IPBL, 7*, 78–86.

Clegg, C., Unsworth, K., Epitropaki, O., & Parker, G. (2002). Implicating trust in the innovation process. *Journal of Occupational and Organizational Psychology, 75*, 409–422. doi:10.1348/096317902321119574

Clement, J., & McDonald. (1996). Medical heuristics: The silent adjudicators of clinical practice. *Annals of Internal Medicine, 124*, 56–62.

Cockburn, A., & Williams, L. (2001). *The costs and benefits of pair programming, Extreme programming examined*. USA: Addison-Wesley.

Coffield, F. (2002). Britain's continuing failure to train: The birth pangs of a new policy. *Journal of Education Policy, 17*(4), 483–497. doi:10.1080/02680930210140275

Cohen, A. (2005). Unsupervised gene/protein named entity normalization using automatically extracted dictionaries. In *Proceedings of the ACL-ISMB Workshop on Linking Biological Literature, Ontologies and Databases: Mining Biological Semantics*, (pp. 17–24).

Cohen, W., & Levinthal, D. (1990). Absorptive capacity: A new perspective on learning and innovation. *Administrative Science Quarterly, 35*(1), 128–152. doi:10.2307/2393553

Collaboration Ontology. (2011). Retrieved from http://www.collaborationontology.com

Collier, N., Nobata, C., & Tsujii, J. (2000). Extracting the names of genes and gene products with a hidden Markov model. In *Proceedings of the Conference on Computational Linguistics (COLING-2000)*, (pp. 201–207).

Collins, M., & Singer, Y. (1999). Unsupervised models for named entity classification. In *Proceedings of Joint SIGDAT Conference on Empirical Methods in Natural Language Processing and Very Large Corpora (EMNLP-1999)*.

Collins, C. J., & Smith, K. G. (2006). Knowledge exchange and combination: The role of human resource practices in the performance of high-technology firms. *Academy of Management Journal, 49*(3), 544–560. doi:10.5465/AMJ.2006.21794671

Cook, J., & Wall, T. (1980). New work attitude measures of trust, organizational commitment and personal need non-fulfillment. *Journal of Occupational Psychology, 53*(1), 39–52. doi:10.1111/j.2044-8325.1980.tb00005.x

Corbin, J., & Strauss, A. (2008). *Basics of qualitative research: Techniques and procedures for developing grounded theory* (3rd ed.). London, UK: Sage Publications.

Corby, O., Dieng-Kuntz, R., Faron-Zucker, C., & Gandon, F. (2006). Searching the Semantic Web: Approximate query processing based on ontologies. *IEEE Intelligent Systems, 21*(1), 20–27. doi:10.1109/MIS.2006.16

Corcho, O., Fernández-López, M., & Gómez-Pérez, A. (2003). Methodologies, tools and languages for building ontologies. Where is their meeting point? *Data & Knowledge Engineering, 46*(1), 41–64. doi:10.1016/S0169-023X(02)00195-7

Corey, K. E., & Wilson, M. (2006). *Urban and regional technology planning: Planning practice in the global knowledge economy*. London, UK: Routledge.

Crang, M. (1997). Analyzing qualitative materials . In Flowerdew, R., & Martin, D. (Eds.), *Methods in human geography: A guide for students doing research projects*. Harlow, MA: Longman.

Cristani, M., Perina, A., Castellani, U., & Murino, V. (2008). Content visualization and management of geo-located image databases . In *Proceedings of Extended Abstracts on Human factors in Computing Systems* (pp. 2823–2828). New York, NY: ACM. doi:10.1145/1358628.1358768

Cross, R., Rice, R., & Parker, A. (2001). Information seeking in social context: Structural influences and receipt of informational benefits. *IEEE Transactions, 31*(4), 438–448.

Csikszentmihalyi, M. (1997). *Creativity: Flow and the psychology of discovery and invention*. New York, NY: HarperCollins Publishers.

Cucerzan, S. (2007). Large-scale named entity disambiguation based on Wikipedia data. In *Proceedings of the 2007 Joint Conference on Empirical Methods in Natural Language Processing and Computational Natural Language Learning (EMNLP-CoNLL-2007)*, (pp. 708–716).

Culotta, A., & Sorensen, J. (2004). Dependency tree kernels for relation extraction. In *Proceedings of the 42nd Annual Meeting on Association for Computational Linguistics (ACL-2004)*, (pp. 423–429).

Cunningham, H. (1999). *JAPE: A Java annotation patterns engine. Research memorandum*. Department of Computer Science, University of Sheffield.

Cunningham, H. (2002). Gate, a general architecture for text engineering. *Computers and the Humanities, 36*(2), 223–254. doi:10.1023/A:1014348124664

Cunningham, H. (2005). Information extraction, automatic . In Brown, K. (Ed.), *Encyclopedia of language and linguistics*.

Curran, J., & Clark, S. (2003). Language independent NER using a maximum entropy tagger. In *Proceedings of Conference on Computational Natural Language Learning (CoNLL-2003)*, (pp. 164–167).

CXO Media Inc. (2008). *CIO 100 2008: Winner detail.* Retrieved May 6, 2011, from http://www.cio.com/cio100/detail/1840

Dale, J., Willmot, S., & Burg, B. (2002). Challenges and deployment of next-generation service environments . In *Proceedings of Paciic Rim Intelligent Multi-Agent Systems.* Tokyo, Japan: Agentcities.

Dash, D. P. (1999). Current debates in action research. *Systemic Practice and Action Research, 12*(5), 457–492. doi:10.1023/A:1022465506555

Davenport, T. (1994). Saving IT's soul: Human-centered information management. *Harvard Business Review, 72,* 119–119.

Davenport, T. H. (1997). *Information ecology.* Oxford, UK: Oxford University Press.

Davenport, T. H. (2005). *Thinking for a living: How to get better performance and results from knowledge workers.* Boston, MA: Harvard Business School Press.

Davenport, T. H., & Prusak, L. (1998). *Working knowledge.* Boston, MA: Harvard Business School Press.

Davenport, T. H., Thomas, R. J., & Cantrell, S. (2002). The mysterious art and science of knowledge-worker performance. *Sloan Management Review, 44*(1), 23–30.

Davis, H. C., Millard, D. E., & Reich, S. (1998). *OHP-communicating between hypermedia aware applications.* In Towards a New Generation of HTTP, A Workshop on Global Hypermedia Infrastructure, Australia.

Davis, F.D. (2004). Improving computer skill training: behavior modeling, symbolic mental rehearsal,and the role of knowledge structures. *The Journal of Applied Psychology, 89,* 509–523. doi:10.1037/0021-9010.89.3.509

De Long, D., & Fahey, L. (2000). Diagnosing cultural barriers to knowledge management. *The Academy of Management Executive, 14*(4), 113–127. doi:10.5465/AME.2000.3979820

de Vreede, G.-J., & Briggs, R. O. (2005). Collaboration engineering: Designing repeatable processes for high-value collaborative tasks. In *Proceedings of the 38th Hawaii International Conference on System Sciences (HICSS).*

de Vreede, G.-J., Vogel, D., Kolfschoten, G. L., & Wien, J. (2003). Fifteen years of gss in the field: a comparison across time and national boundaries. In *Proceedings of the 36th Annual Hawaii International Conference on System Sciences (HICSS).*

de Vreede, G.-J., Kolfschoten, G. L., & Briggs, R. O. (2006). Thinklets: A collaboration engineering pattern language. *International Journal of Computer Applications of Technology, 25*(2/3), 140–154. doi:10.1504/IJCAT.2006.009064

de Zengotita, T. (2004). *Mediated: How the media shapes your world and the way you live in it.* New York, NY: Bloomsbury Publishing.

Delicious. (2011). *Delicious.* Retrieved May 6, 2011, from http://www.delicious.com/

Dempster, A., Laird, N., & Rubin, D. (1977). Maximum likelihood from incomplete data via the EM algorithm. *Journal of the Royal Statistical Society. Series B. Methodological, 39,* 1–38.

Dennis, A. R., Haley, B., & Vandenberg, R. J. (1996). A meta-analysis of effectiveness, efficiency, and participant satisfaction in group support systems research. In *Proceedings of the 17th International Conference on Information System.*

Dennis, A. R., George, J. F., Jessup, L. M., Nunamaker, J. F. Jr, & Vogel, D. R. (1988, December). Information technology to support electronic meetings. *Management Information Systems Quarterly, 12*(4), 591–624. doi:10.2307/249135

Dennis, A. R., Wixom, B. H., & Vandenberg, R. J. (2001, June). Understanding fit and appropriation effects in group support systems via meta-analysis. *Management Information Systems, 25*(2), 167–193. doi:10.2307/3250928

DeSanctis, G., & Gallupe, R. B. (1987). A foundation for the study of group decision support systems. *Management Science, 33*(5), 589–609. doi:10.1287/mnsc.33.5.589

DeSanctis, G., & Poole, M. S. (1994, May). Capturing the complexity in advanced technology use: Adaptive structuration theory. *Organization Science, 5*(2), 121–147. doi:10.1287/orsc.5.2.121

DeVellis, R. F. (2003). *Scale development: Theory and applications* (2nd ed.). Thousand Oaks, CA: Sage Publications, Inc.

Diehl, M., & Stroebe, W. (1991). Productivity loss in idea-generating groups: Tracking down the blocking effect. *Journal of Personality and Social Psychology, 61*(3), 392–403. doi:10.1037/0022-3514.61.3.392

Digg. (2011). *Digg – All news, videos & images.* Retrieved May 6, 2011, from http://www.digg.com/

Dikenelli, O., Erdur, R. C., & Gumus, O. (2005). SEAGENT: A platform for developing Semantic Web based multi agent systems. In *Proceedings of the Fourth International Joint Conference on Autonomous Agents and Multiagent Systems (AAMAS '05),* (pp. 1271-1272). New York, NY.

Do, H.-H., & Rahm, E. (2002). COMA: A system for flexible combination of schema matching approaches. *Proceedings of the 28th International Conference on Very large Data Bases* (pp. 610-621). VLDB Endowment

Doan, A., Madhavan, J., Domingos, P., & Halevy, A. (2002). Learning to map between ontologies on the Semantic Web. *Proceedings of the 11th International World Wide Web Conference* (pp. 662-673). ACM

Doan, A., Madhavan, J., Domingos, P., & Halevy, A. (2004). Ontology matching: A machine learning approach . In Staab, S. (Ed.), *Handbook on ontologies* (pp. 385–516). Springer.

Doddington, G., Mitchell, A., Przybocki, M., Ramshaw, L., Strassel, S., & Weischedel, R. (2004). The automatic content extraction (ace) program: Tasks, data and evaluation. In *Proceedings of the Fourth International Conference on Language Resources and Evaluation (LREC-2004),* (pp. 837–840).

Doreian, P. (2006). Actor network utilities and network evolution. *Social Networks, 28*(2), 137–164. doi:10.1016/j.socnet.2005.05.002

Dörhöfer, S. (2010). *Management und Organisation von Wissensarbeit: Strategie, Arbeitssystem und organisationale Praktiken in wissensbasierten Unternehmen.* Wiesbaden, Germany: VS Verlag für Sozialwissenschaften.

Dostal, W. (2001). *Neue Herausforderungen an Qualifikation und Weiterbildung im Zeitalter der Globalisierung.* Berlin, Germany: Deutscher Bundestag.

Dostal, W., & Reinberg, A. (1999). *Arbeitslandschaft 2010. Teil 2: Ungebrochener Trend in die Wissensgesellschaft. IAB-Kurzbericht, Nr. 10.* Nürnberg, Germany: Institut für Arbeitsmarkt- und Berufsforschung.

Dourish, P. (1996). Consistency guarantees: Exploiting application semantics for consistency management in a collaboration toolkit. In *Proceedings of the ACM, Conference on Computer-Supported Collaborative Work.*

Drucker, P. F. (1969). *The age of discontinuity: guidelines to our changing society.* New York, NY: Harper & Row.

Drucker, P. F. (1991). The new productivity challenge. *Harvard Business Review, 69*(6), 69–79.

Drucker, P. F. (1999). *Management challenges for the 21st century.* New York, NY: Harper.

Duchon, P., Hanusse, N., Lebhar, E., & Schabanel, N. (2006). Could any graph be turned into a small-world? [Elsevier.]. *Theoretical Computer Science, 355*(1), 96–103. doi:10.1016/j.tcs.2005.12.008

Dueck, G. (2007). *Dueck's panopticon: Gesammelte Kultkolumnen.* Berlin, Germany: Springer.

Duque, R., & Bravo, C. (2008). Supporting distributed pair programming with the COLLECE Groupware System: An empirical study. In *Proceedings of XP,* (pp. 232-233).

Durfee, E. (1999). Distributed problem solving and planning . In Weiss, G. (Ed.), *Multiagent systems: A modern approach to distributed artificial intelligence* (pp. 121–164). Cambridge, MA: MIT Press.

Earl, M. (2001). Knowledge management strategies: Toward a taxonomy. *Journal of Management Information Systems, 18*(1), 215–233.

Edmondson, A. (1999, June). Psychological safety and learning behavior in work teams. *Administrative Science Quarterly, 44*(2), 350–383. doi:10.2307/2666999

Ehrig, M., & Sure, Y. (2004). Ontology mapping - An integrated approach. *Proceedings of the 1st European Semantic Web Symposium* (pp. 76-91). Springer.

Ekbal, A., & Bandyopadhyay, S. (2010). Improving the performance of a NER system by post-processing and voting. In *Structural, Syntactic, and Statistical Pattern Recognition, LNCS 5342* (pp. 831–841). Springer.

Ekbal, A., Sourjikova, E., Frank, A., & Ponzetto, S. P. (2010). Assessing the challenge of fine-grained named entity recognition and classification. In *Proceedings of the 2010 Named Entities Workshop*, (pp. 93–101).

Elfors, S., & Svane, Ö. (2008). Action research for sustainable housing: Theoretical and methodological implications of striving for research as a tool for change. *The Journal of Transdisciplinary Environmental Studies*, 7(2), 1–12.

Ellonen, R., Blomqvist, K., & Puumalainen, K. (2008). The role of trust in organisational innovativeness. *European Journal of Innovation Management*, 11(2), 160. doi:10.1108/14601060810869848

Empson, L. (2001). Fear of exploitation and fear of contamination: Impediments to knowledge transfer in mergers between professional service firms. *Human Relations*, 54(7), 839. doi:10.1177/0018726701547003

Epstein, J. M. (1999). Agent-based computational models and generative social science. *Complexity*, 4(5), 41–60. doi:10.1002/(SICI)1099-0526(199905/06)4:5<41::AID-CPLX9>3.0.CO;2-F

Erne, R. (2009a). *Interview transcripts F&E_SW: Data analysis in Atlas.ti V.5.6.3*. Unpublished Manuscript, Stuttgart.

Erne, R. (2009b). *Interview transcripts F&E_PE: Data analysis in Atlas.ti V.5.6.3*. Unpublished Manuscript, Stuttgart.

Erne, R. (2009c). *Interview transcripts consulting. Data analysis in Atlas.ti V.5.6.3*. Unpublished Manuscript. Stuttgart.

Erne, R. (2009d). *Interview transcripts Medizinische Versorgung KH: Data analysis in Atlas.ti V.5.6.3*. Unpublished Manuscript, Stuttgart.

Erne, R. (2009e). *Interview transcripts Forschung & Lehre Univ.: Data Analysis in Atlas.ti V.5.6.3*. Unpublished Manuscript, Stuttgart.

Etzioni, O., Cafarella, M., Downey, D., Popescu, A.-M., Shaked, T., Soderland, S., & Weld, D. (2005). Unsupervised named-entity extraction from the web: an experimental study. *Artificial Intelligence*, 165, 91–134. doi:10.1016/j.artint.2005.03.001

Euzenat, J., & Shvaiko, P. (2007). *Ontology matching*. Berlin, Germany: Springer.

Facebook. (2007). *Facebook | statistics*. Retrieved from http://www.facebook.com /press/info.php?statistics

Facebook. (2010). Open graph protocol. Retrieved from http://developers.facebook.com /docs/opengraph

Facebook. (2011). *Facebook | home*. Retrieved May 6, 2011, from http://www.facebook.com/

Falconer, S. M., & Storey, M.-A. (2007). A cognitive support framework for ontology mapping. *Proceedings of the 6th International The Semantic Web and 2nd Asian Conference on Asia* (pp. 114-127). ACM.

Favela, J., et al. (2004). Empirical evaluation of collaborative support for distributed pair programming. In *Proceedings of CRIWG*, (pp. 215-222).

Fellbaum, C. (Ed.). (1998). *WordNet: An electronic lexical database*. Cambridge, MA: The MIT Press.

Feltovich, P. J. (2006). Studies of expertise from psychological perspectives . In Ericsson, K. A. (Eds.), *The Cambridge handbook of expertise and expert performance* (pp. 41–67). Cambridge, MA: University Press.

Fernandéz, M., Gómez-Pérez, A., & Juristo, N. (1997). *Methontology: From ontological art towards ontological engineering*. Spring Symposium Series, AAAI97 Stanford.

Fitz-enz, J. (2000). *The ROI of human capital: Measuring the economic value of employee performance*. New York, NY: AMACOM.

Fleischman, M., & Hovy, E. (2002). Fine grained classification of named entities. In *Proceedings of Conference on Computational Linguistics (COLING-2002)*.

Florian, R., Ittycheriah, A., Jing, H., & Zhang, T. (2003). Named entity recognition through classifier combination. In *Proceedings of 7th Conference on Natural Language Learning at HLT-NAACL 2003*, (pp. 168–171).

Florida, R. L. (2002). *The rise of the creative class: And how it's transforming work, leisure, community and everyday life.* New York, NY: Basic Books.

FOAF . (2011, January). Retrieved from http://www.foaf-project.org/

Foner, L. (1996). A multi-agent referral system for matchmaking. *Proceedings the First International Conference on the Practical Application of Intelligent Agents and Multi-Agent Technology* (PAAM '96), (pp. 22-24).

Fonseca, B., Golgher, P., Pôssas, B., Ribeiro-Neto, B., & Ziviani, N. (2005). Concept-based interactive query expansion. *Proceedings of the 14th ACM International Conference on Information and Knowledge Management, CIKM 2005* (pp. 696-703). Bremen, Germany: ACM.

Fort, K., Ehrmann, M., & Nazarenko, A. (2009). Towards a methodology for named entities annotation. In *Proceedings of the Third Linguistic Annotation Workshop*, (pp. 142–145).

Forta, B., & Weiss, N. (1999). *Advanced coldFusion 4.0 application development.* QUE.

Franchi, E. (2010). A multi-agent implementation of social networks. *Proceedings of WOA 2010 Undicesimo Workshop Nazionale "Dagli Oggetti agli Agenti"*, Rimini.

Franchi, E., & Poggi, A. (2011). Multi-agent systems and social networks . In Cruz-Cunha, M., Putnik, G. D., Lopes, N., Patrícia, G., & Miranda, E. (Eds.), *Business social networking: Organizational, managerial, and technological dimensions.* Hershey, PA: IGI Global. doi:10.4018/978-1-61350-168-9.ch005

Fukuda, K., Tsunoda, T., Tamura, A., & Takagi, T. (1998). Towards information extraction: identifying protein names from biological papers. In *Proceedings of the Pacific Symposium on Biocomputing (PSB-98).*

Funayama, H., Shibata, T., & Kurohashi, S. (2009). Bottom-up named entity recognition using a two-stage machine learning method. In *Proceedings of the 2009 Workshop on Multiword Expressions (ACL-IJCNLP-2009)*, (pp. 55–62).

Furnas, G., Landauer, T., Gomez, L., & Dumais, S. (1987). The vocabulary problem in human-system communication. *Communications of the ACM, 30*(11), 964–971. doi:10.1145/32206.32212

Fuxman, A., Tsaparas, P., Achan, K., & Agrawal, R. (2008). Using the wisdom of the crowds for keyword generation. In *Proceeding of the 17th International Conference on World Wide Web* (Beijing, China, April 21 - 25, 2008), WWW '08, (pp. 61-70). New York, NY: ACM.

Gall, U., & Hauck, F. J. (1997). Promondia: A Java-based framework for real-time group communication in the Web. In *Proceedings of the 6th International WWW Conference.*

Gandon, F. (2002). *Distributed artificial intelligence and knowledge management: Ontologies and multi-agent systems for a corporate semantic web.* Scientific Philosopher Doctorate Thesis in Informatics, 7th November 2002, INRIA and University of Nice - Sophia Antipolis

Gandon, F., Poggi, A., Rimassa, G., & Turci, P. (2002). Multi-agents corporate memory management system. *Applied Artificial Intelligence Journal, 16*(9-10), 699–720. doi:10.1080/08839510290030453

Ganti, V., Konig, A., & Vernica, R. (2008). Entity categorization over large document collections. In *Proceeding of the 14th ACM SIGKDD International Conference on Knowledge Discovery and Data Mining (KDD-2008)*, (pp. 274–282).

García-Sánchez, F., Fernández-Breis, J. T., Valencia-García, R., Gómez, J. M., & Martínez-Béjar, R. (2006). Combining Semantic Web technologies with multi-agent systems for integrated access to biological resources. *Journal of Biomedical Informatics, 41*(5), 848–859. doi:10.1016/j.jbi.2008.05.007

Garmus, D., & Herron, D. (2000). *Function point analysis: Measurement practices for successful software projects.* Upper Saddle River, NJ: Addison-Weslay.

Gassler, W., Zangerle, E., & Specht, G. (2011). The snoopy concept: Fighting heterogeneity in semistructured and collaborative information systems by using recommendations. *Proceedings of the 2011 International Conference on Collaboration Technologies and Systems (CTS 2011)*, Philadelphia, PE.

Gassler, W., Zangerle, E., Tschuggnall, M., & Specht, G. (2010). SnoopyDB: Narrowing the gap between structured and unstructured information using recommendations. In M. H. Chignell & E. Toms (Ed.), *Proceedings of the 21st ACM Conference on Hypertext and Hypermedia 2010*, (pp. 271–272).

Genesereth, M., & Ketchpel, S. (1994). Software agents. *Communications of the ACM, 37*(7), 47–53. doi:10.1145/176789.176794

Giacometti, A., Marcel, P., & Negre, E. (2008). A framework for recommending OLAP queries. In *Proceeding of the ACM 11th International Workshop on Data Warehousing and OLAP, DOLAP '08.* New York, NY: ACM.

Giunchiglia, F., Yatskevich, M., & Shvaiko, P. (2007). Semantic matching: Algorithms and implementation. *Journal on Data Semantics, 9,* 1–38.

Glaser, B. (1978). *Theoretical sensitivity.* Mill Valley, CA: Sociology Press.

Glaser, B., & Strauss, A. (1967). *The discovery of grounded theory.* Chicago, UK: Aldine.

Gliozzo, A., Giuliano, C., & Rinaldi, R. (2005). Instance filtering for entity recognition. *SIGKDD Explorations Newsletter, 7,* 11–18. doi:10.1145/1089815.1089818

Gluchowski, P., & Kemper, H.-G. (2006). Quo vadis business intelligence. *BI Spektrum, 1,* 12–19.

Goldberg, D., Nichols, D., Oki, B. M., & Terry, D. (1992). Using collaborative filtering to weave an information tapestry. *Communications of the ACM, 35*(12), 61–70. doi:10.1145/138859.138867

Golder, S., & Huberman, B. (2006). Usage pattern of collaborative tagging systems. *Journal of Information Systems, 32*(2), 198–208.

Golder, S., & Huberman, B. A. (2005). *The structure of collaborative tagging systems. Technical report.* HP Labs.

Goldstein, J., & Sabin, R. E. (2006). Using speech acts to categorize email and identify email genres. In *HICSS'06.* IEEE Computer Society. doi:10.1109/HICSS.2006.528

Google. (2011). *YouTube | Broadcast yourself.* Retrieved May 6, 2011, from http://www.youtube.com/

Gray, P. (2001). The impact of knowledge repositories on power and control in the workplace. *Information Technology & People, 14*(4), 368–384. doi:10.1108/09593840110411167

Gronbæk, K., Hem, J., Madsen, O., & Sloth, L. (1993) Designing dexter-based cooperative hypermedia systems. In *Proceedings of the ACM Conference on Hypertext,* (pp. 25-38). USA.

Grønbak, K., Sloth, L., & Orbak, P. (1999). Webvise: Browser and proxy support for open hypermedia structuring mechanisms on the WWW. In *Proceedings of the 8th International World Wide Web Conference, Elsevier,* (pp. 1331-1345).

Gronbak, K., & Will, U. (1998). Towards a common reference architecture for open hypermedia. *Journal of Digital Information, 1*(2).

Grossberg, J. (2007). *Integration between Twitter and Facebook status.* Retrieved from http://www.twitter-sweet.com /2007/9/30/integration-between-twitter-and-facebook-status

Grossmann, R., Pellert, A., & Gotwald, V. (1997). Krankenhaus, Schule, Universität: Charakteristika und Optimierungspotentiale. In R. Grossmann, R. (Eds.), *Besser Billiger Mehr: Zur Reform der Expertenorganisation Krankenhaus, Schule, Universität* (pp. 24-35). Wien, Germany: Springer.

Gruber, H., & Ziegler, A. (1996). Expertise als Domäne psychologischer Forschung. In H. Gruber & A. Ziegler (Hrsg.), *Expertiseforschung: Theoretische und methodische Grundlagen* (pp. 7-16). Opladen: Westdeutscher Verlag.

Gruber, T. (1993). *A translation approach to portable ontology specifications.* Stanford University. Retrieved June 13, 2011, from http://ksl-web.stanford.edu/KSL_Abstracts/KSL-92-71.html

Gruber, T. R. (1993). A translation approach to portable ontologies. *Knowledge Acquisition, 5*(2), 199–220. doi:10.1006/knac.1993.1008

Gruber, T. R. (1995). Toward principles of the design of ontologies used for knowledge sharing. *International Journal of Human-Computer Studies, 43,* 907–928. doi:10.1006/ijhc.1995.1081

Grüninger, M., & Fox, M. (1995). Methodology for the design and evaluation of ontologies. In *ijcai'95, Workshop on Basic Ontological Issues in Knowledge Sharing,* April 13, 1995.

Guarino, N. (1998). Formal ontology and information systems. *Proceedings of the 1ˢᵗ International Conference on Formal Ontologies in Information Systems* (pp. 3–15). IOS-Press.

Guarino, N. (1995). Formal ontology, conceptual analysis and knowledge representation. *International Journal of Human-Computer Studies*, *43*, 625–640. doi:10.1006/ijhc.1995.1066

Gupta, U. G., & Biegel, J. (1990). A rule–based intelligent test case generator. In *Proceedings of AAAI–90 Workshop on Knowledge–Based System Verification, Validation and Testing*. AAAI Press.

Gutenberg, E. (1958). *Einführung in die Betriebswirtschaftslehre*. Wiesbaden, Germany: Gabler.

Guy, I., Jacovi, M., Shahar, E., Meshulam, N., Soroka, V., & Farrell, S. (2008). Harvesting with SONAR: The value of aggregating social network information. In *Proceeding of the Twenty-Sixth Annual SIGCHI Conference on Human Factors in Computing Systems* (Florence, Italy, April 05 - 10, 2008), CHI '08, (pp. 1017-1026). New York, NY: ACM.

Hackman, J. R., & Oldham, G. R. (1975). Development of the job diagnostic survey. *The Journal of Applied Psychology*, *60*, 159–170. doi:10.1037/h0076546

Haeske-Seeberg, H. (2005). *Handbuch Qualitätsmanagement im Krankenhaus – Strategien, Analysen, Konzepte*. Stuttgart, Germany: Kohlhammer Verlag.

Hague, M. J., & Taleb-Bendiab, A. (1998). Tool for management of concurrent conceptual engineering design. *Concurrent Engineering: Research and Applications*, *6*(2), 111–129. doi:10.1177/1063293X9800600203

Hahn, R., Bizer, C., Sahnwaldt, C., Herta, C., Robinson, S., Bürgle, M., & Scheel, U. (2010). *Faceted Wikipedia search. Business Information Systems* (pp. 1–11). Berlin, Germany: Springer-Verlag.

Hall, H. (2001). Input-friendliness: Motivating knowledge sharing across intranets. *Journal of Information Science*, *27*(3), 139–146. doi:10.1177/016555150102700303

Hall, W., Davis, H., & Hutchings, G. (1996). *Rethinking hypermedia: The microcosm approach*. USA: Springer.

Han, X., & Zhao, J. (2009). Named entity disambiguation by leveraging Wikipedia semantic knowledge. In *Proceeding of the 18th ACM Conference on Information and Knowledge Management* (*CIKM-2009*), (pp. 215–224).

Han, J., & Kamber, M. (2006). *Data mining: Concepts and techniques* (2nd ed.). Morgan Kaufmann.

Harrison, N., & Samaon, D. (2002). *Technology management: Text and international cases*. New York, NY: McGraw-Hill.

Harth, A. (2009). VisiNav: Visual Web data search and navigation. *Proceedings of the 20ᵗʰ International Conference on Databases and Expert Systems Applications*, (pp. 214–228). Berlin, Germany: Springer-Verlag.

Harth, A., Hogan, A., Delbru, R., Umbrich, J., ORiain, S., & Decker, S. (2007). SWSE: Answers before links. *Proceedings of Semantic Web Challenge 2007*.

Hartmann, S. (2008). *Überwindung semantischer Heterogenität bei multiplen Data-Warehouse-Systemen*. Bamberg, Germany: University of Bamberg Press.

Hasler Roumois, U. (2007). *Studienbuch Wissensmanagement: Grundlagen der Wissensarbeit in Wirtschafts-, Non- Profit- und Public- Organisationen*. Zürich, Switzerland: Orell-Füssli.

Hauber, R. (2002). *Performance Measurement in der Forschung und Entwicklung: Konzeption und Methodik*. Wiesbaden, Germany: Deutscher Universitäts Verlag.

Hausenblas, M., Troncy, R., Raimond, Y., & Bürger, T. (2009). *Interlinking multimedia: How to apply linked data principles to multimedia fragments*. Paper presented at the Linked Data on the Web Workshop, Amsterdam, Netherlands.

He, H., Wang, H., Yang, J., & Yu, P. S. (2007). Blinks: Ranked keyword searches on graphs. *Proceedings of the 2007 ACM SIGMOD International Conference on Management of Data*, (pp. 305–316). New York, NY: Springer-Verlag.

Heckner, M., Neubauer, T., & Wolff, C. (2008). Tree, funny, to read, Google: What are tags supposed to achieve? A comparative analysis of user keywords for different digital resource types. In *Proceeding of the 2008 ACM Workshop on Search in Social Media* (Napa Valley, California, USA, October 30 - 30, 2008), SSM '08, (pp. 3-10). New York, NY: ACM.

Heim, P., Ertl, T., & Ziegler, J. (2010). Facet graphs: Complex semantic querying made easy . In Aroyo, L. (Eds.), *The Semantic Web: Research and applications, LNCS 6088* (pp. 288–302). Berlin, Germany: Springer-Verlag. doi:10.1007/978-3-642-13486-9_20

Hendler, J. (2001). Agents and the Semantic Web. *IEEE Intelligent Systems, 16*(2), 30–37. doi:10.1109/5254.920597

Hengartner, U., & Meier, A. (2010). *Web 3.0 & Semantic Web: HMD – Praxis der Wirtschaftsinformatik*. Heidelberg, Germany: DPunkt Verlag.

Herman, S. (2004). Produktive Wissensarbeit: Eine Herausforderung . In Hermann, S. (Ed.), *Ressourcen strategisch nutzen: Wissen als Basis für den Dienstleistungserfolg* (pp. 207–228). Stuttgart, Germany: Fraunhofer IRB-Verlag.

Hesse, H.-A. (1998). *Experte, Laie, Dilettant: Über Nutzen und Grenzen von Fachwissen*. Opladen, Germany: Westdeutscher Verlag.

Hevner, A. R., March, S. T., Park, J., & Ram, S. (2004). Design science in information systems research. *Management Information Systems Quarterly, 28*, 75–105.

Heymann, P., Koutrika, G., & Garcia-Molina, H. (2008). Can social bookmarking improve web search? *Proceedings of the First ACM International Conference on Web Search and Data Mining, WSDM 2008* (pp. 195-206). New York, NY: ACM.

Heymann, P., Ramage, D., & Garcia-Molina, H. (2008). Social tag prediction. In *Proceedings of 31st International ACM Conference on Research and Development in Information Retrieval*, (pp. 531-538). New York, NY: ACM.

Hickson, I. (2011). *Server-sent events*. W3C Working Draft. Retrieved from http://www.w3.org /TR/eventsource/

Hildebrand, M., van Ossenbruggen, J., & Hardman, L. (2006). Facet: A browser for heterogeneous Semantic Web repositories. *The Semantic Web-ISWC, 2006*, 272–285. doi:10.1007/11926078_20

Hitzler, R. (1998). Reflexive Kompetenz: Zur Genese und Bedeutung von Expertenwissen jenseits des Professionalismus. In W. K. Schulz (Ed.), *Expertenwissen: Soziologische, psychologische und pädagogische Perspektiven* (pp. 33-47). Opladen, Germany: Leske + Budrich.

Hoernlein, A., Ifland, M., Kluegl, P., & Puppe, F. (2009). CaseTrain: Design and evaluation of a case-based training-system and its comprehensive application in university (Konzeption und Evaluation eines fallbasierten Trainingssystems im universitätsweiten Einsatz (CaseTrain)). *GMS Medizinische Informatik, Biometrie und Epidemiologie, 5*(1).

Hollingshead, A. B. (1995, January). *The workflow reference model* (Tech. Rep.). Workflow Management Coalition.

Holmer, T., Kienle, A., & Wessner, M. (2006). Explicit referencing in learning chats: Needs and acceptance. In W. Nejdl & K. Tochtermann, (Eds.), *Innovative approaches for learning and knowledge sharing*. First European Conference on Technology Enhanced Learning, Springer. Jackson, P. (2001). Making sense of qualitative data. In M. Limb & C. Dwyer, (Eds.), *Qualitative methodologies for geographers*. London, UK: Arnold.

Horibe, F. (1999). *Managing knowledge workers: New skills and attitudes to unlock the intellectual capital in your organization*. Toronto, Canada: John Wiley.

Horley, B., & Lesser, V. (2004). A survey of multi-agent organizational paradigms. *The Knowledge Engineering Review, 19*, 281–316.

Horowitz, B. (2006, February 17). Creators, synthesizers, and consumers. *Elatable: Thoughts on technology (and not) from Bradley Horowitz of Yahoo*. Retrieved from http://www.elatable.com /blog/?p=5

Hotho, A., Jaschke, R., Schmitz, C., & Stumme, G. (2006). *Information retrieval in folksonomies: Search and ranking*. *The Semantic Web: Research and Applications, LNCS 4011* (pp. 411–426). Heidelberg, Germany: Springer.

Howe, N., Strauss, W., & Matson, R. (2000). *Millennials rising: The next great generation.* New York, NY: Vintage Books/Random House, Inc.

Hron, J. (2000). *Motivationale Aspekte von beruflicher Expertise: Welche Ziele und Motive spornen Experten im Rahmen ihrer Arbeit an?* München, Germany: Utz.

Hsu, I. C. (2008). Knowledge sharing practices as a facilitating factor for improving organizational performance through human capital: A preliminary test. *Expert Systems with Applications*, *35*(3), 1316–1326. doi:10.1016/j.eswa.2007.08.012

Hube, G. (2005). *Beitrag zur Beschreibung und Analyse von Wissensarbeit.* Unveröffentlichte Dissertation, Universität Stuttgart.

Huber, B. (1999). Experts in organizations: The power of expertise. In Academy of Business & Administrative Sciences (Ed.), *Globalization and Emerging Economies: International Conference Proceedings*, July 12-14, 1999, Barcelona, Spain. Retrieved December 12, 2009, from http://www.sba.muohio.edu /abas/1999/huberbe.pdf

Huettig, M., Buscher, G., Menzel, T., Scheppach, W., Puppe, F., & Buscher, H. P. (2004). A diagnostic expert system for structured reports, quality assessment, and training of residents in sonography. *Medizinische Klinik*, *99*(3), 117–122. doi:10.1007/s00063-004-1020-y

Huhns, M. N., Singh, M. P., Burstein, M., Decker, K., Durfee, E., & Finin, T. (2005). Research directions for service-oriented multiagent systems. *IEEE Internet Computing*, *9*(6), 65–70. doi:10.1109/MIC.2005.132

Hummon, N. (2000). Utility and dynamic social networks. *Social Networks, 22*(3), 221-249. Elsevier. Jackson, M. O., & Wolinsky, A. (1996). A strategic model of social and economic networks. *Journal of Economic Theory*, *71*, 44–74.

Humphreys, K., Gaizauskas, R., Azzam, S., Huyck, C., Mitchell, B., Cunningham, H., & Wilks, Y. (1998). Univ. of Sheffield: Description of the LaSIE-II system as used for MUC-7. In *Proceedings of the 7th Message Understanding Conference.*

IBM. (1978). *Report on the contents of a sample of programs surveyed.* California: IBM.

IBM. (2009). *Lotus connections - Dogear.* Retrieved from http://www-01.ibm.com /software/lotus/products/connections/dogear.html

Illig, J., Hotho, A., Jäschke, R., & Stumme, G. (2009). A comparison of content-based tag recommendations in folksonomy systems. In *Postproceedings of the International Conference on Knowledge Processing in Practice*, (pp. 1-14). Springer.

Imhoff, C., & White, C. (2011). Self service business intelligence – Empowering users to generate insights . In *TDWI Best Practices Report*. TDWI Research.

Imine, A. (2008). Flexible concurrency control for real-time collaborative editors. In *Proceedings of 28th International Conference on Distributed Computing Systems, IEEE Computer*, (pp. 423-428).

Inmon, W. H. (1996). *Building the data warehouse.* New York, NY: Wiley & Sons.

Ipe, M. (2003). Knowledge sharing in organizations: A conceptual framework. *Human Resource Development Review, 2*(4), 337–359. doi:10.1177/1534484303257985

Isozaki, H., & Kazawa, H. (2002). Efficient support vector classifiers for named entity recognition. In *Proceedings of the Conference on Computational Linguistics (COLING-2002).*

Janis, I. (1982). *Groupthink* (2nd ed.). Boston, MA: Houghton-Mifflin.

Janz, B. D., Colquitt, J. A., & Noe, R. A. (1997). Knowledge worker team effectiveness: The role of autonomy, interdependence, team development, and contextual support variables. *Personnel Psychology, 50*(4), 877–904. doi:10.1111/j.1744-6570.1997.tb01486.x

Janz, B. D., & Prasarnphanich, P. (2003). Understanding the antecedents of effective knowledge management: The importance of a knowledge-centered culture. *Decision Sciences, 34*(2), 351–384. doi:10.1111/1540-5915.02328

Jäschke, R., Eisterlehner, F., Hotho, A., & Stumme, G. (2009). Testing and evaluating tag recommenders in a live system. In D. Benz & F. Janssen (Eds.), *Workshop on Knowledge Discovery, Data Mining, and Machine Learning*, (pp. 44 -51).

Jaschke, R., Hotho, A., Schmitz, C., Ganter, B., & Stumme, G. (2006). Trias - An algorithm for mining iceberg tri-lattices. *Proceedings of the 6th IEEE International Conference on Data Mining, ICDM 2006* (pp. 907-911). Hong Kong: IEEE Computer Society.

Jäschke, R., Marinho, L., Hotho, A., Schmidt-Thieme, L., & Stumme, G. (2007). Tag recommendations in folksonomies. In J. Kok, J. Koronacki, R. Lopez de Mantaras, S. Matwin, D. Mladenic, & A. Skowron, (Eds.), *Proceedings of Knowledge Discovery in Databases*, volume 4702 of *Lecture Notes in Computer Science*, (pp. 506-514). Berlin, Germany: Springer.

Jaschke, R., Hotho, A., Schmitz, C., Ganter, B., & Stumme, G. (2008). Discovering shared conceptualizations in folksonomies. *Web Semantics: Science . Services and Agents on the World Wide Web, 6*, 38–53.

Jennings, N., Corera, J., & Laresgoiti, I. (1995). Developing industrial multi-agent systems. In *Proceedings of the First International Conference on Multi-Agent Systems (ICMAS-95)*, (pp. 423–430).

Jennings, N., Faratin, P., & Lomuscio, A. (2001). Automated negotiation: Prospects, methods and challenges. *Group Decision and Negotiation, 10*(2), 199–215. doi:10.1023/A:1008746126376

Jimeno, A., Jimenez-Ruiz, E., Lee, V., Gaudan, S., Berlanga, R., & Rebholz-Schuhmann, D. (2008). Assessment of disease named entity recognition on a corpus of annotated sentences. *BMC Bioinformatics, 9*(3), 1–10. doi:10.1186/1471-2105-9-S3-S3

Jin, Y., Li, R., Cai, Y., Li, Q., Daud, A., & Li, Y. (2010). Semantic grounding of hybridization for tag recommendation . In Chen, L., Tang, C., Yang, J., & Gao, Y. (Eds.), *Web-Age Information Management* (*Vol. 6184*, pp. 139–150). Lecture Notes in Computer Science Berlin, Germany: Springer. doi:10.1007/978-3-642-14246-8_16

Jung, J. J., & Euzenat, J. (2007). Towards semantic social networks . In Franconi, E., Kifer, M., & May, W. (Eds.), *The Semantic Web: Research and Applications* (*Vol. 4519*, pp. 267–280). Lecture Notes in Computer Science Springer-Verlag. doi:10.1007/978-3-540-72667-8_20

Jung, R., & Winter, R. (2000). Data-Warehousing-Strategie . In *Business-Engineering*. Berlin, Germany: Springer.

Kacholia, V., Pandit, S., Chakrabarti, S., Sudarshan, R. D., & Karambelkar, D. (2005). Bidirectional expansion for keyword search on graph databases. *Proceedings of the 31st International Conference on Very Large Databases 2005*, (pp. 505–516). Trondheim, Norway: VLDB Endowment.

Kalfoglou, Y., & Schorlemmer, M. (2003). IF-Map: An ontology mapping method based on information flow theory. *Journal on Data Semantics, 1*(1), 98–127. doi:10.1007/978-3-540-39733-5_5

Kalogeraki, V., Gunopulos, D., & Zeinalipour-Yazti, D. (2002). A local search mechanism for peer-to-peer networks. *Proceedings of the Eleventh International Conference on Information and Knowledge Management* (*CIKM '02*), 300-307.

Karau, S. J., & Williams, K. D. (1993, October). Social loafing: A meta analytic review and theoretical integration. *Journal of Personality and Social Psychology, 65*(4), 681–706. doi:10.1037/0022-3514.65.4.681

Katasonov, A., & Terziyan, V. (2008). Semantic agent programming language (S-APL): A middleware platform for the Semantic Web. In *Proceedings of the 2008 IEEE International Conference on Semantic Computing (ICSC '08)* (pp. 504-511).

Kautz, H., & Selman, B. (1997). Referral Web: Combining social networks and collaborative filtering. *Communications of the ACM, 40*(3), 63–65. doi:10.1145/245108.245123

Kazama, J., & Torisawa, K. (2007). Exploiting Wikipedia as external knowledge for named entity recognition. In *Proceedings of the 2007 Joint Conference on Empirical Methods in Natural Language Processing and Computational Natural Language Learning (EMNLP-CoNLL-2007)*, (pp. 698–707).

Kazama, J., Makino, T., Ohta, Y., & Tsujii, J. (2002). Tuning support vector machines for biomedical named entity recognition. In *Proceedings of ACL 2003 Workshop on Natural Language Processing in the Biomedical Domain*, (pp. 1–8).

Keller, P. (2007). *Del.icio.us stats*. Retrieved on December 1, 2007, from http://deli.ckoma.net/stats

Kemmis, S. (1993). Action research and social movement: A challenge for policy research. *Education Policy Analysis, 1*(1).

Kemmis, S. (2001). Exploring the relevance of critical theory for action research: Emancipatory action research in the footsteps of Jürgen Habermas . In Reason, P., & Bradbury, H. (Eds.), *Handbook of action research: Participative inquiry and practice.* Thousand Oaks, CA: Sage.

Kennedy, J. C. (2002). Leadership in Malaysia: Traditional values, international outlook. *The Academy of Management Executive (1993), 16*(3), 15-26.

Kennedy, L. S., & Naaman, M. (2008). Generating diverse and representative image search results for landmarks. In *Proceedings of the 17th International Conference on World Wide Web*, (pp. 297-306). New York, NY: ACM.

Kennedy, L., Naaman, M., Ahern, S., Nair, R., & Rattenbury, T. (2007). How flickr helps us make sense of the world: context and content in community-contributed media collections. In *Proceedings of 15th International Conference on Multimedia*, (pp. 631-640). New York, NY: ACM.

Kerkri, E. M., Quantin, C., Allaert, F. A., Cottin, Y., Charve, P., Jouanot, F., & Yetongnon, K. M. (2001). An approach for integrating heterogeneous information sources in a medical data warehouse. *Journal of Medical Systems, 25*(3), 167–176. doi:10.1023/A:1010728915998

Keuken, F. W. (1996). *Management von Akademikerorganisationen*. Hamburg, Germany: Kovac.

Khoussainov, R., & Kushmerick, N. (2005). *Email task management: An iterative relational learning approach*. In CEAS'05.

Kikoski, K., & Kikoski, F. (2004). *The inquiring organization: Tacit knowledge, Conversation and knowledge creation, skills for 21st-century organizations*. Praeger.

Kim, J.-H., Kang, I.-H., & Choi, K.-S. (2002). Unsupervised named entity classification models and their ensembles. In *Proceedings of the Conference on Computational Linguistics* (*COLING-2002*).

Kimball, R., & Ross, M. (2002). *The data warehouse toolkit: The complete guide to dimensional modeling*. New York, NY: John Wiley & Sons, Inc.

Klein, D., Smarr, J., Nguyen, H., & Manning, C. (2003). Named entity recognition with character-level models. In *Proceedings of 7th Conference on Natural Language Learning* (*HLT-NAACL-2003*), (pp. 180–183).

Kleinberg, J. (2000). The small-world phenomenon: An algorithm perspective. *Proceedings of the 32nd ACM Symposium on Theory of Computing* (pp. 163-170).

Kleinberg, J. (2006). Complex networks and decentralized search algorithms. *Proceedings of the International Congress of Mathematicians (ICM)* (Vol. 3, pp. 1-26). Madrid, Spain.

Kleinberg, J., Kumar, R., Raghavan, P., Rajagopalan, S., & Tomkins, A. S. (1999). The web as a graph: Measurements, models, and methods. *Proceedings of the 5th Annual International Conference on Computing and Combinatorics*, (pp. 1-17). Springer-Verlag.

Kleinberg, J. (2002). Small-world phenomena and the dynamics of information. *Advances in Neural Information Processing Systems*, •••, 14.

Kleinert, J. (2000). *Globalisierung, Strukturwandel und Beschäftigung*. Tübingen, Germany: Mohr Siebeck.

Kluegl, P., Atzmueller, M., & Puppe, F. (2009). TextMarker: A tool for rule-based information extraction. In *Proceedings of the Biennial GSCL Conference 2009, 2nd UIMA@GSCL Workshop*, (pp. 233-240). Gunter Narr Verlag.

Knauf, R., Gonzalez, A. J., & Abel, T. (2002). A framework for validation of rule-based systems. *IEEE Transactions on Systems, Man, and Cybernetics. Part B, Cybernetics, 32*(3), 281–295. doi:10.1109/TSMCB.2002.999805

Knoll, S. W., Chelvier, R., & Horton, G. (2007). Formalised online creativity using thinxels. In *Proccedings of the 10th European Conference on Creativity and Innovation (ECCI)*.

Knoll, S. W., Hörning, M., & Horton, G. (2008). A design approach for a universal group support system using thinklets and thinxels. In *Proceedings of the Group Decision and Negotiation Meeting 2008 (GDN)*.

Knoll, S. W., Hörning, M., & Horton, G. (2009). Applying a thinklet and thinxel-based group process modeling language: A prototype of a universal group support system. In *Proceedings of the 42nd Hawaii International Conference on System Sciences (HICSS)*.

Knoll, S. W., Plumbaum, T., Hoffmann, J. L., & De Luca, E. W. (2010). Collaboration ontology: Applying collaboration knowledge to a generic group support system. In *Proceeding of the Group Decision and Negotiation Meeting 2010 (GDN)*.

Knoll, S. W., & Horton, G. (2011). (in press). Formalized collaboration using collaboration engineering: How to improve collaboration with a universal gss. *Group Decision and Negotiation*.

Kobilarov, G., & Dickinson, I. (2008). *Humboldt: Exploring linked data*. Linked Data on the Web Workshop (LDOW 2008), Beijing, China.

Kolfschoten, G. L., Vreede, G.-J. de., & Briggs, R. O. (2008) Computer aided pattern-based collaboration process design: A computer aided collaboration engineering tool. In *Proceedings of the 14th International Workshop on Groupware 2008 (CRIWG)*.

Kolfschoten, G. L., Briggs, R. O., de Vreede, G.-J., Jacobs, P. H. M., & Appelman, J. H. (2006). A conceptual foundation of the thinklet concept for collaboration engineering. *International Journal of Human-Computer Studies, 64*(7), 611–621. doi:10.1016/j.ijhcs.2006.02.002

Kolfschoten, G. L., & de Vreede, G.-J. (2009). A design approach for collaboration processes: A multimethod design science study in collaboration engineering. *Journal of Management Information Systems, 26*(1), 225–256. doi:10.2753/MIS0742-1222260109

Kolfschoten, G. L., de Vreede, G.-J., & Pietron, L. (2010). A training approach for the transition of repeatable collaboration processes to practitioners. *Group Decision and Negotiation, 20*(3), 1–25.

Krause, B., Hotho, A., & Stumme, G. (2008). A comparison of social bookmarking with traditional search. *Proceedings of the 30th European Conf. on IR Research, Advances in Information Retrieval, ECIR 2008, LNCS 4956*, (pp. 101-113). Springer.

Krebel, U. H.-G. (1999). Pairwise classification and support vector machines . In Scholkopf, B., Burges, C., & Smola, A. (Eds.), *Advances in kernel methods - Support vector learning. MIT Press, 1999*.

Krems, J. (1990). *Zur Psychologie der Expertenschaft*. Unveröffentlichte Habilitation, Universität Regensburg.

Krestel, R., Fankhauser, P., & Nejdl, W. (2009). Latent dirichlet allocation for tag recommendation. In *Proceedings of the Third ACM Conference on Recommender Systems*, (pp. 61-68). New York, NY: ACM.

Krishnan, V., & Manning, C. (2006). An effective two-stage model for exploiting non-local dependencies in named entity recognition. In *Proceedings of the 21st International Conference on Computational Linguistics and 44th Annual Meeting of the Association for Computational Linguistics*, (pp. 1121–1128).

Krishnan, V., Narayanashetty, P. K., Nathan, M., Davies, R. T., & Konstan, J. A. (2008). Who predicts better? Results from an online study comparing humans and an online recommender system. In *Proceedings of the 2008 ACM Conference on Recommender Systems* (Lausanne, Switzerland, October 23 - 25, 2008), RecSys '08, (pp. 211-218). New York, NY: ACM.

Krishnarao, A., Gahlot, H., Srinet, A., & Kushwaha, D. (2009). A comparison of performance of sequential learning algorithms on the task of named entity recognition for Indian languages. In *Proceedings of the International Conference on Computational Science (ICCS 2009), LNCS 5544*, (pp. 123–132). Springer.

Kristiina, M., Hanna, K., & Rebecca, P. (2007). Interpersonal similarity as a driver of knowledge sharing within multinational corporations. *International Business Review, 16*, 1–22. doi:10.1016/j.ibusrev.2006.11.002

Krupka, G. R., & Hausman, K. (1998). IsoQuest Inc.: Description of the NetOwl™ extractor system as used for MUC-7. In *Proceedings of the 7th Message Understanding Conference*.

Küngas, P., Rao, J., & Matskin, M. (2004). Symbolic agent negotiation for Semantic Web service exploitation . In Li, Q., Wang, G., & Feng, L. (Eds.), *Advances in Web-Age Imformation Management* (*Vol. 3129*, pp. 458–467). Lecture Notes in Computer Science Springer-Verlag. doi:10.1007/978-3-540-27772-9_46

Kurze, C., Gluchowski, P., & Bohringer, M. (2010). Towards an ontology of multidimensional data structures for analytical purposes. In *HICSS '10: Proceedings of the 2010, 43rd Hawaii International Conference on System Sciences.* Washington, DC: IEEE Computer Society.

Ladkin, D. (2004). Action research . In Seale, C., Gobo, G., Gubrium, J. F., & Silverman, D. (Eds.), *Qualitative research practice.* London, UK: Sage. doi:10.4135/9781848608191.d39

Lafferty, J., McCallum, A., & Pereira, F. (2001). Conditional random fields: Probabilistic models for segmenting and labeling sequence data. In *Proceedings of the International Conference Machine Learning (ICML-2001).*

Lamnek, S. (2005). *Qualitative Sozialforschung: Lehrbuch.* Weinheim, Germany: Beltz.

Lander, S. E. (1997). Issues in multi-agent design systems. *IEEE Expert, 12*(2), 18–26. doi:10.1109/64.585100

Larkin, J. (1980). Expert and novice performance in solving physics problems. *Science, 208*, 1335–1342. doi:10.1126/science.208.4450.1335

Larson, M. S. (1977). *The rise of professionalism: A sociological analysis.* Berkeley, CA: University of California Press.

Lee, J., & Hwang, S. (2008). Ranking with tagging as quality indicators. In *Proceedings of the 2008 ACM Symposium on Applied Computing* (Fortaleza, Ceara, Brazil, March 16 - 20, 2008), SAC '08, (pp. 2432-2436). New York, NY: ACM.

Lee, K., Kim, H., Shin, H., & Kim, H. (2009). Tag sense disambiguation for clarifying the vocabulary of social tags. *Proceedings of IEEE International Conference on Computational Science and Engineering* (pp. 729-734). Los Alamitos, CA: IEEE.

Lee, H., & Choi, B. (2003). Knowledge management enablers, processes, and organizational performance: An integrative view and empirical examination. *Journal of Management Information Systems, 20*(1), 179–228.

Lee, J., Seo, W., Kim, K., & Kim, C.-H. (2010). An owl-based ontological approach to rad modeling of human interactions for business collaboration. *Expert Systems with Applications, 37*(6), 4128–4138. doi:10.1016/j.eswa.2009.11.011

Lee, K.-J., Hwang, Y.-S., Kim, S., & Rim, H.-C. (2004). Biomedical named entity recognition using two-phase model based on SVMs. *Journal of Biomedical Informatics, 37*(6), 393–428. doi:10.1016/j.jbi.2004.08.012

Lehmann, F., & Wille, R. (1995). A triadic approach to formal concept analysis. *Proceedings of the 3rd International Conference on Conceptual Structures: Applications, Implementation and Theory* (pp. 32-43). Springer.

Levy, F., & Murnane, R. J. (2006). *How computerized work and globalization shape human skill demands.* MIT IPC Working Paper, 05-006. Retrieved January 09, 2007, from http://web.mit.edu/ipc/publications/pdf/05-006.pdf

Lewin, K. (1946). Action research and minority problems. *The Journal of Social Issues, 2*, 34–46. doi:10.1111/j.1540-4560.1946.tb02295.x

Liao, W., & Veeramachaneni, S. (2009). A simple semi-supervised algorithm for named entity recognition. In *Proceedings of the NAACL HLT-2009 Workshop on Semi-Supervised Learning for Natural Language Processing,* (pp. 58–65).

Liben-Nowell, D., Novak, J., Kumar, R., Raghavan, P., & Tomkins, A. (2005). Geographic routing in social networks. *Proceedings of the National Academy of Sciences of the United States of America, 102*(33), 11623–11628. doi:10.1073/pnas.0503018102

Lin, H., Davis, J., & Zhou, Y. (2009). An integrated approach to extracting ontological structures from folksonomies. *Proceedings of the 6th European Semantic Web Conference, ESWC 2009, LNCS 5545,* (pp. 654-668). Heidelberg, Germany: Springer.

Lin, Y.-F., Tsai, T.-H., Chou, W.-C., Wu, K.-P., Sung, T.-Y., & Hsu, W.-L. (2004). A maximum entropy approach to biomedical named entity recognition. In *Proceedings of Workshop on Data Mining in Bioinformatics (BIO-KDD04),* (pp. 56–61).

Lipczak, M. (2008). Tag recommendation for folksonomies oriented towards individual users. In *Proceedings of the ECML/PKDD Discovery Challenge Workshop.*

Liu, F., Zhao, J., Lv, B., Xu, B., & Yu, H. (2005). Product named entity recognition based on hierarchical hidden Markov model. In *Proceedings of the Fourth SIGHAN Workshop on Chinese Language Processing,* (pp. 40–47).

Liu, Q., Cui, X., & Hu, X. (2008). An agent-based multimedia intelligent platform for collaborative design. *International Journal of Communications . Network and System Sciences, 3,* 207–283.

LiveJournal. (2010). Retrieved from http://www.livejournal.com

Li, W., & McCallum, A. (2003). Rapid development of Hindi named entity recognition using conditional random fields and feature induction. *ACM Transactions on Asian Language Information Processing, 2*(3), 290–294. doi:10.1145/979872.979879

Ludwig, L. (2005). *Business Intelligence und das Semantic Web: ein Traumpaar.* Retrieved June 13, 2011, from http://www.competence-site.de /corporate-performance-management/ Business-Intelligence-und-das-Semantic-Web-39683

Luo, J., & Xue, X. (2010). Research on information retrieval system based on Semantic Web and multi-agent. In *Proceedings of 2010 International Conference on Intelligent Computing and Cognitive Informatics,* (pp. 207-209). Kuala Lumpur, Malaysia.

Lüpkes, C. (2011). Ad-hoc Datentransformationen für Analytische Informationssysteme. In *Proceedings of the 23rd GI-Workshop on Foundations of Databases,* University of Innsbruck, Obergurgl, Tirol, Austria.

Ma, H., Chandrasekar, R., Quirk, C., & Gupta, A. (2009). Page hunt: Improving search engines using human computation games. *Proceedings of the 32nd International ACM SIGIR Conference on Research and Development in Information Retrieval* (pp. 746-747). ACM.

MacQueen, J. (1967). Some methods for classification and analysis of multivariate observations. In L. M. Le Cam,& J. Neyman (Eds.), *Proceedings of 5th Berkeley Symposium on Mathematical Statistics and Probability,* (pp. 281-297). Berkeley, CA: University of California Press.

Madhavan, J., Berstein, P., & Rahm, E. (2001). Generic schema matching with Cupid. *Proceeedings of the 27th International Conference on Very larged Data Bases* (pp. 48-58). VLDB Endowment.

Maedche, A., Motik, B., Silva, N., & Volz, R. (2002). MAFRA: A mapping framework for distributed ontologies. *Proceedings of the 13th European Conference on Knowledge Engineering and Knowledge Management* (pp. 235-250). Springer.

Malik, F. (2006). *Führen, leisten, leben: Wirksames Management für eine neue Zeit. Komplett überarb. Neuaufl.* Frankfurt, Germany: Campus.

Manevitz, L. M., & Yousef, M. (2002). One-class SVMs for document classification. *Journal of Machine Learning Research, 2,* 139–154.

Manjunath, B. S., Salembier, P., & Sikora, T. (2002). *Introduction to MPEG-7 - Multimedia content description interface.* Chichester, UK: John Wiley & Sons Ltd.

Manola, F., Miller, E., & McBride, B. (2004). RDF primer. *W3C recommendation.*

Mardia, K., Kent, J., & Bibby, J. (1979). *Multivariate analysis.* Academic Press.

Marinho, L. B., & Schmidt-Thieme, L. (2008). Collaborative tag recommendations . In Bock, H. H. (Eds.), *Data analysis, machine learning and applications, studies in classification, data analysis, and knowledge organization* (pp. 533–540). Berlin, Germany: Springer.

Marshall, C., Halaz, F., Rogres, R., & Janssen, W. (1991). Aquanet: A hypertext tool to hold your knowledge in place. In *Proceedings of the 3rd ACM Conference on Hypertext,* (pp. 261-275). USA.

Marshall, C., Shipman, F., & Coombs, J. (1994). VIKI: spatial hypertext supporting emergent structure. In *Proceedings of the 6th ACM Conference on Hypertext,* (pp. 13-23). Scotland.

Mathes, A. (2004). *Folksonomies - Cooperative classification and communication through shared metadata.* Graduate School of Library and Information Science, University of Illinois Urbana-Champaign.

Matskin, M. Kirkeluten, O.J., Krossnes, S. B., & Sæle, O. (2001). Agora: An infrastructure for cooperative work support in multi-agent systems. In T. Wagner & O. F. Rana, (Eds.), *Proceedings of the International Workshop on Infrastructure for Multi-Agent Systems, Lecture Notes in Computer Science, Volume 1887,* (pp. 28-40). Springer-Verlag.

Ma, Y., Zhang, S., Li, Y., Yi, Z., & Liu, S. (2009). An approach for multi-agent coordination based on semantic approximation. *International Journal of Intelligent Information Database Systems, 3*(2), 163–179. doi:10.1504/IJIIDS.2009.025161

Maynard, D., Tablan, V., Ursu, C., Cunningham, H., & Wilks, Y. (2001). Named entity recognition from diverse text types. In *Proceedings of the Conference on Recent Advances in Natural Language Processing (RANLP-2001)*.

McCallum, A., & Li, W. (2003). Early results for named entity recognition with conditional random fields, feature induction and web-enhanced lexicons. In *Proceedings of the Seventh Conference on Natural language learning at HLT-NAACL 2003 - Volume 4*, (pp. 188–191).

McCann, R., Shen, W., & Doan, A. (2008). Matching schemas in online communities: A Web 2.0 approach. *Proceedings of the 18th International Conference on Data Engineering* (pp 110-119). IEEE.

McDermott, R. (1999). Why information technology inspired but cannot deliver knowledge management. *California Management Review, 4*, 103–117.

McKay, J., & Marshall, P. (2001). The dual imperatives of action research. *Information Technology & People, 14*(1), 46–53. doi:10.1108/09593840110384771

McLeod, J., Childs, S., Lappin, J., & Siggers, G. (2010). Investigation into the use of Microsoft SharePoint in UK higher education institutions. *Communications in Computer and Information Science, 110*(5), 335–344. doi:10.1007/978-3-642-16419-4_34

McNiff, J., Lomax, P., & Whitehead, J. (2005). *You and your action research project*. London, UK: Routledge Falmer.

Medelyan, O., Milne, D., Legg, C., & Witten, I. (2009). Mining meaning from Wikipedia. *International Journal of Human-Computer Studies, 67*, 716–754. doi:10.1016/j.ijhcs.2009.05.004

Melrose, M. J. (1996). Got a philosophical match? Does it matter? In Zuber-Skerritt, O. (Ed.), *New directions in action research*. London, UK: Falmer Press. doi:10.4324/9780203392935_chapter_4

Mertens, M. (2011). Wissensbasiertes business intelligence für die Informations-Selbstversorgung von Entscheidungsträgern. In *Proceedings of the 23. GI-Workshop on Foundations of Databases*, University of Innsbruck, Obergurgl, Tirol, Austria.

Mertens, M., Teiken, Y., & Appelrath, H.-J. (2009). Semantische Anreicherung von strukturierten Daten und Prozessen in analytischen Informationssystemen am Beispiel von MUSTANG. In *Proceedings of Forschungskolloquium Business Intelligence 2009 der GI-Fachgruppe 5.8 - Management Support Systems*. Dortmund, Germany: University of Dortmund.

Mesbah, A., & van Deursen, A. (2008). A component- and push-based architectural style for Ajax applications. *Journal of Systems and Software, 81*(12), 2194–2209. doi:10.1016/j.jss.2008.04.005

Meulder, F., & Daelemans, W. (2003). Memory-based named entity recognition using unannotated data. In *Proceedings of the Seventh Conference on Natural language learning at HLT-NAACL-2003 - Volume 4*, (pp. 208–211).

Microsoft. (n.d.). Retrieved from http://msdn.microsoft.com/en-us/library/aa923224.aspx

Mieg, H. A. (2000). Vom ziemlichen Unvermögen der Psychologie, das Tun der Experten zu begreifen: Ein Plädoyer für Professionalisierung als psychologische Kategorie und einen interaktionsorientierten Expertenbegriff . In Silbereisen, R. K., & Reitzlem, M. (Eds.), *Bericht über den 42. Kongress der Deutschen Gesellschaft für Psychologie 2000* (pp. 635–648). Lengerich, Germany: Pabst.

Mieg, H. A. (2001). *The social psychology of expertise: Case studies in research, professional domains, and expert roles*. Mahwah, NJ: Lawrence Erlbaum.

Mika, P. (2005). Flink: Semantic Web technology for the extraction and analysis of social networks. In *Web Semantics: Science, Services and Agents on the World Wide Web, 3*(2-3), 211-223, Elsevier B. V.

Mika, P. (2005). Ontologies are us: A unified model of social networks and semantics. *Proceedings of the 4th International Semantic Web Conference, ISWC 2005, LNCS 3729*, (pp. 522-536). Galway, Ireland: Springer.

Mikheev, A. (1999). A knowledge-free method for capitalized word disambiguation. In *Proceedings of the Conference of Association for Computational Linguistics (ACL-1999)*.

Mikheev, A., Moens, M., & Grover, C. (1999). Named entity recognition without gazetteers. In *Proceedings of 9th Conference of the European Chapter of the Association for Computational Linguistics (EACL-1999)*, (pp. 1–8).

Miller, S., Crystal, M., Fox, H., Ramshaw, L., Schwartz, R., Stone, R., & Weischedel, R., & the Annotation Group. (1998). BBN: Description of the SIFT system as used for MUC-7. In *Proceedings of the 7th Message Understanding Conference*.

Miller, G. (1995). WordNet: A lexical database for English. *Communications of the ACM, 38*, 39–41. doi:10.1145/219717.219748

Millerson, G. (1964). *The qualifying associations: A study in professionalization*. London, UK: Routledge & Kegan Paul.

Minenko, W. (1995). *The application sharing technology*. The X Advisor.

Mitrix, S. R., Davis, J., & Babich, J. (2008). *Web distributed authoring and versioning. RFC 5323*. IETF.

Mittleman, D. D., Briggs, R. O., Murphy, J., & Davis, A. (2008, September). Toward a taxonomy of groupware technologies. In Groupware: Design, Implementation, and Use, LNCS 5411 (pp. 305–317). Berlin, Germany: Springer-Verlag. doi:10.1007/978-3-540-92831-7_25doi:10.1007/978-3-540-92831-7_25

Moëllic, P.-A., Haugeard, J.-E., & Pitel, G. (2008). Image clustering based on a shared nearest neighbors approach for tagged collections. In *Proceedings of the International Conference on Content-Based Image and Video Retrieval*, (pp. 269-278). New York, NY: ACM.

Monsell, S. (2003). Task switching. *Trends in Cognitive Sciences, 7*(3), 134–140. doi:10.1016/S1364-6613(03)00028-7

Montalvo, S., Martınez, R., Casillas, A., & Fresno, V. (2006). Multilingual document clustering: An heuristic approach based on cognate named entities. In *Proceedings of the 21st International Conference on Computational Linguistics and 44th Annual Meeting of the Association for Computational Linguistics*, (pp. 1145–1152).

Moreland, R. (2006). Transactive memory: Learning who knows what io word groups and organizations. *Small groups: Key readings*, 327.

Morello, D., & Burton, B. (2006). *Future worker 2015: Extreme individualization*. Gartner, Inc. Publication.

Morrison, R. (2000). Persistent languages: Introduction and overview. In M. P. Atkinson & R. Welland (Eds.), *Fully integrated data environments: Persistent programming languages, object stores, and programming environments*, (pp. 5-8). Springer. *Mozilla Project*. (n.d.). Retrieved from www.Mozila.org

Morrison, R., & Atkinson, M. P. (1990). Persistent languages and architecture . In Rosenberg, J., & Keedy, J. L. (Eds.), *Proceedings of Security and Persistence* (pp. 9–28). Springer. doi:10.1007/978-1-4471-3178-6_2

Morton, A. (1999). Ethics in action research. *Systemic Practice and Action Research, 12*(2), 219–222. doi:10.1023/A:1022430231458

Mounce, S., Brewster, C., Ashley, R., & Hurley, L. (2010). Knowledge management for more sustainable water systems . In Teller, J., Cutting-Decelle, A.-F., & Billen, R. (Eds.), *COST action C21 - Future of urban ontologies*. Universite de Liege.

Moxley, E., Kleban, J., & Manjunath, B. S. (2008). Spirittagger: A geo-aware tag suggestion tool mined from Flickr. In *Proceedings of the 1st ACM International Conference on Multimedia Information Retrieval*, (pp. 24-30). New York, NY: ACM.

Müller, H., Michoux, N., Bandon, D., & Geissbuhler, A. (2004). A review of content-based image retrieval systems in medical applications - Clinical benefits and future directions. *International Journal of Medical Informatics, 73*(1), 1–23. doi:10.1016/j.ijmedinf.2003.11.024

Muller, J. (1998). Architectures and applications of intelligent agents: A survey. *The Knowledge Engineering Review, 13*(4), 353–380. doi:10.1017/S0269888998004020

MySpace. (2009). *MySpace | A place for friends*. Retrieved from http://www.myspace.com/

Nadeau, D., Turney, P., & Matwin, S. (2006). Unsupervised named-entity recognition: Generating gazetteers and resolving ambiguity. In *Proceedings of the 19th Canadian Conference on Artificial Intelligence*.

Nadeau, D., & Sekine, S. (2007). A survey of named entity recognition and classification. *Lingvisticae Investigationes, 30*, 3–26. doi:10.1075/li.30.1.03nad

Negri, M., & Magnini, B. (2004). Using WordNet predicates for multilingual named entity recognition . In *Proceedings of Global WordNet Conference* (pp. 169–174). GWC.

Network Inference. (2004). *Ontology and data warehousing*. Technology white paper, network Inference, Inc. Retrieved June 13, 2011, from http://me.jtpollock.us/pubs/

Newell, S. (2002). *Managing knowledge work*. Houndmills, UK: Palgrave Macmillan.

Newman, M. E. J. (2010). *Networks: An introduction*. Oxford University Press, 2010.

Nguyen, H., & Cao, T. (2008). Named entity disambiguation: A hybrid statistical and rule-based incremental approach. In *Proceedings of the 3rd Asian Semantic Web Conference on The Semantic Web (ASWC-2008), LNCS 5367,* (pp. 420–433). Springer-Verlag.

Nguyen, V., & Martel, C. (2005). Analyzing and characterizing small-world graphs. *Proceedings of the 16th Annual ACM-SIAM Symposium on Discrete Algorithms* (pp. 311–320). Society for Industrial and Applied Mathematics.

Niederman, F., Beise, C. M., & Beranek, P. M. (1993). Facilitation issues in distributed group support systems. In *Proceedings of the 1993 Conference on Computer Personnel Research* (pp. 299–312). New York, NY: ACM.

Nonaka, I. (1994). A dynamic theory of organizational knowledge creation. *Organization Science, 5*(1), 14–37. doi:10.1287/orsc.5.1.14

Nonaka, I., & Takeuchi, H. (1995). *The knowledge creating company: How Japanese companies create the dynamics of innovation*. New York, NY: Oxford University Press.

Noorderhaven, N., & Harzing, A. W. (2009). Knowledge-sharing and social interaction within MNEs. *Journal of International Business Studies, 40*(5), 719–741. doi:10.1057/jibs.2008.106

North, K. (1999). *Wissensorientierte Unternehmensführung: Wertschöpfung durch Wissen. 2*. Wiesbaden, Germany: Gabler.

North, K., & Gueldenberg, S. (2008). *Produktive Wissensarbeit(er): Antworten auf die Management-Herausforderung des 21. Jahrhunderts*. Wiesbaden, Germany: Gabler.

Noy, N. F., & McGuinness, D. L. (2001). *Ontology development 101: A guide to creating your first ontology*. Stanford University Knowledge Systems Laboratory Technical Report KSL-01-05, March 2001.

Noy, N. F., Griffith, N., & Musen, M. A. (2008). Collecting community-based mappings in an ontology repository. *International Semantic Web Conference* (pp. 371-386). Springer.

Nunamaker, J. F. Jr, Dennis, A. R., Valacich, J. S., Vogel, D., & George, J. F. (1991). Electronic meeting systems to support group work. *Communications of the ACM, 34*(7), 40–61. doi:10.1145/105783.105793

Nunamaker, J. F. Jr, Reinig, B. A., & Briggs, R. O. (2009). Principles for effective virtual teamwork. *Communications of the ACM, 52*(4), 113–117. doi:10.1145/1498765.1498797

Nutter, J. T. (1987). Epistemology . In Shapiro, S. (Ed.), *Encyclopedia of artificial intelligence*. London, UK: John Wiley.

O'Reilly, T. (2005). *What is Web 2.0: Design patterns and business models for the next generation of software*. Retrieved May 6, 2011, from http://www.oreillynet.com/pub/a/oreilly/tim/news/2005/09/30/what-is-web-20.html

OECD. (2006a). *OECD employment outlook. 2006 edition: Boosting jobs and incomes*. Paris, France: Organisation for Economic Co-operation and Development.

OECD. (2006b). *Education at a glance, OECD indicators 2006, indicator A8: Labour force participation by level of educational attainment.* Paris, France: Organisation for Economic Co-operation and Development. Retrieved January 7, 2007, from http://www.oecd.org/document/6/0,2340,en_2649_34515_37344774_1_1_1_1,00

Ogren, P. V., Wetzler, P. G., & Bethard, S. (2008). *ClearTK: A UIMA toolkit for statistical natural language processing.* In UIMA for NLP workshop at Language Resources and Evaluation Conference (LREC).

Oliveira, F. F., Antunes, J. C. P., & Guizzardi, R. S. S. (2007). *Towards a collaboration ontology.* 2nd Workshop on Ontologies and Metamodels in Software and Data Engineering.

ONeil. B. (2007). *Semantics and business metadata.* The Data Administration. Retrieved June 13, 2011, from http://www.tdan.com /view-articles/4934

OrbiTeam Software GmbH. (2005). *Basic support for cooperative work,* Version 4.3 Manual, Retrieved May 2011, from www.orbiteam.de

Oren, E., Delbru, R., & Decker, S. (2006). Extending faceted navigation for RDF data. In Cruz, I. (Eds.), *The Semantic Web - ISWC 2006, LNCS 4273* (pp. 559–572). Berlin, Germany: Springer-Verlag. doi:10.1007/11926078_40

Orlov, L. (2005). *IBM's technology adoption program taps ideas.* IT's Role . In *Innovation series, (Sept. 2005).* Forrester Research.

Osterloh, R. (2010). *Skype with Facebook integration and group video calling.* Retrieved from http://blogs.skype.com /en/2010/10/new_skype.html

Pachet, F. (2008). The future of content is in ourselves. *Computers in Entertainment, 6,* 1–20. doi:10.1145/1394021.1394024

Pallant, J. (2007). *SPSS Survival Manual: A step-by-step guide to data analysis using SPSS for Windows (Version 15)* (3rd ed.). NSW, Australia: Allen Unwin.

Palmer, D., & Day, D. (2006). A statistical profile of the named entity task. In *Proceedings of ACL Conference for Applied Natural Language Processing (ANLP-1997).*

Pan, J., Taylor, S., & Thomas, E. (2009). Reducing ambiguity in tagging systems with folksonomy search expansion. *Proceedings of the 6th Annual European Semantic Web Conference, ESWC 2009* (pp. 669-683). Springer.

Paolucci, M., & Sycara, K. (2003). Autonomous Semantic Web services. *IEEE Internet Computing, 7*(5), 34–41. doi:10.1109/MIC.2003.1232516

Paradi, J. C., Smith, S., & Schaffnit-Chatterjee, C. (2002). Knowledge worker performance analysis using DEA: an application to engineering design teams at Bell Canada. *IEEE Transactions on Engineering Management, 49*(2), 161. doi:10.1109/TEM.2002.1010884

Park, K.-M., Kim, S.-H., Rim, H.-C., & Hwang, Y.-S. (2006). ME-based biomedical named entity recognition using lexical knowledge. *ACM Transactions on Asian Language Information Processing, 5*(1), 4–21. doi:10.1145/1131348.1131350

Parsons, T. (1939). The professions and social structure. *Social Forces, 17*(4), 457–467. doi:10.2307/2570695

Parunak, V. D., Savit, R., & Riolo, R. L. (1998). Lecture Notes in Computer Science: *Vol. 1534. Agent-based modeling vs. equation-based modeling: A case study and users' guide. Multi-Agent Systems and Agent-Based Simulation* (pp. 10–15). Berlin, Germany: Springer Verlag.

Patel, V. L., & Groen, G. J. (1991). The general and specific nature of medical expertise: A critical look . In Ericsson, K. A., & Smith, J. (Eds.), *Towards a general theory of expertise: Prospects and limits* (pp. 93–125). Cambridge, MA: University Press.

Pathirage, P. C., Amaratunga, G. D., & Haigh, R. P. (2007). Tacit knowledge and organisational performance: construction industry perspective. *Journal of Knowledge Management, 11*(1), 115–126. doi:10.1108/13673270710728277

Pattberg, J., & Fluegge, M. (2007). Towards an ontology of collaboration patterns. In *Proceedings of Challenges in Collaborative Engineering 07.*

Pedell, K. L. (1985). Analyse und Planung von Produktivitätsveränderungen. *Zeitschrift für betriebswirtschaftliche . Forschung, 37*(12), 1078–1097.

Penley, L. E., & Hawkins, B. (1985). Studying interpersonal communication in organizations: A leadership application. *Academy of Management Journal, 28,* 309–326. doi:10.2307/256203

Petasis, G., Karkaletsis, V., Grover, C., Hachey, B., Pazienza, M.-T., Vindigni, M., & Coch, J. (2004). Adaptive, multilingual named entity recognition in web pages. In *Proceedings of 2004 European Conference on Artificial Intelligence* (*ECAI-2004*), (pp. 1073–1074).

Pett, M. A., Lackey, N. R., & Sullivan, J. J. (2003). *Making sense of factor analysis: The use of factor analysis for instrument developmet in health care research.* Thousand Oaks, CA: Sage Publications.

Pfadenhauer, M. (2003a). *Professionalität: Eine wissenssoziologische Rekonstruktion institutionalisierter Kompetenzdarstellungskompetenz.* Opladen, Germany: Leske & Budrich.

Pfadenhauer, M. (2003b). Macht – Funktion – Leistung: Zur Korrespondenz von Eliten und Professionstheorien . In Mieg, H. A., & Pfadenhauer, M. (Eds.), *Professionelle Leistung – Professional Performance: Positionen der Professionssoziologie* (pp. 71–87). Konstanz, Germany: UVK.

Pfiffner, M., & Stadelmann, P. (1999). *Wissen wirksam machen: Wie Kopfarbeiter produktiv werden. 2. unveränd.* Bern, Switzerland: Haupt.

Pinto, H. S., & Martins, J. P. (2004, July). Ontologies: How can they be built? *Knowledge and Information Systems, 6*(4), 441–464. doi:10.1007/s10115-003-0138-1

Poggi, A., & Golinelli, G. (1998). Automatic storing and retrieval of large collections of images. In *Proceedings of the 11th International Conference on Industrial & Engineering Applications of Artificial Intelligence & Expert Systems* (IEA/AIE-98), Spain.

Pond, J. (2004). *Distributed configuration management reference guide.* Oracle Publication.

Poole, M. S., & Hollingshead, A. B. (2005). *Theories of small groups.* Thousand Oaks, CA: Sage Publications.

Posner, M. I. (1988). Introduction: What is it to be an expert? In Chi, M. T. H., Glaser, R., & Rees, M. J. (Eds.), *The nature of expertise* (pp. xxix–xxxvi). Hillsdale, NJ: Erlbaum.

Predoiu, L., & Zhdanova, A. V. (2007). Semantic web languages and ontologies . In Freire, M., & Pereira, M. (Eds.), *Encyclopedia of internet technologies and applications* (pp. 512–518). Hershey, PA: IGI Global. doi:10.4018/978-1-59140-993-9.ch072

Preece, A. (1998). Building the right system right. In *Proceedings KAW'98, 11th Workshop on Knowledge Acquisition, Modeling and Management.*

Probst, G., Raub, S., & Romhardt, K. (2010). *Wissen managen: Wie Unternehmen ihre wertvollste Ressource optimal nutzen.* Wiesbaden, Germany: Gabler.

Puppe, F., Atzmueller, M., Buscher, G., Huettig, M., Lührs, H., & Buscher, H. P. (2008). Application and evaluation of a medical knowledge-system in sonography (SonoConsult). In *Proceedings 18th European Conference on Artificial Intelligence,* (pp. 683–687). Patras, Greece.

Puppe, F. (1998). Knowledge reuse among diagnostic problem-solving methods in the shell-kit D3. *International Journal of Human-Computer Studies, 49,* 627–649. doi:10.1006/ijhc.1998.0221

Rabiner, L. (1989). A tutorial on hidden Markov models and selected applications in speech recognition. *Proceedings of the IEEE, 77*(2), 257–286. doi:10.1109/5.18626

Rader, E., & Wash, R. (2008). Influences on tag choices in del.icio.us. In *Proceedings of the ACM 2008 Conference on Computer Supported Cooperative Work* (San Diego, CA, USA, November 08 - 12, 2008), CSCW '08, (pp. 239-248).

Rae, A., Sigurbjörnsson, B., & van Zwol, R. (2010). Improving tag recommendation using social networks. In *Proceedings of 9th International Conference on Adaptivity, Personalization and Fusion of Heterogeneous Information.* Paris, France: CID.

Rajsiri, V., Lorré, J.-P., Bénaben, F., & Pingaud, H. (2008). Collaborative process definition using an ontology-based approach. *Pervasive Collaborative Networks, 283,* 205–212. doi:10.1007/978-0-387-84837-2_21

Raman, T. V. (2009). Toward 2^W, beyond web 2.0. *Communications of the ACM, 52,* 52–59. doi:10.1145/1461928.1461945

Ramirez, Y. W., & Nembhard, D. A. (2004). Measuring knowledge worker productivity: A taxonomy. *Journal of Intellectual Capital*, *5*(4), 602–628. doi:10.1108/14691930410567040

Ratinov, L., & Roth, D. (2009). Design challenges and misconceptions in named entity recognition. In *Proceedings of the 13th Conference on Computational Natural Language Learning* (*CoNLL-2009*), (pp. 147–155).

Raychaudhuri, S., Chang, J., Sutphin, P., & Altman, R. (2002). Associating genes with gene ontology codes using a maximum entropy analysis of biomedical literature. *Genome Research*. (n.d)., 37.

Ray, P. K., & Sahu, S. (1989). The measurement and evaluation of white-collar productivity. *International Journal of Operations & Production Management*, *9*(4), 28–47. doi:10.1108/EUM0000000001235

Reif, G., Groza, T., Scerri, S., & Handschuh, S. (2008). *Final NEPOMUK architecture deliverable D6.2.B*. NEPOMUK Consortium.

Reinberg, A., & Hummel, M. (2002). Zur langfristigen Entwicklung des qualifikationsspezifischen Arbeitskräfteangebots und –bedarfs in Deutschland: Empirische Befunde und aktuelle Projektionsergebnisse. *Mitteilungen aus der Arbeitsmarkt- und Berufsforschung*, *35*(4), 580–600.

Reinberg, A., & Hummel, M. (2005). *Höhere Bildung schützt auch in der Krise vor Arbeitslosigkeit. IAB-Kurzbericht Nr.9*. Nürnberg, Germany: Institut für Arbeitsmarkt- und Berufsforschung.

Renzl, B. (2008). Trust in management and knowledge sharing: The mediating effects of fear and knowledge documentation. *OMEGA - The International Journal of Management Science*, *36*(2), 206-220.

Resnick, P., & Varian, H. (1997). Recommender systems. *Communications of the ACM*, *40*(3), 58. doi:10.1145/245108.245121

Reutelshoefer, J., Haupt, F., Lemmerich, F., & Baumeister, J. (2009). *An extensible semantic wiki architecture*. In SemWiki'09: 4th Workshop on Semantic Wikis.

Rocchio, J. J. (1971). Relevance feedback in information retrieval . In Salton, G. (Ed.), *The SMART Retrieval System: Experiments in Automatic Document Processing* (pp. 313–323). Englewood Cliffs, NJ: Prentice-Hall Series in Automatic Computation.

Roos, J., & Von Krogh, G. (1992). Figuring out your competence configuration. *European Management Journal*, *10*, 422–422. doi:10.1016/0263-2373(92)90006-P

Rosenschein, J. (1982). Synchronization of multi-agent plans. *Proceedings of the National Conference on Artificial Intelligence*, (pp. 115-119).

Roski, R. (2009). *Zielgruppengerechte Gesundheitskommunikation: Akteure – Audience Segmentation – Anwendungsfelder*. Wiesbaden, Germany: VS Verlag.

Rotondo, F. (2010). Future perspectives in ontologies for urban regeneration . In Teller, J., Cutting-Decelle, A.-F., & Billen, R. (Eds.), *COST action C21 - Future of urban ontologies*. Universite de Liege.

Roussey, C. (2005). *Technical report n°1 guidelines to build ontologies: A bibliographic study*. COST Action C21 "Urban Ontologies for an improved communication in urban civil engineering projects" - TOWNTOLOGY Project. Retrieved from http://www.towntology.net/

Rubinstein, J. S., Meyer, D. E., & Evans, J. E. (2001). Executive control of cognitive processes in task switching. *Journal of Experimental Psychology. Human Perception and Performance*, *27*(4), 763–797. doi:10.1037/0096-1523.27.4.763

Russel, S. J., & Norvig, P. (2003). *Artificial intelligence: A modern approach*. Upper Saddle River, NJ: Pearson Education.

Sabater, J., & Sierra, C. (2002). Reputation and social network analysis in multi-agent systems. *Proceedings 1st International Joint Conference on Autonomous Agents and Multiagent Systems (AAMAS '02)*, 1, (pp. 475-482). ACM Press.

Sackmann, S. A. (1991). *Cultural knowledge in organizations: Exploring the collective mind*. Newsbury Park, CA: Sage.

Sackmann, S. A. (2002). *Unternehmenskultur: Erkennen – Entwickeln – Verändern*. Neuwied, Germany: Luchterhand.

Sahin, A. (2007). *A case in effective knowledge management.* Paper presented at the Portland International Conference on Management of Engineering and Technology.

Saleem, M. (2007, July 19). *The power of Digg top users (one year later).* Pronet Advertising. Retrieved May 6, 2011, from http://www.pronetadvertising.com /articles/the-power-of-digg-top-users-one-year-later34409.html

Sampson, M. (2008). *Seamless teamwork: Using Microsoft SharePoint technologies to collaborate, innovate, and drive business in new ways (BP-Other).* Microsoft Press.

Sanchez, W., & Daboo, C. (2008). *WebDAV current principal extension. RFC 5397.* IETF.

Sang, T. K., Erik, F., & de Meulder, F. (2003). Introduction to the CoNLL-2003 shared task: Language-independent named entity recognition. In *Proceedings of the Conference on Computational Natural Language Learning (coNLL-2003)*, (pp. 142–147).

Sangwan, R. (2006). *Global software development handbook.* Boston, MA: Auerbach Publications.

Sasano, M. (2003). Virtual examples for text classification with support vector machines. In *Proceedings of Conference on Empirical Methods in Natural Language Processing (EMNLP-2003)*.

Scerri, S. (2008b). *Semantic email ontology.* Retrieved from http://ontologies.smile.deri.ie /smail

Scerri, S., Gossen, G., & Handschuh, S. (2010b). *Supporting digital collaborative work through semantic technology.* In KMIS'10, Valencia, Spain.

Scerri, S., Gossen, G., Davis, B., & Handschuh, S. (2010a). *Classifying action items for semantic email.* In LREC'10, European Language Resources Association (ELRA).

Scerri, S., Handschuh, S., & Decker, S. (2008b). Semantic email as a communication medium for the Social Semantic Desktop. In *ESWC'08* (pp. 124-138).

Scerri, S., Mencke, M., Davis, B., & Handschuh, S. (2008c). *Evaluating the ontology powering smail - A conceptual framework for semantic email.* In LREC'08.

Schön, D. (1983). *The reflective practitioner: How professionals think in action.* New York, NY: Basic Books.

Schraefel, M. C., Smith, D., Owens, A., Russell, A., Harris, C., & Wilson, M. (2005). The evolving mSpace platform: Leveraging the Semantic Web on the trail of the Memex. *Proceedings of the ACM Hypertext Conference,* (pp. 174–218). New York, NY: ACM.

Schumann, S. (2005). *The IAF handbook of group facilitation: Best practices from the leading organization in facilitation.* San Francisco, CA: Jossey-Bass.

Searle, J. R. (1969). *Speech acts: An essay in the philosophy of language.* Cambridge, UK: Cambridge University Press.

Sekine, S. (1998). Description of the Japanese NE system used for MET-2. In *Proceedings of the 7th Message Understanding Conference.*

Sekine, S., & Eriguchi, Y. (2000). Japanese named entity extraction evaluation - Analysis of results. In *Proceedings of the Conference on Computational Linguistics (COLING-2000)*, (pp. 1106–1110).

Sell, D., Cabral, L., Motta, E., Domingue, J., Hakimpour, F., & Pacheco, R. (2005). A Semantic Web based architecture for analytical tools. In *CEC'05: Proceedings of the Seventh IEEE International Conference on E-Commerce Technology.* Washington, DC: IEEE Computer Society.

Selman, P. (2006). *Planning at the landscape scale.* Oxon, UK: Routledge.

Semantic Web Conference Corpus . (2011). Retrieved from http://data.semanticweb.org/

Seomoz. (2006). *Top 100 Digg users control 56% of Digg's home page content.* Retrieved May 6, 2011, from http://www.seomoz.org /blog/top-100-digg-users-control-56-of-diggs-homepage-content

Settles, B. (2004). Biomedical named entity recognition using conditional random fields and novel feature sets. In *Proceedings of Joint Workshop on Natural Language Processing in Biomedicine and its Applications (JNLPBA-2004)*, (pp. 104–107).

Seymore, K., McCallum, A., & Rosenfeld, R. (1999). Learning hidden Markov structure for information extraction. In *Proceedings of AAAI'99 Workshop on Machine Learning for Information Extraction.*

Shadbolt, N., Hall, W., & Berners-Lee, T. (2006). The Semantic Web revisited. *IEEE Intelligent Systems*, (May/June): 96–101. doi:10.1109/MIS.2006.62

Shah, U., Finin, T., Joshi, A., Cost, R. S., & Matfield, J. (2002). Information retrieval on the Semantic Web. In *Proceedings of the 11th International Conference on Information and Knowledge Management (CIKM '02)*, (pp. 461-468). New York, NY.

Shannon, C. E. (1948, July). October). A mathematical theory of communication. *The Bell System Technical Journal*, 27, 379–423, 623–656.

Shen, D., Zhang, J., Zhou, G., Su, J., & Tan, C.-L. (2003). Effective adaptation of a hidden Markov model-based named entity recognizer for biomedical domain. In *Proceedings of the Meeting of Association for Computational Linguistics (ACL-2003)*.

Shen, H., & Sun, C. (2000). RECIPE: A prototype for Internet-based real-time collaborative programming. In *Proceedings of the Second International Workshop on Collaborative Editing Systems*, USA.

Shen, H., Xia, S., & Sun, C. (2007). Integrating advanced collaborative capabilities into web-based word processors . *Lecture Notes in Computer Science*, 4674, 1–8. doi:10.1007/978-3-540-74780-2_1

Shen, W., & Barthès, J. P. (1997). An experimental environment for exchanging engineering design knowledge by cognitive agents . In *Knowledge Intensive CAD-2* (pp. 19–38). Chapman & Hall.

Shen, W., Norrie, D. H., & Barthès, J. P. (2001). *Multiagent systems for concurrent intelligent design and manufacturing*. London, UK: Taylor and Francis.

Shi, F., Li, J., Tang, L., Xie, G. T., & Li, H. (2009). Actively learning ontology matching via user interaction. *International Semantic Web Conference ISWC2009* (pp. 585-600). Springer.

Shinyama, Y., & Sekine, S. (2004). Named entity discovery using comparable news articles. In *Proceedings of the Conference on Computational Linguistics (COLING-2004)*, (pp. 848–853).

Shvaiko, P., & Euzenat, J. (2008). *Ten challenges for ontology matching. OTM Conferences* (pp. 1164–1182). Springer.

Sigurbjörnsson, B., & van Zwol, R. (2008). Flickr tag recommendation based on collective knowledge. In *Proceedings of the 17th International Conference on World Wide Web*, (pp. 327-336). New York, NY: ACM.

Simile Project. (2011). *Longwell website*. Retrieved February 24, 2011, from http://simile.mit.edu /wiki/Longwell

Siorpaes, K., & Hepp, M. (2008). OntoGame: Weaving the Semantic Web by online games. *Proceedings of the European Semantic Web Conference* (pp. 751-766). Springer.

Siorpaes, K., & Simperl, E. (2010). *Incentives, motivation, participation, games: Human computation for linked data*, (p. 700). Retrieved May 8, 2011, from http://linkeddata.future-internet.eu /images/9/91/FIA2010_Human_Computation_for_Linked_Data.pdf.

Siorpaes, K., Hepp, M., Klotz, A., & Hackl, M. (2008). *myOntology: Tapping the wisdom of crowds for building ontologies*. Unpublished technical report, STI Innsbruck, Austria.

Siorpaes, K., & Simperl, E. (2010). Human intelligence in the process of semantic content creation. *World Wide Web Journal*, 13(1), 33–59. doi:10.1007/s11280-009-0078-0

Smith, J. (1997). *Integrated spatial and feature image systems: Retrieval, analysis and compression*. PhD thesis, Graduate School of Arts and Sciences, Columbia University, New York, NY.

Smith, J., & Smith, F. (1991). ABC: A hypermedia system for artifact-based collaboration. In *Proceedings of the 3rd ACM Conference on Hypertext*, (pp. 179-192).

Song, Y., Yi, E., Kim, E., & Lee, G. (2005). POSBIOTM-NER: A machine learning approach for bio-named entity recognition. *Bioinformatics (Oxford, England)*, 21(11), 2784–2796.

Sonnentag, S. (1996). *Experten in der Software-Entwicklung: Untersuchung hervorragender Leistungen im Kontext intellektueller Teamarbeit*. Unveröffentliche Habilitation, Universität Gießen.

Soriano, J., Fernandez, R., & Jimenez, M. (2009). Characterization and classification of collaborative tools . In St.Amant, K. (Ed.), *IT outsourcing: Concepts, methodologies, tools, and applications* (pp. 1399–1408). Hershey, PA: IGI Global Publication. doi:10.4018/978-1-60566-770-6.ch087

Spahn, M., Kleb, J., Grimm, S., & Scheidl, S. (2008). Supporting business intelligence by providing ontology-based end-user information self-service. In *OBI '08: Proceedings of the First International Workshop on Ontology-Supported Business Intelligenc.* New York, NY: ACM.

Specia, L., & Motta, E. (2007). Integrating folksonomies with the Semantic Web. *Proceedings of the 4th European Semantic Web Conference, ESWC 2007, LNCS 4519,* (pp. 624-639). Innsbruck, Austria: Springer.

Spira, J. B., & Feintuch, J. B. (2005). *The cost of not paying attention: How interruption impacts knowledge worker productivity.* New York, NY: Basex.

Stam, C. (2007). *Knowledge productivity: Designing and testing a method to diagnose knowledge productivity and plan for enhancement.* Unpublished Ph.D. thesis, Universiteit Twente.

Staples, D. S., & Webster, J. (2008). Exploring the effects of trust, task interdependence and virtualness on knowledge sharing in teams. *Information Systems Journal, 18*(6), 617–640. doi:10.1111/j.1365-2575.2007.00244.x

Stelter, B., & Arango, T. (2009, May 4). Losing popularity contest, MySpace tries a makeover. *New York Times.* Retrieved May 6, 2011, from http://www.nytimes.com /2009/05/04/technology/ companies/04myspace.html

Stibbe, R., Güsgen, J., Dierkes, A., & Tilgen, M. (2011). Geocodierungals Instrument zur Marktanalyse. *KU Gesundheitsmanagement, 1,* 29–31.

Strauss, A., & Corbin, J. (1990). *Basics of qualitative research: Techniques and procedures for developing grounded theory.* London, UK: Sage Publications.

Strawson, P. F. (1959). *Individuals: An essay in descriptive metaphysics.* London, UK: Routledge. doi:10.4324/9780203221303

Stubbs, M. (1983). *Discourse analysis.* Blackwell.

Studer, R., Benjamins, V. R., & Fensel, D. (1998). Knowledge engineering: Principles and methods. *Data & Knowledge Engineering, 25*(1-2), 161–197. doi:10.1016/ S0169-023X(97)00056-6

Studer, R., Grimm, S., & Becker, A. (2007). *Semantic Web services – Concepts, technologies and applications.* Berlin, Germany: Springer. doi:10.1007/3-540-70894-4

Stumme, G., & Maedche, A. (2001). FCA-Merge: Bottom-up merging of ontologies. *Proceedings of the Seventeenth International Joint Conference on Artificial Intelligence* (pp. 225–234). Morgan Kaufmann.

Suff, P., & Reilly, P. (2005). *In the know: Reward and performance management of knowledge workers. HR Network Paper, MP47.* Brighton: Institute for Employment Studies.

Sumanth, D. J., Omachonu, V. K., & Beruvides, M. G. (1990). A review of the state-of-the-art research on white collar / knowledge-worker productivity. *International Journal of Technology Management, 5*(3), 337–355.

Sun, J., Gao, J., Zhang, L., Zhou, M., & Huang, C. (2002). Chinese named entity identification using class-based language model. In *Proceedings of the Conference on Computational Linguistics (COLING-2002).*

Sundar, S. S., Oeldorf-Hirsch, A., & Xu, Q. (2008). The bandwagon effect of collaborative filtering technology. In *CHI '08 Extended Abstracts on Human Factors in Computing Systems* (Florence, Italy, April 05 - 10, 2008), CHI '08, (pp. 3453-3458). New York, NY: ACM.

Sveiby, K. E. (1998). *Wissenskapital – das unentdeckte Vermögen: Immaterielle Unternehmenswerte aufspüren, messen und steigern.* Landsberg, Germany: Moderne Industrie.

Sveiby, K.-E. (1997). *The new organizational wealth: Managing and measuring intangible assets.* San Francisco, CA: Berret-Koehler.

Sweller, J. (1983). Development of expertise in mathematical problem solving. *Journal of Experimental Psychology. General, 112,* 639–661. doi:10.1037/0096-3445.112.4.639

Szomszor, M., & Alani, H. OHara, K., & Shadbolt, N. (2008). Semantic modelling of user interests based on cross-folksonomy. *Proceedings of the 7th International Semantic Web Conference, ISWC 2008,* Karlsruhe, Germany.

Takeuchi, K., & Collier, N. (2002). Use of support vector machines in extended named entity recognition. In *Proceedings of 2002 Conference on Natural Language Learning (coNLL-2002),* (pp. 119–125).

Talukdar, P., Brants, T., Liberman, M., & Pereira, F. (2006). A context pattern induction method for named entity extraction. In *Proceedings of the 10ᵗʰ Conference on Computational Natural Language Learning (CoNLL-2006)*, (pp. 141–148).

Tanev, H., & Magnini, B. (2008). Weakly supervised approaches for ontology population. In *Proceeding of the 2008 Conference on Ontology Learning and Population: Bridging the Gap between Text and Knowledge*, (pp. 129–143).

Technorati. (2011). *Technorati: About us*. Retrieved May 6, 2011, from http://technorati.com/about/

Teiken, Y., Rohde, M., & Mertens, M. (2010). MUSTANG: Realisierung eines Analytischen Informationssystems im Kontext der Gesundheitsberichterstattung. In *Informatik 2010: Service Science - Neue Perspektiven für die Informatik, CEUR Workshop Proceedings*, Leipzig, Germany.

Teller, J. (2007). Ontologies for improved communication in urban development projects. *Studies in Computational Intelligence, 61*, 1–14. doi:10.1007/978-3-540-71976-2_1

Teller, J., Tweed, C., & Rabino, G. (Eds.). (2008). *Conceptual models for urban practitioners*. Bologna, Italy: Societa Editrice Esculapio.

Terveen, L. G. (1995). Overview of human-computer collaboration. *Knowledge-Based Systems, 8*(2-3), 67–81. doi:10.1016/0950-7051(95)98369-H

Terziev, I., Kiryakov, A., & Manov, D. (2005). Base-upper-level ontology guidance. *Deliverable D1.8.1 of the EU-IST Project IST-2003-506826 SEKT*. Retrieved May 8, 2011, from http://proton.semanticweb.org/D1_8_1.pdf

Thao, P., Tri, T., Dien, D., & Collier, N. (2007). Named entity recognition in Vietnamese using classifier voting. *ACM Transactions on Asian Language Information Processing, 6*(4), 1–18. doi:10.1145/1316457.1316460

Thoben, W., Rohde, M., Koch, S., Appelrath, H.-J., & Stuber, R. (2010). Konzepte und Technologien für die strategische Planung im Krankenhausmarkt. *Krankenhaus IT Journal, 5*, 26–27.

Tonino, H., Boss, A., de Weerdt, M., & Wittevee, C. (2002). Plan coordination by revision in collective agent based systems. *Artificial Intelligence, 142*(2), 121–145. doi:10.1016/S0004-3702(02)00273-4

Toye, G., Cutkosky, M. R., Leifer, L., Tenenbaum, J., & Glicksman, J. (1993). SHARE: A methodology and environment for collaborative product development. In *Proceedings of 2ⁿᵈ Workshop on Enabling Technologies: Infrastructure for Collaborative Enterprises*, (pp. 33–47).

Trabelsi, C., Ben Jrad, A., & Ben Yahia, S. (2010). Bridging folksonomies and domain ontologies: Getting out non-taxonomic relations. *Proceedings of the 10th IEEE International Conference on Data Mining Workshops, ICDM Workshops 2010* (pp. 369-379). Sydney, Australia: IEEE Computer Society.

Tran, D. T., Wang, H., Rudolph, S., & Cimiano, P. (2009). Top-k exploration of query candidates for efficient keyword search on graph-shaped (RDF) data. *Proceedings of the 25th International Conference on Data Engineering 2009*, Shanghai, China.

Trausan-Matu, S., & Rebedea, T. (2010). Ontology-based analysis of chat conversations: An urban development case . In Teller, J., Cutting-Decelle, A.-F., & Billen, R. (Eds.), *COST action C21 - Future of urban ontologies*. Universite de Liege.

Tsai, R., Wu, S., Chou, W., Lin, Y., He, D., & Hsiang, J. (2006). Various criteria in the evaluation of biomedical named entity recognition. *BMC Bioinformatics, 7*(92).

Tsai, W., & Ghoshal, S. (1998). Social capital and value creation: The role of intrafirm networks. *Academy of Management Journal, 41*, 464–476. doi:10.2307/257085

Tu, K., & Yu, Y. (2005). CMC: Combining multiple schema-matching strategies based on credibility prediction. *Proceedings of the 10th International Conference on Database Systems for Advanced Applications* (pp. 888-893). Springer.

Tummarello, G., Delbru, R., & Oren, E. (2007). Sindice.com: Weaving the open linked data. *Proceedings of the 6th International The Semantic Web and 2nd Asian Conference on Asian Semantic Web Conference*, (pp. 552–565). Berlin, Germany: Springer-Verlag.

Tuomi, D. (2003). The future of knowledge managment. *Lifelong Learning in Europe, 7*(2), 69–79.

UK National Statistics. (2000). *Standard occupational classification 2000 (SOC 2000): Summary of structure*. London, UK National Statistics. Retrieved January 9, 2007, from www.statistics.gov.uk /methods_quality/ ns_sec/ downloads/ SOC2000.doc

UK National Statistics. (2006). *All in employment by socio-economic classification (NS-SEC) (Not seasonally adjusted*. London, UK National Statistics. Retrieved August 20, 2008, from http://www.statistics.gov.uk / STATBASE/ ssdataset.asp?vlnk=7919 US Department of Labor. (2006). *Occupational outlook handbook*. Washington, DC: Bureau of Labor. Retrieved January 09, 2007, from http://www.bls.gov / oco/home.htm

Uschold, M., & Gruninger, M. (1996). Ontologies: Principles, methods and applications. *The Knowledge Engineering Review*, *11*(2), 1–63. doi:10.1017/ S0269888900007797

Uschold, M., & Gruninger, M. (1996). Ontologies: Principles, methods and applications. *The Knowledge Engineering Review*, *11*, 93–136. doi:10.1017/ S0269888900007797

Van Damme, C., Hepp, M., & Siorpaes, K. (2007). FolksOntology: An integrated approach for turning folksonomies into ontologies. In *Proceedings of ESWC 2007 Workshop "Bridging the Gap between Semantic Web and Web 2.0"*, Innsbruck, Austria, (pp. 71-84).

van der Aalst, W. M. P., ter Hofstede, A. H. M., Kiepuszewski, B., & Barros, A. P. (2003). Workflow patterns. *Distributed and Parallel Databases*, *14*, 5–51. doi:10.1023/A:1022883727209

VanGundy, A. B. (1988). *Techniques of structured problem solving*. New York, NY: Van Nostrant Reinhold.

Vapnik, V. (1998). *Statistical learning theory*. Wiley Interscience.

Vesperman, J. (2006). *Essential CVS*. O'Reilly Media.

Vivacqua, A. S., Garcia, A. C. B., & Gomes, A. (2011). BOO: Behavior oriented ontology to describe participant dynamics in collocated design meetings. *Expert Systems with Applications*, *38*(2), 1139–1147. doi:10.1016/j. eswa.2010.05.007

Von Ahn, L., & Dabbish, L. (2004). Labeling images with a computer game. *Proceedings of the 2004 Conference on Human Factors in Computing Systems* (pp. 319-326). ACM.

Von Ahn, L., Dannenberg, R. B., & Crawford, M. (2007). *Tagatune: A game for music and sound annotation*. Paper presented at the International Conference on Music Information Retrieval, Vienna, Austria.

Von Ahn, L., Liu, R., & Blum, M. (2006). Peekaboom: A game for locating objects in images. *Proceedings of the SIGCHI Conference on Human Factors in Computing Systems* (pp. 55-64). ACM.

Von Ahn, L. (2006). Games with a purpose. *IEEE Computer*, *29*(6), 92–94. doi:10.1109/MC.2006.196

von Schroeders, N., & Heller, C. (2009). *Geocoding - Geografische Analyse fürKrankenhäuser*. Kulmbach, Germany: Baumann Fachzeitschriften Verlag.

Voorhoeve, M., & van der Aalst, W. M. P. (1997). Ad-hoc workflow: Problems and solutions. In *DEXA '97 Workshop* (pp. 36-40).

Wallace, J. E. (1995). Organizational and professional commitment in professional and nonprofessional organizations. *Administrative Science Quarterly*, *40*(2), 228–255. doi:10.2307/2393637

Wang, Y., & Patrick, J. (2009). Cascading classifiers for named entity recognition in clinical notes. In *Proceedings of the Workshop on Biomedical Information Extraction*, (pp. 42–49).

Watanabe, Y., Asahara, M., & Matsumoto, Y. (2007). A graph-based approach to named entity categorization in Wikipedia using conditional random fields. In *Proceedings of the 2007 Joint Conference on Empirical Methods in Natural Language Processing and Computational Natural Language Learning* (*EMNLP-CoNLL-2007*), (pp. 649–657).

Weidig, I. (1999). *Arbeitslandschaft 2010 nach Tätigkeiten und Tätigkeitsniveau. Beiträge zur Arbeitsmarkt- und Berufsforschung, Nr. 227*. Nürnberg, Germany: Institut für Arbeitsmarkt- und Berufsforschung.

Weikum, G., Kasneci, G., Ramanath, M., & Suchanek, F. (2009). Database and information-retrieval methods for knowledge discovery. *Communications of the ACM*, *52*(4), 56–64. doi:10.1145/1498765.1498784

Weiss, A. (2005). The power of collective intelligence. *Networker*, *9*, 16–23. doi:10.1145/1086762.1086763

Wellman, M. P., Greenwald, A., Stone, P., & Wurman, P. R. (2002) The 2001 trading agent competition. In *Proceedings of the 14th Innovative Applications of Artificial Intelligence Conference (IAAI-2002)*, (pp. 935-941). Edmonton.

Whittaker, S., & Sidner, C. (1996). Email overload: Exploring personal information management of email . In *CHI '96* (pp. 276–283). New York, NY: ACM. doi:10.1145/238386.238530

Wikipedia. (2011). *Wikipedia: About*. Retrieved May 6, 2011, from http://en.wikipedia.org/wiki/Wikipedia:About

Willke, H. (2001). *Systemisches Wissensmanagement. 2. neu bearb*. Stuttgart, Germany: UTB.

Winkler, D., Biffl, S., & Kaltenbach, A. (2010). Evaluating tools that support pair programming in a distributed engineering environment. In *Proceedings of 14th International Conference on Evaluation and Assessment in Software Engineering (EASE)*.

Winograd, T. (1986). A language/action perspective on the design of cooperative work . In *CSWC '86* (pp. 203–220). New York, NY: ACM Press. doi:10.1145/637095.637096

Wölger, S., Siorpaes, K., Bürger, T., Simperl, E., Thaler, S., & Hofer, C. (2011). *Interlinking data - approaches and tools*. Unpublished technical report, STI Innsbruck, Austria.

Wong, Z., & Aiken, M. (2003). Automated facilitation of electronic meetings. *Information & Management*, *41*(2), 125–134. doi:10.1016/S0378-7206(03)00042-9

Woods, W. A. (1975). What's in a link: Foundations for semantic networks . In Bobrow, D. G., & Collins, A. M. (Eds.), *Representation and understanding: Studies in cognitive science*. London, UK: Academic Press.

Wooldridge, M. J. (2002). *An introduction to multi-agent systems*. John Wiley and Sons.

Wooldridge, M., & Jennings, N. (1995). Intelligent agents: Theory and practice. *The Knowledge Engineering Review*, *10*(2), 115–152. doi:10.1017/S0269888900008122

Workflow Management Coalition. (2008, October). *Workflow process definition interface – XML process definition language* (Tech. Rep. No. WFMC-TC-1025).

Wrobel, S. (1997). An algorithm for multi-relational discovery of subgroups. In *Proceedings of 1st European Symposium on Principles of Data Mining and Knowledge Discovery*, (pp. 78–87). Berlin, Germany: Springer.

Wu, F., & Weld, D. (2007). Autonomously semantifying Wikipedia. *Proceedings of the Sixteenth ACM Conference on Conference on Information and Knowledge Management*, (pp. 41–50). New York, NY: ACM.

Yahoo. (2011). *Flickr: Explore / tags / New York / clusters*. Retrieved May 6, 2011, from http://www.flickr.com /photos/tags/newyork/clusters/

Yahoo. (2011). *Welcome to Flickr*. Retrieved May 6, 2011, from http://www.flickr.com/

Yamamoto, K., Kudo, T., Konagaya, A., & Matusmoto, Y. (2003). Protein name tagging for biomedical annotation in text. In *Proceedings of ACL 2003 Workshop on Natural Language Processing in Biomedicine*.

Yang, Y. F., & Guo, P. (2007). *The estimation of enterprise's human capital operation*. Paper presented at the 2006 International Conference on Management Science and Engineering, ICMSE'06 (13th).

Yi, E., Lee, G. G., Song, Y., & Park, S.-J. (2004). SVM-based biological named entity recognition using minimum edit-distance feature boosted by virtual examples. In *Proceedings of International Joint Conference on Natural Language Processing (IJCNLP-2004)*, *LNCS 3248*, (pp. 807–814).

Yin, R. K. (2009). *Case study research: Design and methods* (4th ed.). Thousand Oaks, CA: Sage.

Yoshida, S., Kamei, K., Ohguro, T., & Kuwabara, K. (2003). Shine: A peer-to-peer based framework of network community support systems. [Elsevier.]. *Computer Communications*, *26*(11), 1199–1209. doi:10.1016/S0140-3664(02)00254-2

Yu, B., & Singh, M. (2003). Searching social networks. *Proceedings of the Second International Joint Conference on Autonomous Agents and Multiagent Systems,* (pp. 65-72).

Zangerle, E., Gassler, W., & Specht, G. (2010). Recommending structure in collaborative semistructured information systems. *Proceedings of the Fourth ACM Conference on Recommender Systems,* (pp. 261–264). New York, NY: ACM.

Zapf, M., Reinema, R., Wolf, R., & Türpe, S. (2002). UNITE - An agent-oriented teamwork environment. *Lecture Notes in Computer Science,* (n.d)., 2521.

Zephram. (2011, January). Retrieved from http://www.zephram.de /?lang=en

Zhang, M., & Hurley, N. (2008). Avoiding monotony: Improving the diversity of recommendation lists. In *Proceedings of the 2008 ACM Conference on Recommender Systems* (Lausanne, Switzerland, October 23 - 25, 2008), RecSys '08, (pp. 123-130). New York, NY: ACM.

Zhang, J., Shen, D., Zhou, G., Su, J., & Tan, C.-L. (2002). Enhancing HMM-based biomedical named entity recognition by studying special phenomena. *Journal of Biomedical Informatics, 12*(6), 411–422.

Zhao, S. (2004). Named entity recognition in biomedical texts using an HMM model. In *Proceedings of the International Joint Workshop on Natural Language Processing in Biomedicine and Its Applications,* (pp. 84–87).

Zhao, S., & Grishman, R. (2005). Extracting relations with integrated information using kernel methods. In *Proceedings of the 43rd Annual Meeting on Association for Computational Linguistics (ACL-2005),* (pp. 419–426).

Zhdanova, A., & Shvaiko, P. (2006). *Community-driven ontology matching.*

Zhou, G., & Su, J. (2002). Named entity recognition using an HMM-based chunk tagger. In *Proceedings of 40th Meeting of Association of Computational Linguistics (ACL-2002),* (pp. 473–480).

Zou, Y., Finin, T., Ding, L., Chen, H., & Pan, R. (2003). Using Semantic Web technology in Multi-Agent systems: A case study in the TAGA Trading agent environment. In *Proceeding of the 5th International Conference on Electronic Commerce (ICEC 2003),* Pittsburgh, PA.

Zuber-Skerritt, O. (1996). Emancipatory action research for organisational change. In Zuber-Skerritt, O. (Ed.), *New directions in action research.* London, UK: Falmer Press.

About the Contributors

Stefan Brüggemann is a quality engineer at Astrium Space Transportation. He is currently working on software quality assurance in agile development projects, and on several CMMI-topics. He received his PhD from the University of Oldenburg in 2011 for his work on consistency control in data quality management, where he utilized semantic technologies for the detection and removal of violations of conditional functional dependencies. Further, he used collaborative technologies to integrate domain experts in quality management. From 2005 to 2011, he was working as a research assistant at OFFIS - Institute for Information Technology in the R&D Division Health. His main topics of interest are: ontology based data quality management in the health market, quality based data integration in data warehouse systems, linked open data, and the semantic web. He is organizer of the international workshops on "Data management and interoperability in the health market" in 2011 and 2010, and was serving as a program committee member of several international conferences, such as ACM SAC SWA 2010-2012 and IMMM 2011-2012.

Claudia d'Amato graduated in Computer Science at the University of Bari on March 2003 with full marks and honors. After almost one year in a software company, she started her research activity in January 2004 winning a grant from the University of Bari for PhD students in Computer Science. She completed her PhD studies in January 2007 and defended the thesis "Similarity-based Learning Methods for the Semantic Web" on May 2007 receiving a full marks evaluation and also a nomination from the Italian Commission for the AI*IA award 2007 as one of the Best Italian PhD theses in Artificial Intelligence. Since April 2004 she is a research assistant at the University of Bari - Computer Science Department and she is investigating on the analysis and the application of Machine Learning (ML) methods to the Semantic Web (SW) domain. The results of the research activities have been applied in several regional, national and European research projects. Claudia d'Amato also collaborated/collaborates with international universities and research organizations. During January-June 2006, February-May 2007, February-April 2008, Claudia d'Amato was visiting researcher at the University of Koblenz-Landau (Germany). In June 2011, Claudia d'Amato was invited researcher at the University of Poznan (Poland). In March-April 2012 was invited researcher at the Fondazione Bruno Kessler, Trento (Italy). The research activity of Claudia d'Amato has been disseminated in 13 journal articles, 8 book chapters, 37 articles in international collections, 18 articles in international workshop collections and 12 articles in national conferences and workshops collections. Claudia d'Amato has been also editor of 12 books/collections and 2 journal special issues. She has served the editorial board of international journals in the field such as the Semantic Web Journal and she has also served the program committee of more than 50 international conferences such as the International and the European Semantic Web Conference

(ISWC, ESWC), the American, European and the International Conference on Artificial Intelligence (AAAI, ECAI, IJCAI), the International and the European Conference on ML (ICML, ECML). In 2008, Claudia d'Amato served as vice-Chair for ISWC and in 2012 as workshop and tutorial chair. She also served as ML track chair at ESWC 2012. Claudia d'Amato has also been organizer of the International Uncertainty Reasoning Workshop at ISWC (URSW 2011-10-09-08,-07) and the International Workshop on Inductive Reasoning and ML on the Semantic Web at ESWC (IRMLeS 2011,-10.-09). Her research activity also received the following credits: Best Paper at ACM SAC'10 - SWA Track for the paper "Recovering Uncertain Mappings through Structural Validation and Aggregation with the MoTo System" and Best best student paper at SEBD07 for the paper "Constraint Hardness for Modelling, Matching and Ranking Semantic Web services". She has been also invited speaker at various international universities, seminars and conferences over the years.

* * *

Rabeeh Abbasi is working as an assistant professor in Department of Computer Science at Quaid-i-Azam University, Islamabad, Pakistan. He received his master's degree from National University of Computer and Emerging Sciences, Islamabad, in 2004 and his PhD at the University of Koblenz-Landau Germany in December 2010. His research focus includes Social Media, Web 2.0 and Data mining.

Martin Atzmueller is a senior researcher at the University of Kassel. He studied Computer Science at the University of Texas at Austin (USA) and at the University of Würzburg (Germany) where he completed his MSc (Diploma) in Computer Science. Martin earned his doctorate (PhD) from the University of Würzburg. He published more than 60 research papers in refereed international journals and conferences, and has been author, co-author, and co-editor of several books. His research areas include data mining, text mining, natural language processing, machine learning, web science, explanation, ubiquitous and collective intelligence, and the social semantic web.

Stephanie Beer is a medical doctor at the University of Wuerzburg. She studied Medicine at the University of Wuerzburg (Germany) and at the University of Madison and Harvard Medical School in Boston (USA). She earned her doctorate (MD) from the University of Wuerzburg. Stephanie performed her training in internal medicine at the University of Wuerzburg. She published more than 15 research papers in refereed international journals and conferences. Her research areas include data mining, text mining, ultrasound and heart failure.

Sadok Ben Yahia is an Associate-Professor at the Computer Sciences department of the Faculty of Sciences of Tunis since October 2002. He obtained his Habilitation to lead researches in Computer Sciences from the Faculty of Sciences of Tunis in July 2008. Currently, He is leading a group of researchers in Tunis, whose research interests include efficient extraction of informative and compact covers of association rules, visualization of association rules and soft computing. He has served in the program committees of over 20 international conferences and has been technical reviewer of different international journals. He has also served is co-guest editor of three international journals special issues. He is currently member of the steering committee of the International Conference on Concept Lattices and their

Applications (CLA) as well as the International French Spoken Conference on Knowledge Extractions and Management. Contact him at sadok.benyahia@fst.rnu.tn.

Federico Bergenti received a Ph.D. in Information Technologies from the University of Parma (Department of Information Engineering) in 2002. From the same University, he obtained a Laurea degree (M.Sc.) in Electronic Engineering in 1998. From October 2007 he is a permanent researcher in Computer Science at the University of Parma and he is affiliated to the Department of Mathematics. Federico's research activity has been mainly devoted to Artificial Intelligence and Software Engineering, with special regard to multi-agent systems. In the field of Artificial Intelligence he has worked on issues related to agent communication languages and their semantics. In the field of Software Engineering, he initially worked on architectures for agent-based middleware; then he concentrated on issues related to reusability and strong decoupling in agent-based systems. More recently, he turned his interests towards agent programming languages; he is particularly interested in approaches that rely on constraint (logic) programming.

Ernesto William De Luca is Head of the Competence Center for Information Retrieval and Machine Learning at the DAI-Lab, Technische Universität Berlin. He has authored more than 40 papers on national and international conferences and journals in the fields of information retrieval, semantic technologies, adaptive systems and other related areas. He chaired the 1st Workshop on Semantic Personalized Information Management (SPIM 2010) at the Language Resources and Evaluation Conference (LREC 2010) and the 2nd Workshop on Personalized Information Management (SPIM2011) at the International Semantic Web Conference 2011 (ISWC 2011). Together with Shlomo Berkovsky and Alan Said, he chaired the Challenge on Context-aware Movie Recommendation (CAMRa2010), as a joint event with the Workshop on Context-aware Recommender Systems (CARS-2010), in conjunction with the ACM Recommender Systems 2010 Conference (RecSys2010) held in Barcelona, Spain on September 30, 2010. He is chairing the Workshop on Context-awareness in Recommendation and Retrieval that will be held in conjunction with the 2011 International Conference on Intelligent User Interfaces that will take place in Palo Alto, California on February 13-16, 2011.

Stephen Dobson is a Research Fellow at Sheffield Business School, Sheffield Hallam University and holds a PhD from the Department of Landscape, University of Sheffield. His research interests include cultural heritage, urban landscape planning and design, 'relational' social research and participatory action research within an organisational context. Stephen has also worked as a corporate researcher in the public sector also spent nine years at the University of York.

Rainer Erne's main interest and research topic in his PhD project at Leeds Metropolitan University is related to the different aspects the Management of Knowledge Workers. On the one hand this interest is based in 15 years of working with knowledge workers as a project manager at IBM Global Services, as a consultant at Vector Consulting, as a trainer and consultant with his own company and as a project manager at Robert Bosch GmbH. On the other hand he has worked academically on this topic in his two master studies in social sciences and in business management as well as in his vocational trainings in PMI and CMMI.

Enrico Franchi received B.Sc. in Mathematics and Computer Science and M.Sc. in Computer Science from the University of Parma. He is currently enrolled in the Ph.D. course in Information Technologies from the same University under the supervision of Dr. Agostino Poggi. His main interests are related to Multi-Agent and distributed systems, social networks, artificial intelligence and software engineering. He is currently investigating the mutual relationships between social networks and multi-agent systems, with a special regard to simulations.

Wolfgang Gassler is a researcher at the University of Innsbruck, Austria. He is member of the research group Databases and Information Systems at the Institute of Computer Science and works in the field of creating, editing and storing knowledge in large-scale environments. Especially the semistructured paradigm (e.g. RDF) which is used in many collaborative environments and upcoming challenges in this area are the main focus of his research. Together with Eva Zangerle he is the main leader in the ongoing reasearch in the area of the Snoopy Concept. His primary research is concerned with the question: how to store RDF data in a fast and distributed way and simultaneously provide efficient user-centred interfaces and high usability.

Brian D. Goodman is a Senior Technical Staff Member and Master Inventor in IBM's Cloud Computing organization delivering architecture, development and end-to-end user experience for IBM's public cloud offerings. He leads a catalyst team of architects, developers, designers and user experience professionals with a focus on cloud patterns for SaaS, orchestration, and data transfer. Prior to that, he focused on identity, grassroots collaboration and social software leading a skunk works team responsible for designing and developing emerging technology that enriches collaboration and productivity. Mr. Goodman was a co-founder and principal architect directing technical enablement for IBM's Technology Adoption Program (TAP). TAP is IBM's program for identifying, developing and transitioning innovation from the laboratory to internal applications and customer implementation. He earned a multi-disciplinary BA degree in computer science, psychology and graphic design from Hampshire College, Amherst, Massachusetts, where his thesis centered on human-computer interface design for early childhood applications.

Salman Iqbal is a Lecturer in Pakistan. Currently, he is doing PhD in HRM from Massey University, Palmerston North, New Zealand. He received a B.E. degree from Pakistan and later M.B.A. from University of Wollongong, Australia. His research interests include HRM, knowledge management and individual capability. During his PhD, he has attended couple of international conferences and presented his work to professional audience in New Zealand. Currently, he is writing Journal articles and book chapters along with his supervisors. Apart from his academic research, he is also writing magazine articles based on Human resource management in New Zealand. He can be contacted at: s.iqbal@massey.ac.nz

Hayati Abdul Jalal holds a master's degree in Human Resource Development from University Putra Malaysia. She is currently a PhD candidate at School of Management, College of Business, and Massey University New Zealand. Her PhD research aims at bringing the role of human capital in the knowledge management equation, as well as identification of an acceptable and desirable organisational culture values for successful knowledge sharing within knowledge based organisations. Her research areas include HRM, knowledge management and cross-cultural management.

Stefan Werner Knoll studied Computational Visualistics at the University of Magdeburg, obtaining his diploma degree in 2006. He has been working at the Computer Science department of the University of Magdeburg since April 2007 as a PhD student in the research field of Collaboration Engineering and computer-supported methods for ideation. In his PhD thesis is to analyse and define requirements for a generic groupware technology that uses the Collaboration Engineering approach. Since 2011, he is working at the TU Delft as a researcher in the EU project: SMART VORTEX. The goal of this project is to provide a technological infrastructure consisting of a comprehensive suite of interoperable tools, services, and methods for intelligent management and analysis of massive data streams to achieve better collaboration and decision making in large-scale collaborative projects concerning industrial innovation engineering.

Tobias Krahn was born 1984 in Leer, Germany. He was always fascinated by computer technology, which is why he started studying computer sciences at Carl von Ossietzky University of Oldenburg in 2006. In his master thesis he focussed on how dimension elements in a multidimensional data model can be filtered by gathering and making use of semantic metadata from external sources like the linked data cloud. He is keen to do his Ph.D., because of his research interest in the domain of business intelligence. Since 2012 he works as Scientific Research Assistant at OFFIS – Institute for Information Technology in the R+D Division Health in the Data Management and Analysis Group.

Matthias Mertens studied computer science at the University of Oldenburg in North Germany until 2008 with the focus on Information Systems and Software Engineering. Since autumn 2008 he works as Scientific Research Assistant at OFFIS – Institute for Information Technology in the R+D Division Health in the Data Management and Analysis Group. The main focus of his work is the development of the Analytical Information System MUSTANG (Multidimensional Statistical Data Analysis Engine) for several domains like Epidemiological Cancer Registration, Family Offices and Health Services Research resp. Hospital Market Analysis. His research interest is especially the area of Self-Service Business Intelligence to empower business users to create ad-hoc and explorative analysis and to generate new insights without the help of power users. Technologically he focuses therefore on the combination of proven BI techniques with concepts and technologies of the social semantic web.

Seyed Morteza Babamir received the B.S. degree in Computer Science from Ferdowsi University of Mashad, Iran, the M.S. degree in Software Engineering, from Tarbiat Modares University, Iran, in 2001 and Ph.D. degree in Software Engineering from Tarbiat Modares University, Iran in 2007. His current research Interests include software modeling and development. Currently, Dr. Babamir is assistant professor of department of computer engineering in University of Kashan. Home page: http://ce.kashanu.ac.ir/babamir

Bilel Moulahi is a master student at the Computer Sciences department of the Faculty of Sciences of Tunis since June 2010. His research interest lies in the area of Data Mining, Semantic Web, Social Web and Information Retrieval. Contact him at moulahi.bilel@gmail.com.

Girish Keshav Palshikar was born on 5th August, 1963. He obtained an M.Sc. (Physics) from Indian Institute of Technology, Bombay in 1985 and an M.S. (Computer Science and Engineering)

from Indian Institute of Technology, Chennai in 1988. Since 1992, he is working as a scientist in Tata Research Development and Design Centre (TRDDC), Pune, India. TRDDC is part of Tata Consultancy Services - a premier software company in India. Girish leads the Machine Learning research group in TRDDC. He has several publications in international journals and conferences. His areas of research include machine learning, data and text mining, artificial intelligence and theoretical computer science. He is married and has one daughter.

Till Plumbaum received the diploma degree in computer science from the Technische Universität Berlin in 2007. He is currently working on a project dealing with semantic recommendations on large datasets. He has authored more than 20 papers on national and international conferences and journals in the fields of user modelling, information retrieval, semantic technologies, adaptive systems and other related areas. He was technical chair of the 1st Workshop on Semantic Personalized Information Management (SPIM 2010) at the Language Resources and Evaluation Conference (LREC 2010). He chaired the 2nd Workshop on Personalized Information Management (SPIM2011) at the International Semantic Web Conference 2011 (ISWC 2011) and the 1st Workshop Social and Adaptive Web at the User Modeling, Adaptation and Personalization Conference (UMAP 2011). His research interests are in the area of machine learning, social networks and especially semantic user modelling.

Agostino Poggi is full professor of Computer Engineering at the Faculty of Engineering of the University of Parma. He coordinates the Agent and Object Technology Lab and his research focuses on agent and object-oriented technologies and their use to develop distributed and complex systems. He is author of more than a hundred of technical papers in refereed journals and conferences and his scientific contribution has been recognized through the "System Research Foundation Outstanding Scholarly Contribution Award" and the "System Innovation Award". Moreover, he is in the editorial board of the following scientific journals: Software Practice & Experience, International Journal of Hybrid Intelligent Systems, International Journal of Agent-Oriented Software Engineering, International Journal of Multiagent and Grid Systems e International Journal of Software Architecture.

Livia Predoiu is a computer scientist and has been a researcher in the areas of Semantic Web Technologies, Information Integration, Knowledge Representation, Knowledge Management and Reasoning since 2004. After having worked at the University of Innsbruck in Austria and at the University of Mannheim in Germany, she currently is affiliated with the University of Magdeburg in Germany and focuses on research around probabilistic information integration in the semantic web and semantic digital archiving. Livia Predoiu has been working in several different national and international research projects and has authored and co-authored about 30 publications in the aforementioned areas. Further information can be found at her website: http://www.uni-magdeburg.de/predoiu/index.html

Frank Puppe has worked full time in the area of computer science and artificial intelligence since 1983, when he earned his master (diplom) degree at Bonn university. Further academic degrees were his PhD at Kaiserslautern university in 1986 and his habilitation at Karlsruhe university in 1991. 1986/87 he had a one Semester deputyship for professor at University of Hamburg and in 1988 a two month

Visiting Appointments at the Clinical Decision Making Group at the MIT Laboratory for Computer Science. Since 1992 he is appointed as full professor at Wuerzburg university. His research interests include knowledge based systems and knowledge engineering, data mining, information extraction, e-learning and human-computer-interfaces. He is involved in several research projects developing respective tools and published 7 books (incl. 2 edited volumes) and about 200 articles.

Elena Simperl works as assistant professor at the Institute of Applied Informatics and Formal Description Methods (AIFB) at the Karlsruhe Institute of Technology (KIT). She holds a PhD in Computer Science from the Free University of Berlin and a Diploma in Computer Science from the Technical University of Munich. She has held research and teaching positions at the Technical University of Munich (2002-2003), the Free University of Berlin (2003-2007), and the Semantic Technology Institute (STI) Innsbruck at the University of Innsbruck (2007-2009) before joining KIT in January 2010. Elena's primary domain of research is semantic technologies. She has been working as a Semantic Web researcher for almost a decade, being involved in over 15 European and national projects in this field, authoring over 75 publications, and serving as chair to several relevant academic conferences and workshops.

Katharina Siorpaes Since May 2011, is working as executive assistant for the Axel Springer daughter Immonet, Hamburg, Germany. In 2008 she co-founded the IT spin-off playence, where she was responsible for product innovation and research until 2011. From 2004 until 2011, Katharina Siorpaes was working as a senior researcher and university assistant at the Semantic Technology Institute (STI) Innsbruck at the University of Innsbruck, Austria. Katharina holds a PhD in computer science from the University of Innsbruck, Austria. She was working on ontology engineering, collaborative ontology engineering, using games for metadata creation, incentives for knowledge acquisition, and the collaborative annotation of multimedia. Among the projects she was involved in are the Austrian funded projects myOntology and etPlanner and the EU funded projects INSEMTIVES, RENDER, ACTIVE, SNML and eFreight. Katharina was also the coordinator of the Austrian FFG COIN project MOUVIZ.

Paul Toulson is an Associate professor; he is a registered industrial/organisational psychologist and has been a member of the College of Business at Massey University since 1985. Prior to that, he was employed in the New Zealand Armed Forces in a variety of appointments as an industrial/organisational psychologist and a personnel director. He is a Life Fellow of the Human Resources Institute of New Zealand and an Associate Fellow of the New Zealand Psychological Society. He was the founding editor of the New Zealand Journal of Human Resources Management. He is currently a member of the Institute's research and publications committee. He is also a member of the Academy of Management. Currently he is he Vice President of the Academic Branch of HRINZ. His research interests are human resource management practices, research methods in human resource management, valuing human resources management, and strategic human resource management. He can be contacted at P.Toulson@massey.ac.nz

Chiraz Trabelsi received the M.S degrees in Computer Science from Faculty of Sciences of Tunis, Tunisia in 2006. She is currently a PhD studen in the Department of Computer Science and Engineering, Faculty of Sciences of Tunis since January 2010. Her research interests include Data Mining, Semantic Web, Social Web and Ontology Engineering. Contact her at chiraz.trabelsi@fst.rnu.tn.

David Tweed is Associate Pro- Vice-Chancellor for executive education in the college of Business at Massey University. He has been involved in SME development for more twenty ten years and has been a practicing researcher for twenty five years. During this time he has been involved in teaching, research and extension activities. He was part of a team that was awarded a three-year FRST contract for $675,000 to investigate the management competencies which facilitate the uptake of new technology by small firms. He has written widely for academic and practitioner audiences including contributions to six books. He can be contacted at d.m.tweed@massey.ac.nz

Stephan Wölger works as researcher and project leader at the Semantic Technology Institute at the University Of Innsbruck. He holds a Master in Computer Science from the University Of Innsbruck and is currently finishing his diploma studies in Law and Business Law. Stephan's primary domain of research is semantic technologies. He has been working as a Semantic Web researcher for almost three years being involved in the European projects ACTIVE and INSEMTIVES, and corresponding publications. In INSEMTIVES he is work package leader. In the near future he will start his PhD studies in Computer Science and Law.

Eva Zangerle is a researcher at the research group Databases and Information Systems at the Institute of Computer Science at the University of Innsbruck, Austria. Eva Zangerle is working in the fields of Recommender Systems, Personalization and Information Systems. She has a significant expertise in the field of recommendations, semistructured data (especially RDF), microblogging and tagging of internet resources. The facilitation of recommender systems aiming at the creation of a common structure within the underlying data and thus enabling powerful search facilities based on structured data are of particular interest to Eva Zangerle.

Index